Ada

Problem Solving and
Program Design

Michael B. Feldman

The George Washington University

Elliot B. Koffman

Temple University

Ada

Problem Solving and Program Design

Addison-Wesley Publishing Company
Reading, Massachusetts · Menlo Park, California
New York · Don Mills, Ontario · Wokingham, England
Amsterdam · Bonn · Sydney · Singapore
Tokyo · Madrid · San Juan · Milan · Paris

Library of Congress Cataloging-in-Publication Data

Feldman, Michael B.
    Ada : problem solving and program design / Michael B.
Feldman, Elliot B. Koffman.
        p.   cm.
    Includes index.
    ISBN 0-201-52279-9
    1. Ada (Computer program language) I. Koffman,
Elliot B.   II. Title.
QA76.73.A35F44   1993
005.13'3—dc20   92-20775
                                                          CIP

ISBN 0-201-52279-9
1 2 3 4 5 6 7 8 9 10–HA–9695949392

Preface

This book is one of the first CS1-oriented works to use Ada as the language of discourse. It is inspired by, and borrows much material from, two recent successful books by Elliot Koffman, *Problem Solving and Structured Programming with Modula-2*, and *Problem Solving and Structured Programming with Pascal (3rd ed.)*. This is not a "conversion," however: Much material is completely overhauled or entirely new, and the order of presentation is significantly different from the earlier works.

As with the earlier works, no previous programming experience is either assumed or required here; this book can genuinely be used by students who are novices. While the book is in general oriented to the first-term (CS1) student of programming, there is more material here than is usually covered in a CS1 course. Chapters 9–14 focus on design methodology, abstract data types, generics, recursion, and dynamic data structures, and therefore can serve well as the core of a CS2-level course.

Familiar Themes

Readers familiar with the Koffman works will find some familiar themes in this book. These are not at all related to the language of discourse of the book, but are rather general teaching devices that have met with success:

- *Complete, compilable programs:* Right from the start, students see full, compilable, executable programs. Each chapter has a number of these; they are captioned *Program x.y* to identify them clearly as compilable programs and not fragments, which are embedded in the text or numbered as figures. Each listing of a main program is immediately followed by a sample execution, to give the student an idea of the expected results.

    A particular advantage of Ada as a teaching language is that the strong standard ensures that program behavior will be nearly independent of the particular compiler or computer being used. The programs in this book are intended to be *entirely* portable, to be compiled and executed on any validated Ada compiler. Testing with several different suppliers' implementations on different computers has convinced us that no portability problems will be encountered with these programs. The only minor exception is our assumption that a math library is available which contains the usual transcendental functions; we cannot solve the problem of disparate names for math libraries.

We are distributing this complete set of over 180 programs and packages, which have been fully tested with several Ada compilers on Unix and IBM-PC systems, in diskette form and plan to make them available over the Internet.

- *Case Studies:* In this series of books, a case study is a program developed from specifications, step-by-step, from a statement of the problem to a complete working program. There are a number of case studies in the present work, some adapted from earlier books, some entirely new here. It is in the case studies that the software design methodology is taught, reinforced, and applied.

- *Syntax Displays:* A syntax display is a brief description, with words and examples, of the syntax and interpretation of a newly introduced structure. These are set apart typographically for ease of use, and codify the language structures as they are first presented. Traditional syntax diagrams are supplied in an appendix.

- *Programming Style Displays:* These are brief discussions, again set apart typographically, offering advice to the student about how to write good programs. Many of these are of course universal and language-independent; many are also Ada-specific.

- *End-of-Section Exercises:* Following most sections there are two kinds of exercises, self-check and programming.

- *End-of-Chapter Exercises:* Each chapter ends with a set of quick-check exercises with answers, review questions, and programming projects.

- *Error Discussions and Chapter Review:* Each chapter ends with a section that discusses common programming errors and a review section that includes a table of new Ada constructs.

General Organization of the Book

The order of presentation in the book has been entirely overhauled to do justice both to modern programming concepts and to the power of Ada. *Each chapter presents a balanced mixture of a number of important language and computing issues.* These are organized in a number of rubrics; most chapter section headings give the main rubric of the section as well as the specific topic, to orient teacher and student alike to flow of material in given rubric from chapter to chapter. The rubrics are as follows:

- *Problem Solving:* Here is where language-independent concepts of program design, algorithm development, etc., are introduced.

- *Control Structures:* Each of these sections focuses on introducing the program-level control structures of Ada: decisions, loops, assignments, etc.

- *Data Structures:* In each of these sections appears a discussion of data types and their uses, in the usual order of scalar types followed by structured or composite (record and array) types.

- *System Structures:* Each of these sections introduces a concept useful in what is often called "programming in the large." These concepts help the student, right from the start, to realize that real-world programs really consist of many smaller pieces built up in systematic fashion. Included under System Structures are such things as functions and procedures, packages, exception handling, and propagation.

  Some educators might consider subprograms and exceptions to be a form of control structure. This is not an incorrect view, but we have chosen here to enforce a clear distinction between inner or "intra-module" control structures like looping and testing, and "inter-module" structures like subroutines and exceptions, which are especially useful in building systems rather than just individual programs.

- *Tricks of the Trade:* These are the universal techniques that all programmers must learn in order to survive productively; debugging techniques, program tracing, documentation techniques, and the like.

- *Case Studies:* These are as described above; in this book the more significant case studies are given visibility with a rubric of their own.

Some points of divergence from the earlier works should be noted here:

We present top-down *design* or *refinement* of a program right from the start, but introduce top-down *implementation*, through procedure stubs and the like, only in Chapter 9, which is later than has previously been the case. In our experience, it is crucial to foster habits of design for *reusability* very early, and this argues for emphasizing packages and the reusable functions and procedures they provide in the first half of the book, treating the use of local procedures, stubs, etc., as a more advanced topic. This helps to ensure that students will not develop the tendency to reference global variables in subprogram bodies, etc. It will never occur to them to try this, because subprograms are introduced first as exported from packages.

Program design is emphasized through example in the first eight chapters. The methodology used is consistent but informal at this stage. After the student has developed an intuitive feeling for how a good program fits together—never having seen a bad one—he or she is ready for Chapter 9, which takes a systematic approach to both top-down and bottom-up implementation, and Chapter 10, which introduces the design of abstract data types.

Functions are presented very early: They are used in Chapter 3 and written in Chapter 4. *Procedure calls* are introduced early in Chapter 2 because input/output in Ada requires them, but procedures are not *written* until Chapter 6. We believe functions are more intuitive than procedures, and, in Ada, cannot have IN OUT ("variable") parameters. Since functions in Ada are not restricted in their result type—arrays and records as well as scalars can be returned—this early exposure to functions will pay off later in encouraging students to use functional notation where possible. Introducing functions early allows us to introduce the writing of packages early (again in Chapter 4).

Enumeration types are introduced very early (Chapter 3). Enumerations are a useful structure for representing a set of values without regard to their internal representation. Students of other languages have a hard time seeing the utility of enumerations, because they are so hard to read and display. In Ada, because the input/output library provides a generic package for Enumeration I/O, reading and displaying enumerations is very easy. Furthermore, enumerations serve as a useful vehicle for motivating generic instantiation (for Enumeration_IO) and attributes (Pos, Val, Succ, Pred) very early in the game.

Records and *arrays* are presented together in Chapter 8, with records first. Other books have introduced arrays of scalars early, with arrays of records as an "advanced" topic. We prefer to allow arrays of records to be as natural as arrays of integers.

Design is covered systematically in Chapters 9 and 10. Chapter 9 treats *procedural abstraction,* with much emphasis on both top-down and bottom-up coding and testing. Chapter 10 covers *abstract data types,* beginning with the view of Calendar as an ADT, and continuing with ADTs for calendar dates, rational numbers, variable-length strings, and employee records. Multidimensional arrays and variant records are introduced in Chapter 11; unconstrained array types are treated along with generics in Chapter 12. Chapter 13 presents an introduction to *recursion.*

The place of recursion in CS1 is not a settled issue; some teachers introduce it early, others late in the course, and still others defer the issue entirely to the second semester. To accommodate the first preference, we have written Sections 13.1–13.5 so that they can be assigned after the WHILE loops and procedures of Chapter 6. Section 13.7, on recursive sorting and searching, can be taught after Chapter 8, where iterative searching and sorting are introduced.

Dynamic data structures, in the form of one-way linked lists and binary trees, as well as subunits and LIMITED PRIVATE types, are introduced in Chapter 14. While many CS1-level courses do not reach these structures, some do; moreover, this chapter rounds out the material presented in Chapters 9–13 and allows the later chapters to be used as the core of a second-level (CS2) course. In addition, the packages and case study in Chapter 14 serve as a useful unification of dynamic data structures, generics, separate subunits, abstract data types, and especially the idea of multiple implementations of a single client interface.

Assertions are introduced in Chapter 6 as structured comments, and used consistently thereafter to document loop invariants and pre- and post-conditions for subprograms. We encourage the development of programs from their documentation; in case studies, the steps of the algorithm and the various assertions are written before the program is developed, and become comments as the program is refined.

We encourage appropriate use of comments but do not get carried away with them; the programs and the book would be far too long if we used industrial-strength comment conventions. Furthermore, students often respond with overkill to teachers' demands for comments, writing foolishness like

```
Count := Count + 1;        -- add 1 to Count
```

Ada Issues

It is important in introducing Ada to beginners (and we assume no previous programming experience, in any language, in this book) to introduce them, step by step, to the power of this rich language without overwhelming them. Here is a list of a number of Ada capabilities and how we have handled them:

- *Numeric Types:* Subtypes are introduced right from the start, in Chapter 3, as a way of specifying ranges of values that are sensible in the application. Where values shouldn't be negative, we always use a positive subtype, for example, and often use a subtype with range constraints where it makes sense not to allow the full range of integer.

   We have avoided the use of new and derived numeric types because the compatibility issues that arise from their use create more problems than they solve for beginners. It is range checking that is important to them, not the esoterica of type compatibility. Since current Ada compilers are not usually well designed for beginning students, the semantic-error diagnostics regarding type clashes, etc., are overwhelming.

   Furthermore, using new or derived numeric types for simple beginning-level numerical problems gives completely counterintuitive results: attempting to use types for distance, rate, and time, for example, to compute the old

   ```
   Distance := Rate * Time;
   ```

   formula leads to type-compatibility grief that no novice should have to endure. On the other hand, a useful numeric type system is introduced in Chapter 10 in the form of a package to handle dimensioned physical quantities using variant records. This example uses the power of variant records effectively, especially combined with Ada's use of constrained and unconstrained variant objects. It goes beyond the usual data processing examples into a useful tool for building mathematical software.

- *Packages and Related Issues:* Using packages is introduced in Chapter 2, with the use of the various sublibraries of Text_IO. In Chapter 3, students learn how to use some of the capabilities of Calendar, which has a richness not often explored even by advanced Ada texts. Calendar is a recurring theme in this book, and is discussed in the abstract data type material in Chapter 10, since Time and the various Time and Duration operations from Calendar serve as a particularly nice predefined example of a private ADT. Also, all students understand times and dates intuitively; there is nothing esoteric about them.

   Also in Chapter 3, use of a simple screen-control package is introduced. Students will need to compile this before they use it, as it is provided with the book and is not part of most compiler distributions. Thus they will learn how to compile a package and understand specifications very early on, even if they don't yet understand the details of the package body, which are discussed at some length in Chapter 7. Screen is used in a number of examples in the book, especially for menu-handling and plotting.

   By Chapter 4, students are writing simple packages; by Chapter 5 they are learning about overload function and procedure names. Private types and operator overloading appear in Chapter 10. We decided to avoid introducing operator overloading earlier because the entire first half of the book scrupulously avoids the USE clause (see below).

   Many packages appear in the book. A number are introduced in Chapters

8–12, including variable-length strings, rational numbers, and metric types. These make good use of operator overloading. Many packages (modules, units) introduced in the earlier Koffman works are no longer necessary because they focus on reading and writing enumerations, an onerous task that comes "free" with Ada!

- *Private and Limited Private Types:* Private types are covered in depth in Chapter 10, in the discussion of abstract data types. Specifically, a number of examples are given of situations in which giving a client access to the details of a type would allow the client inadvertently to violate the integrity of the abstraction. The exported types in this chapter all provide for default initialization so that assignment and equality test are always meaningful operations.

  In Chapter 14, attention is paid to those situations—especially in the use of dynamic data structures—in which assignment and equality test can indeed be used misleadingly, for example, to copy just the headers of lists. The potential for abuse of these operations provides useful justification for limited private types, for objects of which assignment and equality test are prohibited.

- *Subunits and Ada Stubs:* The table-handling packages of Chapter 14 serve as a way to introduce this concept, which is confusing if brought in too early. Besides being an interesting Ada technique for doing top-down testing, the use of subunits serves as a convenient way to present the operations of the packages as individual program displays and files.

- *The* USE *Clause:* This is introduced in Chapter 7. Current Ada industry practice avoids the USE clause for a number of good reasons. We avoid it here, in general, because qualifying all references to package resources helps the student really understand which resources are provided by which libraries. We do introduce USE in Chapter 7 along with the use of Math packages. Since almost all compiler suppliers these days provide a math library, it is safe to assume that Sin and Sqrt are available. Unfortunately, however, there is no standard *name* for the library: Math_Lib, Math, MathLibrary, and Math-Functions are all names seen in the world of Ada compilers.

  A USE statement here is not only permissible but in fact a good use of the "factorization" principle, because a student can tailor his or her programs to the name of the local math library by making the change in only one place at the top of the program, instead of having to change multiple qualified references.

  USE is also useful in taking advantage of the overloading of infix operators. USE is a better solution for novices than the industry-favored device of renaming declarations.

- *Generic I/O Libraries:* Right away in Chapter 2, the student is asked to "tailor" the numeric libraries with the following file (included as a program in the software distribution):

```
WITH Text_IO;
PACKAGE My_Int_IO IS NEW Text_IO.Integer_IO (Num=> Integer);

WITH Text_IO;
PACKAGE My_Flt_IO IS NEW Text_IO.Float_IO (Num=> Float);
```

This places the instances in the student's library; (s)he never has to instantiate these again. This is a better approach than a `Simple_IO` library, since these are the "real" ones; but the student does not need to remember to include an instantiation in all programs (or sit through a possibly longer compilation because of it!). It is in any event good Ada to pre-instantiate libraries for common types.

Creating these two instances works because we are not using new or derived integer and float types in the book.

- *Generics in General:* Some simple uses of generics appear in Chapter 11: a generic sort, a generic vector, and a matrix package. Heavy concentration on generics should wait until CS2.

- *Exceptions:* Discussion of Ada's predefined exceptions occurs in Chapter 2, where compilation and run-time errors in general are introduced. Robust exception handling cannot be taken up until after the control structures have been presented, and so program level exception handling is first discussed in Chapter 5. Robust input loops are presented in Chapter 6, along with a package providing robust input operations. User-defined exceptions are introduced in Chapter 10, as a natural aspect of abstract data types.

- *Lexical Style:* We have followed the lead of Norman Cohen *(Ada as a Second Language)* in using uppercase reserved words. We believe that beginners in programming should learn the structure templates through heavy reinforcement, and the uppercase reserved words make the structure templates stand out.

  Only one statement appears per line. We believe this makes for more modifiable code, and this is a good habit for students to develop.

- *Procedure Parameters:* Named association is used exclusively in the first six chapters, and almost exclusively thereafter. This is not only good Ada but also good pedagogy because the student has a much easier time understanding the formal/actual binding if the two always appear together. It makes procedure call statements rather cumbersome, but we believe the price is worth paying.

- *Initialization Expressions:* Initialization expressions are introduced in Chapter 8, along with record types, and the reader is advised to use initializations to ensure that record fields are always well-defined. With some reluctance we have decided *not* to introduce initialization expressions for *variables*. It is true that a declaration with a static initialization such as

```
X: Float := 57.0;
```

contributes to program readability. However, an initialization such as

```
X: Float := 3.0 + Sqrt(Y);
```

is permitted but should not be used, because an exception raised if `Y` is negative will propagate unexpectedly. Instead of artificially limiting initializations to static expressions, we have simply chosen not to use them at all.

Summary

This book incorporates a great deal of new material intended to introduce the beginning programmer to the power of Ada, while building on the successful pedagogy of the earlier Koffman works. We believe that the completely redesigned presentation order and the kind of new material we have introduced do justice to first courses in computing using Ada.

Acknowledgments

Programs have been tested using Sun-3, Hewlett-Packard 9000-835, and IBM-PC/AT computers at the School of Engineering and Applied Science Computing Facility, The George Washington University, and using Ada compilers from Gem Technologies, Irvine Compiler Corporation, Meridian Software Systems, TeleSoft, and Verdix. Additional development and testing was done during Feldman's sabbatical year at the University of Washington, using Digital Equipment Corporation equipment and Ada implementations from Alsys and New York University.

The authors are indebted to the following educators who served as formal reviewers: Kevin W. Bowyer, Charles B. Engle, Jr., Robert K. Maruyama, Jaime Niño, S. Ron Oliver, Henry Ruston, Larry Sells, and Robert A. Willis, Jr. Much informal help and advice came from Gertrude Levine, John McCormick, Melinda Moran, Richard Pattis, and Frances Van Scoy.

We owe a debt of gratitude to the thousand or so students in the first-year courses at the University of Washington who used this book and its software distribution during the 1992–93 academic year. Thanks to their determination and sharp-eyed reading, numerous typos and a few program bugs were revealed and corrected, and the viability of NYU's Ada/Ed as a robust and friendly teaching system was demonstrated.

The staff at Addison-Wesley, especially Lynne Doran Cote, Andrea Danese, Jim DeWolf, Katherine Harutunian, Ann Kilbride, Barbara Pendergast, Peter Shepard, and Loren Stevens, have been very supportive and friendly through the writing and production stages. Finally, there aren't enough words to thank Ruth, Ben, and Keith Feldman for patiently hanging in through another seemingly interminable book project.

Bethesda, Md.   *M.B.F.*

Philadelphia, Pa.   *E.B.K.*

Contents

1 **Introduction to Computers and Programming** 1

1.1 Electronic Computers Then and Now 1
1.2 Components of a Computer 8
1.3 The Art and Science of Problem Solving 13
1.4 The Software Development Method 14
1.5 Programming Languages 16
1.6 Processing a High-Level Language Program 18
1.7 Using the Computer 20
Chapter Review 22

2 **Introduction to Ada** 25

2.1 About Ada 26
2.2 The "Look" of Ada Programs 28
2.3 System Structures: Tailoring the Text_IO Packages for Numerical Values 33
2.4 Problem Solving: Software Development Illustrated 37
Case Study: Converting Units of Measurement 37
2.5 Data Structures: Declaring Constants and Variables 40
2.6 System Structures: General Form of an Ada Program 45
2.7 Control Structures: Assignment Statements 46

2.8 Control Structures: Input/Output Statements 49
2.9 Programs in Memory 57
2.10 Data Structures: Introduction to Data Types and Expressions 59
Case Study: Finding the Values of a Coin Collection 64
2.11 Tricks of the Trade: Common Programming Errors 68
Chapter Review 73

3 **Problem Solving and Using Packages** 77

3.1 Problem Solving: Top-Down Design 78
Case Study: Finding Area and Circumference of a Circle 79
3.2 Problem Solving: Extending a Problem Solution 83
Case Study: Unit Price of a Pizza 83
3.3 Problem Solving: Structured Programming 87
Case Study: Changing a Flat Tire 88
3.4 Data Structures: Introducing Enumeration Types 91
Case Study: Translating from English to French Color Names 95
3.5 System Structures: The Importance of Packages 97
3.6 System Structures: Using Ada's Calendar Package 98

Case Study: Displaying Today's
Date in "mm/dd/yy" Form   102
Case Study: Displaying Today's
Date in "month dd, yyyy"
Form   105
3.7 System Structures: Using a
Screen-Control Package   107
3.8 Tricks of the Trade: Common
Programming Errors   110
Chapter Review   111

4 Decision Statements; Writing Simple Functions and Packages   113

4.1 Control Structures: Boolean
Expressions and the IF
Statement   114
4.2 Problem Solving: Decision Steps
in Algorithms   120
Case Study: Modified Payroll
Problem   120
Case Study: Finding the
Alphabetically First Letter   123
4.3 Tricks of the Trade: Tracing a
Program or Algorithm   126
4.4 Problem Solving: More
Strategies   128
Case Study: Computing Overtime
Pay   128
Case Study: Computing
Insurance Dividends   130
4.5 Control Structures: The IF
Statement Revisited   133
Case Study: Given Today, Find
Yesterday and Tomorrow   135
4.6 System Structures: Writing
Simple Functions   144
4.7 System Structures: Writing a
Simple Package   148
Case Study: Finding the Largest
and Smallest of Three
Numbers   152
4.8 Tricks of the Trade: Common

Programming Errors   154
Chapter Review   154

5 Repetition in Programs   159

5.1 Control Structures: Counting
Loops and the FOR
Statement   160
Case Study: Sum of
Integers   165
5.2 Problem Solving: Generalizing a
Solution   168
Case Study: General Sum
Problem   168
Case Study: Minimum,
Maximum, and Average of a List
of Numbers   170
5.3 Problem Solving: Repeating a
Program Body   176
Case Study: Multiple-Employee
Payroll Program   177
5.4 Control Structures: Nested
Loops   179
5.5 Data Structures: Subtypes of
Scalar Types   183
5.6 Tricks of the Trade: Debugging
and Testing Programs   193
5.7 System Structures: A Useful
Functions Package and the
Overloading Principle   195
5.8 System Structures: Introducing
Exception Handling   202
5.9 Tricks of the Trade: Common
Programming Errors   204
Chapter Review   204

6 Other Loop Forms; Procedures; Exception Handling   207

6.1 Control Structures: the WHILE
Statement   208
6.2 Problem Solving: Loop
Design   216

6.3 Problem Solving: Assertions and LOOP Invariants 225
Case Study: Money in the Bank 226
6.4 Control Structures: The General LOOP and EXIT Statements 230
6.5 System Structures: Robust Exception Handling 232
6.6 System Structures: Writing Simple Procedures 237
6.7 System Structures: A Package for Robust Input 247
6.8 Tricks of the Trade: Testing with Exception Handling 252
6.9 Tricks of the Trade: Common Programming Errors 252
Chapter Review 253

7 A Systematic Look at Scalar Data Types 259

7.1 Data Structures: Constant Declarations 260
7.2 Data Structures: Numeric Data Types 261
7.3 System Structures: Using an External Math Library: the USE Clause 274
Case Study: Approximating the Value of e 280
7.4 Data Structures: The Boolean Type 284
7.5 Data Structures: The Character Type 292
7.6 Case Study: Testing Whether a Number Is Prime 300
7.7 Control Structures: The CASE Statement 305
7.8 System Structures: A Package to Print a Number in Words 310
7.9 Case Study: Printing a Check in Words 315
7.10 Tricks of the Trade: Common

Programming Errors 318
Chapter Review 319

8 Composite Types: Records and Arrays 325

8.1 Data Structures: Record Types 326
8.2 Control Structures: Records as Operands and Parameters 331
8.3 System Structures: A Package for Calendar Dates 336
8.4 Data Structures: Hierarchical Records 340
8.5 Data Structures: Array Types 344
8.6 Problem Solving: Selecting Array Elements for Processing 351
8.7 Problem Solving: Using Arrays 357
Case Study: Home Budget Problem 357
8.8 Problem Solving: Reading Part of an Array 369
8.9 Data Structures: Arrays with Noninteger Subscripts 371
8.10 Data Structures: Strings in Ada 375
Case Study: Generating Cryptograms 381
8.11 Problem Solving: Searching and Sorting an Array 385
Case Study: Array Search 385
8.12 Case Study: Sorting an Array of Records 393
8.13 Tricks of the Trade: Common Programming Errors 398
Chapter Review 399

9 Programming in the Large: Procedural Abstraction 407

9.1 The Software Life Cycle 408
9.2 Problem Solving: Using

Abstraction to Manage
Complexity   410
9.3 Problem Solving: Refinement
Using Procedural
Abstraction   412
Case Study: A Mother's Day
Greeting   413
Case Study: General Sum
Problem   419
9.4 System Structures: Nested
Procedures and Scope of
Identifiers   424
9.5 Case Studies: Top-Down
Development   429
Case Study: Balancing a
Checkbook   429
Case Study: Summarizing the
Grades on an Exam   437
9.6 System Structures: A Systematic
View of Text Files   445
Case Study: A Histogram Plotting
Program   456
9.7 Tricks of the Trade: Debugging
a Program System   460
9.8 Tricks of the Trade: Common
Programming Errors   461
Chapter Review   462

10 Programming in the Large: Abstract Data Types   467

10.1 System Structures: Abstract Data
Types (ADTs)   468
10.2 System Structures: Using Package
Calendar as an ADT   473
Case Study: World Times   477
10.3 System Structures: Writing an
ADT for Calendar Dates   480
10.4 System Structures: Writing an
ADT for Rational Numbers   491
Case Study: Helping Your Cousin
with Fractions   492
10.5 System Structures: Writing an
ADT for Variable-Length
Strings   503

10.6 Case Study: Printing a Form
Letter—A Simple Mail
Merge   513
10.7 System Structures: Writing an
ADT for Employee Records   519
10.8 Case Study: Employee Inquiry
System   523
10.9 Tricks of the Trade: Common
Programming Errors   524
Chapter Review   525

11 Multidimensional Arrays and Variant Records   529

11.1 Data Structures:
Multidimensional Arrays   530
11.2 Problem Solving: Using
Multidimensional Arrays   536
11.3 Case Study: Analysis of Sales
Trends   539
11.4 Data Structures: Variant
Records   558
11.5 Case Study: Geometric
Figures   565
11.6 Case Study: Metric System   574
11.7 Tricks of the Trade: Common
Programming Errors   583
Chapter Review   583

12 Introduction to Unconstrained Array Types and Generics   589

12.1 Data Structures: Unconstrained
Array Types   590
12.2 Case Study: A General Sorting
Program   594
12.3 Case Study: Mathematical Vectors
and Matrices   599
12.4 System Structures: Generic
Units   605
12.5 Case Study: A Generic Sorting
Program   613

12.6 Case Study: A Generic Vector
Package 618
12.7 Tricks of the Trade: Common
Programming Errors 622
Chapter Review 622

13 Recursion 625

13.1 Problem Solving: The Nature of
Recursion 626
13.2 Tricks of the Trade: Tracing a
Recursive Function 631
13.3 Problem Solving: Recursive
Mathematical Functions 634
13.4 Problem Solving: More Recursive
Programs 638
Case Study: Printing an Array
Backward 639
Case Study: Displaying an Array
in Normal Order 641
Case Study: Discovering Whether
a String Is a Palindrome 644
13.5 Case Study: Towers of
Hanoi 647
13.6 Case Study: Picture Processing
with Recursion 651
13.7 Problem Solving: Recursive
Searching and Sorting 655
Case Study: Binary Search 656
Case Study: Recursive Selection
Sort 662
Case Study: QuickSort 664
13.8 Tricks of the Trade: Common
Programming Errors 670
Chapter Review 671

14 Dynamic Data
Structures 675

14.1 Data Structures: Access Types
and the NEW Operator 676
14.2 Data Structures: Linked
Lists 685
14.3 Problem Solving: Specification of
a Keyed-Table Abstract Data
Type 691
14.4 Data Structures: Implementing
the Keyed Table as a One-Way
Linked List 696
14.5 Case Study: Airline Passenger
List 705
14.6 Data Structures: Multiple-Linked
Lists and Trees 710
14.7 Data Structures: Reimplementing
the Keyed Table as a Search
Tree 716
14.8 Tricks of the Trade: Common
Programming Errors 722
Chapter Review 723

Appendixes

A The Ada Character Set, Delimiters,
and Reserved Words 727
B The Ada Syntax Charts 731
C The Ada Predefined Language
Environment 769
D Specification of the Package
Text_IO 775
E Ada Hints for Pascal Users 781
F Summary of Ada Execution-Time
Exceptions 785

Index 787

Introduction to Computers and Programming

1

1.1 Electronic Computers Then and Now
1.2 Components of a Computer
1.3 The Art and Science of Problem Solving
1.4 The Software Development Method
1.5 Programming Languages
1.6 Processing a High-Level Language Program
1.7 Using the Computer
Chapter Review

I n this chapter, we introduce computers and computer programming. We begin with a brief history of computers and a description of the major components of a computer, including memory, central processor, input devices, and output devices. We also discuss how information is represented in a computer and how it is manipulated.

You are about to begin the study of programming using one of the richest and most interesting programming languages available today: the Ada language. This chapter begins a discussion of the main topics of this book: problem solving, programming, and Ada. We first discuss problem solving with a computer. Then languages for computer programming are described. Finally, we describe the process for creating a program and the roles performed by special programs that are part of a computer system. These programs include the operating system, compiler, editor, and loader.

1.1 Electronic Computers Then and Now

It is difficult to live in today's world without having some contact with computers. Computers are used to provide instructional material in schools, to print transcripts, to send out bills, to reserve airline and concert tickets, to play games, and to help authors write books. Several kinds of computers cooperate in dispensing cash from an automatic teller machine; "embedded" or "hidden" computers help control the ignitions, fuel systems, and transmissions of modern automobiles; at the supermarket, a computer device reads the bar codes on the packages you buy, to total your purchase and help manage the store's inventory. Even a microwave oven has a special-purpose computer built into it.

However, it wasn't always this way. Computers as we know them did not exist at all before the late 1930s, and as recently as the early 1970s, computers were fairly mysterious devices that only a small percentage of our population knew much about. Computer "know-how" turned around when advances in solid-state electronics led to cuts in the size and cost of electronic computers. Today, a personal computer (see Fig. 1.1) that costs less than $3000 and sits on a desk has as much computational power as one that 10 years ago cost more than $100,000 and filled a 9 × 12 room. This price reduction is even more remarkable when we consider the effects of inflation over the last decade. Indeed it is said that if the development of automobiles had progressed at the same rate as that of computers, a luxurious car would cost only a few dollars and travel as fast as the Space Shuttle.

If we take the literal definition for *computer* as a device for counting or computing, then the abacus might be considered the first computer. However, the first electronic digital computer was designed in the late 1930s by Dr. John Atanasoff at the University of Iowa. Atanasoff designed his computer to perform mathematical computations for graduate students.

The first large-scale, general-purpose electronic digital computer, called the ENIAC, was built in 1946 at the University of Pennsylvania with funding

Figure 1.1   IBM Personal Computer with Mouse

supplied by the U.S. Army. The ENIAC was used for computing ballistics tables, for weather prediction, and for atomic energy calculations. The ENIAC weighed 30 tons and occupied a space 30 × 50 feet (see Fig. 1.2).

   Although we are often led to believe otherwise, computers cannot reason as we do. They are basically devices for performing computations at incredible speeds (more than 1 million operations per second) and with great accuracy. However, in order to accomplish anything useful, a computer must be *programmed*, or given a sequence of explicit instructions (the *program*) to carry out.

   To program the ENIAC hundreds of wires and thousands of switches had to be connected in a certain way. In 1946, Dr. John von Neumann of Princeton University proposed the concept of a *stored-program computer*, in which the instructions of a program would be stored in computer memory rather than be set by wires and switches. Because the contents of computer memory can be changed easily, it would not be nearly as difficult to reprogram this computer to perform different tasks as it was to reprogram the ENIAC. Von Neumann's design is the basis of the digital computer as we know it today.

Brief History of Computers

Table 1.1 lists some of the important milestones along the path from the abacus to modern-day electronic computers. We often use the term *first generation* to refer to electronic computers that used vacuum tubes (1939–1958). The *second generation* began in 1958 with the changeover to transistors. The *third generation* began in 1964 with the introduction of integrated circuits. The *fourth generation* began in 1975 with the advent of large-scale integration. Since then, change has come so rapidly that we don't seem to be counting generations anymore. How-

Figure 1.2 The ENIAC Computer (photo courtesy of Unisys Corporation)

Table 1.1 Milestones in the Development of Computers and Programming
Languages

Date	Event
2000 B.C.	The abacus is first used for computations.
1642 A.D.	Blaise Pascal, in France, creates a mechanical adding machine for tax computations. It is unreliable.
1670	In Germany, Gottfried von Leibniz creates a more reliable adding machine, which adds, subtracts, multiplies, divides, and calculates square roots.
1842	Charles Babbage, in England, designs an analytical engine to perform general calculations automatically. Ada Byron, daughter of the poet Lord Byron and known later as Lady Lovelace, assists him in programming this machine.
1890	Herman Hollerith designs a system to record and tabulate data for the decennial U.S. census. The information is stored as holes on cards which are interpreted by machines with electrical sensors. Hollerith starts a company that will eventually become IBM.
1939	John Atanasoff at the University of Iowa, with graduate student Clifford Berry, designs and builds the first digital computer. His project was funded by a grant for $650.
1946	J. Presper Eckert and John Mauchly design and build the Electronic Numerical Integrator and Calculator (ENIAC) at the University of Pennsylvania. It used 18,000 vacuum tubes and cost $500,000 to build.

Table 1.1 *continued*

5

1.1 Electronic
Computers Then
and Now

Date	Event
1946	John von Neumann, at Princeton, proposes that a program be stored in a computer in the same form that data are stored. His proposal, called "von Neumann architecture," is still the basis of most modern computers.
1951	Eckert and Mauchly build the first general-purpose commercial computer, the UNIVAC.
1957	John Backus and his team at IBM complete the first FORTRAN compiler. This is a milestone in the development of programming languages.
1958	The first computer to use the transistor as a switching device, the IBM 7090, is introduced.
1958	Seymour Cray builds the first fully transistorized computer, the CDC 1604, for Control Data Corporation.
1964	The first computer using integrated circuits, the IBM 360, is announced.
1971	The Pascal programming language is introduced by Niklaus Wirth of the Technical University of Zurich.
1975	The first microcomputer, the Altair, is introduced.
1975	The first supercomputer, the Cray-1, is announced.
1975	The U.S. Department of Defense High-Order Language Working Group (HOLWG) is created to find a solution to the DoD's "software crisis." The group's efforts culminate in the adoption of Ada.
1976	Digital Equipment Corporation introduces its popular minicomputer, the VAX 11/780.
1977	Steve Wozniak and Steve Jobs begin producing Apple computers in a garage.
1977	Radio Shack announces the TRS-80, one of the first fully packaged microcomputers to be sold in retail stores, in time for the Christmas season.
1978	Dan Bricklin and Bob Frankston develop the first electronic spreadsheet, called VisiCalc, for the Apple computer.
1979	The preliminary specification of Ada is published by the U.S. government.
1981	IBM introduces the IBM Personal Computer. The business world now acknowledges that microcomputers are "real."
1982	Sun Microsystems introduces its first workstation, the Sun 100.
1983	The Ada language standard is adopted by the government and by the American National Standards Institute (ANSI).
1984	Apple introduces the Macintosh, the first widely available computer with a "graphical user interface" using icons, windows, and a mouse device.
1987	Ada is adopted as an international standard by the International Standards Organization (ISO).
1990	Over 200 different Ada compilers have been validated. Compilers—all handling the same Ada language—are readily available for all categories of computers from laptops to supercomputers.

ever, the late 1970s saw the beginning of the "personal computer revolution" with computers that individuals and families could afford being sold at retail in computer stores.

Categories of Computers

Modern-day computers are classified according to their size and speed. The three major categories of computers are microcomputers, minicomputers, and mainframes.

Many of you have seen or used *microcomputers* such as the IBM Personal Computer (see Fig. 1.1) or the Apple Macintosh (see Fig. 1.3). Microcomputers are also called personal computers because they are usually used by one person at a time and are small enough to fit on or next to a desk. The largest microcomputers, called *workstations* (see Fig. 1.4) are commonly used by engineers to produce engineering drawings and to assist in the design and development of new products. The smallest general-purpose microcomputers are often called *laptops* because they are small enough to fit into a briefcase and are often used on one's lap in an airplane.

Often the term *embedded computer* is used to refer to a computer, usually a microcomputer, built into a larger system and not operated directly by a human user. Embedded computers are found in automobiles, teller machines, cash registers, and so on.

Figure 1.3 Apple Macintosh Computer with Mouse

Figure 1.4 Sun Microsystems Workstation (photo courtesy of Sun Microsystems, Inc.)

Minicomputers are the next larger variety of computers. They generally operate at faster speeds than microcomputers and can store larger quantities of information. Minicomputers can serve several different users simultaneously. The computer you will use to solve problems for the course you are taking might well be a minicomputer—for example, a VAX computer from Digital Equipment Corporation. A small- or medium-sized company might use a minicomputer to perform payroll computations and keep track of its inventory. Engineers often use minicomputers to control a chemical plant or a production process.

The largest computers are called *mainframes.* A large company, government agency, or university would have one or more mainframes at its central computing facility. Mainframes are often used as "number crunchers" to generate solutions to systems of equations that characterize an engineering or scientific problem. A mainframe can solve in seconds equations that might take hours to solve on a minicomputer, days on a microcomputer, or years with a hand calculator. The largest mainframes, called *supercomputers,* are used to solve the most complex systems of equations.

This book was written using an Apple Macintosh microcomputer; the programs were tested on an IBM Personal Computer, a Sun workstation, and a Hewlett-Packard minicomputer.

1.2 Components of a Computer

Despite large variation in cost, size, and capabilities, modern computers are remarkably similar in a number of ways. Basically, a computer consists of the five components shown in Fig. 1.5. The arrows connecting the components show the direction of information flow.

All information that is to be processed by a computer must first be entered into the computer memory via an input device. The information in memory is manipulated by the central processor unit (CPU), and the results of this manipulation are stored in memory. Information in memory can be displayed through an output device. A secondary storage device is often used for storing large quantities of information in a semipermanent form.

Many of you have seen or used a personal computer (see Figs. 1.1 and 1.3). The memory, CPU, and secondary storage devices are usually housed in a single cabinet. The input device is a keyboard, and the output device is a televisionlike monitor or screen. These components and their interaction are described in more detail in the following sections.

Figure 1.5 Components of a Computer

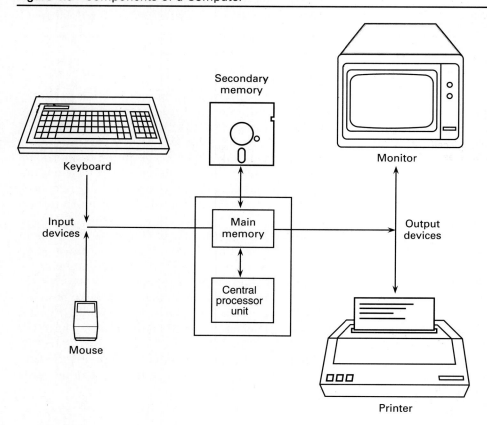

Main Memory

Main memory is used for storing information and programs. All types of information—numbers, names, lists, and even pictures—can be represented and stored in main memory.

The memory of a computer can be pictured as an ordered sequence of storage locations called *memory cells*. To be able to store and retrieve (access) information, there must be some way to identify the individual memory cells. To accomplish this, each memory cell has associated with it a unique *address*, which indicates its relative position in memory. Figure 1.6 shows a computer memory consisting of 1000 memory cells with addresses 0 through 999. Today's personal computers often have around 1 million individual cells; larger computers typically have memories consisting of many millions of cells.

The information stored in a memory cell is called the *contents* of a memory cell. Every memory cell always contains some information, although we may have no idea what that information is. Whenever new information is placed in a memory cell, any information already there is destroyed and can no longer be retrieved. In Fig. 1.6, the contents of memory cell 3 is the number − 26, and the contents of memory cell 4 is the letter H.

Figure 1.6 A Computer Memory with 1000 Cells

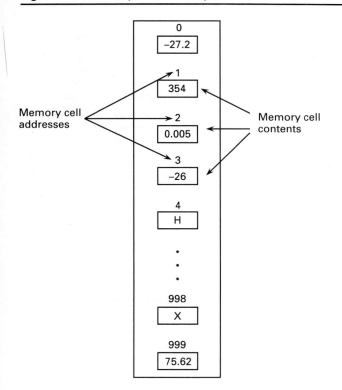

The memory cells shown in Fig. 1.6 are actually aggregates of smaller units called *bytes*. A byte is the amount of storage required to store a single character. The number of bytes in a memory cell depends on the kind of information stored in that cell and varies from computer to computer. A byte is an aggregate of an even smaller unit of storage called a bit; a *bit* is a single binary digit (0 or 1). In most common computers there are eight bits to a byte.

Each value stored in memory is represented by a particular pattern of 0s and 1s. To store a value, the computer sets each bit of a selected memory cell to 0 or 1, thereby destroying what was previously in that bit. Each value is represented by a particular pattern of 0s and 1s. To retrieve a value from a memory cell, the computer copies the pattern of 0s and 1s stored in that cell to another storage area, the *memory buffer register,* where the bit pattern can be processed. The copy operation does not destroy the bit pattern currently in the memory cell. The process described above is the same regardless of the kind of information—character, number, or program instruction—stored in a memory cell.

Central Processor Unit

The *central processor unit* (CPU) performs the actual processing or manipulation of information stored in memory. The CPU can retrieve information from memory. This information can be either data or instructions for manipulating data. The CPU can also store the results of these manipulations back in memory for later use.

The CPU coordinates all activities of the computer. It determines which operations should be carried out and in what order; the control unit then transmits coordinating control signals to the computer components. The CPU also performs a variety of arithmetic operations, including addition, subtraction, multiplication, and division. These arithmetic operations are performed on data that are stored in memory; the computational results are then saved in memory. A typical CPU can perform each arithmetic operation in about 1 millionth of a second. The CPU can also compare information; the operations that are carried out may depend on the results of the comparison.

Input and Output Devices

The manipulative capability of the computer would be of little use to us if we were unable to communicate with the computer. Specifically, we must be able to enter data for a computation into memory. Later, the computational results that are stored in memory can be displayed.

Most of you will be using a *keyboard* (see Fig. 1.7) as an input device and a *monitor* or *display screen* as an output device. A computer keyboard resembles a typewriter keyboard except that it has some extra keys for performing special functions. On the keyboard shown in Fig. 1.7, the row of keys at the top (labeled F1 through F12) are *function keys*. The function performed by each of these keys depends on the program that is executing.

A monitor is similar to a television screen. Some monitors have graphics

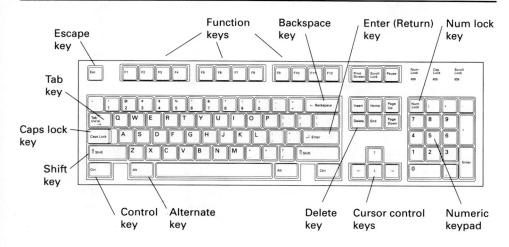

capability (see Fig. 1.3), which enables the output to be displayed as a two-dimensional graph or picture, not just as rows of letters and numbers.

Another common input device is a *mouse* (see Fig. 1.3). A mouse is used to move an electronic pointer called a *cursor* around the screen. The computer user can select an operation pictured on the screen by clicking a button on the mouse when the cursor is over that item.

If you are using a personal computer to develop programs, the keyboard and/or monitor may be built into the computer or connected to it by cables. If you are using a minicomputer or mainframe, you will be communicating with it using a terminal connected to it by a cable or telephone line. The terminal may be a "dumb terminal"—one without its own general-purpose CPU or memory—or a personal computer running a "terminal emulator" program.

The only problem with using a monitor as an output device is that there is no written record of the computation. Once the image disappears from the monitor screen it is lost. If you want *hard-copy* output, then you have to send your computational results to an output device called a *printer* (see Fig. 1.8).

Secondary Memory

Most computers have a limited amount of main memory. Consequently, *secondary memory* provides additional storage capability on most computer systems. For example, a *disk drive,* which stores data on a disk, is a common secondary storage device for today's computers.

There are two kinds of disks: *hard disks* and *floppy disks* (sometimes called *diskettes*); a computer may have one or more drives of each kind. A hard disk cannot normally be removed from its drive, so the storage area on a hard disk is often shared by all users of a computer. On the other hand, each computer user may have his or her own floppy disks that can be inserted in a disk drive as needed. Hard disks can store much more data than floppy disks and operate

Figure 1.8 Printer

much more quickly, but they are also much more expensive. Floppy disks are called "floppy" because the actual recording surface is a flexible piece of magnetically coated plastic; floppy disks are commonly encased in a hard plastic outer shell to protect them from damage (see Fig. 1.9).

Many types of information can be stored on disk, for example, a term paper, a computer program, payroll data from a business, or data from earthquake seismic readings taken by a research center. Each of these collections of information is called a *file*. You must give a file a unique name when you first store it on a disk, so that you can retrieve the file at a later date.

Comparison of Main and Secondary Memory

Main memory is much faster and more expensive than secondary memory. For example, a typical 3.5″ floppy disk holds approximately one megabyte (1 million bytes) of data and costs a dollar or two. The equivalent amount of main memory costs, at this writing, $50 to $100. A typical personal-computer hard disk will store 20 to 100 megabytes and cost at least a few hundred dollars.

The CPU normally transfers data between secondary memory and main memory; it manipulates the data in main memory only. Data in main memory are *volatile*: They disappear when you reset or switch off the computer. Data in secondary memory are *nonvolatile:* They do not disappear when the computer is switched off and are magnetically "erased" only by a program operating under an explicit command from the user. You can remove a floppy disk from

Figure 1.9   Inserting a Floppy Disk into a Disk Drive

the computer and set it aside for later use; the data will remain on the disk until explicitly erased.

Exercises for Section 1.2

Self-Check

1. What are the contents of memory cells 0 and 999 in Fig. 1.6? What memory cells contain the letter X and the fraction 0.005?
2. Explain the purpose of the memory, central processor, and the disk drive and disk. What input and output devices will be used with your computer?

 # 1.3   The Art and Science of Problem Solving

You must be able to solve problems in order to succeed in academics and in the real world. Problem-solving ability is a combination of art and science. The art of problem solving is the transformation of an English description of a problem into a form that permits a mechanical solution. A relatively straightforward example of this process is transforming an algebra word problem into a set of algebraic equations that can then be solved for one or more unknowns.

In the real world, this process is more difficult because problem descriptions are often incomplete, imprecise, or ambiguous. The successful problem solver must be able to ask the right questions in order to clarify the problem and obtain any information missing from the problem statement (this process is called *problem specification*). Next, the problem solver analyzes the problem and attempts to extract its essential features, identifying what is provided (the *problem inputs*) and what is required (the *problem outputs*). The problem solver must also be able to determine whether there are any *constraints* or *simplifying assumptions* that can be applied to facilitate the problem solution. We often cannot solve the most general case of a problem but must make some realistic assumptions that limit or constrain the problem so that it can be solved.

The science part of problem solving involves knowledge of the problem environment, knowledge of the formulas or equations that characterize the environment, and the ability to apply and manipulate these formulas. Using this knowledge, the problem solver develops a series of steps whose successful completion will lead to the problem solution. Once the solution is obtained, the problem solver must verify its accuracy by comparing the computed results with observed results.

1.4 The Software Development Method

Students in many subject areas receive instruction in specific problem-solving methods. For example, business students are encouraged to follow a *systems approach* to problem solving; engineering and science students are encouraged to follow the *engineering and scientific method*. Although these problem-solving methods are associated with very different fields of study, their essential ingredients are quite similar. We will describe one such method below.

This book is concerned with a particular kind of problem solving, namely, developing solutions that use computers to get results. We mentioned earlier that a computer cannot think; therefore, in order to get it to do any useful work, we must provide a computer with a program that is a list of instructions. Programming a computer is a lot more involved than simply writing a list of instructions. Problem solving is an important component of programming. Before we can write a program to solve a particular problem, we must consider carefully all aspects of the problem and then organize its solution.

The collection of programs that runs on a computer is referred to as *software,* as opposed to the term *hardware*, which refers to the collection of physical devices that comprises the computer itself. A *software developer* is somone who is involved with the design and implementation of reliable software systems. This title emphasizes the fact that programmers, like engineers, are concerned with developing practical, reliable solutions to problems. However, the product produced by a software developer is a software system, rather than a physical system.

To highlight the analogy with engineering, some people refer to this method as "software engineering" and to software developers as "software engineers." To emphasize the fact that one need not be an actual engineer or even an engineering student to develop good software, we use instead the terms "software development" and "software developer" in this book.

Steps in the Software Development Method

1. *Requirements specification*—State the problem and gain a clear understanding of what is required for its solution. This sounds easy, but it can be the most critical part of problem solving. A good problem solver must be able to recognize and define the problem precisely. If the problem is not totally defined, you must study the problem carefully, eliminating the aspects that are unimportant and zeroing in on the root problem.
2. *Analysis*—Identify problem inputs, desired outputs, and any additional requirements or constraints on the solution. Identify what information is supplied as problem data and what results should be computed and displayed. Also, determine the required form and units in which the results should be displayed (for example, as a table with specific column headings).
3. *Design*—Develop a list of steps (called an *algorithm*) to solve the problem, and verify that the algorithm solves the problem as intended. Writing the algorithm is often the most difficult part of the problem-solving process. Once you have the algorithm, you should verify that it is correct before proceeding further.
4. *Implementation or coding*—Implement the algorithm as a program. This requires knowledge of a particular programming language. Each algorithm step must be converted into a statement in that programming language.
5. *Testing*—Test the completed program, and verify that it works as expected. Don't rely on just one test case, but run the program using several different sets of data.

The first three steps in the list above are most critical; if they are not done properly you will either solve the wrong problem or produce an awkward, inefficient solution. To perform these steps successfully, it is most important that you read the problem statement carefully before attempting to solve it. You may need to read each problem statement two or three times. The first time, you should get a general idea of what is being asked. The second time, you should try to answer the questions:

What information should the solution provide?
What data do I have to work with?

The answer to the first question will tell you the desired results, or the *problem outputs*. The answer to the second question will tell you the data provided, or the *problem inputs*. It may be helpful to underline the phrases in the problem statement that identify the inputs and outputs.

As indicated above, the design phase is often the most difficult part of the problem-solving process. When you write an algorithm, you should first list the major steps of the problem that need to be solved (called *subproblems*). Don't try to list each and every step imaginable; instead, concentrate on the overall strategy. Once you have the list of subproblems, you can attack each one individually, in this way adding detail or *refining the algorithm*. The process of solving a problem by breaking it up into its smaller subproblems, called *divide and conquer*, is a basic strategy for all kinds of problem-solving activities.

The software development method can be used with any actual programming language; indeed, only the implementation phase really requires detailed knowledge of a language or a particular computer. Even the testing phase is, in industry, often carried out by individuals who do not know programming but specialize in developing good tests of programs.

 ## 1.5 Programming Languages

Writing a computer program requires knowing a system of instructions for the computer. There are many such systems; these have come to be called *programming languages*. Like human languages (often called *natural languages* by computer people), programming languages have vocabularies—or sets of acceptable words—and grammars—or rules for combining words into larger units analogous to sentences and paragraphs.

There is an important distinction between programming languages and natural languages. Because a person can think, he or she can understand or "make sense" of another person's communication, even if the second person's grammar or usage is poor. Because a computer cannot think, it is far less tolerant of a programmer's poor grammar or usage and will usually stop and refuse to proceed until the errors are corrected. This is not as difficult as it may seem: Although natural languages grew over many centuries and are filled with irregularities and strange constructions, programming languages were *designed* by humans expressly to be consistent and regular and are therefore easier to learn and use than natural languages.

Categories of Programming Languages

There are many different programming languages, which fall into three broad categories: machine, assembly, and high-level languages. High-level languages (also called high-order languages, mostly by the U.S. government) are most often used by *programmers* (program writers). One reason for the popularity of high-level languages is that they are much easier to use than machine and assembly languages. Another reason is that a high-level language program is *portable*. This means that it can be executed with little or no modification on many different types of computers. An assembly-language or machine-language program, on the other hand, can execute on only one type of computer.

Some common high-level languages are BASIC, FORTRAN, COBOL, Pascal, C, and Ada. Each of these languages was designed with a specific purpose in mind. FORTRAN is an acronym for FORmula TRANslation, and its principal users have been engineers and scientists. BASIC (Beginners All-purpose Symbolic Instructional Code) was designed in the 1960s to be learned and used easily by students. COBOL (COmmon Business Oriented Language) is used primarily for business data-processing operations. Pascal (named for Blaise Pascal) was designed in the early 1970s as a language for teaching programming. C (whose developers designed B first) combines the power of an assembly language with the ease of use and portability of a high-level language. Ada, the language of this book, was named for Ada Lovelace, the nineteenth-century Englishwoman often credited with being the first programmer. In Chapter 2 we discuss the origins and history of both Ada the person and Ada the language.

One of the most important features of high-level languages is that they allow us to write program statements that resemble English or everyday mathematics. We can reference data that are stored in memory using descriptive names (e.g., Name, Rate) rather than numeric memory cell addresses. We can also describe operations that we would like performed using familiar symbols. For example, in several high-level languages the statement

```
Price = Cost + Profit
```

means add Cost to Profit and store the result in Price.

We can also use descriptive names to reference data in assembly language; however, we must specify more explicitly the operations to be performed on the data. The high-level language statement above might be written as

```
LOAD Cost
ADD Profit
STORE Price
```

in an assembly language.

Machine language is the native tongue of a computer. Each machine language instruction is a *binary string* (string of 0s and 1s) that specifies an operation and the memory cells involved in the operation. The assembly language statements above might be written as

```
0010 0000 0000 0100
0100 0000 0000 0101
0011 0000 0000 0110
```

in a machine language. Obviously, what is easiest for a computer to understand is most difficult for a person to understand and vice versa.

A computer can execute only programs that are in machine language. Consequently, a high-level language program must be translated into machine language before it can be executed. This process is described in the next section.

Exercise for Section 1.5

Self-Check

1. What do you think the high-level language statements below mean?

```
X := A + B + C
X := Y / Z
D := C - B + A
```

1.6 Processing a High-Level Language Program

Before it can be processed, a high-level language program must be entered at the terminal. The program will be stored on disk as a file called the *source file* (see Fig. 1.10). An *editor program* is used to enter and save the program.

Once the source file is saved, it must be translated into machine language. A *compiler* program processes the source file and attempts to translate each statement. Often, one or more statements in the source file will contain a *syntax error*. This means that these statements do not correspond exactly to the syntax (grammar rules) of the high-level language. In this case, the compiler will cause some error messages to be displayed.

At this point, you can make changes to your source file and have the compiler process it again. If there are no more errors, the compiler will create an *object file,* which is your program translated into machine language. The object file and any additional object files (e.g., programs for input and output operations) that may be needed by your program are combined into a *load file* or *executable image* by the *linker* program (in Ada, the linker program is often called the *binder* program). Finally the load file is placed into memory by the *loader* program and executed. The editor, compiler, linker (or binder), and loader programs are part of your computer system. This process is shown in Fig. 1.10.

Executing a Program

To execute a program, the computer control unit must examine each program instruction in memory and send out the command signals required to carry out the instruction. Normally, the instructions are executed in sequence; however, as we will see later it is possible to have the control unit skip over some instructions or execute some instructions more than once. During execution, data can be entered into memory and manipulated in some specified way. Then, the result of this data manipulation will be displayed.

Figure 1.11 shows the effect of executing a payroll program stored in memory. The first step of the program requires entering data into memory that describe the employee. In the second step, the employee data are manipulated by the central processor and the results of computations are stored in memory. In the final step, the computational results may be displayed as payroll reports or employee payroll checks. An example of a program that does this is provided in Chapter 2.

Portability and Compiler Standards

Each high-level language has a language *standard,* which is a document, agreed to by the community of language users and compiler developers, that describes the form and meaning of all its statements. Some languages (Pascal especially) have "dialects," or compiler versions that make additional features available that are not part of the standard. To make a program portable, a programmer must be careful to use only those features that are part of the standard.

Happily, this is easier with Ada than with many other languages, because the standard for Ada is a particularly strong one: Dialects are not allowed, and

Figure 1.10 Preparing a Program for Execution

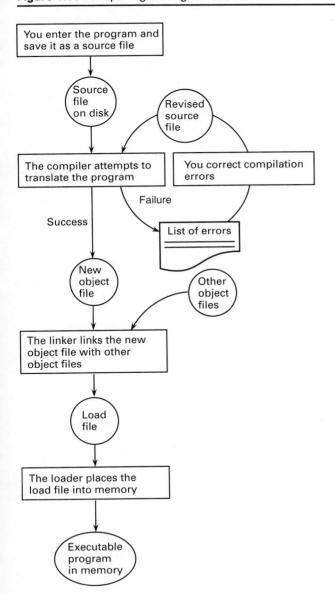

Figure 1.11   Flow of Information during Program Execution

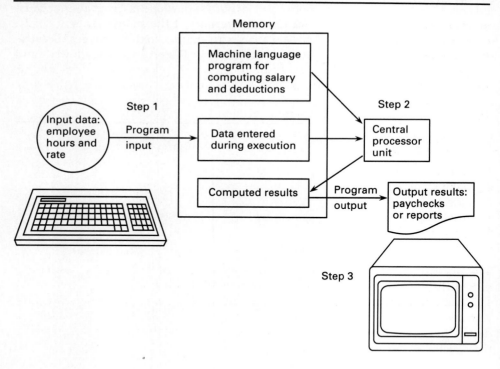

an Ada compiler is subjected to a strenuous set of tests (called *validation tests*) specified by the U.S. Government. Language differences from one Ada compiler to another are so few as to be noticeable only to a very knowledgeable user of Ada (more on this in Chapter 2).

Exercises for Section 1.6

Self-Check

1. What is the role of a compiler? What is a syntax error? In which file would a syntax error be found?
2. What is the difference between the source file and the object file? Which do you create and which does the compiler create? Which one is processed by the linker? What does the loader do?

1.7 Using the Computer

The mechanics of entering a program as a source file and translating and executing it differ somewhat from system to system, although the general process is the same. In this section we describe this general process.

Operating Systems

Some of you will be using a timeshared computer. In this environment many users are connected by terminals to one large, central computer, and all users share the central facilities.

Many of you will be using a personal computer. A personal computer is a smaller, desktop computer that is used by one individual at a time. Regardless of what computer you are using, it will be necessary to interact with a supervisory program within the computer called the operating system. In timeshared computers, it is the responsibility of the operating system to allocate the central resources among many users. Some tasks of the operating system are

1. validating the user's identification and password;
2. making the editor, compiler, or loader available to users;
3. allocating memory and processor time;
4. providing input and output facilities;
5. retrieving needed files; and
6. saving new files that are created.

The operating system on a personal computer performs these tasks as well; the only difference is that often there is no user validation.

Each computer has its own special control language for communicating with its operating system. Although space does not allow us to provide all the details here, we will discuss the general process. Your instructor will provide the specific commands for your system.

Creating a Program or Data File

In order to use an interactive system, it is first necessary to "boot up" a personal computer or "log on" to a timeshared computer. Once you have accomplished one of these tasks, you can begin to create your program.

In most cases, you will use a special program called an editor to enter your Ada program. An *editor* is a program that is used to create and modify program and data files. After accessing the editor, you can start to enter a new Ada program. Once your program is entered, you must save the program as a permanent file on disk. Follow these steps to create and save a program file:

1. log onto a timeshared computer or boot up a personal computer;
2. access the editor program;
3. indicate that you are creating a new file and specify its name;
4. enter each line of your program; and
5. save your program as a permanent file in secondary memory.

Once your program is created and you are satisfied that each line is entered correctly, you can attempt to compile, link (or bind), load, and execute it. Ada usually requires that before you can use the compiler for the first time, you must set up a library. The command to do this depends on the specific compiler, and it is not repeated each time you log on or boot up. The Ada system will create some files or directories on your diskette or file system; they are for use by the compiler and linker, and you should not disturb them!

In any event, if your program will not compile because it contains syntax errors, you will have to edit it to eliminate the syntax errors before going further. To accomplish this you will have to access the editor again, retrieve your program file, make the necessary changes to the Ada program, save the modified program file, and attempt to recompile. Follow these steps to correct and reexecute a program file:

1. reaccess the editor program;
2. get your program file;
3. correct the statements with syntax errors;
4. save your edited program file; and
5. compile, link (or bind), load, and execute the new program file.

A First Ada Program

Now that you have read about the steps in creating, compiling, and executing a program file, you probably want to try one. After getting the detailed instructions for using your class computer, operating system, and Ada compiler, try the program given in Program 1.1. Do not be concerned at this point about what each of the statements in this program means; just enter it exactly as given and take it from there. When the program is executed, the following line should appear on your display screen:

```
Hello there. We hope you enjoy studying Ada!
```

Program 1.1   A First Ada Program

```
WITH Text_IO;
PROCEDURE Hello IS

BEGIN

   Text_IO.Put (Item => "Hello there. ");
   Text_IO.Put (Item => "We hope you enjoy studying Ada!");
   Text_IO.New_Line;

END Hello;
```

 Chapter Review

This chapter described the basic components of a computer: main and secondary memory, the central processor or CPU, and the input and output devices. Remember these important facts about computers:

1. A memory cell is never empty, but its initial contents may be meaningless to your program.

2. The current contents of a memory cell are destroyed whenever new information is placed in that cell.
3. A program must be copied into the memory of the computer before it can be executed.
4. Data cannot be manipulated by the computer until they are first read into memory.
5. A computer cannot think for itself; you must use a programming language to instruct it in a precise and unambiguous manner to perform a task.
6. Programming a computer can be fun—if you are patient, organized, and careful.

✓ *Quick-Check Exercises*

1. The _____ translates a _____ language program into _____.
2. After a program is executed, all program results are automatically displayed. True or false?
3. Specify the correct order for these four operations: execution, linking, translation, loading.
4. A high-level language program is saved on disk as a _____ file or a _____ file.
5. The _____ finds syntax errors in the _____ file.
6. A machine-language program is saved on disk as an _____ file.
7. The _____ is used to create and save the source file.
8. The _____ creates the load file.
9. The _____ program is used to place the _____ file into memory.
10. Computers are becoming (more/less) expensive and (bigger/smaller) in size.
11. The first large-scale, general-purpose electronic computer was called the _____. It (was/was not) a stored-program computer.

Answers to Quick-Check Exercises

1. compiler, high-level, machine language
2. false
3. translation, linking, loading, execution
4. source, program
5. compiler, source
6. object
7. editor
8. linker
9. loader, load
10. less, smaller
11. ENIAC, was not

Review Questions for Chapter 1

1. List at least three types of information stored in a computer.
2. List two functions of the CPU.
3. List two input/output devices and two secondary storage devices.
4. A computer can think. True or false?
5. List the three categories of programming languages.
6. Give three advantages of programming in a high-level language such as Ada.
7. What processes are needed to transform an Ada program to a machine-language program ready for execution?
8. List the five phases in the software development method. Which phases require actual use of a computer?

Introduction to Ada

2

2.1 About Ada

2.2 The "Look" of Ada Programs

2.3 System Structures: Tailoring the Text_IO Packages for Numerical Values

2.4 Problem Solving: Software Development Illustrated

2.5 Data Structures: Declaring Constants and Variables

2.6 System Structures: General Form of an Ada Program

2.7 Control Structures: Assignment Statements

2.8 Control Structures: Input/Output Statements

2.9 Programs in Memory

2.10 Data Structures: Introduction to Data Types and Expressions

2.11 Tricks of the Trade: Common Programming Errors

Chapter Review

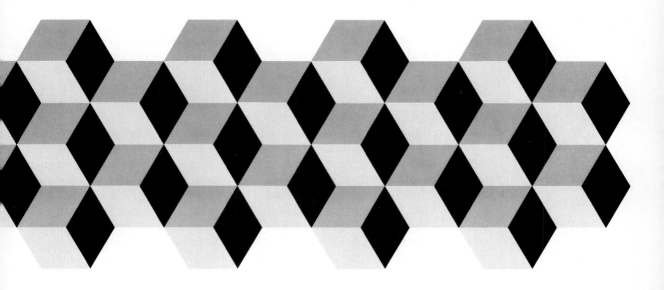

Programming is a problem-solving activity. This means that if you are a good problem solver, you are likely to become a good programmer. Therefore, one important goal of this book is to help you improve your problem-solving ability. We believe that it is beneficial to approach each programming problem in a systematic and consistent way. In this chapter we show you how to apply the software development method introduced in Chapter 1.

In this chapter we also introduce the programming language Ada, starting with a brief discussion of Ada's history and strongest attributes. You will learn a bit about the three important categories of structures in a programming language—*data structures, control structures,* and *system structures*—and examine a few simple Ada programs, applying our software development method along the way.

2.1 About Ada

Ada was developed in the late 1970s and early 1980s at the direction of the United States Department of Defense (DoD). Although it seems hard to believe, in the mid-seventies there were *several hundred languages* in use in defense-oriented computer systems. DoD determined that the use of a modern and strongly standardized programming language might result in more reliable and portable software at lower cost to the taxpayer, and therefore organized a competition for the best design of a new language for its needs.

The result of this competition was a language rich in capabilities for building software systems for general as well as defense purposes. The capabilities of Ada can be organized in a way similar to the way sections are titled in chapters of this book:

- *Control structures* are those structures which allow the programmer to instruct the computer precisely which operations to carry out in which order. Control structures control the sequencing of a program: unconditional sequencing, selection of one or more alternative paths, and repetition or *looping.* In this book you will study all the important control structures of Ada.
- *Data structures* provide ways to organize data—numbers, letters, sequences of letters, records, and other groupings—so that they can be processed by the control structures of the program. Most of the data structures—*scalar types, records,* and *arrays*—of Ada are presented in this book.
- *System structures* provide ways to organize control structures and data structures into units of appropriate size, so that systems of programs can be built reliably and without great difficulty. *Procedures* and *functions* allow grouping of data and control statements into small, cohesive units; *packages* allow procedures, functions, and other resources such as data type declarations, to be organized into larger units or *modules* so that they can be put in libraries for you and others to use in many applications. We consider *exception handling* to be a system structure because exception handling provides a standard way to control the flow of error information from one part of a system to another.

The facilities of Ada also include *tasking*—a powerful capability for building *concurrent programs* (programs containing segments that execute, or appear to execute, simultaneously)—and *representation specifications*—which explicitly associate high-level constructs with the lowest levels of the computer hardware. These two topics are advanced and are not covered in this book; you will learn about them as you continue your education in this interesting language.

The Ada Standard

A *standard* is a document describing a common way to do or build something. Engineering standards developed early in the twentieth century covered the sizes and shapes of mechanical fasteners like nuts and bolts. The ability to attach a nut from one manufacturer to a bolt from another was an important advance in the industrial revolution; the automobile industry owes much of the success of mass production to standards.

In the computer industry, standards have governed the formulation and dimensions of physical media like punched cards and magnetic tape; as computer software has grown and matured since the 1940s, so has the industry's attention to standards for programming languages. A language standard describes the structure of valid and invalid programs in the language and therefore serves as a defining document for users and compiler writers alike.

Some language standards are voluntary and represent a "lowest common denominator" subset of the language facilities. The "subset" nature of these standards makes it difficult to move a program from one compiler to another, even if both theoretically accept the same language. The Ada standard is an exception to this rule: DoD, in the interest of encouraging programs to be written in a truly common language, irrespective of computer or compiler supplier, took measures accordingly.

The reference manual for Ada (usually abbreviated LRM, for Language Reference Manual) became an American National Standard in January 1983, and an international standard under the International Standards Organization in 1987. At this writing, more than 200 different Ada compilers have been *validated*, which means that they have successfully passed a series of several thousand small test programs (known as the Ada Compiler Validation Capability or ACVC) designed to evaluate their conformance to the standard. This unusually high degree of conformance to a language standard means that Ada programs are usually quite easy to "port," or move to a different compiler on the same computer or to a different computer. To an extent unprecedented in the history of computers, Ada compilers all accept the same language.

The Status of Ada

At this writing, Ada is being actively used not only by the defense software industry, whose needs inspired Ada's creation, but also by other important governmental projects like NASA's Space Station and the Federal Aviation Administration air traffic control system. Ada has also been adopted as a language for management information systems, banking systems, steel mills, industrial robotics, medical electronics, telecommunications, and personal-computer software packages.

The name Ada honors Augusta Ada Byron (1815–1852), Countess of Lovelace, the daughter of the English poet Lord Byron. Ada assisted the computer pioneer Charles Babbage in "programming" his early machines; she is therefore sometimes credited with having been the first programmer. In learning Ada you will be learning a computer language that can be used equally well for teaching introductory programming concepts and for developing large practical computer systems. Programs in Ada are relatively easy to read, understand, and maintain (keep in good working order).

The richness of Ada is such that you are learning a language that will serve you very well throughout your career, no matter how large or complex the programs you will need to write. This book introduces you to a large and useful part of the language; you will undoubtedly learn the more advanced features as your experience and interest grows. The standard nature of Ada ensures that you will be able to use everything you learn in this book about Ada, regardless of the computer or Ada compiler you use.

In the rest of this chapter we will provide a brief introduction to Ada. Statements for reading data, performing simple computations, and displaying results will be described.

 ## 2.2 The "Look" of Ada Programs

Before beginning our study of programming with Ada, we will examine three short programs. Don't worry about understanding the details of these programs yet; it is the general "look" of the programs that is of concern now.

■ Example 2.1

Program 2.1 is the Ada program introduced at the end of Chapter 1. This time the lines are numbered for convenience in explaining them to you; when you write a program, you do not number the lines.

Program 2.1 A First Ada Program, with Output

```
 1   WITH Text_IO;
 2   PROCEDURE Hello IS
 3
 4   BEGIN
 5
 6   Text_IO.Put (Item => "Hello there. ");
 7   Text_IO.Put (Item => "We hope you enjoy studying Ada!");
 8   Text_IO.New_Line;
 9
10   END Hello;


Hello there. We hope you enjoy studying Ada!
```

Line 1 informs the compiler that this program will be making use of a *package* called Text_IO. A statement like this almost always precedes the rest of an Ada program file. A fuller explanation of packages will appear in the next section; for now you should know that input and output are done in Ada by means of standard packages. Text_IO is the most used standard package.

Line 2 informs the compiler that this program is to be called Hello (in Ada a program is called a PROCEDURE). Line 3 is left blank just to make the program easier to read. The section of the program between BEGIN (line 4) and END (line 10), called the *body*, or *executable statements section*, contains a list of actions the program is to perform. Each *statement* or action ends with a semicolon. In this program there are three statements, all calling for *output* actions. The statements in lines 6 and 7,

```
Text_IO.Put(Item => "Hello there. ");
Text_IO.Put(Item => "We hope you enjoy studying Ada!");
```

display the strings enclosed in quotes on the screen. The statement in line 8,

```
Text_IO.New_Line;
```

terminates the line displayed on the screen by advancing the *cursor* (a blinking place marker) to the first position of the next line. All these statements are prefixed by Text_IO as our way of indicating to the compiler (and to the reader of this program) that the operations in question are meant to be the ones provided by the Text_IO package. More about this later. ∎

∎ Example 2.2

Program 2.2 is similar to the last one, but with the important difference that the program asks the user (the person running the program) to enter his or her initials, then greets the user with these initials. Lines 4 and 5 identify the names of two memory cells (Initial1, and Initial2) that will be used to store each initial. The section of the program between the reserved word IS (line 2) and the reserved word BEGIN (line 7) is called the *declarative section*, or sometimes just the *declarations*. Generally this section describes *objects* (such as our two memory cells) and *types* (more on this later) to the compiler. If there are no declarations, as in the first program, this section will be empty.

The statements in lines 9 through 12 are all calls to input/output procedures. As before, each statement containing a Text_IO. Put causes some information to be displayed on the video screen during program execution. The statement

```
Text_IO.Put(Item => "Enter your two initials> ");
```

asks the program user to enter two letters. The statements

```
Text_IO.Get(Item => Initial1);
Text_IO.Get(Item => Initial2);
```

cause the program to wait until two letters are entered on the keyboard by the program user. These letters are "read" (stored) into the two memory cells listed, one letter per cell. The last output line of the program is displayed by the

Program 2.2 *Displaying Initials*

```
 1   WITH Text_IO;
 2   PROCEDURE HelloInitials IS
 3
 4      Initiall : Character;
 5      Initial2 : Character;
 6
 7   BEGIN
 8
 9      Text_IO.Put (Item => "Enter your two initials> ");
10      Text_IO.Get (Item => Initiall);
11      Text_IO.Get (Item => Initial2);
12      Text_IO.New_Line;
13
14      Text_IO.Put (Item => "Hello ");
15      Text_IO.Put (Item => Initiall);
16      Text_IO.Put (Item => Initial2);
17      Text_IO.Put (Item => ". We hope you enjoy studying Ada!");
18      Text_IO.New_Line;
19
20   END HelloInitials;
```

```
Enter your two initials> MF

Hello MF. We hope you enjoy studying Ada!
```

Text_IO. Put statements in lines 14 through 18. These statements display the string "Hello ", the two letters just read, and finally the longer greeting message. ∎

■ Example 2.3

Program 2.3 is similar to Program 2.2, except that it reads a person's name instead of just that person's initials. The declaration in line 4 describes a location First_Name able to hold a sequence of *exactly* ten characters (letters, digits, etc.). That is why the prompt in lines 8 through 10 requests an entry of exactly that many letters. ∎

One of the nice things about Ada is that it lets us write program statements that resemble English or everyday mathematics. At this point, you probably can read and understand the sample programs, even though you may not know how to write your own programs. In the following sections you will learn more details about the Ada programs we have looked at so far.

Reserved Words and Identifiers

All of the lines in the preceding programs satisfy the syntax rules for the Ada language. The programs contain several different elements: *reserved words, predefined identifiers, special symbols,* and names for memory cells. Let's look at the first three categories. The reserved words all appear in uppercase; they have

```
 1   WITH Text_IO;
 2   PROCEDURE HelloName IS
 3
 4     First_Name: String(1..10);
 5
 6   BEGIN
 7
 8     Text_IO.Put (Item => "Enter your first name, exactly 10 letters.");
 9     Text_IO.New_Line;
10     Text_IO.Put (Item => "Add spaces at the end if it's shorter.> ");
11     Text_IO.Get (Item => First_Name);
12     Text_IO.New_Line;
13
14     Text_IO.Put (Item => "Hello ");
15     Text_IO.Put (Item => First_Name);
16     Text_IO.Put (Item => ".  We hope you enjoy studying Ada!");
17     Text_IO.New_Line;
18
19   END HelloName;
```

```
Enter your first name, exactly 10 letters.
Add spaces at the end if it's shorter.> Michael

Hello Michael   "." We hope you enjoy studying Ada!
```

special meanings in Ada and cannot be used for other purposes. The reserved words in Programs 2.1 through 2.3 are (in order of appearance)

    WITH PROCEDURE IS BEGIN END

The predefined identifiers also have special meanings, but they can be used by the programmer for other purposes (however, we don't recommend this practice). The predefined identifiers in Programs 2.1 through 2.3 are (in order of appearance)

    Text_IO Put New_Line Character Get String

There are also some symbols (e.g., =, *, =>) that have special meanings in Ada. Appendix A contains a complete list of reserved words and special symbols; Appendix C summarizes the predefined identifiers.

What is the difference between reserved words and predefined identifiers? You cannot use a reserved word as the name of a memory cell, but in certain cases you can use a predefined identifier. Exactly how Ada would treat such a "reused" predefined identifier depends on just which identifier is involved. In any case the result would be very confusing to the reader of the program. Therefore we strongly recommend that you treat predefined identifiers as though they were reserved words and refrain from reusing them.

The other identifiers appearing in the three sample programs are described in more detail in the next sections.

Use of Uppercase and Lowercase

Throughout the text, issues of good program style are discussed in displays like this one. Program style displays provide guidelines for improving the appearance and the readability of your programs. Most programs are examined, studied, and used by someone other than the original author. A program that follows consistent style conventions is easier to read and understand than one that is sloppy or inconsistent. These conventions have no effect whatsoever on the computer; they just make it much easier for humans to understand programs.

In this text, reserved words always appear in uppercase. This is because the reserved words determine the structure and organization of the program. Writing them in uppercase, combined with a consistent indentation style, makes the structure and organization of the program immediately visible to the human eye.

Identifiers are in mixed uppercase and lowercase. The first letter of each identifier is capitalized. If an identifier consists of two or more words (such as `New_Line`), each word is usually capitalized and the words are sometimes separated by an underscore character.

The compiler does not differentiate between uppercase and lowercase in reading your program. You could write the reserved word `BEGIN` as `begin` and the predefined identifier `Character` as `CHARACTER` or even `ChArAcTeR`. The compiler doesn't care, but we do as humans striving for clarity and consistency. The compiler does, however, treat the underscore as a character, so `Two_Words` is different from `TwoWords`.

Your instructor may prefer a different convention; if so, it is prudent to follow it. In the end, what matters most is using a well thought out and consistent programming style.

Programs and Packages

Ada is a language designed for writing real-world programs that can be very large, sometimes numbering hundreds of thousands of statements. Because a single program file of that length would be completely unmanageable for humans and computers alike, Ada is built around the idea of libraries and packages. Using these, sets of commonly used operations can be tested once and then put in a library for others to use. Ada comes with several standard, predefined packages; the first one you have seen is `Text_IO`. Later in the book you will learn how to use other predefined packages and to write packages of your own. For now, keep in mind that almost every Ada program is preceded by at least one `WITH` clause (formally called a *context clause)* of the form

```
WITH Package_Name;
```

`WITH` clauses inform the compiler to which packages it must refer in order to understand the operations you are using. Preceding a program by the context clause

```
WITH Text_IO;
```

informs the compiler that the program will be using this package to read input data from the keyboard and display output data on the monitor. Omitting the context clause would cause one compilation error or more.

2.3 System Structures: Tailoring the Text_IO Packages for Numerical Values

So far, our program examples have used only character and string quantities. Computers are commonly used to work with numbers, so it is time for a numerical example or two. Computer programs use two general kinds of numerical values: *integer* values, such as 0, 2, and −1048, which are "whole numbers" with no fractional part, and *floating-point* values, such as 0.0, 3.14159, and −185.7, which are numbers with fractional parts. *Ada requires us, generally, to keep integer numbers and floating-point numbers separate, and not to mix them in the same calculation.*

In Ada, reading numerical values from the keyboard or a file, and writing or displaying these, are done by using two important pieces of the Text_IO library, called Integer_IO and Float_IO. These are designed to provide a great deal of flexibility in handling different kinds of numerical values; they are implemented as generic packages.

A *generic package* is actually a template or "recipe" for a package which needs to be "tailored" or *instantiated* before it can be used for the first time. You will learn more about this tailoring process later in the book; for now, we need to create tailored versions of Integer_IO and Float_IO, called *instances,* before we can read and write numerical values. Program 2.4 shows an Ada source file that will create instantiated, or tailored, integer and floating-point input/output

Program 2.4 Precompiled Input/Output Libraries

```
-- Precompiled instantiations of Integer_IO and
-- Float_IO for the predefined Integer and Float types

WITH Text_IO;
PACKAGE My_Int_IO IS
  NEW Text_IO.Integer_IO (Num => Integer);

WITH Text_IO;
PACKAGE My_Flt_IO IS
  NEW Text_IO.Float_IO(Num => Float);
```

---

packages called `My_Int_IO` and `My_Flt_IO`. Create a file exactly as given in Program 2.4 and compile it. The compiler will place these two tailored packages in your personal program library, and you will be ready to write `WITH My_Int_IO` or `WITH My_Flt_IO` as in the next few examples. Through the rest of the book, our examples will be making use of these "tailored" packages.

As you can see in Fig. 2.1, `Text_IO` is designed as a large library that has a number of "inner libraries" within it. The main library has a number of operations that don't have to be instantiated; the inner libraries do have to be instantiated. The reason that these inner libraries are generic is not explained at this point in the book; we will return to the issue in Chapter 3 and later. For now, all you need to know is to precede your programs with a context clause,

```
WITH Text_IO;
```

and, if you are reading and writing integer quantities,

```
WITH My_Int_IO;
```

If your program reads and displays floating-point quantities, precede it by

```
WITH My_Flt_IO;
```

It is permissible to have all three context clauses as well, if necessary.

Figure 2.1   Structure of the Text_IO Libraries

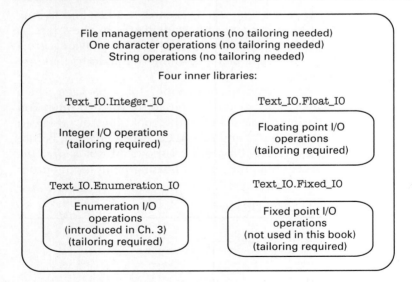

■ Example 2.4

Program 2.5 converts inches to centimeters. The number of inches to be converted is read into the memory cell `Inches` by the statement

```
My_Flt_IO.Get (Item => Inches);
```

```
WITH Text_IO;
WITH My_Flt_IO;
PROCEDURE InchToCM IS

   CM_Per_Inch : CONSTANT Float := 2.54;
   Inches      : Float;
   Centimeters : Float;

BEGIN

   Text_IO.Put (Item => "Enter a length in inches> ");
   My_Flt_IO.Get (Item => Inches);

   Centimeters := CM_Per_Inch * Inches;

   Text_IO.Put (Item => "That equals ");
   My_Flt_IO.Put (Item => Centimeters);
   Text_IO.Put (Item => " centimeters");
   Text_IO.New_Line;

END InchToCM;


Enter a length in inches> 30.5
That equals 7.74700E+01 centimeters
```

The Get statement looks similar to the one in the earlier examples. There are many different Get statements in the input/output libraries; they have in common the fact that each is able to accept keyboard input and store it in a single data element. As before, we write the prefix My_Flt_IO to indicate that we are interested in the Get supplied by our tailored floating-point input/output package.

The statement

```
Centimeters := CM_Per_Inch * Inches;
```

computes the equivalent length in centimeters by multiplying the length in inches by the floating-point constant 2.54 (the number of centimeters per inch); the product is stored in memory cell Centimeters.

The statement My_Flt_IO.Put (Item => Centimeters); displays the value of Centimeters as the floating-point number 7.74700 + 01 in Ada scientific notation. The value printed is equivalent to 7.747×10 or 77.47, as will be explained later.

Suppose the user enters a negative number of inches at the keyboard (say, -1.45)? The program will compute a negative number of centimeters. Whether this is appropriate or not depends on the use we are making of the program. Throughout this book we will be introducing better and better ways of ensuring that user input is appropriate before proceeding to a calculation that may not make sense. At this stage we can only identify the problem; we do not yet have the tools to solve it. ∎

■ **Example 2.5**

Program 2.6 computes the distance of an automobile trip by asking the user to enter the estimated trip time in hours and the average speed in miles per hour. The numbers are nonnegative integer values (type `Natural`). Nonnegative integers are still integers, so we can make use of our tailored integer input/output package `My_Int_IO`, prefixing the `Get` and `Put` operations accordingly.

In Programs 2.5 and 2.6, there are two context clauses (`WITH` clauses) preceding the program. Why do we need both? Because we are displaying prompts to request user input as well as titles to make the output meaningful, we need to use the character-string part of `Text_IO` to do this, in addition to the appropriate numerical input/output package. Ada requires us to supply context clauses for all library packages we are using. ■

In testing this program, we entered positive numbers for the trip time and speed. You might find it interesting to execute the program yourself and enter a negative number. The result will be a message from Ada called an "exception report." Exception reports will be discussed in Section 2.11.

Program 2.6 Finding Distance Traveled

```
WITH Text_IO;
WITH My_Int_IO;
PROCEDURE Distance IS

   How_Long : Natural;
   How_Fast : Natural;
   How_Far  : Natural;

BEGIN

   -- prompt user for hours and average speed
   Text_IO.Put (Item => "How many hours will you be driving? ");
   My_Int_IO.Get (Item => How_Long);
   Text_IO.Put (Item => "At what average speed (miles per hour)? ");
   My_Int_IO.Get (Item => How_Fast);

   -- compute distance driven
   How_Far := How_Fast * How_long;

   -- display results
   Text_IO.Put (Item => "You will travel about ");
   My_Int_IO.Put (Item => How_Far);
   Text_IO.Put (Item => " miles");
   Text_IO.New_Line;

END Distance;


How many hours will you be driving? 3
At what average speed (miles per hour)? 55
You will travel about        165 miles
```

In this textbook, we will provide solutions to a number of case studies of programming problems. We obtain the solutions by following the software development method outlined in Section 1.4. We begin each case study with a statement of the problem. As part of the problem analysis, we will identify the data requirements for the problem, indicating the problem inputs and desired outputs. Next, we will develop and refine the initial algorithm. Finally, we will implement this algorithm as an Ada program. We will provide a sample run of the program, and we will discuss how we might perform a more complete test of the program.

◆ Case Study: Converting Units of Measurement

Problem
You work in a store that imports fabric. Most of the fabric you receive is measured in square meters; however, the store's customers want to know the equivalent amount in square yards. You need to write a program that performs this conversion.

Analysis
The first step in understanding this problem is to determine what you are being asked to do. It should be clear that you must convert from one system of measurement to another, but are you supposed to convert from square meters to square yards, or vice versa? The problem states that you receive fabric measured in square meters, so the problem input is *fabric size in square meters.* Your customers want to know the *equivalent amount in square yards,* which must be your problem output.

   To solve this problem, *with or without a computer,* we need to know the relationship between square meters and square yards. By examining a metric table, we find that 1 square meter equals 1.196 square yards.

   We summarize the data requirements and relevant formulas below. As shown below, we will use the name SquareMeters to identify the memory cell that will contain the problem input and the name SquareYards to identify the memory cell that will contain the program result, or the problem output.

Data Requirements and Formulas

Problem Inputs
SquareMeters—the fabric dimensions in square meters

Problem Outputs
SquareYards—the fabric dimensions in square yards

Case Study: Converting Units of Measurement, continued

Formulas or Relations
1 square meter equals 1.196 square yards

Design
Next, we try to formulate the algorithm that we must follow to solve the problem. We begin by listing the three major steps, or subproblems, of the algorithm.

Algorithm

1. Read the fabric size in square meters.
2. Convert the fabric size to square yards.
3. Display the fabric size in square yards.

In using the term "read" we mean "find out the value of this quantity from the user of the program"; because this quantity will change from run to run, we need to ask the user for its value each time. Generally this is done by instructing the computer to ask the user to enter the value on the computer keyboard; sometimes it is done by reading it from an external disk file (secondary storage). Similarly, in using the term "display" we usually mean "instruct the computer to show the value on the computer monitor."

Next, we decide whether any steps of the algorithm need further refinement or whether they are perfectly clear as stated. Step 1 (reading data) and step 3 (displaying a value) are basic steps and require no further refinement. Step 2 is fairly straightforward, but it might help to add some detail. The refinement of step 2 follows.

Step 2 Refinement
2.1 Multiply the fabric size in square meters by 1.196; the result is the fabric size in square yards.

The complete algorithm with refinements is shown below. The algorithm resembles an outline for a paper. The refinement of step 2, numbered as step 2.1, is indented under step 2. We list the complete algorithm with refinements below to show you how it all fits together.

Algorithm with Refinements

1. Read the fabric size in square meters.
2. Convert the fabric size to square yards.

   2.1 Multiply the fabric size in square meters by 1.196; the result is the fabric size in square yards.

3. Display the fabric size in square yards.

Implementation
To implement the solution, we must write the algorithm as an Ada program that is acceptable to the compiler. Ada's syntax or grammatical rules require

that we first list the problem data requirements—that is, what memory cell names we are using and what kind of data will be stored in each memory cell. Next, we convert each algorithm step into one or more Ada statements. If an algorithm step has been refined, we convert its refinements into Ada statements. You will be able to do this yourself as you learn more about Ada. Program 2.7 shows the program along with a sample execution (the last two lines of the figure).

One thing you might notice in Program 2.7 is a number of lines containing text preceded by two adjacent hyphens or minus signs

```
--Converts square meters to square yards.
```

In Ada, these minus signs denote a program comment. A program comment is like a parenthetical remark in a sentence; its purpose is to provide supplementary information to the person reading the program. A program comment consists of the double minus sign and all subsequent text on the same line. Program comments are ignored by the Ada compiler and are not translated into machine language.

The program consists of two parts: the declaration part and the program body. The declaration part tells the compiler what memory cells are needed in the program; the declaration part is based on the problem data requirements

Program 2.7 Converting Square Meters to Square Yards

```
WITH Text_IO;
WITH My_Flt_IO;
PROCEDURE MetricConversion IS
-- Converts square meters to square yards

   MetersToYards : CONSTANT Float := 1.196; -- conversion constant
   SquareMeters : Float;                     -- input - metric fabric size
   SquareYards: Float;                       -- output - US fabric size

BEGIN

   -- Read the fabric size in square meters
   Text_IO.Put (Item => "Enter the fabric size in square meters > ");
   My_Flt_IO.Get (Item => SquareMeters);

   -- Convert the fabric size to square yards
   SquareYards := MetersToYards * SquareMeters;

   -- Display the fabric size in square yards
   Text_IO.Put (Item => "The fabric size in square yards is ");
   My_Flt_IO.Put (Item => SquareYards);
   Text_IO.New_Line;

END MetricConversion;


Enter the fabric size in square meters > 4.56
The fabric size in square yards is 5.45376000000000E+00
```

identified earlier during the problem analysis. Memory cells are needed for storing the variables `SquareMeters` and `SquareYards`, and for storing the conversion constant `MetersToYards` (whose value is 1.196).

The program body begins with the line

```
BEGIN
```

and contains the Ada statements that are translated into machine language and later executed. In the program body, we find the statements that express the algorithm steps as Ada statements. The statement

```
My_Flt_IO.Get(Item => SquareMeters);
```

reads the data value typed by the program user (in this case, 4.56) into the memory cell named `SquareMeters`. The statement

```
SquareYards := MetersToYards * SquareMeters;
```

computes the equivalent fabric size in square yards by multiplying the size in square meters by 1.196; the product is stored in memory cell `SquareYards`.

Finally, the `Put` statements display a message string, the value of `SquareYards`, and a second message string. The instruction displays the value of `SquareYards` as a real number in Ada scientific notation (5.453800E + 00). The value printed is equivalent to 5.4538×10^0 or 5.4538, as will be explained later. The last program line is

```
END MetricConversion;
```

Testing and Verification

The last two lines of Program 2.7 show one sample run of this program. To verify that the program works properly, we should enter a few more values of square meters. We really don't need to try more than a few test cases to verify that a simple program like this is correct.

As in the previous examples using floating-point quantities, if the user enters a negative number of square meters, the program will compute a negative number of square yards. Since this doesn't make physical sense, we will need a way of ensuring that it does not happen. In Section 2.10 we will offer some first solutions to this.

 ## 2.5 Data Structures: Declaring Constants and Variables

Every program begins with one or more context clauses, followed by a program heading such as

We tell the Ada compiler the names of memory cells used in a program through object (constant and variable) declarations. The programs seen so far contained declarations for constants and variables. The *constant declaration*

```
CM_Per_Inch: CONSTANT Float := 2.54;
```

in Program 2.5 specifies that the identifier `CM_Per_Inch` will be used as the name of the constant 2.54. Identifiers declared in a constant declaration are called *constants*. Only data values that never change (for example, the number of centimeters per inch is always 2.54) should be associated with an identifier that is a constant. Instructions that attempt to change the value of a constant cannot appear in an Ada program.

The *variable declarations*

```
Initiall: Character;
Initial2: Character;
```

in Program 2.2 give the names of two identifiers that will be used to reference data items that are individual characters as denoted by the predefined identifier `Character`. The variable declarations

```
Inches: Float;
Centimeters: Float;
```

in Program 2.5 give the names of two identifiers that will be used to reference data items that are floating-point numbers (for example, 30.0 and 562.57) as denoted by the predefined identifier `Float`. The variable declarations in Program 2.6

```
How_Long: Natural;
How_Fast: Natural;
How_Far: Natural;
```

give the names of three identifers whose values will be nonnegative integers, using Ada's predefined integer type `Natural`. We wish these numbers to be nonnegative because negative time and negative speed do not make good physical sense. We will come back frequently to the question of defining sensible ranges of values for our variables.

An identifier given in a variable declaration statement to the left of the : (colon) symbol is called a *variable*. Variables are used in a program for storing input data items and computational results. The identifier appearing to the right of the : symbol (for example, Integer, Float, Character, or String) tells the Ada compiler the *data type* (for example, an integer number, a floating-point number, a single character, or a sequence of characters) of the data that will be stored in the variable. Data types will be considered in more detail in Section 2.10.

You have quite a bit of freedom in selecting the identifiers, or names of variables and constants, that you use in a program. The syntactic rules are as follows:

1. An identifier must always begin with a letter.
2. An identifier must consist only of letters, digits, and underscores.
3. You cannot use two or more underscore characters in succession; the first character cannot be an underscore.
4. You cannot use an Ada reserved word as an identifier.

Some valid and invalid identifiers are listed below.

Valid identifiers:

```
INITIAL1, initial1, Inches, Centimeters, CM_Per_Inch, hello
```

Invalid identifiers:

```
1LETTER, CONSTANT, BEGIN, Two*Four, Joe's, CM__Per__ Inch
```

Note again that both uppercase and lowercase may be used, but remember the style recommendations from Section 2.2. The syntactic rules do not place a limit on the length of an identifier, except that an identifier may not be more than one line long. Ada requires a declaration for every identifier you create and use in your program (no declaration is required or desirable for predefined identifiers). Identifiers that you create and use are called *user-defined identifiers*.

The names of variables, constants, procedures, packages, package instances, and so on are all identifiers; thus all follow the syntactic rules just given.

The reserved words and identifiers used in Examples 2.1 through 2.5 are shown in Table 2.1 under their appropriate categories.

In this section we introduced the context clause, program heading, constant declaration, and variable declaration. The syntactic form of each of these Ada language constructs is summarized in the following syntax displays. Each display describes the syntactic form of a construct and provides an example.

Table 2.1 Categories of Identifiers in Examples 2.1 through 2.5

Program Names
Hello HelloInitials HelloName InchToCM

Predefined Packages
Text_IO Text_IO.Integer_IO Text_IO.Float_IO

Package Instances
My_Int_IO My_Flt_IO

Operations in Predefined Packages
Put New_Line Get

Variables
Initial1 Initial2 First_Name Inches Centimeters

Constants
CM_Per_Inch

Predefined Types
Character String Integer Float

Context Clause

Form: WITH list of package names;
Example: WITH Text_IO, My_Int_IO;
Interpretation: A context clause informs the compiler that the named package(s) is (are) being used by this program. The compiler will check all references to resources (e.g., procedures) provided by the package(s), making certain that the program is using them correctly.
Note: Context clauses can appear only at the very beginning of a source file. Generally we will give only one package name per context clause; this makes it easier to add or delete context clauses.

Program Heading

Form: PROCEDURE *program name* IS
Example: PROCEDURE Distance IS
Interpretation: A program heading is used to signal the start of a program.

Comment

Form: — *comment*
Example: — This is a comment
Interpretation: A double hyphen indicates the start of a comment; the comment ends at the end of the line. Comments are listed with the program but are otherwise ignored by the Ada compiler. Note that if you write a program statement *following* a comment on the same line, it will be treated by the compiler as part of the comment and therefore it will be ignored!

Constant Declaration

Form: *constant*: CONSTANT *type* := *value*;
Example: Pi: CONSTANT Float :=3.14159;
Interpretation: The specified *value* is associated with the identifier *constant*. The value of *constant* cannot be changed by any subsequent program statements.

Variable Declaration

Form: *variable list*: *type* ;
Example: Initiall, Initial2: Character;

Interpretation: A memory cell is allocated for each *variable* (an identifier) in the *variable list*. The type of data (`Character` in this case) to be stored in each variable is specified between the colon and the semicolon. Commas are used to separate the identifiers in the variable list.

PROGRAM
STYLE

Choosing Identifier Names

It is very important to pick meaningful names for identifiers; they will be easier to understand when used in a program. For example, the identifier `Salary` would be a good name for a variable used to store a person's salary; the identifiers `S` and `Bagel` would be bad choices. There is no restriction on the length of an identifier. However, it is difficult to form meaningful names using fewer than three letters. On the other hand, typing errors become more likely when identifiers are too long. A reasonable rule of thumb is to use names that are between three and ten characters in length. If you mistype an identifier, the compiler will usually detect this as a syntax error and display an *undefined identifier* message during program translation. Sometimes mistyped identifiers resemble other identifiers, so avoid picking names that are similar to each other. Make sure that you do not choose two names that are identical except for their use of case; the compiler will not be able to distinguish between them.

PROGRAM
STYLE

Form of Declarations and Context Clauses

From the syntax displays, you can see that Ada permits several package names to appear in a single context clause, and several variable names to appear in a declaration. Declarations are often changed during the development of a program as variables are added and removed. It is therefore much easier to develop a program (and to read it as well) if each variable and constant is declared in a separate declaration on its own line. All programs in this book follow this style convention, and we recommend that you follow it too.

The same recommendation applies to context clauses: Because any number of context clauses can precede a program, we recommend that each context clause name only a single package and appear on its own line.

Exercises for Section 2.5

Self-Check

1. Should the value of MyPi (3.14159) be stored in a constant or a variable? Why?

2. Which of these are valid Ada identifiers?

```
MyProgram    prog2    Prog#2    2NDone    procedure
"MaxScores"
```

3. Indicate which of the identifiers below are Ada reserved words, predefined identifiers, identifiers, and invalid identifiers.

```
END       Put       BILL                    PROCEDURE SUE'S
Rate      OPERATE   START                   BEGIN     CONSTANT
XYZ123    123XYZ    This__Is__A__Long__One  Y=Z
```

 # 2.6 System Structures: General Form of an Ada Program

To summarize what we have learned so far, the programs shown earlier all have the general form described in Fig. 2.2.

- Each program begins with one or more context clauses followed by a program heading.
- The last line of each program begins with the reserved word END.
- The program heading is followed by declarations, if any, which may appear in any order.
- The reserved word BEGIN signals the start of the *sequence of executable statements* part of the program. The *sequence of executable statements* consists of the program statements that are translated into machine language and executed. The program statements seen so far consist of statements that perform computations and input/output operations. These executable statements are described in the next section.
- The last line in a program has the form END *pname* ; where *pname* is the name of the program.

Figure 2.2 General Form of an Ada Program

```
WITH  package1;
WITH  package2;
   ...
WITH  packageN;
PROCEDURE  pname  IS

  -- declarations (variables, constants, etc.)

BEGIN

  program statement;
  ...
  program statement;

END  pname;
```

- Each declaration and statement in an Ada program ends with a semicolon.
- An Ada statement can extend over more than one line; such a statement cannot be split in the middle of an identifier, a reserved word, a number, or a string. Also, we can write more than one statement on a line, although we will not do so in this book and do not recommend it.

One of the main functions of a computer is to perform computations and display the results of computations. Such operations are specified by the sequence of executable statements that appear in the program body following the reserved word BEGIN. Each statement is translated by the Ada compiler into one or more machine language instructions, which are copied to the object file and later executed. Declarations, on the other hand, describe to the compiler the meaning and purpose of each user-defined identifier. They result in the allocation of some memory space to hold the data values.

PROGRAM
STYLE

Use of Blank Space

The consistent and careful use of blank spaces can significantly enhance the style of a program. A blank space is required between words in a program line (e.g., between PROCEDURE and Distance in Program 2.6). Because extra blanks between words and symbols are ignored by the compiler, you may insert them as desired to improve the style and appearance of a program.

Always leave a blank space after a comma and before and after operators such as *, −, and =.

Indent by two or more spaces all lines except for the first and last lines of the program and the line BEGIN.

Finally, use blank lines between sections of the program.

All of these measures are taken for the sole purpose of improving the style and hence the clarity of the program. They have no effect whatever on the meaning of the program as far as the computer is concerned; however, they make it easier for people to read and understand the program. Be careful not to insert blank spaces where they do not belong. For example, there cannot be a space between the characters : and = that comprise the assignment symbol :=. Also, you cannot put a blank in the middle of an identifier.

 ## 2.7 Control Structures: Assignment Statements

The *assignment statement* is used in Ada to perform computations. The assignment statement

```
Centimeters := CM_Per_Inch * Inches;
```

in Program 2.5 assigns a value to the variable `Centimeters`. In this case, Centimeters is being assigned the result of the multiplication (`*` means multiply) of the constant `CM_Per_Inch` by the variable `Inches`. Valid information must be stored in both `CM_Per_Inch` and `Inches` before the assignment statement is executed. As shown in Fig. 2.3, only the value of `Centimeters` is affected by the assignment statement; `CM_Per_Inch` and `Inches` retain their original values.

Figure 2.3 Effect of `Centimeters := CM_Per_Inch * Inches;`

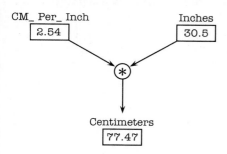

The symbol `:=` is the *assignment symbol* in Ada and should be pronounced "becomes" or "takes the value of" rather than "equals." The `:` and `=` must be adjacent characters with no intervening space. The general form of the assignment statement is shown in the next display.

Assignment Statement

Form:　*result* `:=` *expression* ;
Example: `X := Y + Z + 2.0;`
Interpretation: The variable specified by *result* is assigned the value of *expression*. The previous value of *result* is destroyed. The *expression* can be a single variable or a single constant, or it can involve variables, constants, and operators, some of which are listed in Table 2.2. The variable specified by result must be the same data type as the expression.

Table 2.2 Some Arithmetic Operators

Operator	Meaning
+	addition
−	subtraction
*	multiplication
/	division
**	exponentiation

It is permissible to write assignment statements of the form

```
Sum := Sum + Item;
```

where the variable Sum is used on both sides of the assignment operator. This is obviously not an algebraic equation, but it illustrates something that is often done in programming. This statement instructs the computer to add the current value of the variable Sum to the value of Item; the result is saved temporarily and then stored back into Sum. The previous value of Sum is destroyed in the process as illustrated in Fig. 2.4; however, the value of Item is unchanged.

Figure 2.4 Effect of Sum := Sum + Item;

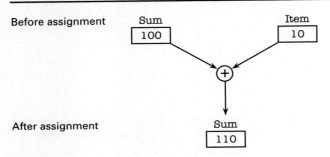

Before assignment

After assignment

Assignment statements can also be written with an expression part that consists of a single variable or value. The statement

```
NewX := X;
```

instructs the computer to copy the value of X into NewX. The statement

```
NewX := -X;
```

instructs the computer to get the value of X, *negate* this value, and store the result in NewX (e.g., if X is 3.5, NewX is −3.5; if X is −17.4, NewX is 17.4). Neither of the assignment statements above changes the value of X.

Exercises for Section 2.7

Self-Check

1. Which of the following are valid Ada assignment statements? Why?

```
X = Y;
A := B - C;
P + Q := R;
G := G;
H := 3 + 4;
H := 3 + K;
T := S * T;
```

2.8 Control Structures: Input/Output Statements

Information cannot be manipulated by a computer unless it is first stored in main memory. There are three ways to place a data value in memory: Associate it with a constant, assign it to a variable, or read it into a variable from the terminal or a file. The first two approaches can be followed only when the value to be stored will be the same every time the program is run. If we wish to be able to store different information each time, then it must be read in as the program is executing (an *input operation*).

As it executes, a program performs computations and assigns new values to variables. The results of a program's execution can be displayed to the program user by an *output operation.*

Input/output operations in Ada are performed by *procedures* that are included in a set of *library packages* supplied with each Ada compiler. We will use procedures from `Text_IO` and the instantiations, or tailored numeric input/output packages, we have called `My_Int_IO` and `My_Flt_IO`; later we will use other parts of the input/output libraries. The specific procedure used to read or display a value is determined by the *type* of that value. For the time being, we will manipulate values of four different types: character, string, floating-point number, and integer. As you write each program, you should be aware of the input/output operations that need to be performed and give the required context clauses. Input/output operations in Ada are done using procedure calls, so we now present a syntax display that shows the form of a call.

Simple Procedure Call Statement

Form: *pname* (*list of parameters*) ;
Example:
```
Text_IO.Put(Item => "Hello.");
Text_IO.New_Line;
```
Interpretation: The *list of parameters* is enclosed in parentheses; each actual parameter value is preceded by the name of that formal parameter.
Note: In the case of input/output operations, the most important parameter—the value to be output or the variable receiving the input—is always called `Item`. There is no special Ada rule that requires this; it is just the name chosen by the designers of `Text_IO`.

As the second example shows, it is possible for a procedure to require no parameters at all. The number, order, and type of parameters are, of course, determined by the writer of the procedure, not by its user.

Performing Input Operations

A *procedure call* statement is used to call or activate an input/output procedure. In Program 2.5, the procedure call statement

```
My_Flt_IO.Get (Item => Inches);
```

reads a *floating-point number* (a number with a decimal point) into the variable Inches. This statement causes the number entered at the keyboard to be stored in the variable Inches, as illustrated in Fig. 2.5. After typing a number, the program user should press the RETURN or ENTER key or the space bar.

Figure 2.5 Effect of `My_Flt_IO.Get(Item=>Inches);`

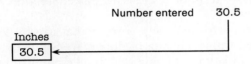

Now recall that in Program 2.2, a user's initials were read. Because each person using the program probably will have different initials, the statements

```
Text_IO.Get (Item => Initial1);
Text_IO.Get (Item => Initial2);
```

are used to read in two letters. These statements cause the next two characters entered at the terminal to be stored in the variables Initial1 and Initial2 (type Character), one character per variable. Figure 2.6 shows the effect of these statements when the letters EK are entered. It may be necessary to press the RETURN key after typing in the data characters above. Some systems will read in these characters as they are typed; others will not begin to read them until after the RETURN key is pressed.

Figure 2.6 Effect of Input of Character Values

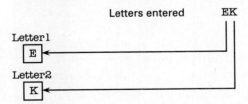

It is interesting to note that the four input characters in Fig. 2.5 comprise a single data value, the number 30.5, which is stored in the variable Inches (type Float). In Program 2.2, each input character represents a separate data value and is stored in a different variable. And in Program 2.3, where a user's name is read, the sequence of exactly ten characters represents a single value. A sequence of one or more characters representing a single input value is commonly called a *token*. The input sequence 30.5 is a floating-point token, the sequence Jane Smith is a string token, and the initials JS represent two single-character tokens.

The procedure My_Int_IO.Get is used to read an *integer* (a number without a decimal point). This number may or may not be preceded by a sign. The variable into which this number is stored must be of integer type.

The number of characters read by an input operation depends on the type of the variable into which the data are placed. Only one character is read for a variable of type Character. In the case of integer and floating-point values, the computer skips over any leading blanks and then continues to read characters until a character that cannot be part of a number is reached (e.g., a blank or a letter) or the RETURN key is pressed.

How does a program user know when to enter the input data and what data to enter? Your program should print a *prompting message* (as explained in the next section, and as the examples have shown) to inform the program user what data to enter and when. The cursor indicates the current position on the video screen. As each character is entered, the cursor advances to the next screen position.

SYNTAX
DISPLAY

Character Get Procedure

Form: Text_IO.Get (Item => *variable*);
Example: Text_IO.Get (Item => Initiall);
Interpretation: The next character pressed on the keyboard is read into *variable* (type Character). A blank counts as a character; a RETURN does not.

SYNTAX
DISPLAY

String Get Procedure

Form: Text_IO.Get (Item => *variable*);
Example: Text_IO.Get (Item => First_Name);
Interpretation: *Variable* must be a variable of type String (low..high), where 1 ≤ low ≤ high. Exactly high − low + 1 characters are read from the keyboard. A RETURN does not count as a character; the computer will wait until exactly the right number of keys, excluding RETURNs, are pressed.

SYNTAX
DISPLAY

Integer Get Procedure

Form: My_Int_IO.Get (Item => *variable*);
Example: My_Int_IO.Get (Item => How_Long);
Interpretation: The next string of numeric characters entered at the keyboard is read into *variable* (type Integer). Any leading blank characters

or RETURNs are ignored. The first nonblank character may be a sign (+ or –) or a digit. The data string is terminated when a nonnumeric character is entered or the space bar or RETURN key is pressed.

Floating-Point Get Procedure

Form: `My_Flt_IO.Get (Item => variable );`

Example: `My_Flt_IO.Get (Item => Inches);`

Interpretation: The next string of numeric characters entered at the keyboard is read into *variable* (type Float). Any leading blank characters or RETURNs are ignored. The first nonblank character may be a sign (+ or –) or a digit; the string of characters must contain a decimal point surrounded by numeric characters. The data string is terminated when a character that cannot be part of a floating-point number is entered or the space bar or RETURN key is pressed.

Performing Output Operations

In order to see the results of a program execution we must have some way of displaying the values of selected variables. In Program 2.5, the statements

```
Text_IO.Put (Item => "That equals ");
My_Flt_IO.Put (Item => Centimeters);
Text_IO.Put (Item => " centimeters.");
Text_IO.New_Line;
```

display the output line

```
That equals 7.62000E+01 centimeters.
```

The procedure `Text_IO.Put` is called twice, first to display the string "That equals" and next to display the string " centimeters.". A string must be enclosed in double quotes. When the `Text_IO.Put` statement is executed the characters enclosed in the quotes are printed, but the quotes are not.

The procedure `My_Flt_IO.Put` displays the value of variable `Centimeters` (type Float) between two strings. The number displayed is 76.2 expressed in *scientific notation*. In normal scientific notation, 7.62×10^1 means multiply 7.62 by 10, or move the decimal point right one digit. Because superscripts cannot be entered or displayed at the terminal, the capital letter E is used in computers to indicate scientific notation.

In Program 2.2, the statements

```
Text_IO.Put (Item => Initial1);
Text_IO.Put (Item => Initial2);
```

display the characters stored in the two variables `Initial1` and `Initial2` (type Character). Each statement causes a single character to be displayed at the current cursor position.

If the variable given to Text_IO.Put is of type String (low..high) as in Program 2.3,

```
Text_IO.Put (Item => First_Name);
```

exactly high − low + 1 characters are displayed.

The procedure My_Int_IO.Put is used to display integer values. Whenever an output operation is performed, the characters to be displayed appear at the current cursor position.

The procedure Text_IO.New_Line is used to segment our program output into lines. Each time Text_IO.New_Line is executed, the cursor is advanced to the first position of the next line on the screen.

Using Prompting Messages to Request Data from the Program User

The statements

```
Text_IO.Put (Item => "Enter your two initials >");
```

and

```
Text_IO.Put (Item => "Enter a length in inches >");
```

are both used to display *prompts* or *prompting messages* in Programs 2.2 and 2.5, respectively. A prompting message is a string that is displayed just before an input operation is performed. Its purpose is to request that the program user enter data; it may also describe the format of the data expected. It is very important to precede each input operation with a Text_IO.Put statement that prints a prompt; otherwise, the program user may have no idea that the program is waiting for data entry or what data to enter.

Formatting Output Values

Program output is usually designed to be read by humans from a screen display or a printed report. It is therefore important that the output be *formatted* or organized in a way that makes it most easily understood. For example, the decimal value 76.2 is much more obvious to most people than the scientific-notation form of the same value, $7.62000E+01$. Also, displays and reports should be organized in nice neat columns so that the information in them is easily digested by the human reader. Programming languages facilitate production of useful reports by providing ways of precisely controlling both the form and the width of output values, especially numerical ones. In the case of Ada, the integer and floating-point Put procedures provide additional *parameters* for output formatting. These are values that are supplied in the procedure call statement.

The integer Put procedure allows one additional parameter called Width, which indicates the number of print positions to be used for the output value. The statement

```
My_Int_IO.Put (Item => How_Far, Width => 4);
```

will *right-adjust* the displayed value of How_Far to four positions. This means that if How_Far is 327, when the value is displayed it will be preceded by one blank. If How_Far is 19, it will be preceded by two blanks; if How_Far is 1024, it will be preceded by no blanks at all.

Now suppose that How_Far is 12000, which would be a very long trip! In that case, the field in the display would be extended to five positions, so that no important information would be lost.

In Program 2.6 the output statement supplied no value for Width at all. Ada permits the omission of procedure parameters, but only if the author of the procedure has supplied a *default* value, which will be used instead. The integer Put comes with a default value for Width, but this value is different from compiler to compiler! This is why in the remaining programs in this book, a value for Width will always be supplied in the procedure call. We recommend that you follow this practice as well, because it makes your programs more portable (independent of a particular compiler).

In the case of floating-point output, Ada provides for three formatting parameters:

Fore, which indicates the number of positions before the decimal point,
Aft, which indicates the number of positions after the decimal point, and
Exp, which indicates the number of positions desired following the E. If
    Exp is 0, no exponent will appear at all; this produces a decimal value,
    rather than a scientific-notation one.

Look again at Program 2.5, where the statement

```
My_Flt_IO.Put (Item=>Centimeters, Fore=>5, Aft=>2, Exp=>0);
```

will produce the value 77.47 preceded by three blanks.

SYNTAX
DISPLAY

> ## Character Put Procedure
>
> **Form:**   Text_IO.Put (Item => *variable*);
> **Example:** Text_IO.Put (Item => Initiall);
> **Interpretation:** The value of *variable* (type Character) is displayed on the screen and the cursor is advanced to the next position.

SYNTAX
DISPLAY

> ## String Put Procedure
>
> **Form:**   Text_IO.Put (Item => *variable*);
> **Example:** Text_IO.Put (Item => First_Name);
> **Interpretation:** *Variable* must be a variable of type String (low..high), where $1 \leq$ low $\leq$ high. Exactly high $-$ low $+ 1$ characters are displayed on the screen, and the cursor is advanced to the first position after the end of the string.

Integer Put Procedure

Form: My_Int_IO.Put (Item => *variable* , Width => *field width*) ;

Example: My_Int_IO.Put (Item => How_Long, Width => 5);

Interpretation: The value of *variable* (type Integer) is displayed, using the next Width positions on the screen. If the value (including sign) occupies less than Width positions, it will be preceded by the appropriate number of blanks; if the value occupies more than Width positions, the actual number of positions is used. If Width is omitted, a compiler-dependent width is used by default.

Floating-Point Put Procedure

Form: My_Flt_IO.Put (Item => *variable* , Fore => *width before point* ,
Aft => *width after point* , Exp => *width of exponent*) ;

Example: My_Flt_IO.Put (Item => Inches, Fore => 5, Aft => 2,
Exp => 0);

Interpretation: The value of *variable* is displayed on the screen. Fore gives the desired number of positions in the integer part (to the left of the decimal point); Aft gives the number of positions in the fractional part (to the right of the decimal point); Exp gives the desired number of positions in the exponent (after the E). If the actual integer part of the value, including sign, occupies fewer than Fore positions, blanks are added on the left. If Exp is 0, no exponent is displayed.

Table 2.3 shows some examples of formatted integer values, and Table 2.4 shows some examples of formatted floating-point values.

Table 2.3   Formatted Integer Values

Value	Width	Displayed Output
234	4	☐234
234	5	☐☐234
234	6	☐☐☐234
−234	4	−234
−234	6	☐☐−234
234	Len	☐☐☐234 (if Len is 6)
234	1	234
234	0	234

Table 2.4 Formatted Floating-Point Values

Value	Fore	Aft	Exp	Displayed Value
3.14159	2	2	0	□3.14
3.14159	1	2	0	3.14
3.14159	3	1	0	□□3.1
3.14159	1	3	0	3.142
3.14159	2	5	0	□3.14159
3.14159	1	3	2	3.142E+00
0.1234	1	2	0	0.12
−0.006	1	2	0	−0.01
−0.006	1	2	2	−6.00E−03
−0.006	1	5	0	−0.00600
−0.006	4	3	0	□□−0.006

SYNTAX
DISPLAY

New_Line Procedure

Form: Text_IO.New_Line (Spacing => *positive number*);

Example: Text_IO.New_Line (Spacing => 3);

Interpretation: If Spacing is 1, the cursor is moved to the first position of the next line of the display. If Spacing is greater than 1, this action is performed Spacing times. If Spacing is omitted, then 1 is used as the default.

Exercises for Section 2.8

Self-Check

1. Correct the syntax errors in the program below and rewrite it so that it follows our style conventions. What does each statement of your corrected program do? What is printed?

```
PROCEDURE SMALL;
    X : Float;
    Y : Foat;
    X : Float;
BEGIN;
    15.0 = Y;
    Z= -Y + 3.5;
    Y + z = x;
    Put(x, Y, z)
end small;
```

2. Provide the statements needed to display the line below.

```
The value of X is ---------- pounds.
```

Display the value of X using ten characters in the space provided.

In this section we will look at a new sample program and see what happens to memory when this program is loaded and then executed.

■ Example 2.6

A payroll program is shown in Program 2.8. This program computes an employee's gross pay and net pay using the algebraic formulas

> gross pay = hours worked × hourly rate
> net pay = gross pay − tax amount

Program 2.8 A Simple Payroll Calculation

```
WITH Text_IO;
WITH My_Flt_IO;
PROCEDURE Payroll IS

   SUBTYPE NonNegFloat IS Float RANGE 0.0 .. Float'Last;

   Tax : CONSTANT NonNegFloat := 25.0;
   Hours : NonNegFloat;
   Rate  : NonNegFloat;
   Gross : NonNegFloat;
   Net   : NonNegFloat;

BEGIN

   Text_IO.Put (Item => "Enter hours worked > ");
   My_Flt_IO.Get (Item => Hours);
   Text_IO.New_Line;
   Text_IO.Put (Item => "Enter hourly rate > ");
   My_Flt_IO.Get (Item => Rate);
   Text_IO.New_Line;

   Gross := Hours * Rate;
   Net := Gross - Tax;

   Text_IO.Put (Item => "Gross pay is $ ");
   My_Flt_IO.Put (Item => Gross, Fore => 6, Aft => 2, Exp => 0);
   Text_IO.New_Line;

   Text_IO.Put (Item => "Net pay is   $ ");
   My_Flt_IO.Put (Item => Net, Fore => 6, Aft => 2, Exp => 0);
   Text_IO.New_Line;

END Payroll;


Enter hours worked > 40.0

Enter hourly rate > 4.50

Gross pay is $    180.00
Net pay is   $    155.00
```

These formulas are written as the Ada assignment statements

```
Gross := Hours * Rate;
Net := Gross - Tax;
```

in the program. New values of Hours and Rate are read each time the program is executed; a constant Tax of $25.00 is always deducted.

Near the top of the program, there is a line reading

```
SUBTYPE NonNegFloat IS Float RANGE 0.0 .. Float'Last;
```

The purpose of this line, called a subtype declaration, is to indicate to the compiler that certain variables and constants will have floating-point values that must not be negative. The variables of the program are declared as being of type NonNegFloat because it does not make sense for an employee's hours worked or hourly wage to be negative. We will return to this question in Section 2.10.

Program 2.8 first reads the data representing hours worked and hourly rate and then computes gross pay as their product. Next, it computes net pay by deducting a constant tax amount of 25.00. Finally, it displays the computed values of gross pay and net pay. Note in the program how the results are formatted. ∎

Memory Area for the Payroll Program

Figure 2.7(a) shows the payroll program loaded into memory and the program memory area before execution of the program body. The question mark in

Figure 2.7 Memory for Payroll Program

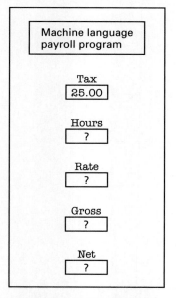

A. Memory before execution

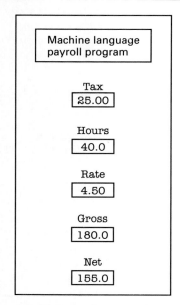

B. Memory after execution

memory cells Hours, Rate, Gross, and Net indicates that these variables are *undefined* (value unknown) before program execution begins. During program execution, the data values 40.0 and 4.50 are read into the variables Hours and Rate, respectively. After the assignment statements shown earlier are used to compute values for Gross and Net, all variables are defined as shown in Fig.2.7(b).

 ## 2.10 Data Structures: Introduction to Data Types and Expressions

First, let's clarify exactly what is meant by a data type in a programming language. A *data type* is a set of values and a set of operations on those values. The data type of the object stored in a particular memory cell determines how the bit pattern in that cell is interpreted. For example, the same bit pattern can represent a type Integer object, a type Character object, a type Float object, or even a program instruction. A *predefined data type* is a data type that is predefined in the programming language (for example Integer, Float, and Character). Besides the standard data types, programmers can define their own data types in Ada. Indeed, defining our own types will be an important part of our study, to be started in Chapter 3.

Character Data Type

Our first predefined type is Character. We have already seen (Example 2.2) that type Character variables can be used to store any single character value. A type Character value mentioned in a program—a *literal*—must be enclosed in single quotes (for example 'A'); however, quotes are not used when character data are entered as tokens. When the Text_IO.Get procedure is used to read character data into a type Character variable, the next character entered at the terminal is stored in that variable. The blank character is entered by pressing the space bar; it is written in a program as the literal ' '.

■ Example 2.7

Program 2.9 first reads and echoes three characters entered at the keyboard. Next, it prints them in reverse order enclosed in asterisks. Each character is stored in a variable of type Character; the character value '*' is associated with the constant Border. The lines

```
Text_IO.Put (Item=>Third);
Text_IO.Put (Item=>Second);
Text_IO.Put (Item=>First);
```

display the three characters in reverse order. As shown in the program output, each character value is printed in a single print position. The second character read in the sample run of Program 2.9 is a blank.   ■

Several operations are defined for character values; the most obvious one

Program 2.9   Reversing the Order of Three Letters

```
WITH Text_IO;
PROCEDURE ReverseLetters IS

   Border : CONSTANT Character := '*';
   First, Second, Third : Character;

BEGIN --- ReverseLetters

   Text_IO.Put(Item => "Enter 3 characters> ");
   Text_IO.Get(Item => First);
   Text_IO.Get(Item => Second);
   Text_IO.Get(Item => Third);
   Text_IO.New_Line;

   Text_IO.Put(Item => Border);
   Text_IO.Put(Item => Third);
   Text_IO.Put(Item => Second);
   Text_IO.Put(Item => First);
   Text_IO.Put(Item => Border);
   Text_IO.New_Line;

END ReverseLetters;


Enter 3 characters> M F

*F M*
```

is *assignment*. An assignment statement can be used to store a literal value into a character constant or variable, or to copy the value of one character variable into another. *Comparison* operations on character values will be introduced in Chapter 4.

Float Data Type

The standard data types in Ada represent familiar objects. For example, the data type Float is the set of real numbers (in the mathematical sense) that can be represented on the computer. Every type Float object in Ada is a real number; however, not all real numbers can be represented in Ada, or in any programming language. Some real numbers are too large or too small, or cannot be represented precisely due to the finite size of a memory cell (more on this in Chapter 7). The normal arithmetic operations (+, −, *, /) for real numbers and the assignment operation (:=) can be performed on type Float objects in Ada. The payroll problem in Section 2.9 is an example of the use of objects of type Float; so is the metric conversion problem discussed in Section 2.4.

Integer Data Type

The other predefined data types that represent numbers are Integer, Natural, and Positive. Type Integer objects in Ada correspond to the integers in mathematics (e.g., −77, 0, 999, +999). However, because of the finite size of a memory cell, not all integers can be represented in Ada, and every Ada compiler has predefined positive and negative limits on type `Integer` values. Quite commonly these limits are -32768 and $+32767$. Type `Natural` objects correspond to the nonnegative integers including 0; type `Positive` objects correspond to the positive integers (excluding 0).

Actually the types `Natural` and `Positive` are *subtypes* of `Integer`: Every positive integer is also an integer. We will have many occasions to use subtypes in this book. Indeed, we already have seen the definition of a subtype of our own. Recall that in Section 2.9, in the payroll program, a line appeared reading

```
SUBTYPE NonNegFloat IS Float RANGE 0.0 .. Float'Last;
```

This line is called a subtype definition; it is necessary because even though Ada supplies us with a predefined nonnegative integer type (`Natural`), it does not provide a similar predefined type for nonnegative floating-point values (languages are not perfect!). We will introduce a discussion of subtypes in Chapter 3 and revisit the subject frequently. For now, be aware that we will use the subtype `NonNegFloat` wherever nonnegative floating-point quantities are necessary.

The basic distinction between type `Float` and the three integer data types is that a number with a decimal point and fractional part can be stored in a type `Float` object, but only whole numbers can be stored in type `Integer`, `Natural`, and `Positive` objects. For this reason, objects of the last three types are more restricted in their use. We often use them to represent a count of items because a count must always be a nonnegative whole number.

What are the operations on integer values? The operations +, −, and * have obvious meanings of sum, difference, and product, respectively. What about division? Dividing one integer by another always gives an integer result, which is the "whole number," or quotient, part of the division. So 3/2 gives a result of 1; 14/4 gives a result of 3, and 2/3 gives a result of 0. The fractional part, or remainder, is lost in the division operation.

Because the remainder is lost in an integer division, Ada provides an operation `REM` that can be applied to two integers. `REM` gives the remainder in the division operation, as you would compute it in a "long division." Here are some examples:

3 `REM` 2 is 1 (dividing 3 by 2 gives a quotient of 1 and a remainder of 1).
14 `REM` 4 is 2 (dividing 14 by 4 gives a quotient of 3 and a remainder of 2).
2 `REM` 3 is 2 (dividing 2 by 3 gives a quotient of 0 and a remainder of 2).

One last operator merits discussion here: The operator `**` is used to represent *exponentiation*, or raising a value to a given power. Given a variable X whose current value is 3,

X `**` 2 is 9 (multiply X by X).
X `**` 3 is 27 (multiply X by X by X).
X `**` 4 is 81 (multiply X by X by X by X).

and so on.

Exponentiation is also defined to raise a floating-point value to a given power. *The power must be an integer, however.* If Y is a floating-point variable with value 1.2, then

> Y ** 2 is 1.44 (multiply 1.2 by 1.2).
> Y ** 3 is 1.728 (multiply 1.2 by 1.2 times 1.2).
> Y ** 1.5 is not allowed by the compiler.

Expressions with Several Operators

Ada allows us to write expressions with many variables and operators; in fact, there is no formal limit at all on the complexity of an expression. We must therefore know the order in which the various parts of an expression are evaluated. We'll take a systematic look at this in Chapter 7. To give you some help in the meantime, let X be 3, Y be 4, and Z be 7. Here's how Ada will evaluate some assignments to the variable W:

> W := X * Y + Z;

will store $(4 \times 3) + 7$ or 19 in W. The result of the multiplication is added to Z. It is as though the expression were written

> W := (X * Y) + Z;

which is also correct Ada and gets the same result. Now

> W := Z + X * Y;

stores $7 + (4 \times 3)$ in W. Again the result of the multiplication is added to Z; this is equivalent to writing

> W := Z + (X * Y);

which, of course, is also correct Ada. The basic rule Ada is following is that multiplications and divisions are done before additions and subtractions, in the absence of parentheses. For example,

> W := X * (Y + Z);

causes $3 \times (4 + 7)$ or 33 to be stored in W. The parentheses force the addition to be done first and the result to be multiplied by X. Consider

> W := X / Y + Z;

which stores $(3/4) + 7$ or 7 in W (remember division of integers!), and

> W := X / (Y + Z);

which stores $3/(4 + 7)$ or 0 in W (again, dividing the integers here gives 0).

Now suppose that we have two or more addition or subtraction operators in the same expression. In this case, the operations are done in left-to-right order.

> W := X − Y + Z;

stores $(3 - 4) + 7$ or 6 in W; the subtraction is done first. If we had written

```
W := X - (Y + Z);
```

the result in W would be $3 - (4 + 7)$ or -8. Again, the parentheses force the addition to be done first. Be sure you understand why

```
W := X - Y - Z;
```

and

```
W : = X - (Y - Z);
```

store -8 and 6, respectively, in W. A similar left-to-right rule applies to multiplication and division operators. Finally, exponentiation is done even before multiplication or division, so the expression

```
Pi * R ** 2
```

is equivalent to

```
Pi * (R ** 2)
```

and not

```
(Pi * R) ** 2
```

PROGRAM
STYLE

Using Parentheses to Write Expressions You Can Understand

Ada has many operators; you will study most of them in this book. The compiler follows very systematic rules (known formally as *precedence and association rules*) in evaluating complicated expressions with many operators; you will see these spelled out in Chapter 7. The compiler "knows exactly what it is doing" and will always get a result that is correct by those rules.

However, a human writer or reader of a program may have trouble sorting out the order of execution of the operations in an expression with more than one or two operators, and the result can sometimes be unpleasantly surprising if the human sorts it out differently than the compiler does. Remembering the precedence and association rules is difficult, and also unnecessary. You should instead use two very simple rules in writing an expression: Keep it as simple as you can, and use a lot of parentheses to indicate both to the compiler and to yourself what the intention of the expression is. Using extra parentheses will save you time in debugging; using too few parentheses to save writing effort is false economy.

Using Integer Objects

The case study below gives an example of manipulating type Integer objects in Ada.

◆ Case Study: Finding the Value of a Coin Collection

Problem

Your little sister has been saving nickels and pennies for quite a while. Because she is getting tired of lugging her piggy bank with her whenever she goes to the store, she would like to trade in her collection for dollar bills and some change. In order to do this, she would like to know the value of her coin collection in dollars and cents.

Analysis

To solve this problem, we must be given the count of nickels and the count of pennies in the collection. The first step is to determine the total value of the collection in cents. Once we have this figure, we can do an integer division using 100 as the divisor to get the dollar value; the remainder of this division will be the loose change that she should receive. In the data requirements below, we list the total value in cents (TotalCents) as a program variable because it is needed as part of the computation process; it is not a required problem output.

Data Requirements

Problem Inputs
Nickels : Natural (the number of nickels)
Pennies : Natural (the number of pennies)

Problem Outputs
Dollars : Natural (the number of dollars she should receive)
Change : Natural (the loose change she should receive)

Additional Program Variables
TotalCents : Natural (the total number of cents)

Relevant Formulas

One nickel equals five pennies.

Design

The algorithm is straightforward and is displayed next.

Initial Algorithm

1. Read in the count of nickels and pennies.
2. Compute the total value in cents.
3. Find the value in dollars and loose change.
4. Display the value in dollars and loose change.

Steps 2 and 3 may need refinement. Their refinement follows.

Step 2 Refinement
2.1. TotalCents is 5 times Nickels plus Pennies.

Step 3 Refinement
3.1. Dollars is the integer quotient of TotalCents and 100.
3.2. Change is the integer remainder of TotalCents and 100.

Coding
Program 2.10 shows the program. The statement

```
TotalCents := 5 * Nickels + Pennies;
```

Program 2.10   Finding the Value of a Coin Collection

```
WITH Text_IO;
WITH My_Int_IO;
PROCEDURE CoinCollection IS

    Pennies    : Natural;       -- input - number of pennies
    Nickels    : Natural;       -- input - number of nickels
    Dollars    : Natural;       -- output - value in dollars
    Cents      : Natural;       -- output - value in cents
    TotalCents : Natural;

BEGIN

    -- prompt user for number of nickels and pennies
    Text_IO.Put (Item => "How many nickels do you have? ");
    My_Int_IO.Get (Item => Nickels);
    Text_IO.Put (Item => "How many pennies do you have? ");
    My_Int_IO.Get (Item => Pennies);
    Text_IO.New_Line;

    -- compute total value in cents
    TotalCents := 5 * Nickels + Pennies;

    -- find the value in dollars and change
    Dollars := TotalCents / 100;
    Cents:= TotalCents REM 100;

    -- display the value in dollars and change
    Text_IO.Put (Item => "Your collection is worth ");
    My_Int_IO.Put (Item => Dollars, Width => 1);
    Text_IO.Put (Item => " dollars and ");
    My_Int_IO.Put (Item => Cents, Width => 1);
    Text_IO.Put (" cents.");
    Text_IO.New_Line;

END CoinCollection;


How many nickels do you have? 30
How many pennies do you have? 77

Your collection is worth 2 dollars and 27 cents.
```

implements algorithm step 2.1 and the statements

```
Dollars := TotalCents / 100;
Change := TotalCents REM 100;
```

implement algorithm steps 3.1 and 3.2.

◆

Note how a value of 1 for the `Width` parameter is used to format the displayed values so that they appear just next to the title text. Can you explain why `Width=>1` accomplishes this?

Literals and Tokens

Objects of a data type can be variables, constants, or literals. A *literal* is a value that appears directly in a program. A type `Float` literal is a number that begins with a digit and contains a decimal point (e.g., `0.112`, `456.0`, `123.456`). A type `Float` literal may have a *scale factor*, which is the capital letter E followed by an optional sign and an integer (e.g., `0.112E3`, `456.0E-2`). The scale factor means "multiply the preceding real number by 10 raised to the power appearing after the letter E (e.g., `0.112E3` is `112.0`, `456.0E-2` is `4.56`). A `Float` literal may be preceded by a + or – sign when it appears in a program. Examples of valid and invalid `Float` literals are shown in Table 2.5.

Table 2.5 Some Valid and Invalid `Float` Literals

Valid `Float` **Literals**	Invalid `Float` **Literals**
`3.14159`	`150` (no decimal point)
`0.005`	`.12345` (no digit before .)
`12345.0`	`16.` (no digit after .)
`15.0E-04` (value is `0.0015`)	`15E-03` (`15` invalid `Float`)
`2.345E2` (value is `234.5`)	`12.5E.3` (`.3` invalid exponent)
`1.2E+6` (value is `1200000`)	`.123E3` (`.123` invalid `Float`)
`1.15E-3` (value is `0.00115`)	

The last valid literal in Table 2.5, `1.15E-3`, has the same value as 1.15×10^{-3} in normal scientific notation where the exponent -3 causes the decimal point to be moved left three digits. A positive exponent causes the decimal point to be moved to the right; the + sign may be omitted when the exponent is positive.

You might be wondering what the difference is between the terms *literal* and *token*. Conventionally, a sequence of characters representing a value is called a literal when it appears within the text of a program, and such a sequence is called a token when it is read from an input device or displayed on an output device.

Exercises for Section 2.10

Self-Check

1. Evaluate the following expressions with 7 and 22 as operands.

   22/7 7/22 22REM7 7REM22

   Repeat this exercise for the pairs of integers:

   15,16   3,23   4, 16

2. Given the declarations

   ```
   Pi : CONSTANT Float :=3.14159;
   MaxI : CONSTANT Integer := 1000;
   ```

   the Float variables X and Y, and the Integer variables A, B, and I, indicate whether each of the following assignments is valid, and if so, what its value is. Assume that A is 3, B is 4, and Y is -1.0.

   a. I := A REM B;
   b. I := (990 - MaxI) / A;
   c. I := A REM Y;
   d. X := Pi * Y;
   e. I := A / B;
   f. X := A / B;
   g. X := A REM (A / B);
   h. I := B / 0;
   i. I := A REM (990 - MaxI);
   j. I := (MaxI - 990) / A;
   k. X := A / Y;
   l. X := Pi ** 2;
   m. X := Pi ** Y;
   n. X := A / B;
   o. I := (MaxI - 990) REM A;
   p. I := A REM 0;
   q. I := A REM (MaxI - 990);

3. If we assume A is 5, B is 2, and Y is 2.0, what values are assigned by the legal statements in Exercise 2?

4. Assume that you have the following integer variables:

   Color, Lime, Straw, Yellow, Red, Orange

   and the following floating-point variables:

   Black, White, Green, Blue, Purple, Crayon

   Evaluate each of the statements below given the following values: Color is 2, Black is 2.5, Crayon is -1.3, Straw is 1, Red is 3, and Purple is 0.3E1.

   a. White := Crayon * 2.5 / Purple;
   b. Green := Black / Purple;
   c. Orange := Color / Red;
   d. Orange := (Color + Straw) / (2*Straw);
   e. Lime := Red / Color + Red REM Color ;
   f. Purple := Straw / Red * Color;

5. Let A, B, C, and X be the names of four Float variables and let I, J, and K be the names of three Integer variables. Each of the statements below

contains a violation of the rules for forming arithmetic expressions. Rewrite each statement so that it is consistent with these rules.

a. `X := 4.0 A * C`

b. `A := AC`

c. `I := 2 * -J`

d. `K := 3(I + J)`

e. `X := 5A / BC`

f. `I := 5J3`

2.11 Tricks of the Trade: Common Programming Errors

One of the first things you will discover in writing programs is that a program often does not run correctly the first time that it is submitted. Murphy's law, "If something can go wrong, it will," seems to have been written with computer programming in mind. In fact, errors are so common that they have their own special name—*bugs*—and the process of correcting them is called *debugging a program*. To alert you to potential problems, a section on common errors appears near the end of each chapter.

When an error is detected, an error message is displayed indicating that you have made a mistake and what the cause of the error might be. Unfortunately, error messages are often difficult to interpret and are sometimes misleading. However, as you gain some experience you will become more proficient at understanding them.

There are two basic categories of error messages: compilation error messages and run-time error messages. *Compilation errors* are detected and displayed by the compiler as it attempts to translate your program. If a statement has a compilation error, then it cannot be translated and your program will not be executed. *Run-time errors* are detected by the computer and are displayed during execution of a program. A run-time error, called an *exception* in Ada, occurs as a result of directing the computer to perform an illegal or inappropriate operation, such as dividing a number by 0 or attempting to store in a variable a number that is outside the acceptable range for that variable (e.g., attempting to store a negative value in a type `Positive` variable). When an exception is raised—that is, when an error occurs—the computer stops executing your program and a diagnostic message is displayed which sometimes indicates the line of your program where the exception was raised.

One of the interesting features of Ada is that it provides a way for programmers to predict the occurrence of exceptions and to *handle* them when they arise. In this manner a programmer can prevent the computer from halting the program. We will return later to the matter of handling exceptions in programs.

Compilation Errors

Program 2.11 is a modification of the payroll program, Program 2.8. The modified program contains errors, which we have purposely put in for illustra-

```
WITH Text_IO;
WITH My_Flt_IO;
PROCEDURE Payroll

   SUBTYPE NonNegFloat IS Float RANGE 0.0 .. Float'Last;

   Tax  : CONSTANT NonNegFloat = 25.0;
   Hours : NonNegFloat;
   Rate  : NonNegFloat;
   Gross : NonNegFloat;

BEGIN

   Text_IO.Put (Item => "Enter hours worked > ");
   My_Flt_IO.Get (Item => Hours);
   Text_IO.New_Line
   Text_IO.Put (Item => "Enter hourly rate > ");
   My_Flt_IO.Get (Item => Rate);
   Text_IO.New_Line;

   Hours * Rate := Gross;
   Net := Gross - Tax;

   Text_IO.Put (Item => "Gross pay is $ ");
   My_Flt_IO.Put (Item => Gross,   Fore => 6, Aft => 2, Exp => 0);
   Text_IO.New_Line;

   Text_IO.Put (Item => "Net pay is   $ ");
   My_Flt_IO.Put (Item => Net,   Fore => 6, Aft => 2, Exp => 0);
   Text_IO.New_Line;

END Payroll;
```

tive purposes. Figure 2.8 shows a *compiler listing* of the payroll program (produced by Irvine Ada on an HP9000-835). You can ask the compiler to create a
listing during translation. The listing shows each line of the source program
(preceded by its line number) and also displays any errors detected by the
compiler. These messages came from the following errors we purposely inserted
in the program:

- missing IS after the program header (line 3)
- use of = instead of := in the constant declaration (line 7)
- missing semicolon after the Text_IO.New_Line statement (line 16)
- assignment statement with transposed variable and expression part (line 21)
- missing declaration for identifier Net (lines 22 and 29)

   The actual format of the listing and error messages produced by your
compiler may differ from Fig. 2.8. In this listing whenever an error is detected,
the compiler prints a line starting with *****>. A caret symbol (^) points to the
position in the preceding line where the error was detected; as we will see in a
moment, this is not necessarily where the error occurred. The error is explained
on the next line.

Figure 2.8 Compilation Listing with Interspersed Error Messages

```
 1 | WITH Text_IO;
 2 | WITH My_Flt_IO;
 3 | PROCEDURE Payroll
 4 |
 5 |   SUBTYPE NonNegFloat IS Float RANGE 0.0 .. Float'Last;
***** >   ^
***** > "paybugs.ada", line 5: Error: Expecting is.
 6 |
 7 |   Tax : CONSTANT NonNegFloat = 25.0;
***** >                                   ^
***** > "paybugs.ada", line 7: Error: Expecting :=.
 8 |   Hours : NonNegFloat;
 9 |   Rate  : NonNegFloat;
10 |   Gross : NonNegFloat;
11 |
12 | BEGIN
13 |
14 |   Text_IO.Put (Item => "Enter hours worked > ");
15 |   My_Flt_IO.Get (Item => Hours);
16 |   Text_IO.New_Line
17 |   Text_IO.Put (Item => "Enter hourly rate > ");
***** >   ^
***** > "paybugs.ada", line 17: Error: Unrecognized statement.
18 |   My_Flt_IO.Get (Item => Rate);
19 |   Text_IO.New_Line;
20 |
21 |   Hours * Rate := Gross;
***** >         ^
***** > "paybugs.ada", line 21: Error: Unrecognized statement.
22 |   Net := Gross - Tax;
***** >   ^
***** > "paybugs.ada", line 22: Error: Undefined variable: net.
23 |
24 |   Text_IO.Put (Item => "Gross pay is $ ");
25 |   My_Flt_IO.Put (Item => Gross, Fore => 6, Aft => 2, Exp => 0);
26 |   Text_IO.New_Line;
27 |
28 |   Text_IO.Put (Item => "Net pay is   $ ");
29 |   My_Flt_IO.Put (Item => Net, Fore => 6, Aft => 2, Exp => 0);
***** >                         ^
***** > "paybugs.ada", line 29: Error: Undefined identifier: net.
30 |   Text_IO.New_Line;
31 |
32 | END Payroll;

32 lines compiled.
6 errors detected.
```

To see how a compiler listing works, look at the first error reported. The error was not detected until after the symbol SUBTYPE was processed by the compiler. At that point the compiler recognized that the word IS was missing (after the program header) and indicated this by displaying the message Expecting IS. In this case, the position of the caret is misleading, as the compiler could not detect the error until it started to process the next statement, which was two lines later in the file.

An error message is displayed after line 7 to indicate an incorrect symbol (= instead of :=). The missing semicolon in line 16 and the transposed assignment statement in line 21 also caused error messages to be displayed. Notice how the compiler did the best it could to tell you what was wrong, but in the case of the missing semicolon it could not, because it tried to interpret the material in lines 16 and 17 as a single statement, which it did not recognize. Remember, the compiler is only a computer program, and is not as good a detective as you are!

One compilation error often leads to the generation of a number of error messages. (These "extra" errors are often called *propagation errors*.) For example, the missing declaration of the variable Net resulted in an error message being displayed each time Net was used in the program. For this reason, it is often a good idea to concentrate first on correcting the errors in the declaration part of a program and then to recompile, rather than to attempt to fix all the errors at once. Many later errors will disappear once the declarations are correct. An undefined variable error occurs if the compiler cannot find the declaration for an identifier referenced in the program body. This can happen because the programmer forgot the declaration or mistyped the name of the identifier. It can also happen if the programmer forgets to supply a WITH for a package needed by the program.

Programmers who are just learning to write Ada programs often forget to write IS and to insert semicolons in the required places. These are two of the most common compilation errors made by beginners, and unfortunately they are also errors which sometimes confuse the compiler hopelessly. Leaving out an IS or a semicolon, or using one where the other is expected, can often lead to an entire sequence of messages (propagation errors), which will all disappear when the original error is corrected. A word to the wise is sufficient!

Another common Ada compilation error is the confusion of single and double quotation marks. You must remember that a *string literal* in Ada is surrounded by *double* quotation marks, but a *single character literal* must be surrounded by *single* quotation marks.

Compilation errors are generally of two kinds: syntax errors and semantic errors. Some Ada compilers distinguish between these in their error messages; others do not. A *syntax error* is one in which the rules of grammar or "sentence structure" are broken. The errors in Fig. 2.8 are in this category. A *semantic error* is one in which no grammatical rule was broken, but rather something was written that didn't make sense. An example of this would be a procedure call whose parameter is of the wrong type. Suppose in displaying Gross, for example, we had written

```
My_Int_IO.Put(Item => Gross, Width => 4);
```

instead of using My_Flt_IO.Put. The procedure expected an integer variable;

we gave it a float variable. Actually, we selected the correct variable but the wrong output procedure, but the compiler didn't know this; it just noticed the mismatch. Another semantic error is intermixing integer and float variables in the same expression.

In languages like Ada with data types, semantic errors occur quite frequently. One of the things you will need to be careful about is making sure that the types of your variables match the expectation of the expression or procedure in which the variables are used. If a procedure expects an integer variable, supplying a float variable won't do; also, you cannot mix integer and float variables in the same expression!

Run-Time Errors

As discussed above, run-time errors are called *exceptions* in Ada. The most common exceptions encountered by beginners are those relating to the ranges of variables in their programs. A range error occurs when a program tries to save an inappropriate value in a variable. This can happen in one of two ways: Either the program itself computes a result that is out of range for the variable in which it will be saved, or the program user enters an out of range value from the keyboard. Ada gives the name `Constraint_Error` to such a range error; Ada uses the term "raising an exception" for reporting the occurrence of such a run-time error.

As an example of the first case, consider Program 2.12. All three variables are declared to be of type `Natural`, which means that none of them is allowed to acquire a negative value. There are no compilation errors in this program, because it breaks no syntax rules. It may seem obvious to you that when this program is executed, it will attempt to save a negative value (–5) in the variable Z, but the compiler cannot predict this runtime error. As you can see in the execution display of Fig. 2.9, the out of range condition is detected when the

Program 2.12   Illustrating a Run-Time Error

```
WITH Text_IO;
WITH My_Int_IO;
PROCEDURE TestRuntimeError IS

   X : Natural;
   Y : Natural;
   Z : Natural;

BEGIN

   X := 5;
   Y := 10;
   Z := X - Y;
   My_Int_IO.Put(Item => Z);
   Text_IO.New_Line;

END TestRuntimeError;
```

program is executed: `Constraint_Error` is raised. Most Ada systems will give you a reasonable explanation of an exception; however, not all systems will tell you the source line number in which the error occurred.

Figure 2.9   Run-Time Error Produced by Program 2.12

```
Ada-runtime:
Exception CONSTRAINT_ERROR raised in testruntimeerror.ada on line 13.
Rangecheck error: -5 not in range 0..32767.
```

As an example of the second case, take another look at the payroll program (Program 2.8), and recall that in this program we required the input to be of type `NonNegFloat`, because negative wages and hours don't make sense in the real world. Figure 2.10 shows what happens if a negative value is entered for the number of hours worked. An exception is raised by the Ada system, and the program halts.

Figure 2.10   Another Ada Run-Time Error

```
Enter hours worked > -5.25

Ada-runtime:
Exception CONSTRAINT_ERROR raised in payroll.ada on line 15.
```

To summarize, Ada's data types and exception system are designed to help you write programs whose results will make sense. In this book we will pay very careful attention to this matter, because it is important and can be very useful to you.

Debugging a program can be time consuming. The best approach is to plan your programs carefully and desk check them beforehand to eliminate bugs before they occur. If you are not sure of the syntax for a particular statement, look it up in the syntax displays in the text, or in Appendix B. Also, take care that your program variables have types that are appropriate and sensible. If you follow this approach, you will save yourself much time and trouble.

 # Chapter Review

In this chapter you have seen how to use the Ada programming language to perform some fundamental operations. You learned how to instruct the computer to read information into memory, perform some simple computations, and display the results of those computations. All of this was done using symbols (punctuation marks, variable names, and special operators such as *, −, and +) that are familiar, easy to remember, and easy to use. You have also learned a bit about data types, a very important concept in developing programs whose results make sense. You do not have to know very much about your computer in order to understand and use Ada.

In the remainder of this text we introduce more features of the Ada language and provide rules for using these features. You must remember throughout that, unlike the rules of English, the rules of Ada are precise and allow no exceptions. The compiler will be unable to translate Ada instructions that violate these rules. Remember to declare every identifier used as a variable or constant and to terminate program statements with semicolons.

New Ada Constructs in Chapter 2

Table 2.6 describes the new Ada constructs introduced in this chapter.

Table 2.6 Summary of New Ada Constructs

Construct	Effect
Context Clause WITH Text_IO;	indicates that package Text_IO is used by the program
Program Heading PROCEDURE Payroll IS	identifies Payroll as the name of the program
Constant Declaration Tax : CONSTANT Float := 25.00;	associates the constant, Tax, with the Float value 25.00
Star : CONSTANT Character := '*';	associates the constant, Star, with the Character value '*'
Variable Declaration X: Float;	allocates a memory cell named X for storage of Float numbers
Me : Integer;	allocates a memory cell named Me for storage of Integer numbers
Assignment Statement Distance := Speed * Time;	assigns the product of Speed and Time as the value of Distance.
Input Statements Text_IO.Get(Item=>Initial);	enters data into the character variable Initial
My_Int_IO.Get(Item=>HowMany);	enters data into the integer variable HowMany
My_Flt_IO.Get(Item=>PayRate);	enters data into the float variable PayRate
Output Statements Text_IO.Put(Item=>Initial);	displays the value of the character variable Initial

Table 2.6 *continued*

Construct	Effect
`My_Int_IO.Put(Item=>HowMany,` `Width=>5);`	displays the value of the integer variable HowMany, using five columns on the display
`My_Flt_IO.Put(Item=>GrossPay,` ` Fore=>4, Aft=>2, Exp=>0);`	displays the value of the float variable GrossPay using four columns before the decimal point and two columns after the decimal point

✓ *Quick-Check Exercises*

1. What value is assigned to X by the following statement?

   ```
   X := 25.0 * 3.0 / 2.5;
   ```

2. What value is assigned to X by the following statement when X is 10.0?

   ```
   X := X - 20.0;
   ```

3. Show the exact form of the output displayed when X is 3.456.

   ```
   Text_IO.Put(Item => "Three values of X are");
   My_Flt_IO.Put(Item => X, Fore => 2, Aft => 1, Exp => 0);
   Text_IO.Put(Item => '*');
   My_Flt_IO.Put(Item => X, Fore => 1, Aft => 2, Exp => 0);
   Text_IO.Put(Item => '*');
   My_Flt_IO.Put(Item => X, Fore => 2, Aft => 3, Exp => 0);
   Text_IO.New_Line;
   ```

4. Show the exact form of the output displayed when N is 345.

   ```
   Text_IO.Put(Item => "Three values of N are");
   My_Int_IO.Put(Item => N, Width => 4);
   Text_IO.Put(Item => '*');
   My_INT_IO.Put(Item => N, Width => 5);
   Text_IO.Put(Item => '*');
   My_INT_IO.Put(Item => N, Width => 1);
   Text_IO.New_Line;
   ```

5. What data type would you use to represent each of the following items: number of children at school, a letter grade on an exam, the average number of school days students are absent each year?

6. Suppose `My_Int_IO.Get` is called twice in succession, for example

   ```
   My_Int_IO.Get(Item => X);
   My_Int_IO.Get(Item => Y);
   ```

   What character(s) may be typed after the first number is entered? What may be typed after the second number is entered?

7. Suppose `Text_IO.Get` is called twice in succession, for example

   ```
   Text_IO.Get(Item => X);
   Text_IO.Get(Item => Y);
   ```

What happens if a blank is entered after the first character? What happens if RETURN is pressed after the first character?

8. What kind of errors does a compilation listing show?

Answers to Quick-Check Exercises

1. 30.0
2. –10.0
3. Three values of X are 3.5*3.46* 3.456
4. Three values of N are 345* 345*345
5. Natural, Character, Float (or NonNegFloat)
6. any number of blanks and/or RETURNs; same
7. the blank will be read into Y; the RETURN will be skipped and the next character (if it is not a RETURN) will be read into Y.
8. Compilation errors: syntax and semantic errors.

Programming Projects

1. Write a program to convert a temperature in degrees Fahrenheit to degrees Celsius. Use the formula

$$\text{Celsius} = (5/9) \times (\text{Fahrenheit} - 32)$$

2. Write a program that reads three data items into variables X, Y, and Z, and then finds and displays their product and sum.
3. Write a program that reads in the weight (in pounds) of an object, and then computes and displays its weight in kilograms and grams. (*Hint:* One pound is equal to 0.453592 kilograms or 453.59237 grams.)
4. Write a program that displays your first initial as a large block letter. (*Hint:* Use a 6 × 6 grid for the letter and print six strings. Each string should consist of a row of *s interspersed with blanks.)
5. A track star competes in a 1-mile race. Write a program that reads in the race time in minutes (Minutes) and seconds (Seconds) for this runner, and then computes and displays the speed in feet per second (FPS) and in meters per second (MPS). (*Hint:* There are 5280 feet in 1 mile and 1 kilometer equals 3282 feet.) Test your program on each of the times below.

Minutes	Seconds
3	52.83
3	59.83
4	00.03
4	16.22

6. A cyclist coasting on a level road slows from a speed of 10 miles per hour to 2.5 miles per hour in one minute. Write a computer program that calculates the cyclist's constant rate of acceleration and determines how long it will take the cyclist to come to rest, given an initial speed of 10 miles per hour (*Hint:* Use the equation $a = (v_f - v_i) / t$, where a is acceleration, t is time interval, v_i is the initial velocity, and v_f is the final velocity.)
7. If a human heart beats on the average of once a second for 78 years, how many times does the heart beat in a lifetime? (Use 365.25 for days in a year.) Rerun your program for a heart rate of 75 beats per minute.

Problem Solving and Using Packages

3

3.1 Problem Solving: Top-Down Design
3.2 Problem Solving: Extending a Problem Solution
3.3 Problem Solving: Structured Programming
3.4 Data Structures: Introducing Enumeration Types
3.5 System Structures: The Importance of Packages
3.6 System Structures: Using Ada's Calendar Package
3.7 System Structures: Using a Screen-Control Package
3.8 Tricks of the Trade: Common Programming Errors
Chapter Review

All your life, you have been solving problems using your own intuitive strategies. Problem solving on a computer requires that you follow a more formal approach. This chapter will help you learn how to analyze a problem and devise an *algorithm*, or list of steps, to describe a possible solution. You will also learn how to verify that a proposed algorithm does indeed solve its intended problem.

In this chapter, we show you how to solve a problem by breaking it into smaller, more manageable subproblems. We also introduce an important concept in data structures, the *enumeration type*, and an important concept in system structures, the *package*. You will see how packages are used by working with a standard Ada package, `Calendar`, which provides date and time services in a way common to all Ada systems.

Finally, you will see how to use a package provided with this book, called `Screen`. This package provides several services for dealing with the terminal screen—namely, clearing the screen, moving the cursor to a specific row–column position, and making the terminal beep.

3.1 Problem Solving: Top-Down Design

In Chapters 1 and 2, we outlined an approach to solving programming problems—the *software development method*—which consists of five separate phases:

1. problem statement / requirements specification,
2. analysis,
3. design,
4. coding, and
5. testing.

During the requirements-specification phase, we determine precisely what problem we are expected to solve and what the program solution is supposed to do. During the analysis phase we identify the problem inputs and outputs and also list any formulas or relationships that might be relevant to the problem solution. During the design phase we write an algorithm that lists the major subproblems. These subproblems are solved separately, and solution details or refinements are added when necessary. During the coding phase we implement the solution in Ada. We first use the program data requirements to construct the declaration part of the solution program. The program body contains the Ada statements that implement the refined algorithm.

The approach to algorithm development followed in the design phase is called *top-down design*. This means that we start with the most abstract formulation of a problem and work down to more detailed subproblems. In this chapter, we will show several ways to facilitate and enhance the top-down approach to programming.

Developing a Program from Its Documentation

If we carefully follow the software development method, introduced in Chapter 2 and reviewed above, we will generate important program documentation as well as a final program. This *program documentation* describes our intentions and thought process as we develop the algorithm and implement the final program. The program documentation contains information about the program data requirements and algorithm. An important part of a program's documentation are the comments included in the program. We should use comments to describe the purpose of each program variable. We should also place a comment that describes each major algorithm step before its implementation in the program body.

Some of you may have access to a word processor, which you can use in writing your problem solution. If you follow the software development method, you can use the documentation developed as a starting point in coding your program. For example, you can begin by duplicating the problem data requirements (part of the analysis phase) in the program declaration part. Then edit these lines to conform to the Ada syntax for constant and variable declarations. To develop the program body, begin with the initial algorithm written as a list of comments. Then, move each algorithm refinement under the alogrithm step that it refines. After the refinements are in place in the program body, you can begin to write actual Ada statements. Place the Ada code for a step that is not refined directly under that step. For a step that is refined, edit the refinement, changing it from English to Ada. We will illustrate this process next.

◆ Case Study: Finding Area and Circumference of a Circle

Problem
Read in the radius of a circle and compute and print its area and circumference.

Analysis
Clearly, the problem input is the circle radius. Two outputs are requested: the circle area and circumference. These variables should be type Float because the inputs and outputs may contain fractional parts.

From our knowledge of geometry, we know the relationship between a circle's radius and its area and circumference; these formulas are listed below along with the data requirements. Note that we have written the English description of each variable as an Ada comment to make it easier to produce the declaration part of our solution program.

Data Requirements

Problem Constant
```
Pi : CONSTANT Float := 3.14159;
```

Problem Inputs

```
Radius : NonNegFloat --radius of a circle
```

Problem Outputs

```
Area : NonNegFloat --area of a circle
Circum : NonNegFloat --circumference of a circle
```

Relevant Formulas

area of a circle $= \pi \times \text{radius}^2$
circumference of a circle $= 2\pi \times \text{radius}$

Design

Once you know the problem inputs and outputs, you should list the steps necessary to solve the problem. It is very important that you pay close attention to the order of the steps. The initial algorithm follows.

Initial Algorithm

1. Read the circle radius.
2. Find the area.
3. Find the circumference.
4. Print the area and circumference.

Algorithm Refinements

Next, we should refine any steps that do not have an obvious solution (for instance, steps 2 and 3).

Step 2 Refinement
2.1. Assign Pi * Radius * Radius to Area.

Step 3 Refinement
3.1. Assign 2 * Pi * Radius to Circumference.

Coding

Program 3.1 is the Ada program so far. The program body consists of the initial algorithm with its refinements. This outline contains the "framework" consisting of PROCEDURE, BEGIN, and END, some declarations, and just comments in the program body. Including the statement

```
NULL;
```

just after the BEGIN in fact makes the program syntactically correct Ada even though it has no other statements. It can be compiled just to check whether the basic framework and declarations are correct.

Program 3.1 Finding the Area and Circumference of a Circle (Framework)

```
PROCEDURE AreaAndCircum IS

   -- Finds and displays the area and circumference of a circle

   SUBTYPE NonNegFloat IS Float RANGE 0.0 .. Float'Last;
   Pi : CONSTANT NonNegFloat := 3.14159;

   Radius        : NonNegFloat; -- input  - radius of a circle
   Area          : NonNegFloat; -- output - area of a circle
   Circumference : NonNegFloat; -- output - circumference of a circle

BEGIN -- AreaAndCircum
   NULL;

   -- 1. Read the circle radius

   -- 2. Find the area
   -- 2.1 Assign Pi * Radius ** 2 to Area

   -- 3. Find the circumference
   -- 3.1 Assign 2.0 * Pi * Radius to Circumference

   -- 4. Display the Area and Circumference

END AreaAndCircum;
```

Null Statement

Form: NULL;
Example:
```
PROCEDURE SmallestAdaProcedure IS
BEGIN
NULL;
END SmallestAdaProcedure;
```
Interpretation: The null statement is used to indicate an "empty" sequence of statements. NULL is sometimes used to satisfy a syntax rule requiring a sequence of statements, even when the sequence is (intentionally) empty.

   To write the final program, we must

- convert the refinements (steps 2.1 and 3.1) to Ada,
- write Ada code for the unrefined steps (steps 1 and 4),
- add the necessary context clauses for input and output,
- delete the NULL statement, and
- delete the step numbers from the comments.
   Program 3.2 is the final program.

Program 3.2   Finding the Area and Circumference of a Circle (Complete)

```
WITH Text_IO;
WITH My_Flt_IO;
PROCEDURE AreaAndCircum IS

  -- Finds and displays the area and circumference of a circle

  SUBTYPE NonNegFloat IS Float RANGE 0.0 .. Float'Last;
  Pi : CONSTANT NonNegFloat := 3.14159;

  Radius        : NonNegFloat; -- input  - radius of a circle
  Area          : NonNegFloat; -- output - area of a circle
  Circumference : NonNegFloat; -- output - circumference of a circle

BEGIN -- AreaAndCircum

  -- Read the circle radius
  Text_IO.Put (Item => "Enter radius > ");
  My_Flt_IO.Get (Item => Radius);

  -- Find the area
  Area := Pi * Radius ** 2;

  -- Find the circumference
  Circumference := 2.0 * Pi * Radius;

  -- Display the Area and Circumference
  Text_IO.Put (Item => "The area is ");
  My_Flt_IO.Put (Item => Area, Fore => 1, Aft => 2, Exp => 0);
  Text_IO.New_Line;
  Text_IO.Put (Item => "The circumference is ");
  My_Flt_IO.Put (Item => Circumference, Fore => 1, Aft => 2, Exp => 0);
  Text_IO.New_Line;

END AreaAndCircum;


Enter radius > 5.0
The area is 78.54
The circumference is 31.42
```

Testing

The sample output shown in Program 3.2 provides a good test of the solution
because it is relatively easy to compute the area and circumference by hand for
a radius value of 5.0. The radius squared is 25.0, so the value of the area
appears correct. The circumference should be ten times π, which is also an easy
number to compute by hand. It would be useful to try another test involving a
radius of 1.0 and a different unit of measurement.

Exercises for Section 3.1

Self-Check

1. Describe the problem inputs and outputs and algorithm for computing an employee's gross salary given the hours worked and hourly rate.
2. Describe the problem inputs and outputs and algorithm for the following problem: Read in a pair of numbers and determine the sum and average of the two numbers.

Programming

1. Write a program for Self-Check question 2.

 ## 3.2 Problem Solving: Extending a Problem Solution

Quite often the solution of one problem turns out to be the basis for the solution to another problem. For example, we can easily solve the next problem by building on the solution to the previous problem.

◆ Case Study: Unit Price of a Pizza

Problem

You and your college roommates frequently order a late-night pizza snack. There are many pizzerias in the area that deliver to dormitories. Because you are on a tight budget, you would like to know which pizza is the best value.

Analysis

To find which pizza is the best value, we must be able to do a meaningful comparison of pizza costs. One way to do this is to compute the unit price of each pizza. The unit price of an item is obtained by dividing the total price of that item by a measure of its quantity. A good measure of quantity is the pizza weight, but pizzas are not sold by weight—they are sold by size (diameter), measured in inches. Consequently, the best that we can do is to use some meaningful measure of quantity based on the pizza diameter. One such measure is the pizza area. So, for our purposes we will define the unit price of a pizza as its price divided by its area.

The data requirements below list the pizza size and price as problem inputs. Although the problem statement does not ask us to display the pizza area, we are listing it as a problem output because the pizza area will give us some idea of how many friends we can invite to share our pizza. The radius (one-half of the diameter) is listed as a program variable because we need it to compute the pizza area, but it is not a problem input or output.

Case Study: Unit Price of a Pizza, continued

Data Requirements

Problem Constant
```
Pi : CONSTANT Float := 3.14159;
```

Problem Inputs
```
Size : NonNegFloat -- diameter of a pizza
Price : NonNegFloat -- price of a pizza
```

Problem Outputs
```
Area : NonNegFloat -- area of a pizza
UnitPrice : NonNegFloat -- unit price of a pizza
```

Relevant Formulas

area of a circle $= \pi \times \text{radius}^2$
radius of a circle $=$ diameter/2
unit price $=$ price/area

Design

We mentioned earlier that we are basing the problem solution on the solution to the Case Study in Section 3.1 (finding the area and circumference of a circle). The initial algorithm is similar to the one shown earlier. The step that computes the circle circumference (step 3) has been replaced with one that computes the pizza unit price.

Initial Algorithm

1. Read in the pizza diameter and price.
2. Compute the pizza area.
3. Compute the pizza unit price.
4. Display the unit price and area.

The algorithm refinements follow. The refinement of step 2 shows that we must compute the pizza radius before we can compute its area.

Step 2 Refinement
2.1. Assign Diameter / 2 to Radius.
2.2. Assign Pi * Radius * Radius to Area.

Step 3 Refinement
3.1. Assign Price / Area to UnitPrice.

Coding

Program 3.3 shows the framework for the Ada program. We will write this program the same way as before: by editing the data requirements to develop the program declaration part and by using the initial algorithm with refinements as a starting point for the program body. Program 3.4 gives the final program.

Program 3.3   Compute the Unit Price of a Pizza (Framework)

```
PROCEDURE Pizzeria IS

   -- Computes and displays the unit price of a pizza

   SUBTYPE NonNegFloat IS Float RANGE 0.0 .. Float'Last;
   Pi : CONSTANT NonNegFloat := 3.14159;

   Diameter  : NonNegFloat; -- input  - diameter of a pizza
   Price     : NonNegFloat; -- input  - price of a pizza
   UnitPrice : NonNegFloat; -- output - unit price of a pizza
   Area      : NonNegFloat; -- output - area of a pizza
   Radius    : NonNegFloat; -- radius of a pizza

BEGIN -- Pizzeria
   NULL;

   -- 1. Read in the pizza diameter and price

   -- 2. Compute the pizza area
   -- 2.1 Assign Diameter/2 to Radius
   -- 2.2 Assign Pi * Radius ** 2 to Area

   -- 3. Compute the pizza unit price
   -- 3.1 Assign Price / Area to UnitPrice

   -- 4. Display the unit price and area

END Pizzeria;
```

Program 3.4   Compute the Unit Price of a Pizza (Complete)

```
WITH Text_IO;
WITH My_Flt_IO;
PROCEDURE Pizzeria IS

   -- Computes and displays the unit price of a pizza

   SUBTYPE NonNegFloat IS Float RANGE 0.0 .. Float'Last;
   Pi : CONSTANT NonNegFloat := 3.14159;

   Diameter  : NonNegFloat; -- input  - diameter of a pizza
   Price     : NonNegFloat; -- input  - price of a pizza
   UnitPrice : NonNegFloat; -- output - unit price of a pizza
   Area      : NonNegFloat; -- output - area of a pizza
   Radius    : NonNegFloat; -- radius of a pizza

BEGIN -- Pizzeria

   -- Read in the pizza diameter and price
   Text_IO.Put (Item => "Size of pizza in inches > ");
```

```
My_Flt_IO.Get (Item => Diameter);
Text_IO.Put (Item => "Price of pizza $");
My_Flt_IO.Get (Item => Price);

-- Compute the pizza area
Radius := Diameter/2.0;
Area := Pi * Radius ** 2;

-- Compute the pizza unit price
UnitPrice := Price / Area;

-- Display the unit price and area
Text_IO.New_Line;
Text_IO.Put (Item => "The pizza unit price is $");
My_Flt_IO.Put (Item => UnitPrice, Fore => 1, Aft => 2, Exp => 0);
Text_IO.New_Line;
Text_IO.Put (Item => "The pizza area is ");
My_Flt_IO.Put (Item => Area, Fore => 1, Aft => 2, Exp => 0);
Text_IO.Put (Item => " square inches.");
Text_IO.New_Line;

END Pizzeria;


Size of pizza in inches > 10.0
Price of pizza $4.50

The pizza unit price is $0.06
The pizza area is 78.54 square inches.
```

Testing

To test this program, run it with a few different pizza sizes. You can verify that the program is working correctly by multiplying the unit price and area. This product should equal the price of the pizza.

◆

Using Comments

Comments make a program more readable by describing the purpose of the program and by describing the use of each identifier. For example, the comment in the declaration

```
Radius: NonNegFloat; -- program input - radius of a circle
```

describes the use of the variable Radius.

You should place comments within the program body to describe the purpose of each section of the program. The top-down programming method we use in this book uses comments in the program framework for each step of the algorithm and its refinements. Some of these comments are turned into program statements as these are written; others remain as program documentation.

You may wish to add other comments to a program to make it easier for yourself and others to understand. Make sure a comment within the program body adds useful descriptive information about what the step does rather than simply restate the step in English. For example, the comment

```
-- Find the area of the circle
Area := Pi * Radius * Radius;
```

is more descriptive than, and therefore preferable to,

```
-- Multiply the Radius by itelf and Pi
Area := Pi * Radius * Radius;
```

Begin each program with a header section that consists of a series of comments specifying:

the programmer's name,
the date of the current version, and
a brief description of what the program does.

If you write the program for a class assignment, you should also list the class identification and your instructor's name. Your instructor may also require other kinds of comments in your program.

A final word on comments: If a program has too few comments, the reader may have difficulty understanding the program. On the other hand, if there are too many comments, finding the program text among the comments will be difficult. Writing effective comments—knowing just how much to write—is a skill that must be practiced.

 # 3.3 Problem Solving: Structured Programming

Structured programming is a disciplined approach to programming that results in programs that are easy to read and understand and are less likely to contain errors. Structured programming was developed in the 1960s, and has become so well accepted since that time that almost nobody attempts to write programs any other way. We hope you agree that the programs written so far are relatively easy to read and understand.

Structured programming comes from a systematic approach to stating co m-plex problem solutions in terms of *sequences* of subtasks, *selections* among several alternative subtasks, and *repetitions* of subtasks. To illustrate that this is a natural approach even if the problem is not being solved on a computer, we consider first an example from everyday life.

Algorithms in Everyday Life

Algorithms are not really unique to the study of computer programming. You have probably been using algorithms to solve problems without being aware of it.

♦ Case Study: Changing a Flat Tire

Problem
You are driving a car with two friends and suddenly get a flat tire. Fortunately, there is a spare tire and jack in the trunk.

Analysis
After pulling over to the side of the road, you might decide to subdivide the problem of changing a tire into the subproblems below.

Algorithm

1. Get the jack and jack up the car.
2. Loosen the lug nuts from the flat tire and remove it.
3. Get the spare tire, place it on the wheel, and tighten the lug nuts.
4. Lower the car.
5. Secure the jack and flat tire in the trunk.

Because these steps are relatively independent, you might decide to assign subproblem 1 to friend A, subproblem 2 to friend B, subproblem 3 to yourself, and so on. If friend A has used a jack before, then the whole process should proceed smoothly; however, if friend A does not know how to use a jack, you need to refine step 1 further.

Step 1 Refinement
1.1. Get the jack from the trunk.
1.2. Place the jack under the car near the flat tire.
1.3. Insert the jack handle in the jack.
1.4. Place a block of wood under the car to keep it from rolling.
1.5. Jack up the car until there is enough room for the spare tire.

Step 1.4 requires a bit of *decision making* on your friend's part. Because the actual placement of the block of wood depends on whether the car is facing uphill or downhill, friend A needs to refine step 1.4.

Step 1.4 Refinement
1.4.1. If the car is facing uphill, then place the block of wood in back of a tire that is not flat; if the car is facing downhill, then place the block of wood in front of a tire that is not flat.

This is actually a *selection* action: One of two alternative actions is selected, depending on a certain condition.

Finally, step 1.5 involves a *repetitive* action: moving the jack handle until there is sufficient room to put on the spare tire. Often, people stop when the car is high enough to remove the flat tire, forgetting that an inflated tire requires more room. It may take a few attempts to complete step 1.5.

Step 1.5 Refinement
1.5.1. Move the jack handle repeatedly until the car is high enough off the ground that the spare tire can be put on the wheel.

The algorithm for changing a flat tire has three categories of action: sequential execution, conditional execution, and repetition. *Sequential execution* simply means to carry out steps 1.1 through 1.5 in the sequence listed. Step 1.4.1 illustrates *selection* in that placement of the block of wood depends on the angle of inclination of the car. Step 1.5.1 illustrates *repetition*.

Control Structures

Structured programming is a way of carrying into computer programs the natural method of systematic problem solving just described. Structured programming utilizes *control structures* to control the flow of statement execution in a program. There are three kinds of control structures: *sequence, selection,* and *repetition* or *iteration*. So far, each program we have looked at has consisted of a sequence of individual statements, and the flow of control has been passed from one statement to the next, beginning with the first statement in the program body and ending with the last statement in the program body.

In the next few chapters, we will introduce some Ada control structures. The control structures of a programming language enable us to group a sequence of related statements into a single structure with one entry point and one exit point. We can then write a program as a sequence of control structures rather than as a sequence of individual statements (see Fig. 3.1).

Motivation for Selection and Repetition Control Structures

So far we have extended the solution to one problem (find a circle radius and circumference) into a second related problem (find the unit price of a pizza). We are not really finished yet because our goal was to be able to do a cost comparison of several pizzas with different prices and sizes in order to determine the best value.

One way to accomplish our larger goal is to run this program several different times, once for each pizza, and record the results. Then we can scan the list of results to determine which pizza has the lowest unit price.

A better solution would be to write a program that repeated the computation steps and also compared unit prices, displaying as its final result the size

Figure 3.1   A Program as a Sequence of Three Control Structures

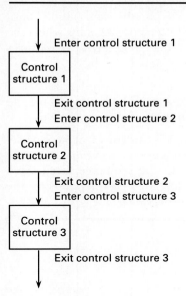

Enter control structure 1

Control
structure 1

Exit control structure 1
Enter control structure 2

Control
structure 2

Exit control structure 2
Enter control structure 3

Control
structure 3

Exit control structure 3

and price of the pizza with the lowest unit price. Let's write an algorithm that will give us this improved solution.

Initial Algorithm for Improved Solution to Pizza Problem

Step 1. For each size of pizza, read in the pizza size and price and compute unit cost. Compare the unit cost just computed with the previous unit costs and save the size and price of the pizza whose unit cost is the smallest so far.

Step 2. Display the size and price of the pizza with the smallest unit cost.

The purpose of step 1 of the algorithm is to perform the cost computation for each individual pizza and somehow save the size and price of the pizza whose unit cost was the smallest. After all costs are computed, step 2 displays the size and price of the pizza that is the best buy.

We don't know how to do step 1 yet in Ada because it involves the use of repetition and selection control structures. However, we can write a refinement of this step that will give you some idea of where we are heading in the next few chapters.

Step 1 Refinement

1.1. Repeat the following steps for each size of pizza:

1.2. Read in the next pizza size and price.

1.3. Compute the unit price.

1.4. If the new unit price is the smallest one so far then save this pizza's size, price, and unit price.

Step 1.1 specifies the *repetition* of a group of steps: step 1.2 (read), step 1.3 (compute), and step 1.4 (compare). We will repeat these steps as many times as necessary until all unit prices are computed. Each time we compute a new unit price, step 1.4 compares it to the others, and the current pizza's size and price are saved if its unit price is smaller than any others computed so far. If the unit price is not the smallest so far, the current pizza's size and price are not saved. Step 1.4 is a *selection* step because it selects between the two possible outcomes—(a) save the pizza's data and (b) do not save the pizza's data.

We will discuss control structures for selection and repetition further in Chapters 4, 5, and 6.

 # 3.4 Data Structures: Introducing Enumeration Types

So far, most of the data types you have seen have been numerical (Integer, Float). In this section you will be introduced to the important concept of enumeration types. An *enumeration type* is defined by a list of values taking the form of identifiers. These types are called enumeration types because their values are *enumerated,* or given in a list. An enumeration type is useful in representing a *fixed set of values* that are not numerical, such as the days of the week, the months of the year, the years in a college career, or the expenditure categories in an accounting program. Ada encourages you to use enumeration types by providing a small but useful set of operations on them, and also an input/output package that makes it easy to read enumeration values from a keyboard or disk file and display them on the screen.

Defining Enumeration Types

In many programming situations, the standard data types and their values are inadequate. For example, in a budget program we might want to distinguish among the following categories of expenditures: entertainment, rent, utilities, food, clothing, automobile, insurance, and miscellaneous. We could always assign an arbitrary code that associates entertainment with a character value of 'e', rent with a character value of 'r', and so on. However, enumeration types allow us to specify the set of values directly. For example, the enumeration type Expenses declared below has eight possible values enclosed in parentheses:

```
TYPE Expenses IS
    (entertainment, rent, utilities, food,
    clothing, automobile, insurance, miscellaneous);

ExpenseKind : Expenses;
```

The variable ExpenseKind (type Expenses) can contain any of the eight values listed after Expenses IS. The values, called *enumeration literals,* associated with an enumeration type are generally identifiers and therefore must conform to the syntax of identifiers. The type declaration must precede any variable declaration that references it.

The enumeration type Day has the values Monday, Tuesday, and so on:

```
TYPE Day IS
    (Monday, Tuesday, Wednesday, Thursday,
    Friday, Saturday, Sunday);
```

SYNTAX
DISPLAY

Enumeration Type Declaration

Form:　　TYPE *enumeration-type* IS (*identifier-list*);
Example: TYPE Class IS (Freshman, Sophomore, Junior, Senior);
Interpretation: A new data type named *enumeration-type* is declared. The enumeration literals, or values associated with this type, are specified in the *identifier-list*. The order in which the enumeration literals are given is important, as it defines an ordering of the literals: Freshman is less than Sophomore; Junior is greater than Freshman.

It is permissible for the same enumeration literal to appear in several enumeration types, just as it is permissible for the same numerical value to appear in several numerical types. It is, for example, possible to define the three types

```
TYPE Traffic_Light_Colors IS
(Red, Yellow, Green);

TYPE Primary_Paint_Colors IS
(Red, Yellow, Blue);

TYPE Primary_TV_Colors IS
(Red, Blue, Green);
```

in the same program without causing difficulties for the compiler.

Enumeration Type Attributes and Operations

The order relationship between the values of an enumeration type is fixed when the type is declared. Each literal has a *position* in the type, given as a value of type Natural. For type Day, the first value in its list (Monday) has position 0, the next value (Tuesday) has position 1, and so on.

An assignment statement can be used to define the value of a variable whose type is an enumeration type. The variable

```
Today     : Day; --current day of the week
Tomorrow  : Day; --day after Today
```

specifies that Today and Tomorrow are type Day and, therefore, can be assigned any of the values listed in the declaration for type Day. Consequently, the assignment statements

```
Today := Friday;
Tomorrow := Saturday;
```

assign the values Friday to variable Today and Saturday to variable Tomorrow.

An important aspect of Ada's type system is the notion of *attributes*. These are characteristics of a type or variable that can be queried by a program. For the case of enumeration types, six important attributes are

- First, which gives the first or lowest value in the type;
- Last, which gives the last or highest value;
- Pos, which, given a value in a type, gives its position in the type;
- Val, which, given a position in a type, gives the value in that position;
- Pred, which, given a value in a type, gives the value that precedes it in the type; and
- Succ, which, given a value in a type, gives the value that follows.

Some examples are given below, assuming that Today is Friday and Tomorrow is Saturday.

```
Day'First is Monday
Day'Last is Sunday
Day'Pos(Monday) is 0
Day'Val(0) is Monday
Day'Pos(Sunday) is 6
Day'Val(6) is Sunday
Day'Pred(Wednesday) is Tuesday
Day'Pred(Today) is Thursday
Day'Succ(Tuesday) is Wednesday
Day'Succ(Today) is Saturday
```

Because enumeration types are not cyclical (i.e., do not "wrap around"), the queries Day'Pred(Monday) and Day'Succ(Sunday) are undefined and would cause a run-time exception—namely, the raising of Constraint_Error— if attempted. Similarly, if indeed Tomorrow had the value Sunday, then Day'Succ(Tomorrow) would cause an exception. Whether the assignment statement

```
Tomorrow := Day'Succ(Today);
```

would cause an exception depends on the value of Today; it cannot cause a compilation error because the value of Today is usually unknown at compilation time.

In the next chapter you will see some examples of how to use careful checking of values in order to prevent exceptions from being raised.

Attribute Query

Form: *type'attribute-name* or *type'attribute-name(value)*
Example:
```
Traffic_Light_Colors'First
Day'Succ(Wednesday)
Day'Pos(Today)
```

Interpretation: An attribute query answers a question regarding certain characteristics of types or variables. For each type, the set of attributes is predefined by the language and cannot normally be changed by the programmer. Note the required presence of the single quote or apostrophe in the attribute query.

Input/Output Operations for Enumeration Types

One of the most convenient Ada features for using enumeration types is a built-in input/output package for reading and displaying enumeration literals. Recall that in Chapter 2 we instantiated or "tailored" the numerical input/output packages, creating instances called My_Int_IO and My_Flt_IO. We needed to do this because the packages are generic. Ada gives us a similar situation for enumeration types. Within Text_IO is a generic package called Enumeration_ IO, which cannot be used immediately. Instances must be created; each instance is tailored to read and display exactly and only the literals in an enumeration type. For example, in a program in which the type Day is defined and the variable declaration Today:Day appears, we could write

```
PACKAGE Day_IO IS NEW Text_IO.Enumeration_IO(Enum=>Day);
```

which would give us the ability to read a value from the keyboard into Today or to display the value of Today on the screen, using procedure calls like

```
Day_IO.Get(Item => Today);
Day_IO.Put(Item => Today, Width => 10);
```

In the case of Get, the exception Data_Error is raised if the value entered on the keyboard is not one of the seven literals in Day. In this manner the input/output system automatically checks the validity of the value entered, making sure that it is a legal value in the enumeration type.

Enumeration Get Procedure

Form: *instance*.Get (Item => *variable*);
Example: Day_IO.Get (Item => Some_Day);
Interpretation: By *instance* we mean an instance of Enumeration_IO for some enumeration type. The next string of characters entered at the keyboard is read into *variable* (of the same enumeration type). Any leading blank characters or RETURNs are ignored. The first nonblank character must be a letter, and the characters must form an identifier. The data string is terminated when a nonidentifier character is entered or the space bar or RETURN key is pressed.

If the identifier read is not one of the literals in the enumeration type for which *instance* was created, Data_Error is raised.

Enumeration Put Procedure

Form: *instance*.Put (Item => *variable* , Width => *field width*,
             Set => Text_IO.Upper_Case, or Text_IO.Lower_Case);

Example: Day_IO.Put (Item => Some_Day, Width => 5,
             Set => Text_IO.Lower_Case);

Interpretation: The value of *variable* (of some enumeration type) is displayed, using the next Width positions on the screen. If the value would occupy less than Width positions, it is followed by the appropriate number of blanks; if the value would occupy more than Width positions, the actual number of positions is used. If Width is omitted, a compiler-dependent width is used by default. The standard values Text_IO.Upper_Case and Text IO.Lower_Case are used to determine the form of the displayed value. If Set is omitted, the value is displayed in uppercase.

◆ Case Study: Translating from English to French Color Names

Problem

Your roommate comes from France, and you are taking a watercolor-painting class together. You would like to have the computer give you some help in remembering the French names of the major colors, so that communication with your roommate will be easier. You'd like to enter an English color name on the keyboard and let the program display the corresponding French name. The English color names are white, black, red, purple, blue, green, yellow, and orange; the French color names are blanc, noir, rouge, pourpre, bleu, vert, jaune, and orange.

Analysis

The French and English colors can be represented by two enumeration types, French_Colors and English_Colors, and can be read and displayed using two instances of Enumeration_IO, which we will call French_Color_IO and English_Color_IO.

Data Requirements

Problem Data Types
English colors, an enumeration type:

```
TYPE English_Colors IS
    (white, black, red, purple, blue, green, yellow, orange);
```

French colors, also an enumeration type:

```
TYPE French_Colors IS
   (blanc, noir, rouge, pourpre, bleu, vert, jaune, orange);
```

Problem Inputs
English color (Eng_Color : English_Colors).

Problem Outputs
French color (Fr_Color : French_Colors).

Design

We were careful to list the French and English colors in the same order, so given an English color, the corresponding French color will be in the same position in the French color type. This gives us the following algorithm.

Initial Algorithm

1. Prompt the user to enter one of the eight English colors, Eng_Color.
2. Find the corresponding French color, Fr_Color.
3. Display the French color.

Algorithm Refinements

The only step needing refinement is step 2. We can find the French color corresponding to a given English one by using the Pos and Val attributes. Since the French and English colors have corresponding positions, we can find the position of the English color in its type, then use that position to find the corresponding value in the French type. To do this we shall need a program variable Position of type Natural to store the color position within its type.

Step 2 Refinement
2.1. Save in Position the position of Eng_Color in its type.
2.2. Save in Fr_Color the corresponding value in the French type.

Coding

The complete program is shown in Program 3.5. The program begins with a context clause for Text_IO. Within the program, the two color types are defined and instances of Enumeration_IO are created to read and display values of these types. Finally, the sequence of statements implements the refined algorithm just developed.

Program 3.5 Translating between English and French Colors

```
WITH Text_IO;
PROCEDURE Colors IS

   TYPE English_Colors IS
      (white, black, red, purple, blue, green, yellow, orange);

   TYPE French_Colors IS
      (blanc, noir, rouge, pourpre, bleu, vert, jaune, orange);
```

```
PACKAGE English_Color_IO IS
    NEW Text_IO.Enumeration_IO (Enum => English_Colors);

PACKAGE French_Color_IO IS
    NEW Text_IO.Enumeration_IO (Enum => French_Colors);

Eng_Color : English_Colors;
Fr_Color  : French_Colors;
Position  : Natural;

BEGIN

    Text_IO.Put (Item => "Please enter an English color > ");
    English_Color_IO.Get (Item => Eng_Color);

    Position := English_Colors'Pos(Eng_Color);
    Fr_Color := French_Colors'Val(Position);

    Text_IO.Put (Item => "The French color is ");
    French_Color_IO.Put (Item => Fr_Color, Set => Text_IO.Lower_Case);
    Text_IO.New_Line;

END Colors;


Please enter an English color > blue
The French color is bleu
```

Exercises for Section 3.4

Self-Check

1. Evaluate each of the following assuming Today (type Day) is Thursday before
   each operation.
   a. Day'Pos(Monday)
   b. Day'Pos(Today)
   c. Day'Val(6)
   d. Today < Tuesday

   e. Day'Succ(Sunday)
   f. Day'Pred(Monday)
   g. Day'Val(0)
   h. Today >= Thursday

3.5 System Structures: The Importance of Packages

Consider the input/output libraries we have been using in this book. Each of
the various Get and Put statements in the earlier examples is really a *procedure
call* statement. A procedure is a kind of system building block, a way of putting
together a group of program statements and treating them as a unit, causing
them to be executed by means of *procedure calls*. In this book you will learn how

to write procedures; in this chapter you will continue just to use procedures written by others.

The Get and Put procedures we have been using were written by another programmer at another time; they were supplied to us as part of a *package* called Text_IO. Just as a procedure is a way of grouping statements, a package is a way of grouping procedures (and other program entities we will introduce later on). It is through the use of packages that procedures can be written and tested for general use (that is, by other programmers) and put in a form in which they can be supplied to others. Ada compilers come with several standard library packages. Text_IO is one of these; in the next section you will see another, called Calendar.

The package concept is one of the most important developments to be found in modern programming languages, such as Ada, Modula-2, Turbo Pascal, C++, and Eiffel. The designers of the different languages have not agreed on what terms to use for this concept: Package, module, unit, and class are commonly used. But it is generally agreed that the package—as it is called in Ada—is the essential programming tool to be used for going beyond the programming of very simple class exercises to what is generally called software engineering, or building real programs of real size for the real world. It is the package that allows us to develop a set of related operations and other entities, especially types, to test these thoroughly, and then to store them in an Ada program library for our future use or even to distribute them to others.

You will work with four kinds of packages in this book:

• standard packages—such as Text_IO, which you have been using, and Calendar, introduced in Section 3.6—which are provided by Ada as part of its standard environment;
• packages provided along with the compiler you are using, such as the math-function package to be introduced in Chapter 7;
• packages supplied along with this book, such as the screen-control package introduced in Section 3.7; and
• packages written as part of your study of this book, such as the packages introduced in Chapters 4, 5, and 6.

Because the package is so important in modern software design, we have introduced its use very early in this book. In the next sections you will see how to use one of Ada's standard packages and one supplied with this book; in the next chapter you will see how to write a very simple package of your own.

3.6 System Structures: Using Ada's Calendar Package

In this section you will see how to use another standard Ada library package, Calendar.

In all Ada packages, the resources provided are listed in an Ada source file called the *package specification*. The package specification plays two roles: It describes the package to the compiler, and it serves as a "contract" with the programmer using it, telling this human user exactly what resources to expect. Some of the different *kinds* of resources provided by a package are

- types and subtypes,
- procedures, and
- functions.

Ada's calendar package provides a number of useful resources relating to dates and times. Figure 3.2 shows a part of the specification for `Calendar`; for clarity we have only listed those services needed in this example. Figure 10.3 gives the entire specification for `Calendar`.

Figure 3.2 Partial Specification of Package Calendar

```
PACKAGE Calendar IS
        -- standard Ada package, must be supplied with compilers
        -- provides useful services for dates and times

        -- type definitions

        TYPE Time IS PRIVATE;

        SUBTYPE Year_Number  IS Integer  RANGE 1901..2099;
        SUBTYPE Month_Number IS Integer  RANGE 1..12;
        SUBTYPE Day_Number   IS Integer  RANGE 1..31;

        FUNCTION Clock RETURN Time;

        FUNCTION Year  (Date : Time)  RETURN Year_Number;
        FUNCTION Month (Date : Time)  RETURN Month_Number;
        FUNCTION Day   (Date : Time)  RETURN Day_Number;

  -- there are many other facilities here;
  -- for clarity, they are omitted from this figure

  . . .

END Calendar;
```

After the first line,

```
PACKAGE Calendar IS
```

which indicates the beginning of a package specification, one type and three subtype declaration statements are given. The line

```
TYPE Time IS PRIVATE;
```

specifies `Time` as a `PRIVATE` type, the details of whose values are not known to the package user. We do not know a `Time` value explicitly because it is an internal value produced by the computer's real-time clock; this internal value represents a year, calendar day, and time of day in a single bit pattern. We will discuss private types in detail later, especially in Chapter 10. For now, you need to know that because `Time` is a `PRIVATE` type, the only way we can use `Time` values is to work with them according to the various operations provided by Calendar; you will see a few of these operations in a short while.

Given a program preceded by a context clause

```
WITH Calendar;
```

then the declaration

```
Right_Now : Calendar.Time;
```

declares a variable capable of holding a time value. The form Calendar.Time is similar to the form Text_IO.New_Line in that the name of the package is used to *qualify* the use of the package resource: Time is a resource provided by Calendar; New_Line is a resource provided by Text_IO.

Returning to the specification of Calendar in Fig. 3.2, the next three lines give declarations for years, months, and days:

```
SUBTYPE Year_Number IS Integer RANGE 1901..2099;
SUBTYPE Month_Number IS Integer RANGE 1..12;
SUBTYPE Day_Number IS Integer RANGE 1..31;
```

Recall from Chapter 2 that a type consists of a set of values and a set of operations on these values, and that a subtype is a subset of the original set of values, together with the full original set of operations. For example, in declaring Month_Number to be a subtype of Integer and giving its range as 1..12, we are saying that any variables of type Month_Number can hold integer values only in the range 1 through 12 inclusive. Similarly, variables of subtype Day_Number can hold integer values in the range 1 through 31 inclusive. All of the operations on integers apply to values of these subtypes, but if an operation attempts to store a value that is outside the declared range, this operation is improper and a Constraint_Error exception will be raised at run time.

In this text we will make frequent use of subtypes; they are a convenient way to inform the compiler—and the reader of a program—that certain variables have ranges that are restricted according to their intended use. Ada can then help us to avoid and recover from errors by checking that variables store numbers only of appropriate size.

The declarations

```
This_Year   : Calendar.Year_Number;
This_Month : Calendar.Month_Number;
This_Day    : Calendar.Day_Number;
```

declare variables of the three subtypes provided by Calendar. Again we have used qualified references; this is done to remind both the compiler and the human reader of the package in which the resources are defined.

Next we consider how to determine the current time of day in Ada. Returning to the Calendar specification in Fig. 3.2, the next line

```
FUNCTION Clock RETURN Time;
```

specifies a *function* called Clock. Given the declaration

```
Right_Now: Calendar.Time;
```

then an assignment statement such as

```
Right_Now := Calendar.Clock;
```

will be compiled into machine instructions that read the computer's internal clock, which delivers the current time of day and stores this time value in the variable `Right_Now`. The expression `Calendar.Clock` is a *function call;* we will see other function calls shortly.

This value is not very useful to us in this form; we cannot display it, for example, because its precise form is not available to us. But as the next three lines of the specification show,

```
FUNCTION Year (Date: Time) RETURN Year_Number;
FUNCTION Month (Date: Time) RETURN Month_Number;
FUNCTION Day (Date: Time) RETURN Day_Number;
```

the package gives us operations to extract the year, month, and day from the internal time value. Each of these operations is a function with a single parameter `Date`, which is of type `Time`. For example, if we declare a variable

```
This_Year : Calendar.Year_Number;
```

then the assignment statement

```
This_Year := Calendar.Year(Date => Right_Now);
```

will store the current calendar year in `This_Year`. Integer operations can be performed on `This_Year`; specifically, its value can be displayed. This function call is analogous to a `Text_IO` procedure call such as

```
Text_IO.Put(Item => FirstInitial);
```

in the sense that a value is being supplied to correspond to the formal parameter. The formal parameter of `Put` is called `Item`; the formal parameter of `Year` is called `Date`.

In using the operations of `Calendar`, we have no knowledge of the details of how they perform. This is of no concern to us; the "contract" embodied in the specification tells us what to expect, and this is all we need to know.

Simple Function Call Statement

Form: *variable* := *fname* (*actual parameters*) ;

Example:

```
Right_Now := Calendar.Clock;
This_Month := Calendar.Month(Date => Right_Now);
```

Interpretation: The list of parameters (if any) is enclosed in parentheses; each actual parameter value is preceded by the name of that formal parameter. The variable must be of the same type as the return type of the function *fname*. The function fname is called, and its returned value is stored in `variable`. During the function execution, the named actual parameters are associated with the corresponding formal parameters.

Note 1: Multiple parameters are separated by commas.

Note 2: The number of actual and formal parameters must be the same. Each actual parameter that is an expression is evaluated when *fname* is called; this value is assigned to the corresponding formal parameter.

Note 3: The type of each actual parameter must agree with the type of the corresponding formal parameter. Ada does not allow, for example, an integer-valued actual parameter to be associated with a float-valued formal parameter.

Note 4: In this book, each actual parameter is listed with the name of the corresponding formal parameter (the two are separated by =>). Therefore, strictly speaking the *order* of the actual parameters does not have to match that of the formal parameters. It is nevertheless good practice to list the actual parameters in an order corresponding to the order of the formal parameters.

Note that as the second example shows, functions can be defined to have no parameters at all. The number, order, and type of the parameters is, of course, determined by the writer of the function, not its user.

◆ Case Study: Displaying Today's Date in "mm/dd/yy" Form

Let's use the knowledge gained in this chapter to solve the problem of displaying today's date.

Problem

Display today's date in the usual American form mm/dd/yy; for example, if today is October 21, 1991, we display 10/21/91. If today is July 8, 1992, we display 7/8/92.

Analysis

Today's date can be obtained from the computer's internal clock using the appropriate Ada calendar facilities to get a time value and then to extract the month, day, and year. These three values can then be formatted to give the desired display.

Data Requirements

Problem Data Types

We need only the type Time and the subtypes Year_Number, Month_Number, and Day_Number provided by the standard package Calendar.

Case Study: Displaying Today's Date in "mm/dd/yy" Form, continued

103

3.6 System
Structures: Using
Ada's Calendar
Package

Problem Inputs
No inputs need to be entered by the user.

Problem Outputs
Today's date, in the form mm/dd/yy.

Design

Initial Algorithm

1. Get the current time value from the computer's clock.
2. Extract the current month, day, and year from the time value.
3. Format and display the date.

Algorithm Refinements

Step 2 Refinement
2.1. Extract the current month from the time value.
2.2. Extract the current day from the time value.
2.3. Extract the current year from the time value.

In step 3, we note that because the year is in the form yyyy (for example, 1989), we need to select the last two digits for formatting.

Step 3 Refinement
3.1. Find the last two digits of the year.
3.2. Format and display the current month, day, and year.

We can illustrate the steps in the problem-solving process with a diagram that shows the algorithm subproblems and their interdependencies. An example of such a diagram, called a *structure chart*, is shown in Fig. 3.3.

Figure 3.3 Structure Chart for Formatting and Displaying Today's Date

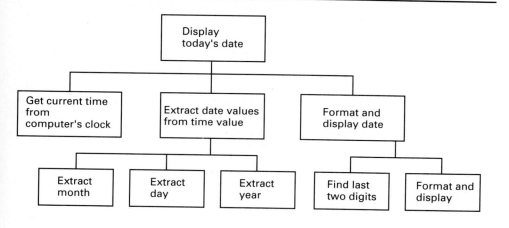

As we trace down this diagram, we go from an abstract problem to a more detailed subproblem. The original problem is shown at the top, or level 0, of the structure chart. The major subproblems appear at level 1. The different subproblems resulting from the refinement of each level 1 step are shown at level 2 and are connected to their respective level 1 subproblem. This diagram shows that the subproblem *Extract date values from time value* is dependent on the solutions to the subproblems *Extract month, Extract day,* and *Extract year.* Because the subproblem *Get current time* is not refined further, there are no level 2 subproblems connected to it.

Structure charts are intended to show the structural relationship between the subproblems. The algorithm (not the structure chart) shows the order in which each step must be carried out to solve the problem.

Coding

Program 3.6 shows the Ada program for this problem. The program begins with the appropriate context clauses, including one for Calendar. Variables for the time, month, day, and year are declared. We need two more declarations:

```
Last_Two_Digits : Natural;
This_Century : CONSTANT Natural := 1900;
```

to allow us to find the last two digits of the year, as you will see in a moment.

Program 3.6 Displaying Today's Date
_____

```
WITH Text_IO;
WITH My_Int_IO;
WITH Calendar;
PROCEDURE TodayDate IS

-- Finds and displays today's date in the form mm/dd/yy
-- The date is gotten from PACKAGE Calendar

   Right_Now   : Calendar.Time;         -- holds internal clock value
   This_Year   : Calendar.Year_Number;  -- holds current year
   This_Month  : Calendar.Month_Number; -- holds current month
   This_Day    : Calendar.Day_Number;   -- holds current day

   Last_Two_Digits : Natural;
   This_century    : CONSTANT Integer := 1900;

BEGIN -- TodayDate

   -- Get the current time value from the computer's clock
   Right_Now := Calendar.Clock;

   -- Extract the current month, day, and year from the time value
   This_Month := Calendar.Month(Date => Right_Now);
   This_Day   := Calendar.Day (Date => Right_Now);
   This_Year  := Calendar.Year (Date => Right_Now);

   -- Format and display the date
   Last_Two_Digits := This_Year - This_Century;
```

Case Study: Displaying Today's Date in "mm/dd/yy" Form, continued

105

3.6 System
Structures: Using
Ada's Calendar
Package

```
Text_IO.Put (Item => "Today's date is ");
My_Int_IO.Put (Item => This_Month, Width => 1);
Text_IO.Put (Item => '/');
My_Int_IO.Put (Item => This_Day, Width => 1);
Text_IO.Put (Item => '/');
My_Int_IO.Put (Item => Last_Two_Digits, Width => 1);
Text_IO.New_Line;

END TodayDate;
```

```
Today's date is 2/11/91
```

In the program body, the statements that get the clock value and extract the month and day were just discussed. Finally, the statement

```
Last_Two_Digits := This_Year - This_Century;
```

finds the last two digits of the year: If the current year is 1990, then `This_Year` gets the value 1990–1900 or 90, as desired.

Finally, the results are formatted and displayed using a sequence of `Put` statements from `Text_IO` and `My_Int_IO`. Notice how the integer values are displayed using a width of 1, to keep them "up against" the slashes.

◆

◆ Case Study: Displaying Today's Date in "month dd, yyyy" Form

This problem is similar to the previous one. In fact, it can be solved just by modifying the previous algorithm. Package `Calendar` gives us only the number of the current month from 1 to 12, so we need to specify the names of the months. We can do this with an enumeration type:

```
TYPE Months IS
   (January, February, March, April, May, June,
   July, August, September, October, November, December);
```

The current month can be displayed using an instance of `Enumeration_IO`, as in the colors program:

```
PACKAGE Month_IO IS NEW Text_IO.Enumeration_IO(Enum => Months);
```

All steps of the algorithm are the same, except for step 3.1. We do not need to select the last two digits of the year, because all four digits will be printed. However, we need to find the name corresponding to the number of the current month. Because the month is given from 1 to 12, and the positions of the names are 0 to 11, subtracting 1 from the month will give us the right position in

Case Study: Displaying Today's Date in "month dd, yyyy" Form, continued

Months, from which we can find the month name using the Val attribute. If
the month name is stored in a variable Month_Name of type Months, we have

```
Month_Name := Months'Val(This_Month - 1);
```

The solution to this problem is shown in Program 3.7.

Program 3.7 Displaying Today's Date in Another Format

```
WITH Text_IO;
WITH My_Int_IO;
WITH Calendar;
PROCEDURE TodayDate2 IS

-- Finds today's date and displays it
--   in the form MONTH dd, yyyy
-- An enumeration type is used for months
-- The date is gotten from PACKAGE Calendar

   TYPE Months IS
       (January, February, March, April, May, June,
        July, August, September, October, November, December);

   PACKAGE Months_IO IS NEW Text_IO.Enumeration_IO(Enum => Months);

   Right_Now  : Calendar.Time;          -- holds internal clock value
   This_Year  : Calendar.Year_Number;   -- holds current year
   This_Month : Calendar.Month_Number;  -- holds current month
   This_Day   : Calendar.Day_Number;    -- holds current day

   Month_Name: Months;

BEGIN -- TodayDate2

   -- Get the current time value from the computer's clock
   Right_Now := Calendar.Clock;

   -- Extract the current month, day, and year from the time value
   This_Month := Calendar.Month(Date => Right_Now);
   This_Day   := Calendar.Day (Date => Right_Now);
   This_Year  := Calendar.Year (Date => Right_Now);

   -- Format and display the date
   Month_Name := Months'Val(This_Month - 1);

   Text_IO.Put (Item => "Today's date is ");
   Months_IO.Put (Item => Month_Name, Set => Text_IO.Upper_Case);
   Text_IO.Put (Item => ' ');
   My_Int_IO.Put (Item => This_Day, Width => 1);
   Text_IO.Put (Item => ',');
   My_Int_IO.Put (Item => This_Year, Width => 5);
   Text_IO.New_Line;

END TodayDate2;
```

```
Today's date is FEBRUARY 11, 1991
```

◆

3.7 System Structures: Using a Screen-Control Package

Ada's Text_IO package provides operations for reading from the terminal keyboard and writing to the screen, but it provides no direct operations for controlling the screen in interesting ways, such as moving the cursor to a given row–column position before writing. Doing this requires an additional package which uses Text_IO to send *control characters* to the teminal; the control characters act as instructions to the terminal instead of data it should display. Because this package, which we will call Screen, is not part of standard Ada, we provide it with this book. The details of just how this package operates are left until Chapter 7, but it is possible for you to use the package without understanding its innards.

A package consists of two files, called the *specification* file and the *body* file. As discussed in Section 3.6, the specification gives the "contract with the user," or list of promised resources. The body delivers the actual source code for the procedures and functions promised by the specification. Because the Text_IO and Calendar packages are supplied in precompiled form by all Ada compilers, we have seen only their specifications; the source code for the bodies is not available to us. Other packages may be supplied to you in source-code form, with both the specification and body files provided. Screen is one of these packages.

Program 3.8 shows the specification for Screen. This package provides two constants, Screen_Width and Screen_Depth, corresponding to the number of columns (usually 80) and rows (usually 24) on the screen. There are also two subtypes, Width and Depth, giving the ranges for valid cursor positions (1..Screen_Depth and 1..Screen_Width respectively).

The package provides three procedures. The first two, Beep and Clear-Screen, take no parameters: A procedure call statement

---

Program 3.8   Specification for Package Screen

```
PACKAGE Screen IS

-- Procedures for drawing pictures on ANSI Terminal Screen

   Screen_Depth : CONSTANT Integer := 24;
   Screen_Width : CONSTANT Integer := 80;

   SUBTYPE Depth IS Integer RANGE 1..Screen_Depth;
   SUBTYPE Width IS Integer RANGE 1..Screen_Width;

   PROCEDURE Beep;
   PROCEDURE ClearScreen;
   PROCEDURE MoveCursor (Column : Width; Row : Depth);

END Screen;
```

```
Screen.Beep;
```

causes the terminal to beep; a procedure call statement

```
Screen.ClearScreen;
```

causes the screen to go blank, erasing all previous information from it. The last procedure, MoveCursor, takes row and column parameters, so that, for example,

```
Screen.MoveCursor (Row => 10, Column => 22);
Text_IO.Put (Item => '*');
```

has the effect of displaying an asterisk in the location of row 10, column 22. Finally,

```
Screen.MoveCursor (Row => 5, Column => 10);
Text_IO.Put (Item => "-----");
```

displays the string ----- in row 5, columns 10 through 14, inclusive.

Program 3.9 gives the body file for this package. You might not understand exactly how the procedures work. Don't worry about this right now; we will return to it in Chapter 7.

Program 3.9 Body of Package Screen

```
WITH Text_IO;
WITH My_Int_IO;
PACKAGE BODY Screen IS

-- Procedures for drawing pictures on ANSI Terminal Screen


  PROCEDURE Beep IS
  BEGIN
    Text_IO.Put (Item => ASCII.BEL);
  END Beep;

  PROCEDURE ClearScreen IS
  BEGIN
    Text_IO.Put (Item => ASCII.ESC);
    Text_IO.Put (Item => "[2J");
  END ClearScreen;

  PROCEDURE MoveCursor (Column : Width; Row : Depth) IS
  BEGIN
    Text_IO.Put (Item => ASCII.ESC);
    Text_IO.Put ('[');
    My_Int_IO.Put (Item => Row, Width => 1);
    Text_IO.Put (Item => ';');
    My_Int_IO.Put (Item => Column, Width => 1);
    Text_IO.Put (Item => 'f');
  END MoveCursor;

END Screen;
```

Preparing to Use a Package

Before a package can be used by other programs, it must be compiled. The specification must be compiled first, then the body. To use the screen package, you must have a copy of the specification and body files available in your computer's file system. If you do not, you must type them in exactly as shown in Programs 3.8 and 3.9, then compile them both. If you subsequently modify the specification file, you must recompile both it and the body, and all other programs that use the package as well. If you do not modify either file, you will not have to recompile it; your Ada compiler's library system will keep it available for use with a context clause

```
WITH Screen;
```

As an example of the use of the screen package, consider Program 3.10, which first clears the screen, then beeps three times, then draws a "smiley face" in the center of the screen. After each beep, there is a statement

```
DELAY 0.1;
```

which causes the computer to wait 0.1 second before sending the next beep. This is done so that even on a very fast computer you will hear three distinct beeps. Figure 3.4 shows the results of executing Smiley.

Figure 3.4 Output from Smiley

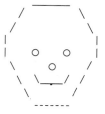

There is one more thing you need to know about Screen. Even though all Ada compilers support the same Ada language, not all Ada programs can show correct output on all terminals, because different kinds of terminals have different characteristics. This package assumes that the terminal you are using responds to ANSI control sequences. Most UNIX and VMS terminals do. So does an IBM-PC or compatible computer, provided that the ANSI.SYS device is listed in the computer's CONFIG.SYS file. If you run Smiley but your screen does not look like Fig. 3.4, see your computer center or teacher to ascertain whether you can use the Screen package.

```
WITH Text_IO;
WITH Screen;
PROCEDURE Smiley IS

-- draws a "smiley face" in the center of the terminal screen

BEGIN -- Smiley

   Screen.ClearScreen;
   Screen.Beep;
   DELAY 0.1;
   Screen.Beep;
   DELAY 0.1;
   Screen.Beep;
   DELAY 0.1;
   Screen.MoveCursor (Row => 7, Column => 34);
   Text_IO.Put (Item =>    "HAVE A NICE DAY!");
   Screen.MoveCursor (Row => 9, Column => 39);
   Text_IO.Put (Item =>    "_____");
   Screen.MoveCursor (Row => 10, Column => 37);
   Text_IO.Put (Item =>    "/        \");
   Screen.MoveCursor (Row => 11, Column => 36);
   Text_IO.Put (Item => "/          \");
   Screen.MoveCursor (Row => 12, Column => 35);
   Text_IO.Put (Item => "|            |");
   Screen.MoveCursor (Row => 13, Column => 35);
   Text_IO.Put (Item => "|  0    0    |");
   Screen.MoveCursor (Row => 14, Column => 36);
   Text_IO.Put (Item => "\    o     /");
   Screen.MoveCursor (Row => 15, Column => 37);
   Text_IO.Put (Item =>    "\ \___/ /");
   Screen.MoveCursor (Row => 16, Column => 38);
   Text_IO.Put (Item =>    "\      /");
   Screen.MoveCursor (Row => 17, Column => 39);
   Text_IO.Put (Item =>    "-----");
   Screen.MoveCursor (Row => 24, Column => 1);

END Smiley;
```

3.8 Tricks of the Trade: Common Programming Errors

When you define enumeration types, keep in mind that the order is important.
Thus

```
TYPE Day IS (Mon, Tue, Wed, Thu, Fri, Sat, Sun);
```

is not the same as

```
TYPE Day IS (Sun, Mon, Tue, Wed, Thu, Fri, Sat);
```

because the positions of the various literals are different in the two types.

When you work with packages that are not part of the Ada system, remember that they may have to be compiled before you can use them. If so, you must compile the specification first, then the body. After the specification is compiled you can compile any program that uses the package, but you cannot link that program until the body is compiled.

 # Chapter Review

In the first part of this chapter we discussed more aspects of problem solving. We reviewed the top-down approach to solving problems and showed how to use the documentation created by following the software development method as the outline of the final program. We also showed how we could extend a solution to one problem to form the basis of the solution for another problem. We discussed how structure charts are used to show relationships between different levels of subproblems or between algorithm steps and their refinements.

We discussed the importance of control structures to structured programming and introduced the three kinds of control structures: sequence, selection, and repetition.

Several guidelines for using program comments were discussed. Well placed and carefully worded comments, and a structure chart, can provide all of the documentation necessary for a program. In the remainder of the chapter, we discussed the representation of the various steps in an algorithm and illustrated the stepwise refinement of algorithms.

In this chapter enumeration types were introduced, along with Ada's standard input/output library for reading and displaying enumeration values. Enumeration types are useful in allowing the programmer to give meaningful names to values such as days of the week, months of the year, colors of the rainbow, and command sets.

This chapter also continued the use of packages, begun in Chapter 2 with the use of the input/output libraries. We discussed Ada's standard package `Calendar` and a package called `Screen`, provided with this book.

New Ada Constructs in Chapter 3

Enumeration type definition:

```
TYPE CompassPoints IS (North, South, East, West);
```

defines a type whose values are enumerated as a list of identifiers

✓ Quick-Check Exercises

1. Does a compiler translate comments?
2. Each statement in a program should have a comment. (True or false?)

3. What is a structure chart?
4. Explain how a structure chart differs from an algorithm.

Answers to Quick-Check Exercises
1. No
2. False
3. A structure chart is a diagram used to show an algorithm's subproblems and their interdependence.
4. A structure chart shows the relationship between subproblems; an algorithm lists the sequence in which subproblems are performed.

Review Questions for Chapter 3

1. Discuss the strategy of top-down design.
2. Provide guidelines for the use of comments.
3. Briefly describe the steps you would take to derive an algorithm for a given problem.
4. The diagram that shows the algorithm steps and their interdependencies is called a _____.

Programming Projects

1. Write a program that clears the screen, then beeps and flashes the word HELP in the center of the screen three times at 1-second intervals. (*Hint:* To "flash" a word, display a word, then display the same number of spaces in the same spot on the screen.)

2. Write a program that displays today's date in the center of the screen.
3. Find out the names of the days of the week in some other language and write a program that translates from those names to the English ones. Revise your program to do the translation in the other direction.

Decision Statements; Writing Simple Functions and Packages

4

4.1 Control Structures: Boolean Expressions and
     the IF Statement
4.2 Problem Solving: Decision Steps in Algorithms
4.3 Tricks of the Trade: Tracing a Program or Algorithm
4.4 Problem Solving: More Strategies
4.5 Control Structures: The IF Statement Revisited
4.6 System Structures: Writing Simple Functions
4.7 System Structures: Writing a Simple Package
4.8 Tricks of the Trade: Common Programming Errors
     Chapter Review

In this chapter we show you how to represent decisions in algorithms by writing steps with two or more alternative courses of action. You will see how to implement conditional execution in Ada by using Boolean conditions and the Ada IF statement. This chapter provides many examples of program fragments containing IF statements.

This chapter also introduces you to the process of writing simple reusable functions and putting them in packages for later use by yourself and others. This continues the practice begun in Chapters 2 and 3, in which each chapter introduces new material that will help you structure small program units, but also shows you immediately how to integrate this new material into larger, system-level units. In this way you will always focus your attention on the two equally important problems of building individual programs and building libraries of programs into systems.

 ## 4.1 Control Structures: Boolean Expressions and the IF Statement

In all the algorithms illustrated so far, each algorithm step is executed exactly once in the order in which it appears. Often we are faced with situations in which we must provide alternative steps that may or may not be executed, depending on the input data. For example, in the simple payroll problem discussed in Chapter 2, a tax of $25 was deducted regardless of the employee's salary. It would be fairer to base the amount deducted on the employee's gross salary. For example, we might want the program to deduct a tax only if the employee's salary exceeds $100. Carrying this one step further, we might want the program to use tax brackets, that is, to deduct one tax percentage for salaries between $100 and $300 and a higher percentage for salaries greater than $300.

Boolean Expressions and Conditions

To achieve this goal, the computer must be able to answer questions such as, "Is gross salary greater than $100?" In Ada, this is accomplished by evaluating a Boolean expression. Assuming that the employee's salary is stored in the float variable Gross, the Boolean expression corresponding to that question is

```
Gross > 100.0
```

There are only two possible values for a Boolean expression: True or False. If Gross is greater than 100.00, the preceding Boolean expression evaluates to True; if Gross is not greater than 100.00, the expression evaluates to False. Chapter 7 examines the operators that can be used on Boolean expressions. For now, we will concentrate on learning how to write and use simple Boolean expressions called conditions.

Most conditions that we use will have one of the following forms:

variable   *relational operator*   *variable*
variable   *relational operator*   *constant*

Relational operators are the familiar symbols

    `<` (less than)
    `<=` (less than or equal to)
    `>` (greater than)
    `>=` (greater than or equal to)
    `=` (equal to)
    `/=` (not equal to)

All these operators should be familiar to you except the last. Ada uses the symbol pair `/=` to express the condition "not equal to." In mathematics, this is usually written $\neq$, but this symbol does not appear on computer keyboards. Also, be careful that you write `>=` and not `=>` for "greater than or equal to"—the latter symbol is used in Ada for other things, such as

```
Text_IO.Put(Item => "Hello");
```

and its mistaken use as a relational operator will lead to a compilation error.

The variables in a Boolean condition can be of `Integer`, `Float`, or enumeration type. In the `Integer` and `Float` cases, the relational operators have their familiar meanings: $3 < 4$, $-17.5 > -30.4$. In the case of enumeration types, the comparisons are with respect to the order in which the values are defined in the type definition. Given two types

```
TYPE Days IS (Mon, Tue, Wed, Thu, Fri, Sat, Sun);
TYPE Colors IS (Red, Orange, Yellow, Green, Blue, Purple);
```

these conditions are all true:

```
Mon < Tue
Wed /= Tue
Wed = Wed
Wed >= Tue

Purple > Red
Yellow < Green
Green >= Yellow
```

The conditions

```
Purple > Fri
3 <= 4.5
Green > 2
```

would cause compilation errors because the two values in each comparison are associated with different types and therefore cannot be compared—it would be like comparing apples and oranges.

If the `Integer` variable `I` is 5, the `Float` variable `X` is 3.9, and the `Days` variable `Today` is `Wed`, then these relations are true:

```
I > 0
X <= 3.9
Today > Tue
```

Finally, we note that the `Character` type is treated as an enumeration type, and the relations are with respect to the alphabetic order. It's actually a bit more complicated than this; we'll come back to it in more detail in Chapter 7.

■ Example 4.1

The relational operators and some sample conditions are shown in Table 4.1. Each condition is evaluated assuming the variable values below.

```
X Power MaxPow Y Item MinItem MomOrDad Num Sentinel
-5 1024  1024  7 1.5  -999.0   'M'      999 999
```
■

Table 4.1 Ada Relational Operators and Sample Conditions

Operator	Condition	Meaning	Value
<=	X <= 0	X less than or equal to 0	true
<	Power < MaxPow	Power less than MaxPow	false
>=	X >= Y	X greater than or equal to Y	false
>	Item > MinItem	Item greater than MinItem	true
=	MomOrDad = 'M'	MomOrDad equal to 'M'	true
/=	MinItem /= Item	MinItem not equal to Item	true
/=	Num /= Sentinel	Num not equal to Sentinel	false

The IF Statement

An Ada programmer can use the IF statement to select among several alternatives. An IF statement always contains a Boolean expression. For example, the IF statement

```
IF Gross > 100.00 THEN
    Net := Gross - Tax;
ELSE
    Net := Gross;
END IF;
```

selects one of the two assignment statements listed. It selects the statement following THEN if the Boolean expression is true (i.e, if Gross is greater than 100.00); it selects the statement following ELSE if the Boolean expression is false (i.e., if Gross is not greater than 100.00).

Figure 4.1 is a graphic description, called a *flow chart,* of the preceding IF statement. Figure 4.1 shows that the condition enclosed in the diamond–shaped box (Gross > 100.00) is evaluated first. If the condition is true, the arrow labeled *True* is followed, and the assignment statement in the rectangle on the right is executed. If the condition is false, the arrow labeled *False* is followed, and the assignment in the rectangle on the left is executed.

The preceding IF statement has two alternatives, but only one will be executed for a given value of Gross. Example 4.2 illustrates that an IF statement can also have a single alternative that is executed only when the condition is true.

Figure 4.1 Two-Alternative IF Statement

117

4.1 Control
Structures: Boolean
Expressions and the
IF Statement

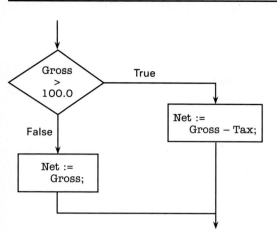

■ Example 4.2

The following IF statement has one alternative, which is executed only when X is not equal to 0. It causes Product to be multiplied by X; the new value is then saved in Product, replacing the old value. If X is equal to 0, the multiplication is not performed. Figure 4.2 is a flow chart of this IF statement.

```
--- Multiply Product by a nonzero X only

IF X /= 0.0 THEN
    Product := Product * X;
END IF;                                                          ■
```

Figure 4.2 Single-Alternative IF Statement

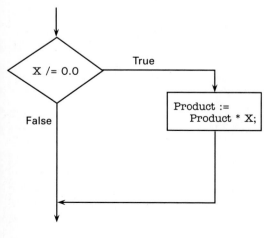

■ Example 4.3

The following IF statement has two alternatives. It displays either Hi Mom or Hi
Dad depending on the character stored in the variable MomOrDad (type Character).

```
IF MomOrDad = 'M' THEN
   Text_IO.Put(Item => "Hi Mom");
   Text_IO.New_Line;
ELSE
   Text_IO.Put(Item => "Hi Dad");
   Text_IO.New_line;
END IF;
```

Notice that the statement sequences may include one or more statements,
all terminated by semicolons, and also that the END IF; is always required
whether the IF statement has one alternative or two.   ■

The forms of the IF statement used so far are summarized in the displays
that follow.

IF Statement (Two Alternatives)

Form:

```
IF condition THEN
   statement sequence T
ELSE
   statement sequence F
END IF;
```

Example:

```
IF X >= 0.0 THEN
   Text_IO.Put(Item => "Positive");
ELSE
   Text_IO.Put(Item => "Negative");
END IF;
```

Interpretation: If the *condition* evaluates to true, then *statement sequence T*
is executed and *statement sequence F* is skipped; otherwise, *statement sequence
T* is skipped and *statement sequence F* is executed.
Note: There is no semicolon after THEN or after ELSE. Inserting a semicolon
here will cause a compilation error.

IF Statement (One Alternative)

Form:

```
IF condition THEN
   statement sequence T
END IF;
```

Example:

```
IF X > 0.0 THEN
    PosProd := PosProd * X;
    CountPos := CountPos + 1;
END IF;
```

Interpretation: If the *condition* evaluates to true, then *statement sequence T* is executed; otherwise, it is skipped.

Formatting the IF Statement

In all the IF statement examples, the statement sequences are indented. If the word ELSE appears, it is entered on a separate line and aligned with the words IF and END IF. The format of the IF statement makes its meaning apparent. This is done solely to improve program readability and is highly recommended; the format used makes no difference to the compiler.

Exercises for Section 4.1

Self-Check

1. Assuming X is 15.0 and Y is 25.0, what are the values of the following conditions?

   X /= Y   X < X   X >= (Y - X)   X = (Y + X - Y)

2. What do the following statements display?
   a.

   ```
   IF 12 < 12 THEN
       Text_IO.Put(Item => "Always");
   ELSE
       Text_IO.Put(Item => "Never");
   END IF;
   ```

   b.

   ```
   Var1 := 15.0;
   Var2 := 25.12;
   IF (2.0*Var1) > Var2 THEN
       Text_IO.Put(Item => "OK");
   ELSE
       Text_IO.Put(Item => "Not OK");
   END IF;
   ```

4.2 Problem Solving: Decision Steps in Algorithms

In the problem that follows, you will see how to improve the payroll program.

◆ Case Study: Modified Payroll Problem

Problem
Modify the simple payroll program to deduct a $25 tax only if an employee earns more than $100 and deduct no tax otherwise.

Analysis
We will analyze this problem using the tools developed in the last chapter. We begin by listing the data requirements and the algorithm.

Data Requirements

Problem Constants
maximum salary without a tax deduction (`TaxBracket = 100.00`)
amount of tax deducted (`Tax = 25.00`)

Problem Inputs
hours worked (`Hours : NonNegFloat`)
hourly rate (`Rate : NonNegFloat`)

Problem Outputs
gross pay (`Gross : NonNegFloat`)
net pay (`Net : NonNegFloat`)

Relevant Formulas
gross pay = hourly rate × hours worked
net pay = gross pay − deductions

Unlike problem inputs, whose values may vary, problem constants have the same values for each run of the program. Each constant value is associated with an identifier (`Tax` and `TaxBracket` above). The program style display following this problem describes the reason for this association.

Design
The structure chart for this algorithm is given in Fig. 4.3, and the initial algorithm follows.

Initial Algorithm

1. Display user instructions.
2. Enter hours worked and hourly rate.
3. Compute gross salary.

4. Compute net salary.
5. Display gross salary and net salary.

Now let's write the refinement of algorithm step 4 as a *decision step*.

Step 4 Refinement
```
4.1. IF Gross > TaxBracket THEN
          Deduct a tax of $25
     ELSE
          Deduct no tax
     END IF;
```

The decision step is expressed in *pseudocode*, which is a mixture of everyday language and Ada used to describe algorithm steps.

Coding
The modified payroll program is shown in Program 4.1. It begins with a multiple-line comment explaining the program's purpose.

Figure 4.3 Structure Chart for Modified Payroll Program

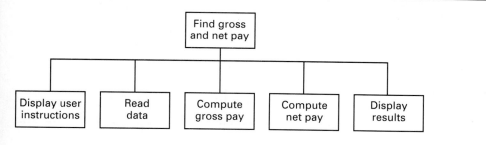

Program 4.1 Modified Payroll Program

```
WITH Text_IO;
WITH My_Flt_IO;
PROCEDURE ModPay IS

-- Computes and displays gross pay and net pay given an hourly
-- rate and number of hours worked. Deducts a tax of $25 if
-- gross salary exceeds $100; otherwise, deducts no tax.

  SUBTYPE NonNegFloat IS Float RANGE 0.0 .. Float'Last;

  TaxBracket : CONSTANT NonNegFloat := 100.00;
                            -- maximum salary for no deduction
  Tax :           CONSTANT NonNegFloat := 25.00;-- tax amount

  Hours : NonNegFloat; -- inputs - hours worked, hourly rate
  Rate:   NonNegFloat;
  Gross:  NonNegFloat; -- outputs - gross pay, net pay
  Net:    NonNegFloat;
```

Case Study: Modified Payroll Problem, continued

```
BEGIN -- ModPay

   -- Enter Hours and Rate
   Text_IO.Put (Item => "Hours worked > ");
   My_Flt_IO.Get (Item => Hours);
   Text_IO.Put (Item => "Hourly rate $");
   My_Flt_IO.Get (Item => Rate);
   Text_IO.New_Line;

   -- Compute gross salary
   Gross := Hours * Rate;

   -- Compute net salary
   IF Gross > TaxBracket THEN
      Net := Gross - Tax;      -- Deduct a tax amount
   ELSE
      Net := Gross;            -- Deduct no tax
   END IF;

   -- Print Gross and Net
   Text_IO.Put (Item => "Gross salary is $");
   My_Flt_IO.Put (Item => Gross, Fore => 1, Aft => 2, Exp => 0);
   Text_IO.New_Line;
   Text_IO.Put (Item => "Net salary is $");
   My_Flt_IO.Put (Item => Net, Fore => 1, Aft => 2, Exp => 0);
   Text_IO.New_Line;

END ModPay;


Hours worked > 40.0
Hourly rate $5.00

Gross salary is $200.00
Net salary is $175.00
```

To test this program, run it with at least two sets of data. One data set should yield a gross salary greater than $100.00, and the other should yield a gross salary less than $100.00. You should also test the program with a data set that yields a gross salary that is exactly $100.00.

◆

Use of Constants

The constants Tax and TaxBracket appear in the preceding IF statement and in Program 4.1. We might have been tempted to insert the constant values (100.00 and 25.00) directly in the IF statement, writing

```
IF Gross > 100.00 THEN
    Net := Gross - 25.00;
ELSE
    Net := Gross;
END IF;
```

There are two reasons why it is better style to use the constants as we did originally. First, the original IF statement is easier to understand because it uses the names Tax and TaxBracket, which are descriptive, rather than numbers, which have no intrinsic meaning. Second, a program written with constants is much easier to modify than one that is not. If the tax bracket and tax value were to change—and tax-related things always change—we would need to change only the constant declaration. If the constant values were inserted directly in the IF statement as just shown above, then we would have to change them not only in the IF statement but in all the other statements in which they appeared. In a program of realistic length, finding all these occurrences would be a tedious and error-prone process. For both reasons, we recommend that you try to avoid dispersing constant values through your programs; instead use constants that are declared by name.

◆ Case Study: Finding the Alphabetically First Letter

Problem
Read three letters and find and display the one that comes first in the alphabet.

Analysis
From our prior experience with conditions and decision steps, we know how to compare two items at a time to see which one is smaller using the relational operator <. We can also use this operator to determine whether one letter precedes another in the alphabet. For example, the condition 'A' < 'F' is true because A precedes F in the alphabet. Because we have no direct way to compare three items, our strategy will be to do a sequence of pairwise comparisons. We will start by comparing the first two letters, finding the smaller of that pair. The result of the second comparison will be the smallest of the three letters.

Data Requirements

Problem Inputs
three letters (Ch1, Ch2, Ch3 : Character).

Problem Outputs
the alphabetically first letter (AlphaFirst : Character).

124

Decision Statements;
Writing Simple
Functions and
Packages

Case Study: Finding the Alphabetically First Letter, continued

Design

Algorithm

1. Read three letters into Ch1, Ch2, and Ch3.
2. Save the alphabetically first of Ch1, Ch2, and Ch3 in AlphaFirst.
3. Display the alphabetically first letter.

Algorithm Refinements

Step 2 can be performed by first comparing Ch1 and Ch2 and saving the alphabetically first letter in AlphaFirst; this result can then be compared to Ch3. The refinement of step 2 follows.

Step 2 Refinement
2.1. Save the alphabetically first of Ch1 and Ch2 in AlphaFirst.
2.2. Save the alphabetically first of Ch3 and AlphaFirst in AlphaFirst.

Figure 4.4 shows the structure chart that corresponds to this algorithm.

Figure 4.4 Structure Chart for Finding Alphabetically First Letter

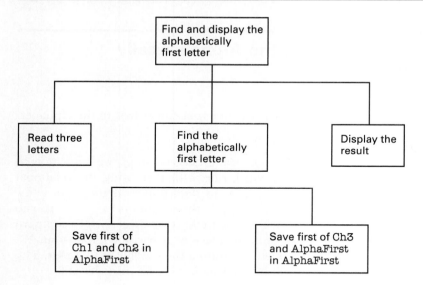

Coding

Program 4.2 shows the desired program. The IF statement with two alternatives saves either Ch1 or Ch2 in AlphaFirst. The IF statement with one alternative stores Ch3 in AlphaFirst if Ch3 precedes the value already in AlphaFirst. Later you will see that IF statements with more than two alternatives are also possible in Ada.

Program 4.2   Finding the Alphabetically First Letter

```
WITH Text_IO;
PROCEDURE FirstLetter IS

-- Finds and prints the alphabetically first letter.

  Ch1, Ch2, Ch3 : Character;    -- input  - three letters
  AlphaFirst    : Character;    -- output - alphabetically first letter

BEGIN -- FirstLetter

  -- Read three letters
  Text_IO.Put (Item => "Enter any three letters, then press RETURN > ");
  Text_IO.Get (Item => Ch1);
  Text_IO.Get (Item => Ch2);
  Text_IO.Get (Item => Ch3);

  -- Save the smaller of Ch1 and Ch2 in AlphaFirst
  IF Ch1 < Ch2 THEN
    AlphaFirst := Ch1;        -- Ch1 comes before Ch2
  ELSE
    AlphaFirst := Ch2;        -- Ch2 comes before Ch1
  END IF;

  -- Save the smaller of Ch3 and AlphaFirst in AlphaFirst
  IF Ch3 < AlphaFirst THEN
    AlphaFirst := Ch3;        -- Ch3 comes before AlphaFirst
  END IF;

  -- Display result
  Text_IO.Put (Item => AlphaFirst);
  Text_IO.Put (Item => " is the first letter alphabetically");
  Text_IO.New_Line;

END FirstLetter;


Enter any three letters, then press RETURN > THE
E is the first letter alphabetically
```

Exercises for Section 4.2

Self-Check

1. What value is assigned to X for each segment below when Y is 15.0?

```
   a. X := 25.0;
      IF Y /= (X - 10.0) THEN
        X := X - 10.0;
      ELSE
        X := X / 2.0;
      END IF;
```

b.
```
IF Y < 15.0 THEN
   X := 5 * Y;
ELSE
   X := 2 * Y;
END IF;
```

Programming

1. Write Ada statements to carry out the steps below.
   a. If Item is nonzero, then multiply Product by Item and save the result in Product; otherwise, skip the multiplication. In either case, display the value of Product.
   b. Store the absolute difference of X and Y in Z, where the absolute difference is (X − Y) or (Y − X), whichever is positive.
   c. If X is zero, add 1 to ZeroCount. If X is negative, add X to MinusSum. If X is greater than zero, add X to PlusSum.

2. Modify the structure chart and program for the first letter problem to find the first of four letters.
3. Write a structure chart and program to find the alphabetically last of three letters.

 # 4.3 Tricks of the Trade: Tracing a Program or Algorithm

A critical step in the design of an algorithm or program is to verify that it is correct before you spend extensive time entering or debugging it. Often a few extra minutes spent in verifying the correctness of an algorithm will save hours of testing time later.

One important technique, a hand trace or desk check (mentioned in Chapter 1), consists of a careful, step-by-step simulation on paper of how the computer would execute the algorithm or program. The results of this simulation should show the effect of each step's execution using data that are relatively easy to process by hand.

As an example, the completely refined algorithm for the smallest letter problem appears next.

Refined Algorithm

1. Read three letters into Ch1, Ch2, and Ch3.
2. Save the alphabetically first of Ch1, Ch2, and Ch3 in AlphaFirst.
   2.1. Save the alphabetically first of Ch1 and Ch2 in AlphaFirst.
       2.1.1. IF Ch1 precedes Ch2 THEN
              2.1.2. AlphaFirst gets Ch1
              ELSE
              2.1.3 AlphaFirst gets Ch2
              END IF;

  2.2 Save the alphabetically first of Ch3 and AlphaFirst in AlphaFirst.
     2.2.1. IF Ch3 precedes AlphaFirst THEN
       2.2.2. AlphaFirst gets Ch3.

3. Display the alphabetically first letter.

Table 4.2 shows a trace of the algorithm for the data string THE. Each step is listed at the left in order of its execution. The values of variables referenced by a step are shown after the step. If a step changes the value of a variable, then the table shows the new value. The effect of each step is described at the far right. For example, the table shows that the step

     Read three letters into Ch1, Ch2, Ch3

stores the letters T, H, and E in the variables Ch1, Ch2, and Ch3.

Table 4.2 Trace of First Letter Algorithm

Algorithm Step	Ch1	Ch2	Ch3	AlphaFirst	Effect
	?	?	?	?	
1. Read three letters	T	H	E		Reads the data
2.1.1 if Ch1 precedes Ch2					Is 'T' < 'H' ? value is false
2.1.3 AlphaFirst gets Ch2				H	'H' is first so far
2.2.1 if Ch3 precedes AlphaFirst					Is 'E' < 'H' ? value is true
2.2.2 AlphaFirst gets Ch3				E	'E' is first
3. Display AlphaFirst					Displays E is the first letter . . .

The trace in Table 4.2 clearly shows that the alphabetically first letter, E, of the input string is stored in AlphaFirst and displayed. In order to verify that the program is correct it would be necessary to select other data that cause the two conditions to evaluate to different combinations of their values. Because there are two conditions and each has two possible values (true or false), there are 2 × 2 or 4 different combinations that should be tried. (What are they?) An exhaustive (complete) desk check of the program would show that it works for all of these combinations.

Besides for the four cases discussed above, you should verify that the program works correctly for unusual data. For example, what would happen if all three letters or a pair of letters were the same? Would the program still provide the correct result? To complete the desk check, it would be necessary to show that the program does indeed handle these special situations properly.

In tracing each case, you must be very careful to execute the program exactly as it would be executed by the computer. A desk check in which you assume that a particular step will be executed a certain way, without explicitly testing each condition and tracing each program step, is of little value.

Exercises for Section 4.3

Self-Check

1. Provide sample data and traces for the remaining three cases of the alphabetically first letter problem. Also, test the special cases where two letters are the same and all three letters are the same. What is the value of the conditions in the latter case?
2. Trace Program 4.1 when Hours is 30.0 and Rate is 5.00. Perform the trace when Hours is 20.0 and Rate is 4.00.

 # 4.4 Problem Solving: More Strategies

Often what appears to be a new problem will turn out to be a variation of one that you have already solved. Consequently, an important skill in problem solving is the ability to recognize that a problem is similar to one solved earlier. As you progress through the course you will start to build up a collection of programs and procedures. Whenever possible, you should try to adapt or reuse parts of a program that have been shown to work correctly.

Extending a Problem Solution

An experienced programmer usually writes programs that can be easily changed or modified to fit other situations. One reason for this is that programmers (and program users) often wish to make slight improvements to a program after having used it. If the original program is designed carefully from the beginning, the programmer will be able to accommodate changing specifications with a minimum of effort. In the next problem, it is possible to insert a new decision step rather than having to rewrite the entire program.

◆ Case Study: Computing Overtime Pay

Problem

You decide to modify the payroll program so that employees who work more than 40 hours a week are paid double for all overtime hours.

Analysis

This problem is an extension of the modified payroll problem solved by Program 4.1. Employees who work more than 40 hours should be paid one rate for the first 40 hours and a higher rate for the extra hours over 40. Employees who work 40 hours or less should be paid the same rate for all hours worked. We can solve this problem by replacing step 3 (compute gross pay) in the original algorithm with a decision step that selects either a straight pay computation or a computation with overtime pay.

Data Requirements

Problem Constants
maximum salary for no tax deduction (TaxBracket = 100.00)
amount of tax deducted (Tax = 25.00)
maximum hours without overtime pay (MaxHours = 40.0)

Problem Inputs
hours worked (Hours : NonNegFloat)
hourly rate (Rate : NonNegFloat)

Problem Outputs
gross pay (Gross : NonNegFloat)
net pay (Net : NonNegFloat)

Design
The critical change to the algorithm involves modifying step 3 of the algorithm. The algorithm is repeated below followed by a new refinement for step 3.

Initial Agorithm
1. Display user instructions.
2. Enter hours worked and hourly rate.
3. Compute gross salary including any overtime pay.
4. Compute net salary.
5. Display gross salary and net salary.

Algorithm Refinements
The new step 3 is refined next.

Step 3 Refinement
3.1. IF no overtime hours were worked THEN
    3.2. Gross gets Hours * Rate
ELSE
    3.3. Compute Gross as (the pay for 40 hours) + (the pay for overtime hours)
END IF;

Coding
As shown below, we should replace the assignment statement in Program 4.1 that computes gross pay by

130

Decision Statements;
Writing Simple
Functions and
Packages

Case Study: Computing Overtime Pay, continued

```
-- Compute gross pay including any overtime pay
IF Hours <= MaxHours THEN
   Gross := Hours * Rate;
ELSE
   Gross := (MaxHours * Rate) + ((Hours - MaxHours) * (2.0 * Rate));
END IF;
```

If the condition Hours <= MaxHours is true, there is no overtime pay, so gross pay is computed as before; otherwise, Gross is computed using the second assignment statement above. The pay for the first 40 hours is added to the pay earned for the overtime hours (Hours - MaxHours).

The assignment statement for step 3.3 involves three arithmetic operators: +, -, and *. As recommended in Section 2.10, we have used parentheses to cause the operators above to be evaluated in the order of subtraction first, multiplication next, and addition last. Consequently, the overtime hours (Hours - MaxHours) are multiplied by 2.0*Rate and added to the value of Max-Hours*Rate computed earlier; the result is the new value of Gross. Modifying Program 4.1 as discussed here is left as an exercise.

Solution by Analogy

Sometimes a new problem is simply an old one presented in a new guise. Each time you face a problem, try to determine whether you have solved a similar problem before; if you have, adapt the earlier solution. This problem-solving strategy requires a careful reading of the problem statement to detect requirements that may be similar to those of earlier problems but worded differently.

◆ Case Study: Computing Insurance Dividends

Problem

Each year an insurance company sends out dividend checks to its policyholders. The dividend amount is a fixed percentage (4.5%) of the insurance premium paid in. If there were no claims made by the policyholder, the dividend rate for that policy is increased by 0.5%. Write a program to compute dividends.

Analysis

This problem is quite similar to the overtime pay problem. Just as there was a bonus pay rate for workers with overtime hours, there is a bonus dividend for policyholders with no claims. We must first read in the input data (number of claims and premium). We then use a decision step to select either the basic dividend computation or the computation with a bonus dividend. (In the overtime pay problem, we followed a similar algorithm by first computing gross pay, then adding in overtime pay when earned.)

Data Requirements

Problem Constants
the fixed dividend rate of 4.5% (FixedRate = 0.045)
the bonus dividend rate of 0.5% (BonusRate = 0.005)

Problem Inputs
premium amount (Premium : NonNegFloat)
number of claims (NumClaims : Natural)

Problem Outputs
dividend amount (Dividend : NonNegFloat)

Design
Figure 4.5 shows the structure chart for this algorithm; the initial algorithm follows.

Figure 4.5   Structure Chart for Insurance Dividend Problem

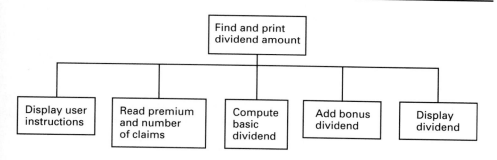

Algorithm
1. Display user instructions.
2. Enter premium amount and number of claims.
3. Compute basic dividend including a bonus dividend when earned.
4. Display total dividend.

Algorithm Refinements
The refinement of step 3 in this problem is similar to the refinement of step 3 in the overtime pay problem. This refinement is shown next.

132

Decision Statements;
Writing Simple
Functions and
Packages

Case Study: Computing Insurance Dividends, continued

Step 3 Refinement
3.1. IF the basic dividend applies THEN
      3.2. Dividend gets Premium * BasicRate
      ELSE
      3.3. Dividend gets basic dividend plus bonus dividend
      END IF;

Coding

The complete program is shown in Program 4.3. The basic dividend rate, 4.5%, is written as the decimal fraction 0.045, and the bonus rate, 0.5%, is written as the decimal fraction 0.005. Because Ada possesses no % operator, decimal fractions are required. All floating-point numbers must begin with a digit; therefore, the zero in front of the decimal point is always required for a floating-point value less than 1.0. The IF statement at the end of the program displays an extra message to policyholders who receive a bonus dividend.

Program 4.3 Computing an Insurance Dividend

```
WITH Text_IO;
WITH My_Int_IO;
WITH My_Flt_IO;
PROCEDURE CompDividend IS

  SUBTYPE NonNegFloat IS Float RANGE 0.0 .. Float'Last;

-- Finds and displays the insurance dividend.

  BasicRate : CONSTANT NonNegFloat := 0.045; -- basic dividend rate 4.5%
  BonusRate : CONSTANT NonNegFloat := 0.005; -- bonus dividend rate 0.5%

  Premium   : NonNegFloat;   -- input  - premium amount
  NumClaims : Natural;       -- input  - number of claims
  Dividend  : NonNegFloat;   -- output - dividend amount

BEGIN -- CompDividend

  -- Enter Premium and NumClaims
  Text_IO.Put (Item => "Premium amount > $");
  My_Flt_IO.Get (Item => Premium);
  Text_IO.Put (Item => "Number of claims > ");
  My_Int_IO.Get (Item => NumClaims);
  Text_IO.New_Line;

  -- Compute dividend using bonus rate when earned
  IF NumClaims /= 0 THEN
    Dividend := Premium * BasicRate;
  ELSE
    Dividend := (Premium * BasicRate) + (Premium * BonusRate);
  END IF;

  -- Display total dividend
  Text_IO.Put (Item => "Total dividend is $");
```

```
  My_Flt_IO.Put (Item => Dividend, Fore => 1, Aft => 2, Exp => 0);
  Text_IO.New_Line;

  IF NumClaims = 0 THEN
    Text_IO.Put(Item => "This includes a bonus dividend for zero claims!");
    Text_IO.New_Line;
  END IF;

END CompDividend;
```

```
Premium amount > $1200.00
Number of claims > 0

Total dividend is $60.00
This includes a bonus dividend for zero claims!
```

Exercises for Section 4.4

Self-Check

1. Rewrite the algorithm for the modified payroll problem so that the computation of gross salary is performed in two steps rather than in one. Compute the base pay for all hours worked first. Then add in an extra amount only if overtime hours were worked.
2. Refer to Program 4.3. Write the step that computes Dividend as two steps. Compute the basic dividend first and then add a bonus dividend only if there were no claims.

Programming

1. Provide the complete program for the overtime pay problem.

4.5 Control Structures: The IF Statement Revisited

In this section we show some more examples of IF statements, and we introduce the multiple-alternative IF statement, which allows more complicated decisions to be made.

More IF Statement Examples

■ Example 4.4

Suppose you are the manager of a clothing boutique and are planning a spring sale. You could use the following IF statement to compute the discounted price of an item. The statement first determines the discount by multiplying the item price and the discount rate (a fraction); next, it deducts the discount. The statement sequence is not executed when the discount rate is zero.

```
IF DiscRate /= 0.0 THEN
   Discount := Price * DiscRate; -- Compute discount amount
   Price := Price - Discount ;    -- Deduct discount from price
END IF;
```
■

■ Example 4.5

In later chapters, you will see that it is useful to be able to order a pair of data values so that the smaller value is stored in one variable (say, X) and the larger value is stored in another (say, Y). The following IF statement rearranges any two values stored in these two variables as just described. If the two numbers are already in the proper order, the statement sequence is not executed.

```
IF X > Y THEN -- switch X and Y
   Temp := X; -- Store old X in Temp
   X := Y;    -- Store old Y in X
   Y := Temp; -- Store old X in Y
END IF;
```

The variables X, Y, and Temp must, of course, all be the same type. Although the values of X and Y are being switched, an additional variable, Temp, is needed for storage of a copy of one of these values. The trace in Table 4.3 illustrates the need for Temp, assuming X and Y have original values of 12.5 and 5.0, respectively. ■

■ Example 4.6

As the manager of a clothing boutique, you want to keep records of your bank transactions. You could use the IF statement below to process a transaction amount (TransAmount) that represents either a payment for goods received (in which case, TransType is 'C') or a cash deposit. In either case, an appropriate message is displayed and the account balance (Balance) is updated.

```
IF TransType = 'C' THEN -- check
   Text_IO.Put (Item => "Check for $");
   My_Flt_IO.Put (Item=>TransAmount, Fore=>1, Aft=>2, Exp=>0);
   Text_IO.New_Line;
   Balance := Balance - TransAmount; -- Deduct check amount
ELSE -- deposit
   Text_IO.Put (Item => "Deposit of $");
   My_Flt_IO.Put (Item=>TransAmount, Fore=>1, Aft=>2, Exp=>0);
   Text_IO.New_Line;
   Balance := Balance + TransAmount; -- Add deposit amount
END IF;
```

The semicolons in the IF statement above are used to terminate the individual statements in each alternative. Note that a semicolon is not used after THEN or ELSE; if it were, the compiler would detect a syntax error. ■

Statement Part	X	Y	Temp	Effect
	12.5	5.0	?	
IF X > Y THEN				12.5 > 5.0 is true
Temp := X;			12.5	Store old X in Temp
X := Y;	5.0			Store old Y in X
Y := Temp;		12.5		Store old X in Y

 Case Study: Given Today, Find Yesterday and Tomorrow

Problem

Read the day of the week from the terminal as a three-letter abbreviation, and display yesterday and tomorrow.

Analysis

Recall from Chapter 3 that the days of the week are best represented as an enumeration type, so the days can be read and displayed by an instance of Enumeration_IO. Yesterday and tomorrow can be found using the successor and predecessor attributes. Because the predecessor of the first day of the week and the successor of the last day of the week are undefined because the type does not "wrap around," we shall need to test for these as special cases.

Data Requirements

Problem Data Types
Days of the week, an enumeration type:

```
TYPE Days IS
    (Mon, Tue, Wed, Thu, Fri, Sat, Sun);
```

Problem Inputs
Today (Today : Days)

Problem Outputs
Yesterday (Yesterday: Days)
Tomorrow (Tomorrow: Days)

Design
The initial algorithm follows.

Initial Algorithm

1. Prompt the user for the current day abbreviation and read it from the keyboard.

136

Decision Statements;
Writing Simple
Functions and
Packages

Case Study: Given Today, Find Yesterday and Tomorrow, continued

2. Find the abbreviations for yesterday and tomorrow.
3. Display the results on the screen.

Algorithm Refinements

Step 2 Refinement

The refinement of step 2 takes into account that in Ada the enumeration types are not cyclic.

2.1. If today is the first day of the week, then yesterday is the last day of the (previous) week; otherwise yesterday is the predecessor of today.

2.2. If today is the last day of the week, then tomorrow is the first day of the (following) week; otherwise tomorrow is the successor of today.

Coding

Program 4.4 gives the complete solution to the problem. If a value is entered which is not one of the seven valid abbreviations, the program terminates with a Data_Error exception. In Section 5.8 we will see how to prevent a program from terminating in this manner.

Program 4.4   Finding Yesterday and Tomorrow

```
WITH Text_IO;
PROCEDURE ThreeDays IS

   TYPE Days IS (Mon, Tue, Wed, Thu, Fri, Sat, Sun);
   PACKAGE Day_IO IS
      NEW Text_IO.Enumeration_IO (Enum => Days);

   Yesterday : Days;
   Today     : Days;
   Tomorrow  : Days;

BEGIN -- ThreeDays

   -- prompt user to enter a day abbreviation
   Text_IO.Put (Item => "Enter the first 3 letters of a day of the week > ");
   Day_IO.Get (Item => Today);

   -- find yesterday
   IF Today = Days'First THEN
      Yesterday := Days'Last;
   ELSE
      Yesterday := Days'Pred(Today);
   END IF;

   Text_IO.Put (Item => "Yesterday was ");
   Day_IO.Put (Item => Yesterday);
   Text_IO.New_Line;

   Text_IO.Put (Item => "Today is ");
   Day_IO.Put (Item => Today);
   Text_IO.New_Line;
```

```
-- find tomorrow
IF Today = Days'Last THEN
   Tomorrow := Days'First;
ELSE
   Tomorrow := Days'Succ(Today);
END IF;

Text_IO.Put (Item => "Tomorrow is ");
Day_IO.Put (Item => Tomorrow);
Text_IO.New_Line;

END ThreeDays;
```

```
Enter the first 3 letters of a day of the week > sat
Yesterday was FRI
Today is SAT
Tomorrow is SUN
```

Multiple-Alternative Decisions

Until now, we have used IF statements to implement decisions involving one or two alternatives. In this section, you will see how the IF statement can be used to implement decisions involving more than two alternatives.

■ Example 4.7

The IF statement below has three alternatives. It causes one of three variables (NumPos, NumNeg, or NumZero) to be increased by 1 depending on whether X is greater than 0, less than 0, or equal to 0, respectively.

```
-- Increment NumPos, NumNeg, or NumZero depending on X
IF X > 0 THEN
   NumPos := NumPos + 1;
ELSIF X < 0 THEN
   NumNeg := NumNeg + 1;
ELSE -- X = 0
   NumZero := NumZero + 1;
END IF;
```

The execution of this IF statement proceeds as follows: The first condition (X > 0) is tested; if it is true, the statement NumPos := NumPos+1 increments NumPos by 1 and the rest of the IF statement is skipped. If the first condition is false, the second condition (X < 0) is tested; if it is true, NumNeg is incremented; otherwise, NumZero is incremented. It is important to realize that the second condition is tested only when the first condition is false. Figure 4.6 diagrams the execution of this statement. Each condition is shown in a diamond-shaped box. If a condition is true, its arrow labeled True is followed. If a condition is false, its arrow labeled False is followed. This diagram shows that one and only one of the statement sequences in a rectangular box will be executed. A trace of the IF statement for X = −7 is shown in Table 4.4. ■

Figure 4.6 Flow Chart of the IF Statement in Example 4.7

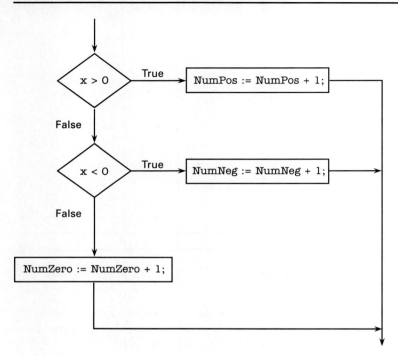

Table 4.4 Trace of IF Statement in Example 4.7 for X = −7

Statement Part	X	Effect
	−7	
IF X > 0 THEN		−7 > 0 is false
ELSIF X < 0 THEN		−7 < 0 is true
NumNeg := NumNeg + 1;	Add 1 to NumNeg	

Multiple-Alternative IF Statement

Form:

IF *expression₁* THEN
    statement sequence₁
ELSIF *expression₂* THEN
    statement sequence₂
     . . .

```
ELSIF expressionₖ THEN
    statement sequenceₖ
ELSE
    statement sequenceₙ
END IF;
```

Example:

```
IF N >0 THEN
    Text_IO.Put(Item=>"Positive");
ELSIF N = 0 THEN
    Text_IO.Put(Item=>"Zero");
ELSE
    Text_IO.Put(Item=>"Negative");
END IF;
```

Interpretation: The expressions (conditions) in a multiple-alternative IF statement are evaluated from top to bottom until a true value is obtained. The statement sequence following the first true expression is executed and the rest of the IF statement is skipped. If every expression is false, then *statement sequenceₙ* (between ELSE and END) is executed.

Notes: At most one statement sequence is executed. If ELSE and *statement sequenceₙ* are present, exactly one statement sequence is always executed. If ELSE and *statement sequenceₙ* are omitted, then no statement sequence is executed when every expression is false.

Also note the spelling required by Ada: ELSIF is spelled without a second E or space; END IF must have a space between END and IF.

Writing a Multiple-Alternative IF Statement

When writing a multiple-alternative IF statement, align the reserved words IF, ELSE, ELSIF, and END IF, and indent each statement sequence consistently. This is done to make the IF statement more readable; indentation is ignored by the compiler.

Order of Conditions

Very often the conditions in a multiple-alternative decision are not mutually exclusive. This means that it may be possible for more than one condition to be true for a given data value. If this is the case, then the order of the conditions becomes very important because only the statement sequence following the first true condition is executed.

■ **Example 4.8**

The table below describes the assignment of grades based on an exam score.

Exam Score	Grade Assigned
90 and above	A
80–89	B
70–79	C
60–69	D
below 60	F

The multiple alternative IF statement below displays the letter grade assigned according to this table. The last three conditions are true for an exam score of 85; however, a grade of B is assigned because the first true condition is Score >= 80.

```
-- correct grade assignment
IF Score >= 90 THEN
    Text_IO.Put (Item=>'A');
ELSIF Score >= 80 THEN
    Text_IO.Put (Item=>'B');
ELSIF Score >= 70 THEN
    Text_IO.Put (Item=>'C');
ELSIF Score >= 60 THEN
    Text_IO.Put (Item=>'D');
ELSE
    Text_IO.Put (Item=>'F');
END IF;
```

The order of conditions can also have an effect on program speed. If we know that low exam scores are much more likely than high scores, it would be faster to test first for scores below 60, next for scores between 60 and 69, and so on. It would, however, be wrong to write the decision as shown next. All passing exam scores (60 or above) would be incorrectly categorized as a grade of D because the first condition would be true and the rest would be skipped.

```
-- incorrect grade assignment
IF Score >= 60 THEN
    Text_IO.Put (Item=>'D');
ELSIF Score >= 70 THEN
    Text_IO.Put (Item=>'C');
ELSIF Score >= 80 THEN
    Text_IO.Put (Item=>'B');
ELSIF Score >= 90 THEN
    Text_IO.Put (Item=>'A');
ELSE
    Text_IO.Put (Item=>'F');
END IF;
```

■

■ **Example 4.9**

You can use a multiple alternative IF statement to implement a *decision table* that describes several alternatives. Let's say you are an accountant setting up a

	Salary Range	Base Tax	Percentage of Excess
1	0.00–1499.99	0.00	15%
2	1500.00–2999.99	225.00	16%
3	3000.00–4999.99	465.00	18%
4	5000.00–7999.99	825.00	20%
5	8000.00–14999.99	1425.00	25%

payroll system for a small firm. Each line of Table 4.5 indicates an employee's salary range and a corresponding base tax amount and tax percentage. Given a salary amount, the tax is calculated by adding the base tax for that salary range, and the product of the percentage of excess and the amount of salary over the minimum salary for that range.

For example, the second line of the table specifies that the tax due on a salary of \$2000.00 is \$225.00 plus 16% of the excess salary over \$1500.00 (i.e., 16% of \$500.00). Therefore, the total tax due is \$225.00 plus \$80.00, or \$305.00.

The IF statement in Fig. 4.7 implements the tax table. If the value of Salary is within the table range (0.00 to 14999.99), exactly one of the statements assigning a value to TAX will be executed. A trace of the IF statement for Salary = \$2000.00 is shown in Table 4.6. The value assigned to Tax is \$305.00, as desired. ∎

Figure 4.7 IF Statement for Table 4.5

```
IF Salary < 0.0 THEN
    Text_IO.Put (Item=>"Error! Negative salary $");
    My_Flt_IO.Put (Item=>Salary, Fore=>1, Aft=>2, Exp=0);
    Text_IO.New_Line;
ELSIF Salary < 1500.00 THEN -- first range
    Tax := 0.15 * Salary;
ELSIF Salary < 3000.00 THEN -- second range
    Tax := (Salary - 1500.00) * 0.16 + 225.00;
ELSIF Salary < 5000.00 THEN -- third range
    Tax := (Salary - 3000.00) * 0.18 + 465.00;
ELSIF Salary < 8000.00 THEN -- fourth range
    Tax := (Salary - 5000.00) * 0.20 + 825.00;
ELSIF Salary < 15000.00 THEN -- fifth range
    Tax := (Salary - 8000.00) * 0.25 + 1425.00;
ELSE
    Text_IO.Put (Item=>"Error! Too large salary $");
    My_Flt_IO.Put (Item=>Salary, Fore=>1, Aft=>2, Exp=0);
    Text_IO.New_Line;
END IF;
```

Table 4.6 Trace of IF Statement in Fig. 4.7 for Salary = $2000.00

Statement Part	Salary	Tax	Effect
	2000.00	?	
IF Salary < 0.0			2000.0 < 0.0 is false
ELSIF Salary < 1500.00			2000.0 < 1500.0 is false
ELSIF Salary < 3000.00			2000.0 < 3000.0 is true
Tax := (Salary − 1500.00)			difference is 500.00
* 0.16			product is 80.00
+ 225.00		305.00	sum is 305.00

PROGRAM
STYLE

Validating the Value of Variables

It is important to validate the value of a variable before you perform computations using invalid or meaningless data. Instead of computing an incorrect tax amount, the IF statement in Fig. 4.7 displays an error message if the value of Salary is outside the range covered by the table (0.0 to 14999.99). The first condition is used to detect negative salaries, and an error message is displayed if Salary is less than zero. All conditions evaluate to False if Salary is greater than 14999.99, and the alternative following ELSE displays an error message.

Nested IF Statements

The statement sequence inside a control statement can contain another control statement. For example, an IF statement can contain another IF or a loop; a loop can contain another loop or an IF, and so on. The second control statement is said to be *nested* inside the first control statement. The inner control statement can itself contain a control statement; in fact, there is no theoretical limit on the depth to which control statements can be nested.

The ability to nest control statements allows us to write very sophisticated programs. In Chapters 5 and 6 we will introduce many examples of IF statements nested inside loops and vice versa. For the time being, consider the following example.

■ Example 4.10

Depending on a student's Grade Point Average (GPA), the following fragment displays one of three messages. If the GPA is less than or equal to 1.5, the painful message following the second ELSE is displayed. If GPA is greater than 1.5, the *inner* IF statement is executed, and a more pleasant message is displayed.

```
IF GPA > 1.5 THEN
    IF GPA < 3.0 THEN
        TextIO.Put(Item => "Progressing satisfactorily");
```

```
    ELSE
        Text_IO.Put (Item => "Made the Dean's List - send money");
    END IF;
ELSE
    Text_IO.Put (Item => "Flunked out");
END IF;
```

The nested statements below have the same effect as the ones above. Again, the inner IF statement is executed when GPA exceeds 1.5.

```
IF GPA <= 1.5 THEN
    Text_IO.Put (Item => "Flunked out");
ELSE
    IF GPA < 3.0 THEN
        Text_IO.Put (Item => "Progressing satisfactorily");
    ELSE
        Text_IO.Put (Item => "Made the Dean's List - send money");
    END IF;
END IF;
```

Nested IF statements can sometimes be confusing to write and to read. Often, a single multiple-alternative IF statement can replace nested IF statements, resulting in a more readable program. Verify for yourself that the IF statement below has the same effect as the earlier nested IF statements.

```
IF GPA <= 1.5 THEN
    Text_IO.Put (Item => "Flunked out");
ELSIF GPA < 3.0 THEN
    Text_IO.Put (Item => "Progressing satisfactorily");
ELSE
    Text_IO.Put (Item => "Made the Dean's List - send money");
END IF;
```

∎

Indentation Conventions for Nested Control Structures

It is a good idea to develop a consistent indentation style for nested control structures. Note in the examples above that the entire nested IF is indented the same amount as the Put following the ELSE.

Developing a consistent indentation style is one way of making your programs clear and easy to read. Many companies have adopted company-wide or project-wide programming style standards that include indentation rules. This makes it easy for programmers to read each other's source code. There is no one "best" indentation rule; the most important principle is consistency.

In this book, we indent each structure several spaces deeper than the structure within which it is nested. The complete program examples use a consistent indentation of two spaces, and the code fragments in the text are usually indented a bit more for added clarity. We recommend an indentation convention similar to that used in the programs. If your teacher states different rules, follow them consistently.

Exercises for Section 4.5

Self-Check

1. Trace the execution of the IF statement in Fig. 4.7 for Salary = 13500.00.
2. What would be the effect of reversing the order of the first two conditions in the IF statement of Fig. 4.7?

Programming

1. Rewrite the IF statement for Example 4.8 using only the relational operator < in all conditions.
2. Implement the decision table below using a multiple-alternative IF statement. Assume that the grade point average is within the range 0.0 through 4.0.

Grade Point Average	Transcript Message
0.0–0.99	Failed semester — registration suspended
1.0–1.99	On probation for next semester
2.0–2.99	(no message)
3.0–3.49	Dean's list for semester
3.5–4.0	Highest honors for semester

4.6 System Structures: Writing Simple Functions

In Chapter 3 you saw how to use some predefined functions in a package, the Month, Day, and Year functions in the package Calendar. This section introduces the very important subject of how to *write* such functions; the next section shows how to put functions in packages for yourself and others to use again later.

Function Specifications

In general, a function is written so as to require the caller to supply some values to it. When called, the function performs its desired computation and then *returns* a result to the calling program. The line indicating the name of the function, the list of expected parameters, and the type of the returned result is called a *function specification*. You saw three such specifications in Chapter 3:

```
FUNCTION Year (Date: Time) RETURN Year_Number;
FUNCTION Month (Date: Time) RETURN Month_Number;
FUNCTION Day (Date: Time) RETURN Day_Number;
```

The specification for Year tells the compiler—and the reader—that this function must be called with one value of type Time, and that it returns a result of type Year_Number to the program that calls it. The other two specifications are similar.

Here is a specification for a function to find the larger of two integer values and return it to the calling program:

```
FUNCTION Maximum(Value1, Value2: Integer) RETURN Integer;
```

Notice that between the parentheses is a list of the expected parameters, and after the word RETURN is the type of the returned result. In this case, the function is to determine which of the two parameters is larger and return it as the result.

Calling a Function

Recall from Chapter 3 that we were able to extract the year from a system-generated time value by writing

```
This_Year := Calendar.Year(Date => Right_Now);
```

where This_Year was declared as a variable of type Calendar.Year_Number and Right_Now was a variable of type Calendar.Time. Notice that between the parentheses is an association of the name of the *formal* parameter (Date) with the variable containing the value of the *actual* parameter (Right_Now).

How could we use our function Maximum in a similar way? Given an integer variable Larger, writing

```
Larger := Maximum(Value1=>24,Value2=>-57);
```

stores the value 24 in the variable Larger, because that is the larger of the two values. Given two integer variables Grade1 and Grade2, writing

```
Grade1 := -24;
Grade2 := 113;
Larger := Maximum(Value1=>Grade1,Value2=>Grade2);
```

stores in Larger the value 113, again because that is the larger value. Notice again how the formal parameters Value1 and Value2 are associated with the actual parameters Grade1 and Grade2, and notice that it is improper to write, for example,

```
Larger := Maximum(Grade1=>Value1,Grade2=>Value2);
```

because Value1 is the formal parameter and Grade1 is the actual. The formal parameter comes first, followed by the actual parameter.

The difference between these two examples is that the function Year already exists (in package Calendar) but the function Maximum does not. We have a specification indicating the name of the function, how it is to be called, and what it returns, but we do not yet actually have a function that will find the larger number.

Function Bodies

To complete our function Maximum we need to write a *function body,* that is, a small program in Ada in a form that the compiler will recognize as a function. Here is the desired function body:

```
FUNCTION Maximum (Valuel, Value2: Integer) RETURN Integer IS
   Result: Integer;
BEGIN
   IF Valuel > Value2 THEN
           Result := Valuel;
   ELSE
           Result := Value2;
   END IF;
   RETURN Result;
END Maximum;
```

This function body has the basic form of an Ada program. There is a header line similar to the first line of a program; this line ends with the word IS. Next there is a section of declarations; here we are declaring only a single program variable Result. Following the word BEGIN is the statement sequence of the function body, and the function body ends with an END. The IF statement in the function body stores in the variable Result the larger of Valuel and Value2. Finally, the value in Result is returned to the calling program as the function result. This value can be stored directly in a variable of the calling program, as in the examples above, or used as part of an expression implementing a larger calculation.

The variable Result is called a *local variable* of the function. Because it is declared inside the function body, it has no existence outside the function body. It is good practice when writing a function to put the variables needed by the function *inside* the function body, so that they are the private property of the function and cannot be seen or disturbed by any other program.

To see an example of how a function is declared as part of a larger program, consider Program 4.5, in which the user is prompted to enter two integer values FirstValue and SecondValue. These values are then passed to the function Maximum, which returns the larger value to the main program. The answer is then displayed. The function Maximum is declared in the declaration part of the main program.

Program 4.5   Finding the Larger of Two Integer Values

```
WITH Text_IO;
WITH My_Int_IO;
PROCEDURE MaxTwo IS

   -- finds the larger of two integer values
   -- using the Maximum function

   FirstValue:  Integer;
   SecondValue: Integer;
   Larger:      Integer;

   -- function specification
   FUNCTION Maximum (Valuel, Value2: Integer) RETURN Integer;

   -- function body
   FUNCTION Maximum (Valuel, Value2: Integer) RETURN Integer IS

      Result: Integer;
```

```
BEGIN -- Maximum

  IF Value1 > Value2 THEN
    Result := Value1;
  ELSE
    Result := Value2;
  END IF;

  RETURN Result;

END Maximum;

BEGIN -- MaxTwo

  Text_IO.Put (Item => "Please enter first integer value > ");
  My_Int_IO.Get (Item => FirstValue);
  Text_IO.Put (Item => "Please enter second integer value > ");
  My_Int_IO.Get (Item => SecondValue);

  Larger := Maximum(Value1=>FirstValue, Value2=>SecondValue);

  Text_IO.Put (Item => "The larger number is ");
  My_Int_IO.Put (Item => Larger, Width => 1);
  Text_IO.New_Line;

END MaxTwo;

Please enter first integer value > 374
Please enter second integer value > -158
The larger number is 374
```

SYNTAX
DISPLAY

Function Specification

Form:

> FUNCTION *fname* (*formal parameters*) RETURN *result type* ;

Example:

> FUNCTION Square (Num : Integer) RETURN Integer;

Interpretation: The function *fname* is declared. The list of *formal parameters* is enclosed in parentheses. The data type of the function result is indicated by the identifier *result type*.

SYNTAX
DISPLAY

Function Body

Form:

> FUNCTION *fname* (*formal parameters*) RETURN *result type* IS
>   *local declaration section*
> BEGIN
>   *statement sequence*
> END *fname*;

Example:

```
FUNCTION Square (Num : Integer) RETURN Integer IS
   Result: Integer;
BEGIN
   Result := Num * Num;
   RETURN Result;
END Square;
```

Interpretation: The function *fname* is declared. The list of *formal parameters* is enclosed in parentheses. The data type of the function result is indicated by the identifier *result type*. Any identifiers declared in the *local declaration section* exist only during the execution of the function. The function body describes the data manipulation to be performed by the function. At least one RETURN statement must be executed each time the function is called.
Note 1: The result type is not restricted in Ada. It may be any type.
Note 2: If there are no parameters, you should omit the formal parameters and parentheses.
Note 3: The first line of the function body must agree exactly with the function specification, except that the specification ends with a semicolon and the first line of the body ends with IS. In fact, the way the line ends is the indication to the compiler whether it should treat the line as a specification or as the first line of a body. It is therefore important not to confuse the two endings, lest you confuse the compiler.

4.7 System Structures: Writing a Simple Package

As you have seen, it is possible to declare a function as part of a program. It is certainly permitted to declare a function like this, and doing so provides an easy way to test the function. However, the real usefulness of functions, and of procedures for that matter, is achieved when they are collected together as a group of related items and placed in a package. A package is compiled and placed in a library, either your own personal program library or, in a group project, the team's library. Once a package is compiled, it—and all the resources in it—are available for use by means of a simple context clause (WITH statement).

Package Specifications and Package Bodies

Recall from Section 3.7 that a package consists of two files: the *specification* and the *body*. The specification is like a "table of contents" for the package, listing all the different resources (e.g., functions and procedures) available in the package; the package body contains the actual Ada code for each of these resources.

In the case of the standard packages (Text_IO and Calendar, for example), the Ada source files are not supplied with the compiler, as these are the private property of the compiler vendor. The executable (precompiled) version of the package body is supplied, along with a precompiled form of the package specification, often called a symbol file. These are usually installed at the same time the compiler is, and are usually available to you without further action on your part.

In the case of programmer-defined packages, it is the programmer's responsibility to write both the specification file and the body file. This book shows a number of programmer-defined packages, for which the Ada source code is given.

A Package Containing Minimum and Maximum Functions

Finding the larger or smaller of two numbers is frequently required in programming. The programming task would be made easier, therefore, if we could write functions once to find the minimum and maximum, then package them up for future use. Our first step is to write a package specification. Remember that the specification is a table of contents to the package. In this case the specification will list the function specifications of the two functions to be provided:

```
PACKAGE MinMax IS
   FUNCTION Minimum (Value1, Value2: Integer) RETURN Integer;
   FUNCTION Maximum (Value1, Value2: Integer) RETURN Integer;
END MinMax;
```

This specification can be compiled as it stands, just to be sure there are no compilation errors.

We now must write the package body. We can incorporate the Maximum function written above. Also, we can write the Minimum function very easily: Given the Maximum function, writing a Minimum function is just a matter of making a change to the inequality in the IF statement:

```
FUNCTION Minimum (Value1, Value2: Integer) RETURN Integer IS
   Result: Integer;
BEGIN
   IF Value1 < Value2 THEN
         Result := Value1;
   ELSE
         Result := Value2;
   END IF;
   RETURN Result;
END Minimum;
```

The package specification is shown again as Program 4.6; Program 4.7 gives the entire package body. Be certain you understand that the package specification contains the function specifications and the package body contains the function bodies.

Program 4.6 Specification for Package MinMax

```
PACKAGE MinMax IS

   -- specifications of functions provided by MinMax package

   FUNCTION Minimum (Value1, Value2: Integer) RETURN Integer;
   FUNCTION Maximum (Value1, Value2: Integer) RETURN Integer;

END MinMax;
```

Program 4.7 Body of Package MinMax

```
PACKAGE BODY MinMax IS

   -- bodies of functions provided by MinMax package

   FUNCTION Minimum (Value1, Value2: Integer) RETURN Integer IS

      Result: Integer;

   BEGIN -- Minimum

      IF Value1 < Value2 THEN
         Result := Value1;
      ELSE
         Result := Value2;
      END IF;

      RETURN Result;

   END Minimum;


   FUNCTION Maximum (Value1, Value2: Integer) RETURN Integer IS

      Result: Integer;

   BEGIN -- Maximum

      IF Value1 > Value2 THEN
         Result := Value1;
      ELSE
         Result := Value2;
      END IF;

      RETURN Result;

   END Maximum;

END MinMax;
```

Package Specification

Form:

```
PACKAGE pname IS

    list of specifications of resources provided by the package

END pname;
```

Example:

```
PACKAGE MinMax IS
    FUNCTION Minimum (Value1, Value2: Integer) RETURN Integer;
    FUNCTION Maximum (Value1, Value2: Integer) RETURN Integer;
END MinMax;
```

Interpretation: The package specification gives a list or "table of contents" of the resources to be provided by the package. These resources can be procedures, functions, and types (see Section 3.6 for an example of a package providing types). The package specification must be compiled before the corresponding body is compiled.

Package Body

Syntax:

```
PACKAGE BODY pname IS

    sequence of function and procedure bodies implementing the resources listed in the
    package specification for pname

END pname;
```

Example: Program 4.7 serves as an example. For brevity we shall not repeat it here.

Interpretation: The resources (functions and procedures) "promised" in the specification must be "delivered" in the corresponding package body. If any are missing, a compilation error will result.

Note: The function and procedure specifications in the package specification must agree *exactly* with the corresponding function and procedure headers in the package body. Specifically, the names, types, and order of parameters must agree exactly. A formal parameter named Value1 in the specification cannot, for example, be called Val1 in the body. Ada compilers are *very* fussy about this: Care taken here will avoid compilation errors.

◆ Case Study: Finding the Largest and Smallest of Three Numbers

Problem
Find the largest and smallest of three numbers to be provided by the user.

Analysis
We cannot directly compare the three numbers, so, as in Program 4.3, we will compare them pairwise.

Data Requirements

Problem Inputs
the three numbers (Num1, Num2, Num3: Integer)

Problem Outputs
the largest and smallest numbers (Largest, Smallest: Integer)

Design
Instead of doing the comparisons directly, we can use the package MinMax to find the larger and smaller of pairs of numbers. Given the three numbers, we can find the smaller of the first two numbers, then find the smaller of this result and the third number. We can apply the same approach to finding the largest number.

Initial Algorithm

1. Prompt the user for the three numbers.
2. Find the largest of the three numbers.
3. Find the smallest of the three numbers.
4. Display the results.

Algorithm Refinements
Steps 2 and 3 can be refined as follows:

Step 2 Refinement
2.1. Let Largest temporarily be the larger of Num1 and Num2.
2.2. Now let Largest be the larger of itself and Num3.

Step 3 Refinement
3.1. Let Smallest temporarily be the smaller of Num1 and Num2.
3.2. Now let Smallest be the larger of itself and Num3.

Coding
The coding is straightforward because our minimum and maximum functions already exist in the package. Assuming that the specification and body for

MinMax have both been successfully compiled, Program 4.8 solves the problem.
Note the context clause

```
WITH MinMax;
```

at the beginning of the program, along with the other context clauses for the
input/output packages.

Program 4.8 A Program That Uses Package MinMax

```
WITH Text_IO;
WITH My_Int_IO;
WITH MinMax;
PROCEDURE MinMaxThree IS

  -- finds the largest and smallest of three integer values
  -- using the Minimum and Maximum functions from package MinMax

  Num1:     Integer;
  Num2:     Integer;
  Num3:     Integer;
  Largest:  Integer;
  Smallest: Integer;

BEGIN -- MinMaxThree

  Text_IO.Put (Item => "Please enter first integer value > ");
  My_Int_IO.Get (Item => Num1);
  Text_IO.Put (Item => "Please enter second integer value > ");
  My_Int_IO.Get (Item => Num2);
  Text_IO.Put (Item => "Please enter third integer value > ");
  My_Int_IO.Get (Item => Num3);

  Largest := MinMax.Maximum(Value1=>Num1, Value2=>Num2);
  Largest := MinMax.Maximum(Value1=>Largest, Value2=>Num3);

  Smallest := MinMax.Minimum(Value1=>Num1, Value2=>Num2);
  Smallest := MinMax.Minimum(Value1=>Smallest, Value2=>Num3);

  Text_IO.Put (Item => "The smallest number is ");
  My_Int_IO.Put (Item => Smallest, Width => 1);
  Text_IO.Put (Item => " and the largest number is ");
  My_Int_IO.Put (Item => Largest, Width => 1);
  Text_IO.New_Line;

END MinMaxThree;


Please enter first integer value > -29
Please enter second integer value > 574
Please enter third integer value > 0
The smallest number is -29 and the largest number is 574
```

Exercises for Section 4.7

Programming

1. Create and test a second version of package `MinMax`. Copy the specification and body of `MinMax`, change the name in both files to `MinMaxFloat`, and modify the functions so that `Float` parameters are used instead of `Integer`. Write a program that tests *both* packages together. (*Hint:* You will need two context clauses.)

4.8 Tricks of the Trade: Common Programming Errors

When writing `IF` statements, remember not to put a semicolon after `THEN` or `ELSE`, and always to put semicolons after the other statements. Also do not forget the required `END IF;` at the end of the entire structure. When writing multiple-alternative `IF` statements, be careful to put the alternatives in an order that is correct for the problem being solved.

When writing a package, be sure that everything you promise in the specification is delivered in the body, and that the parameter list for each function or procedure in the specification matches *exactly* the corresponding procedure or function header in the body. Remember that you must compile the package specification without compilation errors before you can attempt to compile the package body.

If the *body* of a package is changed, but not the *specification*, do not recompile the specification, but just recompile the body and repeat the link step. If you recompile the specification, all programs that use the package will have to be recompiled.

Chapter Review

This chapter introduced you to an important control structure, the `IF` statement, for building decision steps into programs. `IF` statements are of three types: single-alternative, two-alternative, and multiple-alternative. `IF` statements provide a way to build decision making into a program.

You also learned how to write simple user-defined functions, and how to structure a package you are writing. A package consists of a specification file and a body file. The specification gives a "contract with the user," telling both the reader and the compiler what to expect in a package. The body then provides all the things promised by the specification.

New Ada Constructs in Chapter 4

The new Ada constructs introduced in this chapter are described in Table 4.7.

Table 4.7 Summary of New Ada Constructs

Construct	Effect
IF Statement	

One Alternative

```
IF X /= 0.0 THEN
    Product := Product * X;
END IF;
```
Multiplies Product by X only if X is nonzero.

Two Alternatives

```
IF X >= 0 THEN
    My_Int_IO.Put(Item=>X);
    Text_IO.Put(" is positive");
ELSE
    My_Int_IO.Put(Item=>X);
    Text_IO.Put(" is negative");
END IF;
```
If X is greater than or equal to 0, the message " is positive" is displayed; otherwise, the message " is negative" is displayed.

Several Alternatives

```
IF X < 0.0 THEN
    Text_IO.Put(Item=>"negative");
    AbsX := -X;
ELSIF X = 0.0 THEN
    Text_IO.Put(Item=>"zero");
    AbsX := X;
ELSE
    Text_IO.Put(Item=>"positive");
    AbsX := X;
END IF;
```
One of three messages is displayed depending on whether X is negative, positive, or zero. AbsX is set to represent the absolute value or magnitude of X.

Function Specification

```
FUNCTION Sign (X :Float) RETURN Character;
```
Specifies a function.

Function Body

```
FUNCTION Sign (X :Float) RETURN Character IS
    Temp: Character;
BEGIN -- Sign
    IF X >= 0.0 THEN
        Temp := '+';
    ELSE
        Temp := '-';
    END IF;
    RETURN Temp;
END Sign;
```
Returns a character value that indicates the sign ('+' or '-') of its type Float argument.

✓ *Quick-Check Exercises*

1. An IF statement implements _____ execution.
2. What is pseudocode?

3. What values can a Boolean expression have?
4. The relational operator /= means _____.
5. A _____ is used to verify that an algorithm is correct.
6. What value is assigned to Fee by the IF statement below when speed is 75?

```
IF Speed > 35 THEN
    Fee := 20.0;
ELSIF Speed > 50 THEN
    Fee := 40.00;
ELSIF Speed > 75 THEN
    Fee := 60.00;
END IF;
```

7. Answer Quick-Check Exercise 6 for the IF statement below. Which IF statement is correct?

```
IF Speed > 75 THEN
    Fee := 60.0;
ELSIF Speed > 50 THEN
    Fee := 40.00;
ELSIF Speed > 35 THEN
    Fee := 20.00;
END IF;
```

8. What output line(s) are displayed by the statements below when X is 5.53? When X is 9.95?

```
IF X >= 7.5 THEN
    X := 90.0;
    My_Flt_IO.Put(Item=>X, Fore=>2, Aft=>2, Exp=>0);
ELSE
    X := 25.0;
    My_Flt_IO.Put(Item=>X, Fore=>2, Aft=>2, Exp=>0);
END IF;
```

9. Explain the difference between the statements on the left and the statements on the right below. For each of them, what is the final value of X if the initial value of X is 1?

```
IF X >= 0 THEN          IF X >= 0 THEN
    X := X + 1;             X := X + 1;
ELSIF X >= 1 THEN       END IF;
    X := X + 2;         IF X >= 1 THEN
END IF;                     X := X + 2;
                        END IF;
```

Answers to Quick-Check Exercises
1. Conditional
2. A mixture of English and Ada used to describe algorithm steps
3. True and False
4. Not equal
5. Hand trace
6. 20.00, first condition is met
7. 40.00, the one in 7
8. When X is originally 5.53: 25.00; when X is originally 9.95: 90.00
9. A multi-alternative IF statement is on the left; a sequence of IF statements is on the right. X becomes 2 on the left; X becomes 4 on the right.

Review Questions for Chapter 4

1. A decision in Ada is actually an evaluation of a(n) _____ expression.
2. List the six relational operators discussed in this chapter.
3. What should the programmer do after writing the algorithm but before entering the program?
4. Trace the following program fragment and indicate what will be displayed if a data value of 27.34 is entered.

```
Text_IO.Put(Item => "Enter a temperature> ");
My_Flt_IO.Get (Item => Temp);
IF Temp > 32.0 THEN
    Text_IO.Put(Item => "Not Freezing");
ELSE
    Text_IO.Put(Item => "Ice Forming");
END IF;
```

5. Write the appropriate IF statement to compute GrossPay given that the hourly rate is stored in the variable Rate and the total hours worked is stored in the variable Hours. Pay time and a half for more than 40 hours worked.
6. Explain the difference between a package specification and a package body.

Programming Projects

1. Write a program to simulate a state police radar gun. The program should read an automobile's speed and print the message "speeding" if the speed exceeds 55 miles per hour.
2. You need a program that will read a character value and a number. Depending on what is read, certain information will be displayed. The character should be either an S or a T. If an S is read and the number is, say, 100.50, the program will display

   ```
   Send money!   I need $100.50.
   ```

   If a T is read instead of S, the program will display

   ```
   The temperature last night was 100.50 degrees.
   ```

3. Write a program that reads in a room number, its capacity, and the size of the class enrolled so far, and displays an output line showing the classroom number, capacity, number of seats filled and available, and a message indicating whether the class is filled or not. Display the heading below before the output line.

   ```
   Room   Capacity   Enrollment   Empty seats   Filled/Not Filled
   ```

   Display each part of the output line under the appropriate column heading. Test your program with the following classroom data:

Room	Capacity	Enrollment
426	25	25
327	18	14
420	20	15
317	100	90

4. Write a program that will determine the additional state tax owed by an employee. The state charges a 4% tax on net income. Determine net income by subtracting a $500 allowance for each dependent from gross income. Your program will read gross income, number of dependents, and tax amount already deducted. It will then compute the actual tax owed and display the difference between tax owed and tax deducted followed by the message "SEND CHECK" or "REFUND", depending on whether this difference is positive or negative.

5. The New Telephone Company has the following rate structure for long-distance calls:
   a. Any call started after 6:00 P.M. (1800 hours) but before 8:00 A.M. (0800 hours) is discounted 50%.
   b. Any call started after 8:00 A.M. (0800 hours) but before 6:00 P.M. (1800 hours) is charged full price.
   c. All calls are subject to a 4% Federal tax.
   d. The regular rate for a call is $0.40 per minute.
   e. Any call longer than 60 minutes receives a 15% discount on its cost (after any other discount is subtracted but before tax is added).

   Write a program that reads the start time for a call based on a 24-hour clock and the length of the call. The gross cost (before any discounts or tax) should be printed followed by the net cost (after discounts are deducted and tax is added). Use a procedure to display instructions to the program user.

6. Write a program that uses package MinMax to find the smallest and largest of four integers read from the terminal.

Repetition in Programs

5

5.1   Control Structures: Counting Loops and
      the FOR Statement
5.2   Problem Solving: Generalizing a Solution
5.3   Problem Solving: Repeating a Program Body
5.4   Control Structures: Nested Loops
5.5   Data Structures: Subtypes of Scalar Types
5.6   Tricks of the Trade: Debugging and Testing Programs
5.7   System Structures: A Useful Functions Package and the
      Overloading Principle
5.8   System Structures: Introduction to Exception Handling
5.9   Tricks of the Trade: Common Programming Errors
      Chapter Review

Chapters 3 and 4 introduced you to two control structures: *sequence*, in which statements are simply written one after the other, and *selection*, embodied in the IF statement, which allows one of a set of paths to be taken.

The third category of control structure in structured programming is *repetition*, or *iteration*, which allows a section of a program to be repeated, the number of repetitions being determined by some condition. In this chapter, you will see how to specify the repetition of a group of statements (called a *counting loop*) using the FOR statement. You will study how to design counting loops in Ada programs. Two other repetition constructs are introduced in Chapter 6.

Also in this chapter, the important concept of *subtypes* is extended, and you will see how using subtypes of scalar data types—integer, float, character, and enumeration—makes reading and writing programs easier and makes the programs more reliable.

Finally, two important system-structuring ideas are introduced: *overloading* and *exception handling*. Overloading permits several operations with similar behavior to be given the same name, and exception handling provides a method for keeping control when an error arises, instead of returning control automatically to the run-time system.

5.1 Control Structures: Counting Loops and the FOR Statement

Just as the ability to make decisions is a very important programming tool, so is the ability to specify that a group of operations is to be repeated. For example, a company with seven employees will want to repeat the gross pay and net pay computations in its payroll program seven times, once for each employee.

The repetition of steps in a program is called a *loop*. The *loop body* contains the steps to be repeated. Ada provides three control statements for specifying repetition. This chapter examines the FOR statement and previews the WHILE statement. The WHILE statement and the third loop form, the general LOOP statement, are examined in Chapter 6.

The FOR Statement

The FOR statement can be used to specify some forms of repetition quite easily, as shown in the next examples.

■ Example 5.1

The statement

```
FOR Count IN 1..5 LOOP
   Text_IO.New_Line;
END LOOP;
```

has the same effect as the five statements

```
Text_IO.New_Line;
Text_IO.New_Line;
Text_IO.New_Line;
Text_IO.New_Line;
Text_IO.New_Line;
```

The FOR statement above causes the New_Line operation to be performed five times. The FOR statement is used to implement *counting loops,* which are loops where the exact number of loop repetitions can be specified as a variable or constant value. Here, the number of repetitions required was five. The reserved words END LOOP terminate the FOR statement.

The FOR statement specifies that the variable Count should take on each of the values in the range 1 to 5 during successive loop repetitions. This means that the value of Count is 1 during the first loop repetition, 2 during the second loop repetition, and 5 during the last loop repetition. ■

Count is called a *loop control variable* because its value controls the loop repetition. The loop control variable is initialized to 1 when the FOR statement is first reached; after each execution of the loop body, the loop control variable is incremented by 1 and tested to see whether loop repetition should continue.

■ Example 5.2

The following FOR loop displays a sequence of HowMany asterisks. If HowMany has a value of 5, 5 asterisks in a row will be displayed; if HowMany has a value of 27, 27 asterisks will be displayed, and so on.

```
FOR Count IN 1 .. HowMany LOOP
   Text_IO.Put(Item => '*');
END LOOP;
```
■

Unlike other variables, a FOR loop control variable is not declared. A loop control variable may also be referenced in the loop body, but its value cannot be changed. The next example shows a FOR statement whose loop control variable is referenced in the loop body.

■ Example 5.3

Program 5.1 uses a FOR loop to print a list of integer values and their squares. During each repetition of the loop body, the statement Square := Num**2; computes the square of the loop control variable Num; then, the values of Num and NumSquared are displayed. A trace of this program is shown in Table 5.1.

The trace in Table 5.1 shows that the loop control variable Num is initialized to 1 when the FOR loop is reached. After each loop repetition, Num is incremented by 1 and tested to see whether its value is still less than or equal to MaxNum (4). If the test result is true, the loop body is executed again, and the next values of Num and Square are displayed. If the test result is false, the loop is exited. Num is equal to MaxNum during the last loop repetition. After this repetition, the value of Num becomes undefined (indicated by ? in the last table line), and the loop is exited. The variable Num ceases to exist and cannot be referenced

again unless the loop is entered again, in which case the variable is given a new
existence.   ■

Program 5.1 Finding the Squares of the First Four Integers

```
WITH Text_IO;
WITH My_Int_IO;
PROCEDURE Squares IS

  -- Displays a list of integer values and their squares.

  MaxNum : CONSTANT Natural := 4;
  Square : Natural;    -- output - square of Num

BEGIN -- Squares

  Text_IO.Put(Item => "        Num     Num ** 2 ");
  Text_IO.New_Line;
  Text_IO.Put(Item => "        ---     ---------");
  Text_IO.New_Line;

  FOR Num IN 1..MaxNum LOOP
    Square := Num ** 2;
    My_Int_IO.Put (Item => Num, Width => 10);
    My_Int_IO.Put (Item => Square, Width => 10);
    Text_IO.New_Line;
  END LOOP;

END Squares;
```

```
        Num     Num ** 2
        ---     ---------
         1          1
         2          4
         3          9
         4         16
```

Table 5.1 Trace of Program 5.1

Statement	Num	Square	Effect
	?	?	
FOR Num IN 1..MaxNum LOOP	1		Initialize Num to 1
Square := Num**2;		1	Assign 1 * 1 to Square
My_Int_IO.Put(Item=>Num,Width=>10);			Display 1
My_Int_IO.Put(Item=>Square,Width=>10);			Display 1
Increment and test Num	2		2 <= 4 is true
Square := Num**2;		4	Assign 2 * 2 to Square
My_Int_IO.Put(Item=>Num,Width=>10);			Display 2
My_Int_IO.Put(Item=>Square,Width=>10);			Display 4

Table 5.1 *continued*

163

5.1 Control
Structures: Counting
Loops and the FOR
Statement

Statement	Num	Square	Effect
Increment and test Num	3		3 <= 4 is true
Square := Num**2;		9	Assign 3 * 3 to Square
My_Int_IO.Put(Item=>Num,Width=>10);			Display 3
My_Int_IO.Put(Item=>Square,Width=>10);			Display 9
Increment and test Num	4		4 <= 4 is true
Square := Num**2;		16	Assign 4 * 4 to Square
My_Int_IO.Put(Item=>Num,Width=>10);			Display 4
My_Int_IO.Put(Item=>Square,Width=>10);			Display 16
Increment and test Num	?		Exit loop

It is also possible to count backward in a FOR loop. Writing IN REVERSE instead of IN causes the loop control variable to start at its maximum value and be decremented by 1, instead of incremented, in each loop iteration.

■ Example 5.4

Program 5.2 is a modification of Program 5.1. This time the largest number MaxNum is read from the terminal, and the squares are printed from the largest down to the smallest. The loop statement

```
FOR Num IN REVERSE 1..MaxNum LOOP
```

controls the iteration. The value of MaxNum is the number entered at the keyboard. ■

Program 5.2 Finding the Squares in Reverse Order

```
WITH Text_IO;
WITH My_Int_IO;
PROCEDURE ReverseSquares IS

   -- Displays a list of integer values and their squares.

   MaxNum :      Positive;
   NumSquared : Natural;    -- output - square of Num

BEGIN -- ReverseSquares

   Text_IO.Put(Item => "Enter the largest integer you wish to square > ");
   My_Int_IO.Get(Item => MaxNum);

   Text_IO.Put(Item => "       Num      Num ** 2 ");
   Text_IO.New_Line;
   Text_IO.Put(Item => "       ___      ---------");
   Text_IO.New_Line;
```

```
FOR Num IN REVERSE 1..MaxNum LOOP
   NumSquared := Num ** 2;
   My_Int_IO.Put (Item => Num, Width => 10);
   My_Int_IO.Put (Item => NumSquared, Width => 10);
   Text_IO.New_Line;
END LOOP;

END ReverseSquares;
```

```
Enter the largest integer you wish to square > 11
        Num     Num ** 2
        ---     ---------
        11         121
        10         100
         9          81
         8          64
         7          49
         6          36
         5          25
         4          16
         3           9
         2           4
         1           1
```

SYNTAX
DISPLAY

Counting Loops (Simplest Form)

Forms:

```
FOR counter IN 1..repetitions LOOP
     statement sequence
END LOOP;

FOR counter IN REVERSE 1..repetitions LOOP
     statement sequence
END LOOP;
```

Example:

```
FOR I IN 1 .. HowMany LOOP
   My_Int_IO.Put (Item => I, Width => 5);
   Text_IO.New_Line;
END LOOP;
```

Interpretation: The number of times *statement sequence* is executed is determined by the value of *repetitions*. The value of the loop control variable *counter* is set to 1 before the first execution of *statement sequence; counter* is incremented by 1 after each execution of *statement sequence. Repetitions* must be an expression, constant, or variable with an integer value.

If REVERSE is present, as in the second example above, *counter* is initialized to *repetitions* before the first execution of *statement sequence*, then decremented by 1 after each execution of *statement sequence.*

Note: If the value of *repetitions* is less than 1, *statement sequence* will not be executed. No statement within *statement sequence* can change the value of *counter*. The variable *counter* is not declared separately and has no existence outside the loop.

Accumulating a Sum

We can use a counting loop to accumulate the sum of a collection of data values as shown in the next problem.

 ## Case Study: Sum of Integers

Problem
Write a program that finds the sum of all integers from 1 to *N*.

Analysis
In order to solve this problem, it will be necessary to find some way to form the sum of the first N positive integers.

Data Requirements

> *Problem Inputs*
> the last integer in the sum (N : Positive)
>
> *Problem Outputs*
> the sum of integers from 1 to *N* (Sum : Natural)

Design

Initial Algorithm

1. Prompt the user for the last integer (N).
2. Find the sum (Sum) of all the integers from 1 to N inclusive.
3. Display the sum.

Algorithm Refinements

> *Step 2 Refinement*
> 2.0. Set Sum to zero
> 2.1. Add 1 to Sum
> 2.2. Add 2 to Sum
> 2.3. Add 3 to Sum
> . . .
> 2.N. Add N to Sum

For a large value of N, it would be rather time consuming to write this list of steps. We would also have to know the value of N before writing this list; consequently, the program would not be general, as it would work for only one value of N.

Because steps 2.1 through 2.*N* are all quite similar, we can represent each of them with the general step

2.i. Add i to Sum

This general step must be executed for all values of i from 1 to N, inclusive. This suggests the use of a counting loop with i as the loop control variable.

Program Variables
loop control variable—represents each integer from 1 to N (i : Positive).

The variable i will take on the successive values 1, 2, 3, ...,N. Each time the loop is repeated, the current value of i must be added to Sum. We now have a new refinement of step 2.

Step 2 Refinement

2.1.

```
FOR each integer i from 1 to N LOOP
   Add i to Sum
END LOOP;
```

Coding
The complete program is shown in Program 5.3. The statements

```
Sum := 0; -- Initialize Sum to zero
FOR I IN 1 .. N LOOP
   Sum := Sum + I ; -- Add the next integer to Sum
END LOOP;
```

are used to perform step 2. In order to ensure that the final sum is correct, the value of Sum must be initialized to zero (algorithm step 2.0) before the first addition operation. The FOR statement causes the assignment statement Sum := Sum + I; to be repeated N times. Each time, the current value of I is added to the sum being accumulated and the result is saved back in Sum.

Program 5.3   Finding the Sum of the First N Integers

```
WITH Text_IO;
WITH My_Int_IO;
PROCEDURE SumIntegers IS

-- Finds and displays the sum of all positive integers from 1 to N.

  N   : Positive;        -- input - the last integer added
  Sum : Natural;         -- output - the sum being accumulated

BEGIN -- SumIntegers
```

Case Study: Sum of Integers, continued

167

5.1 Control
Structures: Counting
Loops and the FOR
Statement

```
-- Read the last integer, N
Text_IO.Put (Item => "Enter the last integer in the sum > ");
My_Int_IO.Get (Item => N);

-- Find the sum (Sum) of all integers from 1 to N
Sum := 0;          -- Initialize Sum to 0
FOR I IN 1 .. N LOOP
  Sum := Sum + I;    -- Add the next integer to Sum
END LOOP;

-- Display the sum
Text_IO.Put (Item => "The sum of the integers from 1 to ");
My_Int_IO.Put (Item => N, Width => 1);
Text_IO.Put (Item => " is ");
My_Int_IO.Put (Item => Sum, Width => 1);
Text_IO.New_Line;

END SumIntegers;


Enter the last integer in the sum > 25
The sum of the integers from 1 to 25 is 325
```

Note that Sum must be of type Natural, rather than Positive, in order to initialize it to zero.

A trace of the program for a data value of 3 is shown in Table 5.2. The trace verifies that the program performs as desired because the final value stored in Sum is 6 (1+2+3). The loop control variable I ceases to exist after it reaches the value of N (3 in this case). As shown in the table, the statement Sum := Sum + I; is executed exactly three times.

Table 5.2   Trace of Program 5.3

Statement	i	N	SUM	Effect
`Text_IO.PUT(Item=>"Enter..");`	?	?	?	
`My_Int_IO.Get(Item=> N);`		3		Display a prompt
				Read 3 into N
`Sum := 0;`			0	Initialize Sum
`FOR i IN 1 . . N LOOP`	1	3	0	Initialize i to 1
`  Sum := Sum + i`			1	Add 1 to Sum
`Increment and test i`	2	3	1	2 <= 3 is true
`  Sum := Sum + i`			3	Add 2 to Sum
`Increment and test i`	3	3	3	3 <= 3 is true
`  Sum := Sum + i`			6	Add 3 to Sum
`Increment and test i`	?	3	6	Exit loop
`Text_IO.Put(Item=>"The Sum is");`				Display message
`My_Int_IO.Put(Item=>Sum,Width=>1);`			6	Display 6

5.2 Problem Solving: Generalizing a Solution

After you finish a program, someone will often ask a "What if?" question. The person asking the question usually wants to know whether the program would still work if some of the restrictions implied by the problem statement were removed. If the answer is "No," then you may have to modify the program to make it work. Try to anticipate these questions in advance and make your programs as general as possible right from the start. Sometimes this can be as easy as changing a program constant to a problem input.

One question that comes to mind for the last problem is: What if we wanted to find the sum and average of a list of any numbers, not just the sum of the first N integers. Would the program still work? Clearly, the answer to this question is "No." However, it would not be too difficult to modify the program to solve this more general problem.

◆ Case Study: General Sum Problem

Problem
Write a program that finds and displays the sum of a list of numbers.

Analysis
To add any list of numbers, a new variable (`CurrentValue`) is needed to store each value to be summed. The numbers must be provided as input data. Because the numbers are not necessarily positive, we will make `CurrentValue` and `Sum` type `Integer`.

Data Requirements

Problem Inputs
number of items to be summed (`NumValues : Natural`)
temporary storage for each data value to be summed (`CurrentValue: Integer`)

Problem Outputs
sum of the `NumValues` data values (`Sum: Integer`)

Design

Initial Algorithm

1. Prompt the user for the number (`NumValues`) of values to be summed.
2. Prompt the user for each data value and add it to the sum.
3. Display the sum.

Case Study: General Sum Problem, continued

This algorithm is very similar to the earlier one. Step 2 is modified slightly and is refined below.

Algorithm Refinements

Step 2 Refinement
2.1. Initialize Sum to 0.
2.2.

```
FOR each data value LOOP
   Read the data value into CurrentValue and add CurrentValue to Sum.
END LOOP;
```

In this refinement, the variable CurrentValue is used to store each number to be summed. After each number is read into CurrentValue, it is added to Sum. If there are more data items, the loop body is repeated and the next data item replaces the last one in CurrentValue. The number of data values to be summed is read into NumValues before the loop is reached. NumValues determines the number of loop repetitions that are required. A loop control variable is needed to count the data items as they are processed and ensure that all data are summed.

Program Variables

loop control variable—the number of data items added so far (Count : Positive)

Coding

The general program to find the sum of a list of data items is shown in Program 5.4.

Program 5.4   Finding the Sum of a Series of Data Items

```
WITH Text_IO;
WITH My_Int_IO;
PROCEDURE SumItems IS

-- Finds and displays the sum of a list of data items.

  NumValues :     Natural;      -- the number of items to be added
  Sum :           Integer;      -- the sum being accumulated
  CurrentValue : Integer;       -- the next data item to be added

BEGIN -- SumItems

  -- Read the number of items to be summed
  Text_IO.Put(Item => "Enter number of integer items to be summed > ");
  My_Int_IO.Get(Item => NumValues);
  Text_IO.New_Line;

  -- Read each data item and add it to Sum
  Sum := 0;
  FOR Count IN 1 .. NumValues LOOP
    Text_IO.Put(Item => "Integer item no. ");
```

Case Study: General Sum Problem, continued

```
      My_Int_IO.Put(Item => Count, Width => 1);
      Text_IO.Put(Item => " to be summed > ");
      My_Int_IO.Get(Item => CurrentValue);
      Sum := Sum + CurrentValue;
   END LOOP;

   -- Print the sum
   Text_IO.Put(Item => "The Sum is ");
   My_Int_IO.Put(Item => Sum, Width => 1);
   Text_IO.New_Line;

END SumItems;


Enter number of integer items to be summed > 6

Integer item no. 1 to be summed > 4
Integer item no. 2 to be summed > -7
Integer item no. 3 to be summed > 0
Integer item no. 4 to be summed > 24
Integer item no. 5 to be summed > -10
Integer item no. 6 to be summed > 1
The Sum is 12
```

We can further generalize this solution to find the minimum, maximum, and average of a list of data values—for example, the results of a class examination. The average is computed by finding the sum of all the values, then dividing by the number of values. From the previous example, we know how to find the sum. The minimum and maximum can be found at the same time, using our package MinMax.

 ## Case Study: Minimum, Maximum, and Average of a List of Numbers

Problem
Write a program that finds and displays the minimum, maximum, and average of a list of integers.

Analysis
This is quite similar to the previous problem. We can use the variables CurrentValue and Sum as above. As each value is read, it must be added into the sum, but also compared against the current minimum, Smallest, and the current maximum, Largest. The comparisons can be handled by the Minimum and Maximum functions already provided in the MinMax package.

Because each new value, *including the first,* needs to be compared to Smallest and Largest, what initial values should these two variables have? It might be tempting to simply initialize them to zero, like the sum. This would be a mistake: Suppose that all the values to be read happened to be positive? The program would give incorrect results, as it would report that the smallest value was zero, instead of the really smallest value (which in this case would be greater than zero!).

One way to solve this problem is to initialize Smallest to the *largest* possible integer value we will accept from the user. For now, we will just let this be the largest possible value of the type Integer. This way, any value the user could enter would automatically be no larger than this initial value. Luckily, Ada gives us an easy way to discover the largest possible value of Integer: It is an attribute called Integer'Last. (Notice the use of the apostrophe in the syntax.) This value is a large number whose actual value depends on the compiler you are using. Because we also need to find the largest number, we should initialize Largest to the *smallest* possible Integer value, which Ada calls Integer'First.

Data Requirements

Problem Inputs
number of items to be averaged (NumValues : Positive)
temporary storage for each data value (CurrentValue: Integer)

Problem Outputs
minimum of the NumValues data values (Smallest: Integer)
largest of the NumValues data values (Largest: Integer)
average of the NumValues data values (Average: Integer)

Design

Initial Algorithm

1. Prompt the user for the number (NumValues) of values to be summed.
2. Prompt the user for each data value; add it to the sum, check to see if it is a new minimum, and check to see if it is a new maximum.
3. Compute the average of the values.
4. Display the minimum, maximum, and average.

This algorithm is very similar to the earlier one. Step 2 is modified and is refined below; there is a new step 3.

Algorithm Refinements

Step 2 Refinement
2.1. Initialize Sum to 0, Smallest to Integer'Last, and Largest to Integer'First.

2.2.
FOR each data value LOOP
    Read the data value into CurrentValue and add CurrentValue to Sum;
    determine whether the data value is a new minimum or maximum
END LOOP;

In this refinement, the variable CurrentValue is used to store each number to be summed. After each number is read into CurrentValue, it is added to Sum. If there are more data items, the loop body is repeated and the next data item replaces the last one in CurrentValue. The number of data values to be summed is read into NumValues before the loop is reached. NumValues determines the number of loop repetitions required. A loop control variable is needed to count the data items as they are processed and ensure that all data are summed.

We need a further refinement of step 2.2:

Step 2.2 Refinement
2.2
FOR each data value LOOP
    2.2.1 Read the data value into CurrentValue and add CurrentValue to Sum;
    2.2.2 Replace Smallest with the smaller of itself and CurrentValue;
    2.2.3 Replace Largest with the larger of itself and CurrentValue;
END LOOP;

Program Variables

loop control variable—the number of data items added so far (Count : Positive)

Coding

Program 5.5 shows the entire program. Note that this program finds the average as an integer value, by dividing Sum by NumValues. This is because all the numbers are integers and the division throws away the fractional part of the quotient. In Chapter 7 we will examine how to convert between integer and floating-point values.

Program 5.5   Finding Minimum, Maximum, and Average Values

```
WITH Text_IO;
WITH My_Int_IO;
WITH MinMax;
PROCEDURE MinMaxAverage IS

-- Finds and displays the minimum, maximum, and average
-- of a list of data items.
```

```
NumValues:      Positive;    -- the number of items to be averaged
Sum:            Integer;     -- the sum being accumulated
CurrentValue:   Integer;     -- the next data item to be added

Smallest:       Integer;     -- minimum of the data values
Largest:        Integer;     -- maximum of the data values
Average:        Integer;     -- average of the data values

BEGIN -- MinMaxAverage

  -- Read the number of items to be averaged
  Text_IO.Put(Item =>
    "Enter number (at least 1) of integer items to be averaged > ");
  My_Int_IO.Get(Item => NumValues);
  Text_IO.New_Line;

  -- Initialize program variables
  Smallest := Integer'Last;
  Largest := Integer'First;
  Sum := 0;

  -- Read each data item, add it to Sum,
  -- and check if it is a new minimum or maximum
  FOR Count IN 1 .. NumValues LOOP
    Text_IO.Put(Item => "Integer item no. ");
    My_Int_IO.Put(Item => Count, Width => 1);
    Text_IO.Put(Item => " > ");
    My_Int_IO.Get(Item => CurrentValue);

    Sum := Sum + CurrentValue;
    Smallest := Minmax.Minimum(Value1 => Smallest, Value2 => CurrentValue);
    Largest := Minmax.Maximum(Value1 =>  Largest, Value2 => CurrentValue);
  END LOOP;

  -- compute the average; since Sum and NumValues are integers,
  -- the average will be truncated to the next lower integer

  Average := Sum / NumValues;

  -- Display the results
  Text_IO.Put(Item => "The Smallest is ");
  My_Int_IO.Put(Item => Smallest, Width => 1);
  Text_IO.New_Line;
  Text_IO.Put(Item => "The Largest is ");
  My_Int_IO.Put(Item => Largest, Width => 1);
  Text_IO.New_Line;
  Text_IO.Put(Item => "The Average is ");
  My_Int_IO.Put(Item => Average, Width => 1);
  Text_IO.New_Line;

END MinMaxAverage;


Enter number (at least 1) of integer items to be averaged > 7

Integer item no. 1 > -5
Integer item no. 2 > 2
Integer item no. 3 > 29
```

```
Integer item no. 4 > 16
Integer item no. 5 > 0
Integer item no. 6 > -17
Integer item no. 7 > 4
The Smallest is -17
The Largest is 29
The Average is 4
```

Using an External File for Input Data

A modification of Program 5.5 could use an external (disk) file for the input data. In fact, most real-world computer programs make heavy use of external files. The user prepares a file of data using an editor, then uses it later as input to the program. If the program is being developed and debugged, requiring several test runs, preparing the data this way saves having to enter them interactively each time the program is tested. We shall cover this topic more systematically in Chapters 8 and 9; for now, let's just consider how Program 5.5 would be changed to allow an external file for input.

The Get operations we have been working with all assume that input is coming interactively from the keyboard. In fact, each Get (for characters, strings, integers, floating-point quantities, and enumeration literals) has a second form requiring an additional parameter that names a disk file. For example, the input operation to read an integer value from a disk file called, say, TestScores, would be

```
My_Int_IO.Get(File => TestScores, Item => CurrentValue);
```

In general these operations look just like the interactive ones except for the file name. TestScores is an Ada variable, which must be declared as

```
TestScores: Text_IO.File_Type;
```

The type File_Type is provided by Text_IO.

Now suppose that the user prepared the input data with an editor and stored them in a disk file called SCORES.DAT. The program needs a way to associate the name of the file in the program (TestScores in this case) with the name of the file as it is known to the operating system (SCORES.DAT in this case). This is done by means of an operation called Text_IO.Open. In this case the operation would look like

```
Text_IO.Open
(File => TestScores, Mode => Text_IO.In_File, Name => "SCORES.DAT");
```

The parameter Mode indicates whether we are reading from the file (Text_IO.In_File, as in this example) or writing to it (Text_IO.Out_File). Notice also that the operating-system file name must appear in quotes.

It is important to type the name of the file *exactly* as it is listed in the directory you get from the operating system. Many operating systems use *case-sensitive* file names, which means that if the operating system file name is uppercase (e.g., SCORES.DAT) then your parameter in the Open statement must also be uppercase (as in our example); if the operating system file name is in lowercase, your parameter must be also. If you supply to Open a file name that does not exist in your current directory, the Ada exception Name_Error will be raised.

Program 5.6 shows a modification of MinMaxAverage in which input values are read from a file instead of from the terminal keyboard. Notice that there are no prompts, because there is no interactive user entering the data. The file SCORES.DAT, created with an editor, will contain first the number of values to be read, then the actual values, one value per line. The program "logs," or displays on the terminal, the values as they are read from the file and processed; finally the results are displayed as before.

Program 5.6   MinMaxAverage, File Version

```
WITH Text_IO;
WITH My_Int_IO;
WITH MinMax;
PROCEDURE MinMaxAvgFile IS

-- Finds and displays the minimum, maximum, and average
-- of a list of data items.

  NumValues:      Positive;           -- the number of items to be averaged
  Sum:            Integer;            -- the sum being accumulated
  CurrentValue:   Integer;            -- the next data item to be added
  Smallest:       Integer;            -- minimum of the data values
  Largest:        Integer;            -- maximum of the data values
  Average:        Integer;            -- average of the data values
  TestScores:     Text_IO.File_Type;  -- program variable naming the input file

BEGIN -- MinMaxAvgFile

  -- Open the file and associate it with the file variable name
  Text_IO.Open
    (File => TestScores, Mode => Text_IO.In_File, Name => "SCORES.DAT");

  -- Read from the file the number of items to be averaged
  My_Int_IO.Get(File => TestScores, Item => NumValues);
  Text_IO.Put("The number of scores to be averaged is ");
  My_Int_IO.Put(Item => NumValues, Width => 1);
  Text_IO.New_Line;

  -- Initialize program variables
  Smallest := Integer'Last;
  Largest := Integer'First;
  Sum := 0;

  -- Read each data item, log to the screen, add it to Sum,
  -- and check if it is a new minimum or maximum
  FOR Count IN 1 .. NumValues LOOP
    My_Int_IO.Get(File => TestScores, Item => CurrentValue);
```

```
Text_IO.Put("Score number ");
My_Int_IO.Put(Item => Count, Width => 1);
Text_IO.Put(" is ");
My_Int_IO.Put(Item => CurrentValue, Width => 1);
Text_IO.New_Line;

    Sum := Sum + CurrentValue;
    Smallest := Minmax.Minimum(Valuel => Smallest, Value2 => CurrentValue);
    Largest  := Minmax.Maximum(Valuel => Largest, Value2 => CurrentValue);
END LOOP;

-- compute the average; since Sum and NumValues are integers,
-- the average will be truncated to the next lower integer
Average := Sum / NumValues;

-- display the results
Text_IO.Put(Item => "The Smallest is ");
My_Int_IO.Put(Item => Smallest, Width => 1);
Text_IO.New_Line;
Text_IO.Put(Item => "The Largest is ");
My_Int_IO.Put(Item => Largest, Width => 1);
Text_IO.New_Line;
Text_IO.Put(Item => "The Average is ");
My_Int_IO.Put(Item => Average, Width => 1);
Text_IO.New_Line;

END MinMaxAvgFile;


The number of scores to be averaged is 10
Score number 1 is 57
Score number 2 is 22
Score number 3 is 100
Score number 4 is 42
Score number 5 is 37
Score number 6 is 70
Score number 7 is 81
Score number 8 is 92
Score number 9 is 100
Score number 10 is 87
The Smallest is 22
The Largest is 100
The Average is 68
```

 ## 5.3 Problem Solving: Repeating a Program Body

In the discussion of repetition in programs, we mentioned that we would like
to be able to execute the payroll program for several employees in a single run.
We will see how to do this next.

◆ Case Study: Multiple-Employee Payroll Problem

Problem

Modify the payroll program to compute gross pay and net pay for a group of employees.

Analysis

The number of employees must be provided as input data along with the hourly rate and hours worked by each employee. The same set of variables will be used to hold the data and computational results for each employee. The computations will be performed in the same way as before.

Data Requirements

Problem Constants
maximum salary for no tax deduction (TaxBracket = 100.0)
amount of tax deducted (Tax = 25.00)

Problem Inputs
number of employees (NumEmp : Positive)
hours worked by each employee (Hours : NonNegFloat)
hourly rate for each employee (Rate : NonNegFloat)

Problem Outputs
gross pay (Gross : NonNegFloat)
net pay (Net : NonNegFloat)

Design

Algorithm

1. Prompt for the number of employees (NumEmp).
2. FOR each employee LOOP
       Enter payroll data and compute and print gross and net pay.
   END LOOP;

An additional variable is needed to count the number of employees processed and to control the FOR loop in step 2.

Program Variable

loop control variable—counts the employees that are processed:

    (CountEmp : Positive)

The structure chart is shown in Fig. 5.1. (The structure chart for the subproblem "find gross and net pay" was drawn in Fig. 4.3.)

Case Study: Multiple-Employee Payroll Problem, *continued*

Figure 5.1   Structure Chart for Multi-Employee Payroll Problem

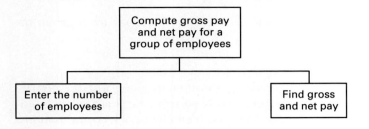

Coding

Program 5.7 gives the entire program. Notice how the code is very similar to that in the original program, with the addition of a few more declarations and the loop construct. Sample output is given for three employees.

Program 5.7   Multi-Employee Payroll Program

```
WITH Text_IO;
WITH My_Int_IO;
WITH My_Flt_IO;
PROCEDURE MultiPay IS

-- Computes and displays gross pay and net pay for a number
-- of employees, given each employee's hourly rate and hours worked.
-- Deducts a tax of $25 if gross salary exceeds $100;
-- otherwise, deducts no tax.

   SUBTYPE NonNegFloat IS Float RANGE 0.0 .. Float'Last;

   TaxBracket : CONSTANT NonNegFloat := 100.00;
                                   -- maximum salary for no deduction
   Tax :        CONSTANT NonNegFloat := 25.00;   -- tax amount

   NumEmp: Positive;

   Hours : NonNegFloat; -- inputs - hours worked, hourly rate
   Rate:   NonNegFloat;
   Gross:  NonNegFloat; -- outputs - gross pay, net pay
   Net:    NonNegFloat;

BEGIN -- MultiPay

   Text_IO.Put ("Please enter number of employees > ");
   My_Int_IO.Get (Item => NumEmp);

   FOR CountEmp IN 1 .. NumEmp LOOP

      -- Enter Hours and Rate
      Text_IO.Put (Item => "Employee number ");
      My_Int_IO.Put (Item => CountEmp, Width => 1);
      Text_IO. New_Line;
```

```
    Text_IO.Put (Item => " Hours worked > ");
    My_Flt_IO.Get (Item => Hours);
    Text_IO.Put (Item => " Hourly rate > ");
    My_Flt_IO.Get (Item => Rate);

    -- Compute gross salary
    Gross := Hours * Rate;

    -- Compute net salary
    IF Gross > TaxBracket THEN
       Net := Gross - Tax;        -- Deduct a tax amount
    ELSE
       Net := Gross;              -- Deduct no tax
    END IF;

    -- Print Gross and Net
    Text_IO.Put (Item => " Gross salary is $");
    My_Flt_IO.Put (Item => Gross, Fore => 1, Aft => 2, Exp => 0);
    Text_IO.Put (Item => "; Net salary is $");
    My_Flt_IO.Put (Item => Net, Fore => 1, Aft => 2, Exp => 0);
    Text_IO.New_Line;

  END LOOP;

END MultiPay;


Please enter number of employees > 3
Employee number 1
  Hours worked > 40.0
  Hourly rate > 6.50
  Gross salary is $260.00; Net salary is $235.00
Employee number 2
  Hours worked > 20.0
  Hourly rate > 4.75
  Gross salary is $95.00; Net salary is $95.00
Employee number 3
  Hours worked > 39.5
  Hourly rate > 7.95
  Gross salary is $314.03; Net salary is $289.03
```

5.4 Control Structures: Nested Loops

In this section, we examine nested loops. Nested loops consist of an outer loop with one or more inner loops. Each time the outer loop is repeated, the inner loops are reentered, their loop control parameters are reevaluated, and all required iterations are performed.

■ **Example 5.5**

Program 5.8 shows a program with two nested FOR loops. The outer loop is
repeated three times (for OuterCounter equals 1, 2, and 3). Each time the outer
loop is repeated, the statements

```
Text_IO.Put (Item => "OUTER");
My_Int_IO.Put (Item => OuterCounter, Width => 10);
Text_IO.New_Line;
```

display the string "OUTER" and the value of OuterCounter (the outer loop
control variable). Next, the inner loop is entered, and its loop control variable
InnerCounter is reset to 1. The number of times the inner loop is repeated
depends on the current value of OuterCounter. Each time the inner loop is
repeated, the statements

```
Text_IO.Put (Item => "INNER");
My_Int_IO.Put (Item => InnerCounter, Width => 22);
Text_IO.New_Line;
```

display the string "INNER" and the value of InnerCounter (the inner loop
control variable).   ■

Program 5.8   Illustrating Nested FOR Loops

```
WITH Text_IO;
WITH My_Int_IO;
PROCEDURE NestLoop IS

-- Illustrates a pair of nested FOR loops.

BEGIN -- NestLoop

  Text_IO.Put(Item => "   OuterCounter InnerCounter");
  Text_IO.New_Line;

  FOR OuterCounter IN 1 .. 3 LOOP

    Text_IO.Put(Item => "OUTER");
    My_Int_IO.Put(Item => OuterCounter, Width => 10);
    Text_IO.New_Line;

    FOR InnerCounter IN 1 .. OuterCounter LOOP
      Text_IO.Put(Item => " INNER");
      My_Int_IO.Put(Item => InnerCounter, Width => 22);
      Text_IO.New_Line;
    END LOOP;

  END LOOP;

END NestLoop;
```

```
        OuterCounter  InnerCounter
OUTER        1
   INNER                   1
OUTER        2
   INNER                   1
   INNER                   2
```

```
OUTER        3
   INNER                    1
   INNER                    2
   INNER                    3
```

In Program 5.8, the outer loop control variable OuterCounter is used as the limit expression that determines the number of repetitions of the inner loop. This is perfectly valid. It is also valid to use the same variable name as the loop control variable of both an outer and an inner FOR loop in the same nest. This is strongly discouraged, however, because it causes the compiler to create two "nested" variables with the same name. Although this is not a problem for the compiler, it certainly is a source of confusion for the human reader of the program!

■ Example 5.6

Program 5.9 prints an isosceles triangle. The program contains an outer loop (loop control variable Row) and two inner loops. Each time the outer loop is

Program 5.9   Draw an Isosceles Triangle

```
WITH Text_IO;
PROCEDURE Triangle IS

-- Draws an isosceles triangle

  NumLines: CONSTANT Integer := 5;
  Blank   : CONSTANT Character := ' ';
  Star    : CONSTANT Character := '*';

BEGIN -- Triangle

  FOR Row IN 1 .. NumLines LOOP      -- draw each row

    FOR LeadBlanks IN REVERSE 1 .. NumLines - Row LOOP
      Text_IO.Put(Item => Blank); -- display leading blanks
    END LOOP;

    FOR CountStars IN 1 .. (2*Row) - 1 LOOP
      Text_IO.Put(Item => Star);   -- display asterisks
    END LOOP;

    Text_IO.New_Line;              -- terminate row

  END LOOP;

END Triangle;


    *
   ***
  *****
 *******
*********
```

repeated, two inner loops are executed. The first inner loop prints the leading blank spaces; the second inner loop prints one or more asterisks.

The outer loop is repeated five times; the number of repetitions performed by the inner loops is based on the value of Row. Table 5.3 lists the inner loop control parameters for each value of Row. As the table shows, four blanks and one asterisk are printed when Row is 1, three blanks and three asterisks are printed when Row is 2, and so on. When Row is 5, the first inner loop is skipped and nine ($2 \times 5 - 1$) asterisks are printed. ∎

Table 5.3 Inner Loop Control Parameters

Row	LeadBlanks	CountStars	Effect
1	REVERSE 1..4	1..1	Displays 4 blanks and 1 star
2	REVERSE 1..3	1..3	Displays 3 blanks and 3 stars
3	REVERSE 1..2	1..5	Displays 2 blanks and 5 stars
4	REVERSE 1..1	1..7	Displays 1 blank and 7 stars
5	REVERSE 1..0	1..9	Displays 0 blanks and 9 stars

Exercises for Section 5.4

Self-Check

1. What is displayed by the following program segments, assuming M is 3 and N is 5?

   a.

```
FOR I IN 1..N LOOP
    FOR J IN 1..I LOOP
        Text_IO.Put(Item => '*');
    END LOOP;
    Text_IO.New_Line;
END LOOP;
```

   b.

```
FOR I IN 1..N LOOP
    FOR J IN 1..M LOOP
        Text_IO.Put(Item => '*');
    END LOOP;
    Text_IO.New_Line;
END LOOP;
```

2. Show the output printed by the nested loops below.

```
FOR I IN 1..2 LOOP
    Text_IO.Put(Item=>"Outer");
    My_Int_IO.Put(Item=>I, Width=>5);
    FOR J IN 1..3 LOOP
        Text_IO.Put(Item=>"Inner ");
        My_Int_IO.Put(Item=>I, Width=>3);
        My_Int_IO.Put(Item=>J, Width=>3);
    END LOOP;
```

```
FOR K IN REVERSE 1..2 LOOP
        Text_IO.Put(Item=>"Inner ");
        My_Int_IO.Put(Item=>I, Width=>3);
        My_Int_IO.Put(Item=>K, Width=>3);
    END LOOP;
END LOOP;
```

Programming

1. Write a program that prints the multiplication table.
2. Write a nest of loops that causes the output below to be printed.

```
1
1 2
1 2 3
1 2 3 4
1 2 3
1 2
1
```

5.5 Data Structures: Subtypes of Scalar Types

One of the most important features of Ada is that it permits the declaration of data types. Many of these data types will be discussed in later chapters. In this section we will discuss the declaration of *subtypes*. Recall that a type is a set of values and a set of operations appropriate for those values. A subtype defines a *subset* of the values associated with the original type, or *base type*; the operations of the subtype are the same as those of the base type. In this section we shall consider how to create subranges of the predefined types Integer, Float, and Character, and of programmer-defined enumeration types like the names of the days in the week. Subtypes are used both to make a program more readable and to enable detection of an attempt to give a variable a value that is unreasonable in the problem environment.

Subtypes of Predefined Scalar Types

So far in this book we have used six different subtypes. The first two are predefined in the Ada language and are thus always available:

```
SUBTYPE Natural IS Integer RANGE 0..Integer'Last;
SUBTYPE Positive IS Integer RANGE 1..Integer'Last;
```

The next three subtypes, introduced in Section 3.5, are predefined, not in the language itself, but in the standard package Calendar, and are therefore available to any program with a context clause WITH Calendar:

```
SUBTYPE Year_Number IS Integer RANGE 1901..2099;
SUBTYPE Month_Number IS Integer RANGE 1..12;
SUBTYPE Day_Number IS Integer RANGE 1..31;
```

Finally, in Section 2.9 we introduced a programmer-defined subtype,

```
SUBTYPE NonNegFloat IS Float RANGE 0.0 .. Float'Last;
```

All these subtypes (and subtypes in general) have a common characteristic. An attempt to assign to a variable a value that is not in the defined set of values will cause a compilation error or warning, if the compiler can detect the attempt. If the compiler cannot detect the attempt, for example because the out-of-range value is computed as the program is executed, then the Constraint_Error exception will be raised.

■ Example 5.7

Subtype declarations begin with the reserved word SUBTYPE. Two subtypes are declared below, as well as some variables:

```
SUBTYPE SmallInt IS Integer RANGE -50..50;
SUBTYPE CapitalLetter IS Character RANGE 'A'..'Z';

X, Y, Z : SmallInt;
NextChar : CapitalLetter;
InDay : Calendar.Day_Number;
Hours_Worked : NonNegFloat;
```

The first subtype, SmallInt, is a subtype with base type Integer. The following sequence of assignment statements will cause Constraint_Error to be raised at run time:

```
X := 26;
Y := 25;
Z := X + Y;
```

Why is there no compilation error? Remember that the compiler does not actually carry out the computation you specify; it only produces an object program, which carries out the computation when it is executed. Even though it may be obvious to you that this simple computation will produce an out-of-range result, it is not obvious to the compiler, so the checking can be done, and the exception raised, only at run time.

CapitalLetter has the base type Character. Any character from A to Z inclusive may be stored in a variable of type CapitalLetter. Constraint_Error will be raised if an attempt is made to store any other character in a variable of type CapitalLetter. For example, the assignment statement

```
NextChar := 'a';
```

causes the exception to be raised because the character a is not included in the subtype CapitalLetter. The compiler might notice this attempted out-of-range assignment, but instead of considering this an outright error, will often give a warning stating that the statement will cause Constraint_Error to be raised at run time.

Month_Number is a subtype with base type Integer. A variable of type Month_Number may be used to keep track of the current date, a value between 1 and 31 inclusive. The statement

```
My_Int_IO.Get(Item => InDay);
```

reads a data value into InDay. Constraint_Error is raised if the data value entered from the keyboard is less than 1 or greater than 31. This is clearly a situation where the compiler cannot guess whether the value entered from the keyboard will be in range or not. ∎

Subtypes of Enumeration Types

Subtypes of programmer-defined types can be defined just as easily as subtypes of predefined types. As an example, consider the month-name type introduced in Section 3.5:

```
TYPE Months IS
    (January, February, March, April, May, June,
    July, August, September, October, November, December);
```

We can define subtypes for three seasons as follows:

```
SUBTYPE Spring IS Months RANGE March .. May;
SUBTYPE Summer IS Months RANGE June .. August;
SUBTYPE Autumn IS Months RANGE September .. November;
```

We cannot easily define a subtype Winter (the months December, January, and February) because unfortunately Ada requires that the values of a subtype be specified in the form of a range and therefore *contiguous*, that is, adjacent in the base type definition. Sometimes a way can be found to work around this, as in the case of the day-names type introduced in Section 4.6:

```
TYPE Days IS
    (Mon, Tue, Wed, Thu, Fri, Sat, Sun);
```

Since Mon through Fri are contiguous, and Sat and Sun are contiguous, we can define subtypes for weekdays and weekend days:

```
SUBTYPE Weekdays IS Days RANGE Mon .. Fri;
SUBTYPE Weekend  IS Days RANGE Sat .. Sun;
```

Unfortunately, this work-around requires the Days type to look different than the "normal" American calendar in which the week starts on Sunday.

SYNTAX
DISPLAY

Subtype Declaration

Form:

```
SUBTYPE subtype-name IS base-type-name RANGE minvalue .. maxvalue;
```

Example:

```
SUBTYPE Uppercase IS Character RANGE 'A'..'Z';
```

Interpretation: A new subtype named *subtype-name* is defined. A variable of type *subtype-name* may be assigned a value from *minvalue* through *maxvalue* inclusive. The values *minvalue* and *maxvalue* must belong to the base type, and *minvalue* must be less than *maxvalue*.

Motivation for Using Subtypes

You may be wondering why we bother with subtypes. They don't seem to provide any new capabilities. However, they do provide additional opportunity for your program to "bomb" because attempting to store an out-of-range value in a variable causes an exception, usually `Constraint_Error`, to be raised. This should happen only as the result of an error by either the programmer or the program user.

The use of subtypes ensures the immediate detection of an out-of-range value. This contributes to a program's reliability and usefulness, because it ensures that variables do not acquire values that are meaningless in the problem being solved (such as a negative number of hours worked in a week).

In this book we use subtypes extensively, especially where it is necessary that a variable be nonnegative.

Compatibility Rules for Types and Subtypes

Ada does not allow a programmer accidentally to mix the types of operands for an operator. This means that the expression V1 + V2 leads to a compilation error such as "type incompatible operands" if V1 is one data type (say, `Integer`) and V2 is another (say, `Float`). However, what if V1 is type `Integer` and V2 is type `SmallInt` (a subtype of `Integer`)? In this case, the expression is valid because `SmallInt` and `Integer` are considered *compatible types*. Ada has simple compatibility rules: Two values are compatible if they have the same type name, if one value's type is a subtype of the other value's type (`Integer` and `SmallInt`, for example), or if their types are subtypes of the same base type (`Positive` and `SmallInt`, for example).

The compatibility relationship between operands determines what operators can be used with the operands. An operator can be used only with operands that are compatible with it and with each other. Assignment of a value to a variable is possible only if the value and the variable are compatible. And an actual parameter supplied to a function or procedure must be compatible with the corresponding formal parameter.

These rules ensure, for example, that a `Float` value is not assigned to an `Integer` variable, that an `Integer` value is not assigned to a `Float` variable, and that an `Integer` value is not supplied to `Text_IO.Put` (which expects a character). On the other hand, a Positive value can be supplied to My_Int_IO.Put (which expects an Integer) because of the subtype relationship.

Type Membership: The Operator IN

An important operator that applies to almost all types in Ada is IN. It can be used to determine whether a given value is a member of a given type's set of values.

■ Example 5.8

Suppose Today is of type Days, and that we have defined the two subtypes Weekdays and Weekend as above. The following IF statement serves as an example of the use of IN:

```
IF Today IN Weekdays THEN
    Text_IO.Put(Item => "Another day, another dollar...");
ELSE
    Text_IO.Put(Item => "We've worked hard, let's play hard!");
END IF;
```

Program 5.10 can be used to determine whether we need to go to work tomorrow. It is based on Program 4.4. Notice the use of the IF statement shown above. ■

Program 5.10   Do We Have to Work Tomorrow?

```
WITH Text_IO;
PROCEDURE WorkDays IS

   -- demonstrates the use of enumeration subtypes
   -- prompts user for a day of week and determines whether
   -- the following day is a weekday or a weekend day

   TYPE Days IS (Mon, Tue, Wed, Thu, Fri, Sat, Sun);
   SUBTYPE WeekDays IS Days RANGE Mon .. Fri;
   SUBTYPE WeekEnd IS Days RANGE Sat .. Sun;
   PACKAGE Day_IO IS
      NEW Text_IO.Enumeration_IO (Enum => Days);

   Today    : Days;
   Tomorrow : Days;

BEGIN -- WorkDays

   -- prompt user to enter a day abbreviation
   Text_IO.Put (Item => "Enter a 3-letter day of the week > ");
   Day_IO.Get (Item => Today);

   -- find tomorrow
   IF Today = Days'Last THEN
     Tomorrow := Days'First;
   ELSE
     Tomorrow := Days'Succ(Today);
   END IF;
```

```
Text_IO.Put (Item => "Tomorrow is ");
Day_IO.Put (Item => Tomorrow);
Text_IO.New_Line;

-- Is Tomorrow a week day or a weekend day?
IF Tomorrow IN Weekdays THEN
   Text_IO.Put (Item => "Another day, another dollar...");
   Text_IO.New_Line;
ELSE
   Text_IO.Put (Item => "We've worked hard, let's play hard!");
   Text_IO.New_Line;
END IF;

Text_IO.Put (Item => "Have a good day tomorrow.");
Text_IO.New_Line;

END WorkDays;


Enter a 3-letter day of the week > fri
Tomorrow is SAT
We've worked hard, let's play hard!
Have a good day tomorrow.
```

As you have seen in this chapter, another use for IN is in counting loops. So far, you have seen only loops whose range is 1..repetitions. Another useful form of the counting loops is to give the name of a type or subtype as the range of the loop. Suppose that SmallInt is defined as above, with a range −50..50, then

```
FOR Counter IN SmallInt LOOP
   My_Int_IO.Put(Item => Counter);
   Text_IO.New_Line;
END LOOP;
```

displays all the values in the type SmallInt (-50, -49, -48...), one at a time.

■ Example 5.9

Program 5.11 displays the addition table for integer values between 0 and 9 (type SmallNatural). For example, the table line beginning with the digit 9 shows the result of adding to 9 each of the digits 0 through 9. The initial FOR loop prints the table heading, which is the operator + and the list of digits from 0 through 9.

Program 5.11 Computing an Addition Table

```
WITH Text_IO;
WITH My_Int_IO;
PROCEDURE AddTable IS

-- Displays an addition table.

   MaxDigit : CONSTANT Natural := 9;              -- largest digit
   SUBTYPE SmallNatural IS Natural RANGE 0 .. MaxDigit;

BEGIN -- AddTable
```

```
        -- Display the table heading.
        Text_IO.Put(Item => "+");
        FOR Right IN SmallNatural LOOP
           My_Int_IO.Put(Item => Right, Width => 3);   -- Display digits in heading
        END LOOP;
        Text_IO.New_Line;                              -- Terminate heading

        -- Display the table body.
        FOR Left IN SmallNatural LOOP

           -- Display each row of the table
           My_Int_IO.Put(Item => Left, Width => 1);    -- Display first addend

           FOR Right IN SmallNatural LOOP
              My_Int_IO.Put(Item => Left + Right, Width => 3);
           END LOOP;

           Text_IO.New_Line;                           -- Terminate table row

        END LOOP;

END AddTable;


+  0  1  2  3  4  5  6  7  8  9
0  0  1  2  3  4  5  6  7  8  9
1  1  2  3  4  5  6  7  8  9 10
2  2  3  4  5  6  7  8  9 10 11
3  3  4  5  6  7  8  9 10 11 12
4  4  5  6  7  8  9 10 11 12 13
5  5  6  7  8  9 10 11 12 13 14
6  6  7  8  9 10 11 12 13 14 15
7  7  8  9 10 11 12 13 14 15 16
8  8  9 10 11 12 13 14 15 16 17
9  9 10 11 12 13 14 15 16 17 18
```

The nested FOR loops are used to print the table body. The outer FOR loop (loop control variable Left) first prints the current value of Left. In the inner FOR loop, each value of Right (0 through 9) is added to Left and the individual sums are printed. Each time the outer loop is repeated 10 additions are performed; a total of 100 sums are printed. ∎

∎ Example 5.10

Program 5.12 shows how this structure can be used to print all the days, weekdays, and weekend days in the week. This program uses three FOR loops, one for the base type Days, and one for each of the two subtypes.

Program 5.12   Illustrating Enumeration Subtypes

```
WITH Text_IO;
PROCEDURE DisplayDays IS

   -- display the days of the week, weekdays, weekend days;
   -- demonstrate enumeration subtypes and how they can be used
   -- to control a loop
```

```
    TYPE Days IS (Mon, Tue, Wed, Thu, Fri, Sat, Sun);
    SUBTYPE WeekDays IS Days RANGE Mon .. Fri;
    SUBTYPE WeekEnd IS Days RANGE Sat .. Sun;
    PACKAGE Day_IO IS
        NEW Text_IO.Enumeration_IO (Enum => Days);

BEGIN -- DisplayDays

    Text_IO.Put (Item => "The days of the week are ");
    FOR Day IN Days LOOP
      Day_IO.Put (Item => Day, Width => 4);
    END LOOP;
    Text_IO.New_Line;

    Text_IO.Put (Item => "The weekdays are ");
    FOR Day IN WeekDays LOOP
      Day_IO.Put (Item => Day, Width => 4);
    END LOOP;
    Text_IO.New_Line;

    Text_IO.Put (Item => "The weekend days are ");
    FOR Day IN WeekEnd LOOP
      Day_IO.Put (Item => Day, Width => 4);
    END LOOP;
    Text_IO.New_Line;

END DisplayDays;


The days of the week are MON TUE WED THU FRI SAT SUN
The weekdays are MON TUE WED THU FRI
The weekend days are SAT SUN
```

Program 5.13 is a modification of Program 5.12, using REVERSE in the FOR loop statement to show how the days can be displayed in reverse order. ∎

Program 5.13 Displaying Subtypes in Reverse Order

```
WITH Text_IO;
PROCEDURE ReverseDisplayDays IS

    -- display the days of the week, weekdays, weekend days;
    -- demonstrate enumeration subtypes and how they can be used
    -- to control a loop running in reverse

    TYPE Days IS (Mon, Tue, Wed, Thu, Fri, Sat, Sun);
    SUBTYPE WeekDays IS Days RANGE Mon .. Fri;
    SUBTYPE WeekEnd IS Days RANGE Sat .. Sun;
    PACKAGE Day_IO IS
        NEW Text_IO.Enumeration_IO (Enum => Days);

BEGIN -- ReverseDisplayDays

    Text_IO.Put (Item => "The days of the week are ");
    FOR Day IN REVERSE Days LOOP
      Day_IO.Put (Item => Day, Width => 4);
    END LOOP;
    Text_IO.New_Line;
```

```
Text_IO.Put (Item => "The weekdays are ");
FOR Day IN REVERSE WeekDays LOOP
   Day_IO.Put (Item => Day, Width => 4);
END LOOP;
Text_IO.New_Line;

Text_IO.Put (Item => "The weekend days are ");
FOR Day IN REVERSE WeekEnd LOOP
   Day_IO.Put (Item => Day, Width => 4);
END LOOP;
Text_IO.New_Line;

END ReverseDisplayDays;
```

```
The days of the week are SUN SAT FRI THU WED TUE MON
The weekdays are FRI THU WED TUE MON
The weekend days are SUN SAT
```

■ Example 5.11

Program 5.14 uses the Screen package from Chapter 3 to draw vertical and horizontal lines on the screen, dividing the screen into four quadrants. We repeat the subtype and constant declarations from Screen here, just to remind you:

```
Screen_Depth : CONSTANT Integer := 24;
Screen_Width : CONSTANT Integer := 80;

SUBTYPE Depth IS Integer RANGE 1..Screen_Depth;
SUBTYPE Width IS Integer RANGE 1..Screen_Width;
```

The loop

```
FOR Count IN Screen.Width LOOP
   Screen.MoveCursor (Row => 12, Column => Count);
   Text_IO.Put (Item => '-');
   Screen.MoveCursor
         (Row => 13, Column => (Screen.Screen_Width – Count) + 1);
   Text_IO.Put (Item => '-');
END LOOP;
```

draws the horizontal separator consisting of two lines of hyphen characters on rows 12 and 13 of the screen. The parameters to the first call of Screen.MoveCursor move the cursor one position to the right in each loop iteration; just to make the program more interesting, the second call moves the cursor one position to the left each time. ■

Program 5.14   Dividing the Screen into Four Pieces
___

```
WITH Text_IO;
WITH Screen;
PROCEDURE FourPieces IS

-- this program divides the screen into four pieces by drawing horizontal
-- and vertical lines. The Screen package is used to position the cursor.
```

```
BEGIN -- FourPieces

   Screen.ClearScreen;

   FOR Count IN Screen.Depth LOOP
      Screen.MoveCursor (Row => Count, Column => 41);
      Text_IO.Put (Item => '|');
      Screen.MoveCursor (Row => (Screen.Screen_Depth - Count) + 1, Column => 42);
      Text_IO.Put (Item => '|');
   END LOOP;

   FOR Count IN Screen.Width LOOP
      Screen.MoveCursor (Row => 12, Column => Count);
      Text_IO.Put (Item => '-');
      Screen.MoveCursor (Row => 13, Column => (Screen.Screen_Width - Count) + 1);
      Text_IO.Put (Item => '-');
   END LOOP;

   Screen.MoveCursor (Row => 24, Column => 1);

END FourPieces;
```

Counting Loops (Type-Name Form)

Forms:

```
FOR counter IN type-name LOOP
   statement sequence
END LOOP;

FOR counter IN REVERSE type-name LOOP
   statement sequence
END LOOP;
```

Example:

```
FOR WhichDay IN Weekdays LOOP
   Day_IO.Put (Item => WhichDay);
   Text_IO.New_Line;
END LOOP;
```

Interpretation: The number of times *statement sequence* is executed is determined by the number of values in the type given by *type-name*, which must be the name of an integer or enumeration type or subtype. The value of the loop control variable *counter* is set to *type-name*'First before the first execution of *statement sequence; counter* is incremented to its successor value after each execution of *statement sequence;* the last execution of *statement sequence* occurs when *counter* is equal to *type-name*'Last. The value of *counter* must not be changed within *statement sequence*. The variable *counter* is not declared separately and has no existence outside the loop.

If REVERSE is present, *counter* is initialized to *type-name*'Last and the iteration is done backward decrementing *counter* to its predecessor value after each execution of *statement sequence*.

Limitations of the FOR Statement

The FOR statement is very powerful and useful, but it has one important limitation: The loop control variable is *always* either incremented (by taking the successor) or decremented (by taking the predecessor). The FOR statement can therefore be used only to loop through *all* the values of a given range. There is no way to count by 2s, for example.

Ada provides two other loop statements, which can be used with arbitrary loop control conditions, not just counting straight through the values of a range. Specifically, we can use either the WHILE loop or the general loop structure, which will be presented in Chapter 6.

 ## 5.6 Tricks of the Trade: Debugging and Testing Programs

Chapter 2 described the general categories of error messages that you are likely to see: compilation errors and run-time errors, or exceptions. It is also possible for a program to execute without generating any error messages, but still produce incorrect results. Sometimes the cause of an exception, or the origin of incorrect results, is apparent and the error can be fixed easily. Often, however, the error is not obvious and may require considerable effort to locate.

The first step in attempting to find a hidden error is to try to determine what part of the program is generating incorrect results. Then insert extra output statements in your program to provide a trace of its execution. For example, if the summation loop in Program 5.4 is not computing the correct sum, you might want to insert extra diagnostic output statements, such as the last five lines in the loop below:

```
FOR Count IN 1 .. NumItems LOOP
    Text_IO.Put (Item=>"Please enter next value to be summed >");
    My_Flt_IO.Get (Item => CurrentValue);
    Sum := Sum + CurrentValue;

    Text_IO.Put (Item => "*****Sum = "); -- diagnostic statements
    My_Int_IO.Put (Item => Sum);
    Text_IO.Put (Item => "*****Count = ");
    My_Int_IO.Put (Item => Count);
    Text_IO.New_Line;
END LOOP;
```

The diagnostic Put statements will display each partial sum that is accumulated and the current value of Count. Each of these statements displays a string of asterisks at the beginning of its output line. This makes it easier to identify diagnostic output in the debugging runs and makes it easier to locate the diagnostic Put statements in the source program. Be careful when inserting extra diagnostic Put statements, as they can be a source of syntax errors.

Once it appears that you have located an error, you will want to take out the extra diagnostic statements. As a temporary measure, it is sometimes advisable to make these diagnostic statements comments by preceding them with comment marks (--). If errors crop up again in later testing, it is easier to remove the comment marks than to retype the diagnostic statements.

Using Debugger Programs

Many computer systems have *debugger programs* available to help you debug an Ada program. The debugger program lets you execute your program one statement at a time (single-step execution) so that you can see the effect of each statement. You can select several variables whose values will be automatically displayed after each statement executes. This allows you to trace the program's execution. Besides printing a diagnostic when a run-time error occurs, the debugger indicates the statement that caused the error and displays the values of the variables you selected.

You can also separate your program into segments by setting *breakpoints* at selected statements. A breakpoint is like a fence between two segments of a program. You can request the debugger to execute all statements from the last breakpoint up to the next breakpoint. When the program stops at a breakpoint, you can select variables to examine, in this way determining whether the program segment executed correctly. If a program segment executes correctly, you will want to execute through to the next breakpoint. If it does not, you may want to set more breakpoints in that segment or perhaps perform single-step execution through that segment.

The debugger is a feature of the operating system or the Ada compilation system, not part of the Ada language. Therefore we cannot give any further details, because they depend on the system you are working on. You should try to find out from your teacher or computer center whether an Ada debugger is available, and if so, how to use it. Debuggers are helpful and can save you a lot of time in debugging a complicated program.

Testing a Program

After all compilation errors have been corrected and the program appears to execute as expected, the program should be tested thoroughly to make sure that it works. Section 4.3 discussed tracing an algorithm and suggested that you provide enough sets of test data to ensure that all possible paths are traced. The same statement is true for the completed program. Make enough test runs to verify that the program works properly for representative samples of all possible data combinations.

5.7 System Structures: A Useful Functions Package and the Overloading Principle

195

5.7 System
Structures: A Useful
Functions Package
and the Overloading
Principle

In Section 4.7 we showed how to write a simple package, `MinMax`, containing functions to find the minimum and maximum of two integer values. Let us rework that package to include two more useful mathematical functions, the sum of integers from 1 to N, and the product of integers from 1 to N. The latter function is called *factorial*.

First we shall rewrite the package specification to name the package `UsefulFunctions` and include specifications for the two new functions. Note in the specification that the sum and factorial functions require parameters of type `Positive` and return `Positive` results. The specifications for the two new functions are given below; Program 5.15 shows the entire package specification.

```
-- sum of integers from 1 to N
FUNCTION Sum (N: Positive) RETURN Positive;

-- product of integers from 1 to N
FUNCTION Factorial (N: Positive) RETURN Positive;
```

Program 5.15 Specification for Package UsefulFunctions

```
PACKAGE UsefulFunctions IS

   -- specifications of functions provided by UsefulFunctions package

   -- minimum and maximum values
   FUNCTION Minimum (Value1: Integer;   Value2: Integer) RETURN Integer;
   FUNCTION Minimum (Value1: Float;     Value2: Float)   RETURN Float;

   FUNCTION Maximum (Value1: Integer;   Value2: Integer) RETURN Integer;
   FUNCTION Maximum (Value1: Float;     Value2: Float)   RETURN Float;

   -- sum of integers from 1 to N
   FUNCTION Sum (N: Positive) RETURN Positive;

   -- factorial, or product of integers from 1 to N
   FUNCTION Factorial (N: Positive) RETURN Positive;

END UsefulFunctions;
```

The Overloading Principle

There is something else noteworthy about the specification in Program 5.15. Function specifications appear for *two* functions called `Minimum` and *two* functions called `Maximum`. Looking at the two `Minimum` functions,

```
FUNCTION Minimum (Valuel, Value2: Integer) RETURN Integer;
FUNCTION Minimum (Valuel, Value2: Float)   RETURN Float;
```

we see that they have the same names but different *parameter profiles;* that is, their input parameters and return types are different. This is an example of *overloading,* which in Ada allows two or more different operations to have the same name, as long as there is enough difference in their parameter profiles so that the compiler can distinguish them.

The advantage of overloading is that operations with similar behavior or functionality can be given similar names. This makes programs easier to write and to read because the programmer is not forced to invent names like `MinimumInteger` and `MinimumFloat` merely because the language requires all subprograms to have distinct names.

Actually, you have been using overloaded operations without realizing it. One example relates to the input/output libraries. Many programs in this book have used procedure calls of the form

```
My_Int_IO.Get (Item => CurrentValue);
```

from the input/output package for integer tokens. On the other hand, in Program 5.6, a procedure call appears

```
My_Int_IO.Get (File => TestScores, Item => CurrentValue);
```

which has the same name, `Get`, but a different parameter profile: The second procedure call includes a file variable; the first does not. There is no "magic" about this, or anything unique to the I/O libraries—it is just an application of the overloading principle.

When the compiler reaches a statement like one of the two above, it can select the appropriate procedure to include in the executable program by examining the parameter profile. If the profile matches one of the procedures made available by context clauses, all is well. If there is no match, a compilation error results. It could be that there are *two* matches; this case also results in a compilation error.

Another example comes from the arithmetic operations we have been doing. An assignment statement such as

```
Result := Result + Count;
```

uses a *different* + depending on whether its operands are `Integer` or `Float`. Indeed, the machine instructions generated by the compiler are quite different for the two numeric types. We could write specifications for the integer and float versions of + that look just like function specifications:

```
FUNCTION "+" (Left: Integer; Right: Integer) RETURN Integer;
FUNCTION "+" (Left: Float;   Right: Float ) RETURN Float;
```

Mathematically, an arithmetic operation is just a special kind of function; writing an operator specification this way just reflects that mathematical fact. There is no problem in naming both of the operations + (the quotes are required

197

5.7 System
Structures: A Useful
Functions Package
and the Overloading
Principle

in this form for syntactic reasons): They have different parameter profiles, so the compiler can distinguish between them.

Specifications of *all* the predefined types and operators in Ada appear in the *Language Reference Manual* in a section called PACKAGE Standard; a version of this very useful description appears in Appendix C. PACKAGE Standard is automatically available to all Ada programs; no context clause is necessary. When the compiler reaches a statement like

```
Result := Result + Count;
```

it examines the types of Result and Count to discover whether a matching + is available. If Result is integer and Count is float, for example, there is no matching + in PACKAGE Standard, so a compilation error arises.

Using Overloading Wisely

Used carefully, overloading can be a very helpful concept in writing Ada programs, because it allows operations to be given meaningful names, and all operations with similar functionality can be given the same name. Clearly, overloading can be abused by using it too much, or by using it to name functions and procedures that do not have similar behavior. This would mislead and confuse the reader of a program and so should be avoided.

Writing the Body of UsefulFunctions

The next step is to provide the package body of UsefulFunctions, which consists of function bodies for the six functions. The body of Sum is adapted from Program 5.3; the body of Factorial can be readily adapted from the body of Sum (note, however, that Result is initialized to 1, not 0). The complete package body appears in Program 5.16.

Program 5.16 Body of Package UsefulFunctions

```
PACKAGE BODY UsefulFunctions IS

  -- bodies of functions provided by UsefulFunctions package

    -- minimum of two Integer values
    FUNCTION Minimum (Value1: Integer; Value2: Integer) RETURN Integer IS

      Result: Integer;

    BEGIN -- Minimum
```

```
        IF Valuel < Value2 THEN
           Result := Valuel;
        ELSE
           Result := Value2;
        END IF;
        RETURN Result;

END Minimum;

-- minimum of two Float values
FUNCTION Minimum (Valuel: Float; Value2: Float) RETURN Float IS

    Result: Float;

BEGIN -- Minimum

    IF Valuel < Value2 THEN
       Result := Valuel;
    ELSE
       Result := Value2;
    END IF;
    RETURN Result;

END Minimum;

-- maximum of two Integer values
FUNCTION Maximum (Valuel: Integer; Value2: Integer) RETURN Integer IS

    Result: Integer;

BEGIN -- Maximum

    IF Valuel > Value2 THEN
       Result := Valuel;
    ELSE
       Result := Value2;
    END IF;
    RETURN Result;

END Maximum;

-- maximum of two Float values
FUNCTION Maximum (Valuel: Float; Value2: Float) RETURN Float IS

    Result: Float;

BEGIN -- Maximum

    IF Valuel > Value2 THEN
        Result := Valuel;
ELSE
        Result := Value2;
END IF;
RETURN Result;

END Maximum;

-- sum of integers from 1 to N
FUNCTION Sum (N: Positive) RETURN Positive IS

    Result: Natural;
```

199

5.7 System
Structures: A Useful
Functions Package
and the Overloading
Principle

```
BEGIN -- Sum

    Result := 0;
    FOR Count IN 1..N LOOP
       Result := Result + Count;
    END LOOP;
    RETURN Result;

END Sum;

-- factorial, or product of integers from 1 to N
FUNCTION Factorial (N: Positive) RETURN Positive IS

    Result: Positive;

BEGIN -- Factorial

    Result := 1;
    FOR Count IN 1..N LOOP
       Result := Result * Count;
    END LOOP;
    RETURN Result;

END Factorial;

END UsefulFunctions;
```

Program 5.17 illustrates the overloading principle in action by finding the maximum of two integers and the maximum of two floats. Notice in this program that UsefulFunctions.Maximum appears to be called twice. In fact, *different* functions are being called, as you can see from the different parameter profiles: In the first call integers are supplied; in the second call floats are supplied.

Program 5.17   Illustration of the Overloading Principle

```
WITH Text_IO;
WITH My_Int_IO;
WITH My_Flt_IO;
WITH UsefulFunctions;
PROCEDURE MaxIntFlt IS

   -- illustrates the overloading principle using the Maximum
   -- functions for both integer and float quantities

   Int1 :      Integer;
   Int2 :      Integer;
   LargerInt : Integer;
   Flt1 :      Float;
   Flt2 :      Float;
   LargerFlt : Float;

BEGIN -- MaxIntFlt

   Text_IO.Put (Item => "Please enter first integer value > ");
```

```
My_Int_IO.Get (Item => Int1);
Text_IO.Put (Item => "Please enter second integer value > ");
My_Int_IO.Get (Item => Int2);

LargerInt := UsefulFunctions.Maximum(Value1=>Int1, Value2=>Int2);

Text_IO.Put (Item => "The larger integer is ");
My_Int_IO.Put (Item => LargerInt, Width => 1);
Text_IO.New_Line;

Text_IO.Put (Item => "Please enter first float value > ");
My_Flt_IO.Get (Item => Flt1);
Text_IO.Put (Item => "Please enter second float value > ");
My_Flt_IO.Get (Item => Flt2);

LargerFlt := UsefulFunctions.Maximum(Value1=>Flt1, Value2=>Flt2);

Text_IO.Put (Item => "The larger float is ");
My_Flt_IO.Put (Item => LargerFlt, Fore => 1, Aft => 2, Exp => 0);
Text_IO.New_Line;

END MaxIntFlt;



Please enter first integer value > -27
Please enter second integer value > 34
The larger integer is 34
Please enter first float value > 29.77
Please enter second float value > 100.34
The larger float is 100.34
```

Finally, Program 5.18 gives a program that prompts the user for an integer between 1 and 10, then displays a table of the sum and factorial of each of the integers from 1 to the number entered.

Program 5.18   A Program That Uses UsefulFunctions

```
WITH Text_IO;
WITH My_Int_IO;
WITH UsefulFunctions;
PROCEDURE SumFact IS

   -- Prompts the user for an integer N from 1 to 10
   -- and displays the sum and factorial of all integers from
   -- 1 to N. Sum and Factorial are gotten from package UsefulFunctions.

   SUBTYPE OneToTen IS Positive RANGE 1..10;

   MaxNum:       OneToTen;    -- input - a value from one to ten
   SumToCount:   Positive;    -- output - sum of integers from one to Count
   ProdToCount:  Positive;    -- output - product of integers from one to Count

BEGIN -- SumFact

   Text_IO.Put (Item => "Please enter an integer from 1 to 10 > ");
   My_Int_IO.Get (Item => MaxNum);
   Text_IO.New_Line;
```

201

5.7 System
Structures: A Useful
Functions Package
and the Overloading
Principle

```
Text_IO.Put(Item => " N    Sum    Factorial");
Text_IO.New_Line;
Text_IO.Put(Item => "  ----------------------");
Text_IO.New_Line;

FOR Count IN 1..MaxNum LOOP
   SumToCount   := UsefulFunctions.Sum (N => Count);
   ProdToCount  := UsefulFunctions.Factorial (N => Count);

   My_Int_IO.Put (Item => Count, Width => 3);
   My_Int_IO.Put (Item => SumToCount, Width => 7);
   My_Int_IO.Put (Item => ProdToCount, Width => 9);
   Text_IO.New_Line;
END LOOP;

END SumFact;
```

```
Please enter an integer from 1 to 10 > 7

N    Sum    Factorial
----------------------
1     1       1
2     3       2
3     6       6
4    10      24
5    15     120
6    21     720
7    28    5040
```

PROGRAM
STYLE

Displaying a Table

Program 5.18 displays a table of output values. The table heading is displayed, before the loop is reached, by the statements

```
Text_IO.Put (Item => " N    Sum    Factorial");
Text_IO.New_Line;
Text_IO.Put (Item => "  ----------------------");
Text_IO.New_Line;
```

The spaces in the first string are used to align the column headings over their respective table values. We have left enough spaces to center the column titles of the respective values. The second string is used to "draw a line" between the column titles and the values. Within the FOR loop, the four statements

```
My_Int_IO.Put (Item => Count, Width => 3);
My_Int_IO.Put (Item => SumToCount, Width => 7);
My_Int_IO.Put (Item => ProdToCount, Width => 9);
Text_IO.New_Line;
```

display three output values on each line of the table, using 19 columns per line.

5.8 System Structures: Introduction to Exception Handling

It is useful to take a close look at Program 5.18 and make a list of the things that could go wrong with its execution.

- The user could enter a value that is a perfectly good integer value but is out of range for the variable MaxNum (for example, the user could enter a 0, a negative number, or a number greater than 10). In this case, the program would terminate with a Constraint_Error, Ada's usual exception for out-of-range conditions.
- The user could enter a value that begins with a nonnumeric character, such as ABC or A1. In this case, the program would terminate with Text_IO.Data _Error, because the input/output system would complain about bad data.
- The user could enter a value that, when passed to Factorial, could produce a result that is simply too large. Some Ada systems, for example on IBM-PC-type computers, use the value 32767 for Integer'Last, because this is the largest integer that will fit in a 16-bit word. Because Factorial(8) is 40320, trying to compute it will cause Numeric_Error to be raised. Numeric_Error is Ada's usual exception for overflow conditions, that is, conditions that would overflow the bounds of the computer's arithmetic system.

As written, Program 5.18 will terminate if any of these conditions arises, and the Ada "run-time system" will display a message. Generally the name of the exception will be displayed, but otherwise the form of the message depends on the compiler.

Ada provides a useful mechanism called *exception handling,* which allows the programmer to "catch" the exception before it goes to the Ada run-time system. The programmer can supply, at the bottom of the program, procedure, or function, a set of statements, called *exception handlers,* indicating what is to be done in case an exception is raised. Later chapters, beginning with Chapter 6, will introduce exception handling systematically; for now, Program 5.19 shows you the general idea. Notice that at the bottom of the program, there is a section:

```
EXCEPTION
    WHEN Constraint_Error =>
          Text_IO.Put(Item => "The input value is out of range.");
          Text_IO.New_Line;
    WHEN Text_IO.Data_Error =>
          Text_IO.Put(Item => "The input value is not well formed.");
          Text_IO.New_Line;
    WHEN Numeric_Error =>
          Text_IO.Put(Item => "The result is too large to compute.");
          Text_IO.New_Line;
END RobustSumFact;
```

Each group of statements beginning with WHEN is called an exception handler. If the program executes normally, then execution stops at the "normal" last statement (the last line before the word EXCEPTION); it is as though the exception handling section were not there. However, if an exception is raised anywhere in the program, execution of the statement causing the exception is halted, and control is passed immediately to the appropriate exception handler. Once the handler's statements have been executed (in this case, displaying a message), the program terminates normally. There is no message displayed by the run-time system; because the program handled its own exception, the run-time system has no need to do so.

How useful is this? We will see in Chapter 6 how exception handling can make programs much less prone to terminate with error messages from the run-time system, and also how exception handling can be used to ensure the validity of user input. In the simple case considered here, the usefulness of exception handling is that it allows the programmer to control the form of the message displayed when the program terminates. This is better than leaving it to the run-time system, the form of whose messages depends on the compiler.

Program 5.19 Illustration of Exception Handling

```
WITH Text_IO;
WITH My_Int_IO;
WITH UsefulFunctions;
PROCEDURE RobustSumFact IS

  -- Prompts the user for an integer N from 1 to 10
  -- and displays the sum and factorial of all integers from
  -- 1 to N. Sum and Factorial are gotten from package UsefulFunctions.

  SUBTYPE OneToTen IS Positive RANGE 1..10;

  MaxNum:       OneToTen;    -- input - a value from one to ten
  SumToCount:   Positive;    -- output - sum of integers from one to Count
  ProdToCount:  Positive;    -- output - product of integers from one to Count

BEGIN -- RobustSumFact

  Text_IO.Put (Item => "Please enter an integer from 1 to 10 > ");
  My_Int_IO.Get (Item => MaxNum);
  Text_IO.New_Line;

  Text_IO.Put(Item => "  N     Sum      Factorial");
  Text_IO.New_Line;
  Text_IO.Put(Item => " ----------------------");
  Text_IO.New_Line;

  FOR Count IN 1..MaxNum LOOP
    SumToCount   := UsefulFunctions.Sum (N => Count);
    ProdToCount  := UsefulFunctions.Factorial (N => Count);

    My_Int_IO.Put (Item => Count, Width => 3);
    My_Int_IO.Put (Item => SumToCount, Width => 7);
    My_Int_IO.Put (Item => ProdToCount, Width => 9);
    Text_IO.New_Line;
  END LOOP;

EXCEPTION

  WHEN Constraint_Error =>
```

```
      Text_IO.Put (Item => "The input value is out of range.");
      Text_IO.New_Line;
    WHEN Text_IO.Data_Error =>
      Text_IO.Put (Item => "The input value is not well formed.");
      Text_IO.New_Line;
    WHEN Numeric_Error =>
      Text_IO.Put (Item => "The result is too large to compute.");
      Text_IO.New_Line;

END RobustSumFact;


Please enter an integer from 1 to 10 > 11
The input value is out of range.
```

 ## 5.9 Tricks of the Trade: Common Programming Errors

Remember that the counter variable in a FOR loop has no existence outside the loop. If you need to remember the value of the counter variable, copy it into a different variable.

 # Chapter Review

We showed how to implement repetition in Ada using the counting loop or FOR statement.

Algorithm and program traces are used to verify that an algorithm or program is correct. Errors in logic can be discovered by carefully tracing an algorithm or program. Tracing an algorithm or program before entering the program in the computer will save you time in the long run.

We also introduced the important concept of subtypes. Subtypes are used both to improve program readability and to enable the detection of out-of-range values. The operators that can be used with a subtype are the same as for its base type.

We also discussed the issue of type compatibility. A subtype is compatible with its base type and with all other subtypes of the same base type. This means that an operator can have one operand whose type is the subtype and one operand whose type is the base type, or indeed another subtype.

Another important concept introduced in this chapter was *overloading*, which in Ada permits several functions or procedures to be given the same name, as long as they have different parameter profiles. This is convenient for giving names to operations, like Minimum, that have similar function regardless of the type on which they operate.

Finally, exception handling was discussed. Exception handling is Ada's way of allowing a program to keep control even in the event of an error.

New Ada Constructs in Chapter 5

The new Ada constructs introduced in this chapter are described in Table 5.4.

Table 5.4 Summary of New Ada Constructs

Construct	Effect
FOR **statement** ```FOR CurMonth IN March..July LOOP My_Flt_IO.Get(Item=>MonthSales); YearSales := YearSales+MonthSales; END LOOP;```	The loop body is repeated for each value of CurMonth from March through July, inclusive. For each month, the value of MonthSales is read and added to YearSales.
Subtype definition `SUBTYPE FDIC_Insured IS Float RANGE 0.0..100000.0;`	declares a subtype of Float in the range 0.0–100000.0

✓ *Quick-Check Exercises*

1. In the following program fragment, how many times do the Put and New_Line statements execute? What is the last value displayed?

```
FOR I IN 1..10 LOOP
  FOR J IN 1..5 LOOP
    My_Int_IO.Put(Item => I * J, Width => 5);
  END LOOP;
  Text_IO.New_Line;
END LOOP;
```

2. In the following program fragment, how many times do the Put and New_Line statements execute? What is the last value displayed?

```
FOR I IN 1..10 LOOP
  FOR J IN 1..I LOOP
    My_Int_IO.Put(Item => I * J, Width => 5);
  END LOOP;
  Text_IO.New_Line;
END LOOP;
```

3. In the following program fragment, what values are displayed?

```
FOR Counter IN 1..5 LOOP
   My_Int_IO.Put(Item => Counter, Width => 5);
END LOOP;
My_Int_IO.Put(Item => Counter, Width => 5);
```

4. In the following program, what values are displayed?

```
WITH My_Int_IO;
PROCEDURE TryIt IS

   Counter: Integer;

BEGIN -- TryIt

   Counter := 1;
   FOR Counter IN 1..5 LOOP
      My_Int_IO.Put(Item => Counter, Width => 5);
   END LOOP;
   My_Int_IO.Put(Item => Counter, Width => 5);

END TryIt;
```

Answers to Quick-Check Exercises
1. The Put statement executes 50 times; the New_Line executes 10 times; the last value displayed is 50.
2. The Put statement executes $1 + 2 + 3 + \ldots + 9 + 10$, or 55 times; the New_Line executes 10 times; the last value displayed is 100.
3. No result is displayed, because the program has a compilation error. The variable Counter cannot be accessed outside of the loop.
4. The values displayed are 1 2 3 4 5 1. The declared variable Counter is a different variable from the one used to control the loop.

Review Questions for Chapter 5

1. Write a FOR statement that runs from 'Z' to 'A' and displays only the consonants. *Hint:* Test each character against the vowels.
2. Write a nested loop that displays the first six letters of the alphabet on a line, the next five letters on the next line, the next four letters on the next line, and so on, down to and including one letter (the letter U) on the last line. Use either uppercase or lowercase letters.
3. Explain the overloading principle. What examples have you seen of its use?

Programming Projects

1. Modify Programming Project 1 of Chapter 4 so that 10 speeds are handled in a single run. Also, print a count of the number of speeding automobiles.
2. Write a program that computes the product of a collection of 15 data values. Your program should ignore values that are 0.
3. Compute and display a table showing the first 15 powers of 2.
4. Write a program that reads in 20 values and displays the number of values that are positive (greater than or equal to 0) and the number that are negative. Also display "more positive" or "more negative" based on the result.

Other Loop Forms; Procedures; Exception Handling

6

6.1 Control Structures: The WHILE Statement
6.2 Problem Solving: Loop Design
6.3 Problem Solving: Assertions and Loop Invariants
6.4 Control Structures: The General LOOP and EXIT Statements
6.5 System Structures: Robust Exception Handling
6.6 System Structures: Writing Simple Procedures
6.7 System Structures: A Package for Robust Input
6.8 Tricks of the Trade: Testing with Exception Handling
6.9 Tricks of the Trade: Common Programming Errors
Chapter Review

6.1 Control Structures: The WHILE Statement

In all the loops used so far, the exact number of loop repetitions required could be determined before the start of loop execution. We used the FOR statement to implement these counting loops.

Ada's FOR loop is limited in that counting can proceed only over a range that is *discrete* (i.e., of an integer or enumeration type). Furthermore, the counter variable is updated by taking its successor (or predecessor if REVERSE is used)—either adding 1 (subtracting 1) if it is an integer counter, or taking the Succ (Pred) attribute if it is an enumeration counter. This means that counting cannot proceed, for example, by 2s. In many programming situations, the exact number of loop repetitions cannot be determined before loop execution begins. It may depend on some aspect of the data that is not known beforehand, but usually can be stated by a condition. For example, we may wish to continue writing checks as long as our bank balance is positive, as indicated by the following pseudocode description.

```
WHILE the balance is still positive LOOP
    Read in the next transaction
    Update and print the balance
END LOOP;
```

The actual number of loop repetitions performed depends on the type of each transaction (deposit or withdrawal) and its amount.

To summarize, there are three kinds of looping problems where the Ada FOR statement cannot be used:

- when the most natural type for the loop control variable is not discrete (e.g., if it is Float);
- when the loop does not step through all the values of a discrete type in forward or reverse order (e.g., only every third value is of interest); and
- when the number of iterations depends on conditions arising during the execution of the loop.

In cases like these there are other alternatives for writing conditional loops in Ada. Ada provides two additional looping statements (WHILE and general LOOP) to implement conditional loops. The WHILE statement is discussed next; the general LOOP statement is introduced later in the chapter.

■ Example 6.1

Program 6.1 displays the odd numbers from 1 to 39 inclusive. Because the step size is not 1, we cannot use a FOR loop for this. A WHILE structure is used instead. A variable OddNumber is declared and used to control the loop. OddNumber is initialized to 1 before the WHILE statement is reached; the WHILE loop heading

```
WHILE OddNumber <= 39 LOOP
```

controls the condition for continuing the loop. Inside the loop body, `OddNumber` is incremented:

```
OddNumber := OddNumber + 2;
```

The loop body is repeated as long as the WHILE condition remains true. This is tested at the top of each iteration. If the condition is false, the loop is ended and control passes to the statement following END LOOP. ∎

Program 6.1   Illustration of a WHILE Loop

```
WITH Text_IO;
WITH My_Int_IO;
PROCEDURE OddNumbers IS

-- Displays odd numbers from 1 to 39 inclusive

  OddNumber : Integer;

BEGIN -- OddNumbers

  OddNumber := 1;
  WHILE OddNumber <= 39 LOOP

    My_Int_IO.Put(Item => OddNumber, Width => 3);
    OddNumber := OddNumber + 2;

  END LOOP;

  Text_IO.New_Line;

END OddNumbers;


  1  3  5  7  9 11 13 15 17 19 21 23 25 27 29 31 33 35 37 39
```

∎ Example 6.2

Program 6.2 displays a table of Celsius and equivalent Fahrenheit temperatures for the range of temperatures from 100 degrees Celsius to –20 degrees Celsius in steps of –10 degrees. The assignment statement

```
Fahrenheit := (1.8 * Celsius) + 32.0;
```

converts each Celsius value in this range to a real Fahrenheit value. You can check this formula by knowing the freezing points (0 and 32 degrees) and boiling points (100 and 212 degrees) in the two systems. Because an integer cannot be multiplied by 1.8 and the step size is not 1, a WHILE statement is used instead of a FOR.

Three Float constants are declared in the program. CStart is the starting value of the Float loop control variable Celsius, CLimit is the limit value, and CStep is the step value. The loop is executed for values of Celsius in the sequence 100.0, 80.0, 90.0, ..., – 10.0, – 20.0. ∎

Program 6.2 Converting from Celsius to Fahrenheit

```
WITH Text_IO;
WITH My_Flt_IO;
PROCEDURE TempTable IS

-- Displays a table of Fahrenheit and
-- equivalent Celsius temperatures.

   CStart : CONSTANT Float := 100.0;    -- initial Celsius temp
   CStep  : CONSTANT Float := -10.0;    -- change in Celsius temp
   CLimit : CONSTANT Float := -20.0;    -- final Celsius temp

   Celsius :        Float;              -- Celsius temp
   Fahrenheit :     Float;              -- Fahrenheit temp

BEGIN -- TempTable

   Text_IO.Put(Item => "Celsius      Fahrenheit");
   Text_IO.New_Line;

   Celsius := CStart;
   WHILE Celsius >= CLimit LOOP

      Fahrenheit := 1.8 * Celsius + 32.0;
      My_Flt_IO.Put(Item => Celsius, Fore => 4, Aft => 0, Exp => 0);
      Text_IO.Put(Item => "           ");
      My_Flt_IO.Put(Item => Fahrenheit, Fore => 3, Aft => 1, Exp => 0);
      Text_IO.New_Line;

      Celsius := Celsius + CStep;
   END LOOP;

END TempTable;
```

```
Celsius     Fahrenheit
 100.0        212.0
  90.0        194.0
  80.0        176.0
  70.0        158.0
  60.0        140.0
  50.0        122.0
  40.0        104.0
  30.0         86.0
  20.0         68.0
  10.0         50.0
   0.0         32.0
 -10.0         14.0
 -20.0         -4.0
```

■ Example 6.3

Program 6.3 traces the progress of a hungry worm approaching an apple. Each time it moves, the worm cuts the distance between itself and the apple by its own body length until the worm is close enough to enter the apple. A WHILE loop is the correct looping structure to use because we have no idea beforehand how many moves are required.

```
WITH Text_IO;
WITH My_Flt_IO;
PROCEDURE WormAndApple IS

-- Displays distances between a worm and an apple. The worm keeps reducing
-- the distance by its body length until it is close enough to bite the apple.

   SUBTYPE NonNegFloat IS Float RANGE 0.0 .. Float'Last;

   WormLength: CONSTANT NonNegFloat := 3.5;    -- worm body length in inches

   InitialDist: NonNegFloat;  -- starting distance of worm from apple
   Distance:    NonNegFloat;  -- distance between worm and apple

BEGIN -- WormAndApple

   Text_IO.Put(Item => "Initial distance (float) between worm and apple > ");
   My_Flt_IO.Get(Item => InitialDist);
   Text_IO.New_Line;

   -- Cut the distance between the worm and the apple by the worm's
   -- body length until the worm is close enough to bite the apple
   Distance := InitialDist;

   WHILE Distance > WormLength LOOP
      Text_IO.Put(Item => "The distance is ");
      My_Flt_IO.Put(Item => Distance, Fore => 4, Aft => 2, Exp => 0);
      Text_IO.New_Line;

      Distance := Distance - WormLength;    -- reduce Distance
   END LOOP;

   -- Display final distance before entering the apple.
   Text_IO.New_Line;
   Text_IO.Put(Item => "Final distance between worm and apple is ");
   My_Flt_IO.Put(Item => Distance, Fore => 4, Aft => 2, Exp => 0);
   Text_IO.New_Line;
   Text_IO.Put(Item => "The worm bites the apple.");
   Text_IO.New_Line;

END WormAndApple;


Initial distance (float) between worm and apple > 12.0

The distance is    12.00
The distance is     8.50
The distance is     5.00

Final distance between worm and apple is    1.50
The worm bites the apple.
```

The assignment statement just before the loop initializes the variable Distance to the starting distance (12.0), which was previously read into
InitialDist. Next, the loop header is reached and the loop repetition condition (or WHILE condition)

Distance > WormLength

is evaluated. Because this condition is true, the loop body (through END LOOP) is executed. The loop body displays the value of Distance, and the statement

```
Distance := Distance - WormLength;     --reduce Distance
```

reduces the value of Distance, thereby bringing the worm closer to the apple. The loop repetition condition is tested again with the new value of Distance (8.5); because 8.5 > 3.5 is true, the loop body displays Distance again, and Distance becomes 5.0. The loop repetition condition is tested a third time; because 5.0 > 3.5 is true, the loop body displays Distance again, and Distance becomes 1.5. The loop repetition condition is tested again; because 1.5 > 3.5 is false, loop exit occurs, and the statements following the loop end are executed.

It is important to realize that the loop is not exited at the exact instant that Distance becomes 1.5. If more statements appeared in the loop body after the assignment to Distance, they would be executed. Loop exit does not occur until the loop repetition condition is retested at the top of the loop and found to be false. ■

Just as in the counting loops in Chapter 5, there are three critical steps in Program 6.3 that involve the loop control variable Distance:

- Distance is initialized to InitialDist before the loop header is reached.
- Distance is tested before each execution of the loop body.
- Distance is updated (reduced by 3.5) during each iteration.

Steps similar to these three steps (initialization, test, and update) must be performed for every WHILE loop. If the first step is missing, the initial test of Distance will be meaningless. The last step ensures that we make progress toward the final goal (Distance <= WormLength) during each repetition of the loop. If the last step is missing, the value of Distance cannot change, so the loop will execute "forever" (an infinite loop). The WHILE loop is described in the next display.

WHILE Statement

Form:

```
WHILE expression LOOP
     statement sequence
END LOOP;
```

Example: Display powers of 2:

```
PowerOf2 := 1;
WHILE PowerOf2 < 10000 LOOP
  My_Int_IO.Put (Item => PowerOf2);
  PowerOf2 := PowerOf2 * 2;
END LOOP;
```

Interpretation: The *expression* (a condition) is tested, and if it is true, the *statement sequence* is executed and the *expression* is retested. The *statement sequence* is repeated as long as (WHILE) the *expression* is true. When the *expression* is tested and found to be false, the WHILE loop is exited and the next program statement after END LOOP is executed.
Note: If the expression evaluates to false the first time it is tested, the statement sequence will not be executed.

■ Example 6.4

It is instructive to compare the two loop forms that we currently know how to write: the FOR loop and the WHILE loop. We can always implement a FOR loop using a WHILE loop, but we cannot always implement a WHILE loop using a FOR loop. The WHILE loop shown below behaves identically to the FOR loop shown above it.

```
FOR i IN 1..5 LOOP
    Square := i * i;
    My_Int_IO.Put (Item => i, Width => 1);
    My_Int_IO.Put (Item => Square, Width => 1);
    Text_IO.New_Line;
END LOOP;

i := 1;
WHILE i <= 5 LOOP
    Square := i * i;
    My_Int_IO.Put (Item => i, Width => 1);
    My_Int_IO.Put (Item => Square, Width => 1);
    Text_IO.New_Line;
    i := i + 1;
END LOOP;
```
■

We can make the following observations about the two loop forms just shown:

1. The statement i := 1; before the WHILE loop initializes i to 1. The initialization of the FOR loop control variable i is specified in the FOR loop header statement.
2. The statement i := i+1; in the WHILE loop body increments i by 1. This step is implicit in the FOR loop.
3. Unlike the FOR statement, in which the counter variable is declared implicitly and has no existence outside the loop body, the loop variable in the WHILE is a "normal" variable: It must be declared, and it is known outside the loop body just like any other variable.

Wherever possible, use a FOR loop, rather than a WHILE loop, to implement a counting loop.

■ Example 6.5

The distance traveled in t seconds by an object dropped from a tower is represented by the formula distance = $1/2 \times gt^2$, where g is the gravitational constant. Program 6.4 displays a table showing the height of a falling object at fixed time intervals after it is dropped from a tower and before it hits the ground. The number of lines in the table depends on the time interval between lines (DeltaT) and the tower height (Tower), both of which are data values. During each iteration, the current elapsed time (t) and the current object height (Height) are displayed. Next, the elapsed time is incremented by DeltaT and the new object height is computed. The message following the table is displayed when the object hits the ground. The sample output shows the result of dropping an object from a tower approximately the height of the Washington Monument (150 meters). ■

Program 6.4   An Object in Free Fall

```
WITH Text_IO;
WITH My_Flt_IO;
PROCEDURE FreeFall IS

-- Displays the height of an object dropped
-- from a tower until it hits the ground.

   SUBTYPE NonNegFloat IS Float RANGE 0.0 .. Float'Last;

   g : CONSTANT NonNegFloat := 9.80665;        -- gravitational constant

   Height: Float;          -- height of object
   Tower:  NonNegFloat;    -- height of tower
   t:      NonNegFloat;    -- elapsed time
   DeltaT: NonNegFloat;    -- time interval

BEGIN -- FreeFall

   -- Enter tower height and time interval.
   Text_IO.Put(Item => "Please enter all values in floating-point form.");
   Text_IO.New_Line;
   Text_IO.Put(Item => "Tower height in meters > ");
   My_Flt_IO.Get(Item => Tower);
   Text_IO.Put(Item => "Time in seconds between table lines > ");
   My_Flt_IO.Get(Item => DeltaT);
   Text_IO.New_Line(Spacing => 2);

   -- Display object height until it hits the ground.
   Text_IO.Put(Item => "        Time        Height");
   Text_IO.New_Line;

   t := 0.0;
   Height := Tower;

   WHILE Height > 0.0 LOOP
      My_Flt_IO.Put(Item => t, Fore => 8, Aft => 3, Exp => 0);
      My_Flt_IO.Put(Item => Height, Fore => 8, Aft => 3, Exp => 0);
      Text_IO.New_Line;
      t := t + DeltaT;
      Height := Tower - 0.5 * g * (t ** 2);
   END LOOP;

   -- Object hits the ground.
   Text_IO.New_Line;
```

```
    Text_IO.Put(Item => "SPLATT!!!");
    Text_IO.New_Line;

END FreeFall;
```

```
Please enter all values in floating-point form.
Tower height in meters > 150.0
Time in seconds between table lines > 0.5


        Time        Height
       0.000       150.000
       0.500       148.774
       1.000       145.097
       1.500       138.968
       2.000       130.387
       2.500       119.354
       3.000       105.870
       3.500        89.934
       4.000        71.547
       4.500        50.708
       5.000        27.417
       5.500         1.674

SPLATT!!!
```

Exercises for Section 6.1

Self-Check

1. What values would be printed if the order of the statements in the loop body of Progam 6.1 were reversed?
2. What is the least number of times that the body of a WHILE loop may be executed?
3. How would you modify the loop in Program 6.3 so that it also determines the number of moves (CountMoves) made by the worm before biting the apple? Which is the loop control variable, Distance or CountMoves?
4. How many times is the loop body below repeated? What is printed during each repetition of the loop body?

```
X := 3;
Count := 0;
WHILE Count < 3 LOOP
    X := X * X;
    My_Int_IO.Put(Item => X);
    Count := Count + 1;
END LOOP;
```

5. Answer Self-Check Exercise 4 if the last statement in the loop is

```
Count := Count + 2;
```

6. Answer Self-Check Exercise 4 if the last statement in the loop body is omitted.

Programming

1. There are 9870 people in a town whose population increases by 10% each year. Write a loop that determines how many years (`CountYears`) it takes for the population to go over 30,000.
2. Write a program that prints a table showing n and 2^n while 2^n is less than 10,000.

 # 6.2 Problem Solving: Loop Design

It is one thing to be able to analyze the operation of loops like those in Programs 6.1 through 6.4 and another to design our own loops. We will attack this problem in two ways. One approach is to analyze the requirements for a new loop to determine what initialization, test, and update of the loop control variable are needed. A second approach is to develop *templates* for loop forms that frequently recur and to use a template as the basis for a new loop. We will discuss loop templates later in this section.

To gain some insight into the design of the loop needed for the worm and apple problem, we should study the comment in Program 6.3 that summarizes the goal of this loop:

```
-- Cut the distance between the worm and the apple by the worm's
-- body length until the worm is close enough to bite the apple
```

In order to accomplish this goal, we must concern ourselves with loop control and loop processing. Loop control involves making sure that loop exit occurs when it is supposed to; loop processing involves making sure the loop body performs the required operations.

To help us formulate the necessary loop control and loop processing steps, it is useful to list what we know about the loop. In this example, if `Distance` is the distance of the worm from the apple, we can make the following observations:

1. Just before the loop begins, `Distance` must be equal to `InitialDist`.
2. During pass i, `Distance` must be less than the value of `Distance` during pass $i - 1$ by the length of the worm (for $i > 1$).
3. Just after loop exit, `Distance` must be between 0 and the worm's body length.

Statement 1 above simply indicates that `InitialDist` is the starting distance of the worm from the apple. Statement 2 says that the distance of the worm from the apple must be cut by the worm's body length during each iteration. Statement 3 derives from the fact that the worm enters the apple when `Distance <= WormLength`. `Distance` cannot be `<= WormLength` until loop exit; if it were, the loop should have been exited at the end of an earlier pass.

Statement 1 by itself tells us what initialization must be performed. Statement 2 tells us how to process `Distance` within the loop body (i.e., reduce it by the worm's length). Finally, statement 3 tells us when to exit the loop. Because `Distance` is decreasing, loop exit should occur when `Distance <= WormLength` is true. These considerations give us the outline below, which is the basis for the WHILE loop shown in Program 6.3. The loop repetition condition, Distance > WormLength, is the opposite of the exit condition, Distance <= WormLength.

1. Initialize Distance to InitialDist
2. WHILE Distance > WormLength LOOP
   3. Display Distance
   4. Reduce Distance by WormLength
   END LOOP;

Working Backward to Determine Loop Initialization

It is not always so easy to come up with the initialization steps for a loop. In some cases, we must work backward from the results that we know are required in the first pass to determine what initial values will produce these results.

■ Example 6.6

Your little cousin is learning the binary number system and has asked you to write a program that displays all powers of 2 that are less than a certain value (say, 10,000). Assuming that each power of 2 is stored in the variable Power, we can make the following observations about the loop.

1. Power during pass i is 2 times Power during pass $i - 1$ (for $i > 1$) .
2. Power must be between 10,000 and 20,000 just after loop exit.

Statement 1 derives from the fact that the powers of a number 2 are all multiples of 2. Statement 2 derives from the fact that only powers less than 10,000 are displayed. From statement 1 we know that Power must be multiplied by 2 in the loop body. From statement 2 we know that the loop exit condition is Power >= 10000, so the loop repetition condition is Power < 10000. These considerations lead us to the following outline:

1. Initialize Power to _
2. WHILE Power < 10000 LOOP
   3. Display Power
   4. Multiply Power by 2
   END LOOP;

One way to complete step 1 is to ask what value should be displayed during the first loop repetition. The value of N raised to the power 0 is 1 for any number N; specifically, 2^0 is 1. Therefore, if we initialize Power to 1, the value displayed during the first loop repetition will be correct.

1. Initialize Power to 1 ■

WHILE Loops with Zero Iterations

The body of a WHILE loop is not executed if the loop repetition test fails (evaluates to false) when it is first reached. To verify that you have the initialization steps correct, you should make sure that a program still generates the correct results for zero iterations of the loop body. If `WormLength` is greater than or equal to the value read into `InitialDist` (say 2.5), the loop body in Program 6.3 would not execute, and the lines below would be correctly displayed:

```
Enter the initial distance between worm and apple: 2.5
The final distance between the worm and the apple is 2.5
The worm bites the apple.
```

Entering an Unspecified Number of Values

Very often we do not know exactly how many data items will be entered before a program begins execution. This may be because there are too many data items to count them beforehand (e.g., a stack of exam scores for a very large class) or because the number of data items provided may depend on how the computation proceeds.

There are two ways to handle this situation using a WHILE loop. One approach is to ask whether there are any more data before each data item is read. The user should enter Y (for yes) or N (for no), and the program would either read the next item (Y) or terminate data entry (N). The Y/N variable is sometimes known as a *flag*. The other way is to terminate data entry when a particular *value* occurs in the data. This value is often called a *sentinel:* It comes at the end of the data.

Flag-Controlled Loop

■ Example 6.7

Let us use this approach to design a loop that accumulates the sum (in `Sum`) of a collection of exam scores. The statements below are true assuming that `MoreData` always contains the value `'Y'` or `'N'`.

1. `Sum` is the sum of all scores read so far.
2. `MoreData` is `'N'` just after loop exit.

From statement 1 we know that we must add each score to `Sum` in the loop body and that `Sum` must initially be 0 in order for its final value to be correct. From statement 2 we know that loop exit must occur when `MoreData` is `'N'`, so the loop repetition condition is `MoreData = 'Y'`. These considerations lead us to the loop form below:

1. Initialize `Sum` to 0
2. Initialize `MoreData` to _____
3. WHILE MoreData = 'Y' LOOP
   4. Read the next score into `Score`
   5. Add `Score` to `Sum`
   6. Read the next value of `MoreData`
   END LOOP;

The loop repetition condition, MoreData = 'Y', derives from the fact that MoreData is either 'Y' or 'N', and loop exit occurs when MoreData is 'N'. To ensure that at least one pass is performed, step 2 should be

2. Initialize MoreData to 'Y'

In the Ada loop below, the value of the type Character variable MoreData controls loop repetition. It must be initialized to 'Y' before the loop is reached. A new character value ('Y' or 'N') is read into MoreData at the end of each loop repetition. The loop processing consists of reading each exam score (into Score) and adding it to Sum. Loop exit occurs when the value read into MoreData is not equal to 'Y'.

```
Sum := 0;
MoreData := 'Y';
WHILE MoreData = 'Y' LOOP
    Text_IO. Put (Item => "Enter the next score > ");
    My_Int_IO.Get (Item => Score);
    Text_IO.New_Line;
    Sum := Sum + Score;
    Text_IO.Put (Item => "Any more data? Enter Y (Yes) or N (No) > ");
    Text_IO.Get (Item => MoreData);
END LOOP;
```

The sample dialogue below would be used to enter the scores 33, 55, and 77. The problem with this approach is that the program user must enter an extra character value, Y, before each actual data item is entered.

```
Enter the next score > 33
Any more data? Enter Y (Yes) or N (No) > Y
Enter next data item > 55
Any more data? Enter Y (Yes) or N (No) > Y
Enter next data item: 77
Any more data? Enter Y (Yes) or N (No) > N
```                                                        ■

Template for Flag-Controlled Loop

The general form of the loop just seen can be used to write other loops as the need arises. This general form is

1. Initialize flag variable to its affirmative value
2. WHILE flag variable is still true LOOP
   ...
   Read new value of flag variable
   END LOOP;

Sentinel-Controlled Loops

A second approach to solving the problem addressed in the last section would be to instruct the user to enter a unique data value, or *sentinel value*, when done. The program would test each data item and terminate when this sentinel value is read. The sentinel value should be carefully chosen and must be a value that could not normally occur as data. This approach is more convenient, because the program user enters only the required data.

■ Example 6.8

The statements below must be true for a sentinel-controlled loop that accumulates the sum of a collection of exam scores.

1. Sum is the sum of all scores read so far.
2. Score contains the sentinel value just after loop exit.

Statement 2 derives from the fact that loop exit occurs after the sentinel is read into Score. These statements lead to the following trial loop form:

Incorrect Sentinel-Controlled Loop

1. Initialize Sum to 0
2. WHILE Score is not the sentinel LOOP
   3. Read the next score into Score
   4. Add Score to Sum
   END LOOP;

Because Score has not been given an initial value, the WHILE condition in step 2 cannot be evaluated when the loop is first reached. One way around this would be to initialize Score to any value other than the sentinel (in step 2) and then read in the first score at step 3. A preferred solution is to read in the first score as the initial value of Score before the loop is reached and then switch the order of the read and add steps in the loop body. The outline for this solution is shown below.

Correct Sentinel-Controlled Loop

1. Initialize Sum to 0
2. Read the first score into Score
3. WHILE Score is not the sentinel LOOP
   4. Add Score to Sum
   5. Read the next score into Score
   END LOOP;

Step 2 reads in the first score, and step 4 adds this score to 0 (initial value of Sum). Step 5 reads all remaining scores including the sentinel. Step 4 adds all scores except the sentinel to Sum. The initial read (step 2) is often called the *priming read*, to draw an analogy with the priming of a pump in which the first cup of water must be poured into a pump before it can begin to pump water out of a well. The Ada implementation shown below uses -1 (value of Sentinel) as the sentinel because all normal exam scores will be nonnegative:

```
Sum := 0;
Text_IO.Put (Item => "When done, enter -1 to stop.");
Text_IO.New_Line;
Text_IO.Put (Item => "Enter the first score > ");
My_Int_IO.Get (Item => Score);
Text_IO.New_Line;
WHILE Score /= Sentinel LOOP
   Sum := Sum + Score;
```

```
      Text_IO.Put (Item => "Enter the next score > ");
      My_Int_IO.Get (Item => Score);
      Text_IO.New_Line;
  END LOOP;
```

Although it may look strange at first to see the statement

```
  My_Int_IO.Get (Item => Score);
```

at two different points in the program, this is a perfectly good programming practice and causes no problems. Note that Score must be Integer, not Natural, because the sentinel value is negative. The following sample dialogue would be used to enter the scores 33, 55, and 77. Compare this with the dialogue shown in Example 6.7.

```
  When done, enter -1 to stop.
  Enter the first score > 33
  Enter the next score > 55
  Enter the next score > 77
  Enter the next score > -1
  The sum of the scores is 165.
```

It is usually instructive (and often necessary) to question what happens when there are no data items to process. In this case, the sentinel value should be entered as the "first score," and loop exit would occur right after the first (and only) test of the loop repetition condition so the loop body would not be executed (i.e., a loop with zero iterations). Sum would retain its initial value of 0, which would be correct.

Template for a Sentinel-Controlled Loop

Sentinel-controlled loops have the general form shown next.

1. Read the first value of input variable
2. WHILE input variable is not equal to the sentinel LOOP

>   . . .

   Read the next value of input variable
  END LOOP;

The sentinel value must be a value that would not be entered as a normal data item. For program readability, we usually store the sentinel value in a constant.

Remembering the Previous Data Value in a Loop

In some situations it is necessary to remember the data value processed during the previous iteration of a loop. For example, some keyboards are "bouncy" and cause multiple occurrences of the same character to be sent when a single key is pressed. Some faculty are forgetful and may enter the same exam score twice in succession. An IF statement nested inside a loop can be used to check whether or not the current data value is the same as the last data value.

■ Example 6.9

Program 6.5 finds the product of a collection of data values. If there are multiple consecutive occurrences of the same data value, only the first occurrence is included in the product. For example, the product of the numbers 10, 5, 5, 5, and 10 is $10 \times 5 \times 10$, or 500. Assuming a new data value is read into NextNum during each loop iteration, we can make the following observations.

1. Product in pass i is the same as Product in pass $i - 1$ if NextNum in pass i is NextNum in pass $i - 1$; otherwise, Product during pass i is NextNum times Product in pass $i - 1$ (for $i > 1$).
2. NextNum is the sentinel just after loop exit.

Statement 1 requires the loop to "remember" the value read into NextNum during the previous iteration. We will introduce a new program variable, PreviousNum, for this purpose. The current value of NextNum should be incorporated in the product only if it is different from the previous value of NextNum (saved in PreviousNum). A trial loop form follows.

Initial Loop Form

1. Initialize Product to _____
2. Initialize PreviousNum to _____
3. Read the first number into NextNum
4. WHILE NextNum is not the sentinel LOOP
    5. IF NextNum is not equal to PreviousNum THEN
            6. Multiply Product by NextNum
       END IF;
    7. Set PreviousNum to NextNum
    8. Read the next number into NextNum
    END LOOP;

For Product to be correct during the first pass, it must be initialized to 1 (step 1). We must also initialize PreviousNum so that the condition in step 4 can be evaluated. To ensure that the first number read into NextNum is incorporated in the product, we must pick a value for PreviousNum that is different from the initial data value. The safest thing to do is to initialize PreviousNum to the sentinel. (Why?) These considerations lead to the following revised loop form.

Revised Loop Form

1. Initialize Product to 1
2. Initialize PreviousNum to the sentinel
3. Read the first number into NextNum
4. WHILE NextNum is not the sentinel LOOP
    5. IF NextNum is not equal to PreviousNum THEN
            6. Multiply Product by NextNum
       END IF;
    7. Set PreviousNum to NextNum
    8. Read the next number into NextNum
    END LOOP;

Within the loop, steps 7 and 8 prepare for the next iteration by saving the previous value of NextNum in PreviousNum before reading the next data value. (What would happen if the order of these two steps were reversed?) ∎

Program 6.5   Product of a Series of Integers

```
WITH Text_IO;
WITH My_Int_IO;
PROCEDURE Multiply IS

-- Finds the product of a collection of non-zero integers. If there
-- are multiple consecutive occurrences of the same value, only the
-- first value is included in the product.

   Sentinel : CONSTANT Natural := 0;  -- sentinel value

   NextNum :        Integer;       -- input - new data item
   PreviousNum : Integer;          -- last data item
   Product :        Integer;       -- output - product of data

BEGIN -- Multiply

   -- Compute product of non-zero, non-repeating data items.
   Product := 1;
   PreviousNum := Sentinel;
   Text_IO.Put (Item => "Enter 0 to stop.");
   Text_IO.New_Line;
   Text_IO.Put (Item => "Enter first number > ");
   My_Int_IO.Get (Item => NextNum);          -- priming read

   WHILE NextNum /= Sentinel LOOP
      -- invariant:
      --No prior value of NextNum is the sentinel and
      --Product in pass i is Product in pass i-1 if NextNum is
      --PreviousNum; otherwise, Product in pass i is NextNum * Product
      --in pass i-1 (for i > 1)

      IF NextNum /= PreviousNum THEN
         Product := Product * NextNum ;        -- compute next product
      END IF;
      PreviousNum := NextNum;                   -- remember previous item
      Text_IO.Put (Item => "Enter next  number > ");
      My_Int_IO.Get (Item => NextNum);          -- read next item
   END LOOP;
   -- assert: NextNum is the sentinel and Product is the product of
   --every value of NextNum such that NextNum /= PreviousNum

   Text_IO.Put (Item => "The product is ");  -- display result
   My_Int_IO.Put(Item => Product, Width => 1);
   Text_IO.New_Line;

END Multiply;


Enter 0 to stop.
Enter first number > 10
Enter next  number > 5
Enter next  number > 5
```

```
Enter next   number >  5
Enter next   number > 10
Enter next   number >  0
The product is 500
```

Program 6.5 illustrates the proper form of a sentinel-controlled loop. The constant Sentinel has the value 0 because it is meaningless to include 0 in a collection of numbers being multiplied. To determine whether or not to execute the loop, each value read into NextNum must be compared to Sentinel. In order for this test to make sense in the beginning, the first data value must be read before the WHILE loop is reached. The next value must be read at the end of the loop so that it can be tested before starting another iteration.

Remember, in a sentinel-controlled loop, the read operation appears twice: before the WHILE header (the priming read) and at the end of the loop body.

PROGRAM
STYLE

A Problem with Sentinel-Controlled Loops

Sentinel-controlled loops are popular, but they do have a disadvantage. We have been stressing the importance of defining subtypes that reflect the range of data that will normally appear. A sentinel, on the other hand, makes sense only if it is a value that does *not* normally appear in the data. Therefore the range of data values must be extended beyond the normal range, to accommodate the sentinel, as we extended the range of Score to be Integer rather than Natural.

The difficulty that arises in extending the range is that an *incorrectly entered* data value may not be caught by Ada. One solution is to use an extra variable of the extended range, just to read the input data. If a value is entered into it that is not the sentinel, that value is copied into the other variable, whose range is that of the normally occurring data. Copying the value will raise Constraint_Error if the value is out of range.

Exercises for Section 6.2

Self-Check

1. What output values are displayed by the loop below for a data value of 5?

```
Text_IO.Put(Item => "Enter an integer> ");
My_Int_IO.Get(Item => X);
Product := X;
Count := 0;
WHILE Count < 4 LOOP
    My_Int_IO.Put(Item => Product, Width => 1);
    Product := Product * X;
    Count := Count + 1;
END LOOP;
```

2. What values are displayed if the call to My_Int_IO.Put comes at the end of the loop instead of at the beginning?

3. Write a program segment that computes $1 + 2 + 3 + \ldots + (N - 1) + N$, where N is a data value. Follow the loop body with an IF statement that compares this value to $(N \times (N + 1)) / 2$ and displays a message indicating whether the values are the same or different. What message do you think will be displayed?

6.3 Problem Solving: Assertions and Loop Invariants

Many program errors occur within loops, so it is important to verify that loops are correct. One verification method is to trace the loop's execution for a variety of different sets of data, making sure that the loop always terminates and that it produces the correct results, even when zero iterations are performed. To help us verify that a loop works properly, we can use special comments, called *assertions* and *loop invariants,* within a loop body. In this section, we introduce some principles of loop verification that will help you in loop design.

A critical part of loop verification is to document the loop using assertions, which are logical statements that are always true. An assertion should be placed just before the loop body (after the WHILE statement), and another one should be placed just after the loop exit.

The assertion that precedes the loop body is called the *loop invariant.* Because the loop invariant is an assertion, it must always be true, even before loop repetition begins. Like the WHILE condition, the loop invariant is evaluated just before each repetition of the loop body. The execution of the loop body may change the value of the WHILE condition from true to false (e.g., just before the loop exit); however, the value of the loop invariant must remain true. In other words, the execution of the loop body must not change the value of the loop invariant.

The loop from Program 6.3 is rewritten below using assertions. Remember that these assertions are inserted to help you or another *human* reader verify the correctness of the loop. Since assertions are just comments, they are ignored by the Ada compiler.

```
-- Cut the distance between the worm and the apple by the worm's
-- body length until the worm is close enough to bite the apple

Distance := InitialDist;

WHILE Distance > WormLength LOOP
-- invariant:
--    Distance <= InitialDist and
--    Distance in pass i is Distance in pass i-1
--       less the worm's length (for i > 1)

  Text_IO.Put(Item => "The distance is ");
  My_Flt_IO.Put(Item => Distance, Fore => 4, Aft => 2, Exp => 0);
  Text_IO.New_Line;

Distance := Distance - WormLength;    -- reduce Distance
END LOOP;
-- assert: Distance <= WormLength
```

The invariant and the assertion following the loop summarize all we know about the loop, and they are similar to our earlier observations:

1. `Distance` must always be less than or equal to `InitialDist`.
2. During each pass, the value of `Distance` is reduced by the worm's body length.
3. `Distance` must be less than or equal to the worm's body length just after loop exit.

■ Example 6.10

The sentinel-controlled loop in Example 6.8 is rewritten below using assertions. Compare the loop invariant with the statements below that summarize the loop properties.

- Sum is the sum of all scores read so far.
- Score is the sentinel just after loop exit.

```
Sum := 0;
Text_IO.Put (Item => "When done, enter -1 to stop.");
Text_IO.New_Line;
Text_IO.Put (Item => Enter the first score > ");
My_Int_IO.Get (Item => Score);

WHILE Score /= Sentinel LOOP
   -- invariant: Sum is the sum of all scores read
   -- and no prior score was the sentinel

   Sum := Sum + Score;
   Text_IO.Put ("Item => Enter the next score > ");
   My_Int_IO.Get (Item => Score);
END LOOP;
-- assert: Score is Sentinel and Sum is the sum of all scores ■
```

Some computer scientists use loop invariants for loop design as well as loop verification. By first writing the loop invariant as a comment inside the loop, they can discern from the invariant what initialization, testing, and processing steps are required. In this book, we will generally document our WHILE and general loops with invariants and end-of-loop assertions.

◆ Case Study: Money in the Bank

Problem

Now that you are finally graduating, your parents have some money to invest in a savings account and they are interested in knowing the best strategy for investment. They would like you to write a program that shows them the value of a certificate of deposit as it increases annually. They would like to use this program for fixed-rate certificates or variable-rate certificates (in which the interest rate changes at the beginning of each year). Whenever it is run, your program should display a table showing the investment year, the annual interest, and the certificate balance at the end of each year until the balance has passed a target amount.

Analysis

What is needed is a program that computes annual interest and new balance using the formulas

> interest = balance x rate
> new balance = old balance + interest

The program should display these values while the new balance is less than the target balance. We can use a single variable (`Balance`) to represent the old and new balance, where the initial value of `Balance` is the deposit amount (`Deposit`). The data requirements for the problem follow.

Data Requirements

Problem Inputs
the deposit amount (`Deposit` : `NonNegFloat`)
the target balance (`TargetBal` : `NonNegFloat`)
the annual interest rate as a fraction (`Rate` : `NonNegFloat`)
an indicator of whether the interest rate is fixed or variable
(`FixedOrVar` : `Character`)

Problem Outputs
the current investment year (`Year` : `Natural`)
the annual balance (`Balance` : `NonNegFloat`)
the annual interest earned (`Interest` : `NonNegFloat`)

The type `Character` variable `FixedOrVar` indicates whether or not the annual interest rate is fixed (value is `'F'`) or varying (value is `'V'`). The algorithm is shown next.

Design

Initial Algorithm

1. Enter the deposit amount, the value of `FixedOrVar`, and the interest rate for a fixed-rate certificate.
2. Display a table showing the year, interest earned, and account balance as long as the balance has not passed the target balance. If the interest rate is variable, read in the new rate at the start of each year before computing the annual interest.

Step 2 requires a loop. Because we don't know how many iterations are needed, we should use a `WHILE` loop. The loop has the following properties:

Case Study: Money in the Bank, continued

1. Year is the number of loop iterations performed so far.
2. Balance is the sum of Deposit plus all prior values of Interest.
3. Balance is between TargetBal and TargetBal + Interest just after loop exit.

These statements suggest the following refinement for step 2 of the algorithm.

Step 2 Refinement
2.1. Initialize Year to 0
2.2. Initialize Balance to Deposit
2.3. Initialize Interest to 0
2.4. WHILE Balance < TargetBal LOOP
    2.5.   Increment Year by 1
    2.6.   IF the interest rate is variable THEN
        2.7.   Read this year's rate
        END IF;
    2.8.   Compute the interest for this year
    2.9.   Compute the new value of Balance
    2.10. Display the table line for the current year
END LOOP;

Coding

The program is Program 6.6. The sample run uses a fixed interest rate.

Program 6.6   Table of Interest on a Savings Account

```
WITH Text_IO;
WITH My_Int_IO;
WITH My_Flt_IO;
PROCEDURE GrowMoney IS

-- Displays a table of interest earned and account balance for each
-- investment year for fixed or varying rate certificates.

   SUBTYPE NonNegFloat IS Float RANGE 0.0 .. Float'Last;

   FixedOrVar : Character;    -- input - indicates fixed or varying rate
   Deposit :    NonNegFloat;  -- input - initial amount of deposit
   Rate :       NonNegFloat;  -- input - annual rate of interest
   TargetBal :  NonNegFloat;  -- input - the target certificate amount
   Balance :    NonNegFloat;  -- output - current certificate amount
   Interest :   NonNegFloat;  -- output - amount of annual interest
   Year :       Natural;      -- output - year of investment

BEGIN -- GrowMoney

   Text_IO.Put (Item => "Enter the deposit amount $");
   My_Flt_IO.Get (Item => Deposit);

   Text_IO.Put (Item => "Enter the desired final balance $");
   My_Flt_IO.Get (Item => TargetBal);
```

```
    Text_IO.Put (Item => "Is the interest rate fixed (F) or variable (V)? ");
    Text_IO.Get (Item => FixedOrVar);

  IF FixedOrVar = 'F' THEN
    Text_IO.Put (Item => "Enter the interest rate as a decimal fraction > ");
    My_Flt_IO.Get (Item => Rate);
  END IF;

  -- Display table heading
  Text_IO.New_Line;
  Text_IO.Put (Item => "Year         Interest          Balance");
  Text_IO.New_Line;

  -- Display the certificate balance for each year.
  Year := 0;
  Balance := Deposit;
  Interest := 0.0;
  WHILE Balance < TargetBal LOOP
      -- invariant:
      --    Balance < TargetBal + Interest and
      --    Balance is the sum of Deposit and all values of Interest

    Year := Year + 1;
    IF FixedOrVar = 'V' THEN
      Text_IO.Put (Item => "Enter rate for year ");
      My_Int_IO.Put (Item => Year, Width => 0);
      Text_IO.Put (Item => " > ");
      My_Flt_IO.Get (Item => Rate);
    END IF;

    Interest := Balance * Rate;
    Balance := Balance + Interest;

    My_Int_IO.Put (Item => Year, Width => 4);
    My_Flt_IO.Put (Item => Interest, Fore => 12, Aft => 2, Exp => 0);
    My_Flt_IO.Put (Item => Balance, Fore => 12, Aft => 2, Exp => 0);
    Text_IO.New_Line;
  END LOOP;
  -- assert: Balance >= TargetBal and
  --Balance is the sum of Deposit and all values of Interest

  Text_IO.New_Line;
  Text_IO.Put (Item => "Certificate amount reaches target after ");
  My_Int_IO.Put (Item => Year, Width => 2);
  Text_IO.Put (Item => " years");
  Text_IO.New_Line;
  Text_IO.Put (Item => "Final balance is $");
  My_Flt_IO.Put (Item => Balance, Fore => 1, Aft => 2, Exp => 0);
  Text_IO.New_Line;

END GrowMoney;


Enter the deposit amount $100.00
Enter the desired final balance $200.00
Is the interest rate fixed (F) or variable (V)? F
Enter the interest rate as a decimal fraction > 0.075
```

Case Study: Money in the Bank, continued

```
Year      Interest      Balance
  1           7.50       107.50
  2           8.06       115.56
  3           8.67       124.23
  4           9.32       133.55
  5          10.02       143.56
  6          10.77       154.33
  7          11.57       165.90
  8          12.44       178.35
  9          13.38       191.72
 10          14.38       206.10

Certificate amount reaches target after 10 years
Final balance is $206.10
```

6.4 Control Structures: The General LOOP and EXIT Statements

There is another kind of loop statement in Ada that is used less frequently than the FOR and the WHILE loops but comes in very handy in certain situations. This is the general LOOP structure. Instead of a loop control construct at the head of the loop (as in the case of the FOR and the WHILE), loop exit occurs when the EXIT statement is reached. There are two common forms of the EXIT statement. The first is EXIT WHEN:

```
EXIT WHEN Distance < 0.5;
```

Here are a WHILE statement and a general LOOP statement that both accomplish the same purpose, which is to compute and display all powers of 2 less than 10,000:

```
Power := 1;
WHILE Power < 10000 LOOP
  My_Int_IO.Put (Item => Power, Width => 5);
  Power := Power * 2;
END LOOP;

Power := 1;
LOOP
  EXIT WHEN Power >= 10000;
  My_Int_IO.Put (Item => Power, Width => 5);
  Power := Power * 2;
END LOOP;
```

The test in the EXIT WHEN loop (Power >= 10,000) is the *complement*, or opposite, of the test used in the WHILE loop. The loop body is repeated *until* the value of Power is greater than or equal to 10,000. Loop repetition stops when the condition is true, whereas in the WHILE loop, repetition stops when the condition is false.

The EXIT WHEN statement is allowed to appear *anywhere* in the loop body. It is most often used if a loop termination condition is more conveniently placed at the end or middle of a loop body instead of at the top, as is required by FOR and WHILE. We will have occasional opportunities to use this structure in later chapters of the book.

The other form of the EXIT statement is an unconditional statement,

```
EXIT;
```

which appears without an explicit condition. A common example of the use of this statement in Ada appears in the next section; it is associated with robust exception handling.

General LOOP Statement

Form:

```
LOOP
    statement sequence₁
    EXIT WHEN condition;
    statement sequence₂
END LOOP;
```

Example:

```
PowerOf2 := 1;
LOOP
    My_Int_IO.PUT (Item => PowerOf2);
    PowerOf2 := PowerOf2 * 2;
    EXIT WHEN PowerOf2 > 10000;
END LOOP;
```

Interpretation: *Statement sequence₁* is executed and *condition* (a Boolean expression) is tested. If *condition* is found to be true, the loop is exited and the next program statement after END LOOP is executed. If *condition* is found to be false, *statement sequence₂* is executed and the loop is repeated. **Note:** EXIT transfers out of the innermost loop in which it appears; that is, if EXIT appears inside a nested loop, only the inner loop is exited.

EXIT Statement

Form:

```
EXIT;
```

Example: An example will appear in the next section.

Interpretation: EXIT is a meaningful statement only within a loop structure. EXIT transfers control to the next statement after the nearest END LOOP.

6.5 System Structures: Robust Exception Handling

A good program should be written so as to predict likely errors and behave accordingly, retaining control instead of "crashing" or just returning control to the operating system. Such a program is called a *robust* program; the property of *robustness* is advantageous in a program. A robust Ada program is one that retains control and behaves predictably even when exceptions are raised.

Program 5.19 was written with an exception-handling section at the end, so that it would display an appropriate message if an input value was out of range or badly formed, or if a result would overflow the computer's arithmetic system. This is only a partial solution, because the program terminates without giving the user another chance to enter an acceptable value. There are many techniques for solving this problem; the one we consider here is the use of Ada exception handlers.

We will get user input by entering a loop that exits only when the input value is acceptable. We will detect out-of-range or badly formed input values using an exception handler form similar to that in Program 5.19. It is necessary to associate the exception handler with the input statement rather than with the entire program. A pseudocode description of the process follows.

Template for a Robust Input Loop, Initial Version

```
LOOP
    Prompt the user for an input value
    Get the input value from the user
    EXIT the loop if and only if no exception was raised on input
    If an exception was raised, notify the user
END LOOP;
```

The first two lines in the loop body should present no problem to you at this point. The last line is coded using an exception handler section like that in Program 5.19. Ada's rules require that an exception handler be associated with a *block* or *frame*, that is, a sequence of statements between a BEGIN and an END. A procedure or function has a block as part of its body; the exception handler in Program 5.19 is associated with that block. Luckily, we can build a block wherever we need one within a program, just by enclosing a group of statements between BEGIN and END. In the pseudocode below (a refinement of the pseudocode above), the entire loop body is considered a block because it is enclosed between BEGIN and END. The structure beginning EXCEPTION is associated with this block.

```
LOOP
    BEGIN
            Prompt the user for an input value
            Get the input value from the user
            EXIT the loop;        -- valid data
        EXCEPTION                 -- invalid data
            Determine which exception was raised and notify the user
    END;
END LOOP;
```

The EXIT statement is associated with the LOOP structure. If control reaches the EXIT—that is, if the input is correct—then loop exit occurs. Control passes to the exception handler if the input is incorrect; after execution of the exception handler, control flows to the END LOOP, which of course causes the loop to be repeated. The only code permitted between EXCEPTION and END is a sequence of one or more exception handlers.

SYNTAX
DISPLAY

Exception Handler

Form:

```
WHEN exception name =>
    sequence of statements
```

Example:

```
WHEN Constraint_Error =>
    Text_IO.Put(Item => "Input number is out of range");
    Text_IO.New_Line;
    Text_IO.Put(Item => "Please try entering it again.");
    Text_IO.New_Line;
```

Interpretation: This structure is valid only in the exception-handler part of a BEGIN/END block. If *exception name* was raised in the block, then *sequence of statements* is executed, after which control passes to the next statement after the block's END.

Note: *Exception name* can be a predefined exception or a programmer-defined exception. We will introduce programmer-defined exceptions in Chapter 9. The predefined exceptions most commonly used follow.

- Constraint_Error—An attempt is made to store a value in a variable that is out of range for that variable, that is, out of the range of the variable's type or subtype.
- Numeric_Error—An attempt is made to carry out an arithmetic operation that violates the arithmetic system of the computer, usually an overflow or a division by 0.
- Text_IO.Data_Error—An attempt is made to read a value which is invalid for the variable being read.

Block with Exception Handler

Form:

```
BEGIN

    normal sequence of statements

EXCEPTION

    WHEN  exception-name₁ =>
               sequence-of-statements₁

    WHEN  exception-name₂ =>
               sequence-of-statements₂

    ...

    WHEN  exception-nameₙ =>
               sequence-of-statementsₙ

END;
```

Example: An example is given in Program 6.7.

Interpretation: If an exception is raised by any statement in *normal-sequence-of-statements,* execution of the statement causing the exception is immediately halted, and control passes to the appropriate exception handler. If the block has no exception handler part, or no exception handler is appropriate (i.e., the exception that was raised is not named in any of the handlers), then control passes out of the block to the statement following the END, and the exception is re-raised at that point.

Note: The last sentence means that if an exception is raised in executing the statements of a function or procedure, and that function or procedure has no exception handler part, the exception is "passed back" to the program that called the function or procedure, and an attempt is made to find an appropriate handler *there.* If the procedure was the main program, the program ends and control passes to the Ada run-time system, which reports the exception to the user.

■ Example 6.11

Program 6.7 shows a robust input handler. The purpose of the program is to add five integers in the range $-10..10$. A subtype SmallInt is declared with this range, then My_Int_IO.Get is used to get input in this range, storing the value in the variable InputValue of type SmallInt. If the value entered is out of range, the attempt to store it in InputValue raises Constraint_Error. The exception handler for Constraint_Error notifies the user that the input is out of range.

Suppose the input entered is not an integer: for example, suppose it is a letter. In this case Text_IO.Data_Error is raised. In this situation the letter is *not* consumed from the input stream. If the program just loops around it will try to read the same letter again, and again, and again, causing an "infinite loop." To prevent this unpleasant occurrence, the handler for Text_IO.Data_ Error contains a statement,

```
Text_IO.Skip_Line;
```

which causes the bad input to be skipped, creating a fresh line for input. Actually, Text_IO.Skip_Line causes all input, up to and including the carriage return with which you end a line, to be skipped.

Suppose a floating-point value—say, 345.67—is entered when an integer is called for. An odd consequence of the design of Text_IO is that the 345 will be accepted as a valid integer, and the decimal point will raise Text_IO.Data_ Error if you try to read another integer. When your program is reading an integer token with My_Int_IO.Get, input stops whenever a character is reached that is not part of an integer token. In this case the decimal point stops input. This is one reason for including the Text_IO.Skip_Line statement in the exception handler. ∎

Program 6.7   An Example of Robust Numeric Input

```
WITH Text_IO;
WITH My_Int_IO;
PROCEDURE ExceptionLoop IS

  MinVal : CONSTANT Integer := -10;
  MaxVal : CONSTANT Integer :=  10;
  SUBTYPE SmallInt  IS Integer RANGE MinVal .. MaxVal;

  InputValue: SmallInt;
  Sum:        Integer;

BEGIN -- ExceptionLoop

  Sum := 0;

  FOR Count IN 1..5 LOOP -- counts the five values we need to read

    LOOP        -- inner loop just to control robust input
       BEGIN    -- block for exception handler

         Text_IO.Put(Item => "Enter an integer between ");
         My_Int_IO.Put(Item => SmallInt'First, Width => 0);
         Text_IO.Put(Item => " and ");
         My_Int_IO.Put(Item => SmallInt'Last, Width => 0);
         Text_IO.Put(Item => " > ");
         My_Int_IO.Get(Item => InputValue);

         EXIT; -- leave the loop only upon correct input

       EXCEPTION
         WHEN Constraint_Error =>
           Text_IO.Put ("Value entered is out of range. Please try again.");
           Text_IO.New_Line;
         WHEN Text_IO.Data_Error =>
           Text_IO.Put ("Value entered not an integer. Please try again.");
           Text_IO.New_Line;
           Text_IO.Skip_Line;
```

```
        END;    -- block for exception handler
      END LOOP;
      -- assert: InputValue is in the range MinN to MaxN

      Sum := Sum + InputValue; -- add new value into Sum
   END LOOP;

   Text_IO.Put (Item => "The sum is ");
   My_Int_IO. Put (Item => Sum, Width => 1);
   Text_IO.New_Line;

END ExceptionLoop;
```

```
Enter an integer between -10 and 10 > 20
Value entered is out of range. Please try again.
Enter an integer between -10 and 10 > -11
Value entered is out of range. Please try again.
Enter an integer between -10 and 10 > x
Value entered not an integer. Please try again.
Enter an integer between -10 and 10 > 0
Enter an integer between -10 and 10 > -5
Enter an integer between -10 and 10 > y
Value entered not an integer. Please try again.
Enter an integer between -10 and 10 > 3
Enter an integer between -10 and 10 > 4
Enter an integer between -10 and 10 > -7
The sum is -5
```

■ Example 6.12

Program 6.8 shows one way to write a robust menu handler, that is, an input handler that displays a range of selections on the screen. This program uses Screen.MoveCursor to control the positioning of the cursor, and DELAY to cause execution to be delayed for a brief period before clearing the screen and prompting the user again.   ■

Program 6.8 Framework for a Menu Handler

```
WITH Text_IO;
WITH My_Int_IO;
WITH Screen;
PROCEDURE MenuHandler IS

   SUBTYPE MenuValues IS Positive RANGE 1..6;
   MenuSelection : MenuValues;

BEGIN -- MenuHandler

   LOOP
     BEGIN -- exception handler block

       Screen.ClearScreen;
       Screen.MoveCursor (Row => 5, Column => 20);
```

```
Text_IO.Put (Item => "Select one of the operations below.");
Screen.MoveCursor (Row => 7, Column => 20);
Text_IO.Put (Item => "1. Compute an Average");
Screen.MoveCursor (Row => 8, Column => 20);
Text_IO.Put (Item => "2. Compute a Standard Deviation");
Screen.MoveCursor (Row => 9, Column => 20);
Text_IO.Put (Item => "3. Find the Median");
Screen.MoveCursor (Row => 10, Column => 20);
Text_IO.Put (Item => "4. Find the smallest and largest values");
Screen.MoveCursor (Row => 11, Column => 20);
Text_IO.Put (Item => "5. Plot the data");
Screen.MoveCursor (Row => 12, Column => 20);
Text_IO.Put (Item => "6. Exit the program");

Screen.MoveCursor (Row => 14, Column => 20);
Text_IO.Put ("Enter a number between 1 and 6 > ");

-- this statement could raise an exception if input is out of range
-- or not an integer value
My_Int_IO.Get (Item => MenuSelection);

-- these statements will be executed only if the input is correct
-- otherwise, control passes to exception handler
Screen.MoveCursor (Row => 17, Column => 20);
Text_IO.Put ("Thank you for correct input.");
EXIT;         -- valid data

    EXCEPTION    -- invalid data

        WHEN Text_IO.Data_Error =>
            Screen.MoveCursor (Row => 17, Column => 20);
            Text_IO.Put (Item => "Value entered is not an integer.");
            Text_IO.Skip_Line;
            DELAY 1.0;
        WHEN Constraint_Error =>
            Screen.MoveCursor (Row => 17, Column => 20);
            Text_IO.Put (Item => "Value entered is out of range.");
            DELAY 1.0;

    END;              -- of exception handler block
END LOOP;

Screen.MoveCursor (Row =>23, Column => 20);
Text_IO.Put (Item => "Correct input entered; do the requested task here");
Screen.MoveCursor (Row => 24, Column => 1);

END MenuHandler;
```

 # 6.6 System Structures: Writing Simple Procedures

In this book you have been using calls to procedures provided by the standard input/output libraries and another package called Screen. In this section you will learn how procedures are written and used.

Writing Procedures

Procedures and functions are both subprograms, but they differ in two important ways. First, a procedure is called with a procedure call statement, as in

```
My_Flt_IO.Put (Item => X, Fore => 3, Aft => 2, Exp => 0);
```

whereas a function is used in an expression, for example

```
Temp := UsefulFunctions.Minimum (Value1 => X, Value2 => Y) + 45;
```

A function returns a result, so that the result can be used in an expression; a procedure does not return a result.

The second important difference is that a function is permitted to have parameters that are passed only *into* the function, whereas a procedure is allowed to have parameters of three kinds, or *modes:*

- *Mode* IN *parameters*—These are passed *into* the procedure and, inside the procedure, are treated as constants and may not be changed (e.g., they may not appear on the left side of an assignment statement).
- *Mode* OUT *parameters*—These are computed in the procedure and passed *out* to the caller; inside the procedure they may not be used for anything else (e.g., they cannot appear on the right side of an assignment statement).
- *Mode* IN OUT *parameters*—These are passed into the procedure, possibly changed by it, and passed back out again.

The determination of a particular parameter's mode is based on the direction of the data flow between the procedure and its calling programs. If the parameter is used to transmit data *to* the procedure, its mode should be IN; if the parameter receives data *from* the procedure, its mode should be OUT.

Mode IN parameters are similar to the parameters of a function and are used to transmit values that will not be changed by the procedure, only used by it. For example, the parameters to the various Put procedures provided by Text_IO are IN parameters, because the data and formatting values are transmitted from the caller to the procedure.

Mode OUT parameters are commonly used in input routines like the Get operations in Text_IO. It may seem strange that an *input* routine should have an OUT parameter, but the input routine receives a value from the terminal or a file and passes it *out* to the program that calls it. The caller receives the input value from the procedure.

Mode IN OUT parameters are used when a procedure will modify its parameters. An example follows.

■ Example 6.13

Here is a procedure specification for a procedure Order, which orders the values in the two variables whose names are supplied to it as actual parameters, placing the smaller of the two values in X and the larger in Y:

```
PROCEDURE Order (X: IN OUT Float; Y: IN OUT Float);
```

A procedure call statement

```
Order (X => Num1, Y => Num2);
```

is intended to order the values in the two floating-point variables Num1 and Num2. Suppose, for example, that Num1 is 3.0 and Num2 is -5.0. After the above call we want Num1 to be -5.0 and Num2 to be 3.0. Ordering pairs of values is a very common operation in programming, especially in sorting applications. Here is the body of procedure Order:

```
PROCEDURE Order (X: IN OUT Float; Y: IN OUT Float) IS

-- Orders a pair of numbers represented by X and Y so that the
-- smaller number is in X and the larger number is in Y.
-- Pre: X and Y are assigned values
-- Post: X has the smaller value and Y has the larger value

   Temp: Float;

BEGIN

   IF X > Y THEN
        -- interchange the values of X and Y
      Temp := X;
      X := Y;
      Y := Temp;
   END IF;

END Order;
```

The variable Temp is a local variable of the procedure, necessary to carry out the interchange. Temp is created when the procedure is called; it is destroyed when the procedure returns to its caller. X and Y must be IN OUT parameters because their values are changed by the procedure. The effect of calling procedure Order is shown in Program 6.9, which carries out a very simple sort of three numbers Num1, Num2, and Num3 by calling Order three times:

```
Order (X => Num1, Y => Num2);
Order (X => Num1, Y => Num3);
Order (X => Num2, Y => Num3);
```

Because each statement contains a different association of *actual parameters* with the *formal parameters* X and Y, a different pair of variables will be ordered each time the procedure is called. Figure 6.1 shows a structure chart for this program. ■

Program 6.9 A Very Simple Sorting Program

```
WITH Text_IO;
WITH My_Flt_IO;
PROCEDURE Sort3Numbers IS

-- Reads three numbers and sorts them
-- so that they are in increasing order.
```

```
Num1 : Float;                    -- a list of three cells
Num2 : Float;
Num3 : Float;

-- procedure specification
PROCEDURE Order (X: IN OUT Float; Y: IN OUT Float);

-- procedure body
PROCEDURE Order (X: IN OUT Float; Y: IN OUT Float) IS

-- Orders a pair of numbers represented by X and Y so that the
-- smaller number is in X and the larger number is in Y.
-- Pre: X and Y are assigned values.
-- Post: X has the smaller value and Y has the larger value.

  Temp : Float;              -- copy of number originally in X

BEGIN  -- Order

  IF X > Y THEN
    -- interchange the values of X and Y
    Temp := X;               -- Store old X in Temp
    X := Y;                  -- Store old Y in X
    Y := Temp;               -- Store old X in Y
  END IF;

END Order;


BEGIN -- Sort3Numbers

  Text_IO.Put(Item => "Enter 3 float numbers to be sorted, one per line.");
  Text_IO.New_Line;
  My_Flt_IO.Get(Item => Num1);
  My_Flt_IO.Get(Item => Num2);
  My_Flt_IO.Get(Item => Num3);

  -- Sort the numbers
  Order (X => Num1, Y => Num2);      -- Order the data in Num1 and Num2
  Order (X => Num1, Y => Num3);      -- Order the data in Num1 and Num3
  Order (X => Num2, Y => Num3);      -- Order the data in Num2 and Num3

  -- Display the results.
  Text_IO.Put(Item => "The three numbers in order are: ");
  My_Flt_IO.Put(Item => Num1, Fore => 5, Aft => 2, Exp => 0);
  My_Flt_IO.Put(Item => Num2, Fore => 5, Aft => 2, Exp => 0);
  My_Flt_IO.Put(Item => Num3, Fore => 5, Aft => 2, Exp => 0);
  Text_IO.New_Line;

END Sort3Numbers;


Enter 3 float numbers to be sorted, one per line.
23.7
-99.4
1.78
The three numbers in order are:   -99.40    1.78    23.70
```

Figure 6.1 Structure Chart for Simple Sort Program

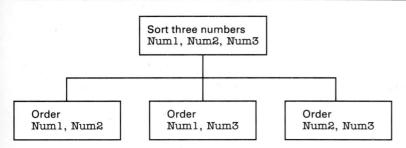

To show the importance of the choice of parameter mode for procedure Order, Fig. 6.2 gives a compilation listing for a modification of Program 6.9 in which the parameter modes have all been changed from IN OUT to IN. Notice that the Ada compiler has marked as errors the lines in Order in which attempts are made to change the IN parameters.

Figure 6.2 Procedure Order with Compilation Errors

```
 1 | WITH Text_IO;
 2 | WITH My_Flt_IO;
 3 | PROCEDURE Sort3Numbers IS
 4 |
 5 | -- Reads three numbers and sorts them
 6 | -- so that they are in increasing order.
 7 |
 8 |    Num1 : Float;           -- a list of three cells
 9 |    Num2 : Float;
10 |    Num3 : Float;
11 |
12 |    -- procedure specification
13 |    PROCEDURE Order (X: IN Float; Y: IN Float);
14 |
15 |    -- procedure body
16 |    PROCEDURE Order (X: IN Float; Y: IN Float) IS
17 |
18 |    -- Orders a pair of numbers represented by X and Y so that the
19 |    -- smaller number is in X and the larger number is in Y.
20 |    -- Pre: X and Y are assigned values.
21 |    -- Post: X has the smaller value and Y has the larger value.
22 |
23 |      Temp : Float;           -- copy of number originally in X
24 |
25 |    BEGIN -- Order
26 |
27 |       IF X > Y THEN
28 |          -- interchange the values of X and Y
29 |          Temp := X;          -- Store old X in Temp
30 |          X := Y;             -- Store old Y in X
***** >              ^
***** > "sort3numbers.ada", line 30: Error: Cannot assign to IN parameter: x.
31 |          Y := Temp;          -- Store old X in Y
***** >              ^
***** > "sort3numbers.ada", line 31: Error: Cannot assign to IN parameter: y.
```

```
32 |    END IF;
33 |
34 |  END Order;
35 |
36 |
37 | BEGIN -- Sort3Numbers
38 |
39 |   Text_IO.Put(Item => "Enter 3 float numbers to be sorted, one per line.");
40 |   Text_IO.New_Line;
41 |   My_Flt_IO.Get(Item => Num1);
42 |   My_Flt_IO.Get(Item => Num2);
43 |   My_Flt_IO.Get(Item => Num3);
44 |
45 |   -- Sort the numbers
46 |   Order (X => Num1, Y => Num2);        -- Order the data in Num1 and Num2
47 |   Order (X => Num1, Y => Num3);        -- Order the data in Num1 and Num3
48 |   Order (X => Num2, Y => Num3);        -- Order the data in Num2 and Num3
49 |
50 |   -- Display the results.
51 |   Text_IO.Put(Item => "The three numbers in order are: ");
52 |   My_Flt_IO.Put(Item => Num1, Fore => 5, Aft => 2, Exp => 0);
53 |   My_Flt_IO.Put(Item => Num2, Fore => 5, Aft => 2, Exp => 0);
54 |   My_Flt_IO.Put(Item => Num3, Fore => 5, Aft => 2, Exp => 0);
55 |   Text_IO.New_Line;
56 |
57 | END Sort3Numbers;

57 lines compiled.
2 errors detected.
```

Preconditions and Postconditions as Comments

The body of procedure Order begins with a lengthy comment that describes its operations. The line

    -- Pre: X and Y are assigned values.

describes the *precondition* for the procedure. This is the condition that the procedure designer assumes will be true before the procedure is called. The line

    -- Post: X has the smaller value and Y has the larger value.

describes the *postcondition* for the procedure. The procedure designer is stating his or her assumptions about the parameters and promising that *if* the preconditions are true just before the procedure is called, then the postcondition will be true after the procedure execution is completed.

Preconditions and postconditions form an informal contract between the subprogram (function or procedure) designer and the subprogram user. The designer promises that the subprogram execution will cause the postcondition to be true if the user calls the subprogram *only* when the preconditions are true. If the procedure is called when a precondition is not true—for example, if X and Y are not defined (i.e., haven't been assigned definite values), then "all bets are off."

The contract is informal because Ada provides no automatic way to ensure that the preconditions are met or to guarantee that the subprogram's execution in fact makes the postcondition true. Explicit preconditions and postconditions are therefore nothing more than documentation, but this documentation is valuable to the user of the subprogram. The use of preconditions and postconditions also aids in verifying the correctness of a program that calls this subprogram. In this book we will generally document our procedures and functions with preconditions and postconditions.

Executing a Procedure with Parameters

Figure 6.3 shows the data areas for the main program and procedure Order immediately after the execution of the procedure call statement

```
Order(X => Num1, Y => Num2);        -- Order the data in Num1 and Num2
```

This diagram shows the data values read into Num1, Num2, and Num3. It also shows that the local variable Temp is considered undefined immediately after the procedure is called.

Figure 6.3 also shows the parameter correspondence specified by the actual parameter list above. The double-headed arrows symbolize the connection between formal parameters X and Y and main program variables Num1 and Num2, respectively.

The execution of the procedure is traced in Table 6.1. The actual parameter represented by each formal parameter is shown in parentheses at the top of the table. Because the value of Num1 is less than that of Num2, the true alternative is skipped and the variable values are unchanged.

Figure 6.3 Parameter Correspondence for Order (Num1, Num2)

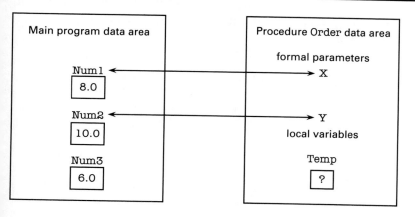

Table 6.1 Trace of Procedure Execution for Order (Num1, Num2)

Statement in Order	X (Num1)	Y (Num2)	Temp	Effect
	8.0	10.0	?	
IF X > Y THEN				8.0 > 10.0 is false; do nothing

The parameter correspondence specified by the procedure call statement

```
Order (X => Num1, Y => Num3);
```

is pictured in Fig. 6.4. This time parameter X corresponds to variable Num1 and parameter Y corresponds to variable Num3. This means that whenever formal parameter Y is referenced in the procedure, the data in main program variable Num3 are actually manipulated.

Figure 6.4 Parameter Correspondence for Order (Num1, Num3)

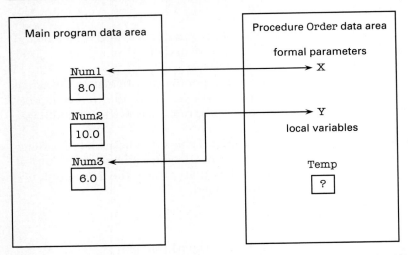

This second execution of the procedure is traced in Table 6.2. The actual parameter represented by each formal parameter is shown in parentheses at the top of the table. The procedure execution switches the values stored in main program variables Num1 and Num3, as desired.

Table 6.2 Trace of Procedure Execution for Order (Num1, Num3)

Statement in Order	X (Num1)	Y (Num3)	Temp	Effect
	8.0	6.0	?	
IF X > Y THEN				8.0 > 6.0 is true
Temp := X;			8.0	save old Num1 in Temp;
X := Y;	6.0			save old Num3 in Num1;
Y := Temp;		8.0		save Temp in Num3.

The Procedure Data Area

Each time a procedure call statement is executed, an area of memory is allocated for storage of that procedure's data. Included in the procedure data area are storage cells for any local variables or constants that may be declared in the procedure. The procedure data area is always erased when the procedure terminates, and it is recreated empty (all values undefined) when the procedure is called again.

Memory cells are allocated in the procedure data area for each formal parameter. These cells are used in different ways for parameters of the three modes.

- For a mode IN parameter, the value of the corresponding actual parameter is placed in this cell when the procedure is called. The compiler will not permit a statement in the procedure to change the value in this cell.
- For a mode OUT parameter, the local cell is initially empty; the procedure computes a value and saves it in this memory cell. The compiler will not allow a statement of the procedure to use this value, only to compute it. After the procedure completes its work, just before it returns to its calling program, the value in the local cell is copied back into the actual parameter in the calling program.
- For a mode IN OUT parameter, the behavior is a combination of the other two. The actual value is copied into the local cell when the procedure is called. Statements of the procedure may change the value in the local cell. Just before the procedure returns to its caller, the value in the local cell is copied back into the actual parameter in the calling program.

If an exception is raised in the procedure's execution and not handled by the procedure, the new values are *not* copied back.

We note that these rules apply to parameters of *scalar* type, which are the only kind we have studied so far. In later chapters you will see that parameter-passing behavior may differ somewhat for parameters of *structured* type (which haven't been introduced yet in this book).

Syntax Rules for Parameter Lists

This section presents the syntax rules for procedure declarations and procedure call statements with parameters. The displays that follow summarize these rules.

SYNTAX
DISPLAY

Procedure Specification (Procedure with Parameters)

Form:

```
PROCEDURE pname (formal-parameters);
```

Example:

```
PROCEDURE Highlight (Ch : IN Character);
```

Interpretation: The procedure *pname* is declared. The *formal parameters* are enclosed in parentheses.

Procedure Body (Procedure with Parameters)

Form:

```
PROCEDURE pname (formal-parameters) IS
    local declaration-section
BEGIN
    statement sequence
END pname;
```

Example:

```
PROCEDURE Highlight (Ch : IN Character) IS

    Border: CONSTANT Character := '*';

BEGIN

    Text_IO.Put (Item => Border);
    Text_IO.Put (Item => Ch);
    Text_IO.Put (Item => Border);

END Highlight;
```

Interpretation: The procedure *pname* is declared. The *formal parameters* are enclosed in parentheses. Any identifiers that are declared in the *declaration-section* are defined only during the execution of the procedure.

The *statement sequence* describes the data manipulation to be performed by the procedure. The formal parameter names are used in place of the actual parameter names in this description.

Procedure Call Statement (Procedure with Parameters)

Form:

pname (*actual-parameters*)

Example:

```
Highlight (Ch => 'A')
```

Interpretation: The *actual-parameters* are enclosed in parentheses; each actual parameter is preceded by the name of the corresponding formal parameter. When procedure *pname* is called into execution, each actual parameter is associated with the corresponding formal parameter.

The formal parameter list determines the form of any actual parameter list that may be used to call the procedure. This form is determined during the translation of the program when the compiler processes the procedure declaration.

Later, when a procedure call statement is reached, the compiler checks the actual parameter list for consistency with the formal parameter list. An actual parameter list may be a list of expressions, variables, or constants separated by commas. The actual parameter list must satisfy the rules shown below.

Rules for Parameter List Correspondence

1. Correspondence between actual and formal parameters is determined by position in their respective parameter lists unless named association is used. These lists must be of the same size. The names of corresponding actual and formal parameters may be, and often are, different.
2. The type of each actual parameter must be compatible with the type of the corresponding formal parameter, that is, either of the same type or of a related subtype.
3. For mode OUT and IN OUT parameters, an actual parameter must be a variable. For mode IN parameters, an actual parameter may be a variable, constant, or expression.

PROGRAMMING STYLE

Named Association in Actual Parameter Lists

In this book, *named association* is used to associate each formal parameter with an actual parameter (the two are separated by =>). This naming is optional in Ada; if it is used, the *order* of the actual parameters does not, strictly speaking, have to match the order of the formal parameters. It is good practice to use named association and also to list the actual parameters in an order corresponding to the order of the formal parameters. In this way, no confusion arises for the reader of the program as to which actual parameter matches which formal parameter.

6.7 System Structures: A Package for Robust Input

Requesting and reading numeric input robustly is a common requirement in programs. It therefore makes sense to consider how we can "package" robust input so that it can just be used, instead of rewritten, for each program needing to do it.

We will do this by analogy with the Text_IO libraries, specifically, the My_Int_IO and My_Flt_IO instances we have been using all along in this book. These standard packages read input values by calls to procedures that are called Get (recall that because of overloading, these procedures can all have the same name provided they have different parameter profiles). We shall write a package, RobustInput, which provides the necessary robust Get operations for integer and floating-point values.

Program 6.10 gives the package specification for RobustInput. There are two procedures, both called Get (this is permitted because of the overloading principle). Here is the one for integer input:

```
PROCEDURE Get (Item : OUT Integer;
    MinVal : IN Integer;
    MaxVal : IN Integer);
```

This procedure will read an integer value from the keyboard and return it to the caller in the actual parameter corresponding to Item. The other two parameters specify the range of acceptable input. The procedure Get for floating-point values is analogous.

Program 6.10 Specification for Package RobustInput

```
PACKAGE RobustInput IS

  -- Package for getting numeric input robustly.

  PROCEDURE Get (Item : OUT Integer;
                MinVal : IN Integer;
                MaxVal : IN Integer);

  -- Gets an integer value in the range MinVal..MaxVal from the terminal
  -- Pre: MinVal and MaxVal are defined
  -- Post: MinVal <= Item <= MaxVal


  PROCEDURE Get (Item : OUT Float;
                MinVal : IN Float;
                MaxVal : IN Float);

  -- Gets a float value in the range MinVal..MaxVal from the terminal
  -- Pre: MinVal and MaxVal are defined
  -- Post: MinVal <= Item <= MaxVal

END RobustInput;
```

Program 6.11 gives the package body for RobustInput. It consists of the bodies of the two procedures promised in the procedure specification. Note that in the body for the integer Get, a subtype is declared corresponding to the range parameters, and a corresponding variable:

```
SUBTYPE TempType IS Integer RANGE MinVal..MaxVal;
TempItem : TempType;     -- temporary copy of MinVal
```

The statement sequence of this procedure is very similar to that of Program 6.9; a loop is used to retain control if an exception is raised. The subtype TempType and variable TempItem are necessary so that if the input value produced by My_Int_IO.Get is out of range, Constraint_Error will be raised.

Program 6.11 Body of Package RobustInput

249

6.7 System
Structures: A
Package for
RobustInput

```
WITH Text_IO;
WITH My_Int_IO;
WITH My_Flt_IO;
PACKAGE BODY RobustInput IS

   PROCEDURE Get (Item : OUT Integer;
                  MinVal : IN Integer;
                  MaxVal : IN Integer) IS

   -- Gets an integer value in the range MinVal..MaxVal from the terminal
   -- Pre: MinVal and MaxVal are defined
   -- Post: MinVal <= Item <= MaxVal

      SUBTYPE TempType IS Integer RANGE MinVal..MaxVal;
      TempItem : TempType;       -- temporary copy of Item

   BEGIN -- Get

      LOOP
        BEGIN        -- exception handler block
          Text_IO.Put(Item => "Enter an integer between ");
          My_Int_IO.Put(Item => MinVal, Width => 0);
          Text_IO.Put(Item => " and ");
          My_Int_IO.Put(Item => MaxVal, Width => 0);
          Text_IO.Put(Item => " > ");
          My_Int_IO.Get(Item => TempItem);
          Item := TempItem;
          EXIT;-- valid data
        EXCEPTION -- invalid data
          WHEN Constraint_Error =>
            Text_IO.Put ("Value entered is out of range. Please try again.");
            Text_IO.New_Line;
            Text_IO.Skip_Line;
          WHEN Text_IO.Data_Error =>
            Text_IO.Put ("Value entered not an integer. Please try again.");
            Text_IO.New_Line;
            Text_IO.Skip_Line;
        END;          -- exception handler block
      END LOOP;
      -- assert: Item is in the range MinVal to MaxVal

   END Get;

   PROCEDURE Get (Item : OUT Float;
                  MinVal : IN Float;
                  MaxVal : IN Float) IS

   -- Gets a float value in the range MinVal..MaxVal from the terminal
   -- Pre: MinVal and MaxVal are defined
   -- Post: MinVal <= Item <= MaxVal

      SUBTYPE TempType IS Float RANGE MinVal..MaxVal;
      TempItem : TempType;       -- temporary copy of Item

   BEGIN -- Get

      LOOP
        BEGIN        -- exception handler block
          Text_IO.Put(Item => "Enter a floating-point value between ");
          My_Flt_IO.Put(Item => MinVal, Fore=> 1, Aft => 2, Exp => 0);
```

```
        Text_IO.Put(Item => " and ");
        My_Flt_IO.Put(Item => MaxVal, Fore=> 1, Aft => 2, Exp => 0);
        Text_IO.Put(Item => " > ");
        My_Flt_IO.Get(Item => TempItem);
        Item := TempItem;
        EXIT;          -- valid data
      EXCEPTION        -- invalid data
        WHEN Constraint_Error =>
          Text_IO.Put ("Value entered is out of range. Please try again.");
          Text_IO.New_Line;
          Text_IO.Skip_Line;
        WHEN Text_IO.Data_Error =>
          Text_IO.Put ("Value entered not floating point. Please try again.");
          Text_IO.New_Line;
          Text_IO.Skip_Line;
      END;             -- exception handler block
    END LOOP;
    -- assert: Item is in the range MinVal to MaxVal

  END Get;

END RobustInput;
```

Finally, Program 6.12 serves to test the package operations. Two integer and two floating-point subtypes are declared; the RobustInput operations are called. This is an example of a "test driver" program, whose purpose is just to test the operations provided by a package.

Program 6.12 A Program That Uses RobustInput

```
WITH RobustInput;
PROCEDURE TestRobustInput IS

  SUBTYPE SmallInt   IS Integer RANGE -10 ..10;
  SUBTYPE LargerInt IS Integer RANGE -100..100;
  SUBTYPE SmallFloat  IS Float RANGE -10.0 ..10.0;
  SUBTYPE LargerFloat IS Float RANGE -100.0..100.0;

  Small: SmallInt;
  SmallF : SmallFloat;
  Larger : LargerInt;
  LargerF : LargerFloat;

BEGIN -- TestRobustInput

  RobustInput.Get(Small,SmallInt'First,SmallInt'Last);
  RobustInput.Get(Larger,LargerInt'First,LargerInt'Last);
  RobustInput.Get(SmallF,SmallFloat'First,SmallFloat'Last);
  RobustInput.Get(LargerF,LargerFloat'First,LargerFloat'Last);

END TestRobustInput;


Enter an integer between -10 and 10 > 11
```

```
Value entered is out of range. Please try again.
Enter an integer between -10 and 10 > -11
Value entered is out of range. Please try again.
Enter an integer between -10 and 10 > 10
Enter an integer between -100 and 100 > 101
Value entered is out of range. Please try again.
Enter an integer between -100 and 100 > 99
Enter a floating-point value between -10.00 and 10.00 > 10.001
Value entered is out of range. Please try again.
Enter a floating-point value between -10.00 and 10.00 > -12.00
Value entered is out of range. Please try again.
Enter a floating-point value between -10.00 and 10.00 > 10
Value entered not floating point. Please try again.
Enter a floating-point value between -10.00 and 10.00 > 0.0
Enter a floating-point value between -100.00 and 100.00 > 5.0003
```

Exercises for Section 6.7

Self-Check

1. The following procedure is like the ones in Program 6.11 but does not have a loop or special block for the exception handlers; the handlers are just written to go with the procedure's BEGIN and END. Is this correct as far as the Ada compiler is concerned? If so, describe the difference in behavior from the original.

```
PROCEDURE Get (Item : OUT Integer;
              MinVal : IN Integer;
              MaxVal : IN Integer) IS

   SUBTYPE TempType IS Integer RANGE MinVal..MaxVal;
   TempItem : TempType;       -- temporary copy of MinVal

BEGIN -- Get

   Text_IO.Put(Item => "Enter an integer between ");
   My_Int_IO.Put(Item => MinVal, Width => 0);
   Text_IO.Put(Item => " and ");
   My_Int_IO.Put(Item => MaxVal, Width => 0);
   Text_IO.Put(Item => " > ");
   My_Int_IO.Get(Item => TempItem);
   Item := TempItem;

EXCEPTION -- invalid data
   WHEN Constraint_Error =>
     Text_IO.Put ("Value entered out of range. Try again.");
     Text_IO.New_Line;
     Text_IO.Skip_Line;
   WHEN Text_IO.Data_Error =>
     Text_IO.Put ("Value entered not an integer. Try again.");
     Text_IO.New_Line;
     Text_IO.Skip_Line;

END Get;
```

6.8 Tricks of the Trade: Testing with Exception Handling

Ada's exception handling provides a powerful tool for designing programs whose behavior is predictable even if its inputs are badly formed or out of range. If exception handling were not available, it would be the programmer's responsibility to validate all incoming data—for example, by checking its range with an IF statement. Indeed, Ada programs can certainly be written this way—with no use of exception handling—but the result would not take advantage of this built-in power.

Even if exception handling is used to advantage, however, the programmer still has several important responsibilities in this area:

- Analyze your program so that you know the places where exceptions may be raised, and be sure to place exception handlers in appropriate blocks in your program. This will ensure that exceptions are not unexpectedly passed back to the calling program or to the run-time system.
- When you test your program, be sure to test it with badly formed or out-of-range data, so that your exception-handling flow is tested. When you are finished testing, you should be confident that you know exactly what your program will do under each set of input conditions. The test data supplied to Program 6.12 shows an example of how this is done.

In summary, Ada's exception handling provides a useful way to take account of unusual circumstances in your program but does not relieve you of the responsibility to design and test carefully, so that your program's behavior will always be predictable.

6.9 Tricks of the Trade: Common Programming Errors

Beginners sometimes confuse IF and WHILE statements because both statements contain a condition. Make sure that you use an IF statement to implement a decision step and a WHILE statement to implement a conditional loop. Remember to terminate each control structure with an END IF or END LOOP. The compiler will detect a syntax error if an END IF or END LOOP is missing.

Be careful when using tests for inequality to control the repetition of a WHILE loop. The loop below is intended to process all transactions for a bank account while the balance is positive:

```
WHILE Balance /= 0.0 LOOP
    UpDate (Balance);
END LOOP;
```

If the bank balance goes from a positive to a negative amount without being exactly 0.0, the loop will not terminate (an infinite loop). The loop below would be safer:

```
WHILE Balance >= 0.0 LOOP
    UpDate (Balance);
END LOOP;
```

Verify that the repetition condition for a WHILE loop will eventually become false. If you use a sentinel-controlled loop, remember to provide a prompt that tells the program user what value to enter as the sentinel. Make sure that the sentinel value cannot be entered as a normal data item.

Keep in mind that exception handlers have to be associated with BEGIN-END blocks, and remember that once a program transfers to an exception handler, control does not automatically return to the statement that caused the exception. If you need to return to that statement (as in the robust input loop), you need to use a LOOP–END LOOP structure to do so.

 Chapter Review

A conditional looping structure, the WHILE statement, was used to implement loops whose repetition is controlled by a condition. The WHILE statement is useful when the exact number of repetitions required is not known before the loop begins. In designing a WHILE loop, we must consider both the loop control and loop processing operations that must be performed. Separate Ada statements are needed for initializing and updating variables appearing in the loop repetition condition.

One common technique for controlling the repetition of a WHILE loop is using a special sentinel value to indicate that all required data have been processed. In this case, an input variable must appear in the loop repetition condition. This variable is initialized when the first data value is read (priming read), and it is updated at the end of the loop when the next data value is read. Loop repetition terminates when the sentinel value is read.

The use of assertions and loop invariants in loop verification and loop design was also introduced. We will use loop invariants to document the processing performed by the loop body.

This chapter also introduced the general LOOP and EXIT statements and showed how they are used in Ada to implement robust input with exception handling.

Writing procedures is an important part of programming, and this technique was also introduced in this chapter. Finally, a package providing robust numeric input operations was developed.

New Ada Constructs in Chapter 6

The new Ada statements introduced in this chapter are described in Table 6.3.

Table 6.3 Summary of New Ada Constructs

Construct	Effect

WHILE **Statement**
```Sum := 0;```
```WHILE Sum <= MaxSum LOOP```
```   Text_IO.Put(Item=>"Next integer > ");```
```   My_Int_IO.Get(Item=>Next);```
```   Sum := Sum + Next;```
```END LOOP;```
	A series of data items is read; their sum is in Sum. This process stops when the accumulated sum exceeds MaxSum.

Procedure with Parameters
```PROCEDURE A (X : IN Float;```
```   Op : IN Character;```
```   XTo3 : IN OUT Float) IS```
 	
```BEGIN --A```
 	
``` IF Op = '*' THEN```
```   XTo3 := X * X * X;```
``` ELSIF Op = '+' THEN```
```   XTo3 := X + X + X;```
``` ELSE```
```   Text_IO.Put(Item => "Invalid");```
``` END IF;```
 	
```END A;```
	Procedure A has two IN parameters and one IN OUT parameter. If Op is '*', then the value returned is X * X * X; otherwise, if Op is '+', then the value returned is X + X + X; otherwise, an error message is printed. A result is returned by assigning a new value to the actual parameter (a variable) that corresponds to parameter XTo3.

Procedure Call Statement ```A (X=>5.5, OP=>'+', XTo3=>Y);```	Calls procedure A. 5.5 is passed into X, '+' is passed into Op, and the value 16.5 is stored in Y.

Exception Handler Block
```BEGIN```
``` X := Y + Z;```
``` Y := A / G;```
```EXCEPTION```
``` WHEN Constraint_Error =>```
```   Text_IO.Put(Item=>"Out of Range");```
``` WHEN Numeric_Error =>```
```   Text_IO.Put(Item=>"Overflow");```
```END;```
	If Y+Z is out of range for X, "Out of Range" is displayed; If G=0, then A cannot be divided by G and "Overflow" is displayed. Control passes to the statement following END.

✓ *Quick-Check Exercises*

1. A WHILE loop is called a _____ loop.
2. A WHILE loop is always used for counting. (True or False?)

3. The priming step for a WHILE loop is what kind of statement? When is it used?
4. The sentinel value is always the last value added to a sum being accumulated in a sentinel-controlled loop. (True or False?)
5. It is an error if a WHILE loop body never executes. (True or False?)

Answers to Quick-Check Exercises
1. Conditional
2. False
3. An input operation, used in a sentinel-controlled loop
4. False, the sentinel should not be processed.
5. False

Review Questions for Chapter 6

1. Define a sentinel value.
2. For a sentinel value to be used properly when reading in data, where should the input statements appear?
3. Write a program called Sum to sum and display a collection of payroll amounts entered at the standard input device until a sentinel value of −1 is entered. Use a WHILE statement.
4. Hand trace the program below given the following data:

```
4.0, 2.0, 8.0, 4.0
1.0, 4.0, 2.0, 1.0
9.0, 3.0, 3.0, 1.0
−22.0, 10.0, 8.0, 2.0

WITH Text_IO;
WITH My_Flt_IO;
PROCEDURE Slope IS

    Sentinel CONSTANT Float := 0.0;
    Slope, y2, y1, x2, x1 : Float;

BEGIN -- Slope
    Text_IO.Put(Item => "Enter four real numbers > ");
    Text_IO.New_Line;
    My_Flt_IO.Get(Item => y2);
    My_Flt_IO.Get(Item => y1);
    My_Flt_IO.Get(Item => x2);
    My_Flt_IO.Get(Item => x1);
    Slope := (y2 - y1) / (x2 - x1);
    WHILE Slope /= Sentinel LOOP
            Text_IO.Put(Item => "Slope is ");
            My_Flt_IO.Put(Item => Slope, Fore=>1, Aft=>2,Exp=>0);
            Text_IO.New_Line;
            Text_IO.Put(Item => "Enter four real numbers > ");
            Text_IO.New_Line;
            My_Flt_IO.Get(Item => y2);
            My_Flt_IO.Get(Item => y1);
            My_Flt_IO.Get(Item => x2);
            My_Flt_IO.Get(Item => x1);
            Slope := (y2 - y1) / (x2 - x1);
    END LOOP;
END Slope;
```

5. Which of the statements below is incorrect?
   a. Loop invariants are used in loop verification.
   b. Loop invariants are used in loop design.
   c. A loop invariant is always an assertion.
   d. An assertion is always a loop invariant.
6. Write a procedure called LetterGrade that has one input parameter called Grade, and that will display the corresponding letter grade using a straight scale (90–100 is an A, 80–89 is a B, etc.).
7. Explain the difference between IN parameters, OUT parameters, and IN OUT parameters.
8. Explain the allocation of memory cells when a procedure is called.
9. Explain the purpose of a robust input loop.

Programming Projects

1. Write a program that will find the product of a collection of data values. Your program should terminate when a 0 value is read.
2. Write a program to read in an integer N and compute Slow $= 1 + 2 + 3 + \ldots + N$ (the sum of all integers from 1 to N). Then compute Fast $= (N \times (N + 1)) / 2$ and compare Fast and Slow. Your program should print both Fast and Slow and indicate whether or not they are equal. (You will need a loop to compute Slow.) Which computation method is preferable?
3. Write a program to read a list of integer data items and find and print the index of the first occurrence and the last occurrence of the number 12. Your program should print index values of 0 if the number 12 is not found. The index is the sequence number of the data item 12. For example, if the eighth data item is the only 12, then the index value 8 should be printed for the first and last occurrence.
4. Write a program to read in a collection of exam scores ranging in value from 1 to 100. Your program should count and print the number of outstanding scores (90–100), the number of satisfactory scores (60–89), and the number of unsatisfactory scores (1–59). Test your program on the following data:

   63 75 72 72 78 67 80 63 75 90 89 43 59 99 82 12 100

   In addition, print each exam score and its category.
5. Write a program to process weekly employee time cards for all employees of an organization. Each employee will have three data items indicating an identification number, the hourly wage rate, and the number of hours worked during a given week. Each employee is to be paid time and a half for all hours worked over 40. A tax amount of 3.625 percent of gross salary will be deducted. The program output should show the employee's number and net pay.
6. Suppose you own a soft-drink distributorship that sells Coke (ID number 1), Pepsi (ID number 2), Canada Dry (ID number 3) and Dr. Pepper (ID number 4) by the case. Write a program to
   a. read in the case inventory for each brand for the start of the week;
   b. process all weekly sales and purchase records for each brand; and
   c. display the final inventory.
   Each transaction will consist of two data items. The first item will be the brand identification number (an integer). The second will be the amount purchased (a positive integer value) or the amount sold (a negative integer value). The weekly

inventory for each brand (for the start of the week) will also consist of two items: the identification and initial inventory for that brand. For now, you may assume that you always have sufficient foresight to prevent depletion of your inventory for any brand. (*Hint*: Your data entry should begin with eight values representing the case inventory. These should be followed by the transaction values.)

7. Redesign the body of Program 6.11 (RobustInput) so that the range of the input data is checked explicitly with an IF statement instead of including a handler for Constraint_Error. Could you eliminate exception handling altogether? (*Hint*: How would you deal with the case of an alphabetic character being entered instead of an integer?)

8. The square root of a number N can be approximated by repeated calculation using the formula

```
NG = .5(LG + (N / LG))
```

where NG stands for next guess and LG stands for last guess. Write a function that implements this process where the first parameter will be a positive float number, the second will be an initial guess of the square root, and the third will be the computed result.

The initial guess will be the starting value of LG. The procedure will compute a value for NG using the formula above. The difference between NG and LG is checked to see whether these two guesses are almost identical. If so, the procedure is exited and NG is the square root; otherwise, the new guess (NG) becomes the last guess (LG) and the process is repeated (i.e., another value is computed for NG, the difference is checked, etc.).

For this program the loop should be repeated until the difference is less than 0.005 (Delta). Use an initial guess of 1.0 and test the program for the numbers: 4.0, 120.5, 88.0, 36.01, 10000.0.

A Systematic Look at Scalar Data Types

7

7.1   Data Structures: Constant Declarations

7.2   Data Structures: Numeric Data Types

7.3   System Structures: Using an External Math Library;
the USE Clause

7.4   Data Structures: The Boolean Type

7.5   Data Structures: The Character Type

7.6   Case Study: Testing Whether a Number Is Prime

7.7   Control Structures: The CASE Statement

7.8   System Structures: A Package to Print a Number in Words

7.9   Case Study: Printing a Check in Words

7.10   Tricks of the Trade: Common Programming Errors
Chapter Review

So far in our programming, we have used six predefined data types: Integer, Natural, Positive, Float, Boolean, and Character. In this chapter, we take a closer look at these data types and discuss the various operations that can be performed on them. All the data types in this chapter are *scalar* data types; that is, only one value can be stored in a single variable. In later chapters, we will study *composite* data types; that is, data types that can be used to store multiple values in a single variable.

In Section 7.3 we introduce another external package, Math, which provides functions for doing common mathematical operations like square root, sine, and cosine. This package is not a standard part of Ada but is usually provided along with the compiler.

This chapter introduces one more control structure, namely the CASE statement. This statement is a convenient alternative to the multi-alternative IF structure in many programs.

Finally, another package is introduced which makes use of much of the material in the chapter. This package provides facilities for displaying the value of an integer in English words. Two examples of its use are given; the second example is a program that displays the amount of a bank check in words.

 # 7.1 Data Structures: Constant Declarations

This chapter begins by reexamining constants in Ada. Each constant declaration has the form

> *identifier* : CONSTANT *type-name* := *expression*;

Strictly speaking, the type name is not always necessary, but for consistency and clarity we will always include it. Each *constant* assumes the value of its *expression* as its value; this value cannot be changed by the program.

■ Example 7.1

Some valid constant declarations follow:

```
Rows :          CONSTANT Positive := 24;
Columns :       CONSTANT Positive := 80;
ScreenSize :    CONSTANT Positive := Rows * Columns;
SpeedOfLight :  CONSTANT Float := 2.998E+5;
```

The constant declaration for ScreenSize uses the previously defined constants Rows and Columns. Rows has the value 24 and Columns has the value 80, so ScreenSize has the value 1920. The constant SpeedOfLight is associated with a floating-point value (299800.0) expressed in scientific notation.

As was mentioned earlier, there are two reasons for using constants. First, the name SpeedOfLight has more meaning to a reader of a program than the value $2.998E+5$. Second, using constants makes it unnecessary to use what are sometimes called "magic numbers" in a program. A magic number is a numerical or other constant value that appears several times, dispersed through a program; a magic number is undesirable because if its value must be changed in a later version of the program, the programmer must somehow find and change all the locations where it appears. If we use a constant instead, we just need to change its declaration and recompile the program, and the change propagates through the program. ■

 ## 7.2 Data Structures: Numeric Data Types

The predefined data types `Integer`, `Natural`, `Positive`, and `Float` are used to represent numeric information. `Integer` variables are used to represent data such as exam scores that are whole numbers; `Float` variables are used to represent numeric data that may have a fractional part. The subtypes `Natural` and `Positive` are used to represent integer values that cannot sensibly be negative; a `Natural` value is allowed to be zero; a `Positive` value is not.

Differences Between Numeric Types

You may be wondering why it is necessary to have so many numeric types. Because a whole number is a special case of one with a fractional part (i.e., the fractional part is zero), the data type `Float` could, in theory, be used for all numerical values. There are two important reasons why, in practice, we do not do this.

First, it is always best to use the most appropriate type for representing the values in a program. This not only makes the program easier for the reader to understand but also makes it possible for the compiler to ensure that the values assigned to a variable are appropriate values and that the operations performed on them are appropriate operations.

Another reason for not using `Float` values exclusively is that on many computers operations involving integers are faster and less storage space is needed to store integers. Also operations with integers are always precise, whereas there may be some loss of accuracy when dealing with floating-point values.

These differences result from the way floating point numbers and integers are represented internally in memory. All data are represented in memory as *binary strings,* strings of 0s and 1s. However, the binary string stored for the `Integer` value 13 is not the same as the binary string stored for the `Float` value 13.0. The actual internal representation used is computer dependent, but it will normally have the format shown in Fig. 7.1. In most computers, floating-point format uses more bits than integer format.

Figure 7.1 Integer and Floating-Point Formats

Integer	Floating-point	
Binary number	Mantissa	Exponent

As Fig. 7.1 shows, integers are represented by standard binary numbers. If you are familiar with the binary number system, you know that the integer 13 is represented as the binary number 01101.

Floating-point format is analogous to scientific notation. The storage area occupied by a real number is divided into two parts: the *mantissa* and the *exponent*. The mantissa is a binary fraction between 0.5 and 1.0 (-0.5 and -1.0 for a negative number). The exponent is a power of 2. The mantissa and exponent are chosen so that the formula

$$real\text{-}number = mantissa \times 2^{exponent}$$

is correct.

Besides the capability of storing fractions, floating-point format can represent a range of numbers considerably larger than can integer format. For example, on the IBM personal computer, floating-point numbers range in value from 10^{-308} (a very small fraction) to 10^{+308}, whereas the range of "normal" integers extends only from -32768 to 32767. In the IBM-PC, a floating-point number uses twice the storage space as an integer (32 bits versus 16).

Numeric Literals

A constant value appearing in an expression is called a *literal*. In Ada, a `Float` literal must have a decimal point in it and at least one digit on either side of the point. A literal may also have a decimal *scale factor*. For example, in the literal 2.998E+5, the scale factor is 10^5; in the literal 3E4, the scale factor is 10^4 (this is another way to write the value 30,000). It is also possible in Ada to use underscores (not commas!) to separate groups of digits, so that 30_000 is a valid `Integer` literal.

Type of an Expression

The type of an expression is determined by the type of its operands, and all operands of an expression must be the same type. For example, in the expression

```
X + 3.5
```

the variable X must be the same type (`Float`) as the literal 3.5; the expression is type `Float`. If I is an `Integer` variable, the expression

```
10 - I
```

is type `Integer`. If I is a `Float` variable, this expression is incorrect and will lead to a compilation error.

Numeric Operators

There are two kinds of arithmetic operators: *monadic* and *dyadic*. A monadic operator takes a single operand; a dyadic operator takes two operands. In Ada, the three monadic operators are +, −, and `ABS`. If X has an integer or float value,

+X returns the same value (essentially it has no effect), −X negates the value (e.g., −(−X)=X) and ABS X returns the absolute value (e.g., ABS 3 = ABS (−3) = 3).

The four dyadic arithmetic operators +, −, *, and / can be used with integer or floating-point operands. The operands must both be Float (or subtypes of Float) or both be Integer (or subtypes of Integer). The division operator / deserves special consideration. If the operands of a division operation are floating-point values, the full result is kept and is also floating point. If the operands of division are integer values, the result is an integer equal to the truncated quotient of M divided by N (i.e., the integer part of the quotient). For example, if M is 7 and N is 2, the value of M/N is the truncated quotient of 7 divided by 2 or 3. On the other hand, if X is 7.0 and Y is 2.0, then X/Y is 3.5.

■ Example 7.2

Table 7.1 shows some examples of valid and invalid expressions involving the integer and floating point division operators. For integer division, the result is always 0 when the magnitude of the first operand is less than the magnitude of the second operand.

■

Table 7.1 The Division Operators

```
 3 / 15 = 0        3 / −15 = 0        3.0 / 15.0 =  0.2
15 /  3 = 5       15 / −3  = −5       15   / 3.0 is invalid (mixed types)
16 /  3 = 5       16 / −3  = −5       16.0 / 3.0 =  5.333...
17 /  3 = 5      −17 /  3  = −5      −17.0 / 3.0 = −5.667...
18 /  3 = 6      −18 / −3  = 6        18.0 / 3.0 =  6.0
```

The remainder operator, REM, and the modulus operator, MOD, can also be used with integer operands. The expression A REM B is equal to the remainder of A divided by B, if A and B are both positive. For example, 7 REM 2 is equal to the remainder of 7 divided by 2, or 1. For positive operands, the MOD operator gives the same results as the REM operator; for negative operands, the results differ. The following relations are satisfied by the REM operator:

```
 A   REM (−B) =    A REM B
(−A) REM   B  = −(A REM B)
```

For the MOD operation, the following identity holds:

```
A MOD B = (A + B) MOD B
```

Table 7.2 shows some typical results for the integer division, REM, and MOD operators. Be sure you understand at least the results for REM; we will not generally use either operator with negative operands.

Note that ABS, REM, and MOD are reserved words that represent operators, and not function names. Thus the expression ABS X is correct without parentheses. In the expression ABS(−3), the parentheses denote that the operator ABS is applied after the operator −.

Table 7.2 Results of Integer Division, REM, and MOD Operators

A	B	A/B	A REM B	A MOD B	A	B	A/B	A REM B	A MOD B
10	5	2	0	0	−10	5	−2	0	0
11	5	2	1	1	−11	5	−2	−1	4
12	5	2	2	2	−12	5	−2	−2	3
13	5	2	3	3	−13	5	−2	−3	2
14	5	2	4	4	−14	5	−2	−4	1
10	−5	−2	0	0	−10	−5	2	0	0
11	−5	−2	1	−4	−11	−5	2	−1	−1
12	−5	−2	2	−3	−12	−5	2	−2	−2
13	−5	−2	3	−2	−13	−5	2	−3	−3
14	−5	−2	4	−1	−14	−5	2	−4	−4

■ Example 7.3

Program 7.1 displays each digit of its input value Decimal in reverse order (e.g., if Decimal is 738, the digits printed are 8, 3, 7). This is accomplished by displaying each remainder (0 through 9) of Decimal divided by 10; the integer quotient of Decimal divided by 10 becomes the new value of Decimal. ■

Program 7.1 Displaying Digits in Reverse Order

```
WITH Text_IO;
WITH RobustInput;
WITH My_Int_IO;
PROCEDURE DisplayDigits IS

-- Displays the digits of Decimal in reverse order.
-- Pre:  Decimal is assigned a value.
-- Post: Each digit of Decimal is displayed, starting with the
--       least significant one.

  SUBTYPE Natural_32767 IS Natural RANGE 0..32_767;

  Base : CONSTANT Natural := 10;    -- number system base
  Decimal : Natural_32767;          -- original number
  Digit :Natural;                   -- each digit

BEGIN  -- DisplayDigits

  RobustInput.Get(Item=>Decimal, MinVal=>0, MaxVal => Natural_32767'Last);

  -- Find and display remainders of Decimal divided by 10
  Text_IO.Put(Item=> "The digits in reverse order are ");
  WHILE Decimal /= 0 LOOP
    -- invariant:
    -- Decimal in pass i is (Decimal in pass i-1) / Base (for i > 1)
    -- and Digit in pass i is (Decimal in pass i-1) REM Base (for i > 1)
    -- and Decimal >= 0

    Digit := Decimal REM Base;      -- Get next remainder
    My_Int_IO.Put(Item => Digit, Width => 1);
    Decimal := Decimal / Base;      -- Get next quotient
```

```
      END LOOP;
      -- assert: Decimal is zero

      Text_IO.New_Line;

END DisplayDigits;
```

```
Enter an integer between 0 and 32767 > 54321
Value entered is out of range. Please try again.
Enter an integer between 0 and 32767 > -15
Value entered is out of range. Please try again.
Enter an integer between 0 and 32767 > x
Value entered not an integer. Please try again.
Enter an integer between 0 and 32767 > 12345
The digits in reverse order are 54321
```

The input value Decimal is used as the loop control variable. Within the WHILE loop, the REM operator is used to assign to Digit the rightmost digit of Decimal, and integer division is used to assign the rest of the number to Decimal. The loop is exited when Decimal becomes 0. Table 7.3 shows a trace of the loop execution for an input value of 43. The digits 3 and 4 are displayed.

Table 7.3   Trace of Execution of DisplayDigits

Statement	Decimal	Digit	Effect
WHILE Decimal /= 0 LOOP	43		43 /= 0 is true
Digit := Decimal REM Base	43	3	Remainder is 3
My_Int_IO.Put (Item=>Digit, Width=>1);		3	Display 3
Decimal := Decimal / Base;	4		Quotient is 4
WHILE Decimal /= 0 LOOP	4		4 /= 0 is true
Digit := Decimal REM Base	4	4	Remainder is 4
My_Int_IO.Put (Item=>Digit, Width=>1);	4		Display 4
Decimal := Decimal / Base;	0		Quotient is 0
WHILE Decimal /= 0 LOOP	0		0 /= 0 is false - exit

Recall from Section 2.10 that Ada provides one more dyadic operator, exponentiation, represented by **. An expression X ** M means "raise X to the Mth power;" that is, multiply X by itself M times. The left operand of ** can be an integer or floating-point value; the right operand must be an integer value. Further, if the left operand is an integer, the right operand must not be negative, because then the result would not be an integer value.

Multiple-Operator Expressions, Revisited

Often a problem requires writing an expression containing more than one operator, as discussed in Section 2.10. In such a case, it is always wise to use parentheses to show exactly which operations apply to which operands. However, to make the result of an expression predictable even if the programmer omits the parentheses, programming languages, including Ada, provide rules for the order of execution of operations. These are called *precedence* and *associativity* rules. For example, in the expression A + B * C, is * performed before + or vice versa? Is the expression X / Y * Z evaluated as (X / Y) * Z or X / (Y * Z)? Understanding these rules will help you understand expressions better.

Some expressions with multiple operators are

```
1.8 * Celsius + 32.0
(Salary - 5000.00) * 0.20 + 1425.00
```

where Celsius and Salary are Float variables. In both these cases, the algebraic rule that multiplication is performed before addition is applicable. The use of parentheses in the second expression ensures that subtraction is done first. The Ada rules for expression evaluation below are based on standard algebraic rules.

Rules for Expression Evaluation

a. All parenthesized subexpressions are evaluated first. Nested parenthesized subexpressions are evaluated inside out, with the innermost subexpression evaluated first.

b. *Operator precedence*—Arithmetic operators in the same subexpression are evaluated in the following order:

**, ABS	first
*, /, REM, MOD	next
+, − (monadic)	next
+, − (dyadic)	last

c. *Left associative*—Operators in the same subexpression and at the same precedence level (such as + and −, or * and /) are evaluated left to right.

Note that in Ada certain combinations of operators *require* parentheses. For example, A**B**C is undefined according to Ada syntax rules; you should write either A**(B**C) or (A**B)**C.

■ Example 7.4

The formula for the area of a circle,

$$a = \pi \times r^2,$$

can be written in Ada as

```
Area := Pi * Radius ** 2 ;
```

where Pi is the constant 3.14159. The *evaluation tree* for this formula is shown in Fig. 7.2. In this tree, the arrows connect each operand with its operator. The order of operator evaluation is shown by the number to the left of each operator; the rules that apply are shown to the right. ■

Area := Pi * Radius ** 2;

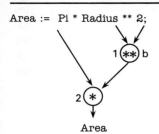

■ Example 7.5

The formula for the average velocity, v, of a particle traveling on a line between points p_1 and p_2 in time t_1 to t_2 is

$$v = \frac{p_2 - p_1}{t_2 - t_1}$$

This formula can be written in Ada as

```
V := (P2 - P1) / (T2 - T1);
```

It is evaluated as shown in Fig. 7.3.   ■

Figure 7.3 Evaluation Tree for Average Velocity

V := (P2 – P1) / (T2 – T1);

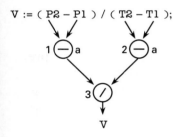

■ Example 7.6

Consider the expression

```
Z - (A + B / 2) + W * Y
```

which contains `Integer` variables only. The parenthesized subexpression (A + B / 2) is evaluated first (Rule a) beginning with B / 2 (Rule b). Once the value of B / 2 is determined, it can be added to A to obtain the value of (A + B / 2). Next the multiplication operation is performed (Rule b) and the value for W * Y is determined. Then the value of (A + B / 2) is subtracted from Z (Rule c), and finally this result is added to W * Y. Figure 7.4 gives an evaluation tree.   ■

Figure 7.4 Evaluation Tree for Z − (A + B / 2) + W * Y

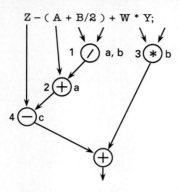

Writing Mathematical Formulas in Ada

There are two problem areas in writing a mathematical formula in Ada; one concerns multiplication, and the other concerns division. In everyday algebra, multiplication is often implied in a mathematical formula by writing the two items to be multiplied next to each other, for example, $a = bc$. In Ada, however, the * operator must always be used to indicate multiplication, as in

```
A := B * C
```

The other difficulty arises in formulas involving division. We normally write the numerator and denominator on separate lines:

$$m = \frac{y - b}{x - a}$$

In Ada, all assignment statements must be written in a linear form; consequently, parentheses are often needed to enclose the numerator and the denominator, and to clearly indicate the order of evaluation of the operators in the expression. The formula above would be written as

```
M := (Y - B) / (X - A);
```

■ Example 7.7

This example illustrates how several mathematical formulas can be written in Ada. Assume all variables except j are Float.

Mathematical Formula	Ada Expression
1. $b^2 - 4ac$	B ** 2 - 4.0 * A * C
2. $a + b - c$	A + B - C
3. $\dfrac{a + b}{c + d}$	(A + B) / (C + D)

Mathematical Formula	Ada Expression
4. $\dfrac{1}{1 + a^2}$	`1.0 / (1.0 + A ** 2)`
5. $a \times -(b + c)$	`A * (-(B + C))`
6. x^j	`X ** J`

■

The points illustrated are summarized as follows:

- Always specify multiplication explicitly by using the operator * where needed (1).
- Use parentheses to control the order of operator evaluation (3, 4).
- Never write two arithmetic operators in succession; they must be separated by an operand or parentheses (5).
- Never mix operand types in an expression (1, 4; note the floating-point constants there). The only exception is the exponentiation operator ** whose right operand must be `Integer` even if its left operand is `Float`. Thus the exponentiation in (1), (4), and (6) is correct.

■ Example 7.8

This example shows the use of the monadic operator `ABS`, which computes the absolute value of its operand. If the value of X is -3.5, the statement

```
Y := 5.7 + ABS(X + 0.5);
```

assigns a value of 8.7 to the `Float` variable Y. The execution of this statement is traced below.

1. The expression argument (X + 0.5) is evaluated as -3.0.
2. The `ABS` operator returns the absolute value of its operand (3.0).
3. The sum of 5.7 and the function result (3.0) are assigned to Y (8.7). ■

Assignment Compatibility

An expression involving floating-point operands can be assigned to a variable only of type `Float` (or a subtype thereof). An expression involving integer operands can be assigned to a variable of type `Integer` (or a subtype thereof). As discussed in Section 5.5, an attempt to assign a value of the wrong type to a variable will result in a compilation error; an attempt to assign an out-of-range value to a variable (e.g., a negative expression result to a `Positive` variable) will result in `Constraint_Error` being raised.

Conversions among Numeric Types

Ada does not allow mixing types in an expression (except in the case of exponentiation, as discussed above). However, Ada does provide a means for performing *explicit conversion* of a value of one type into a value of another. Specifically, Ada allows explicit conversion of float values to integer values and vice versa. This is done using a function-call syntax, where the name of the new type is used as the function. The result of this "function call" is of the new type, unless the result is out of range, in which case `Constraint_Error` is raised as usual.

An integer value always has an exact equivalent in floating-point form, but a floating-point value does not always have an exact integer equivalent. Ada therefore *rounds* such a conversion to the nearest integer value. Suppose we have the following declarations:

```
F: Float;
N: NonNegFloat;
I: Integer;
P: Positive;
T: Natural;
```

Here are some conversions that can be done:

```
F := Float(I);       -- always possible
N := Float(P);       -- always possible
I := Integer(F);     -- always possible; result is rounded
I := Integer(N);     -- always possible, result is rounded

N := NonNegFloat(I); -- raises Constraint_Error if I is negative
T := Natural(F);     -- raises Constraint_Error if F is negative

I := Integer(5.49);  -- result is 5
I := Integer(5.51);  -- result is 6
I := Integer(5.5);   -- result may be 5 or 6, depending on compiler
```

Conversion between two subtypes of `Integer` or two subtypes of `Float` is always possible and will succeed if the result is in range. If `I` happens to be −57, for example, then

```
T := Natural(I);
```

will raise `Constraint_Error`.

■ Example 7.9

If `NumItems` is type `Positive` and `SumOfItems` is type `Float`, the expression

```
SumOfItems / Float(NumItems)
```

divides the value of `SumOfItems` by the floating point equivalent of `NumItems`. This expression is used in the assignment statement below to store the "average value" in `Average`:

```
Average := SumOfItems / Float(NumItems);
```

Note that the expression

```
SumOfItems / NumItems
```

is invalid because the types in the expression do not agree.   ■

Explicit Type Conversion

We now know that Ada allows type conversion to be done explicitly so that floating-point and integer values can be combined in an expression. It is advisable to do this only when it is really necessary. Overuse of such conversions—in the most extreme case, to do all arithmetic in floating point—makes a program much more difficult to understand and also robs you of the assistance you get from Ada in ensuring that appropriate values and operations are used. An occasional explicit conversion—for example, as in the averaging case above—is beneficial, but as in so many other things, moderation is a virtue.

Fixed-Point Types: Type Duration

In addition to the integer and floating-point types we use so much, Ada provides a third kind of numeric type, the *fixed-point type*. We do not make much use of fixed-point types in this book, but one particular predefined fixed-point type is important. Type `Duration` is a fixed-point predefined type and is used by package `Calendar`. Whereas `Calendar.Time` represents *time of day* ("what time is it now?"), `Duration` represents *elapsed time* ("how long before the train leaves?"). A duration value of 1.0 represents the passage of exactly one second; a value of 0.1 represents the passage of a tenth of a second. Package `Calendar` provides a subtype of `Duration` called `Day_Duration` as follows:

```
SUBTYPE Day_Duration IS Duration RANGE 0.0 .. 86_400.0;
```

whose range is chosen to span exactly one day, because 86,400 is the number of seconds in 24 hours. Package `Calendar` also provides a function to retrieve, from a value of type `Calendar.Time`, the number of seconds since midnight on the given day:

```
FUNCTION Seconds (T: Time) RETURN Day_Duration;
```

This function goes along with the `Year`, `Month`, and `Day` functions we used in Section 3.6. All you need to know about `Duration` and `Day_Duration` values is that they are much easier to work with if they are first converted to type `Float`.

■ Example 7.10

Program 7.2 displays the time of day in `hh:mm:ss` form, using European or military 24-hour time. This program uses package `Calendar` to find the time of day. Recall that `Calendar.Clock` returns a value of type `Calendar.Time`. The statement

```
CurrentTime := Calendar.Clock;
```

finds the value of current date/time; the statement

```
SecsPastMidnight := Calendar.Seconds(CurrentTime);
```

extracts the value of seconds since midnight. To work with this, we shall convert it to Float (it's hard to do arithmetic with Duration values), then divide by 60.0 to find the number of minutes past midnight. Because this must be rounded to the next *lower* integer (why?), we subtract 0.5 before converting to Natural:

```
MinsPastMidnight := Natural(Float(SecsPastMidnight)/60.0 - 0.5);
```

We now need to find the hours, minutes, and seconds in the current time. We can find the number of seconds by finding the difference between Secs-PastMidnight and 60 times the number of minutes past midnight. The number of minutes and hours are then easily computed:

```
Secs :=
    Natural(Float(SecsPastMidnight) - 60.0 * Float(MinsPastMidnight));
Mins := MinsPastMidnight REM 60;
Hrs := MinsPastMidnight / 60;
```

As an example of this seemingly complicated calculation, suppose that the current time is 11:55:20 P.M. Knowing that an hour has 3600 seconds and a minute 60, we can easily calculate the value that Calendar.Seconds returns, the number of seconds past midnight, as

$$(3600 \times 23) + (60 \times 55) + 20 = 82800 + 3300 + 20 = 86120$$

We now have to go back the other way, extracting hours, minutes, and seconds. The number of minutes past midnight is

```
Natural((86120.0 / 60.0) - 0.5) = Natural(1434.8) = 1435
```

The number of seconds in the current time is

```
Natural(86120.0 - (60.0 * 1435.0)) = Natural(86120.0-86100.0) = 20
```

The number of hours in the current time is (remember, integer division!)

```
1434 / 60 = 23
```

and the number of minutes is

```
1434 REM 60 = 55
```

You might be wondering why we did not just convert the Seconds value to Natural and do all the arithmetic with integer operations. This is because in some Ada compilers, Integer'Last is 32767, and Seconds values greater than that (such as the value 86120 in our example) would raise Constraint_Error. The program would display the correct time early in the morning, but not late in the afternoon! ∎

Program 7.2 Displaying the Current Time

```
WITH Text_IO;
WITH My_Int_IO;
WITH Calendar;
PROCEDURE TimeOfDay IS

-- displays the current time of day in hh:mm:ss form,
-- using the 24-hour clock. Current time is gotten from Calendar.Clock
```

```
CurrentTime       :  Calendar.Time;
SecsPastMidnight  :  Calendar.Day_Duration;
MinsPastMidnight  :  Natural;
Secs  :              Natural;
Mins  :              Natural;
Hrs   :              Natural;

BEGIN -- TimeOfDay

   CurrentTime := Calendar.Clock;
   SecsPastMidnight := Calendar.Seconds(CurrentTime);
   MinsPastMidnight := Natural(Float(SecsPastMidnight)/60.0 - 0.5);

   Secs :=
      Natural(Float(SecsPastMidnight) - (60.0 * Float(MinsPastMidnight)));
   Mins :=             MinsPastMidnight REM 60;
   Hrs  :=             MinsPastMidnight / 60;

   Text_IO.Put("The current time is ");
   My_Int_IO.Put (Item => Hrs, Width => 1);
   Text_IO.Put (Item => ':');

   IF Mins < 10 THEN
      Text_IO.Put (Item => '0');
   END IF;
   My_Int_IO.Put (Item => Mins, Width => 1);
   Text_IO.Put (Item => ':');

   IF Secs < 10 THEN
      Text_IO.Put (Item => '0');
   END IF;
   My_Int_IO.Put (Item => Secs, Width => 1);
   Text_IO.New_Line;

END TimeOfDay;


The current time is 14:09:22
```

Exercises for Section 7.2

Self-Check

1. Suppose we have the following declarations:

```
F: Float;
N: NonNegFloat;
I: Integer;
T: Natural;
```

and that F is −3.7, and I is −5. Describe the result of each of the following assignment statements.

```
F := Float(I);
I := Integer(F);
I := Integer(N);

N := NonNegFloat(I);
T := Natural(F);
```

```
I := Integer(6.2);
I := Integer(100.88);
I := Integer(9.5);
```

2. Suppose we called `Calendar.Clock` and converted the result to `Integer`. At what time of day would it make a difference whether the maximum value of `Integer` is 32767 or something larger?

7.3 System Structures: Using an External Math Library; the USE Clause

Mathematical functions such as square root, cosine, and exponential are not considered to be a standard part of Ada, and no predefined part of the language provides them. However, most compilers supply a package to do these important operations. The name of this package is not always the same: It may be called `Math_Library`, or `Floating_Point_Math`, or some such name. In this book, we assume that the library is called `Math`; therefore programs using it will include a context clause

```
WITH Math;
```

There is also some variation as to just which functions are included, but it is safe to assume that at least the following functions are provided:

Function	Purpose
Arctan(X)	Returns the angle y in radians satisfying $X = \tan(y)$ where $-\pi/2 <= y <= \pi/2$.
Cos(X)	Returns the cosine of angle X (in radians).
Exp(X)	Returns e^X where $e = 2.71828. \ldots$
Ln(X)	Returns the natural logarithm of X for $X > 0.0$.
Sin(X)	Returns the sine of angle X (in radians).
Sqrt(X)	Returns the square root of X for $X >= 0.0$.

All functions take arguments of type `Float` (or a subtype thereof) and return a value of type `Float`. The arguments for `Ln` and `Sqrt` must be positive. The arguments for `Sin` and `Cos` must be expressed in radians, not degrees.

■ Example 7.11

Program 7.3 displays the square roots of the first 20 positive integers. Notice that the variable `Number` is used as the loop counter, and that its value must be converted to `Float` before it can be used as an argument to `Sqrt`. ■

Program 7.3 Finding Square Roots Using a Math Package
___

```
WITH Text_IO;
WITH My_Int_IO;
```

275

7.3 System
Structures: Using an
External Math
Library; the USE
Clause

```
WITH My_Flt_IO;
WITH Math;
PROCEDURE SquareRoots IS

  -- Illustrates the square root function provided by Math

  MaxNumber : CONSTANT Positive := 20;

BEGIN -- SquareRoots

  Text_IO.Put (Item => "Number Square Root");
  Text_IO.New_Line;
  Text_IO.Put (Item => "------   -----------");
  Text_IO.New_Line;

  FOR Number IN 1..MaxNumber LOOP
    My_Int_IO.Put (Item => Number, Width => 3);
    My_Flt_IO.Put (Item => Math.Sqrt (Float(Number)),
                   Fore => 7, Aft => 5, Exp => 0);
    Text_IO.New_Line;
  END LOOP;

END SquareRoots;
```

Number	Square Root
1	1.00000
2	1.41421
3	1.73205
4	2.00000
5	2.23607
6	2.44949
7	2.64575
8	2.82843
9	3.00000
10	3.16228
11	3.31662
12	3.46410
13	3.60555
14	3.74166
15	3.87298
16	4.00000
17	4.12311
18	4.24264
19	4.35890
20	4.47214

■ Example 7.12

The predefined exponentiation operator in Ada does not apply to floating-point exponents. This means that it is not possible to write x^y directly when x and y are type Float. Some, but not all, math packages provide such an exponentiation operation. However, from the study of logarithms we know that

$$\ln(x^y) = y \times \ln(x)$$

and

$$z = e^{\ln(z)}$$

where e is 2.71828. . . . So we can derive that

$$x^y = e^{(y \times \ln(x))}$$

Assuming that `Exp` and `Ln` are available in `Math`, this formula can be implemented in Ada as

```
XToPowerY := Math.Exp(y * Math.Ln(x))
```
■

The USE Clause

In this book we have been faithful to the convention that all calls to package-provided procedures and functions be prefixed with the name of the package, as in

```
Text_IO.New_Line;
My_Int_IO.Get (Item => Next_Num);
Y := Math.Sqrt (X);
```

Prefixing the name of the package is called *qualification*. There are two main advantages to doing this. First, the reader can tell at a glance exactly which package has provided a given operation. Even in a class project there may be several packages "WITH-ed" by a program, including standard Ada packages, compiler-provided packages like `Math`, and packages you write yourself or are supplied by your teacher. Qualification makes it easy to see, for debugging purposes or for enhancing your program at a later date, just which operations came from which packages. We will discuss the second advantage in a moment.

Ada provides a method for avoiding the need to qualify all references to package-provided operations. This is called the USE clause, looks just like a context clause, and (in this book) is written at the top of a program unit along with the context clause. For example,

```
WITH Math; USE Math;
```

might appear at the top of a program. If a USE clause is present, qualifying the package references is no longer required, although it is certainly still permitted. The two statements

```
Y := Math.Sqrt(X);
Y := Sqrt(X);
```

are both permitted and have the same meaning. An advantage of the USE clause is that expressions can be somewhat more compactly written, but of course the information is lost to the reader as to just which package provided the `Sqrt` operation. An advantage of the USE in the particular case of a package whose *name* varies from compiler to compiler, is that moving a program to a different compiler requires changing only a single mention of the package name in the USE clause, instead of changing every occurrence of the name throughout the program.

This direct information about which package provides which operation is also lost to the compiler if a USE clause is present. This means that the compiler, in translating an unqualified reference to a package operation, must search its tables for *all* the packages mentioned by USE clauses, and this is a tedious and somewhat time-consuming task for the compiler. This is the second advantage of qualified reference: It makes the compiler's job a bit easier.

The Proper Use of USE Clauses

As we have seen, a USE clause has certain advantages, but qualification of all references also has advantages. Many experienced Ada professionals believe that the advantages of qualification outweigh those of USE clauses, and we tend to agree. Generally we will avoid USE clauses, continuing the style with which we have begun the book.

There are certain circumstances, such as the math library, in which the names of the operations are so obvious, and relate so closely to everyday mathematics, that the more compact expression notation is desirable, and in such cases we will write a USE clause. We will also write a USE clause in cases where the name of the package is not standard and may vary from compiler to compiler.

As in the case of type conversions, moderation is a virtue in the use of USE clauses, and we advocate careful, case-by-case consideration of whether the USE or the qualified reference is more advantageous.

■ Example 7.13

The function Sqrt (square root) can be used to compute the roots of a quadratic equation in X of the form

$$aX^2 + bX + c = 0$$

where a, b, and c are type Float. The two roots are expressed in algebraic form as

$$Root_1 = \frac{-b + \sqrt{b^2 - 4ac}}{2a}, \qquad Root_2 = \frac{-b - \sqrt{b^2 - 4ac}}{2a}$$

The Ada implementation is

```
IF Disc > 0.0 THEN
   Root1 := (-b + Sqrt(Disc)) / (2.0 * a);
   Root2 := (-b - Sqrt(Disc)) / (2.0 * a);
END IF;
```

where the variable Disc represents the *discriminant* ($b^2 - 4ac$) of the equation.

■

■ Example 7.14

Program 7.4 draws a sine curve. It uses the Ada function Sin, provided by the math package Math, which returns the trigonometric sine of its parameter, an angle expressed in radians. Because degrees are a more intuitive way to represent angles, the outer FOR loop is executed for values of Angle equal to 0, 18,

36, . . . , 360 degrees. This requires a conversion to radians in order to give Sin a sensible parameter value. For each Angle, the first assignment statement below

```
Radian := Angle * RadPerDegree;
Pad := Natural(Scale * (1.0 + Sin(Radian)));
```

computes the number of radians corresponding to Angle. Then the variable Pad is assigned a value based on Sin(Radian). This value increases from 0 when Sin(Radian) is −1.0 to twice the value of Scale when Sin(Radian) is 1.0. Pad, the limit variable in the inner FOR loop, determines how many blanks precede each character '*' displayed on the screen. In this way, the position of each '*' displayed represents the sine of the current angle. The angle is displayed at the left end of each line; the sine value is also displayed as a floating-point number after each '*'. ∎

Program 7.4 Plotting a Sine Curve Using a Math Package

```
WITH Text_IO;
WITH My_Flt_IO;
WITH Math; USE Math;
PROCEDURE SineCurve IS

-- Plots a sine curve.

  Pi :            CONSTANT Float   := 3.14159;     -- constant Pi
  RadPerDegree :  CONSTANT Float   := Pi / 180.0;  -- radians per degree
  MinAngle :      CONSTANT Float   := 0.0;         -- smallest angle
  MaxAngle :      CONSTANT Float   := 360.0;       -- largest angle
  PlotWidth :     CONSTANT Integer := 40;          -- width of plot
  PlotHeight :    CONSTANT Integer := 20;          -- height of plot
  StepAngle :     CONSTANT Float := (MaxAngle-MinAngle) / Float(PlotHeight);
                                                   -- change in angle
  Star :          CONSTANT Character := '*';       -- symbol being plotted
  Blank :         CONSTANT Character := ' ';       -- blank symbol

  SUBTYPE ColumnRange IS Integer RANGE 0..PlotWidth;

  Angle :         Float;                           -- angle in degrees
  Radian :        Float;                           -- angle in radians
  Scale :         Float;                           -- scale factor
  Pad :           ColumnRange;                     -- size of blank padding

BEGIN -- SineCurve

  Text_IO.Put(Item => "                    Sine curve plot");
  Text_IO.New_Line(2);
  Scale := Float(PlotWidth / 2);
  Angle := MinAngle;

  WHILE Angle <= MaxAngle LOOP

    Radian := Angle * RadPerDegree;
    Pad := Natural(Scale * (1.0 + Sin(Radian)));

    My_Flt_IO.Put(Item =>Angle, Fore => 4, Aft => 0, Exp => 0);
```

279

7.3 System
Structures: Using an
External Math
Library; the USE
Clause

```
-- Display blank padding
Text_IO.Put(Item => Blank);
FOR BlankCount IN 1 .. Pad LOOP
  Text_IO.Put(Item => Blank);
END LOOP;

Text_IO.Put(Item => Star);                    -- Plot * in next column
Text_IO.Put(Item => "          ");
My_Flt_IO.Put(Item =>Sin(Radian), Fore => 1, Aft => 6, Exp => 0);
Text_IO.New_Line;
Angle := Angle + StepAngle;

END LOOP;

END SineCurve;
```

```
                    Sine curve plot

   0.0                       *          0.000000
  18.0                     *              0.309017
  36.0                       *              0.587785
  54.0                         *              0.809017
  72.0                           *              0.951056
  90.0                           *              1.000006
 108.0                           *              0.951057
 126.0                         *              0.809018
 144.0                       *              0.587787
 162.0                     *              0.309019
 180.0                   *          0.000003
 198.0               *          -0.309014
 216.0             *          -0.587783
 234.0           *          -0.809015
 252.0       *          -0.951055
 270.0  *          -1.000005
 288.0  *          -0.951058
 306.0       *          -0.809020
 324.0           *          -0.587789
 342.0               *          -0.309022
 360.0                   *          -0.000005
```

Checking Boundary Values

Example 7.14 states that the value of Pad ranges from 0 to twice Scale as the sine value goes from -1.0 to 1.0. It is always a good idea to check the accuracy of these assumptions; this usually can be done by checking the boundaries of the range as shown below.

```
Sin(Radian) is -1.0, Pad is Natural(Scale * (1.0 + (-1.0)))
Pad is Natural(20.0 * 0.0)
Pad is Natural(0.0) = 0

Sin(Radian) is +1.0, Pad is Natural(Scale * (1.0 + 1.0))
Pad is Natural(20.0 * 2.0)
Pad is Natural(40.0) = 40
```

It is also a good idea to check the boundary values for all loop control variables to see that they make sense. For example, the outer loop control variable, `Angle`, has an initial value of `MinAngle` (`0.0`) and a final value of `MaxAngle` (`360.0`). The inner loop control variable, `BlankCount`, has an initial value of 1 and a final value of `Pad`.

◆ Case Study: Approximating the Value of *e*

Problem

A number of mathematical quantities can be represented using a series approximation, where a series is represented by a summation of an infinite number of terms. For example, the base of the natural logarithms, *e* (whose value is 2.71828. . .), can be determined by evaluating the expression

$$1 + 1/1! + 1/2! + 1/3! + \cdots + 1/n! + \cdots$$

where *n*! is the factorial of *n* as defined below:

$$0! = 1$$
$$n! = n \times (n - 1)! \qquad \text{for } n >= 1$$

Notice that this is just a different, equivalent, way of defining the same `Factorial` that we defined in Section 5.7. Instead of calculating the factorial for each term in the series, we shall use a different method as outlined below.

Analysis

We can get an approximation to the value of *e* by summing the series for a finite value of n. Obviously, the larger the value of n we use, the more accurate will be the computed result. This expression can be represented using *summation notation* as

$$\sum_{i=0}^{n} 1/i!$$

where the first term is obtained by substituting 0 for *i* (1/0! is 1/1), the second term is obtained by substituting 1 for *i* (1/1!), and so on.

Design

A counting loop can be used to implement the formula above easily. The data requirements and algorithm follow.

Data Requirements

Problem Inputs
the number of terms, *n*, in the sum (n : `Positive`)

Problem Outputs
the approximate value of *e* (e: `Float`)

Case Study: Approximating the Value of e, *continued*

281

7.3 System
Structures: Using an
External Math
Library; the USE
Clause

Program Variable
the *i*th term of the series (ithTerm : Float)

Algorithm

1. Read in the value of n
2. Initialize e to 1.0
3. Initialize the *i*th term to 1.0
4. FOR each *i* from 1 to n LOOP
   5. Compute the *i*th term in the series
   6. Add the *i*th term to e
   END LOOP;
7. Display the approximate value of e

Coding

Program 7.5 implements this algorithm. Inside the FOR loop, the statement

```
ithTerm := ithTerm / Float(i);
```

computes the value of the ith term in the series by dividing the previous term by the type Float representation of the loop control variable i. The formula

$$(1 / (i - 1)!) / i = 1 / (i \times (i - 1)!) = 1 / i!$$

shows that this division does indeed produce the next term in the series. Because 0! is 1, ithTerm must be intialized to 1.0. The statement

```
e = e + ithTerm;
```

adds the new value of ithTerm to the sum being accumulated in e. Trace the execution of this loop to satisfy yourself that ithTerm takes on the values 1/1!, 1/2!, 1/3!, and so on, during successive loop iterations.

Program 7.5 Approximating the Value of *e*.

```
WITH Text_IO;
WITH My_Int_IO;
WITH My_Flt_IO;
PROCEDURE eSeries IS

-- Computes the value of e by a series approximation.

   e :        Float;     -- the value being approximated
   ithTerm : Float;      -- ith term in series
   n :        Positive;  -- number of terms in series

BEGIN -- eSeries

   Text_IO.Put(Item => "Enter the number of terms in the series > ");
   My_Int_IO.Get(Item => n);
```

```
-- Compute each term and add it to the accumulating sum.
e := 1.0;                  -- initial sum
ithTerm := 1.0;            -- first term
FOR i IN 1 .. n LOOP
  ithTerm := ithTerm / Float(i);
  e := e + ithTerm;
END LOOP;

-- Print the result.
Text_IO.Put (Item => "The approximate value of e is ");
My_Flt_IO.Put (Item => e, Fore => 1, Aft => 10, Exp => 0);
Text_IO.New_Line;

END eSeries;


Enter the number of terms in the series > 6
The approximate value of e is 2.7180555556
```

Numerical Inaccuracies

One of the problems in processing floating-point numbers is that there is sometimes an error in representing floating-point data. Just as there are certain numbers that cannot be represented exactly in the decimal number system (e.g., the fraction 1/3 is 0.333333...), so there are numbers that cannot be represented exactly in floating-point form. The *representational error* will depend on the number of binary digits (bits) used in the mantissa: The more bits there are, the smaller the error.

The number 0.1 is an example of a real number that has a representational error. The effect of a small error is often magnified through repeated computations. Therefore, the result of adding 0.1 ten times is not exactly 1.0, so the loop below may fail to terminate on some computers.

```
Trial := 0.0;
WHILE Trial /= 1.0 LOOP
    . . .
    Trial := Trial + 0.1;
END LOOP;
```

If the loop repetition test is changed to Trial < 1.0, the loop may execute ten times on one computer and eleven times on another. For this reason, it is best to use integer values—which are always exact—whenever possible in loop repetition tests.

Other problems occur when manipulating very large and very small real numbers. In adding a large number and a small number, the larger number may "cancel out" the smaller number (a *cancellation error*). If X is much larger than Y, then X + Y and X may have the same value (e.g., 1000.0 + 0.0001234 is equal to 1000.0 on some computers).

For this reason, you can sometimes obtain more accurate results by carefully

283

7.3 System
Structures: Using an
External Math
Library; the USE
Clause

selecting the order in which computations are performed. For example, in computing the value of e in the preceding case study, the terms of the series

$$1 + 1/1! + 1/2! + \cdots + 1/n!$$

were generated in left-to-right order and added to a sum being accumulated in e. When n is large, the value of $1/n!$ is very small, so the effect of adding a very small term to a sum that is larger than 2.0 may be lost. If the terms were generated and summed in right-to-left order instead, the computation result might be more accurate.

If two very small numbers are multiplied, the result may be too small to be represented accurately and will become zero. This is called *arithmetic underflow*. Similarly, if two very large numbers are multiplied, the result may be too large to be represented. This is called *arithmetic overflow* and, in Ada, causes Numeric _Error to be raised. Arithmetic underflow and overflow can also occur when processing very large and small integer values.

Exercises for Section 7.3

Self-Check

1. Find out the name of the math library available on your Ada system. List the basic functions available in that library.
2. Rewrite the following mathematical expressions using Ada math functions.
   a. $\sqrt{U + V} \times W^2$
   b. $\log_n (X^Y)$
   c. $\sqrt{X - Y^2}$
   d. $| XY - W/Z |$

3. Evaluate the following expression:

   ```
   Sqrt(ABS(Integer(-15.8)))
   ```

Programming

1. Write a function that computes, for float numbers a and b, $e^{a \times \ln(b)}$. Call this function with several different values of a and b and display the results. Verify for yourself that the results are correct.
2. Using type conversion, write an Ada statement to round any float value X to the nearest two decimal places. (*Hint:* You have to multiply by 100.0 before rounding.)
3. The value of e^x is represented by the series

   $$1 + x + x^2/2! + x^3/3! + \cdots + x^n/n! + \cdots$$

   Write a program to compute and print the value of this series for any x and any n. Compare the result to Exp(x) (Exp should be available in your math library) and print a message O.K. or Not O.K., depending on whether the difference between these results exceeds 0.001. How many terms—that is, what value of n—seems to provide good results without making the computation take too many steps?

7.4 Data Structures: The Boolean Type

We introduced the Boolean data type in Chapter 4. We have used Boolean expressions (expressions that evaluate to True or False) to control loop repetition and to select one of the alternatives in an IF statement. Some examples of Boolean expressions are

```
Gross > TaxBracket
Item /= Sentinel
TranType = 'C'
```

Boolean is one of Ada's predefined types; in fact, it is an enumeration type, defined as

```
TYPE Boolean IS (False, True);
```

The simplest Boolean expression is a Boolean variable or constant. A Boolean variable or constant can be set to either of the Boolean values, False or True. The statement

```
Debug : CONSTANT Boolean := True;
```

specifies that the Boolean constant Debug has the value True; the declarations

```
Switch : Boolean;
Flag : Boolean;
```

declare Switch and Flag to be Boolean variables, that is, variables that can be assigned only the values True and False.

Boolean Operators

A Boolean variable or constant is the simplest form of a Boolean expression (e.g., Switch). We have used the relational operators (=, <, >, etc.) with numeric data to form conditions or Boolean expressions (e.g., Salary < Minsal).

There are four Boolean operators: AND, OR, XOR, and NOT. These operators are used with operands that are Boolean expressions:

```
(Salary < Minsal) OR (NumDepend > 5)
(Temp > 90.0) AND (Humidity > 0.90)
Athlete AND (NOT Failing)
Married XOR CollegeGraduate
```

The first expression can be used to determine whether an employee pays income tax. It evaluates to true if either condition in parentheses is true. The second expression can be used to describe an unbearable summer day: temperature and humidity both above 90. The expression evaluates to true only when both conditions are true. The third expression has two Boolean variables (Athlete and Failing) as its operands. Any individual for whom this expression is true is eligible for intercollegiate sports. The fourth expression evaluates to true if the individual is *either* married *or* a college graduate, but *not both*. It might be useful to a public opinion pollster.

The `Boolean` operators can be used with `Boolean` expressions only. The `Boolean` operators are summarized in Table 7.4, which shows that the `AND` operator yields a true result only when both its operands are true, that the `OR` operator yields a false result only when both its operands are false, and that the `XOR` operator yields a true result only when exactly one of its operands is true. The `NOT` operator has a single operand and yields the *logical complement*, or negation, of its operand.

Table 7.4 Boolean Operators

op1	op2	NOT op1	op1 AND op2	op1 OR op2	op1 XOR op2
false	false	true	false	false	false
false	true	true	false	true	true
true	false	false	false	true	true
true	true	false	true	true	false

Operator Precedence

The precedence of an operator determines its order of evaluation. Table 7.5 shows the precedence of all operators that can occur in an Ada expression.

Table 7.5 Operator Precedence

Operator	Precedence
`**`, `NOT`, `ABS`	highest (evaluated first)
`*`, `/`, `REM`, `MOD`	multiplying operators
`+`, `−`	monadic adding operators
`+`, `−`, `&`	dyadic adding operators (& is concatenation; we will discuss it in Chapter 8)
`<`, `<=`, `=`, `/=`, `>=`, `>`	relational operators
`AND`, `OR`, `XOR`	dyadic logical operators (evaluated last)

■ Example 7.15

The expression

```
X < Y + Z
```

involving the float variables X, Y, and Z is interpreted as

```
X < (Y + Z)
```

because + has higher precedence than <. The expression

```
X < Y OR Z < Y
```

is interpreted as

```
(X < Y) OR (Z < Y)
```

because OR has lower precedence than <. The expression

```
NOT Sunny OR Warm
```

is interpreted as

```
(NOT Sunny) OR Warm
```

because NOT has higher precedence than OR.

As is clear from Table 7.5 and Example 7.15, Ada has many operators, and their relative precedences are often difficult to remember. It is therefore advisable to keep expressions relatively simple and to use parentheses to make clear what you mean. ∎

∎ Example 7.16

The following are all legal Boolean expressions if X, Y, and Z are type Float and Flag is type Boolean. The value of each expression is shown in brackets, assuming that X is 3.0, Y is 4.0, Z is 2.0, and Flag is True.

```
1. (X > Z) AND (Y > Z)                    [True]
2. (X + Y / Z) <= 3.5                     [False]
3. (Y > X) XOR (Y > Z)                    [False]
4. NOT Flag                               [False]
5. (X = 1.0) OR (X = 3.0)                 [True]
6. (0.0 < X) AND (X < 3.5)               [True]
7. (X <= Y) AND (Y <= Z)                 [False]
8. NOT Flag OR ((Y + Z) >= (X - Z))      [True]
9. NOT (Flag OR ((Y + Z) >= (X - Z)))    [False]
```

Expression 1 gives the Ada form of the relationship "X and Y are greater than Z." It is often tempting to write this as

```
X AND Y > Z
```

However, this is an illegal Boolean expression because the float variable X cannot be an operand of the Boolean operator AND. Similarly, expression 5 shows the correct way to express the relationship "X is equal to 1.0 or to 3.0." ∎

Expression 6 is the Ada form of the relationship $0.0 < X < 3.5$; that is, "X is in the range 0.0 to 3.5." Similarly, expression 7 shows the Ada form of the relationship $X <= Y <= Z$; that is, "Y is in the range X to Z, inclusive."

Finally, expression 8 is evaluated in Fig. 7.5; the values given at the beginning of this example are shown above the expression. The expression in Fig. 7.5 is rewritten below with parentheses enclosing the term NOT Flag. Although these parentheses are not required, they do clarify the meaning of the expression and we recommend their use:

```
(NOT Flag) OR ((Y + Z) >= (X - Z))
```

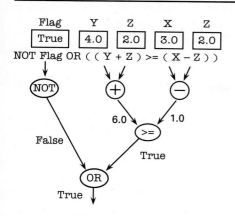

Short-Circuit Boolean Operators

When evaluating Boolean expressions, Ada evaluates both sides of the expression, but in an order not defined by the language. This is not usually a problem; generally we are interested only in the final result of the evaluation. Circumstances do arise, however, when it is desirable to evaluate the right side of an AND only if the left side is true, or the right side of an OR only if the left side is false. Ada provides for this purpose two additional operators, AND THEN and OR ELSE. These are called "short-circuit" operators: The evaluation of the right operand is skipped if evaluating the left operand determines the result of the expression.

■ Example 7.17
Both sides are always evaluated in the expression

```
Flag OR ((Y + Z) /= (X - Z))
```

but in the expression

```
Flag OR ELSE ((Y + Z) /= (X - Z))
```

if the value of Flag is False, then NOT Flag is True, so the expression must evaluate to True regardless of the value of the parenthesized expression following OR (i.e., True OR . . . must always be True). Consequently, the parenthesized expression following OR ELSE is not evaluated when Flag is True. ■

Short-circuit evaluation has important applications. Sometimes it is necessary to omit evaluation of the right operand, lest a run-time error arise.

■ Example 7.18
If *X* is 0, the expression

```
(X /= 0.0) AND (Y / X > 5.0)
```

is False because (X /= 0.0) is False and False AND . . . must always be False. Not only is there no need to evaluate the subexpression (Y / X > 5.0) when X is 0, it is an error to do so: Numeric_Error would be raised because the divisor X is 0. An expression like this must be written

```
(X /= 0.0) AND THEN (Y / X > 5.0)
```

to prevent the right side from being evaluated whenever X is 0. ■

Boolean Assignment Statements

We can write assignment statements that assign a Boolean value to a Boolean variable. The statement

```
Same := X = Y;
```

assigns the value True to the Boolean variable Same when X and Y are equal; otherwise, the value False is assigned. The assignment above has the same effect as the IF statement

```
IF X = Y THEN
    Same := True;
ELSE
    Same := False;
END IF;
```

■ Example 7.19

The assignment statement below assigns the value True to Even if N is an even number:

```
Even := (N REM 2) = 0;
```

This statement assigns a value of True to Even when the remainder of N divided by 2 is 0. (All even numbers are divisible by 2.) ■

Using Boolean Variables as Program Flags

Boolean variables are sometimes used as *program flags* to signal whether or not a special event occurs in a program. The fact that such an event occurs is important to the future execution of the program. A Boolean variable used as a program flag is initialized to one of its two possible values (True or False) and reset to the other as soon as the event being monitored occurs.

■ Example 7.20

In Section 6.8 we developed, for package RobustInput, a procedure for reading an integer value between the values MinVal and MaxVal. That procedure used Ada exception handling to determine whether the input value was in range. Suppose Ada did not have an exception-handling capability (most languages don't). Here is a procedure for reading input within range that has similar behavior but does not use exception handling.

Program 7.6 is a procedure Get that continues to read integer values until a value between its two input parameters, MinVal and MaxVal, is entered. The first data value within range is returned as the procedure result. The Boolean variable Between is used as a program flag to signal whether or not the event "data entry of an integer between MinVal and MaxVal" has occurred. The variable Between is initialized to False before the WHILE loop. Inside the WHILE loop, the assignment statement

```
Between := (N >= MinVal) AND (N <= MaxVal);
```

resets Between to True when a value between MinVal and MaxVal is read into N. The loop is repeated as long as Between is still False. ∎

Program 7.6   Robust Input Without Exception Handling

```
PROCEDURE Get (Item : OUT Integer; MinVal : Integer; MaxVal : Integer) IS

-- Reads an integer between MinVal and MaxVal into Item
-- Pre: MinVal and MaxVal are assigned values.
-- Post: A value between MinVal and MaxVal is read into Item.

  Between : Boolean;    -- program flag -- loop control
  TempN :    Integer;    -- temporary copy to read into

BEGIN -- Get

  -- Keep reading until a valid number is read.
  Between := False;    -- Assume a valid number is not read
  WHILE NOT Between LOOP
    -- invariant:
    --    All prior values of TempN are outside the range MinVal to MaxVal

    Text_IO.Put(Item => "Enter an integer between ");
    My_Int_IO.Put(Item => MinVal, Width => 0);
    Text_IO.Put(Item => " and ");
    My_Int_IO.Put(Item => MaxVal, Width => 0);
    Text_IO.Put(Item => " > ");
    My_Int_IO.Get(Item => TempN);
    Between := (TempN >= MinVal) AND (TempN <= MaxVal);

  END LOOP;
  -- assert: TempN is in the range MinVal to MaxVal

  Item := TempN;

END Get;
```

Reading and Displaying Boolean Values

It is easy to read and display Boolean values in Ada, because Boolean is an enumeration type. All that is necessary is to create an instance of the generic Text_IO.Enumeration_IO to handle the job. Because Boolean is a commonly used predefined type, this instance can be created once and for all in your Ada program library, just as My_Int_IO and My_Flt_IO were created. The lines

```
WITH Text_IO;
PACKAGE Boolean_IO IS NEW Text_IO.Enumeration_IO (Enum => Boolean);
```

are all it takes. You can then supply a context clause

```
WITH Boolean_IO;
```

to use the Get and Put operations for Boolean values.

■ Example 7.21

Two well known laws of logic are called DeMorgan's laws after their discoverer. These two laws state that, for two Boolean variables X and Y, for any combination of values of X and Y,

```
NOT(X OR Y)  = (NOT X) AND (NOT Y)
NOT(X AND Y) = (NOT X) OR  (NOT Y)
```
■

Program 7.7 illustrates the validity of these laws, the use of a Boolean flag to control an input loop, and also the use of Boolean_IO. Program 7.7 prompts the user for values for Boolean variables X and Y. These values must be entered as any enumeration values would, as True or False (the case of the letters does not matter). The sample run shows, by evaluating the four Boolean expressions above, that DeMorgan's laws are true for all combinations of values.

Program 7.7   Demonstration of DeMorgan's Laws and Boolean_IO.

```
WITH Text_IO;
WITH Boolean_IO;
PROCEDURE ShowDeMorgan IS

  -- demonstrates the validity of DeMorgan's Laws, and also Boolean_IO
  -- a Boolean flag is also used to control the input loop

  X          : Boolean;
  Y          : Boolean;
  MoreInput  : Boolean;

BEGIN -- ShowDeMorgan

  MoreInput := True;
  WHILE MoreInput LOOP

    Text_IO.Put(Item => "Please enter True or False value for X > ");
    Boolean_IO.Get (Item => X);
    Text_IO.Put(Item => "Please enter True or False value for Y > ");
    Boolean_IO.Get (Item => Y);

    Text_IO.Put("NOT(X OR Y)        = ");
    Boolean_IO.Put(Item => NOT(X OR Y), Width => 1);
    Text_IO.New_Line;

    Text_IO.Put("(NOT X) AND (NOT Y) = ");
    Boolean_IO.Put(Item => (NOT X) AND (NOT Y), Width => 1);
    Text_IO.New_Line;
    Text_IO.New_Line;
```

```
    Text_IO.Put("NOT(X AND Y)        = ");
    Boolean_IO.Put(Item => NOT(X AND Y), Width => 1);
    Text_IO.New_Line;

    Text_IO.Put("(NOT X) OR (NOT Y)  = ");
    Boolean_IO.Put(Item => (NOT X) OR (NOT Y), Width => 1);
    Text_IO.New_Line;
    Text_IO.New_Line;

    Text_IO.Put(Item=>"Do you wish to try another combination (True/False)? ");
    Boolean_IO.Get (Item => MoreInput);

  END LOOP;

END ShowDeMorgan;


Please enter True or False value for X > false
Please enter True or False value for Y > false
NOT(X OR Y)         = TRUE
(NOT X) AND (NOT Y) = TRUE

NOT(X AND Y)        = TRUE
(NOT X) OR (NOT Y)  = TRUE

Do you wish to try another combination (True/False)? true
Please enter True or False value for X > false
Please enter True or False value for Y > true
NOT(X OR Y)         = FALSE
(NOT X) AND (NOT Y) = FALSE

NOT(X AND Y)        = TRUE
(NOT X) OR (NOT Y)  = TRUE

Do you wish to try another combination (True/False)? true
Please enter True or False value for X > true
Please enter True or False value for Y > false
NOT(X OR Y)         = FALSE
(NOT X) AND (NOT Y) = FALSE

NOT(X AND Y)        = TRUE
(NOT X) OR (NOT Y)  = TRUE

Do you wish to try another combination (True/False)? true
Please enter True or False value for X > true
Please enter True or False value for Y > true
NOT(X OR Y)         = FALSE
(NOT X) AND (NOT Y) = FALSE

NOT(X AND Y)        = FALSE
(NOT X) OR (NOT Y)  = FALSE

Do you wish to try another combination (True/False)? false
```

Using a Global Boolean Constant for Debugging

We mentioned earlier that the programmer should plan for debugging by
including diagnostic print statements in the original code. One way to prevent

the diagnostic print statements from executing during production runs is to declare a global Boolean constant (say Debugging) whose value is True during debugging and False during production runs. The declaration part of the main program will contain the constant declaration

```
Debugging : CONSTANT Boolean := True; -- turn diagnostics on
```

during debugging runs and the constant declaration

```
Debugging : CONSTANT Boolean := False; -- turn diagnostics off
```

during production runs. The diagnostic print statements below will be executed only when Debugging is True (i.e., during debugging runs).

```
IF Debugging THEN
    Text_IO.Put (Item => "Procedure ProcessGoods entered");
    Text_IO.New_Line;
    Text_IO.Put (Item => "Input parameter Salary is ");
    My_Flt_IO.Put (Item => Salary, Fore => 6, Aft => 2, Exp => 0);
    Text_IO.New_Line;
END IF;
```

Exercises for Section 7.4

Self-Check

1. Draw the evaluation tree for expression 9 of Example 7.16.
2. Write the following Boolean assignment statements:
   a. Assign a value of True to Between if the value of N lies between −K and +K, inclusive; otherwise, assign a value of False.
   b. Assign a value of True to UpCase if Ch is an uppercase letter; otherwise, assign a value of False.
   c. Assign a value of True to Divisor if M is a divisor of N; otherwise, assign a value of False.

Programming

1. Write a function that returns a Boolean value indicating whether or not its first parameter is divisible by its second parameter.

7.5 Data Structures: The Character Type

Ada provides a character data type that can be used for the storage of individual characters. Character variables are declared using the data type Character. A character literal consists of a single printable character (letter, digit, punctuation mark, etc.) enclosed in single quotes. A character value may be assigned to a character variable or associated with a constant identifier as shown below.

```
Star : CONSTANT Character := '*';
NextLetter : Character;
```

```
BEGIN
     NextLetter := 'A';
```

The character variable NextLetter is assigned the character value 'A' by the assignment statement above. A single character variable or literal can appear on the right-hand side of a character assignment statement. Character values can also be compared, read, and displayed.

■ Example 7.22

Program 7.8 reads a sentence ending in a period and counts the number of blanks in the sentence. Each character entered after the prompting message is read into the variable Next and tested to see if it is a blank.

The statement

```
Text_IO.Get (Item => Next);
```

appears twice in the program and is used to read one character at a time from the data line because Next is type Character. The WHILE loop is exited when the last character read is a period. ■

Program 7.8   Counting the Number of Blanks in a Sentence

```
WITH Text_IO;
WITH My_Int_IO;
PROCEDURE BlankCount IS

-- Counts the number of blanks in a sentence.

   Blank    :    CONSTANT Character := ' '; -- character being counted
   Sentinel : CONSTANT Character := '.';-- sentinel character

   Next    : Character;              -- next character in sentence
   Count : Natural;                  -- number of blank characters
BEGIN -- BlankCount

   Count := 0;                       -- Initialize Count
   Text_IO.Put(Item => "Enter a sentence ending with a period.");
   Text_IO.New_Line;

   -- Process each input character up to the period
   Text_IO.Get(Item => Next);        -- Get first character
   Text_IO.Put(Item => Next);
   WHILE Next /= Sentinel LOOP
      -- invariant: Count is the count of blanks so far and
      --    no prior value of Next is the sentinel

      IF Next = Blank THEN
         Count := Count + 1;         -- Increment blank count
      END IF;
      Text_IO.Get(Item => Next);     -- Get next character
      Text_IO.Put(Item => Next);
   END LOOP;
   -- assert: Count is the count of blanks and Next is the sentinel

   Text_IO.New_Line;
```

```
Text_IO.Put(Item => "The number of blanks is ");
My_Int_IO.Put(Item => Count, Width => 1);
Text_IO.New_Line;

END BlankCount;
```

```
Enter a sentence ending with a period.
The quick  brown  fox  jumped  over  the lazy  dogs.
The quick  brown  fox  jumped  over  the lazy  dogs.
The number of blanks is 14
```

Using Relational Operators with Characters

In Program 7.8, the Boolean expressions

```
Next = Blank
Next /= Sentinel
```

are used to determine whether two character variables have the same value or different values. Order comparisons can also be performed on character variables using the relational operators <, <=, >, and >=.

To understand the result of an order comparison, we must know something about the way characters are represented internally. Each character has its own unique numeric code; the binary form of this code is stored in a memory cell that has a character value. These binary numbers are compared by the relational operators in the normal way. The character code that is most prevalent is the American Standard Code for Information Interchange (ASCII) code and is shown as the package ASCII in Appendix C.

The printable characters have codes from 32 (code for blank or space) to 126 (code for symbol ~). The other codes represent nonprintable control characters. Sending a control character to an output device causes the device to perform a special operation such as returning the cursor to column one, advancing the cursor to the next line, ringing a bell, and so on.

Some features of the ASCII code are as follows.

- The digits are an increasing sequence of consecutive characters.

  ```
  '0'<'1'<'2'<'3'<'4'<'5'<'6'<'7'<'8'<'9'
  ```

- The uppercase letters are an increasing sequence of consecutive characters.

  ```
  'A'<'B'<'C'< ... <'X'<'Y'<'Z'
  ```

- The lowercase letters are an increasing sequence of consecutive characters.

  ```
  'a'<'b'<'c'< ... <'x'<'y'<'z'
  ```

- The digit characters precede the uppercase letters; the uppercase letters precede the lowercase letters.

  ```
  '0' < '9' < 'A' < 'Z' < 'a' < 'z'
  ```

■ Example 7.23

Let us write a function specified by

```
FUNCTION Cap (InChar : Character) RETURN Character;
```

If InChar is a lowercase letter, then Cap(InChar) returns the corresponding uppercase letter; otherwise Cap(InChar) just returns InChar unchanged. The function body makes use of the Pos (position) and Val (value) attribute functions as well as the fact that all the uppercase letters are "together" in the type Character, as are all the lowercase letters. If InChar is lowercase, its position relative to 'a' is used to find the value of the corresponding uppercase letter. As an example, if InChar is 'g', its position relative to 'a' is 6 (remember, the positions start with 0). The corresponding uppercase value is the value at the same position relative to 'A', namely, 'G'.

```
FUNCTION Cap (InChar : Character) RETURN Character IS

    Temp : Character;

BEGIN

    IF InChar IN 'a' .. 'z' THEN
        Temp := Character'Val(Character'Pos(Inchar)
              - Character'Pos('a') + Character'Pos('A'));
    ELSE
        Temp := InChar;
    END IF;

    RETURN Temp;

END Cap;
```

■

■ Example 7.24

When you enter or display a token of any kind, you are always entering or displaying sequences of characters, because these are the basic unit of information used by keyboards and display devices. A numeric token—for example, 1257—read by, say, My_Int_IO.Get, cannot be placed in an integer variable directly; the sequence of characters must first be converted to a number—in this case a binary integer. This conversion task is generally done by the input/output routines, often with the help of a system utility program. The important thing to realize is that there is always a *program* taking care of this.

You now have the background to learn how such a conversion program works. Let's consider the simple case of reading a positive integer as a sequence of individual characters instead of using My_Int_IO.Get. This enables the program to detect and ignore input errors. For example, if the program user enters a letter instead of a number, this error will be detected and the program will prompt again for a data value. Similarly, if the program user types in $15,400 instead of the number 15400, the extra characters will be ignored.

Program 7.9 is a procedure GetNaturalToken, which reads in a string of characters ending with the sentinel (%) and ignores any character that is not a digit. It also computes the value of the number (of type Natural) formed by the digits only. For example, if the characters $15,43AB0% are entered, the value returned through NumData will be 15430. The procedure uses a temporary TempNum to hold the result as it is accumulated, because NumData is an OUT parameter, which, under Ada's rules, is "write only" and whose value cannot be used within the procedure.

In Program 7.9, the statements

```
Digit := Character'Pos(Next) - Character'Pos('0'); -- Get digit value
TempNum := Base * TempNum + Digit;                  -- Add digit value
```

assign to Digit an integer value between 0 (for character value '0') and 9 (for character value '9'). The number being accumulated in NumData is multiplied by 10, and the value of Digit is added to it. Table 7.6 traces the procedure execution for the input characters 3N5%; the value returned is 35. ∎

Program 7.9 Reading a Token and Converting to Natural

```
PROCEDURE GetNaturalToken (NumData : OUT Natural) IS

-- Reads consecutive characters ending with the symbol %. Computes
-- the integer value of the digit characters, ignoring non-digits.
-- Pre:  None
-- Post: NumData is the value of the digit characters read.

  Base :       CONSTANT Positive := 10;   -- the number system base
  Sentinel : CONSTANT Character := '%';  -- the sentinel character

  TempNum :    Natural;                    -- to compute the numerical value
  Next :       Character;                  -- each character read
  Digit :      Natural;                    -- the value of each numeric character
                                           -- (its ASCII position)

BEGIN -- GetNaturalToken

  -- Accumulate the numeric value of the digits in TempNum
  TempNum := 0;                            -- initial value is zero
  Text_IO.Get(Item => Next);               -- Read first character
  WHILE Next /= Sentinel LOOP
    -- invariant:
    --    No prior value of Next is the sentinel and
    --    if Next is a digit, TempNum is multiplied by Base and
    --    Next's digit value is added to TempNum

    IF (Next >= '0') AND (Next <= '9') THEN
      -- Process digit
      Digit := Character'Pos(Next) - Character'Pos('0'); -- Get digit value
      TempNum := Base * TempNum + Digit; -- Add digit value
    END IF;
    Text_IO.Get(Item => Next);            -- Read next character
  END LOOP;
  -- assert:
  --    Next is the sentinel and
  --    TempNum is the number in base Base formed from the digit
  --    characters read as data

  NumData := TempNum;

END GetNaturalToken;
```

Statement	Next	Digit	TempNum	Effect of Statement
	?	?	?	
`TempNum:= 0;`			0	Initialize TempNum
`Text_IO.Get(Item=>Next);`	`'3'`			Get Character
`WHILE Next/=Sentinel LOOP`	`'3'`			`'3' /= '%'` is True
`IF Next>='0' AND Next<='9'`	`'3'`			`'3'` is a digit
`Digit:=Character'Pos(Next)`		3		Digit value is 3
`    - Character'Pos('0');`				
`TempNum:=Base*TempNum+Digit;`		3	3	Add 3 to 0
`Text_IO.Get(Item=>Next);`	`'N'`			Get Character
`WHILE Next/=Sentinel LOOP`	`'N'`			`'N' /= '%'` is True
`IF Next>='0' AND Next<='9'`	`'N'`			`'N'` is not a digit
`Text_IO.Get(Item=>Next);`	`'5'`			Get Character
`WHILE Next/=Sentinel LOOP`	`'5'`			`'5' /= '%'` is True
`IF Next>='0' AND Next<='9'`	`'5'`			`'5'` is a digit
`Digit:=Character'Pos(Next)`		5		Digit value is 5
`    - Character'Pos('0');`				
`TempNum:=Base*TempNum+Digit;`		5	35	Add 5 to 30
`Text_IO.Get(Item=>Next);`	`'%'`			Get Character
`WHILE Next/=Sentinel LOOP`	`'%'`			`'%' /= '%'` is False

Representing Control Characters

The ASCII character set includes a number of "nonprintable" characters, which are used for controlling input and output devices. These control characters cannot be represented in programs in the usual way (i.e., by enclosing them in quotes). A control character can be specified in Ada using its position in the `Character` type (see Appendix C). For example, `Character'Val(10)` is the line-feed character, and `Character'Val(7)` is the bell character. The statements

```
Text_IO.Put(Item => Character'Val(10));
Text_IO.Put(Item => Character'Val(7));
Text_IO.Put(Item => Character'Val(7));
```

will cause the output device to perform a line feed and then ring its bell twice.

Ada also has a more intuitive way of representing the control characters. These characters are all given names, by declaring them as character constants in a predefined package `ASCII`. The statements

```
Text_IO.Put(Item => ASCII.LF);
Text_IO.Put(Item => ASCII.Bel);
Text_IO.Put(Item => ASCII.Bel);
```

give the same effect as the statements above, using the names of the characters instead of their numerical values. A program that uses the `ASCII` package must of course be preceded by a context clause

```
WITH ASCII;
```

■ **Example 7.25**

A *collating sequence* is a sequence of characters arranged in the order in which they appear in the ASCII character set. The Character type is really an enumeration type; each character's position in this type corresponds to its ASCII value. Program 7.10 prints part of the Ada collating sequence. It lists the characters with values 32 through 90, inclusive. The sequence shown in the sample run is for the ASCII code; the first character displayed is a blank (position 32). ■

Program 7.10   Display Part of the ASCII Collating Sequence

```
WITH Text_IO;
PROCEDURE Collate IS

-- Displays part of the collating sequence.

  MinPos : CONSTANT Positive := 32; -- smallest ASCII position
  MaxPos : CONSTANT Positive := 90; -- largest ASCII position

BEGIN -- Collate

  -- Display characters Character'Val(32) through Character'Val(90)

  FOR NextPos IN MinPos .. MaxPos LOOP
    Text_IO.Put(Item => Character'Val(NextPos));
  END LOOP;
  Text_IO.New_Line;

END Collate;


  !"#$%&'()*+,-./0123456789:;<=>?@ABCDEFGHIJKLMNOPQRSTUVWXYZ
```

■ **Example 7.26**

In Section 3.7 we introduced the package Screen, which we have used several times since. In Section 3.7 we advised you not to worry about the details of the package body; now, having studied the Character type systematically, you are ready to understand those details. Program 7.11 repeats the package body. The procedure Beep contains a statement,

```
Text_IO.Put (Item => ASCII.BEL);
```

which sends the ASCII bell character to the terminal. Instead of displaying this character, the terminal will beep. Procedure ClearScreen contains the statements,

```
Text_IO.Put (Item => ASCII.ESC);
Text_IO.Put (Item => "[2J");
```

which send four characters to the terminal. According to standard American National Standards Institute (ANSI) terminal control commands, this sequence will cause the screen to be erased. Finally, the procedure MoveCursor contains these lines:

```
Text_IO.Put (Item => ASCII.ESC);
Text_IO.Put (Item => "[" );
My_Int_IO.Put (Item => Row, Width => 1);
Text_IO.Put (Item => ';');
My_Int_IO.Put (Item => Column, Width => 1);
Text_IO.Put (Item => 'f');
```

The sequence of characters sent to the terminal by these statements will cause the cursor to be moved to the given row/column position. Suppose Row is 15. Under these circumstances, sending the integer value Row does not cause the terminal to display the characters 15; rather, because these characters are sent in the middle of a control command (preceded by ASCII.ESC and [), the terminal obeys the command and moves the cursor to row 15. The command must end with 'f'. It may seem strange to you, but that is what the ANSI terminal control standard specifies. As you saw in the examples using the screen package, these commands really do cause the terminal to carry out the desired actions. ■

Program 7.11   Repetition of the Body of Package Screen

```
WITH Text_IO;
WITH My_Int_IO;
PACKAGE BODY Screen IS

-- Procedures for drawing pictures on ANSI Terminal Screen

  PROCEDURE Beep IS
  BEGIN
    Text_IO.Put (Item => ASCII.BEL);
  END Beep;

  PROCEDURE ClearScreen IS
  BEGIN
    Text_IO.Put (Item => ASCII.ESC);
    Text_IO.Put (Item => "[2J");
  END ClearScreen;

  PROCEDURE MoveCursor (Column : Width; Row : Depth) IS
  BEGIN
    Text_IO.Put (Item => ASCII.ESC);
    Text_IO.Put ("[");
    My_Int_IO.Put (Item => Row, Width => 1);
    Text_IO.Put (Item => ';');
    My_Int_IO.Put (Item => Column, Width => 1);
    Text_IO.Put (Item => 'f');
  END MoveCursor;

END Screen;
```

Exercises for Section 7.5

Self-Check

1. Evaluate the following:
   a. `Boolean'Pos(True)`
   b. `Boolean'Pred(True)`
   c. `Boolean'Succ(False)`
   d. `Boolean'Pos(True) - Boolean'Pos(False)`

2. Evaluate the following; assume the letters are consecutive characters.
   a. `Character'Pos('D') - Character'Pos('A')`
   b. `Character'Pos('d') - Character'Pos('a')`
   c. `Character'Succ(Character'Pred('a'))`
   d. `Character'Val(Character'Pos('C'))`
   e. `Character'Val(Character'Pos('C')-`
      `Character'Pos('A')+Character'Pos('a'))`
   f. `Character'Pos('7') - Character'Pos('6')`
   g. `Character'Pos('9') - Character'Pos('0')`
   h. `Character'Succ(Character'Succ(Character'Succ('d')))`
   i. `Character'Val(Character'Pos('A') + 5)`

 # 7.6 Case Study: Testing Whether a Number Is Prime

This case study involves the manipulation of type `Natural` data. It also illustrates the use of `Boolean` variables as program flags.

Problem

Write a program that tests a positive integer to determine whether or not it is a prime number.

Analysis

A *prime number* is an integer that has no divisors other than 1 and itself. Examples of prime numbers are the integers 2, 3, 5, 7, and 11. Our program will either display a message indicating that its data value is a prime number, or it will display the smallest divisor of the number if it is not prime. The data requirements follow.

Data Requirements

Problem Inputs
the number to be tested for a prime number (`N : Positive`)

Problem Outputs
the smallest divisor if N is not prime (`FirstDiv : Positive`)

Design

Initial Algorithm

1. Read in the number to be tested for a prime number.
2. Find the smallest divisor > 1 or determine that the number is prime.
3. Display a message that the number is prime or print its smallest divisor.

We will use the Boolean variable `Prime` as a program flag to indicate the result of step 2 as described below. A structure chart is shown in Fig. 7.6.

Figure 7.6   Structure Chart for Prime-Testing Program

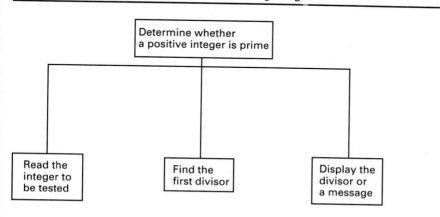

Additional Program Variables

program flag that will be set to `True` if N is prime, `False` otherwise (`Prime : Boolean`)

Step 3 of the algorithm is relatively simple. The refinement for step 3 follows.

Step 3 Refinement

3.1. IF N is prime THEN
      Display a message that N is prime
   ELSE
      Display the first divisor of N
   END IF;

Step 1 is implemented by an invocation of `RobustInput.Get`. Step 2 is performed as described next.

The subtype `SmallPos` includes the positive numbers from 2 to `MaxN` (1000). Variable `FirstDiv` (the first divisor) is type `SmallPos`, and we need to compute the values of `FirstDiv` and `Prime` by determining whether or not N has any divisors other than 1 and itself. If N is an even integer, then it is divisible by 2. Therefore, 2 is the only even integer that can be prime, and 2 is the smallest divisor of all other even integers.

If N is an odd integer, then its only possible divisors are the odd integers less than N. In fact, it can be proved that a number is prime if it is not divisible by any odd integer less than or equal to its square root. These considerations form the basis for the algorithm shown next.

Step 2 Refinement

```
2.1.  IF N = 2 THEN
          2.2. N is a prime number
      ELSIF N is even then
          2.3. 2 is the smallest divisor and N is not prime
      ELSE
          2.4. Test each odd integer between 3 and the square root of N to see
               whether it is a divisor of N
      END IF;
```

Step 2.4 must test each odd integer as a possible divisor of N until a divisor is found. This we do with a WHILE loop that has the following loop invariant:

```
-- invariant:
-- FirstDiv during pass i is 1 + 2 * i (3, 5, 7, ... ) and
-- No prior value of FirstDiv is a divisor of N and
-- FirstDiv is less than or equal to the square root of N
```

Step 2.4 Refinement

```
2.4.1. Assume N is a prime number (i.e., set Prime to True)
2.4.2. Initialize FirstDiv to 3
2.4.3. WHILE Prime is still True and FirstDiv is less than sqrt(N) LOOP
           2.4.4. IF FirstDiv is a divisor of N THEN
                      2.4.5. Set Prime to False (N is not a prime number)
                  ELSE
                      2.4.6. Set FirstDiv to the next odd number
                  END IF;
       END LOOP;
```

Coding

Program 7.12 gives the complete solution. Four test runs are shown.

Program 7.12   Test Whether a Number Is Prime

```
WITH Text_IO;
WITH My_Int_IO;
WITH RobustInput;
WITH Math; USE Math;
PROCEDURE PrimeNumber IS

-- Displays the smallest divisor (other than 1) of the positive N if
-- a divisor exists; otherwise, displays a message that N is prime.

  MaxN : CONSTANT Positive := 1000;              -- largest n to be tested
   SUBTYPE SmallPos IS Positive RANGE 2..MaxN;   -- range of values for n
```

```
N :                 Positive;      -- number being tested as a prime
FirstDiv :          SmallPos;      -- first divisor if found
MaxPossibleDiv :    SmallPos;      -- truncated square root of N
Prime:              Boolean;       -- flag -- signals whether N is prime
                                   -- (True) or not prime (False)

BEGIN -- PrimeNumber

   -- Enter an integer to test for a prime number
   Text_IO.Put(Item => "Enter a number that you think is a prime.");
   Text_IO.New_Line;
   RobustInput.Get (Item => N, MinVal => 2, MaxVal => MaxN);

   -- Find smallest divisor FirstDiv or determine that N is prime.
   -- Set Prime to indicate whether or not N is a prime number.

   -- Finds first divisor (FirstDiv) of N if it exists.
   -- Pre: N is assigned a value.
   -- Post: FirstDiv is the first divisor of N besides 1 and N.
   --       -- Prime is True if a divisor is not found; otherwise,
   --       -- Prime is False.

   IF N = 2 THEN
      Prime := True;                 -- 2 is a prime number
   ELSIF (N REM 2) = 0 THEN          -- N is even
      Prime := False;
      FirstDiv := 2;                 -- 2 is first divisor of even N
   ELSE                              -- N is odd
      Prime := True;                 -- Assume that N is prime
      MaxPossibleDiv := Positive(Sqrt(Float(N)));
      FirstDiv := 3;                 -- Try 3 first

      WHILE Prime AND (FirstDiv <= MaxPossibleDiv) LOOP
      -- invariant:
      -- FirstDiv during pass i is 1 + 2 * i (3, 5, 7, ... ) and
      -- No prior value of FirstDiv is a divisor of N and
      -- FirstDiv is less than or equal to the square root of N

         IF N REM FirstDiv = 0 THEN    -- N is not prime
            Prime := False ;
         ELSE
            FirstDiv := FirstDiv + 2; -- Try next odd number
         END IF;
      END LOOP;
      -- assertion:
      -- Prime is True and FirstDiv > Sqrt(N) or
      -- Prime is False and FirstDiv is the smallest divisor of N

   END IF;

   -- Display first divisor or a message that N is prime
   IF Prime THEN
      My_Int_IO.Put(Item => N, Width => 5);
      Text_IO.Put(Item => " is a prime number");
      Text_IO.New_Line;
   ELSE
      My_Int_IO.Put(Item => FirstDiv, Width => 5);
      Text_IO.Put(Item => " is the smallest divisor of ");
      My_Int_IO.Put(Item => N, Width => 1);
      Text_IO.New_Line;
   END IF;

END PrimeNumber;
```

```
Enter a number that you think is a prime.
Enter an integer between 2 and 1000 > 1000
    2 is the smallest divisor of 1000

Enter a number that you think is a prime.
Enter an integer between 2 and 1000 > 997
  997 is a prime number

Enter a number that you think is a prime.
Enter an integer between 2 and 1000 > 35
    5 is the smallest divisor of 35

Enter a number that you think is a prime.
Enter an integer between 2 and 1000 > 0
Value entered is out of range. Please try again.
Enter an integer between 2 and 1000 > 1001
Value entered is out of range. Please try again.
Enter an integer between 2 and 1000 > 2
    2 is a prime number
```

The program flag Prime is set to indicate whether or not N is a prime number. Prime is initialized to True before any candidate divisors are tested. If a divisor is found, Prime is reset to False and the WHILE loop is exited. If no divisors are found, Prime will remain True and the loop is exited when FirstDiv becomes greater than Sqrt(N).

PROGRAM
STYLE

Removing Unnecessary Computation from Loops

In Program 7.12, the variable MaxPossibleDiv is used to hold the maximum possible divisor and is assigned its value by the statement

```
MaxPossibleDiv := Positive(Sqrt(Float(N)) − 0.5);
```

just before the WHILE loop. The Float is required by Sqrt; the Positive function returns the integral part of the result. Because, if the fractional part happens to be exactly 0.5, it is compiler-dependent whether the rounding is upward or downward, we again ensure downward rounding by subtracting 0.5 from the square root.

If MaxPossibleDiv were not declared as a local variable, the expression above would be included in the WHILE loop condition and would be reevaluated each time the loop was repeated. This is not necessary since the expression value never changes. You should examine loops carefully and move any computations that always generate the same results outside the loop.

Selection of Adequate Test Cases

Several sample runs of the prime number program were shown with Program 7.12. The test values used for N were selected to exercise all parts of the program and to verify that the program works for numbers that are prime as well as for numbers that are not prime. The operation of the program at the boundaries (2 and 1000) was also checked as well as the operation of the program for invalid data values (0 and 1001). A very large prime number (997) was used as a test case as well as odd and even numbers that were not prime. Although many valid data values were not tested, the sample selected is representative and provides a fair indication that the program is correct.

You should use a similar strategy when selecting test data to exercise your programs. Try to avoid choosing sample test data that are similar. Also, select test data that are at or near any boundary values.

Exercises for Section 7.6

Programming

1. Modify TestPrime to print all divisors of N where N may be any positive integer (odd or even). If N is prime, the only divisors printed should be 1 and N.

 # 7.7 Control Structures: The CASE Statement

The CASE statement is used in Ada to select one of several alternatives. It is especially useful when the selection is based on the value of a single variable or a simple expression. The type of this variable or expression must be discrete (integer or enumeration) type or subtype.

■ Example 7.27

The CASE statement

```
CASE MomOrDad IS
   WHEN 'M' =>
         Text_IO.Put (Item => "Hello Mom - Happy Mother's Day");
   WHEN 'D' =>
         Text_IO.Put (Item => "Hello Dad - Happy Father's Day");
   WHEN OTHERS =>
         Text_IO.Put (Item => "invalid character ");
         Text_IO.Put (Item => MomOrDad);
END CASE;
```

has the same behavior as the IF statement below.

```
IF MomOrDad = 'M' THEN
   Text_IO.Put (Item => "Hello Mom - Happy Mother's Day");
ELSIF MomOrDad = 'D' THEN
   Text_IO.Put (Item => "Hello Dad - Happy Father's Day");
ELSE
   Text_IO.Put (Item => "invalid character ");
   Text_IO.Put (Item => MomOrDad);
END IF;
```

The message displayed by the CASE statement depends on the value of the

CASE *selector* MomOrDad. If the CASE selector matches the first CASE *choice*, 'M', the first message is displayed. If the CASE selector matches the second CASE *choice*, 'D', the second message is displayed. Otherwise, the WHEN OTHERS clause is executed.

The WHEN OTHERS choice is necessary whenever the other choices of the CASE statement do not exhaust all possible values of the selector; if it were not present in this case, then (assuming MomOrDad is type Character) a compilation error would arise. ■

■ Example 7.28

The CASE statement below displays a string indicating the value of a variable whose type is the enumeration Days. A statement like this could be used if Ada did not have a standard I/O library to display enumeration values.

```
CASE Today IS
    WHEN Monday =>
            Text_IO.Put (Item => "Monday");
    WHEN Tuesday =>
            Text_IO.Put (Item => "Tuesday");
    WHEN Wednesday =>
            Text_IO.Put (Item => "Wednesday");
    WHEN Thursday =>
            Text_IO.Put (Item => "Thursday");
    WHEN Friday =>
            Text_IO.Put (Item => "Friday");
    WHEN Saturday =>
            Text_IO.Put (Item => "Saturday");
    WHEN Sunday =>
            Text_IO.Put (Item => "Sunday");
END CASE;
```

Seven different choices are shown in this program; the value of ToDay (type Day) is used to select one of these for execution. The seven possible values of ToDay are listed in CASE choices; the task for that CASE choices, a sequence of statements, follows the => ("arrow") symbol. Because all seven values of Today are listed in CASE choices, no WHEN OTHERS is necessary. After the appropriate Text_IO.Put statement is executed, the CASE statement and procedure are exited. ■

■ Example 7.29

The CASE statement below could be used to compute the numeric value of the hexadecimal digit stored in HexDigit (type Character). In the hexadecimal number system, the valid "digits" are the characters '0' through '9' and 'A' through 'F'. The characters '0' through '9' have the numeric value 0 through 9; the characters 'A' through 'F' have the numeric values 10 (for 'A') through 15 (for 'F').

```
CASE HexDigit IS
    WHEN '0'|'1'|'2'|'3'|'4'|'5'|'6'|'7'|'8'|'9' =>
            Decimal := Character'Pos(HexDigit) - Character'Pos('0') ;
    WHEN 'A'|'B'|'C'|'D'|'E'|'F' =>
            Decimal := Character'Pos(HexDigit)-Character'Pos('A') + 10;
```

```
    WHEN OTHERS =>
        Text_IO.Put (Item => "Illegal hexadecimal digit ");
        Text_IO.Put (Item =>HexDigit);
        Text_IO.New_Line;
END CASE;
```

This CASE statement causes the first assignment statement to be executed when HexDigit is one of the digits '0' through '9'; the second assignment statement is executed when HexDigit is one of the letters 'A' through 'F'. If HexDigit is not one of the characters listed above, the WHEN OTHERS alternative executes and displays an error message. ∎

We can use range notation to abbreviate CASE choices. The CASE statement of Example 7.29 is rewritten below using ranges.

```
CASE HexDigit IS
    WHEN '0'..'9' =>
        Decimal := Character'Pos(HexDigit) - Character'Pos('0') ;
    WHEN 'A'..'F' =>
        Decimal := Character'Pos(HexDigit) - Character'Pos('A') + 10;
    WHEN OTHERS =>
        Text_IO.Put (Item => "Illegal hexadecimal digit ");
        Text_IO.Put (Item =>HexDigit);
        Text_IO.New_Line;
END CASE;
```

∎ Example 7.30

A CASE statement can be used in a student transcript program that computes grade point average (GPA). For each case shown, the total points (Points) earned toward the GPA increases by an amount based on the letter grade (Grade); the total credits earned toward graduation (GradCredits) increases by 1 if the course is passed. The expression

```
Character'Pos('A') - Character'Pos(Grade) + 4
```

evaluates to 4 when the Grade is 'A', 3 when Grade is 'B', and so on.

```
CASE Grade IS
    WHEN 'A'..'D' =>
        Points := Points+Character'Pos('A')-Character'Pos(Grade)+4;
        GradCredits := GradCredits + 1;
    WHEN 'P' =>
        GradCredits := GradCredits + 1;
    WHEN 'F'| 'I'| 'W' =>
        Text_IO.Put (Item => "No points to GPA or graduation");
        Text_IO.New_Line;
    WHEN OTHERS =>
        Text_IO.Put (Item => "Illegal grade ");
        Text_IO.Put (Item =>grade);
        Text_IO.New_Line;
END CASE;
```

A grade of A through D earns a variable number of points (4 for an A, 3 for a B, etc.) and one graduation credit; a grade of P earns one graduation credit; and a grade of F, I, or W earns neither graduation credits nor points.

The WHEN OTHERS clause displays an error message if the program user enters a grade that is not listed in a CASE choice. ∎

∎ Example 7.31

Given an enumeration type

```
TYPE Months IS
   (Jan, Feb, Mar, Apr, May, Jun, Jul, Aug, Sep, Oct, Nov, Dec);
```

and variables ThisYear in the range 1901..2099 (the range of Year_Number in Calendar), DaysInMonth of type Positive, and ThisMonth of type Months, this CASE statement saves in DaysInMonth the number of days in ThisMonth:

```
CASE ThisMonth IS
   WHEN Feb =>
         IF (ThisYear MOD 4 = 0) AND
            ((ThisYear MOD 100 /= 0) OR (ThisYear MOD 400 = 0)) THEN
               NumberOfDays := 29;                    -- leap year
         ELSE
               NumberOfDays := 28;
         END IF;
   WHEN Apr | Jun | Sep | Nov =>
         NumberOfDays := 30;
   WHEN Jan | Mar | May | Jul | Aug | Oct | Dec =>
         NumberOfDays := 31;
END CASE;
```

Because all values of ThisMonth are covered in the choices, no WHEN OTHERS is needed. ∎

CASE Statement

Form:
```
CASE selector IS
    WHEN choice₁ =>
            statement sequence₁

    WHEN choice₂ =>
            statement sequence₂

        .
        .
        .
    WHEN choiceₙ =>
            statement sequenceₙ
    WHEN OTHERS =>
            statement sequenceₒ
END CASE;
```

Example:
```
CASE N IS
    WHEN 1 | 2 =>
            Text_IO.Put (Item => "Buckle my shoe");
    WHEN 3 | 4 =>
            Text_IO.Put (Item => "Shut the door");
    WHEN 5 | 6 =>
            Text_IO.Put (Item => "Pick up sticks");
    WHEN OTHERS =>
            Text_IO.Put (Item => "Forget it...");
END CASE;
```

Interpretation: The *selector* expression is evaluated and compared to each of the CASE *choices*. Each *choice* is a list of one or more possible values for the selector. Only one *statement sequence* will be executed; if the selector value is listed in *choice$_i$*, then *statement sequence$_i$* is executed. If the selector value is not listed in any *choice$_i$*, *statement sequence$_O$* is executed. Control is next passed to the first statement following the END CASE.

Note 1: A WHEN OTHERS alternative must be present if the other choices do not cover all possible values in the type of *selector*.

Note 2: A particular *selector* value may appear in, at most, one *choice$_i$*.

Note 3: The type of each value listed in *choice$_i$* must correspond to the type of the selector expression.

Note 4: Any discrete data type is permitted as the selector type.

PROGRAM
STYLE

Comparison of the IF Statement and the CASE Statement

You can use an IF–THEN–ELSIF statement, more general than the CASE statement, to implement a multiple-alternative decision. The CASE statement, however, is more readable and should be used whenever practical.

You should use the CASE statement when each case choice contains a list of values of reasonable size (ten or less). However, if the number of values in a case choice is large or there are large gaps in those values, an IF–THEN–ELSIF structure may be better.

Exercises for Section 7.7

Self-Check

1. Write an IF statement that corresponds to the CASE statement below.

```
CASE X > Y IS
   WHEN True =>
        Text_IO.Put(Item => "X greater");
   WHEN False =>
        Text_IO.Put(Item => "Y greater or equal");
END CASE;
```

Programming

1. Rewrite the CASE statement in Example 7.29 as an IF structure.
2. If type Color is defined as the enumeration type (Red, Green, Blue, Brown, Yellow), write a CASE statement that assigns a value to Eyes (type Color), given that the first two letters of the color name are stored in Letter1 and Letter2.
3. Write a CASE statement that displays a message indicating whether NextCh (type Character) is an operator symbol (+, −, *, =, <, >, /), a punctuation symbol (comma, semicolon, parenthesis, brace, bracket), or a digit. Your

statement should display the category selected. Write the equivalent IF statement.

7.8 System Structures: A Package to Display a Number in Words

The need to display the value of a number in words arises from time to time, for example, in writing checks (indeed, in the next section we will develop such a program). In this section we will develop a package NumToWord, which provides one operation, PutInWords. The specification for this package is given as Program 7.13. The package also provides a subtype Natural16, with range 0..32767. This is called Natural16 because 32767 is the largest integer normally stored in a 16-bit word. Limiting the range of inputs to this range ensures that the package will operate correctly with any Ada system.

Program 7.13 Specification of Package to Display a Number in Words

```
PACKAGE NumToWord IS

   -- procedure to print a positive integer in words. The subtype
   -- Natural16 is provided so that the package will be correct
   -- on all Ada compilers including those for which Natural is 16 bits.

   SUBTYPE Natural16 IS Natural RANGE 0 .. 32767;
   PROCEDURE PutInWords (Item: Natural16);

END NumToWord;
```

The package body uses three local procedures, which are not provided to the user of the package. Two are called Put1Digit and Put2Digits; they display a single-digit number and a two-digit number, respectively. For example, if Number is 9, then

```
Put1Digit (Item => Number);
```

displays nine. If Number is 37, then

```
Put2Digits (Item => Number);
```

displays thirty seven.

Procedure Put2Digits displays an integer value less than 100 in words. Its parameter value is separated into a tens digit (stored in Tens) and a units digit (stored in Units). Once this separation is performed the two digits are printed in words. The data requirements and algorithm for Put2Digits follow.

Data Requirements for Put2Digits

Procedure Inputs
a number less than 100 (Item: Natural)

Procedure Outputs
a two-digit integer printed in words

Local Variables for Put2Digits:
the tens digit (Tens : 0..9)
the units digit (Units : 0..9)

Algorithm for Put2Digits

1. Separate Item into Tens and Units.
2. Display the Tens digit and Units digit in words.

Step 2 of Put2Digits must be able to display integers that are less than 10 (Tens is 0), in the teens (Tens is 1), and above the teens (Tens >= 2). If Tens is 0, only the Units digit is displayed. If Tens is 1, then the string for a number between 10 ('ten') and 19 ('nineteen') is displayed. If Tens is between 2 and 9, then a string ('twenty' through 'ninety') representing the Tens digit is displayed, followed by a string for the Units digit, provided the latter is not 0.

Step 2 Refinement
2.1. CASE Tens OF
WHEN 0 => display the Units digit
WHEN 1 => select and display a string based on the Units digit
WHEN 2 => display 'twenty' and a nonzero Units digit
WHEN 3 => display 'thirty' and a nonzero Units digit
WHEN 4 => display 'forty' and a nonzero Units digit
WHEN 5 => display 'fifty' and a nonzero Units digit
WHEN 8 => display 'eighty' and a nonzero Units digit
WHEN 6 | 7 | 9 => display the Tens digit followed by 'ty '
    and a nonzero Units digit
END CASE;

Given the ability to display one- or two-digit numbers, we can discuss how to display numbers less than 100,000. A three-digit number (in the hundreds) is displayed by separating the Hundreds value, displaying it followed by hundred, then calling Put2Digits to display the rest. For example, 747 is displayed as

```
seven hundred forty seven
```

A four- or five-digit number (in the thousands and tens of thousands) is displayed by separating the thousands, displaying the thousands using Put2Digits, then proceeding as above. For example, 16384 is displayed as

```
sixteen thousand three hundred eighty four
```

The third procedure provided in NumToWord is Call1Digit, which is written just as a convenience for the rest of the package body: Call1Digit calls

PutlDigit if and only if its argument is nonzero. Program 7.14 gives the package body for NumToWord, which consists of four procedures. Program 7.15 demonstrates the utility of the package by prompting a terminal user to enter positive integers in the required range, then displaying these integers in words. The program uses RobustInput to ensure that the input integers are in range.

Program 7.14 Body of Package to Display a Number in Words

```
WITH Text_IO;
PACKAGE BODY NumToWord IS

-- package body for displaying nonnegative integers in words

  SUBTYPE Digit IS Natural RANGE 0..9;

-- local procedures

  PROCEDURE PutlDigit (Item : Digit) IS

  -- Puts its argument in words.
  -- Pre:  Item is assigned a value between 0 and 9.
  -- Post: Item is displayed in words.

  BEGIN -- PutlDigit

    CASE Item IS
      WHEN 0 => Text_IO.Put (Item => "zero");
      WHEN 1 => Text_IO.Put (Item => "one");
      WHEN 2 => Text_IO.Put (Item => "two");
      WHEN 3 => Text_IO.Put (Item => "three");
      WHEN 4 => Text_IO.Put (Item => "four");
      WHEN 5 => Text_IO.Put (Item => "five");
      WHEN 6 => Text_IO.Put (Item => "six");
      WHEN 7 => Text_IO.Put (Item => "seven");
      WHEN 8 => Text_IO.Put (Item => "eight");
      WHEN 9 => Text_IO.Put (Item => "nine");
    END CASE;

  END PutlDigit;

  PROCEDURE CalllDigit (Units : Digit) IS

  -- Calls procedure PutlDigit with parameter Units if
  -- Units is not zero.
  -- Pre:  Units is assigned a value between 0 and 9.
  -- Post: Calls PutlDigit if Units is not 0.

  BEGIN -- CalllDigit
    IF Units /= 0 THEN
      Text_IO.Put(Item => " ");
      PutlDigit (Item => Units);
    END IF;
  END CalllDigit;

  PROCEDURE Put2Digits (Item : Natural16) IS

  -- Puts its argument in words.
  -- Pre:  Item is assigned a value between 0 and 99.
```

```
-- Post: Item is displayed in words.
-- Uses: PutlDigit
```

```
    Tens  : Digit;                              -- tens digit
    Units : Digit;                              -- units digit

  BEGIN -- Put2Digits

    Tens  := Item / 10;                         -- Get tens digit
    Units := Item REM 10;                       -- Get units digit

    CASE Tens IS
      WHEN 0 =>
        PutlDigit (Units);                      -- less than ten
      WHEN 1 =>
        CASE Units IS                           -- in the teens
          WHEN 0 => Text_IO.Put (Item => "ten");
          WHEN 1 => Text_IO.Put (Item => "eleven");
          WHEN 2 => Text_IO.Put (Item => "twelve");
          WHEN 3 => Text_IO.Put (Item => "thirteen");
          WHEN 5 => Text_IO.Put (Item => "fifteen");
          WHEN 8 => Text_IO.Put (Item => "eighteen");
          WHEN 4 | 6 | 7 | 9 =>
            PutlDigit (Units);                  -- Put ...teen
            Text_IO.Put (Item => "teen");
        END CASE;
      WHEN 2 =>
        Text_IO.Put (Item => "twenty");         -- Put twenty ...
        CalllDigit (Units);
      WHEN 3 =>
        Text_IO.Put (Item => "thirty");         -- Put thirty ...
        CalllDigit (Units);
      WHEN 4 =>
        Text_IO.Put (Item => "forty");          -- Put forty ...
        CalllDigit (Units);
      WHEN 5 =>
        Text_IO.Put (Item => "fifty");          -- Put fifty ...
        CalllDigit (Units);
      WHEN 8 =>
        Text_IO.Put (Item => "eighty");         -- Put eighty ...
        CalllDigit (Units);
      WHEN 6 | 7 | 9 =>
        PutlDigit (Tens);                       -- Put ...ty ...
        Text_IO.Put (Item => "ty");
        CalllDigit (Units);
    END CASE;
  END Put2Digits;

PROCEDURE PutInWords (Item: Naturall6) IS

  CopyOfItem: Natural;
  Thousands:  Natural;
  Hundreds:   Natural;

BEGIN

  IF Item = 0 THEN
    PutlDigit (Item => Item);
  ELSE
    CopyOfItem := Item;
    IF CopyOfItem >= 1000 THEN
```

```
          Thousands := CopyOfItem / 1000;
          Put2Digits (Item => Thousands);
          Text_IO.Put (Item => " thousand ");
          CopyOfItem := CopyOfItem REM 1000;
        END IF; .

        IF CopyOfItem >= 100 THEN
          Hundreds := CopyOfItem / 100;
          Put1Digit (Item => Hundreds);
          Text_IO.Put (Item => " hundred ");
          CopyOfItem := CopyOfItem REM 100;
        END IF;

        IF CopyOfItem /= 0 THEN
          Put2Digits (Item => CopyOfItem);
        END IF;
      END IF;

    END PutInWords;

END NumToWord;
```

Program 7.15 Displaying a Number in Words

```
WITH Text_IO;
WITH My_Int_IO;
WITH RobustInput;
WITH NumToWord;
PROCEDURE TestNumToWord IS

  -- program to demonstrate and test NumToWord.PutInWords

  N: NumToWord.Natural16;

BEGIN -- TestNumToWord

  FOR Count IN 1..5 LOOP
    Text_IO.Put (Item => "Integer ");
    My_Int_IO.Put (Item => Count, Width => 1);
    Text_IO.New_Line;
    RobustInput.Get (Item => N,
      MinVal => NumToWord.Natural16'First,
      MaxVal => NumToWord.Natural16'Last);
    NumToWord.PutInWords (Item => N);
    Text_IO.New_Line;
  END LOOP;

END TestNumToWord;
```

```
Integer 1
Enter an integer between 0 and 32767 > 0
zero
Integer 2
Enter an integer between 0 and 32767 > 32767
thirty two thousand seven hundred sixty seven
Integer 3
Enter an integer between 0 and 32767 > 30
thirty
```

```
Integer 4
Enter an integer between 0 and 32767 > 125
one hundred twenty five
Integer 5
Enter an integer between 0 and 32767 > 2048
two thousand forty eight
```

"Extra" Subprograms in Package Bodies

The body for NumToWord contains four procedures, only one of which is listed in the specification. This is perfectly correct Ada: The purpose of the specification is to provide a contract with the user; the purpose of the body is to deliver whatever is promised in the specification. The Ada compiler would complain if a procedure specification appeared in a package specification but a corresponding procedure body did not appear in the package body, because a promise was made that was not fulfilled.

What does it mean if a procedure body appears in the package body but not in the package specification? It simply means that the given procedure is not available to a client program; it is encapsulated or "hidden" in the body. It is available for use only within the package body itself.

In the present situation, the procedures Put1Digit, Put2Digits, and Call1Digit are very narrow in purpose, and exist only to assist the procedure PutInWords in doing its job. They are of little use to other users and so should not be available to them. Therefore these three procedures appear only in the package body. PutInWords, on the other hand, is a general procedure that can be used in many applications, and so it is sensible to make it available to users. It is therefore part of the package's specification, its contract with users.

It might be tempting to list, in a package specification, everything in the corresponding package body. You should resist the temptation and should consider carefully just which procedures, functions, types, variables, and so on, should be provided to the client program. Packages are more general in purpose, more "reusable," if they provide resources that are carefully designed.

 # 7.9 Case Study: Printing a Check in Words

When you first learned to write checks in payment for purchases, you were probably taught to spell out the amount of the check in words on the appropriate line of the check. This case study considers how to write a program to assist you in doing this.

Problem

It is desirable to have a program that writes a check amount in words. Some examples of the desired output are shown below.

Amount	Amount in Words
43.55	forty three dollars and fifty five cents
62.05	sixty two dollars and five cents
15.20	fifteen dollars and twenty cents
0.95	zero dollars and ninety five cents
35.00	thirty five dollars and zero cents
123.45	one hundred twenty three dollars and forty five cents
2001.05	two thousand one dollars and five cents

Analysis

The program must separate the check amount into two integers, `Dollars` and `Cents`. Once this is done, `Dollars` can be printed followed by the string `' dollars and '`, the value of `Cents`, and the string `' cents'`. For the sake of portability, we will restrict the check writing procedure to amounts no greater than $32,767.00. A description of the procedure data requirements follows.

Problem Inputs
check amount as a floating point number (`Check : Float`)

Problem Outputs
description of check amount in words

Local Variables for `DisplayCheck`:
dollar amount (`Dollars : Natural16`)
number of cents (`Cents : Natural16`)

Design

Algorithm for DisplayCheck

1. IF check amount is invalid THEN
2. Display an error message
ELSE
3. Separate check amount into `Dollars` and `Cents`
4. Display `Dollars` in words
5. Display `' dollars and '`
6. Display `Cents` in words
7. Display `' cents'`
END IF;

The structure chart for procedure `DisplayCheck` is shown in Fig. 7.7. Procedure `NumToWord.PutInWords` is called twice: first to print the value of `Dollars` in words and then to print the value of `Cents` in words.

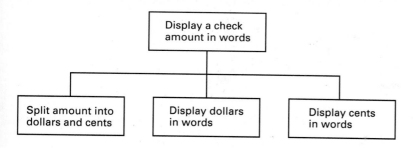

Coding

Program 7.16 implements this algorithm. Package `NumToWord` is used to display the check amount; package `RobustInput` is used to read the input float values and ensure that they are in range.

Program 7.16   Displaying a Check Amount in Words

```
WITH Text_IO;
WITH NumToWord;
WITH RobustInput;
PROCEDURE DisplayCheck IS

-- Displays a check amount in words.
-- Pre:  Check is read from the terminal; amount must be in 0.00 .. 32767.00
-- Post: Displays the value of Check in words.
-- Uses: NumToWord.PutInWords; Text_IO.Put; Text_IO.New_Line;
--       RobustInput.Get;

  MaxCheck : CONSTANT Float := 32767.00;

  SUBTYPE CheckAmount IS Float RANGE 0.0 .. MaxCheck;

  Check :        CheckAmount;               -- amount of check
  Dollars :      NumToWord.Natural16;       -- the dollar amount
  Cents :        NumToWord.Natural16;       -- the cents amount

BEGIN -- DisplayCheck

  Text_IO.Put (Item => "Please enter check amount");
  Text_IO.New_Line;
  RobustInput.Get (Item => Check,
    MinVal => CheckAmount'First, MaxVal => CheckAmount'Last);

  Dollars := NumToWord.Natural16(Check);    -- round downward
  IF Float(Dollars) > Check THEN            -- in case rounding was upward
    Dollars := Dollars - 1;
  END IF;

  Cents := NumToWord.Natural16(100.0 * (Check - Float(Dollars)));

  NumToWord.PutInWords (Item => Dollars); -- Display dollar amount
  Text_IO.Put (Item => " dollar");
  IF Dollars /= 1 THEN
    Text_IO.Put (Item => "s");
```

```
END IF;
Text_IO.Put (Item => " and ");

NumToWord.PutInWords (Item => Cents);    -- Display cents amount
Text_IO.Put (Item => " cent");
IF Cents /= 1 THEN
   Text_IO.Put (Item => "s");
END IF;
Text_IO.New_Line;

END DisplayCheck;
```

```
Please enter check amount
Enter a floating-point value between 0.00 and 32767.00 > 50000.00
Value entered is out of range. Please try again.
Please enter check amount
Enter a floating-point value between 0.00 and 32767.00 > 2001.05
two thousand one dollars and five cents
```

7.10 Tricks of the Trade: Common Programming Errors

A good deal of care is required when working with complicated expressions. It is easy to omit parentheses or operators inadvertently. If an operator or a single parenthesis is omitted, a syntax error will be detected. If a pair of parentheses is omitted, then the expression, although syntactically correct, will compute the wrong value.

Sometimes it is beneficial to break a complicated expression into subexpressions that are separately assigned to *temporary variables*, and then to manipulate these temporary variables. For example, it is easier to write correctly the three assignment statements

```
Temp1 := Sqrt(X + Y);
Temp2 := 1 + Temp1;
Z := Temp1 / Temp2;
```

than the single assignment statement

```
Z := Sqrt(X + Y) / (1 + Sqrt(X + Y));
```

which has the same effect. Using three assignment statements also happens to be more efficient in this case, because the square root operation is performed only once; it is performed twice in the single assignment statement above.

Be careful to use the correct type of operands with each operator. The arithmetic operators can be used only with operands of type Integer, or Float, or subtypes of these. The relational operators can be used with any scalar data type. The Boolean operators can be used only with type Boolean operands.

Make sure that an operator does not have incompatible type operands. The Boolean expression is invalid because it compares an integer to a character value. All operators require compatible operands; make sure that you supply the right type operand to mathematical functions. An example is `Sqrt`, whose argument must be `Float` and nonnegative.

Remember that in a `CASE` statement, there must be enough `CASE` choices to exhaust every possible value of the `CASE` selector variable or expression. If there are not, a `WHEN OTHERS` choice must be provided; otherwise a compilation error will result. If you find that you are writing a large number of `WHEN OTHERS` choices, your case selector variable may be of an inappropriate type (e.g., `Integer` instead of a subtype or enumeration type).

 # Chapter Review

This chapter described how to write arithmetic expressions involving several operators, and introduced a package of mathematical functions called `Math`. Also introduced was the idea of an *explicit type conversion*. Type conversion makes it possible to mix integer and floating-point values in one expression by explicitly converting floats to integers and vice versa.

This chapter also discussed the manipulation of other scalar data types, including the standard types, `Boolean` and `Character`, and presented more detail on programmer-defined subtypes. Several new operators were introduced, including the operators `REM` and `MOD` for manipulating integers and the operators `AND`, `OR`, `XOR`, and `NOT` for manipulating `Boolean` data. Attention was paid to certain attributes of scalar types, such as the `First` and `Last` attributes of subtypes and the `Pos` and `Val` attributes of integer and, especially, enumeration values.

The `CASE` statement was introduced, along with a number of examples of its use. A package was shown that provided facilities for printing the value of numbers in words.

New Ada Constructs in Chapter 7

The new Ada constructs introduced in this chapter are described in Table 7.7.

Table 7.7 Summary of New Ada Constructs

Statement	Effect
Arithmetic Assignment	
`I := J / K + (L + 5) REM N;`	Adds the result (an integer) of `J / K` to the result (an integer) of `(L + 5) REM N`. `J, K, L,` and `N` must all be type `Integer` or an integer subtype.

Table 7.7 *continued*

Statement	Effect
Character Assignment `NextCh := 'A';`	Assigns the character value `'A'` to `NextCh`.
Boolean Assignment `Even := (N REM 2 = 0);`	If `N` is an even number, assigns the value `True` to `Even`; otherwise, assigns the value `False` to `Even`.

```
Case Statement
CASE NextCh IS
   WHEN 'A'|'a' =>
       Text_IO.Put(Item=>"Excellent");
   WHEN 'B'|'b' =>
       Text_IO.Put(Item=>"Good");
   WHEN 'C'|'c' =>
       Text_IO.Put(Item=>"OK");
   WHEN 'D'|'d'|'F'|'f' =>
       Text_IO.Put(Item=>"Poor");
       Probation(WhichStudent => IDNum);
   WHEN OTHERS =>
       Text_IO.Put(Item => "Grade out of Range!");
END CASE;
```

Prints one of four messages based on the value of `NextCh`.

If `NextCh` is `'D','d','F','f'`, procedure `Probation` is also called with `IDNum` as an actual parameter.

✓ *Quick-Check Exercises*

1. The operator _____ means real division, the operator _____ means integer division, and the operator _____ yields the remainder of _____ division.
2. Write a `Boolean` condition that is `True` if `N` divides `M`.
3. Evaluate the `Boolean` expression

   ```
   True AND ((30 REM 10) = 0)
   ```

4. Evaluate the `Boolean` expression

   ```
   False AND (((30 REM 10) / 0) = 0)
   ```

   What occurs when Ada evaluates this expression? Suppose the `AND` were replaced by `AND THEN`?

5. In ASCII, give the values of these expressions:

```
Character'Val(Character'Pos('a'))
Character'Val(Character'Pos('a') + 3)
Character'Val(Character'Pos('z') - 26)
Character'Val(Character'Pos('z') - 32)
```

6. If two variables are type compatible, can one always be assigned to the other?
7. Under what condition can one variable be assigned to another when they are not type compatible?
8. A CASE statement is often used instead of _____.
9. Which of the following can appear in a CASE selector?

   a range of integers, a list of integers, a Float value, a Boolean value, a type Character value, a string value, an enumeration literal

Answers to Quick-Check Exercises
1. / (float operands), / (integer operands), REM, integer
2. (M REM N) = 0
3. True
4. Constraint_Error or Numeric_Error is raised; error won't be detected because in short-circuit evaluation the right side won't be evaluated.
5. 'a', 'd', 'a', 'Z'
6. Yes, if they are the same type or the one getting a new value is the base type and the other is a subtype of that base type. If the one getting a new value is a subtype, the value of the variable being assigned must be in range.
7. A variable of one numeric type can be converted to the other type.
8. A multiple-alternative IF construct
9. All but Float and string

Review Questions for Chapter 7

1. Compare and contrast integer types and floating-point types. What are the advantages and disadvantages of each?
2. What is the result of each of the following operations?

11 REM 2	_____	11 / 2	_____
12 REM -3	_____	12 / -3	_____
27 REM 4	_____	-25 / 4	_____
18 REM 6	_____	-18 / -5	_____

3. What is the result of the expression (3 + 4 / 2) + 8 - 15 REM 4?
4. Write an assignment statement that rounds a floating-point variable Num1 to two digits after the decimal point, leaving the result in Num1.
5. Write a procedure called Change that has one IN parameter C, type NonNegFloat, and four OUT parameters Q, D, N, and P, type Natural. The procedure returns the number of quarters in Q, the number of dimes in D, the number of nickels in N, and the number of pennies in P to make change with the minimum number of coins. C (the change amount) is less than $1.00. (*Hint:* Use the integer division and REM operators.)
6. List and explain three computational errors that can occur in type Float expressions.

7. Write an IF statement that displays True or False according to the following conditions: Either Flag is True or Color is Red, or both Money is Plenty and Time is Up.

8. Write the statement to assign a value of True to the Boolean variable OverTime only if a worker's weekly Hours are greater than 40.

9. Write a Boolean expression using the Character'Pos attribute that determines whether the position of 'a' in ASCII is greater than that of 'Z'. What is the value of this expression?

8. When should an IF statement be used instead of a CASE statement?

9. Write a CASE statement to select an operation based on Inventory. Increment TotalPaper by PaperOrder if Inventory is 'B' or 'C'; increment TotalRibbon by RibbonOrder if Inventory is 'L', 'T', or 'D'; increment TotalLabel by LabelOrder if Inventory is 'A' or 'X'. Do not take any action if Inventory is 'M'.

10. Write the FOR statement that displays the character values of the positive numbers 32 through 126, inclusive. Use OrdNum as the loop control variable. What is the value of OrdNum after completion of the loop?

Programming Projects

1. A company has ten employees, many of whom work overtime (more than 40 hours) each week. The company accountant wants a payroll program that reads each employee's name, hourly rate (rate), and hours worked (hours). The program must compute the gross salary and net pay as follows:

$$gross = \begin{cases} hours \times rate \ (\text{if hours} <\ = 40) \\ 1.5\ rate(hours\ -\ 40)\ +\ 40\ \times\ rate\ (\text{if hours} > 40) \end{cases}$$

$$net = \begin{cases} gross\ (\text{if gross} <= \$65) \\ gross\ -\ (15\ +\ 0.45gross)\ (\text{if gross} > \$65) \end{cases}$$

The program should print each employee's gross salary and net pay. The total amount of the payroll, which can be computed by adding the gross salaries for all employees, should be displayed at the end. Test your program on the following data:

Name	Rate	Hours
Ivory Hunter	6.50	35
Track Star	4.50	10
Smokey Bear	3.25	80
Oscar Grouch	6.00	10
Jane Jezebel	4.65	25
Fat Eddie	8.00	40
Pumpkin Pie	9.65	35
Sara Lee	5.00	40
Human Eraser	6.25	52

2. Write a program to read in a collection of integers and determine whether each is a prime number. Test your program with the four integers 7, 17, 35, and 96. All numbers should be processed in one run.

3. Let n be a positive integer consisting of up to ten digits, $d_{10}d_9 \ldots d_1$. Write a program to list in one column each of the digits in the number n. The rightmost digit, d_1, should be listed at the top of the column. (*Hint:* As computed according to the formula

```
digit = n REM 10
```

what is the value of `digit` if $n = 3704$?)
Test your program for values of n equal to 6, 3704, and 170498.

4. An integer N is divisible by 9 if the sum of its digits is divisible by 9. Use the algorithm developed for Programming Project 3 to determine whether the following numbers are divisible by 9.

```
N = 154368
N = 621594
N = 123456
```

5. Redo Programming Project 4 by reading each digit of the number to be tested into the character variable `Digit`. Form the sum of the numeric values of the digits. (*Hint:* The numeric value of `Digit` (type `Character`) is

```
Character'Pos(Digit) - Character'Pos('0').)
```

6. The interest paid on a savings account is compounded daily. This means that if you start with `StartBal` dollars in the bank, at the end of the first day you will have a balance of

```
StartBal × (1 + rate/365)
```

dollars, where `rate` is the annual interest rate (0.10 if the annual rate is 10 percent). At the end of the second day, you will have

```
StartBal × (1 + rate/365) × (1 + rate/365)
```

dollars, and at the end of N days you will have

```
StartBal × (1 + rate/365)ᴺ
```

dollars. Write a program that processes a set of data records, each of which contains values for `StartBal`, `rate`, and `N`, and computes the final account balance.

7. Compute the monthly payment and the total payment for a bank loan, given:
   a. the amount of the loan,
   b. the duration of the loan in months, and
   c. the interest rate for the loan.

Your program should read in one loan at a time, perform the required computation, and print the values of the monthly payment and the total payment. Test your program with at least the following data (and more if you want).

Loan	Months	Rate
16000	300	12.50
24000	360	13.50
30000	300	15.50
42000	360	14.50
22000	300	15.50
300000	240	15.25

(*Hints:* The formula for computing monthly payment is

$$monthpay = \frac{(ratem \times expm^{months} \times loan}{expm - 1.0)}$$

where

$$ratem = rate / 1200.0 \qquad expm = (1.0 + ratem)$$

You will need a loop to multiply *expm* by itself *months* times. The formula for computing the total payment is

$$total = monthpay \times months.)$$

Composite Types: Records and Arrays

8

8.1   Data Structures: Record Types
8.2   Control Structures: Records as Operands and Parameters
8.3   System Structures: A Package for Calendar Dates
8.4   Data Structures: Hierarchical Records
8.5   Data Structures: Array Types
8.6   Problem Solving: Selecting Array Elements for Processing
8.7   Problem Solving: Using Arrays
8.8   Problem Solving: Reading Part of an Array
8.9   Data Structures: Arrays with Noninteger Subscripts
8.10   Data Structures: Strings in Ada
8.11   Problem Solving: Searching and Sorting an Array
8.12   Case Study: Sorting an Array of Records
8.13   Tricks of the Trade: Common Programming Errors
         Chapter Review

In the programs written so far, each variable was associated with a single memory location. These variables are called *scalar* variables, and their data types are scalar or unstructured types. In this chapter, we will begin the study of *composite types*. A composite type is one that defines a collection of related data values. The items in a variable of a composite type can be processed individually, although some operations can be performed on the structure as a whole.

Ada provides *type constructors,* which can be used to form composite types from simpler types. The type constructors RECORD and ARRAY are introduced in this chapter and some simple cases are explored. More complex and interesting kinds of arrays and records are taken up in Chapters 10, 11, and 12.

A *record* is a data structure containing a group of related data items; the individual components, or *fields*, of a record can contain data of different types. We can use a record to store a variety of information about a person, such as the person's name, marital status, age, date of birth, and so on. Each data item is stored in a separate record field; we can reference each data item stored in a record through its field name. For example, Person.Name references the field Name of the record Person.

An *array* is a data structure used for storage of a collection of data items that are all of the same type (e.g., all the exam scores for a class). Using an array allows us to associate a single variable name (e.g., Scores) with the entire collection of data. This enables us to save the entire collection of data in main memory (one item per memory cell) and to reference individual items easily. For example, the third score in the array Scores would be referenced as Scores(3).

Records make it easier to organize and represent information in Ada; the availability of record structures is a major reason for the popularity of Ada and other modern programming languages.

 # 8.1 Data Structures: Record Types

A *data base* is a collection of information or facts stored in a computer's memory or in a disk file. A data base consists of records, which normally contain information regarding particular data objects. For example, the description of a person, place, or thing would be stored as a record.

Record Type Declaration

Before a record can be created or saved, the record format must be specified by means of a record type declaration.

■ Example 8.1
The staff of our small software firm is growing rapidly. To keep our records more accessible and organized, we decide to store relevant data, such as the descriptive information shown below, in an employee data base.

```
ID : 1234
Name: Caryn Jackson
Gender : Female
Number of Dependents: 2
Hourly Rate: 3.98
Taxable Salary (for 40 hour week): 130.40
```

Noting that the number of dependents should be of type `Natural` and the hourly rate and taxable salary should both be of type `NonNegFloat`, let us give an appropriate type declaration for each piece of information in the first three lines above.

```
NameSize :CONSTANT Positive := 20;

SUBTYPE IDRange IS Positive RANGE 1111..9999;
SUBTYPE NameType IS String(1..NameSize);
TYPE GenderType IS (Female,Male);
```

We next declare a record type `Employee` to store this information. We must specify the name of each field and the type of information stored in each field. We choose the field names in the same way as we choose all other identifiers: The names describe the nature of the information represented.

```
TYPE Employee IS RECORD
    ID : IDRange;
    Name : NameType;
    Gender : GenderType;
    NumDepend : Natural;
    Rate : NonNegFloat;
    TaxSal : NonNegFloat;
END RECORD;
```

The record type is a template that describes the format of each record and the name of each individual data element. A variable declaration is required to allocate storage space for a record. The record variables `Clerk` and `Janitor` are declared next.

```
Clerk : Employee;
Janitor : Employee;
```

The record variables `Clerk` and `Janitor` both have the structure specified in the declaration for record type `Employee`. Thus, the memory allocated for each consists of storage space for six distinct values. Figure 8.1 shows the record variable `Clerk`, assuming the values shown earlier are stored in memory. ∎

Figure 8.1 Record Variable Clerk

Record variable Clerk

ID	1234
Name	Caryn Jackson
Sex	Female
NumDepend	2
Rate	3.98
TaxSal	130.40

As illustrated in the type declaration for `Employee`, each of the fields of a record can be a predefined or user-defined type. There are no limitations on the type of a field, except that the type specification must be the name of a type that has already been declared. The record type declaration is described in the next display.

Record Type Declaration

Form:
```
TYPE rec-type IS RECORD
    F₁ : type₁;
    F₂ : type₂;
      .
      .
      .
    Fₙ : typeₙ;
END RECORD;
```

Example:
```
TYPE Fraction IS RECORD
    Numerator: Integer;
    Denominator: Positive;
END RECORD;
```

Interpretation: The identifier *rec-type* is the name of the record structure being described. Each identifier F_i is a field name; the data type of each field F_i is specified by *type$_i$*.

Note: *type$_i$* may be any predefined or user-defined type. Also, the field names must be unique: No two fields of the same record type may have the same field name.

Manipulating Individual Fields of a Record

We can reference a record field by using a *field selector*, which consists of the record variable name followed by the field name. A period separates the field name and record name.

■ Example 8.2

The data shown in Fig. 8.1 could have been stored in `Clerk` through this sequence of assignment statements:

```
Clerk.ID := 1234;
Clerk.Name := "Carẏn Jackson        ";
Clerk.Gender := Female;
Clerk.NumDepend := 2;
Clerk.Rate := 3.98;
Clerk.TaxSal := Clerk.Rate * 40.0 - Float(Clerk.NumDepend) * 14.40;
```

Once data are stored in a record, they can be manipulated in the same way as other data in memory. For example, the assignment statement above computes the clerk's taxable salary by deducting $14.40 for each dependent from the gross salary (`Clerk.Rate * 40.0`). The computed result is saved in the record field named `Clerk.TaxSal`.

The statements

```
Text_IO.Put(Item => "The clerk is ");
CASE Clerk.Gender IS
WHEN Female => Text_IO.Put (Item => "Ms. ");
WHEN Male => Text_IO.Put (Item => "Mr. ");
END CASE;
Text_IO.Put (Item => Clerk.Name);
```

display the clerk's name after an appropriate title (Ms. or Mr.). For the data above, the output would be

```
The clerk is Ms. Caryn Jackson
```
■

■ Example 8.3

Program 8.1 computes the distance from an arbitrary point on the *x-y* plane to the origin (intersection of the *x-* and *y-*axes). The values of the *x*-coordinate and the *y*-coordinate are entered as data and stored in the fields X and Y of the record variable Point1. The formula used to compute the distance, *d*, from the origin to an arbitrary point (X, Y) is

$$d = \sqrt{X^2 + Y^2}$$

Each coordinate of the record variable Point1 is read separately. Text_IO does not provide operations to read an entire record; we will write our own operations to read records later in this chapter. ■

Program 8.1 Distance from Point to Origin

```
WITH Text_IO;
WITH My_Flt_IO;
WITH Math; USE Math;
PROCEDURE DistOrigin IS

-- Finds the distance from a point to the origin.

   TYPE Point IS RECORD
      X : Float;
      Y : Float;
   END RECORD;

   Point1 : Point;          -- the data point
   Distance : Float;        -- its distance to the origin

BEGIN -- DistOrigin

   Text_IO.Put(Item => "Enter X coordinate (floating point) > ");
   My_Flt_IO.Get(Item => Point1.X);
   Text_IO.Put(Item => "Enter Y coordinate (floating point) > ");
   My_Flt_IO.Get(Item => Point1.Y);
   Distance := sqrt(Point1.X ** 2 + Point1.Y ** 2);
   Text_IO.Put(Item => "Distance to origin is ");
   My_Flt_IO.Put(Item => Distance, Fore=>1,Aft=>2,Exp=>0);
   Text_IO.New_Line;

END DistOrigin;
```

```
Enter X coordinate (floating point) > 3.00
Enter Y coordinate (floating point) > 4.00
Distance to origin is 5.00
```

Abstract Record

We can summarize what we have discussed about records in the following specification for an abstract record.

Specification for Abstract Records

Structure: A record is a collection of related data values of different types. Each data value is stored in a separate field of the record.

Operations: Four basic operations act on a record: store, retrieve, assignment, and equality. The store operation inserts a value into the record field. If R1 is a record with a field named F1 and E is an expression that is compatible with field F1, the statement

```
R1.F1 := E;
```

stores the result of evaluating E in field F1 of record R1. If the field R1.F1 is compatible with variable C (that is, if they have the same type), the statement

```
C := R1.F1;
```

retrieves the value in field F1 of record R1 and copies it into C. Note that it is always permissible, given two record variables R1 and R2 of the same type, to write

```
R1.F1 := R2.F1;
```

An assignment statement can also be used to copy the entire contents of one record to another of the same type. If R1 and R2 are record variables of the same type, the statement

```
R1 := R2;
```

copies all values associated with record R2 to record R1. Finally, the result of the Boolean expression

```
R1 = R2
```

is true if and only if each of the fields of R1 is equal to its corresponding field in R2; the result of the Boolean expression

```
R1 /= R2
```

is true if and only if at least one of the fields of R1 is not equal to its corresponding field in R2.

Exercises for Section 8.1

331

8.2 Control
Structures: Records
as Operands and
Parameters

Self-Check

1. Each part in an inventory is represented by its part number, a descriptive name, the quantity on hand, and price. Define a record type `Part`.
2. A catalogue listing for a textbook consists of the author's name, title, publisher, and year of publication. Declare a record type `CatalogEntry` and variable `Book` and write assignment statements that store the relevant data for this textbook in `Book`.

Programming

1. Modify program `DistOrigin` to find the distance between two points. Use the formula

$$\text{Distance} = \sqrt{(X1 - X2)^2 + (Y1 - Y2)^2)}$$

Store the points in two record variables of type `Point`.

8.2 Control Structures: Records as Operands and Parameters

Because predefined arithmetic and logical operations—except for equality and inequality—can be performed only on individual memory cells, record variables cannot be used as the operands of predefined arithmetic and relational operators. These operators must be used with individual fields of a record, as shown in the previous section.

Copying and Comparing Records

It is possible to copy all the fields of one record variable to another record variable of the same type using a record copy (assignment) statement. If `Clerk` and `Janitor` are both record variables of type `Employee`, the statement

```
Clerk := Janitor;  --copy Janitor to Clerk
```

copies each field of `Janitor` into the corresponding field of `Clerk`. It is also permissible to determine in a single statement whether two records R1 and R2 of the same record type are equal, that is, whether each field of R1 is equal to the corresponding field of R2. For example,

```
IF R1 = R2 THEN
    DoSomething;
ELSE
    DoSomethingElse;
END IF;
```

executes DoSomething if R1 and R2 both contain the same field values, field by field, and DoSomethingElse otherwise.

Passing Records as Parameters

A record can be passed as a parameter to a function or procedure, provided that the actual parameter is of the same type as its corresponding formal parameter. The use of records as parameters can shorten parameter lists considerably because one parameter (the record variable) can be passed instead of several related parameters.

■ Example 8.4

In a grading program, the summary statistics for an exam might consist of the average score, the highest and lowest scores, and the standard deviation. In previous problems these data would be stored in separate variables; however, it makes sense to group them together as a record.

```
SUBTYPE NonNegFloat IS Float RANGE 0.0 .. Float'Last;
SUBTYPE ScoreRange IS Natural RANGE 0..100;

TYPE ExamStats IS RECORD
   Low: ScoreRange;
   High : ScoreRange;
   Average : NonNegFloat;
   StandardDev : NonNegFloat;
END RECORD;

Exam : ExamStats;
```

A procedure that computes one of these results (e.g., Average) could be passed a single record field (e.g., Exam.Average). A procedure that manipulates more than one of these fields could be passed the entire record. An example would be procedure PrintStat shown in Program 8.2. ■

Program 8.2 Procedure PrintStat

```
PROCEDURE PrintStat (Exam : ExamStats) IS

-- Prints the exam statistics.
-- Pre : The fields of record variable Exam are assigned values.
-- Post: Each field of Exam is displayed.

BEGIN -- PrintStat

  Text_IO.Put(Item => "High score: ");
  My_Int_IO.Put(Item => Exam.High, Width => 3);
  Text_IO.New_Line;
  Text_IO.Put(Item => "Low score: ");
  My_Int_IO.Put(Item => Exam.Low, Width => 3);
  Text_IO.New_Line;
  Text_IO.Put(Item => "Average: ");
  My_Flt_IO.Put(Item => Exam.Average, Width => 3);
  Text_IO.New_Line;
  Text_IO.Put(Item => "Standard deviation: ");
  My_Flt_IO.Put(Item => Exam.StandardDev, Width => 3);
  Text_IO.New_Line

END PrintStat;
```

Example 8.5

333

8.2 Control
Structures: Records
as Operands and
Parameters

Before performing a potentially dangerous or costly experiment in the laboratory, we can often use a computer program to simulate the experiment. In computer simulations, we need to keep track of the time of day as the experiment progresses. Because the time in a simulation is simulated, or "pseudo," time, we could create our own time type instead of using the one made available by Calendar. Normally, the time of day is updated after a certain time period has elapsed. The record type TimeRecord is declared below assuming a 24-hour clock.

```
SUBTYPE Hours IS Natural RANGE 0..23;
SUBTYPE Minutes IS Natural RANGE 0..59;
SUBTYPE Seconds IS Natural RANGE 0..59;

TYPE TimeRecord IS RECORD
   Hour : Hours;
   Minute : Minutes;
   Second : Seconds;
END RECORD;
```

Procedure ChangeTime in Program 8.3 updates the time of day, TimeOfDay (type TimeRecord), after a time interval, ElapsedTime, expressed in seconds. Each statement that uses the REM operator updates a particular field of the record represented by TimeOfDay. The REM operator ensures that each updated value is within the required range; the integer division (/) operator converts multiples of 60 seconds to minutes and multiples of 60 minutes to hours. ∎

Program 8.3 Procedure ChangeTime

```
PROCEDURE ChangeTime (ElapsedTime : Natural;
                      TimeOfDay : IN OUT TimeRecord) IS

-- Updates the time of day, TimeOfDay, assuming a 24-hour clock and
-- an elapsed time of ElapsedTime in seconds.
-- Pre : ElapsedTime and record TimeOfDay are assigned values.
-- Post: TimeOfDay is "incremented" by ElapsedTime.

  NewHour : Natural;      -- temporary values
  NewMin  : Natural;
  NewSec  : Natural;

BEGIN -- ChangeTime

  NewSec := TimeOfDay.Second + ElapsedTime;      -- total seconds
  TimeOfDay.Second := NewSec REM 60;             -- seconds rem 60
  NewMin := TimeOfDay.Minute + (NewSec / 60);    -- total minutes
  TimeOfDay.Minute := NewMin REM 60;             -- minutes rem 60
  NewHour := TimeOfDay.Hour + (NewMin / 60);     -- total hours
  TimeOfDay.Hour := NewHour REM 24;              -- hours rem 24

END ChangeTime;
```

Reading a Record

Ada normally uses procedures to read data from the terminal or a file. The Get procedures available in Text_IO are defined only for individual values, not for records. To read a record, we can use a call of the appropriate Get to read each field. It is common to read an entire record at once, so it makes sense to define a procedure for doing this; the body of the procedure will contain the individual Get calls for each record field.

■ Example 8.6

Program 8.4 contains a procedure GetPoint to read a point in the *x-y* plane and a function Distance, which calculates the distance between two points $P_1 = (X_1, Y_1)$ and $P_2 = (X_2, Y_2)$. The formula used to calculate the distance *d* is

$$d = \sqrt{(X_2 - X_1)^2 + (Y_2 - Y_1)^2}$$

The main program requests the coordinates of two points from the user, then calculates and displays the distance between them.   ■

Program 8.4   Distance Between Two Points

```
WITH Text_IO;
WITH My_Flt_IO;
WITH Math; USE Math;
PROCEDURE DistPoints IS

-- Finds the distance from a point to the origin.

  TYPE Point IS RECORD
    X : Float;
    Y : Float;
  END RECORD;

  Point1 : Point;              -- one data point
  Point2 : Point;              -- the other data point


  PROCEDURE GetPoint(Item: OUT Point) IS

  -- reads the X and Y coordinates of a point
  -- Pre: none
  -- Post: the point, Item, is defined with values from the user

  BEGIN

    Text_IO.Put(Item => "Enter X coordinate (floating point) > ");
    My_Flt_IO.Get(Item => Item.X);
    Text_IO.Put(Item => "Enter Y coordinate (floating point) > ");
  , My_Flt_IO.Get(Item => Item.Y);

  END GetPoint;


  FUNCTION Distance(P1 : Point; P2 : Point) RETURN Float IS
```

```
-- calculates the Cartesian distance between two points
-- Pre: P1 and P2 are defined
-- Post: returns the distance

BEGIN

  RETURN Sqrt((P2.X-P1.X) ** 2 + (P2.Y-P1.Y) ** 2);

END Distance;

BEGIN -- DistPoints

  Text_IO.Put(Item => "First Point");
  Text_IO.New_Line;
  GetPoint(Item => Point1);
  Text_IO.Put(Item => "Second Point");
  Text_IO.New_Line;
  GetPoint(Item => Point2);
  Text_IO.Put(Item => "Distance between points is ");
  My_Flt_IO.Put(Item => Distance(Point1, Point2), Fore=>1,Aft=>2,Exp=>0);
  Text_IO.New_Line;

END DistPoints;


First Point
Enter X coordinate (floating point) > 3.00
Enter Y coordinate (floating point) > 4.00
Second Point
Enter X coordinate (floating point) > 9.00
Enter Y coordinate (floating point) > 12.00
Distance between points is 10.00
```

Record Aggregate Assignment

When an entire record must be assigned at one time, it is unnecessary to assign each field in a separate assignment statement. Instead, you can use an *aggregate*. An aggregate is just a list of all the field values in the record, separated by commas and enclosed in parentheses. An aggregate looks like a parameter list in a procedure call: The values can just be listed in sequence (positional association) or given with their names (named association). Generally we will use the latter form, because it is clearer and easier to understand.

A record Clerk of type Employee, as used above, could be filled in with an aggregate assignment as follows:

```
Clerk :=
    (ID => 1234,
    Name => "Caryn Jackson           ",
    Gender => Female,
    NumDepend => 2,
    Rate => 3.98,
    TaxSal => 130.40);
```

We have listed the fields in the order in which they were declared in the type definition, but in fact we could have put them in any order, because the field names help the compiler (and the human reader) make the association. In the aggregate, we could not use the formula used in Example 8.2, that is,

```
TaxSal => Clerk.Rate * 40.0 - Clerk.NumDepend * 14.40;
```

because it depends on the values of other fields in the same record, and the Ada standard does not guarantee that the other fields will have been assigned first. The standard says that all the assignment expressions are evaluated "in some order not specified by the language." This tells us that aggregate assignments will work well only if the assignment expressions are all independent of one another. Otherwise, separate assignment statements should be used.

It is permissible to write an aggregate assignment without specifying the field names, for example,

```
Clerk := (1234,"Caryn Jackson        ", Female, 2, 3.98, 130.40);
```

However, this form, called *positional association*, is not nearly as clear and also requires that the fields be listed exactly in the order in which they appear in the type definition. We will generally use the first, or *named association*, form of record aggregate assignment.

Exercises for Section 8.2

Self-Check

1. What does the program segment below do? Provide the declarations for variables Exam1 and Exam2.

```
PrintStat (Exam1);
Exam2 := Exam1;
Exam2.High := Exam2.High - 5.0;
PrintStat (Exam2);
```

2. If all fields of variable Now (type TimeRecord) are initially zero, how is Now changed by the execution of the program segment below?

```
ChangeTime (ElapsedTime => 3600, TimeOfDay => Now);
ChangeTime (ElapsedTime => 7125, TimeOfDay => Now);
```

Programming

1. Write a code segment that initializes all fields of a variable of type TimeRecord to zero.
2. Write a procedure to read in the data for a record variable of type CatalogueEntry. See Self-Check Exercise 2 at the end of Section 8.1.

 # 8.3 System Structures: A Package for Calendar Dates

In Chapter 3 we discussed some of the uses of Ada's predefined package Calendar. This package provides many facilities for working with dates and times, but it does not provide a way to represent calendar dates in a way suitable for reading and displaying. In this section we develop a specification for a simple package to give us a nicer form for dates, including procedures to read and display dates. In Chapter 9 we will refine this package to make it more capable and robust.

Specification for the Dates Package

We want the `SimpleDates` package to provide a standard representation for the months of the year. We will do this by giving an enumeration type `Months` representing the abbreviated names of the months:

```
TYPE Months IS
     (Jan, Feb, Mar, Apr, May, Jun, Jul, Aug, Sep, Oct, Nov, Dec);
```

We can now make use of this type and the day and year types provided by `Calendar` to define a record type for a date, using the month abbreviation for the month field, as follows:

```
TYPE Date IS RECORD
     Month: Months;
     Day: Calendar.Day_Number;
     Year: Calendar.Year_Number;
END RECORD;
```

We could have defined our own year and month number types, but we chose instead to use types that were already available to us in a predefined Ada package (instead of "reinventing the wheel"). The input program `Get` will read a date in the form

```
OCT 31 1990
```

and the output program `Put` will display dates in this form as well.

One more operation is included: a function `Today` that returns a date record initialized with the date the program is being run. In other words, given a declaration

```
D: SimpleDates.Date;
```

then the statement

```
D := SimpleDates.Today;
```

sets the fields of `D` to today's month, day, and year, respectively. Two things are noteworthy about this function. First, it is an example of a *parameterless* function; it requires no parameters. Second, the return type of the function is a record, namely, one of type `Date`. The full package specification is found in Program 8.5.

Program 8.5 Specification of Package SimpleDates

```
WITH Calendar;
WITH Text_IO;
PACKAGE SimpleDates IS

-- specification for package to represent calendar dates
-- in a form convenient for reading and displaying.
```

```
TYPE Months IS
    (Jan, Feb, Mar, Apr, May, Jun, Jul, Aug, Sep, Oct, Nov, Dec);

TYPE Date IS RECORD
    Month: Months;
    Day:Calendar.Day_Number;
    Year: Calendar.Year_Number;
END RECORD;

PROCEDURE Get(Item: OUT Date);
PROCEDURE Put(Item: IN Date);
FUNCTION Today RETURN Date;

END SimpleDates;
```

Body of the Dates Package

Program 8.6 shows the body of package SimpleDates. There are just two procedures, Get and Put. SimpleDates.Get expects its input to be in the form given above. It is not a robust procedure like the ones in RobustInput (Section 6.7), which prompt the user until correct input is entered; it is more like the predefined Get routines in Text_IO: If anything is wrong with the input, Get simply allows the exception to be passed back to the calling routine.

What can go wrong? The month, day, or year entered by the user can be badly formed or out of range, or the combination of month, day, and year can form a nonexistent date such as Feb 30 1990. A badly formed month, day, or year will result in Text_IO.Data_Error being raised by Months_IO; an out-of-range month or year will result in Constraint_Error being raised. This routine does not discover the case of a nonexistent date; a revised version to be developed in Section 10.3 will correct this shortcoming and add robustness to the package.

The procedure SimpleDates.Put displays a date in the MMM DD YYYY form. Also note how the function Today uses package Calendar to produce today's date and return it to the caller. Program 8.7 shows a test of the SimpleDates package.

Program 8.6   Body of Package SimpleDates

```
WITH Calendar;
WITH Text_IO;
WITH My_Int_IO;
PACKAGE BODY SimpleDates IS

-- body for package to represent calendar dates
-- in a form convenient for reading and displaying.

    PACKAGE Month_IO IS
        NEW Text_IO.Enumeration_IO(Enum => Months);


    PROCEDURE Get(Item: OUT Date) IS
    -- gets a date in the form MMM DD YYYY
    -- Post: returns a date in Item
```

```
BEGIN

   Month_IO.Get(Item => Item.Month);
   My_Int_IO.Get(Item => Item.Day);
   My_Int_IO.Get(Item => Item.Year);

 END Get;


 PROCEDURE Put(Item: IN Date) IS
 -- displays a date in mmm dd yyyy form
 -- Pre: Item is assigned a value
 -- Post: Displays a date in mmm dd yyyy form

 BEGIN

   Month_IO.Put (Item => Item.Month, Width=>1);
   Text_IO.Put(Item => ' ');
   My_Int_IO.Put(Item => Item.Day, Width => 1);
   Text_IO.Put(Item => ' ');
   My_Int_IO.Put(Item => Item.Year, Width => 4);

 END Put;

 FUNCTION Today RETURN Date IS

 -- Finds today's date and returns it as a record of type Date
 -- Today's date is gotten from PACKAGE Calendar

   Right_Now : Calendar.Time;          -- holds internal clock value
   Temp      : Date;

 BEGIN -- Today

   -- Get the current time value from the computer's clock
   Right_Now := Calendar.Clock;

   -- Extract the current month, day, and year from the time value
   Temp.Month := Months'Val(Calendar.Month(Right_Now)- 1);
   Temp.Day := Calendar.Day (Right_Now);
   Temp.Year := Calendar.Year (Date => Right_Now);

   RETURN Temp;

 END Today;

END SimpleDates;
```

Program 8.7 A Test of the SimpleDates Package

```
WITH Text_IO;
WITH SimpleDates;
PROCEDURE TestSimpleDates IS

-- program to test the SimpleDates package

  D: SimpleDates.Date;

BEGIN -- TestSimpleDates
```

```
-- first test the function Today
D := SimpleDates.Today;
Text_IO.Put(Item => "Today is ");
SimpleDates.Put(Item => D);
Text_IO.New_Line;

LOOP

   BEGIN -- block for exception handler
     Text_IO.Put("Please enter a date in MMM DD YYYY form > ");
     SimpleDates.Get(Item => D);
     EXIT; -- only if no exception is raised
   EXCEPTION
     WHEN Constraint_Error =>
       Text_IO.Skip_Line;
       Text_IO.Put(Item => "Badly formed date; try again, please.");
       Text_IO.New_Line;
     WHEN Text_IO.Data_Error =>
       Text_IO.Skip_Line;
       Text_IO.Put(Item => "Badly formed date; try again, please.");
       Text_IO.New_Line;
   END;

END LOOP;
-- assert: at this point, D contains a correct date record

Text_IO.Put(Item => "You entered ");
SimpleDates.Put(Item => D);
Text_IO.New_Line;

END TestSimpleDates;
```

```
Today is MAR 16 1991
Please enter a date in MMM DD YYYY form > mmm dd yyyy
Badly formed date; try again, please.
Please enter a date in MMM DD YYYY form > dec 15 1944
You entered DEC 15 1944
```

Exercises for Section 8.3

Self-Check

1. Can a client program that uses SimpleDates change the day field of a Date
   variable? For example, suppose the variable represents November 30, 1991.
   Can the client program change the 30 to a 31?

 ## 8.4 Data Structures: Hierarchical Records

In solving any programming problem, we must select data structures that enable
us to represent a variety of different kinds of information efficiently in the
computer. The selection of data structures is a very important part of the

problem-solving process. The data structures used can have a profound effect on the efficiency and simplicity of the completed program.

The data-structuring facilities in Ada are quite powerful and general. In the previous examples, all record fields were scalar types or strings. It is possible to declare a record type with fields that are other structured types. We will call a record type with one or more fields that are record types a *hierarchical record*.

We began our study of records by introducing a record type Employee. In this section we will modify that record by adding new fields for storage of the employee's address, starting date, and date of birth. We start with some basic types and constants:

```
StringLength  :  CONSTANT Positive := 20;
ZipCodeLength : CONSTANT Positive := 5;

SUBTYPE IdRange IS Positive RANGE 1111..9999;
SUBTYPE EmpString IS String(1..StringLength);
SUBTYPE ZipString IS String(1..ZipCodeLength);

TYPE GenderType IS (Female, Male);
```

Next we a give modified employee record based on that of Section 8.1, and we define an additional record type, Address.

```
TYPE Employee IS RECORD
    ID : IDRange;
    Name : EmpString;
    Gender : GenderType;
    NumDepend : Natural;
    Rate : NonNegFloat;
    TaxSal : NonNegFloat;
END RECORD;

TYPE Address IS RECORD
    Street : EmpString;
    City :EmpString;
    State : EmpString;
    ZipCode : ZipString;
END RECORD;
```

Finally, here is the declaration of the hierarchical record for an employee, and a declaration of an employee variable. Notice how simple the employee record is, given the component record types; notice also how we have used the Date type provided by the package SimpleDates developed in the previous section.

```
TYPE NewEmployee IS RECORD
    PayData : Employee;
    Home :      Address;
    StartDate : SimpleDates.Date;
    BirthDate : SimpleDates.Date;
END RECORD;

Programmer: NewEmployee;
```

If Programmer is a record variable of type NewEmployee, the hierarchical structure of Programmer can be sketched as shown in Fig. 8.2. This diagram provides a graphic display of the record form. This diagram shows that Programmer is a record with fields PayData, Home, StartDate, and BirthDate.

Figure 8.2 Record Variable Programmer (Type NewEmployee)

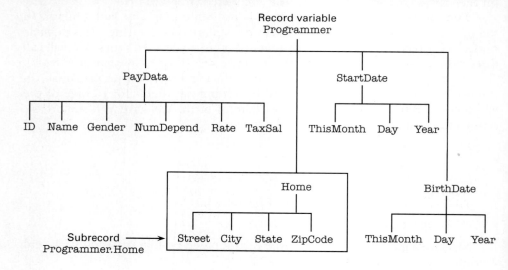

Each of these fields is itself a record (called a *subrecord* of Programmer). The fields of each subrecord are indicated under it.

To reference a field in this diagram, we must trace a complete path to it starting from the top of the diagram. For example, the field selector

```
Programmer.StartDate
```

references the subrecord StartDate (type Date) of the variable Programmer. The field selector

```
Programmer.StartDate.Year
```

references the Year field of the subrecord Programmer.StartDate. The field selector

```
Programmer.Year
```

is incomplete (which Year field?) and would cause a syntax error.

The record copy statement

```
Programmer.StartDate := DayOfYear;
```

is legal if DayOfYear is a record variable of type Date. This statement copies each field of DayOfYear into the corresponding field of the subrecord Programmer.StartDate.

The statements

```
Text_IO.Put(Item => "Year started: ");
My_Int_IO.Put(Item => Programmer.StartDate.Year, Width=>4);
Text_IO.Put(Item => "Month started: ");
My_Int_IO.Put(Item => Programmer.StartDate.Month, Width=>4);
```

display two fields of the subrecord Programmer.StartDate. The statements

```
Text_IO.Put(Item => Programmer.PayData.Name);
Text_IO.Put(Item => "started work in ");
My_Int_IO.Put(Item => Programmer.StartDate.Year, Width=>4);
```

display the line

```
Caryn Jackson         started work in 1985
```

The computation for taxable salary could be written as

```
Programmer.PayData.TaxSal :=
    Programmer.PayData.Rate * 40.0
    - Programmer.PayData.NumDepend * 14.40;
```

Procedure ReadNewEmp in Program 8.9 can be used to read in a record of type NewEmployee. It calls procedures ReadEmployee (see Program 8.8), Dates.Get, and ReadAddress (see Programming Exercise 1, below). The procedure call statement

```
ReadEmployee (Clerk)
```

causes the data read to be stored in record variable Clerk. This procedure uses GenderType_IO to read the gender of the employee; GenderType_IO would need to be defined as an instance of Text_IO.Enumeration_IO.

Program 8.8   Procedure ReadEmployee

```
PROCEDURE ReadEmployee (OneClerk : OUT Employee) IS

-- Reads one employee record into OneClerk.
-- Pre : None
-- Post: Data are read into record OneClerk.

BEGIN -- ReadEmployee

  Text_IO.Put(Item => "ID > ");
  My_Int_IO.Get(Item => OneClerk.ID);
  Text_IO.Put(Item => "Name > ");
  Text_IO.Get(Item => OneClerk.Name);
  Text_IO.Put(Item => "Gender (Female or Male) > ");
  GenderType_IO.Get(Item => OneClerk.Gender);
  Text_IO.Put(Item => "Number of dependents > ");
  My_Int_IO.Get(Item => OneClerk.NumDepend);
  Text_IO.Put(Item => "Hourly rate > ");
  My_Flt_IO.Get(Item => OneClerk.Rate);

END ReadEmployee;
```

Program 8.9   Procedure ReadNewEmp

```
PROCEDURE ReadNewEmp (NewEmp : OUT NewEmployee) IS

-- Reads a record into record variable NewEmp. Uses
```

```
-- procedures ReadEmployee, ReadAddress and SimpleDates.Get.
-- Pre : None
-- Post: Reads data into all fields of record NewEmp.

BEGIN -- ReadNewEmp

  ReadEmployee (NewEmp.PayData);
  ReadAddress (NewEmp.Home);
  SimpleDates.Get (NewEmp.StartDate);
  SimpleDates.Get (NewEmp.BirthDate)

END ReadNewEmp;
```

Exercises for Section 8.4

Self-Check

1. What must be the type of NewAddress if the following statement is correct?

   ```
   Programmer.Home := NewAddress;
   ```

2. Write the field selector needed to reference each field described below.
   a. the programmer's salary
   b. the programmer's street address
   c. the programmer's month of birth
   d. the month the programmer started working

Programming

1. Write the procedure ReadAddress suggested above.

 # 8.5 Data Structures: Array Types

A record contains fields, each of which is potentially of a different type; such a composite type is often called *heterogeneous*. An array, on the other hand, contains elements all of which are of the *same* type; such a type is often called *homogeneous*. This section illustrates the basic operations that can be performed on an array, beginning with a discussion of how to allocate memory space for an array in Ada.

Array Type Declaration

Normally, we begin by describing the structure of an array in an array type declaration. Then we can allocate storage for one or more arrays of that type. The array type FloatArray is declared below, followed by the declaration of array X of type FloatArray:

```
TYPE FloatArray IS ARRAY (1..8) OF Float;
X : FloatArray;
```

Ada associates a collection of eight memory cells with the name X; these memory cells will usually be adjacent to each other in memory. Each element of array X can contain a single Float value, so a total of eight Float values can be stored and referenced using the array name X. (*Note:* The fact that an array's elements are in adjacent memory cells is not required by Ada, but it enables the compiler to get to all elements of an array just by knowing where the first element is stored.)

Referencing Elements of an Array

In order to process the data stored in an array, we must be able to reference each individual element. The array subscript is used to differentiate between elements of the same array. For example, if X is the array with eight elements declared above, then we refer to the elements of the array X as shown in Fig. 8.3.

The *subscripted variable* X(1) (read as X sub 1) may be used to reference the first element of the array X, X(2) the second element, and X(8) the eighth element. The number enclosed in parentheses is the array subscript. As we will see later, the subscript does not have to be a constant.

Figure 8.3   The Eight Elements of the Array X

Array X

X(1)	X(2)	X(3)	X(4)	X(5)	X(6)	X(7)	X(8)
16.0	12.0	6.0	8.0	2.5	12.0	14.0	−54.5

First element / Second element / Third element / Eighth element

■ Example 8.7

Let X be the array shown in Fig. 8.3. Some statements that manipulate this array are shown in Table 8.1.

Table 8.1   Statements That Manipulate Array X

Statement	Explanation
My_Flt_IO.Put(X(1));	Displays value of X(1) or 16.0.
X(4) := 25.0;	Stores value 25.0 in X(4).
Sum := X(1) + X(2);	Stores sum of X(1) and X(2) or 28.0 in Sum.
Sum := Sum + X(3);	Adds X(3) to Sum. The new Sum is 34.0.
X(4) := X(4) + 1.0;	Adds 1.0 to X(4). The new X(4) is 26.0.
X(3) := X(1) + X(2);	Stores sum of X(1) and X(2) or 28.0 in X(3).

The contents of array X is shown in Fig. 8.4 after execution of these statements. Only X(3) and X(4) are changed.   ■

■ Example 8.8

The declaration section for a manufacturing plant operations program is shown below. The type declarations declares HoursRange, EmpRange and Day, and

Figure 8.4 Array X after Modification

Array X

X(1)	X(2)	X(3)	X(4)	X(5)	X(6)	X(7)	X(8)
16.0	12.0	28.0	26.0	2.5	12.0	14.0	–54.5

First
element

Second
element

Third
element

Eighth
element

two array types, EmpArray and DayArray. Two array variables, Vacation and PlantHours, are declared in the variable declaration section.

```
NumEmp : CONSTANT Positive := 10;            -- Number of employees
SUBTYPE EmpRange IS Positive RANGE 1..NumEmp; -- subscript range
SUBTYPE HoursRange IS Float RANGE 0.0..24.0;  -- hours in a day
TYPE Day IS
     (Monday, Tuesday, Wednesday, Thursday, Friday, Saturday, Sunday);

TYPE EmpArray IS ARRAY(EmpRange) OF Boolean;
TYPE DayArray IS ARRAY(Day) OF NonNegFloat;

Vacation : EmpArray;
PlantHours : DayArray;
```

The array Vacation has ten elements (subscripts 1 through NumEmp); each element of array Vacation can store a Boolean value. The contents of this array could indicate which employees were on vacation (Vacation(i) is True if employee i is on vacation). If employees 1, 3, 5, 7, and 9 were on vacation, the array would have the values shown in Fig. 8.5.

Figure 8.5 Array Vacation

Vacation(1)	True
Vacation(2)	False
Vacation(3)	True
Vacation(4)	False
Vacation(5)	True
Vacation(6)	False
Vacation(7)	True
Vacation(8)	False
Vacation(9)	True
Vacation(10)	False

The array PlantHours has seven elements (subscripts Monday through Sunday). The array element PlantHours(Sunday) could indicate how many hours the plant was operating during Sunday of the past week. The array shown in Fig. 8.6 indicates that the plant was closed on the weekend, operating single shifts on Monday and Thursday, double shifts on Tuesday and Friday, and a triple shift on Wednesday.

Figure 8.6 Array PlantHours

347

8.5 Data Structures:
Array Types

PlantHours(Sunday)	0.0
PlantHours(Monday)	8.0
PlantHours(Tuesday)	16.0
PlantHours(Wednesday)	24.0
PlantHours(Thursday)	8.0
PlantHours(Friday)	16.0
PlantHours(Saturday)	0.0

It would be possible to eliminate the declarations for the constant NumEmp and data types EmpRange and EmpArray and just declare the array Vacation as shown below.

```
Vacation : ARRAY (1..10) OF Boolean;
```

There are three advantages to the original set of declarations. First, it is easy to change the declared size of the array Vacation. By simply redefining the constant NumEmp, we change the array size. Second, the subtypes EmpRange and HoursRange and the array types EmpArray and DayArray can be used as type identifiers elsewhere in the program. We will see later that it is convenient to declare arrays and loop control variables using the same subrange types, and the array type names are important in copying and comparing arrays. The third advantage is that the constants NumEmp can be referenced in the program body.

Because a type identifier is not used in the revised declaration of array Vacation, its type is said to be *anonymous*. The compiler gives the array an internal type name, but we do not know the name; the term *anonymous* is chosen by analogy with anonymous authors or poets: They had names, but we don't know the names. In general, you should avoid using anonymous types. ∎

SYNTAX
DISPLAY

Array Type Declaration

Form: TYPE *array-type* IS ARRAY *subscript-type* OF *element-type*;

Example: SUBTYPE WordWidth IS Positive RANGE 1..32;
TYPE BitVector IS ARRAY (WordWidth) OF Boolean;

Interpretation: The identifier *array-type* describes a collection of array elements; each element can store an item of type *element-type*. The *subscript-type* can be any discrete type, that is, any predefined or user-defined integer or enumeration type or subtype. There is one array element corresponding to each value in the *subscript-type*. All elements of an array are of the same *element-type*.

Note 1: The *element-type* can be any predefined or user-defined scalar or composite type.

Note 2: A floating-point type cannot be a *subscript-type* because it is not discrete, as it represents a continuous range of values.
Note 3: It is unwise to use as a subscript type a predefined type with a large range of values (e.g., `Integer`) because doing so would result in arrays with a gigantic number of elements. Generally, our subscript types will be either user-defined subtypes of `Integer` with fairly small ranges, or user-defined enumeration types.

It is important to realize that an array type declaration does not cause allocation of storage space in memory. The array type describes the structure of an array only. Only variables actually store information and require storage. Storage space is not allocated until a variable of this type is declared.

Abstract Array

We can summarize what we have learned about arrays in the following specification for an abstract array.

Specification for Abstract Array

Structure: An array is a collection of elements of the same data type. For each array, a discrete subscript type is specified. There is an array element corresponding to each value in the discrete type.
Operators: Two basic operations act on elements of an array: store and retrieve. The store operation inserts a value into the array. If `A` is an array, `C` is an expression that is compatible with the element type of `A`, and `i` is an expression that is compatible with the subscript type, then the statement

```
A(i) :=C;
```

stores the contents of `C` in element `i` of array `A`. If `C` is a variable that is assignment compatible with the element type of `A`, the statement

```
C := A(i);
```

retrieves element `i` of array `A` and copies its value into `C`. For both of these statements the value of subscript `i` must be in the range of the array subscript type; otherwise, `Constraint_Error` will be raised.

The assignment operator can also be used to copy the contents of one array to another if the arrays are compatible (of the same array type). If `A` and `B` are compatible arrays, the statement

```
A := B;
```

copies all values associated with array `B` to array `A`.

The equality and inequality operators can also be used to compare two arrays if the arrays are compatible (of the same array type). If A and B are compatible arrays, the `Boolean` expression

```
A = B;
```

evaluates to `True` if and only if each element of A is equal to the corresponding element of B, and the `Boolean` expression

```
A /= B;
```

evaluates to `True` if and only if any elements of A are not equal to the corresponding elements of B.

The display above summarizes all the information that we need to know to use an array. We do not need to know how Ada stores the elements of an array in memory or how it implements the *retrieve* and *store* operators above.

Aggregate Array Assignment

As in the case of records, an entire array can be filled with values by three methods:

- assignment to each element with an individual assignment statement, either randomly or sequentially;
- copying one entire array to another with an array assignment statement, as discussed just above; and
- storing values in an entire array using an aggregate, similar to that used in records.

It is the last method that concerns us now. Given an array A of type `TestArray`, the 100 `Float` values could, if they were all known in advance, be stored in A with a single statement such as

```
A := (1.0, 27.0, 35.0, -4.0, 15.0, ...);
```

where the ellipsis must be replaced completely with the other 95 values. This is surely tedious, but it is better than writing 100 separate assignment statements. As in the case of records, named association can also be used:

```
A := (1 => 1.0, 2 => 27.0, ...);
```

where the remaining 97 values also need to be supplied. Whereas in record aggregates we prefer named association, in array aggregates it can be cumbersome because an array can have a large number of elements. In using array aggregates we will generally use positional association unless there is a good reason not to do so.

A common and useful application of array aggregates is to initialize most or all elements of an array with the *same* value. Suppose that our array A were to be "cleared" so that all values were 0. This could be done in a loop:

```
FOR I IN 1..MaxSize LOOP
   A(I) := 0.0;
END LOOP;
```

or with a single aggregate assignment:

```
A := (1..MaxSize => 0.0);
```

The aggregate assignment is certainly more concise, expresses the will of the programmer clearly, and may possibly execute faster. Suppose now that A were to be initialized such that its first 5 elements were as above, but the other 95 were to be 0. The assignment

```
A := (1.0, 27.0, 35.0, -4.0, 15.0, OTHERS => 0.0);
```

does the trick. The OTHERS clause informs the compiler to store 0s in all those elements not expressly listed in the aggregate. If, say, only the first, third, and fifth elements were nonzero, named association could be used:

```
A := (1 => 1.0, 3 => 27.0, 5 => 35.0, OTHERS => 0.0);
```

Finally, the assignment

```
A := (OTHERS => 0.0);
```

fills the entire array with 0s even more concisely: Because no other elements were explicitly filled, the OTHERS applies to all elements.

It is important to remember in using an aggregate that *all* elements of the array must be initialized by the aggregate; otherwise, a compilation error results. OTHERS initializes all elements not otherwise given.

Exercises for Section 8.5

Self-Check

1. What is the difference between the expressions X3 and X(3)?
2. For the following declarations, how many memory cells are reserved for data and what type of data can be stored there? When is the memory allocated— after the type declaration or after the variable declaration?

```
TYPE AnArray IS ARRAY(1..5) OF Character;
Grades : AnArray;
```

3. Write the variable and type declarations for all of the valid arrays below.
   a. subscript type Boolean, element type Float
   b. subscript type 'A'..'F', element type Integer
   c. subscript type Character, element type Boolean
   d. subscript type Integer, element type Float
   e. subscript type Character, element type Float
   f. subscript type Float, element type Character
   g. subscript type Day (enumeration type), element type Float

Programming

351

8.6 Problem Solving:
Selecting Array
Elements for
Processing

1. Given the following declarations:

```
A: ARRAY(1..5) OF Integer;
B: ARRAY(1..5) OF Integer;
C, D: ARRAY(1..5) OF Integer;

TYPE List IS ARRAY (1..5) OF Integer;

E: List;
F: List;
G, H: List;
```

explain why each of the following statements is valid or invalid:

```
A := B;
C := D;
E := F;
G := H;
```

Check your results by writing and compiling a brief program incorporating these statements.

 ## 8.6 Problem Solving: Selecting Array Elements for Processing

Using a Subscript as an Index to an Array

As indicated in the last section, the subscript type of an array may be any discrete type or subtype. In the next few sections, most of the examples will deal with arrays whose subscript type is a subtype of type Positive. We are doing this because it is expedient; you should keep in mind that the features described carry over to other subscript types as well. We will discuss arrays with nonnumeric subscripts in Section 8.9.

Each array reference includes the array name and a subscript enclosed in parentheses. The subscript (sometimes called an *index*) used to reference an array element must be an expression that is compatible with the declared subscript type. Very often, the subscript type is a subtype with a minimum value of 1 (e.g., (1..MaxSize)). Because the minimum subscript value is positive, it must be an expression whose value is in the range specified by the subscript type. For the array Vacation declared in Example 8.8, the allowable subscript values are the positive integers from 1 through 10.

■ Example 8.9

Table 8.2 shows some sample statements involving the array X shown in Fig. 8.3. I is assumed to be a Positive variable with value 6. Make sure you understand each statement.

Table 8.2 Some Sample Statements for Array X

Statement	Explanation
`My_Flt_IO.Put(X(4));`	Displays 8.0 (value of X(4)).
`My_Flt_IO.Put(X(I));`	Displays 12.0 (value of X(6)).
`My_Flt_IO.Put(X(I)+1.0);`	Displays 13.0 (value of 12.0 + 1.0).
`My_Flt_IO.Put(X(I+1));`	Displays 14.0 (value of X(7)).
`My_Flt_IO.Put(X(I+I));`	Illegal attempt to display X(12).
`My_Flt_IO.Put(X(2*I));`	Illegal attempt to display X(12).
`My_Flt_IO.Put(X(2*I-4));`	Displays –54.5 (value of X(8)).
`My_Flt_IO.Put(X(Positive(X(4))));`	Displays value of X(8).
`X(I) := X(I+1);`	Assigns 14.0 (value of X(7)) to X(6).
`X(I-1) := X(I);`	Assigns 14.0 (new value of X(6)) to X(5).
`X(I) - 1 := X(I);`	Illegal assignment statement

The last Put statement uses Positive(X(4)) as a subscript expression. Because this evaluates to 8, the value of X(8) (and not X(4)) is changed. If the value of Positive(X(4)) were outside the range 1 through 8, this would be an illegal subscript expression and Constraint_Error would be raised.

Two different subscripts are used in the last three assignment statements in the table. The first assignment copies the value of X(7) into X(6) (subscripts I+1 and I); the second assignment statement copies the value of X(6) into X(5) (subscripts I and I-1). The last assignment statement causes a syntax error, because there is an expression to the left of the assignment symbol, :=.

In Table 8.2, there are two illegal attempts to display element X(12), which is not in the array. These attempts will result in Constraint_Error being raised. ■

SYNTAX
DISPLAY

> ### Array Reference
>
> **Form:** *name* (*subscript*)
>
> **Example:** X(3*I - 2)
>
> **Interpretation:** The *subscript* must be an expression that is compatible with the *subscript-type* specified in the declaration for array name. If the expression is of the wrong data type, then a "type mismatch" syntax error will be detected; if the value expression depends on values not known at compile time, Constraint_Error will be raised at execution time if the expression value is out of the subscript range.

Using FOR Loops with Arrays

Often we wish to process the elements of an array in sequence, starting with the first. An example would be entering data into the array or displaying its contents. This can be acccomplished using a FOR loop whose loop control variable (e.g., I) is also used as the array subscript (e.g., X(I)). Increasing the value of the loop control variable by 1 causes the next array element to be processed.

■ Example 8.10

The array Cubes declared below can be used to store the cubes of the first ten integers (e.g., Cubes(1) is 1, Cubes(10) is 1000).

```
Size : CONSTANT Positive := 10;
SUBTYPE Index IS Positive RANGE 1..Size;
TYPE IntArray IS ARRAY (Index) OF INTEGER;
Cubes : IntArray;                  -- array of cubes
```

The FOR statement

```
FOR I IN 1 .. Size LOOP
Cubes(I) := I * I * I;
END LOOP;
```

initializes this array as shown in Fig. 8.7.

Figure 8.7 Array Cubes

(1)	(2)	(3)	(4)	(5)	(6)	(7)	(8)	(9)	(10)
1	8	27	64	125	216	343	512	729	1000

A better way to write the FOR loop is

```
FOR I IN Index LOOP
   Cubes(I) := I * I * I;
END LOOP;
```

The behavior of this loop is the same as that of the previous loop: Each element of the array is accessed in sequence. The advantage of writing the loop this way is that, assuming Index is the subscript type of the array, if the bounds of Index are ever changed and the program is recompiled, no other statements will have to change. In cases where an entire array is being referenced in sequence, we will usually use this form of loop control.   ■

■ Example 8.11

Program 8.10 reads an array of values from the terminal, calculates the average of the values, and displays a table of differences, each showing the given value's difference from the average. In this program, the declarations

```
MaxItems : CONSTANT Positive := 8;              -- number of data items

SUBTYPE Index IS Positive RANGE 1..MaxItems;
TYPE FloatArray IS ARRAY (Index) OF Float;

X : FloatArray;                                 -- array of Float numbers
```

allocate storage for an array X with subscripts in the range 1..8. The program

Program 8.10 Table of Differences

```
WITH Text_IO;
WITH My_Int_IO;
WITH My_Flt_IO;
PROCEDURE ShowDiff IS

-- Computes the average value of an array of data and
-- prints the difference between each value and the average.

   MaxItems : CONSTANT Positive := 8;     -- number of data items

   SUBTYPE Index IS Positive RANGE 1..MaxItems;
   TYPE FloatArray IS ARRAY (Index) OF Float;

   X        : FloatArray;                 -- array of data
   Average  : Float;                      -- average value of data
   Sum      : Float;                      -- sum of the data

BEGIN -- ShowDiff

   -- Enter the data.
   Text_IO.Put(Item => "Please enter ");
   My_Int_IO.Put(Item => MaxItems, Width=>0);
   Text_IO.Put(Item => " floating-point numbers > ");
   Text_IO.New_Line;

   FOR I IN Index LOOP
      My_Flt_IO.Get(Item => X(I));
   END LOOP;
   Text_IO.New_Line;

   -- Compute the average value.
   Sum := 0.0;                            -- Initialize SUM
   FOR I IN Index LOOP
      Sum := Sum + X(I);                  -- Add each element to Sum
   END LOOP;

   Average := Sum / FLOAT(MaxItems);   -- Find average value
   Text_IO.Put(Item => "Average value is ");
   My_Flt_IO.Put(Item=>Average, Fore=>5, Aft=>2, Exp=>0);
   Text_IO.New_Line;

   -- Display the difference between each item and the average.
   Text_IO.Put(Item => "Table of differences between X(I) and average");
   Text_IO.New_Line;
   Text_IO.Put(Item => "    I        X(I)        Difference");
   Text_IO.New_Line;

   FOR I IN Index LOOP
      My_Int_IO.Put(Item => I, Width=>4);
      Text_IO.Put(Item => "      ");
      My_Flt_IO.Put(Item=>X(I), Fore=>5, Aft=>2, Exp=>0);
      Text_IO.Put(Item => "      ");
      My_Flt_IO.Put(Item=>X(I)-Average, Fore=>5, Aft=>2, Exp=>0);
      Text_IO.New_Line;
   END LOOP;

END ShowDiff;
```

```
Please enter 8 floating-point numbers >
16.0 12.0 6.0 8.0 2.5 12.0 14.0 -54.5

Average value is      2.00
Table of differences between X(I) and average
   I         X(I)      Difference
   1        16.00        14.00
   2        12.00        10.00
   3         6.00         4.00
   4         8.00         6.00
   5         2.50         0.50
   6        12.00        10.00
   7        14.00        12.00
   8       -54.50       -56.50
```

uses three FOR loops to process the array X. The loop control variable I is also used as the array subscript in each loop.

The first FOR loop

```
FOR I IN Index LOOP
   My_Flt_IO.Get(Item => X(I));
END LOOP;
```

is used to read one data value into each array element (the first item is stored in X(1), the second item in X(2), etc.). The Get procedure is called once for each value of I in the range of Index, that is, from 1 to 8; each call causes a new data value to be read and stored in X(I). The subscript I determines which array element receives the next data value. The sample run causes the array to acquire the values shown in Fig. 8.3.

The second FOR loop is used to accumulate (in Sum) the sum of all values stored in the array; this loop will be traced later. The last FOR loop,

```
FOR I IN Index LOOP
   My_Int_IO.Put(Item => I, Width=>4);
   Text_IO.Put(Item => "    ");
   My_Flt_IO.Put(Item => X(I), Fore=>5, Aft=>2, Exp=>0);
   My_Flt_IO.Put(Item => X(I)-Average, Fore=>5, Aft=>2, Exp=>0);
   Text_IO.New_Line;
END LOOP;
```

is used to display a table showing each array element, X(I), and the difference between that element and the average value, X(I) − Average.

The program fragment

```
Sum := 0.0;                    -- Initialize Sum
FOR I IN Index LOOP
   Sum := Sum + X(I);          -- Add each element to Sum
END LOOP;
```

accumulates the sum of all eight elements of array X in the variable Sum. Each time the FOR loop is repeated, the next element of array X is added to Sum. The execution of this program fragment is traced in Table 8.3 for the first three repetitions of the loop.

Table 8.3 Partial Trace of FOR Loop of Program 8.10

Statement Part	I	X(I)	Sum	Effect
Sum:= 0;			0	Initializes Sum
FOR I := 1 TO MaxItems DO	1	16.0		Initializes I to 1
Sum := Sum + X(I)			16.0	Add X(1) to Sum
increment and test I	2	12.0		2 <= 8 is true
Sum := Sum + X(I)			28.0	Add X(2) to Sum
increment and test I	3	2.5		3 <= 8 is true
Sum := Sum + X(I)			30.5	Add X(3) to Sum

In Program 8.10, the subscripted variable X(I) is an actual parameter for the floating-point Get and Put procedures. It is always necessary to read data into an array one element at a time as shown in this example. In most instances it is also necessary to display one array element at a time. ■

Exercises for Section 8.6

Self-Check

1. Describe the effect of each statement in Table 8.2 assuming I is 5.
2. If an array is declared to have ten elements, must the program use all ten of them?
3. The sequence of statements below changes the initial contents of array X displayed in Fig. 8.3. Describe what each statement does to the array and show the final contents of array X after all statements execute.

```
I := 3;

X(I) := X(I) + 10.0;

X(I - 1) := X(2 * I - 1);

X(I + 1) := X(2 * I) + X(2 * I + 1);

FOR I IN 5 .. 7 LOOP
    X(I) := X(I + 1);
END LOOP;



FOR I IN REVERSE 1..3 LOOP
    X(I + 1) := X(I);
END LOOP;
```

4. Write program statements that will do the following to array X shown in Fig. 8.3.
   a. Replace the third element with 7.0.
   b. Copy the element in the fifth location into the first one.

c. Subtract the first element from the fourth and store the result in the fifth one.

d. Increase the sixth element by two.

e. Find the sum of the first five elements.

f. Multiply each of the first six elements by 2 and place each product in an element of the array AnswerArray.

g. Display all even-numbered elements on one line.

 # 8.7 Problem Solving: Using Arrays

We have written programs that accumulate the sum of all input data items in a single variable. Often, we have different categories of data items, and we might want to accumulate a separate total for each category rather than lump all items together. The problem that follows uses an array to accomplish this. The problem illustrates both random and sequential access of array elements.

◆ Case Study: Home Budget Problem

Problem

Your parents want a program that keeps track of their monthly expenses in each of several categories. The program should read each expense amount, add it to the appropriate category total, and print the total expenditure by category. The input data consists of the category number and amount of each purchase made during the past month.

Analysis

Your parents have selected these budget categories: entertainment, food, clothing, rent, tuition, insurance, and miscellaneous. Seven separate totals are to be accumulated; each total can be associated with a different element of a seven-element array. The program must read each expenditure, determine to which category it belongs, and then add that expenditure to the appropriate array element. When done with all expenditures, the program can print a table showing each category and its accumulated total. As in all programs that accumulate a sum, each total must be initialized to zero. The problem inputs and outputs follow.

Data Type

```
TYPE Categories IS (Entertainment, Food, Clothing, Rent,
    Tuition, Insurance, Miscellaneous);
```

Problem Inputs
each expenditure and its category

Case Study: Home Budget Problem, continued

Problem Outputs
the array of seven expenditure totals (Budget)

Design

Algorithm

1. Initialize all category totals to zero.
2. Read each expenditure and add it to the appropriate total.
3. Display the accumulated total for each category.
   The structure chart in Fig. 8.8 shows the relationship between the three steps. The array Budget is manipulated by all three procedures in the program solution. Procedure Initialize sets up the array; procedure Post stores expenditure information in this array (in accounting terminology, registering a transaction is often called "posting"); this information is displayed by procedure Report.

Figure 8.8 Structure Chart for Home Budget Problem

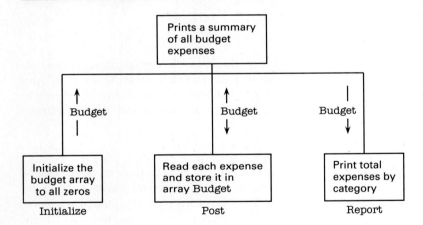

Coding
The main program is shown in Program 8.11 along with several procedures.

Program 8.11 Home Budget Program

```
WITH Text_IO;
WITH My_Flt_IO;
WITH Screen;
PROCEDURE HomeBudget IS

-- Prints a summary of all expenses by budget category.

   MaxExpense : CONSTANT Float := 10_000.00;                -- max expense amount
```

```
TYPE Categories IS (Entertainment, Food, Clothing, Rent,
                    Tuition, Insurance, Miscellaneous);
TYPE Commands IS (E, F, C, R, T, I, M, Q);

PACKAGE Category_IO IS NEW Text_IO.Enumeration_IO(Enum => Categories);
PACKAGE Command_IO IS NEW Text_IO.Enumeration_IO(Enum => Commands);

SUBTYPE Expenses IS Float RANGE 0.00..MaxExpense;    -- expense type
TYPE BudgetArray IS ARRAY (Categories) OF Expenses;  -- array type

Budget : BudgetArray;                    -- array of seven totals

PROCEDURE Initialize (Budget : OUT BudgetArray) IS

-- Initializes array Budget to all zeros.
-- Pre: None
-- Post: Each array element Budget(Category) is 0.00

BEGIN  -- Initialize

  Budget := (OTHERS => 0.00);

END Initialize;


PROCEDURE DisplayTitles IS

-- displays a list of expense categories with their abbreviations

  WhichRow: Screen.Depth;

BEGIN

  Screen.ClearScreen;

  Screen.MoveCursor(Row => 3, Column => 20);
  Text_IO.Put(Item => "Expense Categories");
  Text_IO.New_Line;
  Text_IO.New_Line;

  WhichRow := 5;
  FOR C IN Commands'First..Commands'Pred(Commands'Last) LOOP
    Screen.MoveCursor(Row => WhichRow, Column => 20);
    Command_IO.Put(Item => C, Width => 3);
    Category_IO.Put(Item => Categories'Val(Commands'Pos(C)));
    WhichRow := WhichRow + 1;
  END LOOP;

  Screen.MoveCursor(Row => WhichRow, Column => 20);
  Command_IO.Put(Item => Commands'Last, Width => 3);
  Text_IO.Put(Item => "when data entry is completed");

END DisplayTitles;


PROCEDURE GetCommand(Command: OUT Commands) IS

-- Reads a category command from the terminal
-- Post: a valid Command is returned
```

```
BEGIN

  LOOP
    BEGIN     -- exception handler block
      Screen.MoveCursor(Row => 18, Column => 15);
      Text_IO.Put("Please enter first letter of category > ");
      Command_IO.Get(Item => Command);
      Screen.MoveCursor(Row => 19, Column => 15);
      Text_IO.Put("Category accepted, thank you");
      EXIT;
    EXCEPTION
      WHEN Text_IO.Data_Error =>
        Screen.Beep;
        Screen.MoveCursor(Row => 19, Column => 15);
        Text_IO.Put("Sorry, invalid category!");
        Text_IO.Skip_Line;
    END;       -- exception handler block
  END LOOP;
  -- assert: valid command input received

END GetCommand;


PROCEDURE GetExpense(Expense: OUT Expenses) IS

-- Reads an expense from the terminal
-- Post:  a valid Expense is returned

BEGIN

  LOOP
    BEGIN     -- exception handler block
      Screen.MoveCursor(Row => 20, Column => 15);
      Text_IO.Put("Please enter expense as floating point number > ");
      My_Flt_IO.Get(Item => Expense);
      Screen.MoveCursor(Row => 21, Column => 15);
      Text_IO.Put("Expense accepted, thank you");
      EXIT;
    EXCEPTION
      WHEN Text_IO.Data_Error =>
        Screen.Beep;
        Screen.MoveCursor(Row => 21, Column => 15);
        Text_IO.Put("Sorry, invalid expense! ");
        Text_IO.Skip_Line;
    END;       -- exception handler block
  END LOOP;
  -- assert: valid expense received

END GetExpense;


PROCEDURE Post (Budget : IN OUT BudgetArray) IS

-- Reads each expenditure amount and adds it to the appropriate
-- element of array Budget.
-- Pre:  Each array element Budget(c) is 0.0
-- Post: Each array element Budget(c) is the sum of expense
--          amounts for category c.

  Sentinel : CONSTANT Commands := Q; -- sentinel command
```

```
      NextCommand  :  Commands;          -- command
      NextCategory :  Categories;        -- expenditure category
      NextExpense  :  Expenses;          -- expenditure amount

   BEGIN -- Post

     LOOP
       -- invariant:
       -- no prior value of NextCommand is Sentinel

       GetCommand(Command => NextCommand);
       EXIT WHEN NextCommand = Sentinel;

       NextCategory := Categories'Val(Commands'Pos(NextCommand));
       GetExpense(Expense => NextExpense);
       Budget(NextCategory) := Budget(NextCategory) + NextExpense;
     END LOOP;

   END Post;



   PROCEDURE Report (Budget : IN BudgetArray) IS

   -- Displays the expenditures in each budget category.
   -- Pre:  Each array element Budget(category) is assigned a value.
   -- Post: Each array element Budget(category) is displayed.

     WhichRow: Screen.Depth;

   BEGIN  -- Report

     Screen.ClearScreen;

     Screen.MoveCursor(Row => 3, Column => 20);
     Text_IO.Put(Item => "Category       Expense");
     Text_IO.New_Line;
     Text_IO.New_Line;

     WhichRow := 5;
     FOR Category IN Categories LOOP
       Screen.MoveCursor(Row => WhichRow, Column => 20);
       Category_IO.Put(Item => Category, Width=>13);    -- Print row
       My_Flt_IO.Put(Item=>Budget(Category),
                     Fore=>7, Aft=>2, Exp=>0);
       WhichRow := WhichRow + 1;
     END LOOP;

     Screen.MoveCursor(Row => 23,Column => 1);

   END Report;



BEGIN  -- HomeBudget

  -- prepare terminal screen for data entry
  DisplayTitles;

  -- Initialize array Budget to all zeros.
  Initialize (Budget);
```

```
-- Read and process each expenditure.
Post (Budget);

-- Print the expenditures in each category.
Report (Budget);

END HomeBudget;
```

The main program contains declarations for a constant `NumCategory` and two types (`Categories` and `BudgetArray`) as well as the array `Budget`. The array `Budget` (type `BudgetArray`) appears in each parameter list shown in Program 8.11 and is passed between each procedure and the main program. When passing an entire array, no subscript is used. We will have more to say about the use of arrays as parameters later.

The constant `NumCategory` determines the limit value of the loop control variable in procedure `Report`, which uses the loop control variable `Category`. In procedure `Initialize`, the aggregate assignment

```
Category_IO.Put(Item=>Category, Width=>13);
My_Flt_IO.Put(Item=>Budget(Category), Fore=>10, Aft=>2, Exp=>0);
WhichRow := WhichRow + 1
```

are used to print each category and its associated total. `Category_IO` is, as usual, an instantiation of `Text_IO.Enumeration_IO`.

Procedure `Post` must read each expenditure and add it to the appropriate array element. To read a category, we create an enumeration type for the first letters of the categories, so that the user does not have to type the entire category name:

```
TYPE Commands IS (E, F, C, R, T, I, M, Q);
```

where the type includes an extra command `Q`, which will signal the user's desire to quit the program. `Post` uses the procedures `GetCommand` and `GetExpense` to read valid commands and expenditure values into `NextCommand` and `NextExpense`, respectively. The package `Screen` is used to position the screen cursor properly to require the user to enter input at the bottom of the screen and to send a beep in case of invalid input.

A valid command (other than `Q`) needs to be converted into a category in order to determine the proper array element to update. This is done with the statement

```
NextCategory := Categories'Val(Commands'Pos(NextCommand));
```

as was done with English and French colors in Program 3.2. The assignment statement

```
Budget(NextCategory) := Budget(NextCategory) + Expense;
```

adds the expense amount to whichever element of array Budget is selected by the subscript NextCategory.

Testing

Testing the program with the following transactions:

```
C    25.00
M    25.00
C    15.00
E   675.00
Q
```

should give the following output:

```
Category        Expense

ENTERTAINMENT     675.00
FOOD                0.00
CLOTHING           40.00
RENT                0.00
TUITION             0.00
INSURANCE           0.00
MISCELLANEOUS      25.00
```

As illustrated in the test transactions, it is not necessary for the data to be in order by category.

Allowing for Array Expansion: Designing for Reuse

The enumeration types Categories and Commands are used throughout Program 8.11 to represent the budget categories. This enables us to extend the program easily to handle more budget categories, or to change the entire set of categories, by just rewriting the two types and recompiling the program. Nothing else in the program needs to be changed.

Sequential Versus Random Access to Arrays

Program 8.11 illustrates two common ways of selecting array elements for processing. Often, we need to manipulate all elements of an array in some uniform manner (as in Example 8.10). In situations like this, it makes sense to process the array elements in sequence (sequential access), starting with the first and ending with the last. In procedure Report, this is accomplished by using a FOR loop whose loop control variable is also the array subscript.

In procedure Post the order in which the array elements are accessed is completely dependent on the order of the data. The value assigned to the variable NextCategory determines which element is incremented. This is called *random access* because the order is not predictable beforehand.

Copying and Comparing Arrays

A third way of manipulating an array—accessing the entire array at once—is provided by the assignment (:=), equality (=), and inequality (/=) operations. As in the case of records, it is possible to assign the entire contents of one array to another array provided the arrays are compatible. Arrays follow the same compatibility rules as scalars and records do: Two arrays are compatible if their type names are identical or they are subtypes of the same type. Given the declarations

```
MaxSize : CONSTANT Positive := 100;
SUBTYPE Index IS Positive RANGE 1..MaxSize;
TYPE TestArray IS ARRAY (Index) OF Float;
W : TestArray;
X : TestArray;
Y : TestArray;
```

the assignment statement

```
X := Y;
```

copies each value in array Y to the corresponding element of array X (i.e., Y(1) is copied to X(1), Y(2) to X(2), etc.). Furthermore, the use of = and /= in the fragment

```
IF X = Y THEN
    Text_IO.Put(Item => "Arrays X and Y are equal");
ELSIF W /= Y THEN
    Text_IO.Put(Item => "Arrays W and Y are unequal");
END IF;
```

is quite correct. The additional declaration

```
Z : ARRAY (Index) OF Float;
```

happens to be correct Ada, although we recommend against its use. Z is declared directly as an array, instead of as a variable of an array *type* as X and Y were. The Ada compiler, which tries to establish the type name of every variable, will give Z an internal type name, which our program cannot know. The assignment statements

```
Z := Y;          -- invalid array copy
X := Z;          -- invalid array copy
```

and the IF fragment

```
IF Z = X THEN ...
```

are illegal and result in compilation errors. Even though array Z has the same structure as arrays X and Y, the type of array Z is anonymous and is not compatible with the type of arrays X and Y (type TestArray). Note that the *elements* of Z are compatible with the *elements* of X and Y (they are all Float), and therefore assignments such as

```
Z(3) := Y(5);
X(9) := Z(1);
```

and comparisons such as

```
IF X(9) = Z(1) THEN...
IF Y(3) /= Z(5) THEN ...
```

are legal.

Avoiding Anonymous Array Types

Because using anonymous (unnamed) array types causes difficulties with array assignment and comparison, the use of anonymous (unnamed) types should be avoided, and we avoid it in this book.

Arrays as Parameters

If several elements of an array are being manipulated by a procedure, it is generally better to pass the entire array of data instead of individual array elements. In Program 8.11, the procedure call statements

```
Initialize (Budget);
Post (Budget);
Report (Budget);
```

pass the entire array Budget to each procedure. Budget is declared as an OUT parameter in procedure Initialize, an IN OUT parameter in Post, and an IN parameter in procedure Report.

The rules for manipulating array parameters in a procedure are similar to those for manipulating scalar parameters: IN parameters may not be altered by the procedure; OUT parameters may not be inspected by the procedure, and IN OUT parameters may be inspected or altered at will.

The next two examples illustrate the use of arrays as parameters assuming the declarations below.

```
MaxSize : CONSTANT Positive := 5;
SUBTYPE Index IS Positive RANGE 1..MaxSize;
TYPE TestArray IS ARRAY (Index) OF Float;
X, Y, Z : TestArray;
```

■ Example 8.12

Although it is possible to use a single assignment statement to copy one array to another, no arithmetic on entire arrays is predefined in Ada. For example, the assignment statement

```
Z := X + Y;            -- illegal addition of arrays
```

is invalid because Ada has no predefined operator + that acts on array operands (we will write our own operator to add arrays in Chapter 11). Procedure

AddArray in Program 8.12 can be used to add two arrays of type TestArray. This procedure has the specification

```
PROCEDURE AddArray(A, B: IN TestArray; C: OUT TestArray);
```

The parameter correspondence established by the procedure call statement

```
AddArray (A => X, B => Y, C => Z);
```

is shown in Fig. 8.9. Formal parameter arrays A and B in the procedure correspond to actual arrays X and Y; formal parameter array C corresponds to actual array Z. The procedure results are stored in array Z. After execution of the procedure, Z(1) will contain the sum of X(1) and Y(1), or 3.5; Z(2) will contain 6.7; etc. Arrays X and Y will be unchanged. ■

Program 8.12 Procedure AddArray

```
PROCEDURE AddArray (A, B   : TestArray; C : OUT TestArray) IS

   -- Stores the sum of A(I) and B(I) in C(I).  Array elements
   -- with subscripts in the range Index are summed, element by element.
   -- Pre:  A(I) and B(I) (I in range Index) are assigned values
   -- Post: C(I) := A(I) + B(I) (I in range Index).

BEGIN -- AddArray

   -- Add corresponding elements of each array
   FOR I IN Index LOOP
     C(I) := A(I) + B(I);
   END LOOP;

END AddArray;
```

Figure 8.9 Parameter Correspondence for AddArray(X, Y, Z)

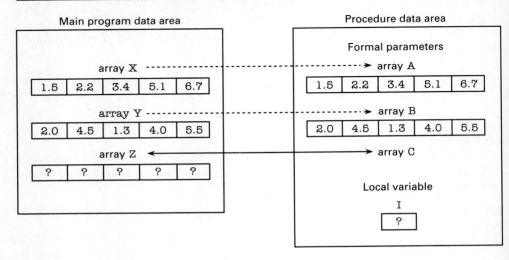

More on the Rules of Parameter Passing

Recall from Section 6.9 that the values of actual scalar IN OUT parameters are always copied into the corresponding formal parameters in the procedure's data area, and that all the OUT and IN OUT results are copied back into the calling program just before the procedure terminates normally and returns to the caller. The rules for structured parameters are somewhat different. The Ada standard allows structured parameters to be copied, as for scalars, but also allows them to be passed more efficiently, simply by copying the *address* of the actual parameter into the location of the corresponding formal parameter in the subprogram's data area. The Ada compiler writer can choose which method to use.

If the latter method (usually called *call by reference*) is used, a modification to an IN OUT parameter will be effective immediately in the calling program, instead of waiting until the procedure returns to its caller. This is because in the latter method, the formal parameter and the actual parameter refer to exactly the same set of locations. Why are the rules different for the scalar and structured cases?

Suppose that an exception is raised in the execution of the procedure, and not handled by an exception handler in that procedure. Ada requires that the procedure terminate abnormally and that the exception be *propagated* (passed back) to the calling program, which could then handle it with its own handler. In this case the scalar OUT or IN OUT parameters will not be copied back, because the procedure didn't terminate normally. This is usually a good thing: The program writer is sure that the original parameter values, not the new ones, remain in the calling program if the procedure does not run to normal completion.

Why not do the same thing with array and record parameters? Arrays and records can be large, and so copying them to and from subprograms could take a large amount of time and space. Ada therefore gives the compiler the option of just passing the address of a structured parameter. Many compilers pass *small* structured parameters by copying, and *large* ones by reference, to try to get the best of both worlds. Although in theory a user does not know which method is being used, it is reasonably safe to assume that a compiler will use reference passing for large structured parameters, and therefore

- there is no large time or space penalty in using arrays or records as parameters; and
- it is wise to assume that, if a subprogram propagates an exception back to the caller, some of the actual parameters may have new values but others may not. It is certain, however, that by the time a procedure returns normally— no exception is raised, or at least it is successfully handled within the procedure—all the parameters will have acquired their new values.

■ Example 8.13

Procedure Exchange in Program 8.13 exchanges the values of its two type Float parameters. The procedure call statement

```
Exchange (X(1), X(2));
```

uses this procedure to exchange the contents of the first two elements (type Float) of array X. The actual parameter X(1) corresponds to formal parameter P; the actual parameter X(2) corresponds to formal parameter Q. This correspondence is shown in Fig. 8.10 for the array X.

It is illegal to use a subscripted variable as a formal parameter. For example, the procedure declaration

```
PROCEDURE Exchange ( X(i), X(j) : IN OUT Float);
```

would cause a syntax error. ∎

Program 8.13 Procedure Exchange

```
PROCEDURE Exchange (P, Q : IN OUT Float) IS

    -- Exchanges the values of P and Q.
    -- Pre: P and Q are assigned values.
    -- Post: P has the value passed into Q and vice-versa.

    Temp : Float;        -- temporary variable for the exchange

BEGIN   -- Exchange

    Temp := P;
    P := Q;
    Q := Temp;

END Exchange;
```

Figure 8.10 Parameter Correspondence for Exchange(X(1),X(2))

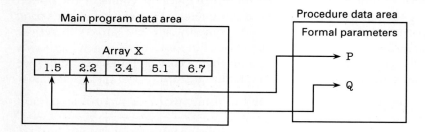

Exercises for Section 8.7

Self-Check

1. When is it better to pass an entire array of data to a procedure rather than individual elements?
2. When is a copy of an entire array made for an array that is a function procedure parameter? What happens to the copy after the procedure executes?

3. Is it acceptable to modify, within a function, an element of an array that is passed as a parameter to that function? What about a procedure?

Programming

1. Write a procedure that assigns a value of True to element I of the output array if element I of one input array has the same value as element I of the other input array; otherwise assign a value of False. If the input arrays have subscript type IndexType, the output array should have the type below:

```
TYPE BoolArray IS ARRAY(IndexType) OF Boolean;
```

 # 8.8 Problem Solving: Reading Part of an Array

Usually we don't know exactly how many elements there will be in an array. For example, if we are processing exam scores, there might be 150 students in one class, 200 in the next, and so on. In this situation, we can declare an array that will accommodate the largest class. Only part of this array will actually be processed for a smaller class.

■ Example 8.14

The array Scores declared below can accommodate a class of up to 250 students. Each array element can contain an integer value between 0 and 100.

```
MaxSize : CONSTANT Positive := 250;
MaxScore : CONSTANT Positive := 100;
SUBTYPE ClassIndex IS Positive RANGE 1..MaxSize;
SUBTYPE ClassRange IS Natural RANGE 0..MaxSize;
SUBTYPE ScoreRange IS Natural RANGE 0..MaxScore;
TYPE ScoreArray IS ARRAY (ClassIndex) OF ScoreRange;

Scores : ScoreArray;
ClassSize : ClassRange;
```

Procedure ReadScores in Program 8.14 reads up to 250 exam scores. It displays a warning message when the array is filled. The actual number of scores read is returned as the value of ClassSize.

Program 8.14 Procedure ReadScores

```
PROCEDURE ReadScores (Scores : OUT ScoreArray;
                      ClassSize : OUT ClassRange) IS

-- Reads an array of exam scores (Scores)
-- for a class of up to MaxSize students.
-- Pre : None
-- Post: The data values are stored in array Scores.
--       The number of values read is stored in ClassSize.

  Sentinel : CONSTANT Integer := -1;  -- Sentinel value
  TempScore : Integer;                -- Temporary storage for a score
  TempSize : ClassRange;
```

```
BEGIN

   Text_IO.Put(Item => "Enter next score after the prompt or -1 to stop.");
   Text_IO.New_Line;

   TempSize := 0;                          -- initial class size
   -- Read each array element until done.
   LOOP
      -- invariant:
      --    No prior value read is Sentinel and
      --    TempSize <= MaxSize

      RobustInput.Get(Item => TempScore,
                      MinVal => Sentinel,
                      MaxVal => ScoreRange'Last);

      EXIT WHEN (TempScore = Sentinel) OR (ClassSize = MaxSize);

      TempSize := TempSize + 1;
      Scores(TempSize) := TempScore;       -- Save the score

   END LOOP;
   -- assert:
   --    Last value read is Sentinel or
   --    TempSize is MaxSize

   IF TempSize = MaxSize THEN
      Text_IO.Put(Item => "Array is filled.");
      Text_IO.New_Line;
   END IF;

   ClassSize := TempSize;

END ReadScores;
```

In any subsequent processing of array Scores, the variable ClassSize should be used to limit the number of array elements processed. Only the subarray with subscripts 1..ClassSize is defined. All array elements with subscripts larger than ClassSize are still undefined and should not be manipulated. ClassSize should be passed as a parameter to any procedure that processes the partially filled array. ∎

Exercises for Section 8.8

Self-Check

1. In procedure ReadScores, what prevents the user from entering more than MaxSize scores?
2. What is the range of data values that can be entered? What is the range of data values that can be stored in the array?
3. Why can't we use a FOR loop instead of a WHILE loop in procedure Read-Scores?

8.9 Data Structures: Arrays with Noninteger Subscripts

The subscript type of each array examined so far was a subrange of the integers. This, of course, is not required in Ada, because the subscript type can be any discrete type or subtype. A number of different array types are described in Table 8.4.

Table 8.4 Some Array Types and Applications

Application

Storing a person's name, up to ten letters

Declarations

```
SUBTYPE NameLength IS Positive RANGE 1..10;
TYPE NameArray IS ARRAY(NameLength) OF Character;
Name : NameArray;
```

Example

```
Name(1) := 'A';
```

Application

Storing Fahrenheit temperatures corresponding to -10 through 10 degrees Celsius

Declarations

```
SUBTYPE CelsiusRange IS Integer RANGE -10..10;
TYPE TemperatureArray IS ARRAY(CelsiusRange) OF Float;
Fahrenheit : TemperatureArray;
```

Example

```
Fahrenheit(-10) := 14.0;
```

Application

Storing the number of times each capital letter occurs

Declarations

```
SUBTYPE UpperCase IS Character RANGE 'A'..'Z';
TYPE LetterCountArray IS ARRAY(UpperCase) OF Natural;
LetterCount : LetterCountArray;
```

Example

```
LetterCount('A') := 0;
```

Application

Storing a set of flags indicating which letters occurred and which did not

Declarations

```
SUBTYPE UpperCase IS Character RANGE 'A'..'Z';
TYPE LetterFoundArray IS ARRAY(UpperCase) OF Boolean;
LetterFound : LetterFoundArray;
```

Example

```
LetterFound('X') := False;
```

Table 8.4 *continued*

Application

Storing the number of `True` answers and `False` answers to a quiz

Declarations
```
TYPE AnswerArray IS ARRAY(Boolean) OF Natural;
Answers : AnswerArray;
```

Example
```
Answers(True) := 15;
```

The array `Name` has 10 elements and can be used to store the letters of a person's name. The array `Fahrenheit` has 21 elements and can be used to store the Fahrenheit temperature corresponding to each Celsius temperature in the range −10 though 10 degrees Celsius. For example, `Fahrenheit(0)` would be the Fahrenheit temperature, 32.0, corresponding to 0 degrees Celsius. Arrays `LetterCount` and `LetterFound` have the same subscript type (i.e., the uppercase letters) and will be discussed in Example 8.16. The array `Answers` has only two elements with subscript values `False` and `True`.

■ Example 8.15

The array `MonthSales`, declared below, could be used to keep track of the amount of sales in each month. The subscript type is `Dates.Month`, so the subscript values are the constants `Jan` to `Dec`.

```
TYPE SalesArray IS ARRAY (SimpleDates.Months) OF Float;
CurrentMonth: SimpleDates.Months;
MonthSales : SalesArray;
CurrentSales : Float;
```

The element type of `SalesArray` is given as `Float`, which can be negative. This is appropriate because in an unusually bad month, the value of returned goods can exceed that of newly sold goods, so the net sales can be negative. The aggregate assignment

```
MonthSales := (OTHERS => 0.0);
```

initializes this array to all zeros. The statement

```
MonthSales(CurrentMonth) := MonthSales(CurrentMonth) + CurrentSales;
```

adds the value of `CurrentSales` to the element of `MonthSales` selected by the subscript `CurrentMonth`. ■

■ Example 8.16

The arrays `LetterCount` and `LetterFound` described in Table 8.4 have the subscript type `UpperCase`. Hence, there is an array element for each uppercase letter. `LetterCount('A')` could be used to count the number of occurrences of the letter A in a line; `LetterFound('A')` could be used to indicate whether or not the letter A occurs. If the letter A occurs, `LetterFound('A')` would be `True`; otherwise, `LetterFound('A')` would be `False`.

Program 8.15 uses the arrays `LetterCount` and `LetterFound` described above to display the number of occurrences of each letter in a line of text. The case of the letter is ignored (e.g., 't' and 'T' are considered the same letter). Only counts greater than 0 are printed.

Program 8.15 Concordance Program

```ada
WITH Text_IO;
WITH My_Int_IO;
PROCEDURE Concordance IS

  -- Finds and displays the number of occurrences of each letter.
  -- The case of each letter is immaterial. Letters with counts
  -- of zero are not displayed.

  Sentinel : CONSTANT Character := '.';

  SUBTYPE UpperCase IS Character RANGE 'A'..'Z';
  SUBTYPE LowerCase IS Character RANGE 'a'..'z';
  TYPE LetterCountArray IS ARRAY (UpperCase) OF Natural;
  TYPE LetterFoundArray IS ARRAY (UpperCase) OF Boolean;

  LetterCount : LetterCountArray;  -- array of counts
  LetterFound : LetterFoundArray;  -- array of flags
  NextChar : Character;            -- each input character

BEGIN -- Concordance

  -- Initialize LetterCount and LetterFound.
  LetterCount := (OTHERS => 0);        -- Initialize counts
  LetterFound := (OTHERS => False);    -- Initialize flags

  -- Read and process each data character.
  Text_IO.Put(Item => "Enter a line of text ending with a period.");
  Text_IO.New_Line;

  LOOP
    Text_IO.Get(Item => NextChar);

    -- Increment the count for each letter character.
    IF NextChar IN UpperCase THEN
      LetterCount(NextChar) := LetterCount(NextChar) + 1;
      LetterFound(NextChar) := TRUE;       -- Set letter flag
    ELSIF NextChar IN LowerCase THEN
      NextChar := Character'Val(Character'Pos(NextChar)
                  - Character'Pos('a') + Character'Pos('A'));
      LetterCount(NextChar) := LetterCount(NextChar) + 1;
      LetterFound(NextChar) := TRUE;       -- Set letter flag
    END IF;
    EXIT WHEN NextChar = Sentinel;
  END LOOP;


  -- Display counts of letters that are in the line.
  Text_IO.New_Line;
  Text_IO.New_Line;
  Text_IO.Put(Item => "Letter      Occurrences");
  Text_IO.New_Line;
  FOR WhichChar IN UpperCase LOOP
```

```
      IF LetterFound(WhichChar) THEN
         Text_IO.Put(Item => "        ");
         Text_IO.Put(Item => WhichChar);
         My_Int_IO.Put(Item => LetterCount(WhichChar), Width => 16);
         Text_IO.New_Line;
      END IF;
   END LOOP;

END Concordance;


Enter a line of text ending with a period.
This is a test of the concordance program.


Letter      Occurrences
   A             3
   C             3
   D             1
   E             3
   F             1
   G             1
   H             2
   I             2
   M             1
   N             2
   O             4
   P             1
   R             3
   S             3
   T             4
```

In Program 8.15, the array LetterFound is not really needed and was included in the example mainly to show an application of an array of Booleans. The condition

```
LetterFound(NextChar)
```

could be written just as easily as

```
LetterCount(NextChar) > 0
```

Writing the condition in this way would eliminate the need for the second array. ∎

Exercises for Section 8.9

Self-Check

1. Describe the following array types, assuming IndexType is a subtype of Integer with range −5..5:
   a. ARRAY (1..20) OF Character;
   b. ARRAY ('0'..'9') OF Boolean;
   c. ARRAY(IndexType) OF Float;
   d. ARRAY (Boolean) OF Character;
   e. ARRAY (Character) OF Boolean;

2. Provide array type definitions for representing the following.
   a. The areas associated with each room in a group of rooms (living-room, dining-room, kitchen, etc.).
   b. The number of students in each grade of an elementary school.
   c. A letter associated with each color in a collection of colors. This letter will be the first letter of the color name.

8.10 Data Structures: Strings in Ada

Until now we have used strings in Ada in a very intuitive way, without much systematic consideration. In this section we will take a somewhat more systematic look at the character string, an important data structure in many applications. Ada provides a predefined type String, which is a certain kind of array of characters. A variable of type String is called a *string variable,* or sometimes just a *string.* The basic ideas are

- a string variable is in fact an array of characters, with a subscript range that must be a subtype of Positive;
- string variables can be compared and assigned like other Ada variables, but their lengths must match exactly;
- it is possible to assign or refer to a part, or *slice,* of a string; and
- strings can be concatenated, or "pasted together," to form longer ones.

Declaring a String Variable

The declarations

```
 NameSize : CONSTANT Positive := 11;
FirstName : String(1..NameSize);
 LastName : String(1..NameSize);
```

allocate storage for two string variables: FirstName and LastName. String variables FirstName and LastName can store 11 characters each (subscript range 1..11). In general, a string variable of type String(1..N) can be used to store a string of up to N characters.

Referencing Individual Characters in a String

We can manipulate individual characters in a string variable in the same way that we manipulate individual elements of an array.

■ Example 8.17

The program fragment below reads 11 characters into string variable First-Name and displays all characters stored in the string.

```
Text_IO.Put(Item => "Enter your first name and an initial,");
Text_IO.Put(Item => " exactly 11 characters > ");

FOR I IN 1..NameSize LOOP
```

```
Text_IO.Get (Item => FirstName(I));
END LOOP;

Text_IO.Put (Item => "Hello ");
FOR I IN 1..NameSize LOOP
Text_IO.Put (Item => FirstName(I));
END LOOP;

Text_IO.Put(Item => '!');
Text_IO.New_Line;
```

A sample run of this program segment is shown below.

```
Enter your first name and an initial, exactly 11 characters >
Jonathon B.
Hello Jonathon B.!
```

Eleven data characters are read into string variable `FirstName` after the prompt in the first line is displayed. The string variable `FirstName` is

(1)	(2)	(3)	(4)	(5)	(6)	(7)	(8)	(9)	(10)	(11)
J	o	n	a	t	h	o	n		B	

The statements

```
FirstName(9) := '''';
FirstName(10) := 's';
```

replace the contents of `FirstName(9)` (the blank character) and `FirstName(10)` (capital B) with the two characters shown above (an apostrophe and the letter s). The `IF` statement

```
IF FirstName(I) = '''' THEN
    Text_IO.Put (Item => "possessive form");
END IF;
```

displays the message `possessive form` when the value of `I` is 9.   ∎

A Character Is Not Compatible with a One-Character String

String variable `OneString`, declared below, is a string of length one.

```
OneString : String(1..1);
NextCh : Character;
```

The assignment statements

```
OneString(1) := NextCh;
NextCh := OneString(1);
```

are valid; they store a copy of `NextCh` in string `OneString`. However, the assignment statements

```
OneString := NextCh;
NextCh := OneString;
```

are invalid; they cause a "type compatibility" compilation error. A string that happens to be only one character long is still of a different type than a character!

Assigning, Comparing, and Displaying Strings

Besides manipulating individual characters in a string variable, we can manipulate the string as a unit. The assignment statement

```
LastName := "Appleseed";
```

appears to store the string value `Appleseed` in the string variable `LastName` declared earlier. This is not true, however: String assignment is correct only if the lengths of the strings on both sides are exactly the same. Because `Appleseed` has only nine letters, the assignment above might cause a warning at compilation time but would always cause `Constraint_Error` to be raised at execution time. If we add two blanks, the assignment will go through as desired:

```
LastName := "Appleseed  ";
```

The string variable LastName is defined as shown below:

(1)	(2)	(3)	(4)	(5)	(6)	(7)	(8)	(9)	(10)	(11)
A	p	p	l	e	s	e	e	d	#	#

where the # characters are used here only to give a visible picture of the blank. The statements

```
Text_IO.Put(Item => LastName);
Text_IO.Put (Item => ', ');
Text_IO. (Item => FirstName);
Text_IO.New_Line;
```

display the output line

```
Appleseed  , Jonathon B.
```

Note the two blanks following the last name!

As with other array types, we can copy the contents of one string variable to another of the same length, and we can compare two strings of the same length. The statement

```
FirstName := LastName;
```

copies the string value stored in `LastName` to `FirstName`; the `Boolean` condition

```
FirstName = LastName
```

is `True` after the assignment but would have been `False` before.

Reading Strings

Ada provides several `Get` procedures in `Text_IO` for entering a string value. The statement

```
Text_IO.Get(FirstName);
```

reads *exactly* 11 characters (including blanks, punctuation, etc.) into the string variable `FirstName`. The data entry operation is *not* terminated by pressing the RETURN key; if only 5 characters are entered before the RETURN is pressed, the computer simply waits for the additional 6 characters! This is a common error made by many Ada beginners, who think their program is "stuck" when nothing seems to happen after RETURN is pressed. In fact, the program is doing just what it was told: Read *exactly* 11 characters. It is not possible to read more than 11 characters into FirstName; the additional characters just stay in the file waiting for the next Get call.

This is an unsatisfying way to read strings, as it provides no way to read a string shorter than the maximum length of the string variable. A better way is to use the Get_Line procedure in Text_IO. Given a variable

```
NameLength : Natural;
```

the statement

```
Text_IO.Get_Line (Item => LastName, Last => NameLength);
```

tries to read 11 characters as before, but if RETURN is pressed before 11 characters are read, reading stops. NameLength is used as an OUT parameter corresponding to Get_Line's formal parameter Last, and after the Get operation, NameLength contains the actual number of characters read. If fewer characters are read than the string can accommodate, the remaining characters in the string are *undefined*.

■ Example 8.18

Given the declarations

```
FirstNameLength : Natural;
LastNameLength  : Natural;
```

the statements

```
Text_IO.Put(Item => "Enter your first name followed by CR > ");
Text_IO.Get_Line(Item => FirstName, Last => FirstNameLength);
Text_IO.Put(Item => "Enter your last name followed by CR > ");
Text_IO.Get_Line(Item => LastName, Last => LastNameLength);
```

can be used to enter string values into the string variables FirstName and LastName. Up to 11 characters can be stored in FirstName and LastName. If the data characters Johnny are entered after the first prompt and the data characters Appleseed are entered after the second prompt, string FirstName is defined as:

(1)	(2)	(3)	(4)	(5)	(6)	(7)	(8)	(9)	(10)	(11)
J	o	h	n	n	y	?	?	?	?	?

and string LastName is defined as

(1)	(2)	(3)	(4)	(5)	(6)	(7)	(8)	(9)	(10)	(11)
A	p	p	l	e	s	e	e	d	?	?

The variables FirstNameLength and LastNameLength will contain 6 and 9, respectively.

■

The first two syntax displays below appeared originally in Section 2.6; they are repeated here for completeness. The third display specifies the Get_Line procedure.

379

8.10 Data Structures: Strings in Ada

Character Get Procedure

Form: Text_IO.Get (Item => *variable*);

Example: Text_IO.Get (Item => Initiall);

Interpretation: The next character pressed on the keyboard is read into *variable* (type Character). A blank counts as a character; a RETURN does not.

String Get Procedure

Form: Text_IO.Get (Item => *variable*);

Example: Text_IO.Get (Item => First_Name);

Interpretation: *Variable* must be a variable of type String (low..high), where $1 \leq$ low $\leq$ high. Exactly high $-$ low $+1$ characters are read from the keyboard. A RETURN does not count as a character; the computer will wait until exactly the specified number of characters are entered.

String Get_Line Procedure

Form: Text_IO.Get_Line (Item => *variable1* , Last => *variable2*);

Example: Text_IO.Get_Line (Item => First_Name, Last => NameLength);

Interpretation: *Variable1* must be a variable of type String (low..high), where $1 \leq$ low $\leq$ high. Get_Line attempts to read high $-$ low+1 characters. Reading stops if RETURN is pressed. After the Get_Line operation, *variable2* contains the actual number of characters read. If the string variable is only partially filled by the operation, the remaining characters are undefined.

String Slicing

The flexibility of string handling in Ada is enhanced by using *string slicing*. This is the ability to store into, or extract, a *slice,* or section, of a string variable just by specifying the bounds of the desired section.

■ **Example 8.19**

Given the string variables `FirstName` and `LastName` as above, the slices

```
FirstName(1..4)
LastName (5..11)
```

refer to the first through fourth characters of `FirstName` and the fifth through eleventh characters of `LastName`, respectively. The statement

```
Text_IO.Put(Item => FirstName(1..FirstNameLength));
```

displays the string `Johnny`. Given declarations

```
WholeNameLength : Natural;
WholeName : String(1..24);
```

the statements

```
WholeNameLength := FirstNameLength + LastNameLength + 2;
WholeName(1..LastNameLength) := LastName(1..LastNameLength);
WholeName(LastNameLength+1..LastNameLength+2) := ", ";
WholeName(LastNameLength+3..WholeNameLength) :=
        FirstName(1..FirstNameLength);
Text_IO.Put(Item => WholeName(1..WholeNameLength));
```

will store in `WholeName`, and display

```
Appleseed, Johnny
```

String Concatenation

One more string operation merits consideration here. The *string concatenation* operator &, applied to two strings S1 and S2, concatenates, or "pastes together," its two arguments. The statement

```
S3 := S1 & S2;
```

stores in S3 the concatenation of S1 and S2. For the assignment to be valid, the length of S3 still must match the sum of the lengths of S1 and S2; if it does not, `Constraint_Error` will be raised, as usual. Continuing with the name example above, `WholeName` can be created more simply using concatenation:

```
WholeNameLength := FirstNameLength + LastNameLength + 2;
WholeName(1..WholeNameLength) :=
    LastName(1..LastNameLength) & ", " &
FirstName(1..FirstNameLength);
```

The result of a concatenation can also be passed directly as a parameter, for example to `Text_IO.Put`:

```
Text_IO.Put(Item =>
    LastName(1..LastNameLength) & ", " &
    FirstName(1..FirstNameLength));
```

◆ Case Study: Generating Cryptograms

Problem
A *cryptogram* is a coded message formed by substituting a code character for each letter of an original message, usually called the *plain text*. The substitution is performed uniformly through the original message; that is, all As might be replaced by Z, all Bs by Y, and so on. We will assume that all other characters, including numbers, punctuation, and blanks between words, remain unchanged.

Analysis
The program must examine each character in the message and replace each character that is a letter by its code symbol. We will store the code symbols in an array `Code` with subscript range `('A'..'Z')` and element type `Character`. The character stored in `Code('A')` will be the code symbol for the letter `'A'`. This will enable us simply to look up the code symbol for a letter by using that letter as an index to the array `Code`. The problem data requirements follow.

Problem Inputs
the array of code symbols (`Code : ARRAY (UpperCase) OF Character`)
the plain text message

Problem Outputs
the encrypted message or cryptogram

Design
The initial algorithm follows; the structure chart is shown in Fig. 8.11.

Figure 8.11   Structure Chart for Cryptogram Generator

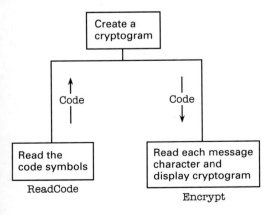

Algorithm

1. Read in the code symbol for each letter.
2. Read the plain text message and display the cryptogram.

The data requirements and algorithms for procedures ReadCode and Encrypt follow. Program 8.16 shows the program and a sample run.

Program 8.16 Cryptogram Generator

```
WITH Text_IO;
PROCEDURE Cryptogram IS

  SUBTYPE Letter IS Character RANGE 'A'..'Z';
  TYPE CodeArray IS ARRAY (Letter) OF Character;
  Code       : CodeArray;                -- array of code symbols

  FUNCTION Cap (InChar : Character) RETURN Character IS

  -- returns an upper-case letter
  -- Pre: InChar is defined
  -- Post: if InChar is a lower-case letter, returns its upper-case
  --    equivalent; otherwise, returns InChar unmodified

  BEGIN -- Cap

    IF InChar IN 'a'..'z' THEN
      RETURN Character'Val(Character'Pos(InChar)
           - Character'Pos('a') + Character'Pos('A'));
    ELSE
      RETURN InChar;
    END IF;

  END Cap;


  PROCEDURE ReadCode (Code : OUT CodeArray) IS

  -- Reads in the code symbol for each letter.
  -- Pre : None
  -- Post: 26 code symbols are read into array Code.

  BEGIN -- ReadCode

    Text_IO.Put(Item => "Enter a code symbol under each letter.");
    Text_IO.New_Line;
    Text_IO.Put(Item => "ABCDEFGHIJKLMNOPQRSTUVWXYZ");
    Text_IO.New_Line;

    -- Read each code symbol into array Code.
    FOR NextLetter IN Letter LOOP
      Text_IO.Get(Item => Code(NextLetter));
    END LOOP;
    Text_IO.Skip_Line;

  END ReadCode;
```

```
PROCEDURE Encrypt (Code : CodeArray) IS

-- Reads a plaintext (unencoded) message and displays its coded version.
-- Pre : The code for letter i is saved in Code(i).
-- Post: Displays the encoded message

   SUBTYPE Line IS String(1..80);

   PlainText  : Line;
   CodedText  : Line;
   HowLong    : Natural;

BEGIN -- Encrypt

   Text_IO.Put(Item => "Enter each character of your message.");
   Text_IO.New_Line;
   Text_IO.Put(Item => "No more than 80 characters, please.");
   Text_IO.New_Line;
   Text_IO.Put(Item => "Enter a CR after your message.");
   Text_IO.New_Line;

   Text_IO.Get_Line (Item => PlainText, Last => HowLong);
   FOR WhichChar IN 1..HowLong LOOP
     IF Cap(PlainText(WhichChar)) IN Letter THEN
       CodedText(WhichChar) := Code(Cap(PlainText(WhichChar)));
     ELSE
       CodedText(WhichChar) := PlainText(WhichChar);
     END IF;
   END LOOP;
   Text_IO.Put (Item => CodedText(1..HowLong));
   Text_IO.New_Line;

END Encrypt;

BEGIN -- Cryptogram

   -- Read in the code symbol for each letter.
   ReadCode (Code);

   -- Read each character and print the cryptogram
   Encrypt (Code);

END Cryptogram;


Enter a code symbol under each letter.
ABCDEFGHIJKLMNOPQRSTUVWXYZ
xyzabcdefghijklmnopqrstuvw
Enter each character of your message.
No more than 80 characters, please.
Enter a CR after your message.
The quick brown fox jumped over the lazy dogs.
qeb nrfzh yoltk clu grjmba lsbo qeb ixwv aldp.
```

Algorithm for ReadCode

1. Display the alphabet.
2. FOR each upper case letter LOOP

Read in the code symbol and store it in array `Code`.
```
END LOOP;
```

Local Type for Encrypt
a string subtype `Line` to hold messages of up to 80 characters

Local Variables for Encrypt
the plain text line (`PlainText : Line`)
the encrypted text (`CodedText : Line`)
the length of the message actually read in (`HowLong : Natural`)

Algorithm for Encrypt

1. Read the plain text message as a string
2. FOR each character in the message LOOP
   3. IF it is a letter THEN
   4. Convert to the corresponding code symbol.
   `END IF;`
`END LOOP;`
5. Display the encrypted message.

In the sample run, the code symbol for each letter is entered directly beneath that letter and read by procedure `ReadCode`. Procedure `Encrypt` generates two columns of output. The encrypted message appears below the plaintext one on the terminal.

Exercises for Section 8.10

Self-Check

1. Suppose that `S1` is `'ABCDE'`, `S2` is `'FGHI'`, and `S3` is declared as `String(1..8)` and has a value `'pqrstuvw'`. Explain what will happen as a result of each of these assignments:

```
S3 := S1 & S2;
S3 := S1(2..4) & S2;
S3(1..5) := S3(4..8);
```

2. Why is it that a space or a comma is not encoded in program `Cryptogram`?

Programming

1. Make changes to the cryptogram program to encode the blank character and the punctuation symbols ,, ;, :, ?, !, and ..
2. Write a procedure that stores the reverse of an input string parameter in its output parameter (for example, if the input string is `'happy      '`, the output string should be `'yppah      '`.) The actual length of the string being reversed should also be an input parameter.

3. Write a program that uses the procedure in Programming Exercise 2 to determine whether or not a string is a palindrome. (A palindrome is a string that reads the same way from left to right as it does from right to left—for instance, 'Level' is a palindrome.)

 # 8.11 Problem Solving: Searching and Sorting an Array

In this section, we will discuss two common problems in processing arrays: searching an array to determine the location of a desired value and sorting an array to rearrange the array elements in sequence. As an example of an array search, we might wish to search the array of exam scores read in by procedure ReadScores (see section 8.8, Program 8.14) to determine which student, if any, got a particular score. An example of an array sort would be rearranging the array elements so that they are in increasing (or decreasing) order by score.

◆ Case Study: Array Search

We repeat the type definitions used in section 8.8 for convenience here:

```
MaxSize  : CONSTANT Positive := 250;
MaxScore : CONSTANT Positive := 100;
SUBTYPE ClassIndex IS Positive RANGE 1..MaxSize;
SUBTYPE ClassRange IS Natural RANGE 0..MaxSize;
SUBTYPE ScoreRange IS Natural RANGE 0..MaxScore;
TYPE ScoreArray IS ARRAY (ClassIndex) OF ScoreRange;

Scores : ScoreArray;
ClassSize : ClassRange;
```

We can search an array for a particular score (called the search target) by examining each array element and testing to see whether it matches the target score. If a match occurs, we have found the target and can return its subscript as the search result. If a match does not occur, we should continue searching until either we get a match or we test all array elements. The data requirements and algorithm for a search function follow.

Data Requirements

Function Inputs

```
Scores : ScoreArray        -- the array to be searched
ClassSize : ClassRange     -- the number of elements in Scores
Target : ScoreRange        -- the score being searched for
```

Function Result

the subscript of the first element containing Target or zero if Target was not found.

Algorithm for Search

1. Start with the first array element.
2. WHILE the current element does not match the target
   AND the current element is not the last element LOOP
   3. Advance to the next element.
   END LOOP;
4. IF the current element matches the target THEN
   5. Return its subscript.
   ELSE
   6. Return zero.
   END IF;

Local Variable for Search

```
CurrentScore : ClassIndex;    -- subscript of the current element
```

The WHILE loop in step 2 compares each array element to the target. Loop exit occurs if there is a match or if the element being tested is the last element. After loop exit, the IF statement defines the function result by repeating the last comparison.

Coding

Program 8.17 shows function Search.

The WHILE loop condition compares the array element selected by CurrentScore to the target. If they are equal, loop exit occurs. If they are unequal and the last element has not been reached, CurrentScore advances to the next array element.

Loop exit occurs when the target is found or the last element is reached. After loop exit, the If statement returns the subscript (CurrentScore) of the current element if Target was found; otherwise, it returns zero.

Program 8.17 Function Search

```
FUNCTION Search (Scores: ScoreArray; ClassSize: ClassRange;
                 Target: ScoreRange) RETURN ClassRange IS

   -- Searches for Target in array Scores
   -- Pre : ClassSize and subarray Scores(1..ClassSize) are defined
   -- Post: Returns the subscript of Target if found;
   --     otherwise, returns 0

   CurrentScore: ClassIndex;        -- array subscript


BEGIN -- Search

   -- Compare each value in Scores to Target until done
   CurrentScore := 1;               -- Start with the first record
   WHILE (Scores(CurrentScore) = Target) AND (CurrentScore <= ClassSize) LOOP
   -- invariant:
   -- CurrentScore <= ClassSize + 1 and
   -- no prior array element was Target
```

```
        CurrentScore := CurrentScore + 1; -- advance to next score

   END LOOP;
   -- assertion: Target is found or last element is reached.

   -- Define the function result.
   IF Scores(CurrentScore) = Target THEN
      RETURN CurrentScore;
   ELSE
      RETURN 0;
   END IF;

END Search;
```

Sorting an Array

In Section 6.7 we discussed a simple sort operation involving three numbers. We performed the sort by examining pairs of numbers and exchanging them if they were out of order. There are many times when we would like to sort the elements in an array, for example, to display a grade report in alphabetical order or in order by score.

This section discusses a fairly intuitive (but not very fast) algorithm called the *selection sort*. To perform a selection sort of an array with N elements (subscripts 1..N), we locate the largest element in the array, and then switch the largest element with the element at subscript N, thereby placing the largest element at position N. Then we locate the largest element remaining in the subarray with subscripts 1..N–1, and switch it with the element at subscript N–1, thereby placing the second largest element at position N–1. Then we locate the largest element remaining in subarray 1..N–2 and switch it with the element at subscript N–2, and so on.

Figure 8.12 traces the operation of the selection sort algorithm. The diagram on the left shows the original array. Each subsequent diagram shows the array after the next largest element is moved to its final position in the array. The subarray in the darker area represents the portion of the array that is sorted after each exchange occurs. Note that it will require, at most, N–1 exchanges to sort an array with N elements. The algorithm follows.

Figure 8.12   Trace of Selection Sort

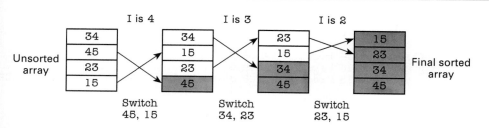

Selection Sort Algorithm

1. FOR PositionToFill IN REVERSE 2..N LOOP
   2. Find the largest element in subarray 1..PositionToFill.
   3. IF the largest element is not at subscript PositionToFill THEN
      Exchange the largest element
      with the one at subscript PositionToFill.
      END IF;
   END LOOP;

The refinement of step 2 also contains a FOR loop and is shown next.

Step 2 Refinement
2.1. Save PositionToFill as the position of the largest so far in the subarray
2.2. FOR ItemToCompare IN REVERSE 1..PositionToFill-1 LOOP
   2.3. IF the element at ItemToCompare is bigger than largest so far THEN
      Save ItemToCompare as the position of the largest so far.
      END IF;
   END LOOP;

Coding

Procedure SelectSort in Program 8.18 implements the selection sort algorithm. Local variable IndexOfMax holds the location of the largest exam score found so far in the current subarray. After each execution of the inner FOR loop, procedure Switch is called to exchange the elements with subscripts IndexOfMax and PositionToFill, provided that the element at PositionToFill is not the next largest element. After the execution of SelectSort, the elements of the array Scores are in decreasing order.

Program 8.18 serves as a test of SelectSort by initializing the first 11 elements of the array to nonzero values, setting ClassSize to 11, then calling SelectSort to sort the array and displaying the result. As an exercise you can put SelectSort together with ReadScores (Program 8.14) into a program to read the score values from the terminal.

Program 8.18   Test of Procedure SelectSort

```
WITH Text_IO;
WITH My_Int_IO;
PROCEDURE SortScores IS

-- Test program for procedure SelectSort
-- Sorts and displays an array of test scores
-- The array is initialized with eleven non-zero scores.

  MaxSize  : CONSTANT Positive := 250;
  MaxScore : CONSTANT Positive := 100;

  SUBTYPE ClassIndex IS Positive RANGE 1..MaxSize;
  SUBTYPE ClassRange IS Natural  RANGE 0..MaxSize;
  SUBTYPE ScoreRange IS Natural  RANGE 0..MaxScore;

  TYPE ScoreArray IS ARRAY (ClassIndex) OF ScoreRange;
```

```
   Scores : ScoreArray;
   ClassSize : ClassRange;

PROCEDURE Exchange(Score1, Score2: IN OUT ScoreRange) IS

-- exchanges two values of type ScoreRange
-- Pre: Score1 and Score2 are defined
-- Post: the values of Score1 and Score2 are interchanged

   TempScore: ScoreRange;

BEGIN

   TempScore := Score1;
   Score1    := Score2;
   Score2    := TempScore;

END Exchange;


PROCEDURE SelectSort(Scores: IN OUT ScoreArray; ClassSize: IN ClassRange) IS

   IndexOfMax: ClassRange;

BEGIN

   FOR PositionToFill IN REVERSE 2..ClassSize LOOP

      -- Find the element in subarray 1..PositionToFill
      -- with largest Score
      IndexOfMax := PositionToFill;
      FOR ItemToCompare IN REVERSE 1..PositionToFill - 1 LOOP
        IF Scores(ItemToCompare) > Scores(IndexOfMax) THEN
           IndexOfMax := ItemToCompare;
        END IF;
      END LOOP;
      -- assert: element at IndexOfMax is largest in subarray

      IF IndexOfMax /= PositionToFill THEN
        Exchange(Scores(PositionToFill),Scores(IndexOfMax));
      END IF;

   END LOOP;

END SelectSort;


PROCEDURE DisplayScores(Scores: ScoreArray; ClassSize: ClassRange) IS

BEGIN

   FOR I IN 1..ClassSize LOOP
     My_Int_IO.Put(Item => I, Width => 3);
     Text_IO.Put(Item => "  ");
     My_Int_IO.Put(Item => Scores(I), Width => 4);
     Text_IO.New_Line;
   END LOOP;

END DisplayScores;


BEGIN -- SortScores
```

```
ClassSize := 11;
Scores := (75, 25, 100, 62, 79, 80, 85, 75, 91, 67, 68, OTHERS => 0);

Text_IO.Put(Item => "Original Test Array:");
Text_IO.New_Line;
Text_IO.New_Line;
DisplayScores(Scores => Scores, ClassSize => ClassSize);
Text_IO.New_Line;

SelectSort(Scores => Scores, ClassSize => ClassSize);
Text_IO.New_Line;
Text_IO.Put(Item => "Sorted Test Array:");
Text_IO.New_Line;
Text_IO.New_Line;
DisplayScores(Scores => Scores, ClassSize => ClassSize);
Text_IO.New_Line;

END SortScores;


Original Test Array:

    1    75
    2    25
    3   100
    4    62
    5    79
    6    80
    7    85
    8    75
    9    91
   10    67
   11    68


Sorted Test Array:

    1    25
    2    62
    3    67
    4    68
    5    75
    6    75
    7    79
    8    80
    9    85
   10    91
   11   100
```

Analysis of Search and Sort: Big-O Notation

There are many algorithms for searching and sorting arrays. Because arrays can have a very large number of elements, the time required to process all the elements of an array can become significant, so it is important to have some idea of the relative efficiency of different algorithms. It is difficult to get a precise measure of the performance of an algorithm or program. For this reason, we normally try to approximate the effect on an algorithm of a change in the number of items, N, that it processes. In this way, we can see how an algorithm's execution time increases with N, so we can compare two algorithms by examining their growth rates.

For example, if we determine that the expression

$$2N^2 + N - 5$$

expresses the relationship between processing time and N, we say that the algorithm is an $O(N^2)$ algorithm where O is an abbreviation for *Order of Magnitude*. (This notation is called *Big-O Notation*.) The reason that this is an $O(N^2)$ algorithm instead of an $O(2N^2)$ algorithm or an $O(N^2 + N - 5)$ is that we are interested in only the fastest growing term (the one with the largest exponent) and we ignore constants.

To search an array of N elements for a target, we have to examine all N elements when the target is not present in the array. If the target is in the array, then we only have to search until we find it. However, it could be anywhere in the array, and it is equally likely to be at the beginning of the array as at the end of the array. So on average, we have to examine $N/2$ array elements to locate a target value that is in an array. This means that an array search is an $O(N)$ process, so the growth rate is *linear*.

To determine the growth rate of a sorting algorithm, we normally focus on the number of array element comparisons that it requires. To perform a selection sort on an array with N elements requires $N - 1$ comparisons during the first pass through the array, $N - 2$ comparisons during the second pass, and so on. Therefore, the total number of comparisons is represented by the series

$$1 + 2 + 3 + \cdots + (N - 2) + (N - 1)$$

The value of this series is expressed in closed form as

$$\frac{N \times (N - 1)}{2} = \frac{N^2}{2} - \frac{N}{2}$$

Therefore, selection sort is an $O(N^2)$ process and the growth rate is *quadratic* (proportional to the square of the number of elements).

What difference does it make whether an algorithm is an $O(N)$ process or an $O(N^2)$ process? Table 8.5 evaluates N and N^2 for different values of N. A doubling of N causes N^2 to increase by a factor of 4. Since N increases much more slowly with N, the performance of an $O(N)$ algorithm is not as adversely affected by an increase in N as is an $O(N^2)$ algorithm.

Because in this book we will be using relatively small arrays in our programming, algorithm efficiency is not a major concern. Analyzing the performance of algorithms is, however, an important subject about which you will study a great deal as you progress in your education, because knowing how to compute the expected big O of an algorithm can, for large arrays and other data structures, make the difference between writing a program whose running time is acceptable and one that may run for weeks or months.

Table 8.5 Table of Values of N and N^2

N	N²
2	4
4	16
8	64
16	256
32	1024
64	4096
128	16384
256	65536
512	262144

Exercises for Section 8.11

Self-Check

1. What happens in function Search if the last student score matches the target? Why can't we use the condition CurrentScore <= ClassSize in the WHILE condition?

2. Another technique for searching an array is to introduce a program flag, say Found, that is initially False and is set to True inside a search loop if the target value is found. Loop repetition continues as long as Found is still False and all elements have not been tested. After loop exit, the value of Found determines whether the current subscript or zero is returned as the function result. Write the procedure body.

3. Trace the execution of the selection sort on the list below. Show the array after each exchange occurs. How many exchanges are required? How many comparisons?

   10 55 34 56 76 5

4. How could you get the scores in descending order (largest score first)? What changes would be needed to sort the array Class by student name instead of score?

5. When looking for the largest element in subarray Scores(1..i-1), explain why the program will be a bit faster if we start the search with the last element (i.e., IndexOfMax := i-1) rather than the first element.

Programming

1. Write a procedure to count the number of students with a passing grade on the exam (60 or higher).

2. Another method of performing the selection sort is to place the smallest value in position 1, the next smallest in position 2, and so on. Write this version.

8.12 Case Study: Sorting an Array of Records

Our study of arrays began with a statement that the element type of an array can be any type, including a structured type like a record. In this section we consider how to sort an array of records.

Declaring an Array of Records

We begin with a set of declarations similar to the ones in the previous section. The new declarations define a subtype StudentName as a string of (exactly) 20 characters, a type ScoreRecord as a record containing a student's name and a test score, and a type ScoreArray as an array of these records.

```
MaxSize  : CONSTANT Positive := 250;
MaxScore : CONSTANT Positive := 100;

SUBTYPE StudentName IS String(1..20);
SUBTYPE ClassIndex  IS Positive RANGE 1..MaxSize;
SUBTYPE ClassRange  IS Natural RANGE 0..MaxSize;
SUBTYPE ScoreRange  IS Natural RANGE 0..MaxScore;

TYPE ScoreRecord IS RECORD
    Name: StudentName;
    Score: ScoreRange;
END RECORD;

TYPE ScoreArray IS ARRAY (ClassIndex) OF ScoreRecord;

Scores : ScoreArray;
ClassSize : ClassRange;
```

These declarations mean that each element of Scores is a record with two fields. We can store values in an element of the array by combining subscripting with field selection:

```
Scores(27).Name  := "Jones, Mary          ";
Scores(27).Score := 79;
```

Note that the string representing the name must be *exactly* 20 characters long, and therefore we have included the extra blanks as required. Figure 8.13 shows a diagram of this array structure, with the first three records occupied.

Reading Records from a File

In fact, arrays of records are more often filled by reading fields from an external file. Program 8.19 is a revised version of Program 8.18. The procedure GetRecords assumes that a file of type Text_IO.File_Type has been created, either by another Ada program or by a human using a text editor. In this file, each line consists of a student name and a score. In creating such a file, one must be careful to provide exactly 20 characters in the student name. Assuming

Figure 8.13 An Array of Records

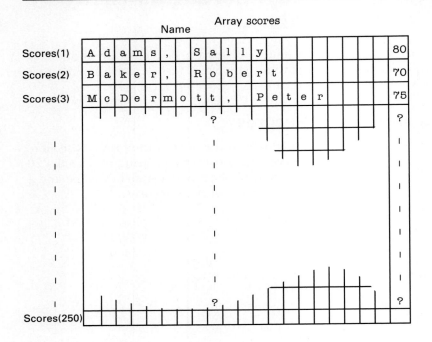

that the person who created this file was careful and that all the data in the file are valid, the two fields in each student record are read from the file by

```
Text_IO.Get(File => TestScores, Item => Scores(WhichStudent).Name);
My_Int_IO.Get(File => TestScores, Item => Scores(WhichStudent).Score);
```

This procedure is similar to Program 5.6 in its use of file operations from Text_IO.

Program 8.19 Sorting a File of Test Score Records

```
WITH Text_IO;
WITH My_Int_IO;
WITH SimpleDates;
PROCEDURE SortScoreFile IS

-- Sorts and displays an array of test score records
-- The records are read from a file SCORES.DAT

  MaxSize : CONSTANT Positive := 250;
  MaxScore : CONSTANT Positive := 100;

  SUBTYPE StudentName IS String(1..20);
  SUBTYPE ClassIndex IS  Positive RANGE 1..MaxSize;
  SUBTYPE ClassRange IS  Natural  RANGE 0..MaxSize;
  SUBTYPE ScoreRange IS  Natural  RANGE 0..MaxScore;
```

```
TYPE ScoreRecord IS RECORD
   Name:  StudentName;
   Score: ScoreRange;
END RECORD;

TYPE ScoreArray IS ARRAY (ClassIndex) OF ScoreRecord;

Scores : ScoreArray;
ClassSize : ClassRange;

PROCEDURE GetRecords(Scores: OUT ScoreArray; ClassSize: OUT ClassRange) IS

   TestScores: Text_IO.File_Type; -- program variable naming the input file
   TempSize:    ClassRange;
   TempRecord: ScoreRecord;

BEGIN -- GetRecords

   -- Open the file and associate it with the file variable name
   Text_IO.Open
     (File => TestScores, Mode => Text_IO.In_File, Name => "SCORES.DAT");

   -- Read each data item
   -- and store it in the appropriate element of Scores

   TempSize := 0;                          -- initial class size
   -- Read each array element until done.
   WHILE (NOT Text_IO.End_Of_File(TestScores)) AND (TempSize < MaxSize) LOOP
      -- invariant:
      --    Records remain in the file and
      --       TempSize <= MaxSize

      Text_IO.Get(File => TestScores, Item => TempRecord.Name);
      My_Int_IO.Get(File => TestScores, Item => TempRecord.Score);

      TempSize := TempSize + 1;
      Scores(TempSize) := TempRecord;      -- Save the score

   END LOOP;
   -- assert:
   --    End of file reached or
   --       TempSize is MaxSize

   IF TempSize = MaxSize THEN
      Text_IO.Put(Item => "Array is filled.");
      Text_IO.New_Line;
   END IF;

   ClassSize := TempSize;
   Text_IO.Close(File => TestScores);

END GetRecords;


PROCEDURE Exchange(Student1, Student2: IN OUT ScoreRecord) IS

   TempRecord: ScoreRecord;

BEGIN -- Exchange

   TempRecord := Student1;
```

```
      Student1 :=   Student2;
      Student2 :=   TempRecord;

END Exchange;


PROCEDURE SelectSort(Scores:    IN OUT ScoreArray;
                     ClassSize: IN ClassRange) IS

  IndexOfMax: ClassRange;

BEGIN -- SelectSort
  FOR PositionToFill IN REVERSE 2..ClassSize LOOP

    -- Find the element in subarray 1..PositionToFill with largest Score
    IndexOfMax := PositionToFill;
    FOR ItemToCompare IN REVERSE 1..PositionToFill-1 LOOP
      IF Scores(ItemToCompare).Score > Scores(IndexOfMax).Score THEN
        IndexOfMax := ItemToCompare;
      END IF;
    END LOOP;
    -- assert: element at IndexOfMax is largest in subarray
    IF IndexOfMax /= PositionToFill THEN
      Exchange(Scores(PositionToFill),Scores(IndexOfMax));
    END IF;

  END LOOP;

END SelectSort;


PROCEDURE DisplayScores(Scores: ScoreArray; ClassSize: ClassRange) IS

BEGIN -- DisplayScores

  FOR I IN 1..ClassSize LOOP
    My_Int_IO.Put(Item => I, Width => 3);
    Text_IO.Put(Item => "  ");
    Text_IO.Put(Item => Scores(I).Name);
    My_Int_IO.Put(Item => Scores(I).Score, Width => 4);
    Text_IO.New_Line;
  END LOOP;

END DisplayScores;


BEGIN -- SortScoreFile

  Text_IO.Put(Item => "Today is ");
  SimpleDates.Put(Item => SimpleDates.Today);
  Text_IO.New_Line;

  GetRecords(Scores => Scores, ClassSize => ClassSize);
  Text_IO.Put(Item => "Original Test File:");
  Text_IO.New_Line;
  Text_IO.New_Line;
  DisplayScores(Scores => Scores, ClassSize => ClassSize);

  SelectSort(Scores => Scores, ClassSize => ClassSize);
  Text_IO.New_Line;
  Text_IO.Put(Item => "Sorted Test File:");
  Text_IO.New_Line;
```

```
Text_IO.New_Line;
DisplayScores(Scores => Scores, ClassSize => ClassSize);
Text_IO.New_Line;

END SortScoreFile;
```

```
Today is MAR 17 1991
Original Test File:

    1   Jones, Mary          75
    2   Hubbard, Kathy       99
    3   Andersen, Lars       80
    4   Quayle, Dan          21
    5   Rogers, Roy          34
    6   Evans, Dale          76
    7   Kissinger, Henry    100

Sorted Test File:

    1   Quayle, Dan          21
    2   Rogers, Roy          34
    3   Jones, Mary          75
    4   Evans, Dale          76
    5   Andersen, Lars       80
    6   Hubbard, Kathy       99
    7   Kissinger, Henry    100
```

Sorting the File of Records

Given the SelectSort procedure from Program 8.18, sorting the file of records
is easy. Instead of using the "whole" array element as the key, or basis of
comparison, the score field of each array element is used. In the sort procedure
itself, only a single line needs to be modified: The line that compares two array
elements needs to be changed to

```
IF Scores(ItemToCompare).Score > Scores(IndexOfMax).Score THEN
```

After the execution of procedure SelectSort, the student records will be
ordered by exam score (record with smallest score first).

The revised version of SelectSort appears as a procedure in Program
8.19, with the necessary changes made to accommodate the fact that we are
using a file of score records instead of an array of scores.

Exercises for Section 8.12

Programming

1. Modify Program 8.19 so that the array is sorted by the students' names
   instead of by the test scores.
2. Combine procedures SelectSort and ReadScores, and function Search,
   into a program to read a set of scores from the terminal, sort the array, and
   then determine whether any student got a score of 75 on the test.

8.13 Tricks of the Trade: Common Programming Errors

When programmers use records, their most common compilation error is incorrectly specifying the record field to be manipulated. The full field selector (record variable and field name) must be used unless the entire record is to be manipulated. Copying one record to another or comparison of two records can be done only if the two records are of the same type. Passing a record as a parameter to a procedure or function can be done only if the actual parameter has the same type as the formal. When records are read, or written at the terminal, each field must be processed separately.

Similarly, in using arrays the most common compilation errors come from type inconsistencies. Remember that two arrays must have the same type name to be assigned or compared, and that an array passed as an actual parameter must have the same type as the formal parameter.

The most common run-time error when arrays are used is the exception `Constraint_Error`, raised when the subscript value is outside the allowable range for the array being processed. Most often, this error is caused by an incorrect subscript expression, a loop parameter error, or a nonterminating loop. Before you spend considerable time debugging, you should carefully check all suspect subscript calculations for out-of-range errors. You can check most easily by inserting diagnostic output statements in your program in order to print subscript values that might be out of range.

If an out-of-range subscript occurs inside a loop, you should make sure that the loop is terminating properly. If the loop control variable is not being updated as expected, the loop may be repeated more often than required. This could happen, for example, if the update step came after the loop end statement or if the loop begin and end were erroneously omitted.

You should also doublecheck the subscript values at the loop boundaries. If these values are in range, it is likely that all other subscript references in the loop will be in range as well. Using the form

FOR *SubscriptVariable* IN *IndexType* LOOP

instead of writing the bounds explicitly helps to ensure that the subscript variable stays in bounds, because the loop body cannot modify it.

As with all Ada data types, make sure that there are no type inconsistencies. The subscript type and element type used in all array references must correspond to the types specified in the array declaration.

A variable of type `String(1..N)` is a string variable of length N (a constant). A string variable of length N can be assigned a string value consisting of exactly N characters. If a string value that is too short or too long is assigned to a string variable, `Constraint_Error` is generally raised at run time; the error may not have been detected by the compiler. If one string variable is assigned to another, they must both be the same length. You can use array slicing to ensure that the lengths agree. Also keep in mind that if S is a string of length 1, then

```
     S := 'A';
```

399"
Chapter Review

is not valid because S is a string and 'A' is a character.

When reading a string, do not forget that the Text_IO.Get procedure for strings reads exactly the number of characters called for by the string length. If you enter fewer characters, even if you press RETURN, the program will wait for you to enter the remaining characters.

 # Chapter Review

In this chapter we studied the record data structure. Records were shown to be useful for organizing a collection of related data items of different types. We were able to create some very general data structures to model our "real world" data organization through the use of hierarchical records.

In processing records, we learned how to reference each individual component through the use of a field selector consisting of the record variable name and field name separated by a period.

Each individual component of a record must be manipulated separately in an input or output operation or in an arithmetic expression. However, it is permissible to assign one record variable to another record variable of the same type (record copy statement), to compare two records of the same type for equality or inequality, and to pass a record as a parameter to a procedure or function.

This chapter also introduced a data structure called an array, a convenient facility for naming and referencing a collection of like items. We discussed how to declare an array type and how to reference an individual array element by placing a subscript in parentheses, following the array name.

The FOR statement enables us to reference easily the elements of an array in sequence. We used FOR statements to initialize arrays, to read and print arrays, and to control the manipulation of individual array elements in sequence.

We also learned how to allocate storage for a string variable and how to store a string value in a string variable. We saw that operations such as comparison, slicing, assignment, concatenation, and display are performed easily on a string variable because the entire string can be processed as a unit rather than element by element.

New Ada Constructs in Chapter 8

The new Ada constructs introduced in this chapter are described in Table 8.6.

Table 8.6 Summary of New Ada Constructs

Statement	Effect
Record Declaration	
SUBTYPE PartID IS Positive RANGE 1111.9999;	A record type Part is de-

Table 8.6 *continued*

Statement	Effect
| ```
TYPE Part IS RECORD
  ID : PartID;
  Quantity : Integer;
  Price : Float;
END RECORD;

Nuts, Bolts : Part;
``` | clared with fields that can store two integers and a float number. Nuts and Bolts are record variables of type Part. |
| **Record Reference**<br>```
Total Cost := Nuts.Quantity
              * Nuts.Price;
``` | Multiplies two fields of Nuts. |
| ```
My_Int_IO.Put(Item=>Bolts.ID);
``` | Displays ID field of bolts. |
| Record Copy<br><br>```
Bolts := Nuts;
``` | Copies record Nuts to Bolts. |
| ```
Record Aggregate Assignment
Bolts := (ID=>2234, Quantity=>53, Price=>0.09);
``` | Assigns values to all fields of Bolts. |
| **Record Compare**<br>```
IF Nuts = Bolts THEN
``` | Compares Nuts to Bolts. |
| Array Declaration<br><br>```
TYPE IntArray IS
  ARRAY (1..10) OF Integer;

Cube, Count : IntArray
``` | The data type describes an array with 10 type Integer elements. Cube and Count are arrays with this structure. |
| ```
SUBTYPE Index IS Integer RANGE 0..10;

Name: ARRAY (Index) OF Character;
``` | The data type Index is the range used as the Index type for Name, an array of characters. |
| **Array Reference**<br>```
FOR I IN 1 .. 10 LOOP
  Cube(I) := I * I * I;
END LOOP;
``` | Saves $I^3$ in the Ith element of array Cube. |
| ```
IF Cube(5) > 100 THEN
``` | Compares Cube(5) to 100. |
| ```
My_Int_IO.Put (Item=>Cube(1),Width=>5);
My_Int_IO.Put (Item=>Cube(2),Width=>5);
``` | Displays the first two cubes. |
```

Table 8.6 *continued*

401

Chapter Review

Statement	Effect
Array Aggregate Assignment	
`Count := (3=>29,5=>17,OTHERS => 1);`	Sets all elements of `Count` to 1 except `Count(3)` and `Count(5)`.
Array Copy	
`Count := Cube;`	Copies contents of array `Cube` to array `Count`.
Array Comparison	
`IF Count /= Cube THEN`	Compares each element of `Count` to the corresponding element of `Cube`.
`IF Count(1..5) = Cube(6..10)`	Compares slices of `Count` and `Cube`.
String Declaration	
`Name : String(1..11);`	Declares a string variable (`Name`) of length 11.
String Assignment	
`Name := "Daffy Duck"`	Saves "Daffy Duck" in array `Name`.
String Concatenation	
`Name := "Jane" & " " & "Jones"`	Saves "Jane Jones" in array `Name`.
String Input	
`Text_IO.Get_Line(Item=>Name,Last=>L);`	Reads a string into `Name`. Stops if all characters of `Name` are filled or if the end of the input line is reached. The number of characters read is returned in `L`.

✓ *Quick-Check Exercises*

1. What is the primary difference between a record and an array? Which would you use to store the catalogue description of a course? Which would you use to store the names of students in the course?
2. What is a field selector?
3. When can you use the assignment operator with record operands? When can you use the equality operator?

4. If `AStudent` has the record type declared below, provide a program segment that displays the initials of student.

```
TYPE Student IS RECORD
   First: String(1..20);
   Last : String(1..20);
   Age: Natural;
   Score: Natural;
   Grade : Character;
END RECORD;
```

5. How many fields are there in a record of type `Student`?
6. If an `Integer` uses two bytes of storage and a character one, how many bytes of storage are occupied by a variable of type `Student`?
7. Write a procedure that displays a variable of type `Student`.
8. What is a composite structure?
9. Which predefined types cannot be array subscript types? Array element types?
10. Can values of different types be stored in an array?
11. If an array is declared to have ten elements, must the program use all ten?
12. When can the assignment operator be used with an array as its operands? Answer the same question for the equality operator.
13. The two methods of array access are _____ and _____.
14. The _____ loop allows us to access the elements of an array in _____ order.

Answers to Quick-Check Exercises

1. The values stored in an array must all be the same type; the values stored in a record do not have to be the same type. Record for catalogue item; array for list of names.
2. Used to select a particular record field for processing
3. When the records are the same type; when the records are the same type
4. `Text_IO.Put (Item=>AStudent.First(1));`
   `Text_IO.Put (Item=>AStudent.Last(1));`
5. 5
6. 45
7.
```
PROCEDURE WriteStudent (OneStu : Student) IS
BEGIN
   Text_IO.Put (Item=>"Student is ");
   Text_IO.Put (Item=>OneStu.First);
   Text_IO.Put (Item=>' ');
   Text_IO.Put (Item=>OneStu.Last);
   Text_IO.Put (Item=>"; age is ");
   My_Int_IO.Put (Item => OneStu.Age, Width=>1);
   Text_IO.Put (Item=>"; score is ");
   My_Int_IO.Put (Item => OneStu.Score, Width=>1);
   Text_IO.Put (Item=>"; grade is ");
   Text_IO.Put (Item=>OneStu.Grade);
   Text_IO.New_Line;
END WriteStudent;
```

8. A composite structure is a grouping of related values in main memory.
9. Float; all can be element types.
10. No
11. No

12. If the arrays are the same type
13. Direct and sequential
14. FOR, sequential

Review Questions for Chapter 8

1. Declare a record called Subscriber, which contains the fields Name, StreetAddress, MonthlyBill (how much the subscriber owes), and which paper the subscriber receives (Morning, Evening, or Both).

2. Write an Ada program to enter and then display the data in record Competition declared below.

```
StringSize: CONSTANT Positive := 20;

TYPE OlympicEvent IS RECORD
    Event: String(1..StringSize);
    Entrant: String(1..StringSize);
    Country : String(1..StringSize);
    Place : Integer
END RECORD;

Competition: OlympicEvent;
```

3. Declare the proper data structure to store the following student data: GPA, Major, Address (consisting of StreetAddress, City, State, and ZipCode), and Class-Schedule (consisting of up to six class records, each of which has Description, Time, and Days fields). Use whatever data types are most appropriate for each field.

4. a. Identify the error in the following program.

```
PROCEDURE P IS

    TYPE AnArray IS ARRAY(1..8) OF Integer;

    X: AnArray;
    I: Integer;

BEGIN

    FOR I IN 1..9 LOOP
      X(I) := I;
    END LOOP;

END P;
```

   b. When will the error be detected? What will the error be?

5. Declare an array of floats called Week that can be referenced by using any day of the week as a subscript, where Sunday is the first subscript.

6. Identify the error in the following Ada program.

```
PROCEDURE P IS

    TYPE FloatArray IS ARRAY (Character) OF Float;

    X : FloatArray;
    I : Integer;
```

```
BEGIN
   I := 1;
   X(I) := 8.384;
END P;
```

7. Is the following Ada program valid?

```
PROCEDURE P IS

   TYPE FloatArray IS ARRAY (1..8) OF Float;

   X : FloatArray;
   I : Integer;

BEGIN
   I := 1;
   X(I) := 8.384;
END P;
```

8. What are two common ways of selecting array elements for processing?
9. Write an Ada program segment to print out the index of the smallest and the largest numbers in an array X of 20 integers with values from 0 to 100. Assume array X already has values assigned to each element.
10. The parameters for a procedure are two arrays (type FloatArray) and an integer representing the length of the arrays. The procedure copies the first array in the parameter list to the other array in reverse order using a loop structure. Write the procedure.

Programming Projects

1. A number expressed in scientific notation is represented by its mantissa (a fraction) and its exponent. Write a procedure that reads two character strings representing numbers in Ada scientific notation and stores each number in a record with two fields. Write a procedure that displays the contents of each record as a floating-point value. Also write a procedure that computes the sum, product, difference, and quotient of the two numbers. (*Hint:* The string −0.1234E20 represents a number in scientific notation. The fraction −0.1234 is the mantissa, and the number 20 is the exponent.)
2. Write a program to read N data items into two arrays X and Y of size 20. Store the product of corresponding elements of X and Y in a third array Z, also of size 20. Display a three-column table showing the arrays X, Y and Z. Then compute and display the square root of the sum of the items in Z. Make up your own data, with N less than 20.
3. Assume for the moment that your computer has the very limited capability of being able to read and display only a single decimal digit at a time, and to add together two integers consisting of one decimal digit each. Write a program to read in two integers of up to ten digits each, add these numbers together, and display the result. Test your program on the following numbers.

```
X =   1487625
Y =     12783

X =  60705202
Y =  30760832
```

```
X =   1234567890
Y =   9876543210
```

(*Hints:* Store the numbers X and Y in two arrays X and Y of size 10, one decimal digit per element (type Character). If the number is less than 10 digits in length, enter enough leading zeros (to the left of the number) to make the number 10 digits long.

```
                    array X
[1] [2] [3] [4] [5] [6] [7] [8] [9] [10]
 0   0   0   1   4   8   7   6   2   5

                    array Y
[1] [2] [3] [4] [5] [6] [7] [8] [9] [10]
 0   0   0   0   0   1   2   7   8   3
```

You will need a loop to add together the digits in corresponding array elements, starting with the element with subscript 10. Don't forget to handle the carry if there is one! Use a Boolean variable Carry to indicate whether or not the sum of the last pair of digits is greater than 9.)

4. Write a program for the following problem. You are given a collection of scores for the last exam in your computer course. You are to compute the average of these scores, and then assign grades to each student according to the following rule. If a student's score is within 10 points (above or below) of the average, assign the student a grade of Satisfactory. If the score is more than 10 points higher than the average, assign the student a grade of Outstanding. If the score is more than 10 points below the average, assign the student a grade of Unsatisfactory. (*Hint:* The output from your program should consist of a labeled three-column list containing the name, exam score, and grade of each student.)

5. It can be shown that a number is prime if there is no smaller prime number that divides it. Consequently, in order to determine whether *N* is prime, it is sufficient to check only the prime numbers less than *N* as possible divisors. Use this information to write a program that stores the first 100 prime numbers in an array. Have your program display the array after it is done.

6. The results of a true–false exam given to a computer science class has been coded for input to a program. The information available for each student consists of a student identification number and the students' answers to ten true–false questions. The available data are as follows:

Student identification	Answer string
0080	FTTFTFTTFT
0340	FTFTFTTTFF
0341	FTTFTTTTTT
0401	TTFFTFFTTT
0462	TTFTTTFFTF
0463	TTTTTTTTTT
0464	FTFFTFFTFT
0512	TFTFTFTFTF
0618	TTTFFTTFTF
0619	FFFFFFFFFF
0687	TFTTFTTFTF
0700	FTFFTTFFFT
0712	FTFTFTFTFT
0837	TFTFTTFTFT

Write a program that first reads in the answer string representing the 10 correct answers (use FTFFTFFTFT as data). Next, for each student, read the student's data and compute and store the number of correct answers for each student in one array, and store the student ID number in the corresponding element of another array. Determine the best score, Best. Then print a three-column table displaying the ID number, score, and grade for each student. The grade should be determined as follows: If the score is equal to Best or Best − 1, give an A; if it is Best − 2 or Best − 3, give a C. Otherwise, give an F.

7. The results of a survey of the households in your township have been made available. Each record contains data for one household, including a four-digit integer identification number, the annual income for the household, and the number of members of the household. Write a program to read the survey results into three arrays and perform the following analyses.

a. Count the number of households included in the survey and print a three-column table displaying the data read in. (You may assume that no more than 25 households were surveyed.)

b. Calculate the average household income, and list the identification number and income of each household that exceeds the average.

c. Determine the percentage of households having incomes below the poverty level. The poverty level income can be computed using the formula

$$p = \$6500.00 + \$750.00 \, (m - 2)$$

where m is the number of members of each household. This formula shows that the poverty level depends on the number of family members, m, and that the poverty level increases as m gets larger.

Test your program on the following data.

Identification number	Annual income	Household members
1041	$12,180	4
1062	13,240	3
1327	19,800	2
1483	22,458	8
1900	17,000	2
2112	18,125	7
2345	15,623	2
3210	3,200	6
3600	6,500	5
3601	11,970	2
4725	8,900	3
6217	10,000	2
9280	6,200	1

8. Assume a set of sentences is to be processed. Each sentence consists of a sequence of words, separated by one or more blank spaces. Write a program that will read these sentences and count the number of words with one letter, two letters, and so on, up to ten letters.

9. Write an interactive program that plays the game of Hangman. Read the word to be guessed into string Word. The player must guess the letters belonging to Word. The program should terminate when either all letters have been guessed correctly (player wins) or a specified number of incorrect guesses have been made (computer wins). (*Hint:* Use a string Solution to keep track of the solution so far. Initialize Solution to a string of symbols '*'. Each time a letter in Word is guessed, replace the corresponding '*' in Solution with that letter.)

Programming in the Large: Procedural Abstraction

9

9.1   The Software Life Cycle
9.2   Problem Solving: Using Abstraction to Manage Complexity
9.3   Problem Solving: Refinement Using Procedural Abstraction
9.4   System Structures: Nested Procedures and Scope of
        Identifiers
9.5   Case Studies: Top-Down Development
9.6   System Structures: A Systematic View of Text Files
9.7   Tricks of the Trade: Debugging a Program System
9.8   Tricks of the Trade: Common Programming Errors
        Chapter Review

This chapter is the first of two that present a systematic consideration of large-scale programming, often called *programming in the large*. The discussion will focus on some principles of software development that have proved useful for designing large program systems. You will also learn more about *abstraction* and its use in programming.

In this chapter we will discuss *procedural abstraction* as a technique to aid in the refinement of programs. We will introduce the notion of *top-down development* and discuss two methods of testing programs, *top down* and *bottom up*. Most programmers and programming teams in fact use a blend of these methods.

You will also see more examples of how to use files of data with your programs. You will be able to enter program data from data files and save program output on output files. Using data files frees you from having to reenter test data continually while debugging a program. Using output files enables you to save output on disk rather than simply to view it on the screen.

9.1 The Software Life Cycle

Programming in college is somewhat different from programming in the real world. In college, you are generally given the problem specification by an instructor. Sometimes the problem specification is ambiguous or incomplete, and interaction between the instructor and the class is necessary so the students can pin down the details.

In the real world, the initial specification for a software product (a large program system) may also be incomplete. The specification is clarified through extensive interaction between the prospective users of the software and its designers (often called *system analysts*). Through this interaction, the software designers determine precisely what the users want the proposed software to do, and the users determine what to expect from the software product. Although it may seem like common sense to proceed in this manner, very often a "final" software product does not perform as expected. The reason is usually a communication gap between those responsible for the product's design and its eventual users; generally, both parties are at fault when the software fails to meet expectations.

One cause of the communication gap is that software users often are not familiar enough with computers and their capabilities to know if their requests are reasonable or how to specify what they want. Software designers, on the other hand, often assume that they are the best judges of what the user really wants; they are quick to interpret a user's incomplete or unclear specification as a "blank check" to do what they think best. To avoid these problems, it is imperative that a complete, written description of the *requirements specification* for a new software product be generated at the beginning of the project and that both users and designers sign the document.

The analysis process begins as soon as the requirements specification is completed. As we have seen in previous chapters and case studies, the most important part of the analysis is determining the inputs to, and outputs from, the system being developed.

The next stage is the design. A major part of this stage is decomposing the complete software system into a set of subsystems. Each subsystem is further decomposed into a set of smaller program units, packages, and procedures. It is important to determine whether any of these can be reused from existing systems, or from available libraries.

Another critical part of the design process is determining the software's internal data representation. In college programming, the instructor often recommends or requires a particular data type or data structure. In the real world, the programmer must choose the internal representation that will lead to the most efficient and effective solution.

Once the design is complete, it is *coded*, that is, it is implemented as a program in a particular programming language. Some programmers may have been involved with the design; others, however, are new to the project. For this reason, it is critical that the software design be carefully documented in a report that contains structure charts and high-level pseudocode. Part of the coding task involves removing all apparent program bugs (debugging) and performing preliminary tests on each procedure, module, subsystem, and system. Once the bugs are removed, the coding and debugging phase is complete, and it is time to test the software product exhaustively.

In college programming, you design, code, debug, and test your programs yourself. Testing a program in a college environment often consists of making several sample runs. Because you are the programmer and also do the testing and are responsible for correcting any bugs, the testing process often is not as complete as it should be. Once you are satisfied that the program is correct, you hand it in to the instructor and go on to something else.

In the "real world," testing is a more rigorous process that is usually performed by a group other than the programmers; the users of the software product should be involved in the testing phase. It is important to identify bugs early, because the software that controls a rocket or processes payroll checks must be absolutely free of errors before its first use.

On the other hand, it is a maxim in computing that "testing shows only the *presence* of bugs, not the *absence* of bugs." Complex programs require complex and rigorous testing to find as many bugs as possible, but unfortunately it is impossible to test every possible state of a complex program. For these reasons, it is important to develop a testing strategy that is as effective as possible, but also to have a well managed process for correcting errors that arise after the formal testing phase is over.

A software product usually must continue to perform effectively over a long period, sometimes in a changing environment. This requirement may cause periodic updating of the program. If the purpose of the update is to correct newly discovered errors, the update process is usually called *maintenance;* if the purpose is to incorporate changes—for example, revised tax laws or new features desired by the users—the update process is called *enhancement*.

To summarize, the *software life cycle* described above consists of at least the following phases:

1. Requirements specification
2. Analysis
3. Design
4. Coding and debugging
5. Testing
6. Operation (sometimes called production)
7. Maintenance

This cycle is iterative. During the design phase, problems may arise that make it necessary to modify the requirements specification. Any such changes require approval of the users. Similarly, during coding it may become necessary to reconsider decisions made in the design phase. Again, any changes must be approved by the system designers and users.

Estimates vary as to the percentage of time spent in each phase. For example, a typical system may require a year to proceed through the first three phases, three months of testing, then four years of operation and maintenance. So you can see why it is important to design and document software in such a way that it can be easily understood and maintained by a variety of users.

You may be wondering what relevance all of this has to your current course. Those of you who are majoring in computer science will, in later courses, participate in the design of large program systems. Consequently, a major goal of your first course is to prepare you to work on increasingly large and more complex problems. Some of the techniques may seem out of place or unnecessary to solve the simpler problems assigned in this class, but it is important that you learn and practice these techniques now so you will be able to apply them later.

Exercises for Section 9.1

Self-Check

1. Name the phases of the software life cycle. Which phase is the longest?

 ## 9.2 Problem Solving: Using Abstraction to Manage Complexity

Beginning programmers often find it difficult to get started on a problem. They are often reluctant to start writing the code for a program until they have worked out the solution to every detail. Of course, preplanning and concern for detail are commendable, but these normally positive work habits can be overdone to the extent that they block the problem-solving process. To make problem solving flow as smoothly as possible, use the strategy of "divide and conquer" to decompose a problem into more manageable subproblems.

Procedural Abstraction

Abstraction is a powerful technique that helps programmers deal with complex issues in a piecemeal fashion. The dictionary defines *abstraction* as the act or process of separating the inherent qualities or properties of something from the actual physical object to which they belong. An example of the use of abstraction is our description in Chapter 1 of a memory cell as a storage location for a data value. We are not concerned with the details of the physical structure of memory and memory cells; we don't need to know them to use a memory cell in programming.

Procedural abstraction is the philosophy that procedure development should separate the concern of *what* is to be achieved by a procedure from the details of *how* it is to be achieved. In other words, you can specify what you expect a procedure to do, then use that procedure in the design of a problem solution before you know how to implement the procedure.

It is also advisable to develop and test your program *incrementally*, which is to say a bit at a time. There are two strategies for doing this in a systematic way: *top down* and *bottom up*. In top-down development, having worked out a preliminary design and refinement of your program into procedures, you code at least a substantial part of the main program (which is often little more than a series of procedure calls), and then test the overall program flow using miniature, limited-function versions of your procedures, called *stubs*. You then implement the full procedures one at a time, testing them as you go. This is called top-down programming because you fill in detail, then test, starting with the main program and going downward into lower and lower levels of procedures.

In bottom-up development, you start again from your preliminary design, but this time you write the procedures one at a time and test each one using a very simple main or "test driver" program whose only function is to help you test and debug the procedure. This is called bottom-up programming because you start with the lower-level procedures and work your way back up to the main program. Generally, programmers do a combination of top-down and bottom-up testing.

Data Abstraction and Software Components

The discussion above is centered on the idea of developing *one* program, *one* time, to solve *one* problem. Refinement is used to break the problem down into smaller pieces and develop procedures to aid in solving it.

The experience of the last two decades has shown us that we should also focus on developing reusable software components, analogous to the hardware components in our computers, that are so generally useful that they can just be "plugged in" to aid in the solution of *many* problems, not just one. You have seen a number of such components already: the math library discussed in Chapter 7, the screen and robust input packages we developed in earlier chapters. Indeed, the calendar and IO packages supplied with Ada compilers are all examples of reusable components. Chapter 10 will round out our discussion of programming in the large with a systematic presentation of the development of a kind of software component, *abstract data types*.

Programming Teams

It is rare for a large software project to be implemented by a single programmer. Most often, a large project is assigned to a team of programmers. It is important for team members to coordinate beforehand the overall organization of the project.

Each team member is responsible for a set of procedures, some of which are accessed by other team members. After the initial organization meeting, each team member provides the others with a specification for each procedure that he or she is implementing. The specification is similar to the documentation provided for each procedure in this text. It consists of a brief statement of the purpose of the procedure, its preconditions and postconditions, and its formal parameter list. This information is all that a potential user of the procedure needs to know to call it correctly.

In a top-down development situation, one team member acts as "librarian" by assuming responsibility for determining the status of each procedure in the system. Initially, the *library of procedures* consists of a stub for each procedure. As a new procedure is completed and tested, its updated version replaces the version currently in the library. The librarian keeps track of the date that each new version of a procedure was inserted in the library and makes sure that all programmers are using the latest version of any procedure.

Ada actually provides a method for top-down team development of a program. This method is called *subunits;* although we are not using subunits in this book, you should be aware that Ada offers this capability.

The Ada feature that we do use heavily in this book is the package, which is Ada's methods for developing reusable components. In a team situation, one part of the team might be responsible for developing one or more reusable components. Once the package specifications for the components have been written, the other part of the team that *uses* these components can start writing and compiling their programs while the component team develops the package bodies.

 ## 9.3 Problem Solving: Refinement Using Procedural Abstraction

Let us take a systematic look at procedural abstraction as a way of refining a program. We start with a very simple example and move to some more complex ones.

◆ Case Study: A Mother's Day Greeting

Problem

Mother's Day is coming, and you would like to do something special for your mother. You decide to write an Ada program to display the message HI MOM in large capital letters.

Analysis

You can interpret this problem in more than one way. You could simply display HI MOM as it appears on this line, but that would not be too impressive. It would be more interesting to use large block letters, as shown in Fig. 9.1. Because program output tends to run from the top of the screen downward, it is easier to display the letters in a vertical column rather than across the screen.

Figure 9.1   Mother's Day Message

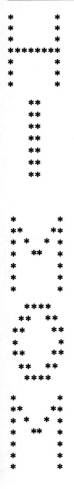

Design

Initial Algorithm

1. Display the word HI in block letters.
2. Display two blank lines.
3. Display the word MOM in block letters.

Algorithm Refinements

The obvious refinements for each step are shown next.

> ***Step 1 Refinement***
> 1.1. Display the letter H.
> 1.2. Display the letter I.
>
> ***Step 3 Refinement***
> 3.1. Display the letter M.
> 3.2. Display the letter O.
> 3.3. Display the letter M.

A structure chart for this problem is shown in Fig. 9.2.

Figure 9.2   Structure Chart for Mother's Day Message

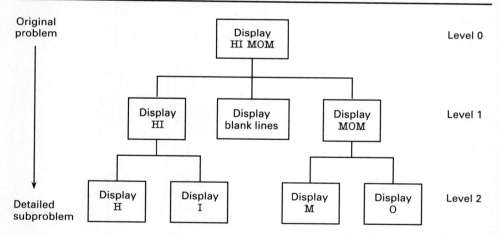

As we trace down this diagram, we go from an abstract problem to a more detailed subproblem. The original problem is shown at the top, or level 0, of the structure chart. The major subproblems appear at level 1. The different subproblems resulting from the refinement of each level 1 step are shown at level 2 and are connected to their respective level 1 subproblem. The right side of this diagram shows that the solution of the subproblem *Display MOM* is dependent on the solutions to the subproblems *Display M* and *Display O*. Because the subproblem *Display two blank lines* is not refined further, there are no level 2 subproblems connected to it.

Case Study: A Mother's Day Greeting, continued

415

9.3 Problem Solving:
Refinement Using
Procedural
Abstraction

Coding

Let us develop this program top down. We first write the main program and its two level 1 procedures, as shown in Program 9.1. Note that the two procedures are *stubs:* They do not actually write HI or MOM in large letters, but only announce that they have been called. We now compile and test the program thus far, giving the indicated output.

Program 9.1 Version 1 of Mother's Day Greeting

```
WITH Text_IO;
PROCEDURE HiMom IS

   PROCEDURE Display_HI IS
   BEGIN
     Text_IO.Put(Item => "Display_HI called.");
     Text_IO.New_Line;
   END Display_HI;

   PROCEDURE Display_MOM IS
   BEGIN
     Text_IO.Put(Item => "Display_MOM called.");
     Text_IO.New_Line;
   END Display_MOM;

BEGIN

   Display_HI;
   Display_MOM;

END HiMom;


Display_HI called.
Display_MOM called.
```

Now we can refine Display_HI and Display_MOM. The refined program is shown as Program 9.2. Note that we have chosen to write the lower-level procedures *lower* in the file than the higher-level ones. This would be fine except that Ada requires that all procedures be declared before they are called, so we need to provide the procedure specification lines

```
PROCEDURE Display_H;
PROCEDURE Display_I;
PROCEDURE Display_M;
PROCEDURE Display_O;
```

to declare these procedures to the compiler. We can then write calls to them and fill in the necessary procedure bodies below. Compiling and testing Program 9.2 gives the output shown with the program.

Program 9.2 Version 2 of Mother's Day Greeting

```
WITH Text_IO;
PROCEDURE HiMom IS

  PROCEDURE Display_H;
  PROCEDURE Display_I;
  PROCEDURE Display_M;
  PROCEDURE Display_O;

  PROCEDURE Display_HI IS
  BEGIN
    Text_IO.Put(Item => "Display_HI called");
    Text_IO.New_Line;
    Display_H;
    Display_I;
    Text_IO.New_Line;
  END Display_HI;

  PROCEDURE Display_MOM IS
  BEGIN
    Text_IO.Put(Item => "Display_MOM called");
    Text_IO.New_Line;
    Display_M;
    Display_O;
    Display_M;
    Text_IO.New_Line;
  END Display_MOM;

  PROCEDURE Display_H IS
  BEGIN
    Text_IO.Put(Item => "Display_H called");
    Text_IO.New_Line;
  END Display_H;

  PROCEDURE Display_I IS
  BEGIN
    Text_IO.Put(Item => "Display_I called");
    Text_IO.New_Line;
  END Display_I;

  PROCEDURE Display_M IS
  BEGIN
    Text_IO.Put(Item => "Display_M called");
    Text_IO.New_Line;
  END Display_M;

  PROCEDURE Display_O IS
  BEGIN
    Text_IO.Put(Item => "Display_O called");
    Text_IO.New_Line;
  END Display_O;

BEGIN

  Display_HI;
  Display_MOM;

END HiMom;
```

Case Study: A Mother's Day Greeting, continued

417

9.3 Problem Solving:
Refinement Using
Procedural
Abstraction

```
Display_HI called
Display_H called
Display_I called

Display_MOM called
Display_M called
Display_O called
Display_M called
```

Finally, now that the overall structure is well understood and tested, the lowest-level procedures can be implemented. Program 9.3 shows only the code for Display_H; the rest of the procedures are obvious given this one.

Program 9.3   Version 3 of Mother's Day Greeting

```
WITH Text_IO;
PROCEDURE HiMom IS

  PROCEDURE Display_H;
  PROCEDURE Display_I;
  PROCEDURE Display_M;
  PROCEDURE Display_O;

  PROCEDURE Display_HI IS
  BEGIN
    Text_IO.Put(Item => "Display_HI called");
    Text_IO.New_Line;
    Display_H;
    Display_I;
  END Display_HI;

  PROCEDURE Display_MOM IS
  BEGIN
    Text_IO.Put(Item => "Display_MOM called");
    Text_IO.New_Line;
    Display_M;
    Display_O;
    Display_M;
  END Display_MOM;

  PROCEDURE Display_H IS
  BEGIN
    Text_IO.Put(Item => "*       *");      Text_IO.New_Line;
    Text_IO.Put(Item => "*       *");      Text_IO.New_Line;
    Text_IO.Put(Item => "*       *");      Text_IO.New_Line;
    Text_IO.Put(Item => "*********");      Text_IO.New_Line;
    Text_IO.Put(Item => "*       *");      Text_IO.New_Line;
    Text_IO.Put(Item => "*       *");      Text_IO.New_Line;
    Text_IO.Put(Item => "*       *");      Text_IO.New_Line;
    Text_IO.New_Line;
  END Display_H;

  PROCEDURE Display_I IS
```

```
BEGIN
  Text_IO.Put(Item => "Display_I called");
  Text_IO.New_Line;
END Display_I;

PROCEDURE Display_M IS
BEGIN
  Text_IO.Put(Item => "Display_M called");
  Text_IO.New_Line;
END Display_M;

PROCEDURE Display_O IS
BEGIN
  Text_IO.Put(Item => "Display_O called");
  Text_IO.New_Line;
END Display_O;

BEGIN

  Display_HI;
  Text_IO.New_Line;
  Text_IO.New_Line;
  Display_MOM;

END HiMom;
```

```
Display_HI called
*       *
*       *
*       *
********
*       *
*       *
*       *

Display_I called


Display_MOM called
Display_M called
Display_O called
Display_M called
```

Finally, when all the lower-level procedures have been coded fully, the tracing statements can be removed from the higher-level ones, and running the resultant program gives the desired Mother's Day greeting.

A more pleasing greeting can be displayed horizontally on the screen by making a modification to this program. We change the letter display procedures to accept two parameters, a row and a column for the upper-left corner of the letter. A call of Display_H becomes, for example,

```
Display_H(Row => 5, Column => 2);
```

and the code for this procedure can be refined to

Case Study: A Mother's Day Greeting, continued

419

9.3 Problem Solving:
Refinement Using
Procedural
Abstraction

```
PROCEDURE Display_H (WhichR: Screen.Row; WhichC: Screen.Column) IS
BEGIN

    Display_String(R=>WhichR,   C=>WhichC, Item => "*        *");
    Display_String(R=>WhichR+1, C=>WhichC, Item => "*        *");
    Display_String(R=>WhichR+2, C=>WhichC, Item => "*        *");
    Display_String(R=>WhichR+3, C=>WhichC, Item => "**********");
    Display_String(R=>WhichR+4, C=>WhichC, Item => "*        *");
    Display_String(R=>WhichR+5, C=>WhichC, Item => "*        *");
    Display_String(R=>WhichR+6, C=>WhichC, Item => "*        *");

END Display_H;
```

This new procedure calls a still lower one, `Display_String`, which just displays a string starting from a given upper-left corner:

```
PROCEDURE Display_String (R: Screen.Row; C: Screen.Column; S: String)
IS
BEGIN

    Screen.MoveCursor(Row => R, Column => C);
    Text_IO.Put(Item => S);

END Display_String;
```

Implementing this last revision of the program is left as an exercise.

◆ Case Study: General Sum Problem

Problem
Write a program to find and display the sum of a list of data items.

Problem Inputs
number of data items to be summed (`NumItems : Natural`)
each data item (`Item : Float`)

Problem Outputs
sum of data items (`Sum : Float`)

Algorithm

1. Read the number of items (`NumItems`).
2. Read each item and add it to the sum (`Sum`).
3. Display the sum.

Step 2 is the only step needing refinement. Rather than refine it now, we will implement it later as procedure `FindSum`.

The structure chart is drawn in Fig. 9.3. The data flow between subproblems is documented in this chart. Downward-pointing arrows indicate inputs to a subproblem; upward pointing arrows indicate outputs from a subproblem. The variables involved in the data transfer are listed inside the arrow.

Case Study: General Sum Problem, continued

Figure 9.3 Structure Chart with Data Flow Information

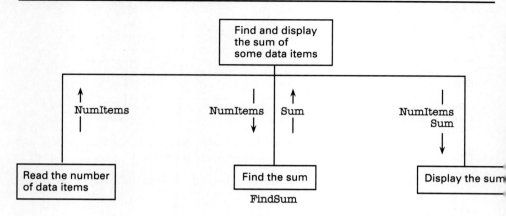

Because the step "Read the number of items" defines the value of the variable NumItems, NumItems is an output of this step. Procedure FindSum needs this value in order to know how many data items to read; consequently, NumItems is an input to procedure FindSum. The procedure result, Sum, is an output of FindSum. Sum must be provided as an input to the step that displays the program result.

Once the data flow information has been added to the structure chart, the main program can be written even if the details of the procedures are not yet known. For example, we know from the data flow information in Fig. 9.3 that the procedure call statement

```
FindSum (N => NumItems, Sum => Sum);
```

may be used to call FindSum. We also know that NumItems should be an IN parameter and Sum should be an OUT parameter.

The program is shown as Program 9.4. All the variables that appear in the structure chart should be declared in the main program.

Program 9.4 Illustration of a Procedure Stub

```
WITH Text_IO;
WITH My_Int_IO;
WITH My_Flt_IO;
PROCEDURE SumItems IS

-- Finds and prints the sum of a list of data items.

   NumItems : Natural;   -- the number of items to be added
   Sum      : Float;     -- the sum being accumulated
```

Case Study: General Sum Problem, continued

421

9.3 Problem Solving:
Refinement Using
Procedural
Abstraction

```
  PROCEDURE FindSum (N    : IN Natural; Sum : OUT Float) IS

  -- Finds the sum of a list of N data items.
  -- Pre:  N is assigned a value.
  -- Post: N data items are read and their sum is stored in Sum.

  -- this is a temporary stub for FindSum

  BEGIN -- FindSum

    Text_IO.Put(Item => "FindSum called");
    Text_IO.New_Line;
    Sum := 0.0;

  END FindSum;

BEGIN -- SumItems

  -- Read the number of items to be summed
  Text_IO.Put(Item => "How many items will be summed? ");
  My_Int_IO.Get(Item => NumItems);

  -- Find the sum of a list of data items
  FindSum (N => NumItems, Sum => Sum);

  -- Print the sum
  Text_IO.Put(Item => "The Sum is ");
  My_Flt_IO.Put(Item => Sum, Fore=>1, Aft=>2, Exp=>0);
  Text_IO.New_Line;

END SumItems;
```

```
How many items will be summed? 10
FindSum called
The Sum is 0.00
```

The declaration for procedure FindSum shown in this program is called a *stub*. Including this declaration enables the main program to be compiled, checked for syntax errors, and even run before FindSum is written. However, the program will not yet generate meaningful results because the value returned by the stub for FindSum is always zero.

We already know how to perform the summation operation, so it will be an easy matter to write procedure FindSum, and replace the stub with it, as shown in Program 9.5.

Program 9.5 SumItems with Procedure FindSum Completely Written

```
WITH Text_IO;
WITH My_Int_IO;
WITH My_Flt_IO;
PROCEDURE SumItems IS
```

Case Study: General Sum Problem, continued

```
-- Finds and prints the sum of a list of data items.

   NumItems : Natural;    -- the number of items to be added
   Sum      : Float;      -- the sum being accumulated

   PROCEDURE FindSum (N    : IN Natural; Sum : OUT Float) IS

   -- Finds the sum of a list of N data items.
   -- Pre:  N is assigned a value.
   -- Post: N data items are read and their sum is stored in Sum.

Item  : Float;          -- the next data item to be added

   BEGIN -- FindSum
     -- Read each data item and add it to Sum
     Sum := 0.0;
     FOR Count IN 1..N LOOP
       Text_IO.Put(Item => "Next number to be summed (float)> ");
       My_Flt_IO.Get(Item => Item);
       Sum := Sum + Item;
     END LOOP;
   END FindSum;

BEGIN -- SumItems

   -- Read the number of items to be summed
   Text_IO.Put(Item => "How many items will be summed? ");
   My_Int_IO.Get(Item => NumItems);

   -- Find the sum of a list of data items
   FindSum (N => NumItems, Sum => Sum);

   -- Print the sum
   Text_IO.Put(Item => "The Sum is ");
   My_Flt_IO.Put(Item => Sum, Fore=>1, Aft=>2, Exp=>0);
   Text_IO.New_Line;

END SumItems;
```

```
How many items will be summed? 6
Next number to be summed > 1.0
Next number to be summed > -3.5
Next number to be summed > 2.0
Next number to be summed > 0.0
Next number to be summed > 10.5
Next number to be summed > -7.5
The Sum is 2.50
```

Because Item is used only within procedure FindSum, it is declared as a local variable in FindSum.

Top-Down and Bottom-Up Testing

In Program 9.4, a stub is substituted for procedure FindSum presumably because FindSum is not yet written. When a team of programmers is working on a problem, this is a common practice. Obviously, not all procedures will be ready at the same time. Still, it would be useful to test and debug those that are available.

The stub for FindSum displays a message and assigns a value of zero to its output parameter Sum. The message provides a trace of procedure execution. Assigning a value of zero to the output parameter enables the rest of the program system to be tested. This process is called *top-down testing*.

Suppose that FindSum is actually being developed by a different programmer. It can be tested separately by writing a short "driver" program to call it and print the actual value assigned to its output parameter. It is easier to locate and correct errors when dealing with a single procedure rather than when dealing with a complete program system. Once we are confident that FindSum works properly, we can substitute it for its stub in the program system. The process of separately testing individual procedures before inserting them in the program system is called *bottom-up testing*.

By following a combination of top-down and bottom-up testing, the programming team can be fairly confident that the complete program system will be relatively free of errors when it is finally put together. Consequently, the final debugging sessions should proceed quickly and smoothly.

Exercises for Section 9.3

Self-Check

1. Often in developing a program top down, it turns out that procedures are written that are usable beyond the current program. For example, the Mother's Day greeting program included a number of procedures to display individual letters. These could be useful in other programs. How would you approach the problem of saving these procedures for reuse?

Programming

1. Modify the Mother's Day greeting program, as suggested in this section, so that the large letters appear horizontally in a row across the screen, instead of vertically.

 ## 9.4 System Structures: Nested Procedures and Scope of Identifiers

In Program 9.5, procedure FindSum is *nested* or contained in program SumItems. It is also possible for one subprogram (procedure or function) to be nested within another. For example, procedure PrintLine is nested within procedure Triangle in Program 9.6. It is important that you understand the effects of nesting, because most programming languages allow it. Therefore we will explain nesting and show a few examples of its effects; but nesting subprograms inside other subprograms is not done as frequently these days as it once was, and we recommend against doing it. Generally in this book, subprograms are contained within either main programs or within package bodies, not within other subprograms; this is the style we recommend that you follow.

Program 9.6   Illustration of a Nested Procedure

```
WITH Text_IO;
PROCEDURE TestTriangle IS

   PROCEDURE Triangle (NumRows : IN Natural) IS

   -- Prints a triangle by displaying lines of increasing length.
   -- The number of lines is determined by NumRows.
   -- Pre: NumRows is assigned a value.
   -- Post: A triangle is displayed.
   -- Requirements: Calls procedure PrintLine to display each line.
```

```
PROCEDURE PrintLine (NumStars : IN Natural) IS

  -- Prints a row of asterisks. The number of
  -- asterisks printed is determined by NumStars.
  -- Pre:  NumStars is assigned a value.
  -- Post: A row of asterisks is displayed.

    Star : CONSTANT Character := '*';   -- symbol being printed

  BEGIN -- PrintLine

    -- Print a row of asterisks
    FOR CountStar IN 1 .. NumStars LOOP
      Text_IO.Put(Item => Star);
    END LOOP;
    Text_IO.New_Line;

  END PrintLine;

BEGIN -- Triangle

  -- Print lines of increasing length
  FOR Row IN 1 .. NumRows LOOP
   PrintLine (NumStars => Row);
  END LOOP;

END Triangle;

BEGIN -- TestTriangle

  Triangle(NumRows => 6);

END TestTriangle;



*
**
***
****
*****
******
```

Each procedure in a nest of procedures has its own declaration part and body; there is also a declaration part and body for the main program. A procedure's parameter list is included in its declaration part.

Figure 9.4 displays the organization of procedures in program Nested. Each box represents a procedure or program *block*. A block consists of the declaration part and body of a program or procedure.

Procedures Outer and Too are nested within the main program block. Procedure Inner is shown nested within the block for Outer.

Figure 9.4 Procedure Nesting

```
PROCEDURE Nested IS

    X, Y : Float;  <------- scope of Y

    PROCEDURE Outer (X : IN OUT Float) IS

       M, N : Integer;  <----------- scope of M

    PROCEDURE Inner (Z : Float) IS <--------------- scope of Z

       N, O : INTEGER;
    BEGIN -- Inner
       .......
    END Inner;

    BEGIN -- Outer
       .......
    END Outer;

    PROCEDURE Too IS

       Blank: CONSTANT Character := ' ';  <---------- scope of Blank

    BEGIN -- Too
       .......
    END Too;

    BEGIN --Nested
       .......
    END Nested;
```

Scope of Identifiers

It is important to understand that Ada permits a subprogram to reference identifiers that are not declared locally. The Ada scope rules below tell us where an identifier may be referenced.

Ada Scope Rules

1. The scope of an identifier is the block in which it is declared. Therefore, an identifier declared in procedure P may be referenced in procedure P and all procedures enclosed in (nested in) procedure P.
2. If an identifier I declared in procedure P is redeclared in some inner procedure Q enclosed in P, then procedure Q and all its enclosed procedures are excluded from the scope of I declared in P.

According to rule 1, the *scope of an identifier* is the block in which it is declared. The scope of the constant Blank in Fig. 9.4 is the block for procedure

Too; therefore, `Blank` may be referenced only in procedure `Too`. The scope of a procedure's formal parameters is the same as for all identifiers declared in that procedure.

With regard to Fig. 9.4, because procedure `Inner` is nested in procedure `Outer`, the scope of an identifier declared in procedure `Outer` includes the block for procedure `Inner`. Therefore an identifier declared in `Outer` (e.g., variable `M`) may be referenced in the body of either procedure.

Rule 2 takes effect when there are multiple declarations of the same identifier. This rule will be discussed in the next section.

Because all procedures are nested within the main program block, an identifier declared in the main program may be referenced anywhere in the program system. For this reason, main program variables are called *global variables*.

Although global variables may be referenced in procedures, experience has shown this to be a very dangerous practice. If a procedure references a global variable, then it is possible for the value of that variable to be changed when the procedure is executed (this is called a *side effect*). Often, there is no documentation to indicate that the procedure manipulates a global variable; consequently, it may be difficult to find a statement in a procedure that is responsible for assigning an incorrect or unexpected value to a global variable.

The formal parameter list and local declarations for a procedure explicitly document the data that will be manipulated. We will continue generally to manipulate only identifiers (including parameters) that are declared locally in a procedure. The only exceptions will be global constants and type identifiers. It is alright to reference a global constant in a procedure because Ada does not allow the value of a constant to be changed. Hence there can't be a side effect when a global constant is referenced.

Multiple Declarations of Identifiers

An identifier may be declared only once in a given procedure; however, the same identifier may be declared in more than one procedure. In Fig. 9.4, for example, `X` is declared as a global variable in the main program and as a formal parameter in procedure `Outer`. Consequently, when `X` is referenced in the program system there may be some question in our minds as to which declaration takes precedence.

Scope rule 2 states that procedures `Outer` and `Inner` are excluded from the scope of global variable `X` because `X` is declared as a formal parameter of `Outer`. Therefore, when `X` is referenced in the body of procedure `Outer` or `Inner`, formal parameter `X` is manipulated. When `X` is referenced anywhere else in the program system, global variable `X` is manipulated. In general, the declaration that takes precedence is the closest declaration with a scope that includes the point of reference. This will always be a local declaration if one exists.

If an identifier is not declared locally, then a declaration in an outer block containing the point of reference is used. For example, if identifier `N` is referenced in procedure `Inner` or procedure `Outer`, the corresponding local declaration for identifier `N` is used. If identifier `M` is referenced in procedure `Inner` where it is not declared locally, the declaration for variable M in procedure Outer is used. A reference to identifier M in either the main program body or procedure Too would cause an "identifier not declared" compilation error.

Table 9.1 shows the meaning of each valid reference to an identifier in the blocks of Fig. 9.4. Procedure names have been included with other identifiers in this table. They will be discussed in the next section.

Table 9.1   Valid Identifier References for Fig. 9.4

Block	Meaning of Each Identifier
Inner	Z (parameter of Inner) N, O (local variables) M (variable declared in Outer) X (parameter of Outer) Inner (procedure declared in Outer) Y (variable declared in Nested) Outer (procedure declared in Nested)
Outer	X (parameter of Outer) M, N (local variables) Inner (local procedure) Y (variable declared in Nested) Outer (procedure declared in Nested)
Too	Blank (local constant) X, Y (global variables) Outer (procedure declared in Nested) Too (procedure declared in Nested)
Nested	X, Y (global variables) Outer (procedure declared in Nested) Too (procedure declared in Nested)

Procedure Calls

Because procedure names are identifiers, the Ada scope rules specify where a procedure may be referenced or called. Procedures Outer and Too are global identifiers (declared in the main program), so they may be called by any of the procedures or by main, with one exception: Because the declaration of Outer precedes that of Too, Outer cannot call Too. Procedure Inner is declared in procedure Outer, so it may be called only by procedure Outer or by Inner itself. A procedure calling itself is known as a *recursive procedure call;* recursive calling will be taken up in Chapter 13.

As things stand now, a call to Inner in the body of procedure Too or the main program body would cause an "identifier is undeclared" compilation error. If we declare procedure Inner in the main program instead of inside procedure Outer, then both the main program and procedure Too will be able to call

Inner. We could allow Outer to call Too by preceding the declaration of Outer by a specification of Too:

```
PROCEDURE Too;
```

This satisfies Ada's rule that a procedure must be declared (at least by a specification) before a statement in which it is called is valid.

Even this simple example of nesting illustrates the possible confusion that can arise from nesting subprograms inside other subprograms. We recommend strongly that you avoid potential confusion by avoiding nesting. Including subprograms only in the main program or in package bodies will ensure that procedures have a simple set of other procedures and variables that they can reference.

Exercises for Section 9.4

Self-Check

1. Explain why variable N declared in Outer cannot be referenced by the main program, procedure Inner, or procedure Too.
2. What would be the effect of executing the body of Inner shown below?

```
BEGIN --Inner
  X := 5.5;
  Y := 6.6;
  M := 2;
  N := 3;
  O := 4;
END Inner;
```

3. If the statement sequence above were also the body of Outer, Too, or Nested, then some of the assignment statements would give rise to compilation errors. Identify the incorrect statements and indicate the effect of executing all the others in each block.

 # 9.5 Case Studies: Top-Down Development

In this section the top-down design process will be demonstrated in solving two problems. The program solutions will be implemented in a stepwise manner, starting at the top of the structure chart or with the main program.

◆ Case Study: Balancing a Checkbook

Problem

You have just received a new personal computer and would like to write a program to help balance your checkbook. The program will read your initial checkbook balance and each transaction (check or deposit). It will print the new balance after each transaction and a warning message if the balance becomes negative. At the end of the session, the starting and final balances should be printed along with a count of the number of checks and deposits processed.

Analysis

After the starting balance is read, each transaction will be read and processed separately. We can use a simple code ('C' or 'D') to distinguish between checks and deposits. The transaction amount will be a positive floating-point number. The starting balance must be available at the end, so we will save it in variable StartBal and use a different variable (CurBal) to keep track of the current balance.

Problem Inputs
starting checkbook balance (StartBal : NonNegFloat)
transaction data
type of transaction (TranType : Character)
amount of transaction (Amount : Float)

Problem Outputs
current balance after each transaction (CurBal : Float)
number of checks (NumCheck : Natural)
number of deposits (NumDep : Natural)

Design

Algorithm

1. Display the instructions and read the starting balance.
2. For each transaction: Read the transaction, update and display the current balance, and increment the count of checks or deposits.
3. Display the starting and final balance and the number of checks and deposits processed.

The structure chart for this algorithm is shown in Fig. 9.5. The level 1 subproblems will be written as procedures Instruct, Process, and Report, respectively. The data flow information shows that StartBal is read by Instruct and passed to Process. Procedure Process defines the program results (CurBal, NumCheck, NumDep); these results are passed to Report and displayed.

The variables shown in the structure chart should be declared in the main program because each variable must be declared at the highest level in which it appears in the structure chart. Variables that are passed between the main program and a level 1 procedure must be declared in the main program.

The data flow information is used to write the parameter lists in Program 9.7. Procedures Instruct and Report consist of input/output statements only,

Figure 9.5 Structure Chart (Levels 0 and 1) for Checkbook Problem

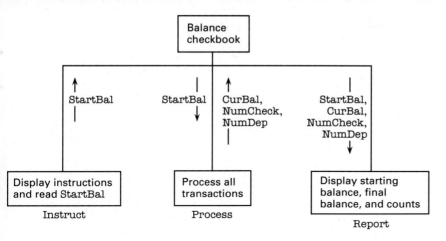

so they are written now. Because procedure Process requires further refinement, it is written as a stub.

Procedure Process performs step 2 of the algorithm, which is repeated below.

Program 9.7 Checkbook Program with Stub for Process

```
WITH Text_IO;
WITH My_Int_IO;
WITH My_Flt_IO;
PROCEDURE CheckBook IS

  -- Reads the starting balance for a checking account and processes
  -- all transactions. Prints the new balance after each transaction
  -- is processed. Also prints a count of the total number of checks
  -- and deposits processed.

  StartBal  : Float;          -- input - starting balance
  CurBal    : Float;          -- output - current balance
  NumCheck  : Natural;        -- output - number of checks
  NumDep    : Natural;        -- output - number of deposits

PROCEDURE Instruct (StartBal : OUT Float) IS

  -- Displays the instructions and reads the starting balance.
  -- Pre: None
  -- Post: User instructions are displayed and StartBal is read in.

BEGIN  -- Instruct

  Text_IO.Put(Item => "Balance your checking account!");
  Text_IO.New_Line;
```

```
      Text_IO.New_Line;
      Text_IO.Put(Item => "Enter C (Check), D (Deposit), or Q (Quit)");
      Text_IO.New_Line;
      Text_IO.Put(Item => "after prompt C, D, or Q: ");
      Text_IO.New_Line;
      Text_IO.Put(Item => "Enter a positive number after prompt Amount $");
      Text_IO.New_Line;
      Text_IO.New_Line;
      Text_IO.Put(Item => "Begin by entering your starting balance $");
      My_Flt_IO.Get(Item => StartBal);

    END Instruct;


    PROCEDURE Process (StartBal : IN Float;
                       CurBal   : IN OUT Float;
                       NumCheck : IN OUT Natural;
                       NumDep   : IN OUT Natural) IS

    -- Processes each transaction. Reads each transaction, updates and
    -- prints the current balance and increments the count of checks or
    -- deposits.
    -- Pre:  StartBal is assigned a value.
    -- Post: CurBal is StartBal plus deposits and minus withdrawals.
    --       NumCheck is the count of checks.
    --       NumDep is the count of deposits.
    -- Uses: ReadTran, Update, and DisplayTran

      TranType : Character;      -- transaction type (check or deposit)
      Amount : Float;            -- transaction amount

    BEGIN -- Process stub

      Text_IO.Put(Item => "Procedure Process entered.");
      Text_IO.New_Line;
      CurBal := StartBal;
      NumCheck := 0;
      NumDep := 0;

    END Process;


    PROCEDURE Report (StartBal : IN Float;
                      CurBal   : IN Float;
                      NumCheck : IN Natural;
                      NumDep   : IN Natural) IS

    -- Prints the starting and final balances and the count of checks
    -- and deposits.
    -- Pre: StartBal, CurBal, NumCheck, and NumDep are assigned values.
    -- Post: Program results are displayed.

    BEGIN -- Report

      Text_IO.New_Line;
      Text_IO.Put(Item => "Starting balance was $");
      My_Flt_IO.Put(Item => StartBal, Fore=>1, Aft=>2, Exp=>0);
      Text_IO.New_Line;
      Text_IO.Put(Item => "Final    balance is  $");
      My_Flt_IO.Put(Item => CurBal , Fore=>1, Aft=>2, Exp=>0);
      Text_IO.New_Line;
```

```
        Text_IO.Put(Item => "Number of checks written: ");
        My_Int_IO.Put(Item => NumCheck, Width=>1);
        Text_IO.New_Line;
        Text_IO.Put(Item => "Number of deposits made : ");
        My_Int_IO.Put(Item => NumDep, Width=>1);
        Text_IO.New_Line;

    END Report;


BEGIN -- CheckBook
  -- Display user instructions and read StartBal
  Instruct (StartBal);

  -- Process each transaction
  Process (StartBal, CurBal, NumCheck, NumDep);

  -- Print starting and final balances and count of checks/deposits
  Report (StartBal, CurBal, NumCheck, NumDep);

END CheckBook;



Balance your checking account!

Enter C (Check), D (Deposit), or Q (Quit)
after prompt C, D, or Q:
Enter a positive number after prompt Amount $

Begin by entering your starting balance $1000.00
Procedure Process entered.

Starting balance was $1000.00
Final    balance is  $1000.00
Number of checks written: 0
Number of deposits made : 0
```

Algorithm for Process

For each transaction: Read the transaction, update and display the current balance, and increment the count of checks or deposits.

A WHILE loop is needed to control the processing. Assuming that we do not know how many transactions will occur, we can use a sentinel-controlled loop that compares the transaction code to a sentinel value. The loop properties follow.

- Curbal is StartBal plus all transactions that are deposits and minus all transactions that are checks.
- NumCheck is the count of checks so far.
- NumDep is the count of deposits so far.
- The transaction code is the sentinel just after loop exit.

These statements suggest the refinement below.

Refinement of Algorithm for Process

1. Initialize NumCheck and NumDep to zero
2. Initialize CurBal to StartBal
3. Read the first transaction
4. WHILE the transaction code is not the sentinel LOOP
   5. Update CurBal and increment NumCheck or NumDep
   6. Display CurBal and the transaction
   7. Read the next transaction
   END LOOP

The structure chart for Process is shown in Fig. 9.6. Procedure ReadTran performs steps 3 and 7, Update performs step 5, and DisplayTran performs step 6. Two new variables, TranType and Amount, should be declared as local variables in procedure Process. Variables passed between a level 1 and level 2 procedure should be declared in the level 1 procedure. The identifiers CurBal, NumCheck, and NumDep are declared already as formal parameters of Process.

Figure 9.6 Structure Chart for Procedure Process

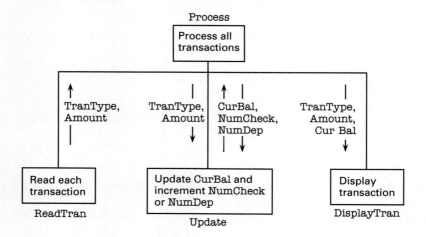

Local Variables for Process
the transaction type (TranType : Character)
the transaction amount (Amount : Float)

The procedure structure prescribed by this structure chart and the earlier one is summarized in Fig. 9.7.

Figure 9.7 Procedure Structure for Checkbook Problem.

```
PROCEDURE CheckBook
    PROCEDURE Instruct
    PROCEDURE Process
    PROCEDURE ReadTran
    PROCEDURE Update
    PROCEDURE DisplayTran
    PROCEDURE Report
```

Procedure `Process` processes all transactions. `Process` calls `ReadTran` to read each transaction, `Update` to process the transaction just read, and `DisplayTran` to display the result.

Procedure `DisplayTran` should contain a nested IF statement that differentiates between checks and deposits. When `TranType` is `'C'`, the inner IF statement is executed and is used to detect an overdrawn account (`CurBal` is negative).

Procedure `Update` should consist of an IF statement that implements the decision table shown in Table 9.2. Program 9.8 gives procedure `Process` and the other procedures it uses. As an exercise, you can finish coding of the lower-level procedures and integrate them and `Process` into the main program. Your test output should agree with the sample run of program `CheckBook` shown in Fig. 9.8.

Table 9.2 Decision Table for Update

Condition	Desired Action
TranType = 'D'	Increment NumDep, add Amount to CurBal
TranType = 'C'	Increment NumCheck, subtract Amount from CurBal

Program 9.8 Procedure Process with Specifications of Lower-Level Procedures

```
-- specifications of lower-level procedures used by Process

PROCEDURE ReadTran (TranType : IN OUT Character; Amount    : OUT Float);

PROCEDURE Update (TranType : IN Character;
                  Amount   : IN Float;
                  CurBal   : IN OUT Float;
                  NumCheck : IN OUT Natural;
                  NumDep   : IN OUT Natural);

PROCEDURE DisplayTran (TranType : IN Character;
                       Amount   : IN Float;
                       CurBal   : IN Float);
```

```
PROCEDURE Process (StartBal : IN Float;
                   CurBal   : IN OUT Float;
                   NumCheck : IN OUT Natural;
                   NumDep   : IN OUT Natural) IS

-- Processes each transaction. Reads each transaction, updates and
-- prints the current balance and increments the count of checks or
-- deposits.
-- Pre:  StartBal is assigned a value.
-- Post: CurBal is StartBal plus deposits and minus withdrawals.
--       NumCheck is the count of checks.
--       NumDep is the count of deposits.
-- Uses: ReadTran, Update, and DisplayTran
  Sentinel: Character;
  TranType : Character;      -- transaction type (check or deposit)
  Amount : Float;            -- transaction amount

BEGIN -- Process

  -- Initialize counters to zero and CurBal to StartBal
  NumCheck := 0;
  NumDep := 0;
  CurBal := StartBal;

  -- Read first transaction
  ReadTran (TranType, Amount);

  -- Process each transaction until done
  WHILE TranType /= Sentinel LOOP
    Update (TranType, Amount, CurBal, NumCheck, NumDep);
    DisplayTran (TranType, Amount, CurBal);
    ReadTran (TranType, Amount);
  END LOOP;

END Process;
```

Figure 9.8   Sample Run of Checkbook Balancing Program

```
Balance your checking account!
Enter C (Check), D (Deposit), or Q (Quit)
after prompt C, D, or Q:

Enter a positive number after prompt Amount $

Begin by entering your starting balance $1000.00

C, D, or Q: D
Amount $100.00
Depositing $ 100.00 Balance of $ 1100.00

C, D, or Q: C
Amount $1200.00
Check for $ 1200.00 Balance of $-100.00
Warning! Your account is overdrawn.

C, D, or Q: X
Amount $500.00
Invalid transaction type X -- transaction ignored.
```

```
C, D, or Q: D
Amount $500.00
Depositing $ 500.00 Balance of $ 400.00


C, D, or Q: Q

Starting balance was $ 1000.00
Final balance is $400.00
Number of checks written: 1
Number of deposits made : 2
```

The program system for the checkbook problem is a good illustration of stepwise design and top-down testing. It uses procedures to implement each of the subproblems shown in the structure chart. Each procedure is relatively short and has a purpose that is simple, well defined, and easy to understand.

The main program at the bottom of Program 9.7 contains three procedure call statements. The second procedure call statement

```
Process (StartBal, CurBal, NumCheck, NumDep);
```

is used to process all transactions. Procedure `Process` calls procedures `ReadTran`, `Update`, and `DisplayTran` to perform the read, update, and display operations, respectively.

The variables `TranType` and `Amount` are declared in `Process` because they are used only by `Process` and the level 2 procedures, which receive `TranType` as a parameter. The constants `Sentinel`, `Check`, and `Deposit` are declared globally, because they must be referenced in the level 2 procedures.

◆ Case Study: Summarizing the Grades on an Exam

Problem

We wish to write a grading program that will determine the number of exam scores that fall into each of three categories: outstanding, satisfactory, and unsatisfactory. The program will also print the high score on the exam. The program user must specify the minimum satisfactory and outstanding scores, and enter each student's name and exam score.

Analysis

The program must start by reading in the scale for the exam. The main processing step must read each student's data, categorize each score, and find the largest score. We will begin by describing the data requirements and the algorithm.

Problem Inputs
minimum satisfactory score (`MinSat : Natural`)
minimum outstanding score (`MinOut : Natural`)
each student's initials (`Name1, Name2 : Character`)
each student's score (`Score : Natural`)

Problem Outputs
highest score (`High : Natural`)
number of outstanding scores (`NumOut : Natural`)
number of satisfactory scores (`NumSat : Natural`)
number of unsatisfactory scores (`NumUns : Natural`)

Design

Algorithm

1. Read in the exam scale.
2. Read each student's initials and score, categorize each score, and find the high score.
3. Print the number of scores in each category and the high score.

Step 2 is the main processing step and requires further refinement. Rather than do this now, we will examine the structure chart for the problem shown in Fig. 9.9. All level 1 subproblems will be implemented as procedures (ReadScale, DoScores, and Report from left to right). The data flow information shows that the scale boundary values (MinSat, MinOut) are defined by

Figure 9.9 Structure Chart for Grader

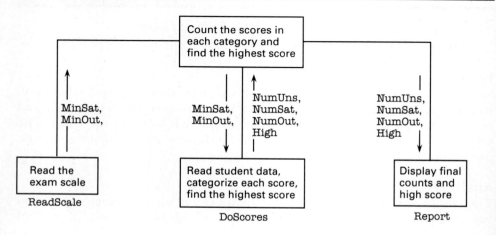

procedure `ReadScale` and passed into procedure `DoScores`. Procedure `DoScores` determines all required output values (`NumUns`, `NumSat`, `NumOut`, and `High`); these values are then passed into `Report` to be printed.

The variables shown in the structure chart are all declared in the main program (see Program 9.9). The data flow information is used to write the parameter lists in the main program. Because procedure `DoScores` requires further refinement before it can be completed, it is written as a stub. Procedure `DoScores` performs step 2 of the original algorithm.

Program 9.9 Grading Program with Stub for Procedure DoScores

```
WITH Text_IO;
WITH My_Int_IO;
PROCEDURE Grader IS

-- Reads an exam scale and uses it to find the number of students who
-- received outstanding, satisfactory, and unsatisfactory grades on an
-- exam. Also, finds the high score on the exam.

  MinSat : Natural;     -- in - boundaries for satisfactory category
  MinOut : Natural;
  NumUns : Natural;     -- out - counters for each category
  NumSat : Natural;
  NumOut : Natural;
  High   : Natural;     -- out - high score so far

  Sentinel : CONSTANT Character := '*';  -- sentinel value
  MinScore : CONSTANT Natural   := 0;    -- lowest possible score

  PROCEDURE ReadScale (MinSat : OUT Natural; MinOut : OUT Natural) IS

  -- Reads the exam scale.
  -- Pre: None
  -- Post: MinSat and MinOut are read in.

  BEGIN -- ReadScale

    -- Enter the exam scale
    Text_IO.Put(Item => "Enter the minimum satisfactory score: ");
    My_Int_IO.Get(Item => MinSat);
    Text_IO.Put(Item => "Enter the minimum outstanding  score: ");
    My_Int_IO.Get(Item => MinOut);

  END ReadScale;


  PROCEDURE DoScores (MinSat : IN Natural;
                      MinOut : IN Natural;
                      NumUns : IN OUT Natural;
                      NumSat : IN OUT Natural;
                      NumOut : IN OUT Natural;
                      High   : IN OUT Natural) IS

  -- Reads each student's initials and score, categorizes each score,
  -- and finds the high score.
  -- Pre: MinSat and MinOut are assigned values.
```

```
-- Post: NumUns, NumSat, and NumOut are the counts of scores in
--        each category. High is the highest score.
-- Uses: ReadStu, Categorize, and CheckHigh

   Score : Natural;                          -- each exam score
   First : Character;                        -- student's initials
   Last  : Character;

BEGIN -- DoScores stub

  Text_IO.Put(Item => "Procedure DoScores entered");
  Text_IO.New_Line;
  -- Initialize category counters and High
  NumUns := 0;
  NumSat := 0;
  NumOut := 0;
  High   := 0;

END DoScores;


PROCEDURE Report (NumUns : IN Natural; NumSat : IN Natural;
                  NumOut : IN Natural; High   : IN Natural) IS

-- Prints the final counts and the high score.
-- Pre: NumUns, NumSat, NumOut, and High are assigned values.
-- Post: The program results are displayed.

BEGIN -- Report

  Text_IO.New_Line;
  Text_IO.Put(Item => "Number of    outstanding scores: ");
  My_Int_IO.Put(Item => NumOut, Width => 3);
  Text_IO.New_Line;
  Text_IO.Put(Item => "Number of    satisfactory scores: ");
  My_Int_IO.Put(Item => NumSat, Width => 3);
  Text_IO.New_Line;
  Text_IO.Put(Item => "Number of unsatisfactory scores: ");
  My_Int_IO.Put(Item => NumUns, Width => 3);
  Text_IO.New_Line;
  Text_IO.New_Line;
  Text_IO.Put(Item => "High score on exam: ");
  My_Int_IO.Put(Item => High, Width => 3);
  Text_IO.New_Line;

END Report;


BEGIN -- Grader

  -- Enter the exam scale
  ReadScale (MinSat, MinOut);

  -- Read and categorize all scores and find the high score
  DoScores (MinSat, MinOut, NumUns, NumSat, NumOut, High);

  -- Print count of scores in each category and the high score
  Report (NumUns, NumSat, NumOut, High);

END Grader;
```

```
Enter the minimum satisfactory score: 65
Enter the minimum outstanding  score: 90
Procedure DoScores entered

Number of    outstanding  scores:0
Number of    satisfactory scores:0
Number of unsatisfactory scores:0
```

Algorithm for DoScores

Read each student's initials and score, categorize each score, and find the high score.

This time we will use a sentinel-controlled WHILE loop that compares a student's initials to a sentinel value. The loop properties follow.

- NumUns is the count of unsatisfactory scores.
- NumSat is the count of satisfactory scores.
- NumOut is the count of unsatisfactory scores.
- High is the high score so far.
- The student's initials are the sentinel just after loop exit.

These properties suggest the refinement below.

Algorithm for DoScores

1. Initialize NumUns, NumSat, and NumOut to zero.
2. Initialize High to lowest possible score.
3. Read first student's initials and score.
4. WHILE the student's initials are not the sentinel LOOP
   5. Increment NumUns, NumSat, or NumOut.
   6. Set High to current score if it is highest so far.
   7. Read the next student's initials and score.
   END LOOP

Step 5 can be implemented as a multiple-alternative decision, as outlined in Table 9.3. This step will be performed by procedure Categorize.

Table 9.3 Decision Table for Step 5 of DoScores

Score	Action
Below MinSat	Score is unsatisfactory; increment NumUns
MinSat to MinOut−1	Score is satisfactory; increment NumSat
Above MinOut−1	Score is outstanding; increment NumOut

In order to accomplish step 6 (check for highest score so far), the program must compare each score to the highest score so far (saved in High). If the current score is larger than the highest score so far, then it becomes the new highest score. The "priming step" is to initialize High to the lowest possible score (zero) so that High is always set to the first score during pass 1.

Now that the algorithm for DoScores is refined, we can draw the structure chart (see Fig. 9.10) that describes this step and its subproblems. Each subproblem is implemented as a procedure. The structure chart shows that Score is an output of procedure ReadStu and an input to procedures Categorize and CheckHigh. Because Categorize must increment a category counter, the counters are input/output parameters for this subproblem. Because High may be modified by CheckHigh, it is also an input/output parameter.

Figure 9.10   Structure Chart for Procedure DoScores

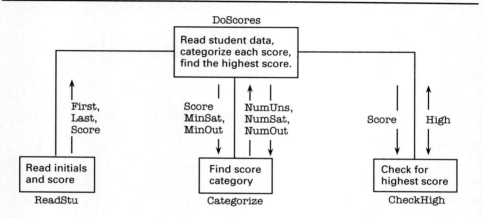

The procedure structure prescribed by this structure chart and the earlier one is summarized in Fig. 9.11. Procedure DoScores is shown as Program 9.10. First, Last, and Score are declared as local variables in DoScores; Sentinel and MinScore are local constants. Procedure DoScores begins by initializing all category counters and High to zero. It calls ReadStu to read each student's initials and score and calls CheckHigh to check for the highest score so far.

Figure 9.11   Procedure Structure for Grading Problem

```
PROCEDURE Grader
   PROCEDURE  ReadScale
   PROCEDURE  DoScores
   PROCEDURE  ReadStu
   PROCEDURE  Categorize
   PROCEDURE  CheckHigh
   PROCEDURE  Report
```

Program 9.10 Procedure DoScores and Its Lower-Level Procedures

```
-- procedure specifications for lower-level procedures

PROCEDURE ReadStu (First : IN OUT Character;
                   Last  : IN OUT Character;
                   Score : OUT Natural);

PROCEDURE Categorize (Score  : IN Natural;
                      MinSat : IN Natural;
                      MinOut : IN Natural;
                      NumUns : IN OUT Natural;
                      NumSat : IN OUT Natural;
                      NumOut : IN OUT Natural);

PROCEDURE CheckHigh (Score : IN Natural; High : IN OUT Natural);


PROCEDURE DoScores (MinSat : IN Natural;
                    MinOut : IN Natural;
                    NumUns : IN OUT Natural;
                    NumSat : IN OUT Natural;
                    NumOut : IN OUT Natural;
                    High   : IN OUT Natural) IS

-- Reads each student's initials and score, categorizes each score,
-- and finds the high score.
-- Pre: MinSat and MinOut are assigned values.
-- Post: NumUns, NumSat, and NumOut are the counts of scores in
--       each category. High is the highest score.
-- Uses: ReadStu, Categorize, and CheckHigh

   Score : Natural;                       -- each exam score
   First : Character;                     -- student's initials
   Last  : Character;

BEGIN -- DoScores
   -- Initialize category counters and High
   NumUns := 0;
   NumSat := 0;
   NumOut := 0;
   High   := MinScore;

   -- Categorize each score and find High
   ReadStu (First, Last, Score);          -- Read first student's data
   WHILE First /= Sentinel LOOP
     -- Categorize Score and increment appropriate counter
     Categorize (Score, MinSat, MinOut, NumUns, NumSat, NumOut);
     CheckHigh (Score, High);             -- Check for high score
     ReadStu (First, Last, Score);        -- Read next student's data
   END LOOP;
END DoScores;
```

The output statements in the WHILE loop of procedure DoScores echo print each student's initials and score. A blank string, Pad, is displayed at the beginning of each output line so that it will be easy to distinguish the program output from the input data. Next, procedure DoScores calls procedure Categorize to find the category of each score. The multiple alternative decision in `Categorize` prints the score category and increments a counter.

As in the checkbook problem, we have left completion of this case study as an exercise. After you have finished the program, check its output against the sample run shown in Fig. 9.12.

Figure 9.12   Sample Run of Program Grader

```
Enter the minimum satisfactory score: 75
Enter the minimum outstanding score: 90

Enter two initials or **: EK
Enter score: 100
    Outstanding

Enter two initials or **: RK
Enter score: 75
    Satisfactory

Enter two initials or **: HH
Enter score: 89
    Satisfactory

Enter two initials or **: **

Number of outstanding scores: 1
Number of satisfactory scores: 2
Number of unsatisfactory scores: 0

High score on exam: 100
```

Exercises for Section 9.5

Self-Check

1. What would be the effect of transposing the parameters `MinSat` and `MinOut` in the call to procedure `DoScores` or `ReadScale` in Program 9.10? Would the compiler detect this error?

Programming

1. Complete and test the checkbook-balancing program as suggested in this section.
2. Complete and test the exam-grading program as suggested in this section.
3. Modify the checkbook program so that a penalty amount of $15.00 is deducted for each overdrawn check and a count of overdrawn checks is maintained and printed next to each overdrawn check. Reset the count of overdrafts to zero whenever the balance becomes positive.

4. What would happen if the person using this program became confused and switched the data values entered for `MinSat` and `MinOut`? Rewrite procedure `ReadScale` so that it checks for this error and takes corrective action if it occurs.

 # 9.6 System Structures: A Systematic View of Text Files

Up to this point, we have written most programs as interactive programs; in other words, each program reads all input data from the keyboard and displays all outputs on the screen. This mode of operation is fine for small programs. However, as you begin to write larger programs, you will see that there are many advantages to using disk files for program input and output.

You can create a data file using a text editor in the same way you create a program file. Once the data file is entered in computer memory, you can carefully check and edit each line before you save it as a disk file. When you enter data interactively, you do not have the opportunity to examine and edit the data.

After the data file is saved on disk, you can instruct your program to read data from the data file rather than from the keyboard. Recall from Chapter 2 that this mode of program execution is called batch mode. Because the program data are supplied before execution begins, prompting messages are not required in batch programs. Instead, batch programs must contain display statements that echo print data values, thereby providing a record of the data that are read and processed in a particular run.

Besides giving you the opportunity to check for errors in your data, using data files has another advantage. Because a data file can be read many times, during debugging you can rerun the program as often as you need to, without retyping the test data each time.

You can also instruct your program to write its output to a disk file rather than display it on the screen. When output is written to the screen, it disappears after it scrolls off the screen and cannot be retrieved. However, if program output is written to a disk file, you can use an operating system command such as TYPE *filename* (VAX/VMS and MS-DOS) or cat *filename* (UNIX) to list file *filename* as often as you wish, or look at it with your editor. You can also get a hard copy of a disk file by sending it to the printer.

Finally, you can use the output file generated by one program as a data file for another program. For example, a payroll program may compute employee salaries and write each employee's name and salary to an output file. A second program that prints employee checks could use the output of the payroll program as its data file.

Ada's Package Specification for Text Files

You know already that in Ada, input and output are done with packages; Text _IO is the one we are using in this book. It is interesting to note that the input/output system, because it is a package, is described with a package specification. An excerpt of the Text_IO specification dealing with files appears as Fig. 9.13. Except for some formatting differences, to take into account our case conventions in this book, this specification is just as it appears in the Ada standard. Notice that a file is defined as a type:

```
TYPE File_Type IS LIMITED PRIVATE;
```

We have seen PRIVATE before, but not LIMITED PRIVATE. The latter term is used to designate a type that behaves like a private type—the client program cannot directly access details of objects of that type—but is even more restricted: The assignment and equality-checking operations are taken away. A type of this kind has *no* predefined operations; all client-accessible operations must be defined in the package specification.

Refer to this partial specification as you read the remainder of this section. Many more operations are defined in the specification than we will ever be using in this book, but it is helpful to know that the Ada standard defines all the operations in such a clear fashion as a package specification. The full specification for Text_IO, which runs for a number of pages, appears in Appendix D.

Figure 9.13   Section of Text_IO Dealing with Text Files

```
WITH IO_Exceptions;
PACKAGE Text_IO IS

  TYPE File_Type IS LIMITED PRIVATE;

  TYPE File_Mode IS (In_File, Out_File);

  ...

  -- File Management

  PROCEDURE Create(File : IN OUT File_Type;
                   Mode : IN File_Mode := Out_File;
                   Name : IN String := "";
                   Form : IN String := "");

  PROCEDURE Open(File : IN OUT File_Type;
                 Mode : IN File_Mode; Name : IN String;
                 Form : IN String := "");

  PROCEDURE Close(File : IN OUT File_Type);
  PROCEDURE Delete(File : IN OUT File_Type);
  PROCEDURE Reset(File : IN OUT File_Type; Mode : IN File_Mode);
  PROCEDURE Reset(File : IN OUT File_Type);

  FUNCTION Mode(File : IN File_Type) RETURN File_Mode;
  FUNCTION Name(File : IN File_Type) RETURN String;
  FUNCTION Form(File : IN File_Type) RETURN String;
```

```
FUNCTION Is_Open(File : IN File_Type) RETURN Boolean;

-- Control of default Input and Output Files

PROCEDURE Set_Input(File : IN File_Type);
PROCEDURE Set_Output(File : IN File_Type);

FUNCTION Standard_Input RETURN File_Type;
FUNCTION Standard_Output RETURN File_Type;

FUNCTION Current_Input RETURN File_Type;
FUNCTION Current_Output RETURN File_Type;

-- Specification of Line and Page lengths

PROCEDURE Set_Line_Length(File : IN File_Type; To : IN Count);
PROCEDURE Set_Line_Length(To : IN Count);

PROCEDURE Set_Page_Length(File : IN File_Type; To : IN Count);
PROCEDURE Set_Page_Length(To : IN Count);

FUNCTION Line_Length(File : IN File_Type) RETURN Count;
FUNCTION Line_Length RETURN Count;

FUNCTION Page_Length(File : IN File_Type) RETURN Count;
FUNCTION Page_Length RETURN Count;

-- Column, Line, and Page Control

PROCEDURE New_Line(File : IN File_Type; Spacing : IN Positive_Count := 1);
PROCEDURE New_Line(Spacing : IN Positive_Count := 1);

PROCEDURE Skip_Line(File : IN File_Type; Spacing : IN Positive_Count := 1);
PROCEDURE Skip_Line(Spacing : IN Positive_Count := 1);

FUNCTION End_of_Line(File : IN File_Type) RETURN Boolean;
FUNCTION End_of_Line RETURN Boolean;

PROCEDURE New_Page(File : IN File_Type);
PROCEDURE New_Page;

PROCEDURE Skip_Page(File : IN File_Type);
PROCEDURE Skip_Page;

FUNCTION End_of_Page(File : IN File_Type) RETURN Boolean;
FUNCTION End_of_Page RETURN Boolean;

FUNCTION End_of_File(File : IN File_Type) RETURN Boolean;
FUNCTION End_of_File RETURN Boolean;

PROCEDURE Set_Col(File : IN File_Type; To : IN Positive_Count);
PROCEDURE Set_Col(To : IN Positive_Count);

PROCEDURE Set_Line(File : IN File_Type; To : IN Positive_Count);
PROCEDURE Set_Line(To : IN Positive_Count);

FUNCTION Col(File : IN File_Type) RETURN Positive_Count;
FUNCTION Col RETURN Positive_Count;

FUNCTION Line(File : IN File_Type) RETURN Positive_Count;
FUNCTION Line RETURN Positive_Count;
```

```
FUNCTION Page(File : IN File_Type) RETURN Positive_Count;
FUNCTION Page RETURN Positive_Count;

-- Character Input-Output

PROCEDURE Get(File : IN File_Type; Item : OUT Character);
PROCEDURE Get(Item : OUT Character);
PROCEDURE Put(File : IN File_Type; Item : IN Character);
PROCEDURE Put(Item : IN Character);

-- String Input-Output

PROCEDURE Get(File : IN File_Type; Item : OUT String);
PROCEDURE Get(Item : OUT String);
PROCEDURE Put(File : IN File_Type; Item : IN String);
PROCEDURE Put(Item : IN String);

PROCEDURE Get_Line(File : IN File_Type;
                   Item : OUT String; Last : OUT natural);
PROCEDURE Get_Line(Item : OUT String; Last : OUT natural);
PROCEDURE Put_Line(File : IN File_Type; Item : IN String);
PROCEDURE Put_Line(Item : IN String);

   . . .

END Text_IO;
```

Reading and Writing Files with Text_IO

Several previous examples have used files for their input and output. This section gives a systematic explanation of how to get an Ada program to read from a data file and to write program results to an output file with Text_IO.

A *text file* is a collection of characters stored under the same name in secondary memory (that is, on a disk). A text file has no fixed size. To mark the end of a text file, the computer places a special character, called the *end-of-file* character (denoted as `<eof>`), following the last character in a text file. The Ada literature usually refers to this marker as the *file terminator*. Its exact form depends on the operating system.

As you create a text file using an editor program, you press the RETURN key to separate the file into lines. Each time you press RETURN, another special character, called the *end-of-line* character (denoted as `<eol>`), or *line terminator*, is placed in the file.

Here is the contents of a text file that consists of two lines of letters, blank characters, and punctuation. Each line ends with `<eol>`, and `<eof>` follows the last `<eol>` in the file. For convenience in scanning the file's contents, we have listed each line of the file as a separate line. In the actual file stored on disk, the characters are stored in consecutive storage locations, with each character occupying a single storage location. The first character of the second line (the letter I) occupies the next storage location following the first `<eol>`.

```
This is a text file!<eol>
It has two lines.<eol><eof>
```

A text file can also contain numeric data or mixed numeric and character data. Here is a text file that consists of numeric data and blank characters. Each number is stored on disk as a sequence of digit characters; blank characters separate numbers on the same line.

```
1234    345<eol>
999    -17<eol><eof>
```

The Keyboard and the Screen as Text Files

In interactive programming, Ada treats data entered at the keyboard as if they were read from the predefined file called Text_IO.Standard_Input. Pressing the RETURN key enters the <eol> in this file. In interactive mode, we normally use a sentinel value to indicate the end of data rather than attempt to enter <eof> in system file Text_IO.Standard_Input. We could use <eof>, however. Its keyboard representation depends on the operating system; control-d and control-z are often used.

Similarly, displaying characters on the screen is equivalent to writing characters to system file Text_IO.Standard_Output. The New_Line procedure places the <eol> in this file, resulting in the cursor moving to the start of the next line of the screen. Both Text_IO.Standard_Input and Text_IO.Standard_Output are text files because their individual components are characters.

The End_of_Line and End_of_File Functions

Both <eol> and <eof> are different from the other characters in a text file because they are not data characters; in fact, the Ada standard doesn't even specify what they should be, because their form depends on the operating system. Many of the Ada Get operations skip over the line terminators. However, if an Ada program attempts to read <eof>, the exception Text_IO.End_Error is raised.

If we can't read or write these characters in the normal way, how do we process them? Text_IO provides two functions that enable us to determine whether the next character is <eol> or <eof>. The function Text_IO.End_of_Line returns a value of True if the next character is <eol>; the function Text_IO.End_of_File returns a value of True if the next character is <eof>. The algorithm below uses the End_of_Line and End_of_File functions to control the processing of a data file.

Template for Processing a Text File, Character by Character

```
WHILE NOT Text_IO.End_of_File (data file) LOOP

    WHILE NOT Text_IO.End_of_Line (data file) LOOP
            process each character in the current line
    END LOOP;
    -- assert: the next character is <eol>

    process the <eol> character

END LOOP;
-- assert: the next character is <eof>
```

If the data file is not empty, the initial call to End_of_File returns a value of False, and the computer executes the inner WHILE loop. This loop processes each character in a line up to (but not including) the <eol>. For the two-line character data file shown above, the first execution of the WHILE loop processes the first line of characters:

```
This is a text file!
```

When the next character is <eol>, the End_of_Line function returns True, so the inner WHILE loop is exited. The <eol> is processed immediately after loop exit, and the outer WHILE loop is repeated.

Each repetition of the outer WHILE loop begins with a call to the End_of_File function to test whether the next character is the <eof> character. If it is, the End_of_File function returns True, so the outer loop is exited. If the next character is not <eof>, the End_of_File function returns False, so the inner loop executes again and processes the next line of data up to <eol>. For the file above, the second execution of the inner WHILE loop processes the second line of characters:

```
It has two lines.
```

After the second <eol> is processed, the next character is <eof>, so the End_of_File function returns True, and the outer WHILE loop is exited. We use this algorithm later in a program that duplicates a file by copying all its characters to another file.

SYNTAX
DISPLAY

End_of_Line Function (for Text Files)

Form: Text_IO.End_of_Line(*filename*)
Interpretation: The function result is True if the next character in file *filename* is <eol>; otherwise, the function result is False.
Note: If *filename* is omitted, the file is assumed to be Text_IO.Standard_Input (usually the terminal keyboard).

SYNTAX
DISPLAY

End_of_File Function (for Text Files)

Form: Text_IO.End_of_File(*filename*)
Interpretation: The function result is True if the next character in file *filename* is <eof>; otherwise, the function result is False.
Note: If *filename* is omitted, the file is again assumed to be Text_IO.Standard_Input. If a read operation is attempted when End_of_File (*filename*) is True, Text_IO.End_Error is raised.

Declaring a Text File

Before we can reference a text file in a program, we must declare it just like any other data object. For example, the declarations

```
InData  : Text_IO.File_Type;
OutData : Text_IO.File_Type;
```

identify InData and OutData as text file variables of type Text_IO.File_Type.

Directory Names for Files

To read or write a text file with an Ada program, we must know the file's *directory name,* or *external name,* which is the name used to identify it in the disk's directory. A disk's directory lists the names of all files stored on the disk. A file's directory name must follow whatever conventions apply on your particular computer system. For example, some systems (MS-DOS, for example) limit you to a file name that consists of eight characters, a period, and a three-letter extension. Many programmers use the extension .DAT or .TXT to designate a text file.

You need to communicate to the operating system the directory names of any files you are using so that the system knows the correspondence between file variables and directory names. This process varies from computer to computer. Your instructor will give you the details for your particular system.

Preparing a File for Input or Output

Before a program can use a file, the file must be prepared for input or output. At any given time, a file can be used for either input or output, but not both simultaneously. If a file is being used for input, then its components can be read as data. If a file is being used for output, then new components can be written to the file.

The procedure call statement

```
Text_IO.Open(File => InData,Mode => Text_IO.In_File,Name =>
"SCORES.DAT");
```

prepares file InData for input by associating it with the disk file SCORES.DAT and moving its file position pointer to the beginning of the file. The *file position pointer* selects the next character to be processed in the file. The file SCORES.DAT must have been previously created and located in the current disk directory; if it is not available, the exception Text_IO.Name_Error is raised.

The procedure call statement

```
Text_IO.Create(File=>OutData,Mode=>Text_IO.Out_File,Name=>"TEST.OUT");
```

prepares file OutData for output. If no file TEST.OUT is saved on disk, a file that is initially empty (that is, TEST.OUT has no characters) is created. If a file TEST.OUT is already saved on disk, it is deleted and a new one is created.

To read and process a file a second time in the same program run, first close it by performing an operation such as

```
Text_IO.Close(File => OutData);
```

and then reopen it for input. A program can read and echo print (to the screen) an output file it creates by calling the `Close` procedure with the newly created file as its parameter. An `Open` operation prepares this file for input, and your program can then read data from that file.

Reading and Writing a Text File

You've learned how to declare a text file and how to prepare one for processing. All that remains is to find out how to instruct the computer to read data from an input file or to write program results to an output file.

If `NextCh` is a type `Character` variable, we know that the procedure call statement

```
Text_IO.Get (Item => NextCh);
```

reads the next data character typed at the keyboard into `NextCh`. This is really an abbreviation for the procedure call statement

```
Text_IO.Get (File => Text_IO.Standard_Input, Item => NextCh);
```

which has the same effect. The statement

```
Text_IO.Get (File => InData, Item => NextCh);
```

reads the next character from file `InData` into `NextCh`, where the next character is the one selected by the file position pointer. The computer automatically advances the file position pointer after each read operation. Remember to open `InData` for input before the first read operation.

In a similar manner, the procedure call statements

```
Text_IO.Put (Item => NextCh);
Text_IO.Put (File => Text_IO.Standard_Output, Item => NextCh);
```

display the value of `Ch` on the screen. The statement

```
Text_IO.Put (File => OutData, Item => NextCh);
```

writes the value of `Ch` to the end of file `OutData`. Remember to open `OutData` for output before the first call to procedure `Put`.

■ Example 9.1

It is a good idea to have a backup or duplicate copy of a file in case the original file data are lost. Program 9.11 is an Ada program that copies one file to another; it is similar in function to the file-copying command provided by the operating system. Program `CopyFile` copies each character in file `InData` to file `OutData`.

The nested `WHILE` loops in Program 9.11 implement the algorithm first shown above. The data file, `InData`, is the argument in the calls to functions

Program 9.11   A Program to Copy One Text File to Another

453

9.6 System
Structures: A
Systematic View of
Text Files

```
WITH Text_IO;
PROCEDURE CopyFile IS

  -- program copies its input file TEST.DAT into its output file TEST.OUT
  -- then closes TEST.OUT, re-opens it for input,
  -- and displays its contents on the screen.

  InData  : Text_IO.File_Type;
  OutData : Text_IO.File_Type;
  NextCh  : Character;

BEGIN -- CopyFile

  Text_IO.Open(File=>InData, Mode=>Text_IO.In_File, Name=>"TEST.DAT");
  Text_IO.Create(File=>OutData, Mode=>Text_IO.Out_File, Name=>"TEST.OUT");

  WHILE NOT Text_IO.End_of_File(File => InData) LOOP
    WHILE NOT Text_IO.End_of_Line(File => InData) LOOP

      Text_IO.Get(File => InData, Item => NextCh);
      Text_IO.Put(File => OutData, Item => NextCh);

    END LOOP;

    Text_IO.Skip_Line(File => InData);
    Text_IO.New_Line(File => OutData);
  END LOOP;

  Text_IO.Close(File => InData);
  Text_IO.Close(File => OutData);
  Text_IO.Open(File=>InData, Mode=>Text_IO.In_File, Name=>"TEST.OUT");

  WHILE NOT Text_IO.End_of_File(File => InData) LOOP
    WHILE NOT Text_IO.End_of_Line(File => InData) LOOP

      Text_IO.Get(File => InData, Item => NextCh);
      Text_IO.Put(Item => NextCh);

    END LOOP;

    Text_IO.Skip_Line(File => InData);
    Text_IO.New_Line;
  END LOOP;

  Text_IO.Close(File => InData);

EXCEPTION

  WHEN Text_IO.Name_Error =>
    Text_IO.Put(Item => "File TEST.DAT doesn't exist in this directory!");
    Text_IO.New_Line;

END CopyFile;
```

End_of_Line and End_of_File. As long as the next character is not <eol>, the statements

```
Text_IO.Get (File => InData, Item => NextCh);
Text_IO.Put (File => OutData, Item => NextCh);
```

read the next character of file InData into NextCh, then write that character to file OutData.

If the next character is <eol>, the inner WHILE loop is exited and the statements

```
Text_IO.Skip_Line (File => InData);
Text_IO.New_Line (File => OutData);
```

are executed. The Text_IO.Skip_Line procedure does not read any data, but simply advances the file position pointer for InData past the <eol> to the first character of the next line. The second statement writes the <eol> to file OutData. After the <eol> is processed, function End_of_File is called again to test whether there are more data characters left to be copied.

It is interesting to contemplate the effect of omitting either the Skip_Line or the New_Line statement. If the New_Line is omitted, the <eol> will not be written to file OutData whenever the end of a line is reached in file InData. Consequently, OutData will contain all the characters in file InData, but on one (possibly very long) line. If the Skip_Line is omitted, the file position pointer will not be advanced and the <eol> will still be the next character. Consequently, End_of_Line (InData) will remain True, the inner loop is exited immediately, and another <eol> is written to file OutData. This continues "forever," or until the program is terminated by its user, or until its time limit is exceeded.

After copying the file, the program closes TEST.OUT, reopens it for input, and displays its contents on the screen; the algorithm in the second part of the program is nearly identical to that in the first part. ∎

A common source of error is forgetting to use a file name with End_of_Line or End_of_File. In this case, the system uses file Text_IO.Standard_Input. A similar error is forgetting to use a file name with Get or Put. Normally, no error diagnostic is displayed, because there is nothing illegal about this; the computer simply assumes the keyboard or screen is intended instead of the disk file. The cause of the incorrect behavior of the program is therefore not obvious.

Behaviors of the Various Get Operations in Text_IO

Learning to write input operations correctly is one of the most difficult tasks for a beginner in any programming language, including Ada. It is important to realize that Text_IO provides many different Get operations. We most frequently use four types: Get for a single character (as we used in Example 9.1), Get and Get_Line for strings (as we used in Section 8.10), and Get for numeric and enumeration values. Each of these behaves slightly differently with respect to blanks and line terminators in a file (including Standard_Input). Here is a summary of their behaviors; we have used the "short form" for reading from the terminal, but the behavior is identical if a file is used.

- Get(Item : OUT Character) first skips any line terminators, then reads *one* character from the input file. A blank counts as a character.
- Get(Item : OUT String) first determines the length of the string and attempts to perform *exactly* that number of character Get operations. It follows that line terminators are skipped. In fact, even if each character in the input is immediately followed by a line terminator (i.e., all the lines are one character long), all the characters are read and all the line terminators are skipped.
- Get_Line (Item : OUT String; Last : OUT Natural) reads characters (including blanks) up to the length of the string. Reading stops if the string's length is longer than the current line, that is, if a line terminator is encountered. The line terminator is then skipped, that is, the equivalent of a Skip_Line is executed. If the input line is longer than the string, the remaining characters in the line remain available for the next input operation.
- Get (Item : numeric or enumeration type) skips over any leading blanks, tab characters, and line terminators, then reads characters as long as they continue to meet the syntax of a literal of the desired type. The character that causes reading to stop remains available for the next input operation.

This operation can cause trouble if you are not careful: Suppose that you are trying to read an integer value and accidentally type a few numeric digits followed by a letter or punctuation character. This last character will cause reading to stop *but remain available*; the already-read numeric digits make up a valid integer literal, so the typing error will not be discovered until the *next* input operation, which will probably not expect that character and raise Text_IO.Data_Error. Be careful!

Now is the time to take another look at the procedures in package Robust_Input (Section 6.8) to be certain you understand exactly how they work to prevent such a situation from arising.

Operating System Redirection of Standard Files

Many popular operating systems, including UNIX and MS-DOS, have a feature that allows the standard input and output files—normally the keyboard and screen, respectively—to be "redirected" or temporarily reassigned to disk files. This feature, which is independent of Ada or any other programming language, allows you, for example, to tell a program that normally gets its input interactively to get it instead from a given file. Similarly, a program that normally writes its output to the screen can be told to put all that output in a file instead. In UNIX or MS-DOS, if you have an Ada program called MyProg, say, which uses keyboard Get calls, executing the operating system-level command

```
MyProg <FileOne.dat
```

causes MyProg to take all its standard input from FileOne.dat instead of the keyboard. (This assumes that FileOne.dat has been created and filled with data.) Executing the command

```
MyProg <FileOne.dat >FileTwo.dat
```

causes the program, without any change in its source code, to read its input from `FileOne.dat` and write its output to `FileTwo.dat`. This is a handy technique, used in writing many operating system commands. It doesn't work well if the program is highly interactive, with a lot of prompting, because the prompts go to the output file while the input comes from the input file, untouched by human hands! The next Case Study will show a program that does not prompt but uses keyboard `Get` calls; its input data can be entered either from the keyboard or by redirection.

◆ Case Study: A Histogram-Plotting Program

Researchers in linguistics or cryptography (the study of secret codes) are often interested in the frequency of occurrence of the various letters in a section of text. A particularly useful way to summarize the number of occurrences is the *histogram* or *bar graph*, in which a bar is drawn for each letter, the length of the bar corresponding to the relative frequency of occurrence.

Problem
Write a program that draws a histogram for the frequency of occurrence of the letters of the alphabet. Uppercase and lowercase letters are to be counted separately; nonletter characters can be ignored.

Analysis
This program is a variation of the concordance program, Program 8.15, developed in Section 8.7. Instead of getting input as a single line from the terminal, this program will read a text file by using input redirection, compute the number of occurrences of each of the 52 (lowercase and uppercase) letters, and draw an appropriately tall vertical bar on the screen for each of the 52 letters. A sample screen dump, produced by running the program with its own source file used as input, is shown in Fig. 9.14.

Design

Algorithm
The initial algorithm for this program is

1. Initialize all letter counters to 0.
2. Read the input file character by character. For each character that is a letter, increment the appropriate letter counter.
3. Plot the results on the screen.

   We leave it to the student to fill in the algorithm refinements.

Coding
Program 9.12 gives the program for this case study. A procedure `Plot` takes care of plotting the vertical bars on the screen, from bottom to top. Its param-

Case Study: A Histogram-Plotting Program, continued

457

9.6 System
Structures: A
Systematic View of
Text Files

Figure 9.14 Output from Histogram Program for Its Own Source File

```
              Scale: 1 star = 9 occurrences

     *
     *
     *
     *
     *
     *                    *
     *                    *
     *         *   *   *
     *         *   *   *
 *   *         *   *   *
 *   *   *     *   *   *
 * * **     ** ***          *
 * * **     ** ***          *
 * * **   * **  ***         *              *
 * * **   * *** ****        *   *      *   **
 * * **   * *** **** **     * *    *  * ***   **   *
 * *** **   ***** **** **    * *  **   * *** ****  *
 ********   ***** ******** ****** **   ***** **** *
 ********************************************************
abcdefghijklmnopqrstuvwxyzABCDEFGHIJKLMNOPQRSTUVWXYZ
```

Program 9.12 A Histogram-Plotting Program

```
WITH Text_IO;
WITH My_Int_IO;
WITH Screen;
PROCEDURE Histogram IS

-- Plots a histogram on the screen consisting of vertical bars.
-- Each bar represents the frequency of occurrence of a given
-- alphabet letter in the input file.
-- The input file is assumed to be Standard_Input; use input redirection
-- if you wish to use a disk file instead.

  SUBTYPE UpperCase IS Character RANGE 'A'..'Z';
  SUBTYPE LowerCase IS Character RANGE 'a'..'z';
  TYPE List IS ARRAY(Character RANGE <>) OF integer;
  Uppers     : List(UpperCase);
  Lowers     : List(LowerCase);

  NextCh     : Character;
  Scale      : Natural;
  MaxCount   : Natural := 0;
  WhichCol   : Screen.Width;


  PROCEDURE Plot(WhichCol   : Screen.Width;
                 BottomRow  : Screen.Depth;
                 HowMany    : Screen.Depth;
                 WhichChar  : Character) IS
```

```
-- draws one vertical bar on the screen
-- Pre: WhichCol, BottomRow, HowMany, and WhichChar are defined
-- Post: draws a bar in column WhichCol, using character WhichChar
--       to do the plotting. The bottom of the bar is given by
--       BottomRow; the bar contains HowMany characters.

BEGIN -- Plot

  FOR Count IN 0 .. Howmany - 1 LOOP

    Screen.MoveCursor(Column => WhichCol, Row => BottomRow - Count);
    Text_IO.Put(Item => WhichChar);

  END LOOP;

END Plot;

BEGIN -- Histogram

  -- initialize letter-counter arrays
  Uppers := (OTHERS => 0);
  Lowers := (OTHERS => 0);

  -- read each character in the file; update letter counters
  WHILE NOT Text_IO.End_Of_File LOOP
    WHILE NOT Text_IO.End_Of_Line LOOP

      Text_IO.Get(NextCh);
      CASE NextCh IS
        WHEN UpperCase =>
          Uppers(NextCh) := Uppers(NextCh) + 1;
          IF Uppers(NextCh) > MaxCount THEN
            MaxCount := Uppers(NextCh);
          END IF;
        WHEN LowerCase =>
          Lowers(NextCh) := Lowers(NextCh) + 1;
          IF Lowers(NextCh) > MaxCount THEN
            MaxCount := Lowers(NextCh);
          END IF;
        WHEN OTHERS =>
          NULL;
      END CASE;

    END LOOP;
    Text_IO.Skip_Line;
  END LOOP;

  Scale := MaxCount / 20 + 1;

  Screen.ClearScreen;
  Screen.MoveCursor(Row => 1, Column => 15);
  Text_IO.Put(Item => "Scale: 1 star = ");
  My_Int_IO.Put(Item => Scale, Width => 1);
  Text_IO.Put(Item => " occurrences");
  Screen.MoveCursor(Row => 22, Column => 4);
  Text_IO.Put(Item => "abcdefghijklmnopqrstuvwxyzABCDEFGHIJKLMNOPQRSTUVWXYZ"
  WhichCol := 4;

  FOR C IN LowerCase LOOP
```

Case Study: A Histogram-Plotting Program, *continued*

459

9.6 System
Structures: A
Systematic View of
Text Files

```
  IF Lowers(c) /= O THEN
    Plot(WhichCol, 21, Lowers(C) / scale + 1, '*');
  END IF;
  WhichCol := WhichCol + 1;

END LOOP;

FOR C IN UpperCase LOOP

  IF Uppers(C) /= O THEN
    Plot(WhichCol, 21, Uppers(C) / scale + 1, '*');
  END IF;
  WhichCol := WhichCol + 1;

END LOOP;

Screen.MoveCursor(Row => 24, Column => 1);

END Histogram;
```

eters are the column in which the bar is desired, the bottom row of the column, the height of the column, and the character to be used for plotting the bar. `Screen.MoveCursor` is used to move the cursor from the bottom of the column to the top, plotting a character at each point.

The main program counts the occurrences of each letter as was done in the concordance program (Program 8.15), with one essential difference: A record must be kept of the maximum number of occurrences. This is done because a column can be no more than 20 rows high, so the height of the columns must be scaled to the maximum. For example, if no letter occurs more than 60 times in the file, a 20-row column corresponds to approximately 60 occurrences. Each dot in the column then corresponds roughly to 3 occurrences of that letter; the number of occurrences of each letter, then, is divided by 3 to get the height of the column; 1 is added so that if there are any occurrences at all of a given letter, that column will be at least 1 row tall.

Exercises for Section 9.6

Self-Check

1. Suppose that the name of a text file given as a parameter to `Text_IO.Open` is not a valid file name, or that the file cannot be found in the current directory. What happens? When does it happen?

Programming

1. "Hard-wiring" the name of a file into a program is usually considered to be poor programming style, because it limits the flexibility of the program.

Rewrite `CopyFile` (Program 9.11) so that the names of the input and output files are read as strings from the keyboard.

2. Rewrite `CopyFile` (Program 9.11) so that redirection is used to get the names of the input and output files.

 # 9.7 Tricks of the Trade: Debugging a Program System

As the number of subprograms and statements in a program system grows, the possibility of error also increases. If each subprogram is kept to a manageable size, then the likelihood of error will increase much more slowly. It will also be easier to read and test each subprogram. Finally, limiting your use of global variables will minimize the chance of harmful side effects, which are always difficult to locate.

Whenever possible, test each subprogram separately by writing a short driver program that contains all necessary declarations. The body of the driver program should assign values to the input and input/output parameters, call the subprogram, and display the subprogram results.

Even before all subprograms are written, you can test the main program flow by substituting stubs for the missing subprograms. If you do this, make sure that any output parameters are defined in the stub.

When developing a package, keep in mind that carefully designing and coding the specification saves work later, because once the specification and a test client program are compiled, it is not necessary to recompile them as you progressively replace stubs in the package body with full subprograms.

Debugging Tips for Program Systems

A list of suggestions for debugging a program system follows.

1. Carefully document each subprogram parameter and local identifier using comments. Also describe the subprogram operation using comments.
2. Leave a trace of execution by printing the subprogram name as it is entered.
3. Display the values of all input and input/output parameters upon entry to a subprogram. Check that these values make sense.
4. Display the values of all output parameters after returning from a procedure. Verify that these values are correct by hand computation. Make sure that all input/output and output parameters are declared as `IN OUT` or `OUT` parameters, respectively.

It is a good idea to plan for debugging as you write each subprogram rather than after the fact. Include the output statements required for steps 2 through

4 in the original Ada code for the subprogram. When you are satisfied that the subprogram works as desired, you can remove the debugging statements. One efficient way to remove them is to change them to comments by preceding them with --. If you have a problem later, you can remove these symbols, thereby changing the comments to executable statements.

 ## 9.8 Tricks of the Trade: Common Programming Errors

Much of this chapter focused on the writing of procedures and their use in stepwise development. Many opportunities for error arise when you use procedures with parameter lists. The proper use of parameters is difficult for beginning programmers to master. One obvious error occurs when the actual parameter list does not have the same number of parameters as the formal parameter list. A compilation error will indicate this problem.

Each actual parameter must be the same data type as its corresponding formal parameter. An actual parameter that correponds to a variable formal parameter must be a variable. A violation of either of these rules will result in a compilation error.

A procedure result should be returned to the calling program by assigning a value to an OUT or IN OUT parameter. Remember that a value cannot be assigned to an IN parameter within the body of the procedure.

The Ada scope rules determine where an identifier may be referenced. If an identifier is referenced outside its scope, a compilation error will result. It is good programming style to limit your use of nesting to procedures nested in the main program or in a package body, not in another procedure.

File processing in any programming language can be difficult to master; Ada is no exception. The name, which will be used as a file variable in the program, will usually differ from the actual directory name of the associated disk file. All file names must be declared as variables (type Text_IO.File_Type), and associated with the corresponding disk file using a Text_IO.Create or Text_IO.Open procedure call statement.

The Text_IO.Get procedures can be used only after a file (other than standard input) has been opened for input. Similarly, the Text_IO.Put procedure can be used only after a file (other than standard output) has been created for output. Be sure to specify the file name as the first Get or Put parameter; otherwise, standard input (keyboard) or standard output (screen) is assumed. Text_IO.End_Error is raised if a Get operation is performed when the file position pointer for a file has passed the last file component. Also, when you use function Text_IO.End_Of_Line or Text_IO.End_Of_File to control data entry, don't forget to include the name of the data file as the function argument.

Chapter Review

This chapter discussed programming in the large through procedural abstraction. You learned about the software life cycle, the various phases of software development. Much of the chapter focused on the use of procedures in stepwise development.

Two common techniques for testing programs and procedures are top-down testing and bottom-up testing. In top-down testing, the program is developed by writing the main program first, and testing its use of lower-level procedure calls by writing procedure stubs, the details of which are filled in as refinement progresses. In bottom-up testing, a lower-level procedure is written in full and then tested by a very simple driver program that tests only the behavior of the procedure. The procedure is then integrated into the main program system. Program testing in the real world is often a blend of the two techniques.

This chapter also elaborated on the use of procedure parameters for passing data to and from procedures. The parameter list provides a highly visible communication path between the procedure and the calling program. By using parameters, we can cause different data to be manipulated by a procedure each time we call it. This makes it easier to reuse the procedure in another program system.

We discussed the scope of identifiers. An identifier may be referenced anywhere within the block that declares it. If one block is nested inside another and an identifier is declared in the outer block, then the identifier's meaning in the inner block is determined by its declaration in the outer block. If the identifier is declared in both blocks, then its meaning in the inner block is determined by its declaration in the inner block.

A global variable is one that is declared in the main program; a local variable is one that is declared in a procedure. A local variable is defined only during the execution of the procedure; its value is lost when the procedure is done.

You also learned how to instruct a program to read its data from a data file rather than from the keyboard and how to save the output generated by a program as a file on disk. Both techniques make it easier to debug large programs, because test data can be prepared in advance and read repeatedly by a program in successive test runs, instead of needing to be entered each time the program is restarted.

New Ada Constructs in Chapter 9

The new Ada constructs introduced in this chapter are given in Table 9.4

Table 9.4 New Ada Constructs

File Declaration, Open and Close	Effect
`MyInput: Text_IO.File_Type;` `MyOutput: Text_IO.File_Type;`	Declares two files.
`Text_IO.Open (File=>MyInput,Mode=>Text_IO.In_File,` `  Name=>"mydata.dat");`	Attempts to open a data file for input.

Table 9.4 *continued*

463

Chapter Review

File Declaration, Open and Close	Effect
`Text_IO.Open (File=>MyOutput,Mode=>Text_IO.Out_File,` `   Name=>"testoutput.dat");`	Attempts to open a data file for output.
`Text_IO.Close(File=>MyInput);`	Closes the file.

End of File and End of Line Functions	
`IF Text_IO.End_Of_File(File=>MyInput) THEN`	True if we are at the end of the file.
`IF Text_IO.End_Of_Line(File=>MyInput) THEN`	True if we are at the end of the current line in the file.

✓ *Quick-Check Exercises*

1. The phases of the software life cycle, listed in arbitrary order, are testing, design, requirements specification, operation, maintenance, analysis, and coding and debugging. Place them in the correct order.
2. In which phases are the users of a software product likely to be involved?
3. In which phases are the programmers and the analysts likely to be involved?
4. Which phases last the longest?
5. The _____ operation prepares a file for input, and the _____ operation prepares it for output.
6. A _____ separates a _____ file into lines, and the _____ appears at the end of a file.
7. What happens if a program attempts to read past the file terminator in a file?
8. What happens if a given file on disk cannot be found by a program?
9. What happens if a program attempts to write to a file that is open for input (or read from a file that is open for output)?

Answers to Quick-Check Exercises
1. Requirements specification, analysis, design, coding and debugging, testing, operation, maintenance
2. Requirements specification, testing, operation, maintenance
3. All phases
4. Operation and maintenance
5. `Open`, `Create`
6. Line terminator or <eol>, text, file terminator or <eof>
7. `Text_IO.End_Error` is raised.
8. `Text_IO.Name_Error` is raised.
9. `Text_IO.Mode_Error` is raised.

Review Questions for Chapter 9

1. List three advantages to using files for input and output as opposed to the standard input and output you have used thus far in this course.
2. Where are files stored?
3. Explain why a file may have two distinct names. What conventions are followed for choosing each name? Which name appears in the file variable declaration? Which name appears in an operating system command?
4. Write a loop that reads up to ten integer values from a data file and displays them on the screen. If there are not ten integers in the file, the message That's all, folks should be displayed after the last number.

Programming Projects

1. Write a program to read in a collection of positive integers and print all divisors of each, except for 1 and the number itself. If the number has no divisors, print a message indicating that it is prime.
2. Each month, a bank customer deposits $50 into a savings account. The account earns 6.5 percent interest, calculated on a quarterly basis (one-fourth of 6.5 percent every three months). Write a program to compute the total investment, total amount in the account, and the interest accrued for each of the 120 months of a ten-year period. Assume that the rate is applied to all funds in the account at the end of a quarter, regardless of when the deposits were made.

   Display all values accurate to two decimal places. The table displayed by your program should begin as follows:

   ```
   MONTH    INVESTMENT    NEW AMOUNT    INTEREST    TOTAL SAVINGS
   1            50.00         50.00        0.00          50.00
   2           100.00        100.00        0.00         100.00
   3           150.00        150.00        2.44         152.44
   4           200.00        202.44        0.00         202.44
   5           250.00        252.44        0.00         252.44
   6           300.00        302.44        4.91         307.35
   7           350.00        357.35        0.00         357.35
   ```

3. Read in a positive integer value and determine the following information about it.
   a. Is it a multiple of 7, 11, or 13?
   b. Is the sum of the digits odd or even?
   c. What is the square root value?
   d. Is it a prime number?

   You should have at least four procedures and label all output. Test your program with the following values:

   104, 3773, 13, 121, 77, and 3075

4. Write a program that reads several lines from a data file and writes each word of the file on a separate line of an output file, followed by a count of the number of letters in that word. After all lines are processed, the program should display the number of words processed and data lines read. Assume that words are separated by one or more blanks. Include a procedure, SkipBlanks, that skips over a sequence of blanks between words.
5. Whatsamata U. offers a service to its faculty in computing grades at the end of each

semester. A program processes three weighted test scores and calculates a student's average and letter grade (an A is 90–100, a B is 80–89, etc.). The program reads the student data from a file and writes each student's name, test score, average, and grade to an output file.

Write a program to provide this valuable service. The data will consist first of the three test weights, then a series of student records, each of which consists of the student's name, ID number (four digits), and the three test scores. Calculate the weighted average for each student and the corresponding grade. This information should be printed along with the initial three test scores. The weighted average for each student is equal to

```
weight1 * grade1 + weight2 * grade2 + weight3 * grade3
```

For summary statistics, print the highest average, the lowest average, the average of the averages, the median average, and the total number of students processed. The median is that average obtained by the "middle" student when the file is sorted by weighted average. To find this, it will be necessary to read the file into an array and store each student's average in a field of the memory record. In this way the array can be sorted.

Some sample data follow:

```
0.35  0.25  0.40
Mouse, Minnie 1014 100 76 88
Duck, Donald 2234 90 85 65
```

6. An employee time card is represented as one long string of characters. Write a program that processes a collection of these strings stored on a data file and writes the results to an output file. The data string for each employee takes up 42 positions:

Positions	Data
1–10	Employee's last name
11–20	Employee's first name
21	C for city office or S for suburban office
22	U for union or N for nonunion
23–26	Employee's identification number
27	Blank
28–29	Number of regular hours (a whole number)
30	Blank
31–36	Hourly rate (dollars and cents)
37	Blank
38–39	Number of dependents
40	Blank
41–42	Number of overtime hours (a whole number)

a. Compute gross pay using the formula

Gross = regular hours × rate + overtime hours × 1.5 × rate

b. Compute net pay by subtracting the following deductions:

Federal tax = 0.14 × (gross − 13 × dependents)
Social Security = 0.052 × gross
City tax = 4% of gross if employee works in the city
Union dues = 6.75% of gross for union member

Programming in the Large: Abstract Data Types

10

10.1 System Structures: Abstract Data Types (ADTs)

10.2 System Structures: Using Package Calendar as an ADT

10.3 System Structures: Writing an ADT for Calendar Dates

10.4 System Structures: Writing an ADT for Rational Numbers

10.5 System Structures: Writing an ADT for Variable-Length Strings

10.6 Case Study: Printing a Form Letter—a Simple Mail Merge

10.7 System Structures: Writing an ADT for Employee Records

10.8 Case Study: Employee Inquiry System

10.9 Tricks of the Trade: Common Programming Errors

Chapter Review

This chapter completes the discussion on programming in the large begun in Chapter 9. Recall that in Chapter 9 we focused on developing a single program for a single application. In this chapter we consider the question of building reusable software components, or software building blocks that can be used by many programs. These fall into several categories; the one we take up here is called *abstract data types*.

An abstract data type (ADT) is a package whose specification provides a type and a set of operations on that type. In this chapter you will see how package `Calendar` should be viewed as an ADT, and you will use a number of its operations for the first time.

Also in this chapter you will learn to write ADTs, and you will see the details of three useful reusable components: calendar dates, rational numbers or fractions, and variable-length strings. A fourth ADT, implementing operations on employee records, is presented as an example of a miniature database system.

 ## 10.1 System Structures: Abstract Data Types (ADTs)

To analyze the solution to a case study, we first list its data requirements and the algorithm. Then, we use procedural abstraction to design and implement the algorithm. The next step is to analyze a problem's data requirements.

Data abstraction is a powerful programming tool, taking procedural abstraction a step further. It is the conceptual approach of combining a data type with a set of operations on that data type. Furthermore, data abstraction is the philosophy that we can use such data types without knowing the details of their representation in the underlying computer system. Just as procedural abstraction enables us to focus on *what* a procedure does without worrying about *how* it does it, data abstraction enables us to consider the data objects needed and the operations that must be performed on those objects, without being concerned with unnecessary details.

You have already practiced data abstraction—you have used the `Float` data type to represent decimal numbers, without knowing much about the internal representation of that data type on a computer. In fact, floating-point representations vary considerably from one computer to another. In some cases there are no hardware instructions for floating-point arithmetic; it is all done with calls to subroutines. The point is that you have used floating-point literals, variables, and operations with confidence, without knowing or even caring how they are represented. The specification for the Ada data type `Float` is shown in the following display.

Specification for Data Type Float

Elements: The elements are real numbers whose range depends on the number of bits used for storage. For example, for Digital Equipment Corporation's VAX-11 computer, the range of positive real numbers is `0.29E-38` to `1.70E310`. Because a digital computer can represent only a finite number of quantities in a given number of bits, not all real numbers in this range can be represented. Indeed, an infinite number of real numbers cannot be represented. However, `Float` serves as a useful approximation to the real numbers. Type `Float` literals are written as decimal numbers with an optional scale factor. There must be a decimal point and at least one digit before and after the decimal point in each `Float` literal.

Operators: The arithmetic operators are ABS, +, -, *, /, and **. The relational operators are <=, <, =, /=, >, and >=. Assignment using := is also predefined.

Ada's Specification for Predefined Types: Package Standard

As it happens, Ada has a convenient way of specifying all the predefined types— `Integer`, `Float`, `Boolean`, `Character`, and so on—and their operations. Because Ada programmers learn very quickly to understand package specifications, the designers of the language chose to specify these things with a package specification! This package specification, called `Standard`, appears as Appendix C. Figure 10.1 shows the section of `Standard` that describes `Float`. Notice that the arithmetic and relational operators are specified as functions. For example,

```
FUNCTION "+" (Left, Right : Float) RETURN Float;
```

tells us concisely that "+" takes two `Float` operands and returns a result of type `Float`. Mathematically, an operator is really just a certain kind of function, so this notation is appropriate. You will see later in this chapter that Ada also gives *you* the ability to specify new operators in this manner.

Figure 10.1 Section of Package Standard Describing Float

```
PACKAGE Standard IS

   . . .

   -- Section of package Standard that defines the type Float and its
   -- operations. Excerpted and reformatted from the Ada Standard Appendix C.

   TYPE Float IS Implementation_Defined;
   -- "Implementation_Defined" means that the Standard does not specify
   -- the details, because they depend on the computer's arithmetic system.
```

```
-- The predefined operators for this type are as follows:

FUNCTION "="  (Left, Right : Float) RETURN Boolean;
FUNCTION "/=" (Left, Right : Float) RETURN Boolean;
FUNCTION "<"  (Left, Right : Float) RETURN Boolean;
FUNCTION "<=" (Left, Right : Float) RETURN Boolean;
FUNCTION ">"  (Left, Right : Float) RETURN Boolean;
FUNCTION ">=" (Left, Right : Float) RETURN Boolean;

FUNCTION "+"  (Right : Float) RETURN Float;
FUNCTION "-"  (Right : Float) RETURN Float;
FUNCTION "ABS"(Right : Float) RETURN Float;

FUNCTION "+"  (Left, Right : Float) RETURN Float;
FUNCTION "-"  (Left, Right : Float) RETURN Float;
FUNCTION "*"  (Left, Right : Float) RETURN Float;
FUNCTION "/"  (Left, Right : Float) RETURN Float;

FUNCTION "**" (Left : Float; Right : Integer) RETURN Float;

. . .

END Standard;
```

As another example from package Standard, consider Fig. 10.2, which shows the specification for the predefined type Integer. Notice the style in which all the familiar integer operations are listed.

Figure 10.2 Section of Package Standard Describing Integer

```
PACKAGE Standard IS

-- This is the section of the package Standard that describes
-- the predefined type Integer.
-- Excerpted and reformatted from the Ada Standard, Appendix C.

   . . .

   TYPE Integer IS implementation_defined;

-- The predefined operators for this type are as follows:

FUNCTION "="  (Left, Right : Integer) RETURN Boolean;
FUNCTION "/=" (Left, Right : Integer) RETURN Boolean;
FUNCTION "<"  (Left, Right : Integer) RETURN Boolean;
FUNCTION "<=" (Left, Right : Integer) RETURN Boolean;
FUNCTION ">"  (Left, Right : Integer) RETURN Boolean;
FUNCTION ">=" (Left, Right : Integer) RETURN Boolean;

FUNCTION "+"   (Right : Integer) RETURN Integer;
FUNCTION "-"   (Right : Integer) RETURN Integer;
FUNCTION "ABS" (Right : Integer) RETURN Integer;

FUNCTION "+"   (Left, Right : Integer) RETURN Integer;
FUNCTION "-"   (Left, Right : Integer) RETURN Integer;
FUNCTION "*"   (Left, Right : Integer) RETURN Integer;
FUNCTION "/"   (Left, Right : Integer) RETURN Integer;
FUNCTION "REM" (Left, Right : Integer) RETURN Integer;
FUNCTION "MOD" (Left, Right : Integer) RETURN Integer;
```

```
FUNCTION "**"    (Left : Integer; Right : Integer) RETURN Integer;

    . . .

END Standard;
```

The Nature of an ADT

An abstract data type, or ADT, is really just a formal name for what Ada calls a *type:* a set of values and a set of operations that are appropriately applied to those values.

A program that uses an abstract data type is called a *client program.* A client program can declare and manipulate objects of the data type and use the data type's operators without knowing the details of the internal representation of the data type or the implementation of its operators; these details are hidden from the client program (this is called *information hiding* by computer scientists). In this way we separate the *use* of the data and operators (by the client program) from the *representation* of the type and *implementation* of the operators (by the abstract data type). This provides several advantages. It allows us to implement the client program and abstract data type independently of each other. If we decide to change the implementation of an operator (function procedure) in the abstract data type, we can do this without affecting the client program. Finally, because the internal representation of a data type is hidden from its client program, we can even change the internal representation at a later time without modifying the client program.

An ADT is an important kind of *reusable software component.* ADTs are written so as to be usable by a variety of client programs. An ADT need have no knowledge of the client programs that will use it; the client programs need have no knowledge of the internal details of the ADT. Ideally, ADTs are thought of as analogous to the various integrated electronic components used in modern computers and other devices: One needs to understand only the interface to an ADT to "plug it in" to a program, the way electronic components are plugged into a circuit board.

ADTs facilitate programming in the large because they reside in ever-larger libraries of program resources. Having large libraries of general resources available makes the client programs much simpler because their writers do not have to "reinvent the wheel." The modern software industry is devoting much time and effort to the development of component libraries; your study of ADTs will give you a taste of how this development is done.

In brief, ADTs are built in Ada using packages. The remainder of this chapter introduces concepts of ADTs and discusses four ADTs in particular: the predefined package Calendar, and four user-written packages for calendar dates, rational numbers, variable-length strings, and employee records.

The Structure of an ADT

Abstract data types are a general concept in programming, independent of any particular programming language. An ADT consists of the specification of one or more data types and a set of operations applicable to the type or types. Generally the type is a composite type, often a record of some kind. The operations can be classified into several classes:

- *Constructor:* A constructor creates, or constructs, an object of the type by putting its component parts together into a unified whole.
- *Selector:* A selector selects a particular component of an object.
- *Inquiry:* An inquiry operation asks whether an object has a particular property, for example, whether it is empty.
- *Input/output:* As usual, an input/output operation is the communication link between the value of an object and the world outside the program, usually a human operator at the terminal or a disk file or printer.

Ada Features for ADTs

Ada provides many capabilities to help us develop ADTs. Here is a summary of the abstraction features we use in this book. We will make use of the first five in this chapter; the last two will be used to advantage in Chapters 11 and 12.

- Ada provides *subtypes*. This feature allows us to define a class of numeric or enumeration values and attach range constraints to it. This allows the compiler to make certain that we never assign an out-of-range value to a variable.
- Ada provides *record field initialization*. This allows us to define a record type in such a way that each field in each variable of that type is initialized to a predetermined value.
- Ada provides *packages*. As we have seen throughout this book, a package is an ideal way of grouping together resources—types, functions, procedures, important constants, and so on—and making them available to client programs. A package specification acts as a "contract" between the writer of the package and the writer of the client program. Furthermore, the compiler checks to make sure that the contract is followed: Everything promised in the specification must be delivered in the package body, and client programs must use the package resources correctly, for example by calling procedures only with the correct parameters.
- Ada provides *private types*. The private type capability enables us to write a package that provides a new type to client programs, in such a way that the client program cannot accidentally misuse values of the type by referencing information that is most properly kept private, that is, restricted for the internal use of the package body only.
- Ada provides *operator overloading*. This allows us to write new arithmetic and comparison operators for new types, and use them just as we use the predefined operators.
- Ada provides *user-defined exceptions*. This enables the writer of a package to provide exceptions to client programs, in order to signal to a client when it has done something inappropriate with the package. The writer of the client program can write exception handlers for user-defined exceptions that work

exactly like the handlers we write for the predefined exceptions like `Constraint_Error`.

- Ada provides *attributes* like the `First` and `Last` attributes we have used frequently thus far. Attributes make it possible to write subprograms that manipulate data structures without knowing all their details. This is especially useful in the case of arrays, where a subroutine that manipulates an array parameter can be written without knowing the array bounds: All it needs to do is inquire about the array bounds by asking for the `First` and `Last` attributes. This will be used to great advantage in Chapter 12.

- Finally, Ada provides *generic definition*. Generic definition allows us to write subprograms and packages that are so general that they do not even have to know all the details of the types they manipulate; these types can be passed to the generic unit as parameters when the generic unit is instantiated. We have seen generic instantiation so far only with respect to the `Text_IO` libraries. Chapter 12 will introduce more about generics and show you how to write generic units of your own.

Exercises for Section 10.1

Self-Check

1. Explain the various kinds of operations in an ADT.

10.2 System Structures: Using Package Calendar as an ADT

Before learning to write ADTs, it is helpful to study an existing one in detail. We have used the predefined package `Calendar` in a number of previous examples in this book, without paying much attention to the fact that `Calendar` serves as an excellent example of a well thought out ADT. It happens that `Calendar` is always provided with an Ada compiler (indeed, it *must* be provided), and our own ADTs will often be written in the style of `Calendar`. Systematic study of `Calendar` will teach you a lot about the design of ADTs and prepare you to start writing your own.

Resources Provided by Calendar

Package `Calendar` uses a type `Duration`, which is actually defined in package `Standard`, not here. `Duration` is a measure of *elapsed* time: One duration unit is exactly equal to one elapsed second. Note that this is not the same as the time of day. Time of day, often called "wall clock" time in computing applications, gives a particular instant of time: 12:05 P.M. on January 25, 1980, for example. `Duration` measures the *passage* of time: Two minutes, or 120 seconds, elapse between 12:05 P.M. and 12:07 P.M. on the same day. Time of day is one of the resources provided by `Calendar`, in the form of a type `Time`.

The purpose of Calendar is to provide a useful number of operations on time-of-day values. Figure 10.3 shows the entire specification of package Calendar, which we have copied straight from the Ada standard, making changes only in the formatting and comments in the specification.

Figure 10.3 Full Specification of Package Calendar

```
PACKAGE Calendar IS

   -- standard Ada package, must be supplied with compilers
   -- provides useful services for dates and times

   -- type definitions

   TYPE Time IS PRIVATE;

   SUBTYPE Year_Number  IS Integer RANGE 1901..2099;
   SUBTYPE Month_Number IS Integer RANGE 1..12;
   SUBTYPE Day_Number   IS Integer RANGE 1..31;
   SUBTYPE Day_Duration IS Duration RANGE 0.0..86_400;
   -- Duration is a predefined (standard) fixed-point type;
   -- Day_Duration range is the number of seconds in 24 hours


   -- constructor operation

   -- constructs a Time value from its components; note that the
   -- default for Seconds is 0.0, so if Seconds value isn't given,
   -- the time is assumed to be at midnight

   FUNCTION Time_Of (Year     : Year_Number;
                     Month    : Month_Number;
                     Day      : Day_Number;
                     Seconds  : Day_Duration:=0.0) RETURN Time;


   -- selector operations

   FUNCTION Year    (Date : Time) RETURN Year_Number;
   FUNCTION Month   (Date : Time) RETURN Month_Number;
   FUNCTION Day     (Date : Time) RETURN Day_Number;
   FUNCTION Seconds (Date : Time) RETURN Day_Duration;

   -- splits a Time value into its component parts

   PROCEDURE Split (Date     : IN Time;
                    Year     : OUT Year_Number;
                    Month    : OUT Month_Number;
                    Day      : OUT Day_Number;
                    Seconds  : OUT Day_Duration);

   -- read the computer's clock to get the current time of day

   FUNCTION Clock RETURN Time;

   -- arithmetic and comparison operations

   -- note that only the "sensible" operations are defined.
   -- this is possible because Time is a private type with no
   -- predefined operations except := and =
```

```
FUNCTION "<"  (Left, Right : Time)        RETURN Boolean;
FUNCTION "<=" (Left, Right : Time)        RETURN Boolean;
FUNCTION ">"  (Left, Right : Time)        RETURN Boolean;
FUNCTION ">=" (Left, Right : Time)        RETURN Boolean;

FUNCTION "+" (Left : Time;       Right : Duration)  RETURN Time;
FUNCTION "+" (Left : Duration; Right : Time)      RETURN Time;
FUNCTION "-" (Left : Time;       Right : Duration)  RETURN Time;
FUNCTION "-" (Left : Time;       Right : Time)      RETURN Duration;


-- exported exceptions

-- Time_Error is raised by Time_Of if its actual parameters
-- don't form a proper date, and also by "+" and "-" if they
-- can't return a date whose year number is in range,
-- or if "-" can't return a value that is in the
-- range of the type Duration.

Time_Error : EXCEPTION;

PRIVATE

-- implementation-dependent (the details depend on the computer's
-- internal clock structure, and are not important because Calendar
-- provides all the operations we need)

END Calendar;
```

The first line of code in `Calendar` is a partial type definition:

```
TYPE Time IS PRIVATE;
```

The definition is completed at the bottom of the figure, below the word `PRIVATE`. Ada provides certain rules for the use of private types. First, variables of the type may be declared; for example,

```
MyBirthday : Calendar.Time;
  LastWeek : Calendar.Time;
```

are permissible declarations. Second, one variable of a private type may be assigned the value of another variable of the same type, and two variables of a private type may be compared for equality or inequality. For example,

```
LastWeek := MyBirthday;
IF LastWeek /= MyBirthday THEN...
```

are both valid operations. *No other operations are predefined.* Indeed, one of the purposes of private types is to allow the writer of a package to define *exactly* those operations he or she deems appropriate.

Following the definition of `Time` are four subtype declarations. Three of these give the acceptable ranges for year, month, and day values; the fourth specifies the number of duration units, or seconds, in a 24-hour day: 86,400. The Ada standard says that any time value from midnight on January 1, 1901, to midnight on December 31, 2099, must be treated as a unique valid value by

Calendar; furthermore, two consecutive time values must not differ by more than 20 milliseconds.

Time is treated as a private type for two reasons. First, the internal representation of a time value is dependent on the form the hardware clock uses for time values. Second, not all operations make sense for time values. If Time were treated as just some sort of integer value, for example, we could multiply two times together; however, multiplying 3 P.M. by 4 P.M. is meaningless! Making Time a private type allowed the designers of Ada to control precisely the set of sensible operations on Time values. What are these operations?

To use time values well, the client program must be able to create time values, for example, by supplying a month, a day, and a year. Calendar provides a function Time_Of for this purpose. An operation like Time_Of, which *constructs* a value of the new type from its component parts, is called a *constructor* operation. There are also five *selector* operations: Year, Month, Day, Seconds, and Split, which allow the client program to select various components of a time value in a useful form (integer and duration values). The first four of these operations are functions that return individual components; Split is a procedure that produces all four components in a single call. The next operation is Clock, which returns the current time of day as a Time value.

We know from the discussion above that each time value is unique; also, time values are *monotonically increasing;* that is, as time progresses, each new value is greater than the previous one. This conforms to our real-world view of time and the concepts of "earlier" and "later." Because time is monotonically increasing—*totally ordered* is another mathematical term with similar meaning—we can confidently compare two values. As for any private type, Ada already provides equality and inequality operators, so Calendar provides the others: <, <=, >, and >=. Notice that these are specified as functions; they can be used in function form, for example,

```
IF Calendar."<="(RightNow, AnotherTime) THEN...
```

or as normal infix operators, for example,

```
IF RightNow <= AnotherTime THEN...
```

The latter form is permitted *only* if a USE Calendar appears at the top of the program.

To do computations with time values, Ada provides some arithmetic operations. Only those operations that make sense are provided by the package, as follows:

```
FUNCTION "+" (Left : Time; Right : Duration) RETURN Time;
FUNCTION "+" (Left : Duration; Right : Time) RETURN Time;
FUNCTION "-" (Left : Time; Right : Duration) RETURN Time;
FUNCTION "-" (Left : Time; Right : Time)     RETURN Duration;
```

For example, adding two times together makes no sense (what does it mean to add 3 P.M. to 4 P.M.?); it is therefore not possible to do so with Calendar operations. It does make sense to add a duration to a time; for example, 3 P.M. plus one hour is 4 P.M. The two "+" operations are provided to ensure that the time value can appear on the right or the left. Finally, the subtraction operations are sensible ones: Subtracting 3 P.M. from 4 P.M. gives one elapsed hour; subtracting two hours from 7 A.M. gives 5 A.M. These operations serve as an excellent example of the usefulness of private types in ensuring that a client cannot perform meaningless operations, or operations that do not make physical sense.

The final line of code in the specification defines an exception `Time_Error`. This exception is raised whenever a `Time_Of` call would return an invalid time value, for example, if 2 (February), 30, and 1990 were supplied as parameters: February 30 does not exist. `Calendar` also understands leap years, so `Time_Error` would be raised if 2, 29, and 1991 were supplied to `Time_Of`, because 1991 is not a leap year. `Time_Error` is also raised if the subtraction operator is given two times that are so far apart that the computer cannot represent the number of elapsed seconds that separate them.

◆ Case Study: World Times

As an example of the use of `Calendar`, consider the problem of determining the time in other time zones around the world.

Problem
Write a program to allow the user to enter the abbreviation of one of a set of cities and display the current time in that city.

Analysis
Given a table of city codes and the number of time zones separating each from the user's home time zone, we can use `Calendar` to find the current local time, then add or subtract the appropriate number of seconds to find the time elsewhere.

Data Requirements for World Time

Problem Inputs

```
City : Cities
```

Design

Algorithm for World Time

1. Read the value of `City` from the keyboard.
2. Find the current local time.
3. Find the time in `City` by using the time zone offset table.
4. Display the local time and the time in `City`.

Coding
Program 10.1 gives the program for `WorldTime`. Type `Cities` gives a list of city names or abbreviations; a procedure `ReadCity` reads a city name robustly,

refusing to permit an invalid city to be entered; and a procedure `DisplayTime` is used to display a time value in a useful form. `DisplayTime` is a modification of `TimeOfDay`, developed earlier in Program 7.2.

Program 10.1 Time Around the World

```
WITH Text_IO;
WITH My_Int_IO;
WITH Calendar;
PROCEDURE WorldTime IS

   TYPE Cities IS (Paris, London, Rio, Caracas, DC,
                    Chicago, Denver, Seattle, Honolulu);

   PACKAGE City_IO IS NEW Text_IO.Enumeration_IO(Cities);

   TYPE TimeDiffs IS ARRAY (Cities) OF Integer;

   -- table of time differences from DC; modify this table if you are
   -- not located in the Eastern U.S. time zone
   Offsets : CONSTANT TimeDiffs :=
      (Paris => +6, London => +5, Rio => +2, Caracas => -1, DC => 0,
       Chicago => -1, Denver => -2, Seattle => -3, Honolulu => -5);

   TimeHere  : Calendar.Time;
   TimeThere : Calendar.Time;
   There     : Cities;

   FUNCTION AdjustTime(T: Calendar.Time; City: Cities;
                        OffsetTable: TimeDiffs) RETURN Calendar.Time IS

   -- given a time value, finds the corresponding time in a given time zone
   -- Pre: T, City, and OffsetTable are initialized
   --       T represents a time in the local time zone
   --       OffsetTable represents the time zone offsets from the local zone
   -- Post: returns the adjusted time

   BEGIN -- AdjustTime

     RETURN Calendar."+"(T, Duration(OffsetTable(City) * 3600));

   END AdjustTime;


   PROCEDURE ReadCity(City : OUT Cities) IS

   -- reads a city name from the terminal, robustly
   -- Pre: none
   -- Post: City contains a valid city name

   BEGIN -- ReadCity

     LOOP
       BEGIN      -- exception handler block
         Text_IO.Put(Item => "Enter a city name, please > ");
         City_IO.Get(Item => City);
         EXIT;   -- good input data
       EXCEPTION -- bad input data
         WHEN Text_IO.Data_Error =>
```

Case Study: World Times, continued

479

10.2 System
Structures: Using
Package Calendar as
an ADT

```
              Text_IO.Skip_Line;
              Text_IO.Put(Item => "Invalid city name; please try again.");
              Text_IO.New_Line;
         END;          -- exception handler block
      END LOOP;

   END ReadCity;


   PROCEDURE DisplayTime(T: Calendar.Time) IS

   -- displays a Calendar.Time value in hh:mm:ss form
   -- Pre: T is defined
   -- Post: displays the Seconds part of T in hh:mm:ss form

      SecsPastMidnight : Calendar.Day_Duration;
      MinsPastMidnight : Natural;
      Secs             : Natural;
      Mins             : Natural;
      Hrs              : Natural;

   BEGIN -- DisplayTime

      SecsPastMidnight := Calendar.Seconds(T);
      MinsPastMidnight := Natural(Float(SecsPastMidnight)/60.0 - 0.5);
      Secs :=
         Natural(Float(SecsPastMidnight) - 60.0 * Float(MinsPastMidnight));
      Mins :=              MinsPastMidnight REM 60;
      Hrs :=               MinsPastMidnight / 60;

      My_Int_IO.Put (Item => Hrs, Width => 1);
      Text_IO.Put (Item => ':');
      IF Mins < 10 THEN
         Text_IO.Put (Item => '0');
      END IF;
      My_Int_IO.Put (Item => Mins, Width => 1);
      Text_IO.Put (Item => ':');
      IF Secs < 10 THEN
         Text_IO.Put (Item => '0');
      END IF;
      My_Int_IO.Put (Item => Secs, Width => 1);

   END DisplayTime;

BEGIN -- WorldTime

   ReadCity(City => There);
   TimeHere := Calendar.Clock;
   TimeThere := AdjustTime(T=>TimeHere, City=>There, OffsetTable=>Offsets);

   Text_IO.Put(Item => "Current local time is ");
   DisplayTime(T => TimeHere);
   Text_IO.New_Line;
   Text_IO.Put(Item => "Current time in ");
   City_IO.Put(Item => There, Width => 1);
   Text_IO.Put(Item => " is ");
   DisplayTime(T => TimeThere);
   Text_IO.New_Line;

END WorldTime;
```

```
Enter a city name, please > NewYork
Invalid city name; please try again.
Enter a city name, please > Seattle
Current local time is 12:48:50
Current time in SEATTLE is 9:48:50
```

The function `AdjustTime` does the work of computing the new time. It contains a table of offsets, or number of time zones away from local time. `Calendar."+"` is used to add or subtract the appropriate number of seconds:

```
RETURN Calendar."+"(T, Duration(OffsetTable(City) * 3600));
```

The array `Offsets` gives the time zone differences; the number of seconds is computed by multiplying the number of time zones by 3600 (the number of seconds in an hour), then converting to type `Duration`.

It is important to note that on most computers, `Calendar.Clock` gives the current *local* time, not some universal time value. The array `Offsets` is initialized to the offsets from the authors' home time zone, the Eastern zone; you will have to change the table values if you are running this program in another zone. An exercise suggests an approach to solving this problem in a more robust manner.

Exercises for Section 10.2

Programming

1. Write a program that tests the operations in package `Calendar`. Try to add two times together, for example. Also investigate what happens when `Time_Of` is called with parameters that would lead to an invalid time value (February 30, for example, or February 29, 1991). Does `Calendar` behave correctly, as the specification suggests?

10.3 System Structures: Writing an ADT for Calendar Dates

Section 10.2 illustrated the use of an ADT. It is now time to consider how we might *write* an ADT of our own.

In Chapter 8 we developed a package `SimpleDates` for representing, reading, and displaying calendar dates. A difficulty with that package is that the user can enter and store a meaningless date (February 30, for example). In this section we improve the package so that it is more robust and offers more capabilities.

Specification for the Improved Dates Package

The specification for our improved package appears in Program 10.2. We represent a date using the same record form as in SimpleDates, but now it is a private type so that a client program does not manipulate the fields directly. This prevents the user from storing an invalid date in a date variable.

Program 10.2   Specification for Robust Dates Package

```
WITH Calendar;
WITH Text_IO;
PACKAGE Dates IS

 -- specification for package to represent calendar dates
 -- in a form convenient for reading and displaying.

   TYPE Months IS
      (Jan, Feb, Mar, Apr, May, Jun, Jul, Aug, Sep, Oct, Nov, Dec);

   TYPE Formats IS
      (Full,           -- February 7, 1991
       Short,          -- 07 FEB 91
       Numeric,        -- 2/7/91
       Julian);        -- 91038

   SUBTYPE Year_Number  IS Calendar.Year_Number;
   SUBTYPE Day_Number   IS Calendar.Day_Number;

   TYPE Date IS PRIVATE;

   -- constructors

   FUNCTION Today                         RETURN Date;
   FUNCTION Date_Of(Year  : Year_Number;
                    Month : Months;
                    Day   : Day_Number) RETURN Date;

   -- exported exception

   Date_Error : EXCEPTION;

   -- selectors

   FUNCTION Year (D: Date) RETURN Year_Number;
   FUNCTION Month(D: Date) RETURN Months;
   FUNCTION Day  (D: Date) RETURN Day_Number;


   -- input/output

   PROCEDURE Get(Item: OUT Date);
   PROCEDURE Put(Item: IN Date; Format: IN Formats);

   PROCEDURE Get(File: IN Text_IO.File_Type; Item: OUT Date);
   PROCEDURE Put(File: IN Text_IO.File_Type;
                 Item: IN Date; Format: IN Formats);

PRIVATE
```

```
TYPE Date IS RECORD
   Month: Months;
   Day:   Calendar.Day_Number;
   Year:  Calendar.Year_Number;
END RECORD;

END Dates;
```

We define two subtypes Year_Number and Month_Number as "nicknames" for the ones provided by Calendar, and an enumeration type, Formats, as follows:

```
TYPE Format IS (Full, Short, Numeric, Julian);
```

which we will use in the output procedure to determine which of the four following forms will be used to display a date:

```
February 4, 1991
04 FEB 91
2/4/91
91035
```

The last format is the only one that is not entirely obvious. This form is called "Julian," named for the ancient Roman emperor Julius Caesar, who developed the 365/366-day calendar, a variant of which we still use. This date format is often used in data processing: the first two digits are the last two digits of the year; the last three digits are the sequential day in the year. January 1, 1991, is 91001; December 31, 1991, is 91365. Naturally, all sequential days after February 28 are different in leap years than in non-leap years.

Because Date is a private type, a client program has no direct access to its fields. Therefore we need to supply constructors Today as in Simple_Dates, and Date_Of by analogy with the Time_Of constructor in Calendar. Further, we need selectors Year, Month, and Day, by analogy with the corresponding ones in Calendar, each of which selects and returns the given component of the date record. Also by analogy with Calendar, we provide an exception Date _Error, raised when Date_Of would produce a meaningless date like February 30 or June 31.

Finally, there are two Get and two Put procedures. By analogy with Text_IO, there are terminal-oriented and file-oriented versions of each.

Private Type Definition

Form:

```
PACKAGE PackageName IS
   ...
   TYPE TypeName IS PRIVATE;
   ...
```

```
      PRIVATE
        TYPE TypeName IS
          full type definition (usually a record)
      END PackageName;
```

Example:

```
PACKAGE Rationals IS
 . . .
    TYPE Rational IS PRIVATE;
 . . .
PRIVATE
    TYPE Rational IS RECORD
      Numerator: Integer;
      Denominator: Positive;
    END RECORD;
END PackageName;
```

Interpretation: A private type can be defined only in a package specification. The first occurrence of *TypeName* defines it as a private type; the full type definition appears at the end of the specification, in the private section.

User-Defined Exception

Form:

```
ExceptionName : EXCEPTION;
```

Example:

```
ZeroDenominator: EXCEPTION;
```

Interpretation: Exceptions are usually defined in a package specification. The exception can be raised by an operation in the corresponding package body by the statement

```
RAISE ExceptionName ;
```

A client program can have an exception handler for this exception, of the form

```
WHEN ExceptionName =>
```

Body of the Improved Dates Package

Program 10.3 shows the body of package Dates. Because Calendar already knows how to validate a date, the constructor function Date_Of just uses Calendar. Time_Of to do this. If Time_Of does not raise Time_Error, the date is valid. The selectors Year, Month, and Day should be obvious, and Today works just as

Program 10.3 Body of Robust Dates Package

```
WITH Calendar;
WITH Text_IO;
WITH My_Int_IO;
PACKAGE BODY Dates IS

-- body for package to represent calendar dates
-- in a form convenient for reading and displaying.

  PACKAGE Month_IO IS
    NEW Text_IO.Enumeration_IO(Enum => Months);

  FUNCTION Today RETURN Date IS

    -- Finds today's date and returns it as a record of type Date
    -- Today's date is gotten from PACKAGE Calendar

      Right_Now : Calendar.Time;              -- holds internal clock value
      Temp      : Date;

  BEGIN -- Today

      -- Get the current time value from the computer's clock
      Right_Now := Calendar.Clock;

      -- Extract the current month, day, and year from the time value
      Temp.Month := Months'Val(Calendar.Month(Right_Now)- 1);
      Temp.Day := Calendar.Day (Right_Now);
      Temp.Year := Calendar.Year (Date => Right_Now);

      RETURN Temp;

  END Today;

  FUNCTION Date_Of(Year : Year_Number;
                   Month : Months;
                   Day : Day_Number) RETURN Date IS

  -- constructs a date given year, month, and day.
  -- Pre: Year, Month, and Day are initialized
  -- Post: returns the corresponding Date record, or raises Date_Error
  --        if the date would be invalid

    Temp: Calendar.Time;

  BEGIN -- Date_Of

    Temp := Calendar.Time_Of(Year=>Year,
                             Month=>Months'Pos(Month)+1, Day=>Day);
    -- assert: M, D, and Y form a sensible date if Time_error not raised

    RETURN (Month => Month, Year => Year, Day => Day);
    -- assert: a valid date is returned

  EXCEPTION

    WHEN Calendar.Time_Error =>
      RAISE Date_Error;

  END Date_Of;

  FUNCTION Year (D: Date) RETURN Year_Number IS
```

```
  BEGIN
    RETURN D.Year;
  END Year;

  FUNCTION Month (D: Date) RETURN Months IS
  BEGIN
    RETURN D.Month;
  END Month;

  FUNCTION Day (D: Date) RETURN Day_Number IS
  BEGIN
    RETURN D.Day;
  END Day;

  PROCEDURE Get(File: IN Text_IO.File_Type; Item: OUT Date) IS
  -- gets a date in the form MMM DD YYYY
  -- Post: returns a date in Item

    M:      Months;
    D:      Calendar.Day_Number;
    Y:      Calendar.Year_Number;

  BEGIN

    Month_IO.Get (File => File, Item => M);
    My_Int_IO.Get(File => File, Item => D);
    My_Int_IO.Get(File => File, Item => Y);
    -- assert: M, D, and Y are well-formed and in range
    --         otherwise one of the Get's would raise an exception

    Item := Date_Of (Month => M, Year => Y, Day => D);
    -- assert: Item is a valid date if Date_Error not raised

  EXCEPTION

    WHEN Text_IO.Data_Error =>
      RAISE Date_Error;
    WHEN Constraint_Error =>
      RAISE Date_Error;
    WHEN Date_Error =>
      RAISE Date_Error;

  END Get;


  PROCEDURE WriteShort(File: IN Text_IO.File_Type; Item: IN Date) IS

    Last2Digits : Natural;

  -- writes a date in dd MMM yy form to a file
  -- Pre: Item is assigned a value
  -- Post: Writes a date in dd MMM yy form

  BEGIN

    Last2Digits := Item.Year MOD 100;

    IF Item.Day < 10 THEN
      Text_IO.Put(File => File, Item => '0');
    END IF;
    My_Int_IO.Put(File => File, Item => Item.Day, Width => 1);
    Text_IO.Put(File => File, Item => ' ');
    Month_IO.Put (File => File, Item => Item.Month, Width => 1);
```

```
      Text_IO.Put(File => File, Item => ' ');
      IF Last2Digits < 10 THEN
        Text_IO.Put(File => File, Item => '0');
      END IF;
      My_Int_IO.Put(File => File, Item => Last2Digits, Width => 1);

END WriteShort;

PROCEDURE WriteFull(File: IN Text_IO.File_Type; Item: IN Date) IS

-- writes a date in full Monthname dd, yyyy form
-- Pre: Item is assigned a value
-- Post: Writes a date in Monthname dd, yyyy form

BEGIN

  CASE Item.Month IS
    WHEN Jan =>
      Text_IO.Put(File => File, Item => "January");
    WHEN Feb =>
      Text_IO.Put(File => File, Item => "February");
    WHEN Mar =>
      Text_IO.Put(File => File, Item => "March");
    WHEN Apr =>
      Text_IO.Put(File => File, Item => "April");
    WHEN May =>
      Text_IO.Put(File => File, Item => "May");
    WHEN Jun =>
      Text_IO.Put(File => File, Item => "June");
    WHEN Jul =>
      Text_IO.Put(File => File, Item => "July");
    WHEN Aug =>
      Text_IO.Put(File => File, Item => "August");
    WHEN Sep =>
      Text_IO.Put(File => File, Item => "September");
    WHEN Oct =>
      Text_IO.Put(File => File, Item => "October");
    WHEN Nov =>
      Text_IO.Put(File => File, Item => "November");
    WHEN Dec =>
      Text_IO.Put(File => File, Item => "December");
  END CASE;

  Text_IO.Put(File => File, Item => ' ');
  My_Int_IO.Put(File => File, Item => Item.Day, Width => 1);
  Text_IO.Put(File => File, Item => ", ");
  My_Int_IO.Put(File => File, Item => Item.Year, Width => 1);

END WriteFull;

PROCEDURE WriteNumeric(File: IN Text_IO.File_Type; Item: IN Date) IS

-- writes a date in mm/dd/yy form to a file
-- Pre: Item is assigned a value
-- Post: Writes a date in mm/dd/yy form

  Last2Digits : Natural;

BEGIN

  Last2Digits := Item.Year MOD 100;

  My_Int_IO.Put (File => File,
                 Item => Months'Pos(Item.Month)+1, Width => 1);
```

```
      Text_IO.Put(File => File, Item => '/');
      My_Int_IO.Put(File => File, Item => Item.Day, Width => 1);
      Text_IO.Put(File => File, Item => '/');
      IF Last2Digits < 10 THEN
        Text_IO.Put(File => File, Item => '0');
      END IF;
      My_Int_IO.Put(File => File, Item => Last2Digits, Width => 1);

END WriteNumeric;

PROCEDURE WriteJulian(File: IN Text_IO.File_Type; Item: IN Date) IS

-- writes a date in yyddd form to a file
-- Pre: Item is assigned a value
-- Post: Writes a date in yyddd form

   Last2Digits : Natural;
   JulianDay: Natural;

   TYPE NumberOfDays IS ARRAY (Months) OF Positive;
   NonLeapDays : CONSTANT NumberOfDays :=
     (31, 28, 31, 30, 31, 30, 31, 31, 30, 31, 30, 31);
   LeapDays : CONSTANT NumberOfDays :=
     (31, 29, 31, 30, 31, 30, 31, 31, 30, 31, 30, 31);

BEGIN

   Last2Digits := Item.Year MOD 100;
   JulianDay := Item.Day;

   IF Item.Month > Months'First THEN
     IF (Item.Year MOD 400 = 0)
        OR ((Item.Year MOD 4 = 0) AND (Item.Year MOD 100 /= 0)) THEN
        FOR Mon IN Months'First..Months'Pred(Item.Month) LOOP
          JulianDay := JulianDay + LeapDays(Mon);
        END LOOP;
     ELSE
        FOR Mon IN Months'First..Months'Pred(Item.Month) LOOP
          JulianDay := JulianDay + NonLeapDays(Mon);
        END LOOP;
     END IF;
   END IF;

   IF Last2Digits < 10 THEN
     Text_IO.Put(File => File, Item => "0");
   END IF;
   My_Int_IO.Put(File => File, Item => Last2Digits, Width => 1);

   IF JulianDay < 10 THEN
     Text_IO.Put(File => File, Item => "00");
   ELSIF JulianDay < 100 THEN
     Text_IO.Put(File => File, Item => "0");
   END IF;
   My_Int_IO.Put(File => File, Item => JulianDay, Width => 1);

END WriteJulian;

PROCEDURE Put(File: IN Text_IO.File_Type;
              Item: IN Date; Format: IN Formats) IS
BEGIN
   CASE Format IS
     WHEN Short =>
       WriteShort(File => File, Item => Item);
```

```
                    WHEN Full =>
                       WriteFull(File => File, Item => Item);
                    WHEN Numeric =>
                       WriteNumeric(File => File, Item => Item);
                    WHEN Julian =>
                       WriteJulian(File => File, Item => Item);
                 END CASE;
              END Put;

              PROCEDURE Get(Item: OUT Date) IS
              BEGIN
                 Get(File => Text_IO.Standard_Input, Item => Item);
              END Get;

              PROCEDURE Put(Item: IN Date; Format: IN Formats) IS
              BEGIN
                 Put(File => Text_IO.Standard_Output, Item => Item, Format => Format);
              END Put;

           END Dates;
```

it did in `SimpleDates`, calling the appropriate `Calendar` operations to produce the date.

The procedure `Dates.Get` reads a date a bit more robustly than its counterpart in `SimpleDates`. If the date read is ill-formed (month, day, or year is not of the proper form), or if the combination would yield a meaningless date, then `Date_Error` is raised and must be handled by the client program. This is analogous to the way in which the various `Get` procedures in `Text_IO` raise `Data _Error` for ill-formed or out-of-range input.

The procedure `Dates.Put` displays a date in one of the four forms given above, depending upon the value of the parameter `Format`. `Put` calls one of four local procedures, `WriteFull`, `WriteShort`, `WriteNumeric`, and `Write–Julian`, depending on a `CASE` statement to select the appropriate one. `WriteShort` and `WriteNumeric` are based on `Today` (Program 3.6) and `Today2` (Program 3.7); the other two need explanation.

`WriteFull` uses a `CASE` statement to write the appropriate month name, depending on the month field of the date record. It would have been nice to use an enumeration type for the full names of the months, because `Enumeration _IO` is so easy to use. Unfortunately, the `Put` procedure in `Enumeration_IO` displays or writes the enumeration literal either in uppercase letters or in lowercase ones; there is no way to get it to display just the first letter as an uppercase letter. Because in American correspondence we always capitalize just the first letter of the month, we need to use the `CASE` statement to control the precise form of the string displayed.

`WriteJulian` needs to compute the sequential day of the year. To do this, it makes reference to two tables, `NonLeapDays` and `LeapDays`, which give the number of days in each month in non-leap years and in leap years. These tables are arrays indexed by the `Months`. The variable `JulianDay` is initialized to the day field of the date; then a loop is used to add in the number of days in each of the months preceding the current one. The loop for a non-leap year situation is

```
FOR Mon IN Months'First..Months'Pred(Item.Month) LOOP
   JulianDay := JulianDay + NonLeapDays(Mon);
END LOOP;
```

Now how do we determine whether the year field represents a leap year? According to the Gregorian calendar—a modification of Caesar's adopted in the sixteenth century—a leap year is divisible by 4. However, to compensate for the small difference between a normal year and the time it takes the earth to revolve once around the sun, a century year like 1900 is *not* a leap year. Well, almost. If the century year is divisible by 400, then it is a leap year all the same. In other words, three century years out of four are *not* leap years, but the fourth one is. We can use the following condition to determine whether the year field Item.Year is a leap year:

```
IF (Item.Year MOD 400 = 0) OR
   (Item.Year MOD 4 = 0) AND (Item.Year MOD 100 /= 0) THEN --leap year
```

PROGRAM
STYLE

Procedures in a Package Body but Not in the Specification

It is worth noting that the four procedures WriteFull, WriteShort, WriteNumeric, and WriteJulian appear *only* in the package body; they are *not* given in the specification. This is quite intentional: These procedures are not intended for use by the client program; their only purpose is to refine the procedure Put, which is indeed intended for the client.

When you design a package, you should consider very carefully just which operations to give to the client, list these in the specification, and implement them in the body. It is, of course, a compilation error to list a procedure or function in the specification and *not* put a corresponding body in the package body. This is because the specification is a contract that makes promises to the client that the body must fulfill. However, it is *not* an error to write procedures or functions in the body but not in the specification. Indeed, it is often quite desirable to do this, as the Dates example illustrates.

Program 10.4 shows a test of the Dates package. The program displays the current date in all four formats, then asks the user to enter a date and displays that date all four ways.

Program 10.4   Test of Dates Package

```
WITH Text_IO;
WITH Dates;
PROCEDURE TestDates IS

  D: Dates.Date;

BEGIN -- TestDates
```

```
-- first test the function Today
D := Dates.Today;
Text_IO.Put(Item => "Today is ");
Text_IO.New_Line;
Dates.Put(Item => D, Format => Dates.Short);
Text_IO.New_Line;
Dates.Put(Item => D, Format => Dates.Full);
Text_IO.New_Line;
Dates.Put(Item => D, Format => Dates.Numeric);
Text_IO.New_Line;
Dates.Put(Item => D, Format => Dates.Julian);
Text_IO.New_Line;

LOOP

   BEGIN -- block for exception handler
     Text_IO.Put("Please enter a date in MMM DD YYYY form > ");
     Dates.Get(Item => D);
     EXIT; -- only if no exception is raised
   EXCEPTION
     WHEN Dates.Date_Error =>
       Text_IO.Skip_Line;
       Text_IO.Put(Item => "Badly formed date; try again, please.");
       Text_IO.New_Line;
   END;

END LOOP;
-- assert: at this point, D contains a correct date record

Text_IO.Put(Item => "You entered ");
Text_IO.New_Line;
Dates.Put(Item => D, Format => Dates.Short);
Text_IO.New_Line;
Dates.Put(Item => D, Format => Dates.Full);
Text_IO.New_Line;
Dates.Put(Item => D, Format => Dates.Numeric);
Text_IO.New_Line;
Dates.Put(Item => D, Format => Dates.Julian);
Text_IO.New_Line;

END TestDates;


Today is
23 MAR 91
March 23, 1991
3/23/91
91082
Please enter a date in MMM DD YYYY form > feb 30 1990
Badly formed date; try again, please.
Please enter a date in MMM DD YYYY form > mmm dd yyyy
Badly formed date; try again, please.
Please enter a date in MMM DD YYYY form > Jan 22 1983
You entered
22 JAN 83
January 22, 1983
1/22/83
83022
```

Exercises for Section 10.3

Self-Check

1. Explain the advantages of making the data record a private type.

Programming

1. Write a short program that attempts to access a field of a date record directly. Explain the result you get.
2. Expand Program 10.4 so that the user has a chance to enter a number of dates. Use this to test the dates package with a number of test cases that will show whether Dates is behaving correctly for all inputs.
3. Suppose that package Calendar did not have a date-validating operation. Rewrite the body of Dates so that a date supplied to Date_Of is validated by your package, raising Date_Error if the date would be meaningless. Do not use Calendar.Time_Of to do this.

 # 10.4 System Structures: Writing an ADT for Rational Numbers

This section explains how to specify and implement an abstract data type for doing arithmetic with fractions or rational numbers. A *rational number* is a number with a *numerator* and a *denominator*. For example, the rational number *a/b* has a numerator *a* and and a denominator *b*; the rational number 2/3 has a numerator 2 and a denominator 3.

As you learned in school when you studied fractions, every integer is also equivalent to a rational number: The integer 4 is equivalent to the rational 4/1. You also learned that a rational number cannot have a denominator of zero, but a numerator of zero is fine. There are certain applications where fractions are useful, for example, where we want to represent the number 1/3 exactly and not as the floating-point approximation 0.3333. . . . Although programming languages usually have built-in support for integers and floats, they usually do not support rationals directly.

An *improper rational* is a rational number whose numerator is larger than its denominator, for example, 5/3. The name "improper" is historical; there is nothing "wrong" with a rational that's improper. Also, each rational is algebraically equivalent to many others. For example,

$$\frac{2}{3} = \frac{4}{6} = \frac{6}{9} = \cdots = \frac{24}{36} = \cdots$$

A rational whose numerator and denominator have no common divisors is called "reduced," or sometimes "in lowest terms." An example of a rational in lowest terms is 2/3; the others in the series can all be "reduced" to 2/3.

◆ Case Study: Helping Your Cousin with Fractions

Problem

Your cousin in junior high school is studying fractions and is interested in whether a computer can "do fractions." You wish to show your cousin that a computer program can indeed handle rational numbers.

Analysis

To be useful, the problem solution should provide for creating, reading, and displaying a rational number, and for extracting the numerator and denominator parts. The package should also contain operations for performing rational arithmetic (addition, subtraction, multiplication, and division). It is also useful to provide operations for comparing two rationals: =, /=, <, >, <=, and >=. This is a problem for which an abstract data type is a good solution, because an ADT provides a type (in this case Rational) and a set of operations applicable to that type.

Design

We will construct an abstract data type package to represent the data structure for a rational number with operators for each of the tasks listed above. We will represent each rational quantity as a record with numerator and denominator fields, and we will make the rational type PRIVATE so as to prevent client programs from directly manipulating the fields.

We can use Ada's predefined assignment, equality, and inequality for rationals, but this is meaningful only if we store all rationals in lowest terms. To understand why, remember that Ada's predefined equality compares two records by checking whether each field of one record is equal to the corresponding field of the other. If each comparison yields a true result, the overall equality is true. If our design did not require rationals to be in lowest terms, then the equality check would return incorrect results; for example, 2/3 = 6/9 is true in the "real world" but would be false in our system. However, if 6/9 were never actually stored in our system, but replaced with its reduced equivalent, 2/3, this problem could not arise.

To reduce a rational to lowest terms, we first find the greatest common divisor, or GCD, of the absolute values of its numerator and denominator, then divide both numerator and denominator by this value. To find the GCD of two positive integers M and N, we use an ancient algorithm called Euclid's algorithm.

Algorithm for GCD

1. Divide M by N and store the remainder in R
2. WHILE R /= 0 LOOP
   Set the value of M to that of N
   Set the value of N to that of R
   Divide M by N and store the remainder in R
   END LOOP;

Case Study: Helping Your Cousin with Fractions, continued

493

10.4 System
Structures: Writing
an ADT for Rational
Numbers

3. The result is in N.

Now we can find the sum and product of rationals. The sum of two rationals X and Y is the result of reducing

$$\frac{(\text{Numer}(X) \times \text{Denom}(Y)) + (\text{Denom}(X) \times \text{Numer}(Y))}{\text{Denom}(X) \times \text{Denom}(Y)}$$

to lowest terms. For example,

$$\frac{1}{6} + \frac{2}{3} = \frac{3 + 12}{18} = \frac{15}{18} = \frac{5}{6}$$

The product of two rationals X and Y is the result of reducing

$$\frac{\text{Numer}(X) \times \text{Numer}(Y)}{\text{Denom}(X) \times \text{Denom}(Y)}$$

to lowest terms.

In comparing two rationals, we "cross-multiply" the numerators and denominators. Thus $X < Y$ is determined by the Boolean expression

```
(Numer(X) × Denom(Y)) < (Numer(Y) × Denom(X))
```

Coding

The package specification for the abstract data type Rationals appears as Program 10.5.

Program 10.5 Specification for Package Rationals

```
PACKAGE Rationals IS

-- Specification of the abstract data type for representing
-- and manipulating rational numbers.

  TYPE Rational IS PRIVATE;

--Operators

  FUNCTION "/" (X : Integer; Y : Integer) RETURN Rational;

    -- constructor: returns a rational number in lowest terms
    -- Pre : X and Y are defined
    -- Post: returns a rational number
    --    If Y > 0, returns Reduce(X,Y)
    --    If Y < 0, returns Reduce(-X,-Y)
    --    If Y = 0, raises ZeroDenominator

  ZeroDenominator: EXCEPTION;

  FUNCTION Numer (R : Rational) RETURN Integer;
  FUNCTION Denom (R : Rational) RETURN Positive;
```

```
--  selectors: return the numerator and denominator of a rational number R
--  Pre: R is defined
--  Post: Numer returns the numerator of R; Denom returns the denominator


PROCEDURE Get (Item : OUT Rational);

--  Reads a pair of integer values into rational number Item.
--  Pre : none
--  Post: The first integer number read is the numerator of Item;
--        the second integer number is the denominator of Item.
--        "/" is called to produce a rational in reduced form.


PROCEDURE Put (Item : IN Rational);

--  Displays rational number Item.
--  Pre : Item is assigned a value.
--  Post: displays the numerator and denominator of Item.


FUNCTION "+"(R1 : Rational; R2 : Rational) RETURN Rational;
FUNCTION "-"(R1 : Rational; R2 : Rational) RETURN Rational;
FUNCTION "*"(R1 : Rational; R2 : Rational) RETURN Rational;
FUNCTION "/"(R1 : Rational; R2 : Rational) RETURN Rational;

--  constructors: return the rational sum, difference, product,
--     and quotient of rational numbers R1 and B
--  Pre : R1 and R2 are assigned values
--  Post: return the rational sum, difference, product, and
--     quotient of R1 and R2.


FUNCTION "<" (R1 : Rational; R2 : Rational) RETURN Boolean;
FUNCTION ">" (R1 : Rational; R2 : Rational) RETURN Boolean;
FUNCTION "<="(R1 : Rational; R2 : Rational) RETURN Boolean;
FUNCTION ">="(R1 : Rational; R2 : Rational) RETURN Boolean;

--  inquiry operators: comparison of two rational numbers
--  Pre : R1 and R2 are assigned values
--  Post: return R1 < R2, R1 > R2, R1 <= R2, and R1 >= R2, respectively


PRIVATE

--  A record of type Rational consists of a pair of integer values
--  such that the first number represents the numerator of a rational
--  number and the second number represents the denominator.

  TYPE Rational IS
    RECORD
      Numerator    : Integer := 0;
      Denominator  : Positive := 1;
    END RECORD; -- Rational

END Rationals;
```

A Detailed Look at Package Rationals

Let us consider the rational-number package in depth. The first declaration in Program 10.5 is that of the type being exported to the client program. The type Rational is declared to be PRIVATE so that client programs are prevented from directly referencing the internal details of a variable of type Rational.

The private type definition is completed at the bottom of the specification, in the PRIVATE section. A Rational quantity is a record with an Integer field, Numerator, and a Positive field, Denominator. We require the denominator to be positive so that it can never be zero.

Returning to the beginning of the specification, the first operator given is a *constructor* "/". This function takes two Integer arguments X and Y and returns a reduced rational number equivalent to x/y. Here we are taking advantage of the fact that Ada allows us to return a record as the result of a function. Note that the inputs to "/" can both be negative; the constructor will always return a positive denominator by multiplying numerator and demominator by −1 if necessary.

A client of the package can create a rational number by calling "/". Given the declaration

```
R: Rationals.Rational;
```

then the assignment

```
R := Rationals."/"(2, −4)
```

creates a record with −1 in the numerator and 2 in the denominator.

The next two operators are *selector* functions Numer and Denom, which, given a rational, return the values stored in its numerator and denominator, respectively. The next two operators are input/output operators that read and display rational quantities. These are implemented as procedures called Get and Put for consistency with all the other input/output operations predefined by Ada in Text_IO. The next four operators specify the four required arithmetic operations for rational quantities. They are specified as operators "+", "−", "*", and "/" by analogy with the corresponding operators for the predefined integer and float types you saw in package Standard. Also specified are the comparison operators "<", ">", "<=", and ">=" to fulfull the requirements of the problem.

Defining operators in this manner is called "operator overloading." Recall the similar group of operators in Calendar; it makes no difference whether the operators are provided by a predefined package like Calendar or by a user-defined package like Rationals. Operators are really nothing more than functions with an unusual syntax, appearing between their parameters instead of preceding them. Because function names can be overloaded, so can operator names. Operator overloading allows us to write operations that are mathematical in nature using the familiar mathematical symbols.

It is important to understand that Ada allows us to overload *only* those operator symbols already available in the language; we cannot, for example, define a new operator "?", because "?" is not already an operator in Ada. Also bear in mind that, for reasons beyond the scope of this book to explain, it is *not* possible under most circumstances to define our own operator "=". It is similarly prohibited (and will cause a compilation error) to overload "/=" and the two membership operators "IN" and "NOT IN".

Generally, ADT's can be written so that Ada's predefined "=" and "/=" work correctly. This is the case with Calendar and also with Rationals, and will be so in the other ADT packages we develop in this book.

After the package specification above is written, programmers can implement and compile (but not link or execute) client programs that use the abstract data type Rational. The next step is to implement in the package body all the operations promised by the specification. If stubs are available for the operations, the client programs can be compiled and executed to test the overall flow of control. Once the package body is completed, the client programs can be executed in a meaningful way. Program 10.6 shows a partially completed package body for the abstract data type, with addition and multiplication fully implemented and stubs for subtraction and division. Also, the function "<" is fully implemented but the other comparison operations are left as stubs. Completing the operations is left as an exercise.

Program 10.6   Body of Rational Number ADT

```
WITH Text_IO;
WITH My_Int_IO;
PACKAGE BODY Rationals IS

-- Body of the abstract data type for representing
-- and manipulating rational numbers.

-- local function GCD

  FUNCTION GCD(M: Positive; N: Positive) RETURN Positive IS

    -- finds the greatest common divisor of M and N
    -- Pre: M and N are defined
    -- Post: returns the GCD of M and N, by Euclid's Algorithm

    R : Natural;
    TempM: Positive;
    TempN: Positive;

  BEGIN -- GCD

    TempM := M;
    TempN := N;

    R := TempM REM TempN;

    WHILE R /= O LOOP
      TempM := TempN;
      TempN := R;
      R := TempM REM TempN;
    END LOOP;

    RETURN TempN;

  END GCD;
```

-- Operators

497

10.4 System
Structures: Writing
an ADT for Rational
Numbers

```
FUNCTION "/" (X : Integer; Y : Integer) RETURN Rational IS

-- constructor: returns a rational number in lowest terms
-- Pre : X and Y are defined
-- Post: returns a rational number
--    If Y > 0, returns Reduce(X,Y)
--    If Y < 0, returns Reduce(-X,-Y)
--    If Y = 0, raises ZeroDenominator

  G: Positive;

BEGIN

  IF Y = 0 THEN
    RAISE ZeroDenominator;
  ELSE

    G := GCD(ABS X, ABS Y);
    IF Y > 0 THEN
      RETURN (Numerator => X/G, Denominator => Y/G);
    ELSE
      RETURN (Numerator => (-X)/G, Denominator => (-Y)/G);
    END IF;

  END IF;

END "/";


FUNCTION Numer (R : Rational) RETURN Integer IS
BEGIN
  RETURN R.Numerator;
END Numer;

FUNCTION Denom (R : Rational) RETURN Positive IS
BEGIN
  RETURN R.Denominator;
END Denom;

-- selectors: return the numerator and denominator of a rational number R
-- Pre: R is defined
-- Post: Numer returns the numerator of R; Denom returns the denominator


PROCEDURE Get (Item : OUT Rational) IS

-- Reads a pair of integer values into rational number Item.
-- Pre : none
-- Post: The first integer number read is the numerator of Item;
--       the second integer number is the denominator of Item.
--       "/" is called to produce a rational in reduced form.

  N: Integer;
  D: Integer;

BEGIN -- Get

  My_Int_IO.Get(Item => N);
  My_Int_IO.Get(Item => D);
  Item := N/D;

END Get;
```

```
PROCEDURE Put (Item : IN Rational) IS

-- Displays rational number Item.
-- Pre : Item is assigned a value.
-- Post: displays the numerator and denominator of Item.

BEGIN -- Put

  My_Int_IO.Put(Item => Numer(Item), Width => 1);
  Text_IO.Put(Item => '/');
  My_Int_IO.Put(Item => Denom(Item), Width => 1);

END Put;

FUNCTION "+"(R1 : Rational; R2 : Rational) RETURN Rational IS
  N: Integer;
  D: Positive;
BEGIN
  N := Numer(R1) * Denom(R2) + Numer(R2) * Denom(R1);
  D := Denom(R1) * Denom(R2);
  RETURN N/D;  -- compiler will use fraction constructor here!
END "+";

FUNCTION "*"(R1 : Rational; R2 : Rational) RETURN Rational IS
  N: Integer;
  D: Positive;
BEGIN
  N := Numer(R1) * Numer(R2);
  D := Denom(R1) * Denom(R2);
  RETURN N/D;  -- compiler will use fraction constructor here!
END "*";

FUNCTION "-"(R1 : Rational; R2 : Rational) RETURN Rational IS
BEGIN -- stub
  RETURN 1/1;
END "-";

FUNCTION "/"(R1 : Rational; R2 : Rational) RETURN Rational IS
BEGIN -- stub
  RETURN 1/1;
END "/";

-- constructors: return the rational sum, difference, product,
--    and quotient of rational numbers R1 and B
-- Pre : R1 and R2 are assigned values
-- Post: return the rational sum, difference, product, and
--    quotient of R1 and R2.


FUNCTION "<" (R1 : Rational; R2 : Rational) RETURN Boolean IS
BEGIN
  RETURN Numer(R1) * Denom(R2) < Numer(R2) * Denom(R1);
END "<";

FUNCTION ">" (R1 : Rational; R2 : Rational) RETURN Boolean IS
BEGIN -- stub
  RETURN True;
END ">";

FUNCTION "<=" (R1 : Rational; R2 : Rational) RETURN Boolean IS
BEGIN -- stub
  RETURN True;
END "<=";
```

```
FUNCTION ">=" (R1 : Rational; R2 : Rational) RETURN Boolean IS
BEGIN -- stub
   RETURN True;
END ">=";

-- inquiry operators: comparison of two rational numbers
-- Pre : R1 and R2 are assigned values
-- Post: return R1 < R2, R1 > R2, R1 <= R2, and R1 >= R2, respectively


END Rationals;
```

Once the package is completed, your cousin can execute client programs that use the abstract data type for rational arithmetic. Program 10.7 shows a client program that uses abstract data type Rationals. TestRational1 uses the data type Rational and five of its operators. The body of TestRational1 begins by assigning values to the rational numbers A and B, then reading data into rational numbers C and D. Next, the sum A+B and the product C*D are saved in E and F, respectively, and displayed. Finally, the sum A+E*F is displayed, which shows that the result of one operation can be used as an input to another.

Program 10.7   Test of Package Rationals

```
WITH Text_IO;
WITH Rationals;
PROCEDURE TestRational1 IS

--- Tests the package Rationals

  A: Rationals.Rational;
  B: Rationals.Rational;
  C: Rationals.Rational;
  D: Rationals.Rational;
  E: Rationals.Rational;
  F: Rationals.Rational;

BEGIN -- TestRational1

  A := Rationals."/"(1,3);
  B := Rationals."/"(2, -4);
  Text_IO.Put(Item => "A = ");
  Rationals.Put(Item => A);
  Text_IO.New_Line;
  Text_IO.Put(Item => "B = ");
  Rationals.Put(Item => B);
  Text_IO.New_Line;

  -- Read in rational numbers C and D.
  Text_IO.Put(Item => "Enter rational number C as 2 integers > ");
  Rationals.Get(Item => C);
  Text_IO.Put(Item => "Enter rational number D as 2 integers > ");
```

```
      Rationals.Get(Item => D);
      Text_IO.New_Line;

      E := Rationals."+"(A,B);                        -- form the sum
      Text_IO.Put(Item => "E = A + B is ");
      Rationals.Put(Item => E);
      Text_IO.New_Line;

      F := Rationals."*"(C,D);                        -- form the product
      Text_IO.Put(Item => "F = C * D is ");
      Rationals.Put(Item => F);
      Text_IO.New_Line;

      Text_IO.Put(Item => "A + E * F is ");
      Rationals.Put(Item => Rationals."+"(A, Rationals."*"(E,F)));
      Text_IO.New_Line;

   END TestRational1;
```

```
A = 1/3
B = -1/2
Enter rational number C as 2 integers > 2 3
Enter rational number D as 2 integers > 3 8

E = A + B is -1/6
F = C * D is 1/4
A + E * F is 7/24
```

Program 10.8 shows a modification of our client program which shows the advantage of sometimes using the USE clause, which allows unqualified references to package capabilities. In Program 10.7, where there is no USE, the rational addition operation is written

```
E := Rationals."+"(A,B);
```

but in TestRational2 it is written

```
E := A + B;
```

One of the advantages of Ada's permitting operator symbols like "+" to be defined as functions is that they can be used in expressions in infix form, as in the above line. When the expressions get more complex, this makes programs even more readable. Compare the line

```
Rationals.Put(Item => Rationals."+"(A, Rationals."*"(E,F)));
```

from Program 10.7 with the corresponding line in Program 10.8:

```
Rationals.Put(Item => A + E * F);
```

This is, however, possible only if a USE clause appears in the client program. Otherwise, the operator must not only be qualified (as in Rationals."+") but also must be used as a prefix function call like any other function call. Show by testing Program 10.8 that its behavior is the same as that of Program 10.7.

Program 10.8   Another Test of Package Rationals

501

10.4 System
Structures: Writing
an ADT for Rational
Numbers

```
WITH Text_IO;
WITH Rationals;
USE Rationals;
PROCEDURE TestRational2 IS

-- Tests the package Rationals, this time with USE clause

  A: Rationals.Rational;
  B: Rationals.Rational;
  C: Rationals.Rational;
  D: Rationals.Rational;
  E: Rationals.Rational;
  F: Rationals.Rational;

BEGIN -- TestRational1

  A := 1/3;
  B := 2/(-4);
  Text_IO.Put(Item => "A = ");
  Rationals.Put(Item => A);
  Text_IO.New_Line;
  Text_IO.Put(Item => "B = ");
  Rationals.Put(Item => B);
  Text_IO.New_Line;

  -- Read in rational numbers C and D.
  Text_IO.Put(Item => "Enter rational number C as 2 integers > ");
  Rationals.Get(Item => C);
  Text_IO.Put(Item => "Enter rational number D as 2 integers > ");
  Rationals.Get(Item => D);
  Text_IO.New_Line;

  E := A + B;                    -- form the sum
  Text_IO.Put(Item => "E = A + B is ");
  Rationals.Put(Item => E);
  Text_IO.New_Line;

  F := C * D;                    -- form the product
  Text_IO.Put(Item => "F = C * D is ");
  Rationals.Put(Item => F);
  Text_IO.New_Line;

  Text_IO.Put(Item => "A + E * F is ");
  Rationals.Put(Item => A + E * F);
  Text_IO.New_Line;

END TestRational2;
```

Operator Overloading

Form:

```
FUNCTION " OpSymbol " (Formal1 : Type1 ; Formal2 : Type2)
    RETURN ReturnType ;
```

Examples:

```
FUNCTION "<=" (Rl : Rational; R2 : Rational) RETURN Boolean;
FUNCTION "+" (Rl : Rational; R2 : Rational) RETURN Rational);
```

Interpretation: The function, defined in a package P will be associated with the operator *OpSymbol* and can be called from a client program in one of two ways. If X is of type *ReturnType*, then

> X := *Actual1 OpSymbol Actual2;*

can be used if a USE statement appears in the client program; otherwise,

> X := P. *"OpSymbol"(Actual1, Actual2);*

is required.

Notes:

1. The quotation marks around the operator are required in the second form above, and not allowed in the first case.
2. The operators "=", "/=", "IN" and "NOT IN" cannot be overloaded.
3. The precedence of the operator cannot be changed by an overload, for example, any "+" operator will have lower precedence than any "*" operator.

PROGRAM
STYLE

The USE Clause Again

When reading Program 10.8, note that the USE clause would also have allowed us to write unqualified references to all the other operations in Rationals, but that we chose to leave most of the qualified references (for example, the Rationals.Put statements) as they were. This shows that qualified references are still *permitted* even though a USE appears.

Most Ada experts advise that qualified references should be used wherever possible, because they clarify programs by always indicating the name of the package whose operation is being called. These same experts often advocate *never* writing a USE clause, because then qualified references are optional. In this book, we use the USE where appropriate—for example, to make infix ADT operators possible—but we also use qualified reference in most cases, even where a USE is present and the qualification is optional.

PROGRAM
STYLE

Advantages of Private Types

A client program that uses ADT Rationals does not need to know the actual internal representation of data type Rational (i.e., a record with two fields). The client can call an operator function of ADT Rationals to perform an operation (e.g., rational addition) without having this knowledge. In fact, it is better to hide this information from the client program to prevent the client from directly manipulating the individual fields of a rational variable.

It is advantageous for a client program not to have direct access to the representation of a rational quantity for three reasons:

- It is easier to write and read a client program that treats a rational quantity just like a predefined one, that is, without being cluttered with direct reference to implementation details.
- The client program cannot directly store values in the fields of a rational variable. For example, storing 4 and 12, respectively, in these fields would violate the package's assumption that all rationals are stored in reduced form.
- If we change the representation—for example, to an array of two elements instead of a record—the client program does not have to be modified in any way, only recompiled.

There is a fourth advantage, which would apply if the type represented something more sophisticated, say a database record of some kind. Each record might contain information for "internal use only," that is, for use only by the data management program itself, not for use by clients. Making the record PRIVATE ensures that the entire record structure is not made available to the client, only that information which the ADT designer chooses to supply via the ADT operations. This is an important advantage for large, complicated, and secure applications.

Exercises for Section 10.4

Programming

1. Complete the body of Rationals implementing those operations left as stubs, then modify one or both test programs so that the package is fully tested. Be sure to test conditions that cause the ZeroDenominator exception to be raised.

10.5 System Structures: Writing an ADT for Variable-Length Strings

As we have seen, Ada does not have any predefined support for variable-length character strings. The predefined type String is nothing but a character array and needs to be declared with a fixed length. On the other hand, it is common in applications to use string objects with a fixed *maximum* length but a variable *actual* length. If we just use Ada string objects, there is nothing built into Ada to keep track of how many useful characters there are in the string at any given moment.

We can use Ada's package capability to design and build what we need to support variable-length strings. Let us create an ADT VStrings in which each string variable has a fixed maximum or physical length (say, eighty characters) but a variable actual or logical length. Program 10.9 shows a package specifi-

Program 10.9 Specification for Package VStrings

```
WITH Text_IO;
PACKAGE VStrings IS

   -- Specification for ADT to handle strings of variable length 1-80 chars.

   MaxLength          : CONSTANT Integer := 80;
   SUBTYPE Index IS Integer RANGE 0 .. MaxLength;

   TYPE    VString IS PRIVATE;

   -- exceptions

   StringOverflow   : EXCEPTION;
   EmptyString      : EXCEPTION;
   InvalidArguments : EXCEPTION;

   -- operators

   -- constructors

   FUNCTION MakeVString(S : String) RETURN VString;
   FUNCTION MakeVString(C : Character) RETURN VString;
   FUNCTION EmptyVString RETURN VString;
   -- construct a VString
   -- Pre: parameters are defined
   -- Post: returns a VString as desired.
   --    Raises StringOverflow if S is longer than MaxLength characters

   -- selectors

   FUNCTION Length(S : VString) RETURN Index;
   FUNCTION Value(S : VString) RETURN String;
   FUNCTION Head(S : VString) RETURN Character;
   -- return the length, the string part, and the first character respectively
   -- Pre: parameters are defined
   -- Post: returns the desired value
   --    Head raises EmptyString if S is empty

   -- inquiry

   FUNCTION IsEmpty(S : VString) RETURN Boolean;
   -- tests whether the string is 0 characters long
   -- Pre: S is defined
   -- Post: returns True if S is empty, False otherwise
   -- concatenation

   FUNCTION "&" (S1, S2 : VString) RETURN VString;
   FUNCTION "&" (S1 : VString; C : Character) RETURN VString;
   FUNCTION "&" (C : Character; S1 : VString) RETURN VString;
   FUNCTION "&" (S1 : VString; S : String) RETURN VString;
   FUNCTION "&" (S : string; S1 : VString) RETURN VString;
   -- these five operators support concatenation of VStrings
   -- Pre: all parameters are defined
   -- Post: each operator returns the concatenation of its arguments,
   --    or raises StringOverflow if the result would be longer than
   --    MaxLength characters

   -- lexical comparison

   FUNCTION "<" (S1, S2 : VString) RETURN Boolean;
```

```
FUNCTION "<=" (S1, S2 : VString) RETURN Boolean;
FUNCTION ">" (S1, S2 : VString) RETURN Boolean;
FUNCTION ">=" (S1, S2 : VString) RETURN Boolean;
-- these four operators compare VStrings, lexically
-- Pre: S1 and S2 are defined
-- Post: carries out the desired comparison, returning True or False


-- search

FUNCTION Locate(Sub : VString; Within : VString) RETURN Index;
FUNCTION Locate(Sub : String; Within : VString) RETURN Index;
FUNCTION Locate(C : Character; Within : VString) RETURN Index;
-- these three operators search for Sub in Within
-- Pre: Sub and Within are defined
-- Post: returns the index of the first character of Sub in Within;
--    returns 0 if Sub is not present in Within

FUNCTION Tail(S : VString) RETURN VString;
-- returns a string similar to S but with the first character removed
-- Pre: S is defined
-- Post: returns a string like S but with the first character removed;
--    raises EmptyString if S is empty

FUNCTION SubString(S : VString; Start, Size : Index) RETURN VString;
-- returns a string containing Size characters, whose value is the
-- Size-character substring starting at position Start in S.
-- Pre: parameters are defined
-- Post: raises InvalidParameters if Start > Length(S),
--    or Size > Length(S), or Start + Size -1 > Length(S)


-- input/output

PROCEDURE Get_Line(Item : OUT VString);
PROCEDURE Put(Item : VString);

PROCEDURE Get_Line(File: Text_IO.File_Type; Item : OUT VString);
PROCEDURE Put(File: Text_IO.File_Type; Item : VString);
PRIVATE

  TYPE VString IS RECORD
    CurrentLength : Index := 0;
    StringPart : String(1 .. MaxLength) := (OTHERS => ASCII.NUL);
  END RECORD;

END VStrings;
```

cation for VStrings. Looking at this specification we see that its structure is similar to the structure of Calendar and Rationals: The type VString provided by this package is a private type. As before, we know that Ada already gives us assignment and equality operators for such types; any additional operators need to be provided by us in the package. Here is the type definition for VString:

```
TYPE VString IS RECORD
   CurrentLength : Index := 0;
   StringPart : String(1..MaxLength) := (OTHERS => ASCII.NUL);
END RECORD;
```

A diagram of a string S1 containing John Brown's body is given in Fig. 10.4. In the type definition we are making use of the ability Ada provides to initialize fields of a record to a known value. This means that every time a VString variable is declared, we can be sure that its current length is set to zero and all its other characters are set to something predictable. It is conventional to use the ASCII character ASCII.Nul for this predictable value; this character is used for almost nothing else in programming. (We do not use the blank character, which is a different ASCII value, for this, so that we can embed blanks in our variable-length strings with no ambiguity.) We make the VString type private so that a client program cannot tinker with the string part of a variable (say, by adding a character to the end) without adjusting the length field.

Figure 10.4 A Variable-Length String

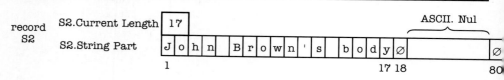

What operations should apply to VStrings? First of all, we need a constructor to create a VString from a normal Ada string. We call this operation MakeVString, and in fact we use overloading to define *two* MakeVString operations so that VStrings can be made from single characters as well as from strings. Given a declaration and a statement

```
S : VStrings.VString;
T : VStrings.VString;
...
S := VStrings.MakeVString("Do you like Ada?");
```

the variable S, after the assignment, will have a CurrentLength value of 16 (the length of the string literal), and a StringPart value of the letters in Do you like Ada? followed by 64 (80 − 16) ASCII.Nul characters.

Next we need selectors so that a client program can get the string length and string value back from a VString object. We call these selectors Length and Value, respectively.

Another useful operation on VStrings is concatenation, represented by the infix operator "&". Ada already provides string concatenation; we will use the built-in operations to build our own operation that works with VStrings instead of strings. As an example, the concatenation of two VStrings, S1 and S2, returns a VString with the useful characters of S1 (not the nulls!) followed by those of S2. So the function call

```
VStrings."&"(VStrings.MakeVString("ABC"),VStrings.MakeVString("DEF"))
```

or the simpler form (if USE VStrings appears at the top of the client program)

```
MakeVString("ABC") & MakeVString("DEF")
```

returns a VString with length 6 and value "ABCDEF". Assuming that USE is present, the statement

```
T := S & MakeVString(" I do.");
```

stores in the string part of T the characters

```
Do you like Ada? I do.
```

and a CurrentLength value of 22 (16 + 6).

For convenience, we define in fact *five* overloaded operators for concatenation, all called "&", so that a client program can, without extra calls to MakeVString, concatenate normal Ada strings and characters with VStrings.

```
FUNCTION "&" (S1, S2 : VString) RETURN VString;

FUNCTION "&" (S1 : VString; C : Character) RETURN VString;
FUNCTION "&" (C : Character; S1 : VString) RETURN VString;

FUNCTION "&" (S1 : VString; S : String) RETURN VString;
FUNCTION "&" (S : String; S1 : VString) RETURN VString;
```

As was the case with time values in Calendar, the pairs of operations are necessary to ensure that either parameter can appear on the left or right. The statement

```
T := "I have a question. " & T;
```

returns the VString with string part

```
I have a question. Do you like Ada? I do.
```

and length value 41. As is always the case with overloading, the compiler can discern which operation you mean by looking at its parameters and return type: Here we have a string on the left and a VString on the right, so the last of the five operations is selected.

The list of operations includes some comparison operations, needing no explanation except to point out that the comparison assumes "dictionary" or "lexical" order, so that "BCD" < "BCDE" (obvious) but also "BCD" < "CD" (perhaps less obvious). As it happens, operations similar to these are also predefined for normal Ada strings.

As we know, equality checking is provided by Ada for all types, including private ones. Does equality work correctly for VStrings? The answer is yes: Built-in equality always compares the *entire* data objects. By this principle, Ada states that two Vstrings are equal if and only if the length fields are equal *and* the string parts are equal. All 80 positions are compared! You can appreciate the advantage of preinitializing all characters in a VString to something predictable, namely, ASCII.Nul.

A number of additional operators are in the specification: Head(S), which returns the first character of its VString argument, and Tail(S), which returns a Vstring equivalent to S with its first character removed. Other useful operations are three Locate functions, which search a target VString for the presence of another given character, string, or VString, returning the position in the target where the substring begins, or 0 if the substring can't be found in the target. Finally, we have SubString(S, Start, Size), which returns the VString substring of length Size, counted from position Start of S. For example,

```
Locate("BC",MakeVString("ABCDEF"))
```

returns 2,

```
Locate('G',MakeVString("AB"))
```

returns 0 because 'G' isn't in "AB", and

```
Locate("Ada", T)
```

returns 32. The statement

```
S := SubString(T, 10, 8)
```

stores in S a VString with length 8 and string part question.

In Program 10.10 we give the body of this package. The various operations make quite heavy use of string slicing; you should study them carefully. Notice also how the exceptions EmptyString, StringOverflow, and InvalidArguments are used to signal a client program that violates an assumption of the package, for example, one that tries to concatenate two 42-character VStrings.

Program 10.10 Body of Package VStrings

```
WITH Text_IO;
PACKAGE BODY VStrings IS

  FUNCTION Length(S : VString) RETURN Index IS
  BEGIN
    RETURN S.CurrentLength;
  END Length;

  FUNCTION Value(S : VString) RETURN String IS
  BEGIN
    IF S.CurrentLength = 0 THEN
      RETURN "";
    ELSE
      RETURN S.StringPart(1 .. S.CurrentLength);
    END IF;
  END Value;

  FUNCTION Tail(S : VString) RETURN VString IS
  BEGIN
    IF S.CurrentLength = 0 THEN
      RAISE EmptyString;
    ELSIF S.CurrentLength = 1 THEN
      RETURN MakeVString("");
    ELSE
      RETURN MakeVString(S.StringPart(2 .. S.CurrentLength));
    END IF;
  END tail;

  FUNCTION Head(S : VString) RETURN Character IS
```

```
  BEGIN
    IF S.CurrentLength = 0 THEN
      RAISE EmptyString;
    ELSE
      RETURN S.StringPart(1);
    END IF;
  END head;

  FUNCTION IsEmpty(S : VString) RETURN Boolean IS
  BEGIN
    RETURN S.CurrentLength = 0;
  END IsEmpty;

  FUNCTION MakeVString(S : String) RETURN VString IS
    Temp : VString;
  BEGIN
    IF S'Length > MaxLength THEN
      RAISE StringOverflow;
    END IF;
    Temp.CurrentLength := S'Length;
    Temp.StringPart(1 .. S'Length) := S;
    RETURN Temp;
  END MakeVString;

  FUNCTION EmptyVString RETURN VString IS
  BEGIN
RETURN MakeVString("");
  END EmptyVString;

  FUNCTION MakeVString(C : Character) RETURN VString IS
    Temp : VString;
  BEGIN
    Temp.CurrentLength := 1;
    Temp.StringPart(1) := C;
    RETURN Temp;
  END MakeVString;

  FUNCTION "&" (S1, S2 : VString) RETURN VString IS
    Temp : VString;
  BEGIN

    IF S1.CurrentLength + S2.CurrentLength > MaxLength THEN
      RAISE StringOverflow;
    ELSIF IsEmpty(S1) THEN
      Temp := S2;
    ELSIF IsEmpty(S2) THEN
      Temp := S1;
    ELSE
      Temp := MakeVString(Value(S1) & Value(S2));
    END IF;

    RETURN Temp;

  END "&";

  FUNCTION "&" (S1 : VString; C : Character) RETURN VString IS
  BEGIN
    RETURN S1 & MakeVString(C);
  END "&";

  FUNCTION "&" (C : Character; S1 : VString) RETURN VString IS
  BEGIN
```

```
      RETURN MakeVString(C) & S1;
END "&";

FUNCTION "&" (S1 : VString; S : String) RETURN VString IS
BEGIN
   RETURN S1 & MakeVString(S);
END "&";

FUNCTION "&" (S : String; S1 : VString) RETURN VString IS
BEGIN
   RETURN MakeVString(S) & S1;
END "&";

FUNCTION "<=" (S1, S2 : VString) RETURN Boolean IS
BEGIN
   RETURN Value(S1) <= Value(S2);
END "<=";

FUNCTION "<" (S1, S2 : VString) RETURN Boolean IS
BEGIN
   RETURN Value(S1) < Value(S2);
END "<";

FUNCTION ">=" (S1, S2 : VString) RETURN Boolean IS
BEGIN
   RETURN Value(S1) >= Value(S2);
END ">=";

FUNCTION ">" (S1, S2 : VString) RETURN Boolean IS
BEGIN
   RETURN Value(S1) > Value(S2);
END ">";

FUNCTION Locate(Sub : String; Within : VString) RETURN Index IS

   Result : Index;
   LSub: Index;
   LWithin : Index;

BEGIN

   LSub := Sub'Length;
   LWithin := Within.CurrentLength;
   Result := 0;
   IF LSub > 0
     AND LWithin > 0
     AND LSub <= LWithin THEN

     FOR Start IN 1 .. (LWithin - LSub + 1) LOOP
       IF Sub = Within.StringPart(Start .. (Start + LSub - 1)) THEN
         Result := Start;
         RETURN Result;
       END IF;
     END LOOP;
   END IF;

   RETURN Result;

END Locate;

FUNCTION Locate(Sub : VString; Within : VString) RETURN Index IS
BEGIN
   RETURN Locate(Value(Sub), Within);
END Locate;
```

```
FUNCTION Locate(C : Character; Within : VString) RETURN Index IS

   Temp : String(1..1);

BEGIN

   Temp(1) := C;
   RETURN Locate(Temp, Within);

END Locate;

FUNCTION SubString(S : VString; Start, Size : Index) RETURN VString IS
BEGIN

   IF Start          > Length(S) OR
      Size           > Length(S) OR
      Start+Size-1 > Length(S) THEN
     RAISE InvalidArguments;
   ELSE
     RETURN MakeVString(S.StringPart(Start..Start+Size-1));
   END IF;

END SubString;

PROCEDURE Get_Line(File : Text_IO.File_Type; Item : OUT VString) IS

   -- reads a VString object from File, using Text_IO.Get_Line
   -- reading stops if a line terminator is encountered, or if
   -- MaxLength characters have been read.

   S     : String(1..MaxLength);
   Count : Natural;

   BEGIN

   Text_IO.Get_Line(File => File, Item => S, Last => Count);
   IF Count > 0 THEN
     Item := MakeVstring(S(1..Count));
   ELSE
     Item := EmptyVstring;
   END IF;

END Get_Line;

PROCEDURE Get_Line(Item : OUT VString) IS
BEGIN
   Get_Line(File => Text_IO.Standard_Input, Item => Item);
END Get_Line;

PROCEDURE Put(File: Text_IO.File_Type; Item : VString) IS
BEGIN
   Text_IO.Put(File=>File, Item=>Value(Item));
END Put;

PROCEDURE Put(Item : VString) IS
BEGIN
   Put(File=>Text_IO.Standard_Output, Item=>Item);
END Put;

END VStrings;
```

The ADT VStrings is useful to have available; we shall use it several times in this and the remaining chapters. Program 10.11 shows a test of some of the operations in the package—specifically the file-oriented operations. As an exercise, you can extend this program to test the other operations.

Program 10.11 A Test of the VStrings Package

```
WITH Text_IO;
WITH VStrings;
PROCEDURE TestVStrings IS

  -- program copies its input file TEST.DAT into its output file TEST.OUT
  -- then closes TEST.OUT, re-opens it for input,
  -- and displays its contents on the screen.

  InData  : Text_IO.File_Type;
  OutData : Text_IO.File_Type;
  S       : VStrings.VString;

BEGIN -- TestVstrings

  Text_IO.Open(File=>InData, Mode=>Text_IO.In_File, Name=>"TEST.DAT");
  Text_IO.Create(File=>OutData, Mode=>Text_IO.Out_File, Name=>"TEST.OUT");

  WHILE NOT Text_IO.End_of_File(File => InData) LOOP

    Vstrings.Get_Line(File => InData, Item => S);
    Vstrings.Put(File => OutData, Item => S);
    Text_IO.New_Line(File => OutData);

  END LOOP;

  Text_IO.Close(File => InData);
  Text_IO.Close(File => OutData);
  Text_IO.Open(File=>InData, Mode=>Text_IO.In_File, Name=>"TEST.OUT");


  WHILE NOT Text_IO.End_of_File(File => InData) LOOP

    Vstrings.Get_Line(File => InData, Item => S);
    Vstrings.Put(Item => S);
    Text_IO.New_Line;

  END LOOP;

  Text_IO.Close(File => InData);

EXCEPTION

  WHEN Text_IO.Name_Error =>
    Text_IO.Put(Item => "File TEST.DAT doesn't exist in this directory!");
    Text_IO.New_Line;

END TestVStrings;



This is the first line of the file;
this is the second line; the third and fourth lines are blank.


And this is the fifth and last line.
```

Exercises for Section 10.5

513

10.6 Case Study:
Printing a Form
Letter—A Simple Mail
Merge

Self-Check

1. Draw a diagram of a VString with your full name stored in it. Write a call to VStrings.SubString showing how your last name could be retrieved.

Programming

1. Extend Program 10.11 to test and demonstrate the remaining operations of VStrings. Be sure you include tests for conditions that will raise exceptions, to be certain that the exceptions are raised properly.

10.6 Case Study: Printing a Form Letter—A Simple Mail Merge

This case study uses procedural abstraction as well as many of the facilities we have developed in this chapter and elsewhere in the book. Specifically, text files and the VStrings and Dates packages are used to advantage, as well as the Screen package we have been using for screen control. This program is a simple example of a *mail merge* program, often used to produce form letters, each of which appears personalized with the recipient's name and address. Sometimes different letter bodies, or different intermixed paragraphs, are used according to the characteristics of the recipient.

Problem

We would like a program that can help in writing job application letters. Each of a number of letters will be sent in turn to an output file for any final editing and printing.

Analysis

Each letter consists of a heading, salutation, body, and closing. The heading, salutation, and first line of the body will be different for each letter, but the body and closing will be the same. The names and addresses of the job contacts will be entered interactively; the body of the letter will be stored in a file. We assume the letter body—50 lines or less, each no more than 80 characters long—will be created with an editor.

Design

The program first opens the letter file and reads it into an array of variable-length strings. Then the interactive data-entry procedure takes over, reading and validating the data for each addressee and writing his or her entire letter to the output file. Processing continues until the user enters a sentinel to quit. The program uses VStrings to do the string processing and Dates to create and write today's date into the output file for each letter. Screen is used to control the cursor position on the screen, and also to cause the terminal to beep when a response is needed from the user.

We will use three local procedures: InitializeLetter, Preamble, and WriteBody. InitializeLetter reads the letter file; Preamble enters the data for the part of the letter that is individualized and writes it to the output file; WriteBody copies the letter body to the output file. The structure chart is shown in Fig. 10.5; the main program body is shown as Program 10.12.

Figure 10.5   Structure Chart for FormLetter

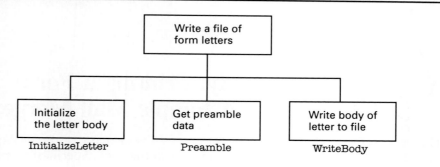

Program 10.12   Form Letter Generation Program

```
WITH Text_IO;
WITH Screen;
WITH Dates;
WITH VStrings; USE Vstrings;
PROCEDURE FormLetter IS

   -- Writes a job application letter to an output file. The data
   -- for the letter preamble is read from the keyboard; the letter
   -- body is copied from a data file to the output file.

   MaxLines : CONSTANT Positive := 50;
   SUBTYPE LetterRange IS Positive RANGE 1..MaxLines;
   TYPE LetterBody IS ARRAY(LetterRange) OF VStrings.VString;
   Letter       : LetterBody;
   LetterLength : LetterRange;
   LetterIn     : Text_IO.File_Type;
   LetterOut    : Text_IO.File_Type;

   OutFileName : VStrings.VString;
   Response    : Character;
   Blanks      : CONSTANT String(1..10) := (OTHERS => ' ');

   PROCEDURE InitializeLetter IS

      InFileName : VStrings.VString;

   BEGIN
```

```
    Text_IO.Put(Item => "Enter name of letter body file > ");
    VStrings.Get_Line(Item => InFileName);
    Text_IO.Open(File=>LetterIn, Mode=>Text_IO.In_File,
            Name=>VStrings.Value(InFileName));

  LetterLength := 1;
  WHILE NOT Text_IO.End_of_File (File=>LetterIn) LOOP
    VStrings.Get_Line(File=>LetterIn, Item=>Letter(LetterLength));
    LetterLength := LetterLength + 1;
  END LOOP;

  Text_IO.Close(File=>LetterIn);

END InitializeLetter;


PROCEDURE Preamble IS

-- Writes a preamble for a job application letter to an output file.
-- Pre : None
-- Post: Writes the heading, salutation, and first sentence of a
--       job application letter.

  Title         : VStrings.VString;
  FirstName     : VStrings.VString;
  LastName      : VStrings.VString;
  Company       : VStrings.VString;
  Address       : VStrings.VString;
  CityStZip     : VStrings.VString;
  DatePadding : CONSTANT String(1..50) := (OTHERS => ' ');

BEGIN -- Premable
  -- Enter all data
  Screen.ClearScreen;
  Screen.MoveCursor(Row=>3, Column=>1);
  Text_IO.Put(Item => Blanks & "Today is             -> ");
  Dates.Put(Item => Dates.Today, Format => Dates.Full);
  Text_IO.New_Line;
  Text_IO.Put(Item => Blanks & "Employer title       -> ");
  VStrings.Get_Line(Item => Title);
  Text_IO.Put(Item => Blanks & "First Name & Initial -> ");
  VStrings.Get_Line(Item => FirstName);
  Text_IO.Put(Item => Blanks & "Employer last name   -> ");
  VStrings.Get_Line(Item => LastName);
  Text_IO.Put(Item => Blanks & "Company name         -> ");
  VStrings.Get_Line(Item => Company);
  Text_IO.Put(Item => Blanks & "Street address       -> ");
  VStrings.Get_Line(Item => Address);
  Text_IO.Put(Item => Blanks & "City, State, and ZIP -> ");
  VStrings.Get_Line(Item => CityStZip);

  -- write preamble to output file
  Text_IO.Put(File=>LetterOut,Item => DatePadding);
  Dates.Put(File=>LetterOut, Item => Dates.Today, Format=>Dates.Full);
  Text_IO.New_Line(File=>LetterOut);
  Text_IO.New_Line(File=>LetterOut);
  VStrings.Put(File=>LetterOut,
    Item => Title & ' ' & FirstName & ' ' & LastName);
  Text_IO.New_Line(File=>LetterOut);
  VStrings.Put(File=>LetterOut, Item => Company);
  Text_IO.New_Line(File=>LetterOut);
  VStrings.Put(File=>LetterOut, Item => Address);
  Text_IO.New_Line(File=>LetterOut);
```

```
        VStrings.Put(File=>LetterOut, Item => CityStZip);
        Text_IO.New_Line(File=>LetterOut);
        Text_IO.New_Line(File=>LetterOut);
        VStrings.Put(File=>LetterOut,
          Item => "Dear " & Title & ' ' & LastName & ':');
        Text_IO.New_Line(File=>LetterOut);
        Text_IO.New_Line(File=>LetterOut);
        VStrings.Put(File=>LetterOut,
          Item => "        I am interested in applying for a job at "
            & Company & '.');
        Text_IO.New_Line(File=>LetterOut);
        Text_IO.New_Line(File=>LetterOut);

      END Preamble;

      PROCEDURE WriteBody IS

      -- Copies the body of a job application letter from a data file
      -- to an output file.
      -- Pre : The output file is opened.
      -- Post: Writes the letter body to the output file.

      BEGIN -- WriteBody
        -- Copy each line until done
        FOR Line IN 1..LetterLength LOOP
          VStrings.Put(File=>LetterOut,Item=>Letter(Line));
          Text_IO.New_Line(File=>LetterOut);
        END LOOP;
      END WriteBody;

  BEGIN -- FormLetter

    Text_IO.Put(Item => "Enter name of letter output file > ");
    VStrings.Get_Line(Item => OutFileName);
    Text_IO.Create(File=>LetterOut, Mode=>Text_IO.Out_File,
                   Name=>VStrings.Value(OutFileName));
    InitializeLetter;
    Response := 'Y';

    LOOP
      Preamble;
      WriteBody;

      LOOP
        Screen.Beep;
        Screen.MoveCursor(Row => 20, Column => 1);
        Text_IO.Put(Blanks & "More Letters? (Y or N) ");
        Text_IO.Get(Item => Response);
        Text_IO.Skip_Line;
        EXIT WHEN (Response = 'y') OR (Response = 'Y') OR
                  (Response = 'n') OR (Response = 'N');
      END LOOP;
      -- assert: response is valid

      Text_IO.New_Page (File => LetterOut);
      EXIT WHEN (Response = 'n') OR (Response = 'N');
    END LOOP;
    -- assert: response was 'n' or 'Y'

    Text_IO.Close(File=>LetterOut);
  END FormLetter;
```

Procedure `InitializeLetter` reads the body of the letter into the array `Letter`, using `VStrings.Get_Line` to get the variable-length string for each line from the file. Notice also that `VStrings.Get_Line` is used to ask the terminal user to enter the name of the input file. This shows that `Text_IO.Open` (and the other file operations in Ada) can use any string as the file name, including one entered at execution time. Of course, the file has to exist; otherwise, it makes no sense to use it as an input file, and an exception is raised by `Text_IO`. A sample file called `BODY.DAT` is shown as Fig. 10.6.

Figure 10.6 Sample File of Body of Form Letter

```
     I am a a good student and a great athlete, and have a sparkling but
easygoing personality. Upon request, I can give you a list of references,
all of whom will say I am the greatest thing since sliced bread.

     Thank you very much for your consideration.



                              Sincerely yours,



                              Jay Gatsby
```

Procedure `Preamble` reads the strings needed for the letter heading and salutation. One screen of the data entry process is shown in the sample run in Fig. 10.7. After data entry, the strings read into `Title` (Mr., Ms., Prof., etc.), `FirstName`, `LastName`, `Company`, `Address`, and `CityStZip` are written to the output file in the form shown in Fig. 10.8.

Figure 10.7 Data Entry Screen for Form Letter Program

```
          Today is                -> March 26, 1991
          Employer title          -> Mr.
          First Name & Initial -> Thomas V.
          Employer last name   -> Watson
          Company name            -> IBM Corporation
          Street address          -> 1 Main St.
          City, State, and ZIP -> Armonk, NY 10234




          More Letters? (Y or N) y
```

Figure 10.8 Output File from Sample Run of FormLetter

```
                                              March 26, 1991

Mr. Thomas V. Watson
IBM Corporation
1 Main Street
Armonk, NY 10234

Dear Mr. Watson:

    I am interested in applying for a job at IBM Corporation.

    I am a a good student and a great athlete, and have a sparkling but
easygoing personality. Upon request, I can give you a list of references,
all of whom will say I am the greatest thing since sliced bread.

    Thank you very much for your consideration.


                                          Sincerely yours,


                                          Jay Gatsby



(skip to new page)
                                              March 26, 1991

Governor Ann Richards
Texas Governor's Staff
The State House
Austin, TX 78600

Dear Governor Richards:

    I am interested in applying for a job at Texas Governor's Staff.

    I am a a good student and a great athlete, and have a sparkling but
easygoing personality. Upon request, I can give you a list of references,
all of whom will say I am the greatest thing since sliced bread.

    Thank you very much for your consideration.


                                          Sincerely yours,


                                          Jay Gatsby


(skip to new page)
```

Procedure `Preamble` uses `VStrings.Get_Line` to enter each data string; `Dates.Today` and `Dates.Put` are used to produce today's date, display it, and write it to the output file. Again `VStrings.Get_Line` is used to ask the user to enter the name of the output file. Procedure `WriteBody` copies the body of the letter from the array Letter to the output file, using VStrings.Put to do the writing.

The main program for FormLetter is simple because we have used procedural abstraction to structure the tasks it needs to do, but also in large part because we have been able to use three ADTs to assist us.

10.7 System Structures: Writing an ADT for Employee Records

In this section we will develop an ADT for employee records that could be used in a larger database application. Recall from Section 8.1 that we defined a record type called Employee. We repeat the type definitions here, modifying the record type so that all fields are initialized.

```
NameSize :CONSTANT Positive := 20;

SUBTYPE IDRange IS Positive RANGE 1111..9999;
SUBTYPE PayRange IS Float RANGE 0.0..1_000_000.0;
SUBTYPE NameType IS String(1..NameSize);
TYPE GenderType IS (Female,Male);

TYPE Employee IS RECORD
    ID : IDRange := IDRange'Last;
    Name : NameType := (OTHERS => ' ');
    Gender : GenderType := Female;
    NumDepend : Natural := 0;
    Rate : PayRange := 0.0;
    TaxSal : PayRange := 0.0;
END RECORD;
```

To make it easier and more reliable for client programs to use records of this type, it makes sense to put these type definitions and a number of operations in a package, which we will call Employees.

Program 10.13 shows the specification of this package. Note that the constant NameSize; the subtypes IDRange and NameType, and the types GenderType and Employee are provided in the specification. For reasons discussed several times in this chapter, the record type Employee is PRIVATE so that client programs do not have direct access to the field names or structure of the record.

Program 10.13 Specification for Employee Record ADT

```
PACKAGE Employees IS

-- specification for ADT package to handle Employee records

-- constant and type definitions

NameSize: CONSTANT Positive := 20;

SUBTYPE IDRange IS Positive RANGE 1111..9999;
SUBTYPE PayRange IS Float RANGE 0.0..1_000_000.0;
SUBTYPE NameType IS String(1..NameSize);
TYPE    GenderType IS (Female, Male);
```

```
TYPE Employee IS PRIVATE;

-- operations

-- constructor

FUNCTION MakeEmployee (ID: IDRange;
                       Name: NameType;
                       Gender: GenderType;
                       NumDepend: Natural;
                       Rate: PayRange;
                       TaxSal: PayRange)  RETURN Employee;

-- constructs an Employee record from its field values
-- Pre: all input parameters are defined
-- Post: returns a value of type Employee

-- selectors

FUNCTION RetrieveID        (OneEmp: Employee) RETURN IDRange;
FUNCTION RetrieveName      (OneEmp: Employee) RETURN NameType;
FUNCTION RetrieveGender    (OneEmp: Employee) RETURN GenderType;
FUNCTION RetrieveNumDepend (OneEmp: Employee) RETURN Natural;
FUNCTION RetrieveRate      (OneEmp: Employee) RETURN PayRange;
FUNCTION RetrieveTaxSal    (OneEmp: Employee) RETURN PayRange;

-- retrieve individual fields of an Employee record
-- Pre: OneEmp is defined
-- Post: each selector retrieves its desired field


-- input/output operations

PROCEDURE ReadEmployee (Item: OUT Employee);

-- reads an Employee record from the terminal
-- Pre: none
-- Post: Item contains a record of type Employee

PROCEDURE DisplayEmployee (Item: IN Employee);

-- displays an Employee record on the screen
-- Pre: Item is defined
-- Post: displays the fields of Item on the screen

PRIVATE

   TYPE Employee IS RECORD
      ID:        IDRange := IDRange'Last;
      Name:      NameType := (OTHERS => ' ');
      Gender:    GenderType := Female;
      NumDepend: Natural := 0;
      Rate:      PayRange := 0.0;
      TaxSal:    PayRange := 0.0;
   END RECORD;

END Employees;
```

Because a client program cannot get into the details of an employee record, the ADT package must provide a set of constructor and selector operations. These are shown in the specification as the constructor MakeEmployee and the selectors RetrieveName, RetrieveGender, RetrieveNumDepend, RetrieveRate, and RetrieveTaxSal. Also provided are input/output procedures ReadEmployee and DisplayEmployee. The body of this package is given in Program 10.14. All operations are fully implemented except for DisplayEmployee, which is left as a stub. Completing this procedure and writing a program to test the package is left as an exercise. Also left as an exercise is provision of file-oriented input/output operations.

Program 10.14 Body of Employee Record ADT

```
WITH Text_IO;
WITH My_Flt_IO;
WITH My_Int_IO;
PACKAGE BODY Employees IS

  PACKAGE GenderType_IO IS NEW Text_IO.Enumeration_IO(Enum => GenderType);

  -- body of ADT package to handle Employee records

  -- operations

  -- constructor

  FUNCTION MakeEmployee (ID: IDRange;
                         Name: NameType;
                         Gender: GenderType;
                         NumDepend: Natural;
                         Rate: PayRange;
                         TaxSal: PayRange)  RETURN Employee IS

  -- constructs an Employee record from its field values
  -- Pre: all input parameters are defined
  -- Post: returns a value of type Employee

    TempRecord: Employee;

  BEGIN -- MakeEmployee

    TempRecord := (ID => ID, Name => Name, Gender => Gender,
                   NumDepend => NumDepend, Rate => Rate, TaxSal => TaxSal);
                   RETURN TempRecord;

  END MakeEmployee;

  -- selectors
  -- retrieve individual fields of an Employee record
  -- Pre: OneEmp is defined
  -- Post: each selector retrieves its desired field

  FUNCTION RetrieveID (OneEmp: Employee) RETURN IDRange IS
  BEGIN
    RETURN OneEmp.ID;
  END RetrieveID;
```

```
FUNCTION RetrieveName (OneEmp: Employee) RETURN NameType IS
BEGIN
   RETURN OneEmp.Name;
END RetrieveName;

FUNCTION RetrieveGender (OneEmp: Employee) RETURN GenderType IS
BEGIN
   RETURN OneEmp.Gender;
END RetrieveGender;

FUNCTION RetrieveNumDepend (OneEmp: Employee) RETURN Natural IS
BEGIN
   RETURN OneEmp.NumDepend;
END RetrieveNumDepend;

FUNCTION RetrieveRate (OneEmp: Employee) RETURN PayRange IS
BEGIN
   RETURN OneEmp.Rate;
END RetrieveRate;

FUNCTION RetrieveTaxSal (OneEmp: Employee) RETURN PayRange IS
BEGIN
   RETURN OneEmp.TaxSal;
END RetrieveTaxSal;


-- input/output operations

PROCEDURE ReadEmployee (Item: OUT Employee) IS

-- reads an Employee record from the terminal
-- Pre: none
-- Post: Item contains a record of type Employee

BEGIN -- ReadEmployee

   Text_IO.Put(Item => "ID > ");
   My_Int_IO.Get(Item => Item.ID);
   Text_IO.Put(Item => "Name > ");
   Text_IO.Get(Item => Item.Name);
   Text_IO.Put(Item => "Gender (Female or Male) > ");
   GenderType_IO.Get(Item => Item.Gender);
   Text_IO.Put(Item => "Number of dependents > ");
   My_Int_IO.Get(Item => Item.NumDepend);
   Text_IO.Put(Item => "Hourly rate > ");
   My_Flt_IO.Get(Item => Item.Rate);

END ReadEmployee;

PROCEDURE DisplayEmployee (Item: IN Employee) IS

-- displays an Employee record on the screen
-- Pre: Item is defined
-- Post: displays the fields of Item on the screen

BEGIN -- stub for DisplayEmployee

   Text_IO.Put(Item => "DisplayEmployee entered.");
   Text_IO.New_Line;

END DisplayEmployee;

END Employees;
```

Programming

1. Complete the body of the procedure `DisplayEmployee` and write a program to test the package `Employees`.
2. Add to package `Employees` two procedures, `GetEmployee` and `PutEmployee`, that read and write employee records using a disk file.

 # 10.8 Case Study: Employee Inquiry System

To show a useful application of the package `Employees`, we introduce a case study involving an interactive query system that allows the user to build a file of employee records, then read that file into an array and answer queries about employees in the file.

Problem

We have a company with no more than 100 employees. We wish to store their basic information in a computer file and be able to do the following kinds of operations:

- build an employee file on disk;
- read the file into main memory and write it back out to disk;
- given an employee ID, search for and display that employee's record;
- given an employee ID, change some of the other fields of the employee's record: name, number of dependents, rate, taxable salary;
- delete a record when an employee leaves the company;

Analysis

Because we already have a package that can handle employee records, our task now is to build an interactive query program. This should be a menu-driven program to allow the functions listed above.

Design

Much of the detailed design and coding of this case study is left as an exercise. This discussion will give you some hints about how to proceed.

To build a menu-driven inquiry program, refer to the home budget case study of Section 8.7. The disk file should be read into an array of records, by analogy with Section 8.12; searching the array for a given employee follows from Section 8.11.

Given the single constructor and field-by-field selector operations provided by package `Employees`, the best way to change a single field in the record is to retrieve all fields with the appropriate selectors, then construct a new record with just the desired field or fields modified. An alternative is to modify the package with some new constructor operations, each of which modifies a single field of its record parameter.

Finally, because the records are kept in the array in no particular order, the easiest way to delete a record with a given array subscript is just to copy the *last* record in the array into that position, then to decrement the variable in which you keep track of how many records are present. That is, if there are 20 records in the 100-element array, and you wish to delete record number 7, just copy record number 20 into position 7, and change the number of records to 19.

Coding

Coding this case study is left as an exercise.

Exercises for Section 10.8

Programming

1. Complete the case study in this section by doing a detailed design, structure chart, algorithm specification, and coding for the menu-driven inquiry program.

 # 10.9 Tricks of the Trade: Common Programming Errors

The most common error in writing and using overloaded operators in Ada is to misunderstand when the operator must be placed in quotation marks. Quotation marks are required if the operator is used in prefix form (e.g., `Rationals."+"(R1,R2)`) and not permitted if the operator is used in infix form (e.g., `R1 + R2`). Infix form is of course allowed only in the presence of a USE statement to eliminate the need for qualification.

In writing an exception handler for a package-defined exception, do not forget that the exception name must be qualified unless a USE is present, for example,

```
EXCEPTION
   WHEN Rationals.ZeroDenominator =>
```

A common design error in writing ADTs is to put too much in the specification. Often an ADT has extra functions or procedures in the body, used only by other operations in the body and not intended to be used by client programs. Putting specifications for these in the package specification provides them to the client, whether or not this was intended.

Chapter Review

In this chapter you studied abstract data types, or ADTs, implemented in Ada as packages. ADTs are characterized by a type and a set of operations applicable to that type. In Ada, the type in an ADT package is often declared as PRIVATE, which prevents a client program from directly accessing the values stored in variables of the type, requiring instead that the client use package-provided operations.

Operator overloading is another useful Ada feature introduced here. If the ADT is a mathematical type for which addition, for example, is appropriate, this addition operation can be called "+". Similarly, a comparison operation implementing "less than" for the new type can be called "<".

Yet another important concept used in this chapter is the package-provided exception. An exception can be defined to report an unusual condition, such as a client action that violates an assumption of the package. If an exception is provided in the package specification, a client program can handle it with a normal Ada exception handler. Exception handling is thus no different for package-provided exceptions than it is for predefined ones.

New Ada Constructs in Chapter 10

The new constructs introduced in this chapter are given in Table 10.1.

Table 10.1 New Ada Constructs

Construct	Effect

Private Type Definition
`PACKAGE ComplexNumbers IS`
 	
  `TYPE Complex IS PRIVATE;`
 	
`. . .`
 	
`PRIVATE`
 	
  `TYPE Complex IS RECORD`
    `RealPart: Float;`
    `ImaginaryPart: Float;`
  `END RECORD;`
 	
`END ComplexNumbers;`
	Defines a type Com-plex which has no predefined opera-tions other than copying and equal-ity.
	The type definition is completed here in the PRIVATE section.

Table 10.1 *continued*

Construct	Effect
User-Defined Exception `SomethingIsWrong: EXCEPTION;`	Usually placed in a package specification, defines an exception that can be raised by an operation in the package body and handled by an exception handler in the client program.
Operator Overloading `FUNCTION "+"(Left, Right: Rational) RETURN Rational;`	Creates an additional meaning for the operator.

✓ *Quick-Check Exercises*

1. A _____ operation selects a particular component of an ADT object, a _____ creates an ADT object from its component parts, and a _____ operation asks whether an ADT object has a given property.
2. The syntax for an exception handler depends on whether the exception is a predefined one or a user-defined one (True/False).
3. List all the operator symbols in Ada that can be overloaded. List the ones that cannot.

Answers to Quick-Check Exercises
1. Selector, constructor, inquiry
2. False–the syntax is exactly the same.
3. `+, −, *, /, **, MOD, REM, ABS, AND, OR, NOT, XOR, &, <, <=, >,` and `>=` all can be overloaded; `=, /=, IN,` and `NOT IN` cannot be.

Review Questions for Chapter 10

1. Explain the rules for private types. Which operations can be done on objects of a private type?
2. Suppose we wrote, and included in `Rationals`, an operation called `"*"` that actually *added* its operands instead of multiplying them. Would this be legal in Ada? Explain. Even if it is legal, give some reasons why it is not a good idea to do this.
3. Explain how the package `VStrings` makes programming with strings easier, by comparing it to the standard string support in Ada. Can you think of any disadvantages of using `VStrings`?

Programming Projects

1. The WorldTime program presented in Section 10.2 has a limitation: The array of time-zone offsets must be completely redefined if the program user is not in the Eastern U.S. time zone. In many applications, time-zone offsets are computed with respect to Greenwich Mean Time, often referred to as GMT or Zulu. This is the local time in Greenwich, England. Modify WorldTime so that Zulu is used as the "zero point" for the offsets. (Encyclopedias and almanacs usually describe the various official time zones around the world; so do amateur radio guides.) Because your computer's clock normally reports only local time, your program will need to find out from the user in which time zone he or she is located before it can compute the time elsewhere.

2. Write a program that asks the user to enter a group of rational numbers from the keyboard, reads these numbers into an array, then sorts them and displays the largest, smallest, median, and average values.

3. Write and test a function that could be added to package VStrings, and that deletes a substring from a VString object. The specification for this function is

   ```
   FUNCTION Delete(Sub: IN Vstring; From: IN VString) RETURN VString;
   ```

   If the string Sub is present somewhere in the string From, the function returns a VString value equal to From with Sub deleted from it; otherwise, Delete just returns From. This function can be written using operations provided by VStrings, without having access to the details of VString. (*Hint:* Locate will find the location of the beginning of the substring. Because Length returns the length of the substring, you can view the string From as having three parts: the part at the beginning of the string, the substring Sub, and the remainder. The first and last parts can be extracted, then concatenated, using VString operations.)

4. Modify the mail merge program so that the names of the input and output files are entered from the keyboard. (*Hint:* Use VStrings to store the file names, then pass the string part of the VStrings to the Create and Open calls.)

5. Refer to Section 8.4 on hierarchical records. Develop an ADT to handle address records. Given the ADTs for address records, employee records (Section 10.8), and dates (Section 10.3), develop an ADT that uses these to provide operations on the hierarchical employee records described in Section 8.4, and modify the inquiry system of Section 10.8 so that hierarchical employee records can be manipulated by the terminal user.

Multidimensional Arrays and Variant Records

11

11.1 Data Structures: Multidimensional Arrays

11.2 Problem Solving: Using Multidimensional Arrays

11.3 Case Study: Analysis of Sales Trends

11.4 Data Structures: Variant Records

11.5 Case Study: Geometric Figures

11.6 Case Study: Metric System

11.7 Tricks of the Trade: Common Programming Errors
Chapter Review

So far, the arrays we have seen have been one-dimensional ones, and the record structures have been fairly simple. In this chapter we look at more interesting and complex structured types.

A multidimensional array has, as the name suggests, more than one dimension. Instead of being a linear collection of elements, it may have the "shape" of a rectangle (two-dimensional) or even a rectangular solid or cube (three-dimensional). In fact, there is in theory no limit to the number of dimensions an array type can have, although it is rare to see an example with more than three. Multidimensional arrays give us the ability to structure information in useful tabular forms.

A variant record is one with several different possible structures, instead of just one structure as we saw in Chapter 8. The structure of the record is determined, at execution time, by the value of a special field called the *discriminant* field; CASE constructs are used both to declare the record type and to process variables of the type.

The chapter contains three major case studies: analysis of sales trends, geometric figures, and dimensioned quantities for use in programs modeling physical situations.

 # 11.1 Data Structures: Multidimensional Arrays

■ Example 11.1

One two-dimensional object we are all familiar with is a tic-tac-toe board. The declarations

```
TYPE GameSymbol IS (X, O, E); -- for Tic Tac Toe; E indicates empty
TYPE BoardArray IS ARRAY (1..3,1..3) OF GameSymbol;

Empty      : CONSTANT GameSymbol := E;
TicTacToe : BoardArray;
```

allocate storage for the array `TicTacToe`. This array has nine storage cells arranged in three rows and three columns. A single enumeration value may be stored in each cell. `TicTacToe` is a two-dimensional array as pictured in Fig.11.1.

Figure 11.1 A Tic-Tac-Toe Board Stored as Array TicTacToe

```
      Column

        1  2  3

    1   X  O  E

Row 2   O  E  O  <----- TicTacToe(2,3)

    3   X  X  X
```

This array has nine elements, each of which must be referenced by specifying a row subscript (1, 2, or 3) and a column subscript (1, 2, or 3). Each array element contains a character value. The array element `TicTacToe(2,3)` pointed to in Fig. 11.1 is in row 2, column 3 of the array; it contains the enumeration value O. The diagonal line consisting of array elements `TicTacToe(1,1)`, `TicTacToe(2,2)`, and `TicTacToe(3,3)` represents a win for player X; each cell contains the value X. ■

Array Type Declaration (Multidimensional)

Form: TYPE *multidim* IS ARRAY (*subscript₁*, *subscript₂*, ... , *subscriptₙ*) OF *element-type*;

Example: TYPE YearByMonth IS ARRAY (1900..1999, Month) OF Real;
          TYPE Election IS ARRAY (Candidate,Precinct) OF Integer;

Interpretation: *Subscript$_i$* represents the *subscript-type* of dimension *i* of array type *multidim*. The *subscript-type* may be any discrete type, that is, integer or enumeration type or subtype. The *element-type* may be any predefined type or a previously defined scalar or composite data type.

Although we will focus our discussion on arrays with two and three dimensions, there is no limit on the number of dimensions allowed in Ada. However, there may be a limit imposed by the particular implementation you are using. The amount of memory space allocated for storage of a multidimensional array can be quite large, as it is the *product* of the ranges.

■ Example 11.2

The array `Table` declared below

```
Table : ARRAY (1..7, 1..5, 1..6) OF Float;
```

consists of three dimensions: the first subscript may take on values from 1 to 7; the second, from 1 to 5; and the third, from 1 to 6. A total of $7 \times 5 \times 6$, or 210, floating-point numbers may be stored in the array `Table`. All three subscripts must be specified in each reference to array `Table` (e.g., `Table(2,3,4)`). ■

Storage of Multidimensional Arrays

Most Ada implementations store multidimensional arrays in adjacent memory cells to simplify accessing the individual elements. The elements of a two-dimensional array are often stored in order by row (i.e., first row 1, then row 2, and so on). This is called *row-major order*. To access a particular array element, the compiler computes the offset of that element from the first element stored. To perform this computation the compiler must know the size of each element in bytes and the number of elements per row. Both values are available from the array type declaration.

For example, the array `TicTacToe` would be stored in row-major form as shown in Fig. 11.2. There are three elements per row and each element occupies one byte of storage. The offset for element `TicTacToe(i,j)` is computed from the formula

$$\text{Offset} = (i - 1) \times 3 + (j - 1)$$

This formula gives a value of 0 as the offset for element `TicTacToe(1,1)` and a value of 5 as the offset for element `TicTacToe(2,3)`.

Not all compilers use a row-major form for a multidimensional array; all Fortran compilers, for instance, store arrays in a column-by-column, or column-major, form. It is interesting to note that the Ada standard does not require a particular way of storing these structures: an Ada compiler can use row-major, column-major, or some other, unusual, form. Usually there is no particular reason for you to know the storage method; it is an abstraction just as floating-point numbers are.

Figure 11.2 Array TicTacToe in Memory, Row-Major Form

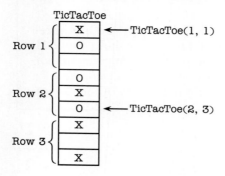

Manipulation of Two-Dimensional Arrays

A row subscript and a column subscript must be specified to reference an element of a two-dimensional array. The type of each of the two subscripts must be compatible with the corresponding subscript type specified in the array declaration. Assuming that `Game_IO` is an instance of `Text_IO.Enumeration_IO` for values of type `GameSymbol`, the loop

```
FOR Column IN 1 .. 3 LOOP
   Game_IO.Put (Item => TicTacToe(1,Column));
END LOOP;
```

displays the first row of array `TicTacToe` (`TicTacToe(1,1)`, `TicTacToe(1,2)`, and `TicTacToe(1,3)`) on the current output line. The loop

```
FOR Row IN 1 .. 3 LOOP
   Game_IO.Put (Item => TicTacToe(Row, 2));
   Text_IO.New_Line;
END LOOP;
```

displays the second column of TicTacToe (TicTacToe(1,2), TicTacToe(2,2); and TicTacToe(3,2)) in a vertical line.

■ Example 11.3
We can use aggregates in multidimensional arrays just as we did in one-dimensional arrays. We can use an aggregate assignment

```
TicTacToe := (1..3 => (1..3 => EMPTY));
```

or even

```
TicTacToe := (OTHERS => (OTHERS => EMPTY));
```

The double aggregate indicates that for each of the rows, all the columns are to be set to Empty.   ■

We can use nested loops to access all elements in a multidimensional array in a predetermined order. In the next examples, the outer loop control variable determines the row being accessed, and the inner-loop control variable selects each element in that row.

■ Example 11.4
Procedure DisplayBoard in Program 11.1 displays the current status of a tic-tac-toe board. A sample output of this procedure is shown in Fig. 11.3.   ■

Program 11.1   Procedure DisplayBoard
_____

```
PROCEDURE DisplayBoard (TicTacToe : BoardArray) IS

-- Displays the status of a tic-tac-toe board (array TicTacToe).
-- Pre : Array TicTacToe is defined.
-- Post: Displays each element of array TicTacToe.

BEGIN -- DisplayBoard
  Text_IO.Put(Item => "--------");
  Text_IO.New_Line;
  FOR Row IN 1 .. 3 LOOP
    -- Display all columns of current row
    FOR Column IN 1 .. 3 LOOP
      Text_IO.Put(Item => "|");
      Game_IO.Put(Item => TicTacToe (Row,Column));
    END LOOP;
    Text_IO.Put(Item => "|");
    Text_IO.New_Line;
    Text_IO.Put(Item => "--------");
    Text_IO.New_Line;
  END LOOP;

END DisplayBoard;
```
_____

Figure 11.3 Sample Output of DisplayBoard

```
 _____
| X| 0| E|
 _____
| 0| X| 0|
 _____
| X| E| X|
 _____
```

■ Example 11.5

Function IsFilled in Program 11.2 returns a value of True if a tic-tac-toe board is all filled up; it returns a value of False if there is at least one cell that contains the value Empty. We are assuming that all cells are initialized to Empty before the game begins. To move to a particular cell, the current player replaces the constant Empty in that cell with an X or an 0. Function IsFilled could be called before making a move to determine whether there were any possible moves left. The IF statement

```
IF IsFilled(TicTacToe) THEN
    Text_IO.Put(Item => "Game is a draw!");
    Text_IO.New_Line;
END IF;
```

displays an appropriate message when there are no moves.   ■

Program 11.2 Function IsFilled

```
FUNCTION IsFilled (TicTacToe : BoardArray) RETURN Boolean IS

-- Tests whether the array TicTacToe is filled.
-- Pre : Elements of array TicTacToe are assigned values.
--       An empty cell contains the value Empty
-- Post: Returns True if array is filled; otherwise,
--       returns False.

BEGIN -- IsFilled

  -- Set BoardFilled to False and return if any cell is empty.
  FOR Row IN 1 .. 3 LOOP
    FOR Column IN 1 .. 3 LOOP
      IF TicTacToe(Row,Column) = Empty THEN
        RETURN False        -- board is not filled
      END IF;
    END LOOP;
  END LOOP;
  -- assertion: No empty cells were found.

  RETURN True;                   -- board is filled

END IsFilled;
```

Procedure EnterMove in Program 11.3 is used to enter a move into the array
TicTacToe. EnterMove calls procedure Robust_Input.Get (see Program 6.10)
twice to enter a pair of values into the move coordinates, MoveRow and
MoveColumn. If the cell selected by these coordinates is empty, its value is reset
to the character stored in Player (X or 0). ■

Program 11.3   Procedure EnterMove

```
PROCEDURE EnterMove (Player : GameSymbol;
                     TicTacToe : IN OUT BoardArray) IS

-- Stores an X or 0 (identity of Player) in the array TicTacToe.
-- Pre : Player is "X" or "0" and array TicTacToe has at least
--       one empty cell.
-- Post: The value of Player is stored in the empty cell of
--       TicTacToe whose coordinates are read in; the rest
--       of array TicTacToe is unchanged.
-- Uses: RobustInput.Get, Text_IO.Put, Text_IO.New_Line;

  MoveRow     : Positive;    -- coordinates of selected cell
  MoveColumn  : Positive;

BEGIN  -- EnterMove

  LOOP
    Text_IO.Put(Item => "Enter your move row and then the column");
    Text_IO.New_Line;
    RobustInput.Get (MinVal => 1, MaxVal => 3, Item => MoveRow);
    RobustInput.Get (MinVal => 1, MaxVal => 3, Item => MoveColumn);

    IF TicTacToe(MoveRow, MoveColumn) = Empty THEN
      EXIT;
    ELSE
      Text_IO.Put(Item => "Cell is occupied - try again");
      Text_IO.New_Line;
    END IF;
  END LOOP;
  -- assertion: A valid move is entered

  TicTacToe(MoveRow, MoveColumn) := Player;   -- Define cell

END EnterMove;
```

Exercises for Section 11.1

Self-Check

1. Declare a three-dimensional array type where the first subscript consists of
   letters from 'A' to 'F', the second subscript consists of integers from 1 to
   10, and the third consists of the user-defined type Day. Floating-point numbers will be stored in the array. How many elements can be stored in an
   array with this type?

2. Assuming the declarations below

```
TYPE MatrixType IS ARRAY (1..5, 1..4) OF Float;
Matrix : MatrixType,
```

answer the following questions.

a. How many elements are there in array `Matrix`?

b. Write a statement to display the element in row 3, column 4.

c. Assuming row-major storage, what is the offset for this element?

d. What formula is used to compute the offset for `Matrix(i, j)`?

e. Write a loop that computes the sum of elements in row 5.

f. Write a loop that computes the sum of elements in column 4.

g. Write a nested loop structure that computes the sum of all array elements.

h. Write nested loops that display the array after it has been rotated 90 degrees counterclockwise. Your program segment should display column 4 as the first output line, column 3 as the second output line, and so on.

Programming

1. Write a function that determines whether either player has won a game of tic-tac-toe. The function should first check all rows to see if one player occupies all the cells in that row, then all columns, and then the two diagonals. The function should return a value from the enumeration type (`NoWinner`, `XWins`, `YWins`).

 ## 11.2 Problem Solving: Using Multidimensional Arrays

The subscript type for each dimension of the multidimensional array `TicTacToe` is a subrange of type `Integer`. It is not necessary for all the subscript types to have the same base type. The arrays in the next example have a different subscript type for each dimension.

■ Example 11.7

A university offers 50 courses at each of five campuses. The registrar's office can conveniently store the enrollments of these courses in the array `Enroll` declared below.

```
MaxCourse : CONSTANT Positive := 50;  -- maximum number of courses
SUBTYPE Course IS Positive RANGE 1..MaxCourse;

TYPE Campus IS (Main, Ambler, Center, Delaware, Montco);
TYPE CourseByCampus IS ARRAY (Course, Campus) OF Natural;

Enroll : CourseByCampus;
```

This array consists of 5 × 50 = 250 elements, as shown in Fig. 11.4. `Enroll(1, Center)` represents the number of students in course 1 at `Center` campus.

Figure 11.4   Two-dimensional Array Enroll

537

11.2 Problem
Solving: Using
Multidimensional
Arrays

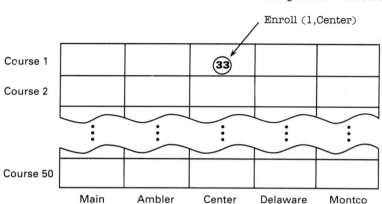

If the registrar wanted to break down this enrollment information according to student rank, a three-dimensional array with 1000 elements would be
required. This array is declared below and shown in Fig. 11.5.

```
MaxCourse : CONSTANT Positive := 50;  -- maximum number of courses
SUBTYPE Course IS Positive RANGE 1..50;
```

Figure 11.5   Three-dimensional Array ClassEnroll

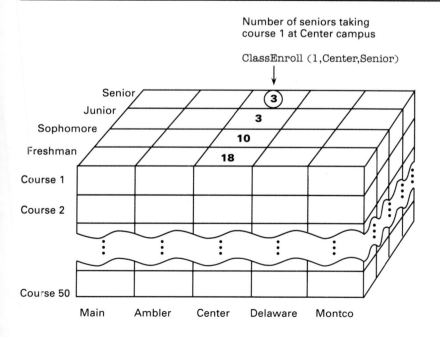

```
TYPE Campus IS (Main, Ambler, Center, Delaware, Montco);
TYPE Rank IS (Freshman, Sophomore, Junior, Senior);

TYPE CourseByCampusByRank IS ARRAY (Course, Campus, Rank) OF Natural;

ClassEnroll : CourseByCampusByRank;

Total       : Natural; -- student totals
```

The subscripted variable ClassEnroll(1, Center, Senior) represents the number of seniors taking course 1 at Center campus. ∎

■ Example 11.8

We can again use aggregates to initialize the entire three-dimensional array to zero, which would need to be done at the beginning of a university registration cycle, for example.

```
ClassEnroll := (OTHERS => (OTHERS => (OTHERS => 0)));
```
∎

■ Example 11.9

The program segment

```
Total := 0;
FOR ClassRank IN Rank LOOP
    Total := Total + ClassEnroll(1, Center, ClassRank);
END LOOP;
```

computes the total number of students of all ranks in course 1 at Center campus. The program segment

```
Total := 0;
FOR CurCampus IN Campus LOOP

    FOR ClassRank IN Rank LOOP
      Total := Total + ClassEnroll(1, CurCampus, ClassRank);
    END LOOP;

END LOOP;
```

computes the total number of students in course 1 (regardless of rank or campus). Finally, the total enrollment is computed by the program segment

```
Total := 0;
FOR CurCourse IN Courses LOOP

    FOR CurCampus IN Campus LOOP

      FOR ClassRank IN Rank LOOP
        Total := Total + ClassEnroll(CurCourse,CurCampus, ClassRank);
      END LOOP;

    END LOOP;

END LOOP;
```
∎

Self-Check

1. Declare a three-dimensional array that can be used to keep track of the number of students in the math classes (Math1, Algebra, Geometry, Algebra2, Trigonometry, Calculus) at your old high school according to the grade level and gender of the students. How many elements are in this array?

2. Extend row-major order to three dimensions and show how the array ClassEnroll might be stored in row-major form. What would be the offset for the array element ClassEnroll(1,Center,Senior) and the general formula for ClassEnroll(i,j,k)?

Programming

1. Redefine MaxCourse as 5 and write program segments that perform the following operations:
   a. Enter the enrollment data.
   b. Find the number of juniors in all classes at all campuses. Students will be counted once for each course in which they are enrolled.
   c. Find the number of sophomores on all campuses who are enrolled in course 2.
   d. Compute and display the number of students at Main campus enrolled in each course and the total number of students at Main campus in all courses. Students will be counted once for each course in which they are enrolled.
   e. Compute and display the number of upper-class students in all courses at each campus, as well as the total number of upper-class students enrolled. (Upper-class students are juniors and seniors.) Again, students will be counted once for each course in which they are enrolled.

 # 11.3 Case Study: Analysis of Sales Trends

At this point you have learned quite a lot about Ada and programming. Knowledge of arrays and records will enable you to write fairly sophisticated programs. In this case study, we will develop a general program that might be used by a company to analyze sales figures. We will use data abstraction to solve this problem, focusing on the data structures and their operators.

Sales Analysis Problem

Problem
The HighRisk Software Company has employed us to develop a general sales analysis program that they can market to a number of different companies.

This program will be used to enter and display sales figures in a variety of formats. The program will be *menu-driven,* which means that each user will be given a choice of a number of different options to perform. The menu format appears in Fig. 11.6.

Figure 11.6   Menu for Sales Analysis Program

```
Menu for Sales Analysis Program
  0. Get help.
  1. Enter sales data.
  2. Update sales data.
  3. Display sales data as a two-dimensional table.
  4. Compute annual sales totals.
  5. Tabulate monthly sales totals.
  6. Display annual sales totals.
  7. Display monthly sales totals.
  8. Display largest annual sales amount and year sold.
  9. Display largest monthly sales amount and month sold.
 10. Graph annual sales data by year.
 11. Graph monthly sales data by month.
 12. Exit the program.
```

Analysis

The operations to be peformed are listed in the menu. The main program will repeatedly display this menu and perform the user's choice. The most difficult part of the problem is choosing the appropriate data structures and writing operators to perform each of the operations above.

Data Requirements

Problem Inputs
the selected option (Choice : Natural)
the table of sales data (Sales)

Problem Outputs
the updated sales table displayed as a matrix (Sales)
the annual sales totals displayed in a table and as a bar graph (SumByYear)
the monthly sales totals displayed in a table and as a bar graph (SumByMonth)

Design

There are three major data structures: a table of sales data organized by year and month, a collection of annual sales totals, and a collection of monthly sales totals. Menu choices 1 through 5 are performed on the complete table of sales data; menu choices 6, 8, and 10 are performed on the annual sales totals; and menu choices 7, 9, and 11 are performed on the monthly sales totals.

Data Type Specification

We can consider each data object and its associated operators as an abstract data type. We provide specifications for the annual sales totals and the sales table next; the specification for monthly sales totals would be very similar to the specification for annual sales totals.

Specification of Annual Sales Totals Data Type

Structure

The record for annual sales totals, SumByYear, consists of a collection of Float values, one for each year. There are also two integer values representing the starting and ending year.

Operators

DisplayYear (SumByYear): Displays a value for each year of the range covered.

MaxByYear (SumByYear, LargeAmount OUT, LargeYear OUT): Finds the largest annual sum (LargeAmount) and its year (LargeYear).

GraphYear (SumByYear): Displays the annual sums in a bar graph

The collection of annual sales totals can be stored in a record SumByYear, of type YearSums. This record has an array field, Sums, with type Float elements and subscript type YearRange. For instance, SumByYear.Sums(1989) will contain the total of all sales in 1989. It also has two fields of type YearRange, FirstYear and LastYear, which specify the range of years covered (MinYear <= FirstYear <= LastYear <= MaxYear). Here are the declarations for the AnnualTotals data structures:

```
MinYear : CONSTANT Dates.Year_Number := 1985;
MaxYear : CONSTANT Dates.Year_Number := 1990;
SUBTYPE YearRange IS Dates.Year_Number RANGE MinYear..MaxYear;

TYPE YearArray IS ARRAY (YearRange) OF Float;
TYPE YearSums IS RECORD -- all fields are initialized by default

   FirstYear : YearRange := MinYear;
   LastYear  : YearRange := MaxYear;
   Sums      : YearArray := (OTHERS => 0.0);

END RECORD; -- YearSums
```

It is very important to understand the default initialization of the record fields in these declarations. FirstYear is initialized to MinYear; LastYear is initialized to MaxYear, and the Volume array is initialized to all zero values. Every variable of type SalesRecord will automatically be initialized in this way. This ensures that the values in any SalesRecord variable will always be well defined. If the user of the package should call one of the operators, even before a SalesRecord variable has been set by a call to one of the SalesTable operators, the results are still reasonable, and no "garbage" is ever used in a computation.

Figure 11.7 shows the memory allocated to a record SumByYear of type YearSums.

Specification of Annual Sales Totals Data Type

The collection of monthly sales totals can be stored in a one-dimensional array, SumByMonth, of type Float elements with subscript type Dates.Months. For

Figure 11.7   Record SumByYear

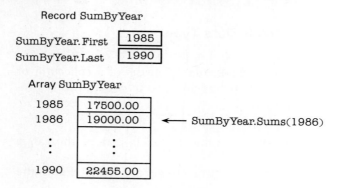

Record SumByYear

instance, `SumByMonth(Jan)` will contain the total of all sales in January. Completing the design of the monthly sales summary is left as an exercise.

Specification of Sales Table Data Type

Structure

The sales table, `Sales`, consists of a collection of `Float` values organized by year and month. There is one value for each month in the range of years covered. There are also two integer values representing the starting year and ending year.

Operators

`EnterSales (Sales OUT)`: Reads and saves the range of years covered and one sales amount for each month of the year.
`UpdateSales (Sales IN OUT)`: Modifies one or more entries in the sales table.
`DisplaySales (Sales)`: Displays the data in the sales table.
`TabYear (Sales, SumByYear OUT)`: Computes and stores the annual totals.
`TabMonth (Sales, SumByMonth OUT)`: Computes and stores the monthly totals.

The complete sales table stores a sales amount (type `Float`) for each month of a given year range (`MinYear..MaxYear`). The sales data can be stored in a two-dimensional array organized by year and month. This array will be part of a record, `Sales`, which also stores the first year (`First`) and last year (`Last`) for which sales data are available (`MinYear <= First <= Last <= Maxyear`). Here are the declarations for the type `SalesTable`.

```
TYPE SalesArray IS
   ARRAY (AnnualTotals.YearRange, Dates.Months) OF Float;

TYPE SalesRecord IS RECORD -- all fields initialized by default
```

```
      FirstYear : AnnualTotals.YearRange := AnnualTotals.YearRange'First;
      LastYear  : AnnualTotals.YearRange := AnnualTotals.YearRange'Last;
      Volume    : SalesArray := (OTHERS => (OTHERS => 0.0));

   END RECORD; -- SalesRecord
```

An object of type SalesRecord will accommodate sales data for the number of years in the subrange AnnualTotals.YearRange.

Figure 11.8 shows a sketch of the memory area allocated to the record variable Sales. There is storage space for two Integer values (Sales.First and Sales.Last) and an array of 72 (6 rows by 12 columns) type Float values. Note again that we have initialized all the fields of this record to known values.

Figure 11.8 Record Sales

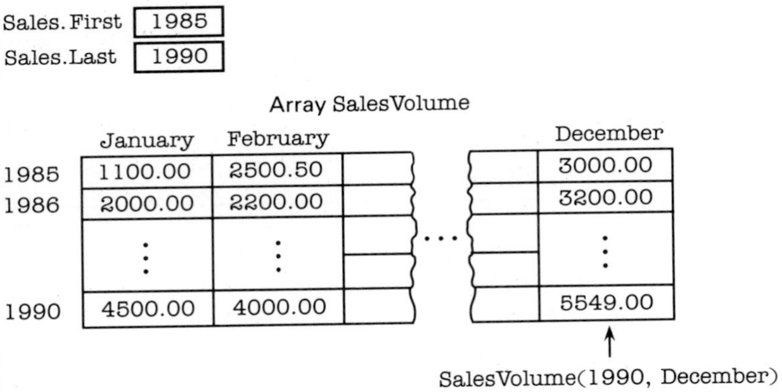

SalesVolume(1990, December)

Design Overview for Main Program

Now that we know the form of the major data objects and their operators, we can proceed with the design of the main program. The main program must allocate storage space for the data structures being manipulated, display the menu of choices, read each choice, and call the relevant operator procedure(s). The additional data requirements for the main program follow.

Program Variables

a variable of type SalesTable.SalesRecord
a variable of type AnnualTotals.YearSums
a variable of type MonthlyTotals.MonthSums

Algorithm for Main Program

Note that all variables are preinitialized in the type definitions

1. LOOP
   2. Display the menu.
   3. Read the user's choice.
   4. Perform the user's choice, updating Sales, SumByYear, SumByMonth, and the program flags.
      EXIT WHEN user is done
END LOOP;

Coding the Sales Analysis System

Let us develop this system in a bottom-up fashion. We shall implement the three abstract data types as three packages, AnnualTotals, MonthlyTotals, and SalesTable. The data structures in the first two packages are independent of SalesTable, but SalesTable uses them. Therefore AnnualTotals and MonthlyTotals can and will be coded and tested before SalesTable is even written. Programs 11.4, 11.5, and 11.6 give the package specifications for these three packages; Fig. 11.9 diagrams the dependencies between the various packages used in the program system for SalesAnalysis.

Program 11.4 Specification for Annual Totals Package

```
WITH Dates;
PACKAGE AnnualTotals IS

-- Package Specification for abstract data type for a table of sales
-- data summarized by year. The operations performed
-- include: displaying the sales data, finding the maximum yearly
-- sales, and plotting a bar graph by year.

  -- Data Types

  MinYear : CONSTANT Dates.Year_Number := 1985;
  MaxYear : CONSTANT Dates.Year_Number := 1990;
  SUBTYPE YearRange IS Dates.Year_Number RANGE MinYear..MaxYear;

  TYPE YearArray IS ARRAY (YearRange) OF Float;
  TYPE YearSums IS RECORD -- all fields are initialized by default
    FirstYear : YearRange := MinYear;
    LastYear  : YearRange := MaxYear;
    Sums      : YearArray := (OTHERS => 0.0);
  END RECORD; -- YearSums

  -- operators

  PROCEDURE DisplayYear (SumByYear : IN YearSums);

  -- Displays sales totals by year. Sums are retrieved from array SumByYear.
  -- Pre : SumByYear.Sums(i) contains sales totals for year i.
  -- Post: SumByYear.First and SumByYear.Last are defined and elements
  --       SumByYear.Sums(First) through SumByYear.Sums(Last) are displayed.
```

```
PROCEDURE MaxByYear (SumByYear   : IN YearSums;
                     LargeAmount : OUT Float;
                     LargeYear   : OUT YearRange);

-- Finds the largest value in array SumByYear.Sums
-- Pre : Records SumByYear is defined
-- Post: Returns the largest value in array SumByYear.Sums through
--       LargeAmount, and its corresponding year through LargeYear.

PROCEDURE GraphYear (SumByYear: IN YearSums);

-- Displays a graph of array SumByYear.Sums.
-- Pre : Record SumByYear is defined.
-- Post: Displays a bar graph such that the size of the bar drawn for
--       each element of array SumByYear.Sums is proprtional to its value.
-- calls: MaxByYear

END AnnualTotals;
```

Program 11.5   Specification for Monthly Totals Package

```
WITH Dates;
PACKAGE MonthlyTotals IS

-- Package Specification for abstract data type for a table of sales
-- data summarized by month. The operations performed
-- include: displaying the sales data, finding the maximum monthly
-- sales, and plotting a bar graph by month.

  -- Data Types

  TYPE MonthArray IS ARRAY (Dates.Months) OF Float;
  TYPE MonthSums IS RECORD -- all fields are initialized by default
    FirstMonth: Dates.Months := Dates.Months'First;
    LastMonth : Dates.Months := Dates.Months'Last;
    Sums      : MonthArray := (OTHERS => 0.0);
  END RECORD; -- MonthSums

  -- operators

  PROCEDURE DisplayMonth (SumByMonth : IN MonthSums);

  -- Displays sales totals by month. Sums are retrieved from array SumByMonth.
  -- Pre : SumByMonth.Sums(i) contains sales totals for month i.
  -- Post: SumByMonth.First and SumByMonth.Last are defined and elements
  -- SumByMonth.Sums(First) through SumByMonth.Sums(Last) are displayed.

  PROCEDURE MaxByMonth (SumByMonth  : IN MonthSums;
                        LargeAmount : OUT Float;
                        LargeMonth  : OUT Dates.Months);

  -- Finds the largest value in array SumByMonth.Sums
  -- Pre : Records SumByMonth is defined
  -- Post: Returns the largest value in array SumByMonth.Sums through
  --       LargeAmount, and its corresponding month through LargeMonth.
```

```
          PROCEDURE GraphMonth (SumByMonth: IN MonthSums);

          -- Displays a graph of array SumByMonth.Sums.
          -- Pre : Record SumByMonth is defined.
          -- Post: Displays a bar graph such that the size of the bar drawn for
          --       each element of array SumByMonth.Sums is proprtional to its value.
          -- calls: MaxByMonth

     END MonthlyTotals;
```

Program 11.6 Specification for Sales Analysis Table

```
WITH Dates;
WITH MonthlyTotals;
WITH AnnualTotals;
PACKAGE SalesTable IS

-- Package Specification for abstract data type for a table of sales
-- data organized by year and month. The operations performed
-- include: reading the sales data, updating sales, displaying the data,
-- and tabulating sums by year or month.

   -- Data Types

   TYPE SalesArray IS ARRAY (AnnualTotals.YearRange, Dates.Months) OF Float;
   TYPE SalesRecord IS RECORD -- all fields initialized by default
     FirstYear : AnnualTotals.YearRange := AnnualTotals.YearRange'First;
     LastYear : AnnualTotals.YearRange := AnnualTotals.YearRange'Last;
     Volume    : SalesArray := (OTHERS => (OTHERS => 0.0));
   END RECORD; -- SalesRecord


   -- operators

   PROCEDURE EnterSales (Sales : OUT SalesRecord);

   -- Reads the sales data into the record Sales.
   -- Pre : None
   -- Post: The fields FirstYear and LastYear are defined and
   --       sales data are read into array Volume for each month of
   --       years FirstYear..LastYear.


   PROCEDURE UpdateSales (Sales : IN OUT SalesRecord);

   -- Reads the sales data into the record Sales.
   -- Pre : Record Sales is defined
   -- Post: Reads year, month, and value for each update and
   --       stores the new value in array Sales.Volume


   PROCEDURE DisplaySales (Sales : IN SalesRecord);

   -- Displays the sales data.
   -- Pre : Record Sales is defined.
   -- Post: Displays two-dimensional table of sales volume by
   --       month for years FirstYear..LastYear.


   PROCEDURE TabYear (Sales : IN SalesRecord;
                      SumByYear : OUT AnnualTotals.YearSums);
```

```
--- Tabulates sales totals by year. Sums are stored in
--- array SumByYear.
--- Pre : Record Sales is defined.
--- Post: Elements SumByYear(FirstYear-MinYear) through
---       SumByYear(LastYear-MinYear) are tabulated.


PROCEDURE TabMonth (Sales : IN SalesRecord;
                    SumByMonth : OUT MonthlyTotals.MonthSums);

--- Tabulates sales totals by month. Sums are stored in
--- array SumByMonth.
--- Pre : Record Sales is defined.
--- Post: Elements SumByMonth(Jan..Dec) are tabulated for
---       the years FirstYear..LastYear.


END SalesTable;
```

Figure 11.9   Package Dependency Diagram for Sales Analysis

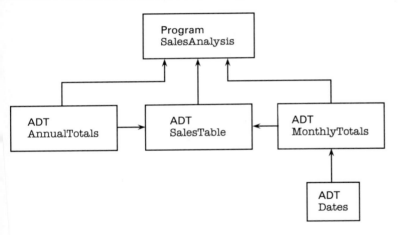

We need to prepare one thing before coding the packages. Because we are going to be reading and displaying values of type Dates.Months, we will need an instance of Text_IO.Enumeration_IO to assist us. This is a very simple file, similar to the My_Int_IO and My_Flt_IO instances we have been using right along in this book.

```
WITH Text_IO;
WITH Dates;
PACKAGE Month_IO IS NEW Text_IO.Enumeration_IO(Enum => Dates.Months);
```

Now a package, or program, needing to read or write month abbreviations, can simply include a context clause

```
WITH Month_IO;
```

at the top of the program.

Coding the Operators for the Annual Totals ADT

Program 11.7 shows the package body for the annual totals abstract data type. Procedure DisplayYear simply displays the values in array field Sums (a one-dimensional array) and is left as an exercise.

Program 11.7 Body of Annual Totals Package

```
WITH Text_IO;
WITH My_Int_IO;
WITH My_Flt_IO;
WITH Dates;
PACKAGE BODY AnnualTotals IS

-- Package Body for abstract data type for a table of sales
-- data summarized by year. The operations performed
-- include: displaying the sales data, finding the maximum yearly
-- sales, and plotting a bar graph by year.

  -- operators

  PROCEDURE DisplayYear (SumByYear : IN YearSums) IS

  -- Displays sales totals by year. Sums are retrieved from array SumByYear.
  -- Pre : SumByYear.Sums(i) contains sales totals for year i.
  -- Post: SumByYear.FirstYear and SumByYear.LastYear are defined and elements
  --       SumByYear.Sums(FirstYear) through SumByYear.Sums(LastYear)
  --       are displayed.

  BEGIN -- stub for DisplayYear

    Text_IO.Put(Item => "Procedure DisplayByYear entered.");
    Text_IO.New_Line;

  END DisplayYear;

  PROCEDURE MaxByYear (SumByYear   : IN YearSums;
                       LargeAmount : OUT Float;
                       LargeYear   : OUT YearRange) IS

  -- Finds the largest value in array SumByYear.Sums
  -- Pre : Records SumByYear is defined
  -- Post: Returns the largest value in array SumByYear.Sums through
  --       LargeAmount, and its corresponding year through LargeYear.

    TempMax  : Float;
    TempYear : YearRange;

  BEGIN

    TempYear := SumByYear.FirstYear;
    TempMax  := SumByYear.Sums(SumByYear.FirstYear);

    -- find largest value in array field Sums
    FOR CurYear IN SumByYear.FirstYear+1 .. SumByYear.LastYear LOOP
      -- invariant:
      --    TempMax contains largest amount so far and
      --    SumByYear.Sums(TempYear) is equal to TempMax
```

```
      IF SumByYear.Sums(CurYear) > TempMax THEN
         -- save largest amount so far.
         TempMax := SumByYear.Sums(CurYear);
         TempYear := CurYear;
      END IF;

   END LOOP;

   LargeAmount := TempMax;
   LargeYear   := TempYear;

END MaxByYear;

PROCEDURE GraphYear (SumByYear: IN YearSums) IS

-- Displays a graph of array SumByYear.Sums.
-- Pre : Record SumByYear is defined.
-- Post: Displays a bar graph such that the size of the bar drawn for
-- each element of array SumByYear.Sums is proportional to its value.
-- calls: MaxByYear

   Star        : CONSTANT Character := '*';
   ScreenWidth : CONSTANT Positive := 50;

   LargeAmount : Float;       -- largest value plotted
   Increment   : Float;       -- amount represented by each point
   PlotVal     : Float;
   LargeYear   : YearRange;

BEGIN -- GraphYear
   -- define scale for horizontal axis
   MaxByYear (SumByYear, LargeAmount, LargeYear);
   Increment := LargeAmount / Float(ScreenWidth);

   -- plot bar graph
   Text_IO.New_Line;
   Text_IO.Put (Item => "Year|     Sales in Dollars"); -- heading
   Text_IO.New_Line;

   FOR CurYear IN SumByYear.FirstYear .. SumByYear.LastYear LOOP
      My_Int_IO.Put(Item => CurYear, Width => 4);
      Text_IO.Put(Item => '|');
      -- plot points until value plotted exceeds element value
      IF SumByYear.Sums(CurYear) /= 0.0 THEN
         PlotVal := Increment;
         WHILE PlotVal <= SumByYear.Sums(CurYear) LOOP
            Text_IO.Put(Item => Star);
            PlotVal := PlotVal + Increment;
         END LOOP;
      END IF;
      Text_IO.New_Line;
   END LOOP;

   -- draw horizontal scale
   Text_IO.Put(Item => "0.00^        ^        ^        ^            ^");
   Text_IO.Put(Item =>        "         ^");
   My_Flt_IO.Put(Item => LargeAmount, Fore=>5, Aft=>2, Exp=>0);
   Text_IO.New_Line;
   Text_IO.Put(Item => "      Each point represents ");
   My_Flt_IO.Put(Item => Increment, Fore=>5, Aft=>2, Exp=>0);
   Text_IO.New_Line;

END GraphYear;

END AnnualTotals;
```

Procedure MaxByYear returns through LargeAmount the largest value in the array field Sums. It does this by saving the largest value found so far (starting with Sums(SumByYear.First)) in parameter LargeAmount. Each time an array element containing a larger value is found, its value is stored in LargeAmount and its subscript is stored in LargeYear.

Procedure GraphYear draws a bar chart for the array field Sums. First GraphYear calls MaxByYear to determine the largest annual sales total. Next, it divides this value by the constant PlotWidth (value is 50) to get the value represented by each point plotted. For each year being displayed, the WHILE loop in GraphYear continues to plot points until the value plotted exceeds the sales total for that year. Hence, the largest value will be plotted as a bar of length PlotWidth; all other bars will be smaller.

We can now test the available operators using a very simple test program, which is shown as Program 11.8. The program just stores some values in the array using an aggregate assignment (this is sometimes called "hard wiring" test data).

```
SumByYear := (FirstYear => 1985, LastYear => 1988,
            Sums => (1985 => 50000.00,
                     1986 => 5437.00,
                     1987 => 0.0,
                     1988 => 132.00,
                     OTHERS => 0.0));
```

After the array is initialized with some values, the operators are called in turn.

Writing the package body for MonthlyTotals is quite easy; it is similar to YearlyTotals, given the specification in Program 11.6; writing this body and a test program, which would be similar to TestAnnualSums, is left as an exercise.

Program 11.8 Test of Annual Sums ADT

```
WITH AnnualTotals;
PROCEDURE TestAnnualSums IS

   -- test program to test the operations in package AnnualTotals

   SumByYear : AnnualTotals.YearSums;

BEGIN

   SumByYear := (FirstYear => 1985, LastYear => 1988,
               Sums => (1985 => 50000.00,
                        1986 => 5437.00,
                        1987 => 0.0,
                        1988 => 132.00,
                        OTHERS => 0.0));
   AnnualTotals.DisplayYear (SumByYear);
   AnnualTotals.GraphYear(SumByYear);

END TestAnnualSums;
```

```
Procedure DisplayByYear entered.
```

11.3 Case Study:
Analysis of Sales
Trends

```
Year|        Sales in Dollars
1985|*****************************************************
1986|*****
1987|
1988|
0.00^       ^          ^          ^          ^          ^50000.00
     Each point represents 1000.00
```

Coding the Operators for the Sales Table ADT

Program 11.9 shows the package body for the sales table ADT. Procedure
EnterSales reads data into array Sales.Volume. EnterSales first calls
RobustInput.Get twice to read in the range of years covered. Next, a pair of
nested FOR loops enters the sales data. Procedure Month_IO.Put displays the
current month name as a prompt.

Program 11.9   Body for Sales Table ADT

```
WITH Text_IO;
WITH My_Int_IO;
WITH My_Flt_IO;
WITH AnnualTotals;
WITH MonthlyTotals;
WITH RobustInput;
WITH Dates;
WITH Month_IO;
PACKAGE BODY SalesTable IS

  -- Package body for abstract data type for a table of sales
  -- data organized by year and month. The operations performed
  -- include: reading the sales data, displaying the data,
  -- tabulating sums by year or month.

  -- Operators

  PROCEDURE EnterSales (Sales : OUT SalesRecord) IS

  -- Reads the sales data into the record Sales.
  -- Pre : None
  -- Post: The fields FirstYear and LastYear are defined and
  --       sales data are read into array Volume for each month of
  --       years FirstYear..LastYear.

    TempFirst : AnnualTotals.YearRange;
    TempLast  : AnnualTotals.YearRange;

  BEGIN -- EnterSales
    -- Enter first and last years of sales data.
    Text_IO.Put(Item => "Enter first year of sales data: ");
```

```
      Text_IO.New_Line;
      RobustInput.Get(MinVal=>AnnualTotals.MinYear,
                      MaxVal=>AnnualTotals.MaxYear, Item=>TempFirst);
      Sales.FirstYear := TempFirst;

      Text_IO.Put(Item => "Enter last year of sales data: ");
      Text_IO.New_Line;
      RobustInput.Get(MinVal=>AnnualTotals.MinYear,
                      MaxVal=>AnnualTotals.MaxYear, Item=>TempLast);
      Sales.LastYear := TempLast;

      -- Enter table data.
      FOR CurYear IN TempFirst .. TempLast LOOP
        Text_IO.Put(Item => "For year ");
        My_Int_IO.Put(Item => CurYear, Width=>4);
        Text_IO.New_Line;
        Text_IO.Put(Item => "Enter sales amount (Float) for each month or 0.0");
        Text_IO.New_Line;
        FOR CurMonth IN Dates.Months LOOP
          Month_IO.Put(Item=>CurMonth, Width=>3);
          Text_IO.Put(Item => " $");
          My_Flt_IO.Get(Item => Sales.Volume(CurYear, CurMonth));
        END LOOP;
        Text_IO.New_Line;
      END LOOP;

END EnterSales;

PROCEDURE UpdateSales (Sales : IN OUT SalesRecord) IS

-- Reads the sales data into the record Sales.
-- Pre : Record Sales is defined
-- Post: Reads year, month, and value for each update and
--       stores the new value in array Sales.Volume

   NewYear    : AnnualTotals.YearRange;
   NewMonth   : Dates.Months;
   NewAmount  : Float;
   MoreChar   : Character;

BEGIN

   Text_IO.Put(Item => "Enter year, month, and amount for each update.");
   Text_IO.New_Line;
   LOOP
     Text_IO.Put(Item => "For year - ");
     My_Int_IO.Get(Item => NewYear);
     Text_IO.Put(Item => "For Month ");
     Month_IO.Get(Item => NewMonth);
     Text_IO.Put(Item => "Enter Amount $");
     My_Flt_IO.Get(Item => NewAmount);
     Sales.Volume(NewYear, NewMonth) := NewAmount;
     Text_IO.Put(Item => "Any more changes? Enter Y (Yes) or N (No) > ");
     Text_IO.Get(Item => MoreChar);
     EXIT WHEN (MoreChar = 'n') OR (MoreChar = 'N');
   END LOOP;

END UpdateSales;

PROCEDURE ShowHalf (Sales : IN SalesRecord;
                    FirstMonth, LastMonth : IN Dates.Months) IS
```

```
-- Displays the sales amounts by year for each of the months from
-- FirstMonth to LastMonth.
-- Pre : Array Sales and FirstMonth and LastMonth are defined.
-- Post: Displays sales volumes in a table whose rows are
--       FirstYear..LastYear and whose columns are FirstMonth..
--       LastMont.

BEGIN -- ShowHalf
   -- Print table heading for 6 months of each year.
   Text_IO.Put(Item => "Year        ");
   FOR CurMonth IN FirstMonth .. LastMonth LOOP
     Month_IO.Put(Item=>CurMonth, Width=>11);        -- Print month names
   END LOOP;
   Text_IO.New_Line;                                 -- End the heading

   -- Print sales figures for 6 months of each year.
   FOR CurYear IN Sales.FirstYear .. Sales.LastYear LOOP
     My_Int_IO.Put(Item => CurYear, Width=>4);
     Text_IO.Put(Item => "  ");
     FOR CurMonth IN FirstMonth .. LastMonth LOOP
       My_Flt_IO.Put (Item=>Sales.Volume(CurYear, CurMonth),
                      Fore=>6, Aft=>2, Exp=>0);
       Text_IO.Put(Item => "  ");
     END LOOP;
     Text_IO.New_Line;
   END LOOP;
END ShowHalf;


PROCEDURE DisplaySales (Sales : IN SalesRecord) IS

-- Displays the sales data.
-- Pre : Record Sales is defined.
-- Post: Displays two-dimensional table of sales volume by
--        month for years FirstYear..LastYear.

-- Due to line length limits,
-- the first 6 months and last 6 months of each year are shown in
-- separate tables.  Uses ShowHalf to display each table.

BEGIN -- DisplaySales
   -- Display first 6 months of array Sales.
   ShowHalf (Sales, Dates.Jan, Dates.Jun);
   Text_IO.New_Line;

   -- Display last 6 months of array Sales.
   ShowHalf (Sales, Dates.Jul, Dates.Dec);
END DisplaySales;


PROCEDURE TabYear (Sales : IN SalesRecord;
                   SumByYear : OUT AnnualTotals.YearSums) IS

-- Tabulates sales totals by year. Sums are stored in
-- array SumByYear.
-- Pre : Record Sales is defined.
-- Post: Elements SumByYear(FirstYear-MinYear) through
--       SumByYear(LastYear-MinYear) are tabulated.

   Sum : Float;                       -- sum for each year
```

```
BEGIN -- TabYear
  -- Find each annual total.
  FOR CurYear IN Sales.FirstYear .. Sales.LastYear LOOP
    -- Accumulate sum for 12 months
    Sum := 0.0;
    FOR CurMonth IN Dates.Months LOOP
      Sum := Sum + Sales.Volume(CurYear, CurMonth);
    END LOOP;
    SumByYear.Sums(CurYear) := Sum;
  END LOOP;
END TabYear;


PROCEDURE TabMonth (Sales : IN SalesRecord;
                    SumByMonth : OUT MonthlyTotals.MonthSums) IS

-- Tabulates sales totals by month. Sums are stored in
-- array SumByMonth.
-- Pre : Record Sales is defined.
-- Post: Elements SumByMonth(Jan..Dec) are tabulated for
--       the years FirstYear..LastYear.

BEGIN -- TabMonth stub
  Text_IO.Put(Item => "Procedure TabMonth entered.");
  Text_IO.New_Line;
END TabMonth;


END SalesTable;
```

Procedure UpdateSales can be used to change an incorrect sales table value or to add new values at a later time. The program user must enter the year, month, and sales amount for each table entry being updated. Month_IO. Get is used to obtain a value of type Dates.Months.

Most screens are not wide enough to display the sales data for all 12 months of a year. Consequently, DisplaySales calls ShowHalf twice: first to print the sales figures for the first 6 months and then to print the last 6 months. ShowHalf begins by displaying the 6 months covered as column headings. Next, a pair of nested FOR loops displays the sales figures for those 6 months of each year.

Procedure TabYear accumulates the sum of each row of the sales table and stores it in the appropriate element of array SumByYear. Procedure TabMonth is written as a stub, and its completion is left as an exercise.

Program 11.10 shows a simple test program for SalesTable. You can use this as a framework to test other operations in the sales table package.

We have developed a system of packages that could work correctly with many different-looking main programs. This is one of the advantages of data abstraction. Further, we have tested each of the packages as it was written, without even considering the detailed structure of the intended main program. If this project were developed by a team, each team member could write and test a different package. This is a nice example of bottom-up testing.

```
WITH AnnualTotals;
WITH MonthlyTotals;
WITH SalesTable;
PROCEDURE TestSalesTable IS

    -- simple test program for the operations in package SalesTable

    Sales : SalesTable.SalesRecord;
    SumByYear : AnnualTotals.YearSums;
    SumByMonth : MonthlyTotals.MonthSums;

BEGIN -- TestSalesTable

    SalesTable.DisplaySales(Sales);
    SalesTable.UpdateSales(Sales);
    SalesTable.DisplaySales(Sales);

    SalesTable.TabYear(Sales, SumByYear);
    SalesTable.TabMonth(Sales, SumByMonth);

    AnnualTotals.DisplayYear (SumByYear);
    AnnualTotals.GraphYear(SumByYear);

    MonthlyTotals.DisplayMonth (SumByMonth);
    MonthlyTotals.GraphMonth(SumByMonth);

END TestSalesTable;
```

Year	JAN	FEB	MAR	APR	MAY	JUN
1985	0.00	0.00	0.00	0.00	0.00	0.00
1986	0.00	0.00	0.00	0.00	0.00	0.00
1987	0.00	0.00	0.00	0.00	0.00	0.00
1988	0.00	0.00	0.00	0.00	0.00	0.00
1989	0.00	0.00	0.00	0.00	0.00	0.00
1990	0.00	0.00	0.00	0.00	0.00	0.00

Year	JUL	AUG	SEP	OCT	NOV	DEC
1985	0.00	0.00	0.00	0.00	0.00	0.00
1986	0.00	0.00	0.00	0.00	0.00	0.00
1987	0.00	0.00	0.00	0.00	0.00	0.00
1988	0.00	0.00	0.00	0.00	0.00	0.00
1989	0.00	0.00	0.00	0.00	0.00	0.00
1990	0.00	0.00	0.00	0.00	0.00	0.00

```
Enter year, month, and amount for each update.
For year - 1990
For Month jul
Enter Amount $100.00
Any more changes? Enter Y (Yes) or N (No) > n
```

Year	JAN	FEB	MAR	APR	MAY	JUN
1985	0.00	0.00	0.00	0.00	0.00	0.00
1986	0.00	0.00	0.00	0.00	0.00	0.00
1987	0.00	0.00	0.00	0.00	0.00	0.00
1988	0.00	0.00	0.00	0.00	0.00	0.00
1989	0.00	0.00	0.00	0.00	0.00	0.00
1990	0.00	0.00	0.00	0.00	0.00	0.00

Year	JUL	AUG	SEP	OCT	NOV	DEC
1985	0.00	0.00	0.00	0.00	0.00	0.00
1986	0.00	0.00	0.00	0.00	0.00	0.00
1987	0.00	0.00	0.00	0.00	0.00	0.00
1988	0.00	0.00	0.00	0.00	0.00	0.00
1989	0.00	0.00	0.00	0.00	0.00	0.00
1990	100.00	0.00	0.00	0.00	0.00	0.00

```
Procedure TabMonth entered.
Procedure DisplayByYear entered.

Year|     Sales in Dollars
1985|
1986|
1987|
1988|
1989|
1990|*****************************************************
0.00^        ^          ^          ^          ^          ^      100.00
      Each point represents     2.00

Procedure DisplayByMonth entered.

Month|     Sales in Dollars
JAN  |
FEB  |
MAR  |
APR  |
MAY  |
JUN  |
JUL  |
AUG  |
SEP  |
OCT  |
NOV  |
DEC  |
0.00 ^        ^          ^          ^          ^          ^        0.00

      Each point represents     0.00
```

Writing and Testing the Sales Analysis Main Program

Developing the menu-driven main program is left as an exercise; it should be menu-driven in the manner of the home budget program in Section 8.7. The main loop of the program will incorporate a CASE statement with alternatives for each of the menu options; each alternative will just execute the appropriate operator from one of the three packages.

To give you an idea of its behavior, a sample run of the intended program is shown in Fig. 11.10. To save space, only part of the data entry process and only the first menu display are shown. The options selected are 1, 2, 4, 6, 8, 10, and 12. Note that because all the data structures are preinitialized, the preconditions for all the options are satisfied automatically; at worst, if operations are done out of sequence, there will be a lot of zero values and empty plots, but because zero is a valid sales amount this is not a problem at all.

To test this program completely, you should enter year values that are outside the expected range to make sure that this does not cause a fatal progam error.

Figure 11.10   Sample Run of the Sales Analysis Program

```
Menu for Sales Analysis Program

 0. Get help.
 1. Enter sales data.
 2. Update sales data.
 3. Display sales data as a two-dimensional table.
 4. Compute annual sales totals.
 5. Tabulate monthly sales totals.
 6. Display annual sales totals.
 7. Display monthly sales totals.
 8. Display largest annual sales amount and year sold.
 9. Display largest monthly sales amount and month sold.
10. Graph annual sales data by year.
11. Graph monthly sales data by month.
12. Exit the program.

Enter a number between 0 and 12> 1
Enter first year of sales data.
Enter a number between 1900 and 1999> 1987
Enter last year of sales data.
Enter a number between 1987 and 1999> 1988

For year 1987, enter sales amount for each month or 0.0
   January  $1000.00
   February $    0.00
   March    $ 700.00
   ...

For year 1988, enter sales amount for each month or 0.0
   January  $500.00
   February $400.00
   March    $400.00
   ...

Enter a number between 0 and 12> 2
Enter year, month, and amount for each update.
For year - Enter a number between 1987 and 1988> 1987
For month - Enter a number between 1 and 12 > 2
Enter amount $600.00
Any more changes? Enter Y (Yes) or N (No) > N

Enter a number between 0 and 12> 3
Table of Sales Volume by Year and Month

Year    Jan       Feb       Mar       Apr       May       Jun
1987   1000.00    600.00    700.00    800.00    950.00   1000.00
1988    500.00    400.00    400.00    900.00   1000.00     55.00

Year    Jul       Aug       Sep       Oct       Nov       Dec
1987    500.00    500.00    900.00    600.00    950.50   1000.00
1988    300.00    800.00    750.00    900.00    600.00    300.00

Enter a number between 0 and 12> 4
Annual sums tabulated.
```

```
Enter a number between 0 and 12> 6
Table of Sales Totals by Year

        Year      Sales
        1987      9500.50
        1988      6905.00

Enter a number between 0 and 12> 8
Largest annual sum is $9500.50 in year 1987

Enter a number between 0 and 12> 10

Year|     Sales in Dollars
1987|****************************************************
1988|*************************************
0.00^        ^          ^            ^           ^            ^9500.50
     Each point represents      190.00

Enter a number between 0 and 12> 12
Exit program? Enter Y (Yes) or N (No): Y
Sales analysis completed.
```

Exercises for Section 11.3

Self-Check

1. Why is the procedure ShowHalf necessary?

Programming

1. Complete and test the monthly totals package for the case study.
2. Complete and test the menu-driven main program for the case study.

 ## 11.4 Data Structures: Variant Records

Each of the record types we have used so far has been such that all records of the type have exactly the same form and structure. It is possible and often very useful, however, to define record types that have some fields that are the same for all variables of that type (*fixed part*) and some fields that may be different (*variant part*).

For example, we might want to include additional information about an employee based on the employee's pay status. There are three categories in a particular company: One group (professionals) receives a fixed monthly salary, one group (sales) receives a fixed weekly salary plus a commission on their sales, and the third group (clerical) receives an hourly wage and is paid weekly based on number of hours worked. A pay record for a given pay period has a fixed part giving the employee's ID and name, the ending date of the pay period, and a variant part giving the pay information according to the pay status.

Here is a declaration of this variant record type:

```
SUBTYPE NameLength IS Positive RANGE 1..20;
SUBTYPE NameString IS String(NameLength);
SUBTYPE IDRange IS Positive RANGE 1000..9999;
SUBTYPE PayRange IS Float RANGE 0.00..10000.00;
SUBTYPE NonNegFloat IS Float RANGE 0.00..Float'Last;
SUBTYPE WorkHours   IS Float RANGE 0.0..168.0;
SUBTYPE CommissionPercentage IS Float RANGE 0.00..0.50;


TYPE PayCategories IS (Unknown, Professional, Sales, Clerical);


TYPE PayRecord (PayStatus : PayCategories := Unknown) IS RECORD
    ID        : IDRange;
    Name      : NameString;
    PayPeriod : Dates.Date;

    CASE PayStatus IS
        WHEN Professional =>
            MonthSalary : PayRange;
        WHEN Sales =>
            WeekSalary  : PayRange;
            CommRate    : CommissionPercentage;
            SalesAmount : NonNegFloat;
        WHEN Clerical =>
            HourlyWage  : PayRange;
            HoursWorked : WorkHours;
        WHEN Unknown =>
            NULL;
    END CASE;

END RECORD;
```

The line at the beginning of the record declaration,

```
TYPE PayRecord (PayStatus : PayCategories := Clerical) IS RECORD
```

indicates to the compiler that the record is a record with a variant part, and that the *discriminant* field, which indicates which of several variants is present, is PayStatus. The discriminant is a special field that looks like a parameter of a procedure; indeed, it has many of the aspects of a parameter in that the record is *parametrized,* or varies, according to the value of the discriminant. The reason for having a value Unknown used as a default will be explained shortly.

The fixed part of a record always precedes the variant part. The variant part begins with the phrase

```
CASE PayStatus IS
```

and declares the different forms the variant part can have. The NULL case indicates that there is no variant part for PayStatus equal to Unknown. There are three different pay records, each of a different variant.

For each variable of type PayRecord, the compiler will usually allocate sufficient storage space to accommodate the largest of the record variants shown in Fig. 11.11. However, *only one of the variants is defined at any given time; this particular variant is determined by the discriminant field value.*

Figure 11.11 Four Variants of a Variant Record

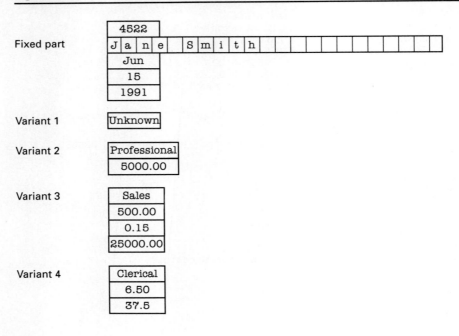

Fixed part

| 4522 |
| Jane Smith |
| Jun |
| 15 |
| 1991 |

Variant 1

Unknown

Variant 2

Professional
5000.00

Variant 3

Sales
500.00
0.15
25000.00

Variant 4

Clerical
6.50
37.5

■ Example 11.10

Because the value of Jill.PayStatus is Professional, then only the variant field MonthSalary may be correctly referenced; all other variant fields are undefined. The program fragment

```
Text_IO.Put("Jill's full name is ");
Text_IO.Put(Jill.Name);
Text_IO.New_Line;
Text_IO.Put("and her monthly salary is $");
My_Flt_IO.Put(Jill.MonthSalary, Fore => 1, Aft => 2, Exp => 0);
Text_IO.New_Line;
```

displays the lines

```
Jill's full name is Jill Smith
and her monthly salary is $2500.00
```
■

In Ada, the compiler and run-time system are very careful to check the consistency of the discriminant value with the references to fields in the record. If, at execution time, an attempt is made to access a field that is not defined in the current variant (i.e., current discriminant value of the same record), Constraint_Error is raised. For this reason, a CASE statement is often used to process the variant part of a record. By using the discriminant field as the CASE selector, we can ensure that only the currently defined variant is manipulated.

The fragment in Fig. 11.12 displays the data stored in the variant part of a record CurrentEmp. The value of CurrentEmp.PayStatus determines what information will be displayed. ■

Figure 11.12 Displaying a Variant Record

```
Text_IO.Put(Item => "Employee ID ");
My_Int_IO.Put(Item => CurrentEmp.ID, Width => 4);
Text_IO.New_Line;
Text_IO.Put(Item => "Employee Name ");
Text_IO.Put(Item => CurrentEmp.Name);
Text_IO.New_Line;
Text_IO.Put(Item => "Pay Period Ending ");
Dates.Put(Item => CurrentEmp.PayPeriod, Format => Numeric);
Text_IO.New_Line;

CASE CurrentEmp.PayStatus IS

  WHEN Unknown =>
    Text_IO.Put(Item => "Unknown pay status!");
    Text_IO.New_Line;

  WHEN Professional =>
    Text_IO.Put("Monthly Salary is $");
    My_Flt_IO.Put
      (Item=>CurrentEmp.MonthSalary, Fore=>1, Aft=>2, Exp=>0);
    Text_IO.New_Line;

  WHEN Sales =>
    Text_IO.Put("Weekly Salary is $");
    My_Flt_IO.Put
      (Item=>CurrentEmp.WeekSalary, Fore=>1, Aft=>2, Exp=>0);
    Text_IO.New_Line;
    Text_IO.Put("Commission percent is ");
    My_Flt_IO.Put
      (Item=>CurrentEmp.CommRate, Fore=>1, Aft=>2, Exp=>0);
    Text_IO.New_Line;
    Text_IO.Put("Sales this week $");
    My_Flt_IO.Put
      (Item=>CurrentEmp.SalesAmount, Fore=>1, Aft=>2, Exp=>0);
    Text_IO.New_Line;

  WHEN Clerical =>
    Text_IO.Put("Hourly wage is $");
    My_Flt_IO.Put
      (Item=>CurrentEmp.HourlyWage, Fore=>1, Aft=>2, Exp=>0);
    Text_IO.New_Line;
    Text_IO.Put("Hours worked this week ");
    My_Flt_IO.Put
      (Item=>CurrentEmp.HoursWorked, Fore=>1, Aft=>2, Exp=>0);
    Text_IO.New_Line;

END CASE;
```

The syntax for a record with fixed and variant parts is described in the following syntax display.

Record Type with Variant Part

Form: TYPE *rec-type* (*discriminant* : *disc_type* := *default*) IS RECORD
       ID_1 : $type_1$;
       ID_2 : $type_2$;
       .
       .   *fixed part*
       .

       ID_n : $type_n$;

       CASE *discriminant* IS
         WHEN *value_1* =>
            field-list_1;
         WHEN *value_2* =>
            field-list_2;
         .
         .   *variant part*
         .
         WHEN *value_n* =>
            field-list_n;
         WHEN OTHERS =>
            others-field-list;
       END CASE;

    END RECORD;

Example: TYPE Face (Bald : Boolean) IS RECORD
      Eyes : Color;
      Height: Inches;
      CASE Bald IS
         WHEN True =>
           WearsWig : Boolean;
         WHEN False =>
           HairColor : Color;
      END CASE;
    END RECORD;

Interpretation: The *field-list* for the fixed part is declared first. The variant part starts with the reserved word CASE. The identifer *discriminant* is the name of the discriminant field of the record; the discriminant field name is separated by a colon from its type (*disc-type*), which must be type Boolean, an enumeration type, or a subrange of a discrete type.

The CASE values (*value_1*, *value_2* ,..., *value_k*) are lists of values of the discriminant field as defined by *discriminant-type*. *Field-list_i* describes the record fields associated with *value_i*. Each element of *field-list_i* specifies a field name and its type.

Note 1: All field names must be unique. The same field name may not appear in the fixed and variant parts or in two field lists of the variant part.

Note 2: An empty field list (no variant part for that CASE label) is indicated by NULL instead of a field list.

Note 3: As in all CASE forms, all values of the discriminant must be covered by WHEN clauses. Values not covered otherwise can be covered by a WHEN OTHERS clause.

Note 4: If := *default* is omitted from the discriminant declaration, all variables of the type must be constrained at the time they are declared; that is, a value for the discriminant must be supplied. If the default is present, unconstrained variables may be declared, that is, variables without an explicit discriminant value.

Constrained and Unconstrained Variant Records

Ada has very strict rules to guarantee two things:

* the discriminant of a variant record is always defined, that is, always has some value; and
* the discriminant value is always consistent with the actual data stored in the record.

The first condition is ensured by requiring that if a default value for the discriminant is *not* present in the record declaration, *all* declarations of variables must supply a value for the discriminant. In the pay status case above, a default of Unknown is supplied; therefore it is possible to declare a record without a discriminant value, as in

```
CurrentEmp : PayRecord;
```

Supplying a discriminant value is not prohibited, however:

```
AnotherEmp : PayRecord(PayStatus=>Professional);
```

is allowed. In the case of the Face record above, it would be a compilation error to declare

```
JohnsFace : Face;
```

and in this case a discriminant value is *required:*

```
JohnsFace : Face(Bald=>False);
```

An *unconstrained* record variable is one that has a default discriminant value, and none is supplied in the variable declaration. It is permissible to change the discriminant value of an unconstrained record at execution time, under rules to be specified in the next section. This means that the variable CurrentEmp can hold a professional employee at one moment, a sales employee at another. This is a common use of variant records in data processing.

A *constrained* record variable is one whose discriminant value is supplied when the variable is declared. Both AnotherEmp and the second JohnsFace are constrained. It is *not* permitted to change the discriminant value of a constrained record at execution time; this means that we are "stuck" with the discriminant value. AnotherEmp is constrained because we chose to make it so even though the discriminant has a default; JohnsFace is constrained because we have no choice, because no default is supplied for Bald. JohnsFace cannot take into account his losing his hair at a later date.

Storing Values into Variant Records

Ada's rules for variant records may seem cumbersome, but the rules are designed to guarantee that the contents of a variant record are always consistent. Here are the basic rules for storing values into a variant record variable:

- Any field of the variable may be selected and *read* individually, by a field selector, at any time.
- Any field of the variable may be selected and *changed* individually (say, by an assignment statement) *except* a discriminant field; if the change is not consistent with the current discriminant value, Constraint_Error is raised.
- The discriminant field of a *constrained* record cannot be changed under any circumstances.
- The discriminant field of an *unconstrained* record can be changed, but only if the *entire* record is changed at the same time. There are two ways to do this: Use a record aggregate, or copy another record.

A common application of variant records is to read the value of a discriminant from the terminal or a file, then create a record variable with that variant. By the rules above, the value cannot be stored directly into the discriminant. It, and the other fields of the record, must be held in temporary variables and stored *as a unit* into the variant record using an aggregate.

PROGRAM
STYLE

Declaring Variant Records

We recommend that variant record type declarations usually have a default value supplied for the discriminant. Otherwise, all variables of that type will have to be constrained when they are declared, and much of the flexibility of variant records—especially their ability to change structure at execution time—will be lost.

Operations on Variant Records

As always in Ada, assignment and equality testing are defined for variant records. However, certain rules apply:

- A variant record value can always be assigned to an *unconstrained* variable of the same record type. This is possible because it is permissible to change the discriminant of an unconstrained variable.
- A variant record value can be assigned to a *constrained* variable of the same record type *only* if the discriminant values match. This restriction follows

from the fact that the discriminant value of a constrained variable cannot be changed, ever.

- Two variant record values can be compared for equality only if the discriminant values agree; otherwise Constraint_Error is raised.

Exercises for Section 11.4

Self-Check

1. How many bytes of storage are required for each of the variants of PayRecord? You will probably have to check your Ada compiler documentation to determine the storage required by each of the fields comprising this record.

Programming

1. Write a procedure to display a record of type Face as declared in the previous syntax display.

 # 11.5 Case Study: Geometric Figures

Problem

We want to write a program that will determine the area and perimeter for a variety of geometric figures.

Analysis

Here are the data requirements for this problem.

Data Requirements

Problem Inputs
An enumeration value representing the kind of figure (Shape : FigKind)
The relevant characteristics for the figure selected

Problem Outputs
The figure area (Area : NonNegFloat)
The figure perimeter (Perimeter : NonNegFloat)

Design

To solve this problem, we will create an abstract data type that represents a geometric figure and contains operators for entering the figure's characteristics, computing its perimeter, computing its area, and displaying its characteristics. Because the characteristics for a figure are related, we would like to save them in a record. However, the characteristics for each figure shape are different, so we must use a record with a variant part. In this case, the fixed part of the record will contain its area and perimeter, which are computed automatically as the figure is read.

Data Types

```
SUBTYPE NonNegFloat IS Float RANGE 0.0 .. Float'Last;
TYPE FigKind IS (Rect, Square, Circle);

TYPE Figure (FigShape : FigKind := Rect) IS RECORD
 Area : NonNegFloat := 0.0;
 Perimeter : NonNegFloat := 0.0;
 CASE FigShape IS
   WHEN Rect =>
     Width : NonNegFloat := 0.0;
     Height : NonNegFloat := 0.0;
   WHEN Square =>
     Side : NonNegFloat := 0.0;
   WHEN Circle =>
     Radius : NonNegFloat := 0.0;
 END CASE;
END RECORD; -- Figure
```

Initial Algorithm

1. Determine the type of the figure.
2. Read in the figure characteristics.
3. Compute the area of the figure.
4. Compute the perimeter of the figure.
5. Display the complete record for the figure.

Coding the Package Specification

The package specification appears as Program 11.11. We have defined the data type Figure as a PRIVATE type. Why? If the client program had access to the details of the record representing the figure, it could, for example, change the Perimeter field by simply plugging in a new number. Because the figure would

Program 11.11 Package Specification for Geometry

```
PACKAGE Geometry IS

-- Defines an abstract data type for a geometric figure.
-- Operators include constructors for rectangles, circles, and squares,
-- selectors for area and perimeter, and input/output operations

-- Data Types

  SUBTYPE NonNegFloat IS Float RANGE 0.0 .. Float'Last;
  TYPE FigKind IS (Rect, Square, Circle);

  TYPE Figure (FigShape : FigKind := Rect) IS PRIVATE;

-- Operators

  FUNCTION MakeRect (Width, Height : NonNegFloat) RETURN Figure;

    -- constructor: creates a rectangular figure from its height and width
    -- Pre : Width and Height are defined
```

```
   -- Post: returns a figure of type Rect


   FUNCTION MakeCircle (Radius : NonNegFloat) RETURN Figure;

   -- constructor: creates a circular figure from its radius
   -- Pre : Radius is defined
   -- Post: returns a figure of type Circle


   FUNCTION MakeSquare (Side : NonNegFloat) RETURN Figure;

   -- constructor: creates a square figure from its side
   -- Pre : Side is defined
   -- Post: returns a figure of type Side


   PROCEDURE ReadFigure (OneFig : OUT Figure);

   -- Enters data into OneFig.
   -- Pre : None
   -- Post: The discriminant and characteristics of OneFig are defined.


   FUNCTION Perimeter (OneFig : Figure) RETURN NonNegFloat;

   -- selector: returns perimeter of OneFig.
   -- Pre : The discriminant and characteristics of OneFig are defined.
   -- Post: Returns perimeter


   FUNCTION Area (OneFig : Figure) RETURN NonNegFloat;

   -- selector: returns Area of OneFig.
   -- Pre : The discriminant and characteristics of OneFig are defined.
   -- Post: Returns area of OneFig.


   PROCEDURE DisplayFigure (OneFig : IN Figure);
   --
   -- Displays the characteristics of OneFig.
   -- Pre : All fields of OneFig are defined.
   -- Post: Displays each field of OneFig.
PRIVATE

   TYPE Figure (FigShape : FigKind := Rect) IS RECORD
     Area : NonNegFloat := 0.0;
     Perimeter : NonNegFloat := 0.0;
     CASE FigShape IS
       WHEN Rect =>
         Width : NonNegFloat := 0.0;
         Height : NonNegFloat := 0.0;
       WHEN Square =>
         Side : NonNegFloat := 0.0;
       WHEN Circle =>
         Radius : NonNegFloat := 0.0;
     END CASE;
   END RECORD; -- Figure

END Geometry;
```

no longer make geometric sense, this action would violate the abstraction. Note the syntax for declaring a PRIVATE type with a variant: The discriminant appears first in the partial declaration and later in the complete declaration in the PRIVATE part of the specification.

The following design decisions make the data type safe from accidental misuse:

1. The data type is declared PRIVATE to keep client programs from prying into, and changing, fields of the record such as the area and the perimeter, or changing the length of the side without changing the area and perimeter fields accordingly.
2. All fields of the type are initialized to 0.0 by default, so that every variable of the type is automatically well defined (a figure with sides of 0.0 also has area and perimeter of 0.0).
3. The area and perimeter are calculated automatically when the figure is constructed, because these are uniquely determined by the other characteristics.

The operations in the package are three constructors, MakeRect, MakeCircle, and MakeSquare, which construct the appropriate variant given the relevant characteristics, two selectors Area and Perimeter, which return these characteristics of the figure, and two input/output operations, ReadFigure and DisplayFigure.

A client program can declare variables of type Figure in either constrained or unconstrained form:

```
SomeShape : Figure;
```

can hold, at different moments, a circle, a square, or a rectangle; it is unconstrained. However,

```
BigSquare : Figure (FigShape => Square);
```

can hold only a square, because it is constrained; that is, we plugged a discriminant value into the declaration of the variable and are now "locked in" to that value.

Coding the Package Body

Program 11.12 shows the package body for Geometry. The constructor procedures create the appropriate variant of the record from the relevant components, then calculate the area and perimeter. Local functions ComputeArea and ComputePerimeter are used to assist. These are not given in the specification. The user can find out the area and perimeter by calling the appropriate selector, whose code is straightforward.

Procedure ReadFigure reads in the enumeration value denoting the kind of figure, reads the data required for the kind of figure indicated by the discriminant field, and calls the appropriate constructor. The other operators are straightforward and are shown in Program 11.12.

In each procedure, a CASE statement controls the processing of the data in the variant part. Procedures ComputePerimeter and ComputeArea define their

```
WITH My_Flt_IO;
WITH Text_IO;
WITH RobustInput;
PACKAGE BODY Geometry IS

-- Defines an abstract data type for a geometric figure.
-- Operators include constructors for rectangles, circles, and squares,
-- selectors for area and perimeter, and input/output operations

  PACKAGE FigKind_IO IS NEW Text_IO.Enumeration_IO (Enum => FigKind);

  Pi : CONSTANT Float := 3.14159;
  MaxSize : CONSTANT Float := 1_000_000.00;

-- Data type Figure is declared in the package specification

-- Local procedure ReadShape is used only within the package,
-- therefore it is not exported (does not appear in the spec).

  PROCEDURE ReadShape (Item : OUT FigKind) IS

    TempItem: FigKind;

  BEGIN -- ReadShape

    LOOP
      BEGIN
        Text_IO.Put(Item => "Enter a shape: rect, circle, square > ");
        FigKind_IO.Get(Item => TempItem);
        Item := TempItem;
        EXIT;
      EXCEPTION
        WHEN Text_IO.Data_Error =>
          Text_IO.Put ("Value not a valid shape. Please try again.");
          Text_IO.New_Line;
          Text_IO.Skip_Line;
      END;
    END LOOP;
    -- assert: Item is rect, circle, or square

  END ReadShape;

-- local functions, not exported in the spec

  FUNCTION ComputePerimeter (OneFig : Figure) RETURN NonNegFloat IS

  -- Computes Perimeter of OneFig.
  -- Pre : The discriminant and characteristics of OneFig are defined.
  -- Post: Returns Perimeter

  BEGIN -- ComputePerimeter

    CASE OneFig.FigShape IS
    WHEN Rect =>
      RETURN 2.0 * (OneFig.Width + OneFig.Height);
    WHEN Square =>
      RETURN 4.0 * OneFig.Side;
    WHEN Circle =>
      RETURN 2.0 * Pi * OneFig.Radius;
    END CASE;
```

```
                    END ComputePerimeter;


                    FUNCTION ComputeArea (OneFig : Figure) RETURN NonNegFloat IS

                    -- Computes Area of OneFig.
                    -- Pre : The discriminant and characteristics of OneFig are defined.
                    -- Post: Returns Area of OneFig.

                    BEGIN -- ComputeArea

                      CASE OneFig.FigShape IS
                        WHEN Rect =>
                          RETURN OneFig.Width * OneFig.Height;
                        WHEN Square =>
                          RETURN OneFig.Side ** 2;
                        WHEN Circle =>
                          RETURN Pi * OneFig.Radius ** 2 ;
                      END CASE;

                    END ComputeArea;

                  -- Exported Operators

                    FUNCTION MakeRect (Width, Height : NonNegFloat) RETURN Figure IS

                    -- constructor: creates a rectangular figure from its height and width
                    -- Pre : Width and Height are defined
                    -- Post: returns a figure of type Rect

                      Temp : Figure(FigShape => Rect);

                    BEGIN -- MakeRect

                      Temp.Height    := Height;
                      Temp.Width     := Width;
                      Temp.Area      := ComputeArea(Temp);
                      Temp.Perimeter := ComputePerimeter(Temp);

                      RETURN Temp;

                    END MakeRect;


                    FUNCTION MakeCircle (Radius : NonNegFloat) RETURN Figure IS

                    -- constructor: creates a circular figure from its radius
                    -- Pre : Radius is defined
                    -- Post: returns a figure of type Circle

                      Temp: Figure (FigShape => Circle);

                    BEGIN -- MakeCircle

                      Temp.Radius    := Radius;
                      Temp.Area      := ComputeArea(Temp);
                      Temp.Perimeter := ComputePerimeter(Temp);

                      RETURN Temp;

                    END MakeCircle;
```

```
FUNCTION MakeSquare (Side : NonNegFloat) RETURN Figure IS

-- constructor: creates a square figure from its side
-- Pre : Side is defined
-- Post: returns a figure of type Square

  Temp: Figure (FigShape => Square);

BEGIN -- MakeSquare

  Temp.Side      := Side ;
  Temp.Area      := ComputeArea(Temp);
  Temp.Perimeter := ComputePerimeter(Temp);

  RETURN Temp;

END MakeSquare;


FUNCTION Perimeter (OneFig : Figure) RETURN NonNegFloat IS

-- selector: returns Perimeter of OneFig.
-- Pre : The discriminant field and characteristics of OneFig are defined.
-- Post: Returns Perimeter

BEGIN -- Perimeter

  RETURN OneFig.Perimeter;

END Perimeter;


FUNCTION Area (OneFig : Figure) RETURN NonNegFloat IS

-- selector: returns Area of OneFig.
-- Pre : The discriminant field and characteristics of OneFig are defined.
-- Post: Returns Area

BEGIN -- Area

  RETURN OneFig.Area;

END Area;


PROCEDURE ReadFigure (OneFig : OUT Figure) IS

  Shape  : FigKind;
  Height : NonNegFloat;
  Width  : NonNegFloat;
  Side   : NonNegFloat;
  Radius : NonNegFloat;

BEGIN -- ReadFigure

  -- Read the shape character and define the discriminant
  ReadShape(Shape);

  -- Select the proper variant and read pertinent data
  CASE Shape IS
    WHEN Rect =>
```

```
      Text_IO.Put(Item => "Enter width.");
      Text_IO.New_Line;
      RobustInput.Get(Item => Width, MinVal => 0.0, MaxVal => MaxSize);
      Text_IO.Put(Item => "Enter height.");
      Text_IO.New_Line;
      RobustInput.Get(Item => Height, MinVal => 0.0, MaxVal => MaxSize);
      OneFig := MakeRect(Width, Height);

    WHEN Square     =>
      Text_IO.Put(Item => "Enter length of side.");
      Text_IO.New_Line;
      RobustInput.Get(Item => Side, MinVal => 0.0, MaxVal => MaxSize);
      OneFig := MakeSquare(Side);

    WHEN Circle     =>
      Text_IO.Put(Item => "Enter circle radius.");
      Text_IO.New_Line;
      RobustInput.Get(Item => Radius, MinVal => 0.0, MaxVal => MaxSize);
      OneFig := MakeCircle(Radius);

  END CASE;

END ReadFigure;


PROCEDURE DisplayFigure (OneFig : IN Figure) IS

-- Displays the characteristics of OneFig.
-- Pre : All fields of OneFig are defined.
-- Post: Displays each field of OneFig.

BEGIN -- DisplayFigure

  -- Display shape and characteristics
  Text_IO.Put(Item => "Figure shape: ");
  FigKind_IO.Put(Item => OneFig.FigShape, Width => 1);
  Text_IO.New_Line;

  CASE OneFig.FigShape IS
    WHEN Rect =>
      Text_IO.Put(Item => "height = ");
      My_Flt_IO.Put(Item => OneFig.Height, Fore=>1, Aft=>2, Exp=>0);
      Text_IO.Put(Item => "; width = ");
      My_Flt_IO.Put(Item => OneFig.Width, Fore=>1, Aft=>2, Exp=>0);

    WHEN Square =>
      Text_IO.Put(Item => "side = ");
      My_Flt_IO.Put(Item => OneFig.Side, Fore=>1, Aft=>2, Exp=>0);

    WHEN Circle =>
      Text_IO.Put(Item => "radius = ");
      My_Flt_IO.Put(Item => OneFig.Radius, Fore=>1, Aft=>2, Exp=>0);

  END CASE;

  Text_IO.Put(Item => "; perimeter = ");
  My_Flt_IO.Put(Item => OneFig.Perimeter, Fore=>1, Aft=>2, Exp=>0);
  Text_IO.Put(Item => "; area = ");
  My_Flt_IO.Put(Item => OneFig.Area, Fore=>1, Aft=>2, Exp=>0);
  Text_IO.New_Line;
```

```
END DisplayFigure;

END Geometry;
```

respective fields in the data structure. Program 11.13 shows a brief and straight-forward test program for the package.

Exercises for Section 11.5

Programming

1. Add the variant

```
RightTriangle : (Base, Height : Real);
```

to Figure and modify the operators to include triangles. Use the formulas

$$\text{Area} = 1/2 \text{ Base} \times \text{Height}$$
$$\text{Hypotenuse} = \sqrt{\text{Base}^2 + \text{Height}^2}$$

where Base and Height are the two sides that form the right angle.

Program 11.13 Test Program for Package Geometry

```
WITH Text_IO;
WITH My_Int_IO;
WITH My_Flt_IO;
WITH Geometry;
PROCEDURE TestGeometry IS

   -- program to test package Geometry

   MyFig : Geometry.Figure;              -- a figure

BEGIN -- TestGeometry

   FOR TestTrial IN 1..3 LOOP

      Text_IO.New_Line;
      Text_IO.Put(Item => "     Trial #");
      My_Int_IO.Put(Item => TestTrial, Width => 1);
      Text_IO.New_Line;
      Geometry.ReadFigure (OneFig => MyFig);
      Geometry.DisplayFigure (OneFig => MyFig);
      Text_IO.Put(Item => "Perimeter is ");
      My_Flt_IO.Put(Item=>Geometry.Perimeter(MyFig),Fore=>1,Aft=>2,Exp=>0);
      Text_IO.New_Line;
      Text_IO.Put(Item => "Area is ");
      My_Flt_IO.Put(Item => Geometry.Area (MyFig), Fore=>1, Aft=>2, Exp=>0);
      Text_IO.New_Line;

   END LOOP;

END TestGeometry;
```

```
        Trial #1
Enter a shape: rect, circle, square > triangle
Value not a valid shape. Please try again.
Enter a shape: rect, circle, square > rect
Enter width.
Enter a floating-point value between 0.00 and 1000000.00 > 3.0
Enter height.
Enter a floating-point value between 0.00 and 1000000.00 > 5.0
Figure shape: RECT
height = 5.00; width = 3.00; perimeter = 16.00; area = 15.00
Perimeter is 16.00
Area is 15.00

        Trial #2
Enter a shape: rect, circle, square > circle
Enter circle radius.
Enter a floating-point value between 0.00 and 1000000.00 > 4.0
Figure shape: CIRCLE
radius = 4.00; perimeter = 25.13; area = 50.27
Perimeter is 25.13
Area is 50.27

        Trial #3
Enter a shape: rect, circle, square > square
Enter length of side.
Enter a floating-point value between 0.00 and 1000000.00 > 5.0
Figure shape: SQUARE
side = 5.00; perimeter = 20.00; area = 25.00
Perimeter is 20.00
Area is 25.00
```

11.6 Case Study: Metric System

In many science and engineering problems that model situations in the physical world, the *dimensions* of a quantity are important. Vehicles travel *distances,* moving with certain *velocities*. Objects have *mass*. In the physical world, only certain operations on dimensioned quantities make sense:

- the area of a figure is given by multiplying two lengths;
- multiplying a velocity by a time gives a distance; multiplying a velocity by another velocity gives no meaningful physical result;
- adding one velocity to another, or one length to another, is appropriate, but adding a velocity to a length is not physically meaningful.

In writing modeling programs, we don't get much help from our programming languages in making certain that operations on dimensioned quantities make physical sense. Through package `Calendar`, Ada gives certain assurances that operations on times and elapsed times are meaningful, but that is as far as Ada goes directly. This case study shows how variant records can be used to give a useful representation of dimensioned quantities. Ada's constrained variant records, combined with operator overloading and private types, can be used to great advantage to save a client program from debugging difficulties stemming from mistakes in operations on dimensioned quantities.

Problem

Develop a means of representing dimensioned quantities so that only physically sensible operations are allowed.

Analysis

We will develop a representation of the metric system's mass, length, and time dimensions. In the physical world, the following rules hold:

- Adding and subtracting dimensioned quantities makes sense only if the two quantities have the same dimensions.
- Multiplying and dividing dimensioned quantities is permitted, but the result of a complex calculation must be a physically meaningful quantity. For example,

      (Area * area * area) / (area * length)

- is meaningful because it results in a quantity with volume dimensions.
- Assignment is meaningful only if the dimensions agree on both sides of the assignment.
- Equality and other comparison operations are meaningful only if the dimensions agree; that is, "You can't compare apples and oranges."

Design

We will develop an abstract data type `Metric` for a physical quantity; to do this, we will store the dimensions of the quantity in the three discriminants of a variant record.

Coding the Package Specification

The package specification for `MetricSystem` is given in Program 11.14. Note the way in which the type `Metric` is defined: at the top of the specification, the following lines appear:

```
TYPE     Metric(Mass, Length, Time : Integer) IS PRIVATE;

SUBTYPE Scalar   IS Metric(0, 0, 0);

SUBTYPE Mass     IS Metric(1, 0, 0);
SUBTYPE Length   IS Metric(0, 1, 0);
SUBTYPE Time     IS Metric(0, 0, 1);

SUBTYPE Accel    IS Metric(0, 1, -2);
SUBTYPE Area     IS Metric(0, 2, 0);
SUBTYPE Distance IS Metric(0, 1, 0);
SUBTYPE Velocity IS Metric(0, 1, -1);
SUBTYPE Volume   IS Metric(0, 3, 0);
```

Type `Metric` is a variant record with *three* discriminants for each of the three dimensions. Note that no defaults are given for the discriminants! This is done so that no variable can be unconstrained. It does not make sense for a variable representing length, for example, to change into one representing mass: Physical quantities simply do not change their dimensions!

```
PACKAGE MetricSystem IS

-- This is the specification of the package MetricSystem.
-- Type definition

   TYPE    Metric(Mass, Length, Time : Integer) IS PRIVATE;

   SUBTYPE Scalar   IS Metric(0, 0, 0);

   SUBTYPE Accel    IS Metric(0, 1, -2);
   SUBTYPE Area     IS Metric(0, 2, 0);
   SUBTYPE Length   IS Metric(0, 1, 0);
   SUBTYPE Distance IS Metric(0, 1, 0);
   SUBTYPE Mass     IS Metric(1, 0, 0);
   SUBTYPE Time     IS Metric(0, 0, 1);
   SUBTYPE Velocity IS Metric(0, 1, -1);
   SUBTYPE Volume   IS Metric(0, 3, 0);


   Gram      : CONSTANT Metric;
   METER     : CONSTANT Metric;
   SEC       : CONSTANT Metric;
   Square_M  : CONSTANT Metric;
   Cubic_M   : CONSTANT Metric;
   M_per_Sec : CONSTANT Metric;
   M_per_Sec2 : CONSTANT Metric;

-- dyadic operator to produce a dimensioned quantity from a scalar
-- Value

   FUNCTION "*" (Left : Float; Right : Metric) RETURN Metric;

-- The monadic operators are passed a single variable, Right, of
-- type Metric. Right can be of any subtype of Metric. The
-- result is of the same subtype.

   FUNCTION "+" (Right : Metric) RETURN Metric;
   FUNCTION "-" (Right : Metric) RETURN Metric;
   FUNCTION "abs" (Right : Metric) RETURN Metric;


-- The dyadic operators are passed two variables, Left and Right, of
-- any subtype of Metric (not necessarily the same). The
-- result type depends on the operation and subtypes of the
-- variables passed.


-- "+" and "-" require two variables of the same subtype,
-- they return a variable of the same type passed

   FUNCTION "+" (Left, Right : Metric) RETURN Metric;
   FUNCTION "-" (Left, Right : Metric) RETURN Metric;


-- "*" and "/" require variables of any subtype
-- of Metric. The subtype of the variable returned depends on
-- the types passed and how the operation combines the units.

   FUNCTION "*" (Left, Right : Metric) RETURN Metric;
   FUNCTION "/" (Left, Right : Metric) RETURN Metric;
```

```
--   "<", "<=", ">", ">=" all require two variables of the same
--   subtype and return a boolean variable

FUNCTION "<"  (Left, Right : Metric) RETURN Boolean;
FUNCTION "<=" (Left, Right : Metric) RETURN Boolean;
FUNCTION ">"  (Left, Right : Metric) RETURN Boolean;
FUNCTION ">=" (Left, Right : Metric) RETURN Boolean;

--   Value returns the Float Value of a variable of
--   a subtype of Metric

FUNCTION Value(Left : Metric) RETURN Float;

Dimension_Error : EXCEPTION;

PRIVATE

   TYPE Metric(Mass, Length, Time : Integer) IS RECORD
     Value : Float := 0.0;
   END RECORD;

   Gram        : CONSTANT Metric := (1, 0,  0, 1.0);
   METER       : CONSTANT Metric := (0, 1,  0, 1.0);
   SEC         : CONSTANT Metric := (0, 0,  1, 1.0);
   Square_M    : CONSTANT Metric := (0, 2,  0, 1.0);
   Cubic_M     : CONSTANT Metric := (0, 3,  0, 1.0);
   M_per_Sec   : CONSTANT Metric := (0, 1, -1, 1.0);
   M_per_Sec2  : CONSTANT Metric := (0, 1, -2, 1.0);

END MetricSystem;
```

The type is made PRIVATE so that we can precisely control which operations are available and how they operate. We have also declared a number of subtypes representing some of the more common physical dimensions. In supplying discriminant values, we have made all these subtypes *constrained*. A variable of type Length will always represent a length.

The discriminant values correspond to the physical dimensions: a length value has dimension length[1] and no mass or time component; a volume value has dimension length × length × length, or length[3]; a velocity value has dimensions length/time, or length[1] and time[-1].

There are also several constants partially declared here:

```
   Gram        : CONSTANT Metric;
   Meter       : CONSTANT Metric;
   Sec         : CONSTANT Metric;
   Square_M    : CONSTANT Metric;
   Cubic_M     : CONSTANT Metric;
   M_per_Sec   : CONSTANT Metric;
   M_per_Sec2  : CONSTANT Metric;
```

This is done to allow a client program to label numerical values in expressions:

```
   Speed: Velocity;

   Speed := 35.7 * M_per_Sec;
```

Looking at the private part of the specification, we see the completion of the type definition and the constant declarations:

```
PRIVATE

   TYPE Metric(Mass, Length, Time : Integer) IS RECORD
     Value : Float := 0.0;
   END RECORD;

   Gram       : CONSTANT Metric := (1, 0, 0, 1.0);
   METER      : CONSTANT Metric := (0, 1, 0, 1.0);
   SEC        : CONSTANT Metric := (0, 0, 1, 1.0);
   Square_M   : CONSTANT Metric := (0, 2, 0, 1.0);
   Cubic_M    : CONSTANT Metric := (0, 3, 0, 1.0);
   M_per_Sec  : CONSTANT Metric := (0, 1, -1, 1.0);
   M_per_Sec2 : CONSTANT Metric := (0, 1, -2, 1.0);
```

The record Metric actually has only a fixed part, a Float value, and no variant part. This is an unusual use of variant records, but it works because of Ada's strict rules about operations on constrained variables. The constants simply give "unit" values for each of the dimensions, so that multiplying them by other values does not change those values.

The operations of Metric_System are similar to the ones already available for Float, as given in package Standard. The only operation worthy of note is the first one, which permits values to be given dimensions:

```
FUNCTION "*" (Left : Float; Right : Metric) RETURN Metric;
```

It was this operation that was used above in the assignment to Speed. Finally, an exception Dimension_Error is provided to signal a client program if it attempts a physically meaningless operation such as adding a length to a time.

Coding the Package Body

Program 11.15 shows the body of the package Metric_System. The operations are repetitive and straightforward, requiring no explanation except to point out the local function SameDimensions, which compares the three dimensions of its two parameters. This function is called by many other operations in the package body.

Program 11.15   Body of Package MetricSystem

```
PACKAGE BODY MetricSystem IS

--  This is the implementation of the package MetricSystem.


   -- local function to check whether its arguments have the same dimensions

   FUNCTION SameDimensions(Left, Right :Metric) RETURN Boolean IS
   BEGIN
      RETURN (Left.Length = Right.Length) AND
             Left.Mass = Right.Mass)         AND
             (Left.Time = Right.Time);
   END SameDimensions;
```

```
--  "*" returns a Metric Value gotten by multipying a scalar by a
--  Metric

FUNCTION "*" (Left : Float; Right : Metric) RETURN Metric IS
BEGIN
   RETURN (Right.Mass, Right.Length, Right.Time, Left * Right.Value);
END "*";

--  Value returns the Float Value of a variable of
--  a subtype of Metric

FUNCTION Value(Left : Metric) RETURN Float IS
BEGIN
   RETURN Left.Value;
END Value;

--  The monadic operators are passed a single variable, Right, of
--  type Metric. Right can be of any subtype of Metric. The
--  result is of the same subtype.

FUNCTION "+" (Right : Metric) RETURN Metric IS
BEGIN
   RETURN Right;
END "+";

FUNCTION "-" (Right : Metric) RETURN Metric IS
BEGIN
   RETURN (Right.Mass, Right.Length, Right.Time, -Right.Value);
END "-";

FUNCTION "ABS" (Right : Metric) RETURN Metric IS
BEGIN
   RETURN (Right.Mass, Right.Length, Right.Time, ABS(Right.Value));
END "ABS";


--  The dyadic operators are passed two variables, Left and Right, of
--  any subtype of Metric (not necessarily the same). The
--  result type depends on the operation and subtypes of the
--  variables passed.

--  "+" and "-" require two variables of the same subtype;
--  they return a variable of the same type passed

FUNCTION "+" (Left, Right : Metric) RETURN Metric IS
BEGIN
   IF SameDimensions(Left, Right) THEN
      RETURN (Left.Mass, Left.Length, Left.Time, Left.Value + Right.Value);
   ELSE
      RAISE Dimension_Error;
   END IF;
END "+";

FUNCTION "-" (Left, Right : Metric) RETURN Metric IS
BEGIN
   IF SameDimensions(Left, Right) THEN
      RETURN (Left.Mass, Left.Length, Left.Time, Left.Value - Right.Value);
   ELSE
      RAISE Dimension_Error;
   END IF;
END "-";
```

```
--  "*" and "/" require variables of any subtype
--  of Metric. The subtype of the variable returned depends on
--  the types passed and how the operation combines the units.

FUNCTION "*" (Left, Right : Metric) RETURN Metric IS
BEGIN
  RETURN (Left.Mass + Right.Mass, Left.Length + Right.Length,
          Left.Time + Right.Time, Left.Value * Right.Value);
END "*";

FUNCTION "/" (Left, Right : Metric) RETURN Metric IS
BEGIN
  RETURN (Left.Mass - Right.Mass, Left.Length - Right.Length,
          Left.Time - Right.Time, Left.Value / Right.Value);
END "/";


--  "<", "<=", ">", ">=" all require two variables of the same
--  subtype and return a Boolean variable

FUNCTION "<" (Left, Right : Metric) RETURN Boolean IS
BEGIN
  IF SameDimensions(Left, Right) THEN
    RETURN Left.Value < Right.Value;
  ELSE
    RAISE Dimension_Error;
  END IF;
END "<";

FUNCTION "<=" (Left, Right : Metric) RETURN Boolean IS
BEGIN
  IF SameDimensions(Left, Right) THEN
    RETURN Left.Value <= Right.Value;
  ELSE
    RAISE Dimension_Error;
  END IF;
END "<=";

FUNCTION ">" (Left, Right : Metric) RETURN Boolean IS
BEGIN
  IF SameDimensions(Left, Right) THEN
    RETURN Left.Value > Right.Value;
  ELSE
    RAISE Dimension_Error;
  END IF;
END ">";

FUNCTION ">=" (Left, Right : Metric) RETURN Boolean IS
BEGIN
  IF SameDimensions(Left, Right) THEN
    RETURN Left.Value >= Right.Value;
  ELSE
    RAISE Dimension_Error;
  END IF;
END ">=";

END MetricSystem;
```

Testing the Package

Finally, Program 11.16 shows a short program to test some operators in the package. Notice how the exception blocks are used to report whether an exception was raised without causing the program to terminate. You are encouraged to use this program as a basis for writing your own test programs and applications of MetricSystem.

Program 11.16   Test Program for Package MetricSystem

```
WITH Text_IO;
WITH My_Flt_IO;
WITH MetricSystem; USE MetricSystem;
PROCEDURE TestMetric IS

  -- test some of the operations of the metric system package

  V   : Velocity;
  T   : Time;
  D   : Length;
  A   : Area;
  Vol : Volume;

BEGIN -- TestMetric

  -- these operations should all work correctly

  V := 23.0 * M_per_Sec;
  T := 3600.0 * Sec;

  D := V * T;

  Text_IO.Put("Distance = Rate * Time works as advertised");
  Text_IO.New_Line;
  Text_IO.Put("Distance is ");
  My_Flt_IO.Put(Item => Value(D), Fore => 1, Aft => 2, Exp => 0);
  Text_IO.Put(" meters.");
  Text_IO.New_Line;
  Text_IO.New_Line;

  D := 3.0 * Meter;
  A := D * D;

  Text_IO.Put("Area = Distance * Distance works as advertised");
  Text_IO.New_Line;
  Text_IO.Put("Area is ");
  My_Flt_IO.Put(Item => Value(A), Fore => 1, Aft => 2, Exp => 0);
  Text_IO.Put(" square meters.");
  Text_IO.New_Line;
  Text_IO.New_Line;

  Vol := A * D;

  Text_IO.Put("Volume = Area * Distance works as advertised");
  Text_IO.New_Line;
  Text_IO.Put("Volume is ");
  My_Flt_IO.Put(Item => Value(Vol), Fore => 1, Aft => 2, Exp => 0);
  Text_IO.Put(" cubic meters.");
  Text_IO.New_Line;
  Text_IO.New_Line;
```

```
D := D + D;

Text_IO.Put("Distance = Distance + Distance works as advertised");
Text_IO.New_Line;
Text_IO.Put("Distance is ");
My_Flt_IO.Put(Item => Value(D), Fore => 1, Aft => 2, Exp => 0);
Text_IO.Put(" meters.");
Text_IO.New_Line;
Text_IO.New_Line;

BEGIN -- block for exception handler
  D := D * D;
  Text_IO.Put("Distance = Distance * Distance worked, but should not");
  Text_IO.New_Line;
EXCEPTION
  WHEN Constraint_Error =>
    Text_IO.Put("Constraint Error Raised on Distance = Distance * Distance");
    Text_IO.New_Line;
  WHEN Dimension_Error =>
    Text_IO.Put("Dimension Error Raised on Distance = Distance * Distance");
    Text_IO.New_Line;
END; -- exception block

BEGIN -- block for exception handler
  D := T + D;
  Text_IO.Put("Distance = Time + Distance worked, but should not");
  Text_IO.New_Line;
EXCEPTION
  WHEN Constraint_Error =>
    Text_IO.Put("Constraint Error Raised on Distance = Time + Distance");
    Text_IO.New_Line;
  WHEN Dimension_Error =>
    Text_IO.Put("Dimension Error Raised on Distance = Time + Distance");
    Text_IO.New_Line;
END; -- exception block

END TestMetric;
```

```
Distance = Rate * Time works as advertised
Distance is 82800.00 meters.

Area = Distance * Distance works as advertised
Area is 9.00 square meters.

Volume = Area * Distance works as advertised
Volume is 27.00 cubic meters.

Distance = Distance + Distance works as advertised
Distance is 6.00 meters.

Constraint Error Raised on Distance = Distance * Distance
Dimension Error Raised on Distance = Time + Distance
```

◆◆ 11.7 Tricks of the Trade: Common Programming Errors

When you use multidimensional arrays, make sure the subscript for each dimension is consistent with its declared type. If any subscript value is out of range, Constraint_Error will be raised, of course.

If you use nested FOR loops to process the array elements, make sure that loop control variables used as array subscripts are in the correct order. The order of the loop control variables determines the sequence in which the array elements will be processed.

Understanding variant records is not always easy. In defining variant record structures, remember that the only way to allow for changing the variant stored in a variant record variable is to supply a default value for the discriminant. This action makes the variable unconstrained.

In using variant record variables, keep in mind that the value of the discriminant field determines the form of the variant part that is currently defined; attempting to manipulate any other variant will cause either a compilation error or the raising of Constraint_Error. It is the programmer's responsibility to ensure that the correct variant is being processed; consequently, a variant record should always be manipulated in a CASE statement with the discriminant field used as the CASE selector to ensure that the proper variant part is being manipulated.

Chapter Review

Multidimensional arrays were used to represent tables of information and game boards. Nested loops are needed to manipulate the elements of a mutidimensional array in a systematic way. The correspondence between the loop-control variables and the array subscripts determines the order in which the array elements are processed.

Also in this chapter, we introduced variant records. A variant record is one that can have one of several structures, depending on the value of a special field called the discriminant. We used variant records to represent employee records, geometric figures, and dimensioned quantities in the metric system.

New Ada Constructs in Chapter 11

The new Ada constructs introduced in this chapter are described in Table 11.1.

Table 11.1 Summary of New Ada Constructs

Construct	Effect
Declaring Multidimensional Arrays	

```
SUBTYPE Weeks IS Positive RANGE 1..52;
TYPE Days IS
  (Mon,Tue,Wed,Thu,Fri,Sat,Sun);
```
YearMatrix describes a two-dimensional array with 52 rows and 7 columns (days of the week).

```
TYPE YearMatrix IS
  ARRAY(Weeks,Days) OF Float;
Sales : YearMatrix;
```
Sales is an array of this type and can store 364 float numbers.

Array References
```
Sales := (OTHERS=>(OTHERS=>0.0));
```
Initializes all elements of Sales to zero.

```
My_Flt_IO.Put(Item=>Sales(3, Mon));
```
Displays the element of Sales for Monday of week 3.

```
My_Flt_IO.Get(Item=>Sales(1, Sun));
```
Reads the value for the first Sunday into Sales.

```
TotalSales := 0.0;
FOR Week IN Weeks LOOP
  FOR Today IN Days LOOP
    TotalSales := TotalSales + Sales(Week,Today);
  END LOOP;
END LOOP;
```
Finds the total sales for the entire year.

Variant Record Declaration
```
TYPE KidKind IS (Girl, Boy);
TYPE Child(Sex: KidKind:=Girl) IS RECORD
  First: Character;
  Last: Character;
  Age: Natural;

  CASE Sex IS
    WHEN Girl =>
      Sugar: Float;
      Spice: Float;
    WHEN Boy =>
      Snakes: Integer;
      Snails: Integer;
      Tails: Integer;
  END CASE;

END RECORD;
```
A record type with a variant part is declared. The discriminant is an enumeration value. Each record variable can store two characters and an integer. One variant part can store two float values, and the other can store three integer values.

Table 11.1 *continued*

585

Chapter Review

Construct	Effect
`Kid : Child;`	Kid is a `Child` record.

Referencing a Record Variant

```
CASE Kid.Sex IS
  WHEN Girl =>
    Text_IO.Put(Item => "Lbs. of sugar>");
    My_Flt_IO.Get(Item=>Kid.Sugar);
  WHEN Boy =>
    Text_IO.Put(Item=>"No. of snakes>");
    My_Int_IO.Get(Item=>Kid.Snakes);
END CASE;
```

Uses a CASE statement to read data into the variant part of the record Kid.
If discriminant is Girl, reads a value into the field Kid.Sugar; if the discriminant is Boy, reads a value into the field Kid.Snakes.

✓ *Quick-Check Exercises*

1. How many subscripts can an array have in Ada?
2. What is the difference between row-major and column-major order? Which does Ada use?
3. What does row-major order mean when an array has more than two subscripts?
4. What control structure is used to process all the elements in a multidimensional array?
5. Write a program segment to display the sum of the values (type Float) in each column of a two-dimensional array, Table, with data type ARRAY (1..5, 1..3) OF Float. How many column sums will be displayed? How many elements are included in each sum?
6. Write the type declaration for an array that stores the batting averages by position (Catcher, Pitcher, FirstBase, etc.) for each of 15 baseball teams in each of two leagues (American and National).
7. When should you use a variant record?
8. Explain the use of the discriminant field. Can a variant record have more than one discriminant field?
9. Explain the difference between a constrained variant record and an unconstrained one.

Answers to Quick-Check Exercises

1. There is no specific limit; however, the size of the array is limited by the memory space available, and multidimensional arrays require memory equal to the product of the dimensions, which can be quite large.
2. In row-major order the first row of the array is placed at the beginning of the memory area allocated to the array. It is followed by the second row, and so on. In column-major order, the first column is placed at the beginning of the array memory area. The Ada standard does not specify an ordering, but many compilers use row-major order.
3. If an array Table has N subscripts, the array elements are placed in memory in the

order Table(1,1,...,1,1), Table(1,1,...,1,2), Table(1,1,...,1,3), and so on. Then the next-to-last subscript is changed and the elements Table(1,1,...,2,1), Table(1,1,...,2,2), Table(1,1,...,2,3), ... are placed. The first subscript will be the last one that changes.

4. Nested FOR loops

5.
```
ColumnSum := 0.0;
FOR Column IN 1..3 LOOP
   ColumnSum := 0.0;
   FOR Row IN 1..5 LOOP
      ColumnSum := ColumnSum + Table(Row,Col);
   END LOOP;
   Text_IO.Put(Item=>"Sum for column ");
   My_Int_IO.Put(Item=>Column, Width=>1);
   Text_IO.Put(Item=>"is ");
   My_Int_IO.Put(Item=>ColumnSum);
END LOOP;
```

Three column sums, five elements added per column

6.
```
TYPE Position IS (Pitcher, Catcher, FirstBase, SecondBase, ThirdBase,
   ShortStop, LeftField, CenterField, RightField);
TYPE League IS (American, National);
SUBTYPE Teams IS Positive RANGE 1..15;
TYPE BAArray IS ARRAY (League, Teams, Position) OF Float;
```

7. When an object has some fields that are always the same and a small number of fields that may be different.

8. The discriminant field is a special field of a variant record, used to distinguish between the variants. A record may have more than one discriminant.

9. A constrained variant record is one in which the discriminant is given a value when the variable is declared, which "locks in" the variant. An unconstrained record is one in which a default value was supplied for the discriminant. In an unconstrained record variable, the variant can change over the life of the variable.

Review Questions for Chapter 11

1. Define row-major order and column-major order. For an array type whose three dimensions are (1..4), (2..3), and (5..7), draw storage layouts for both row-major and column-major order.

2. Write the variant declaration for Supplies, which consist of either Paper, Ribbon, or Labels. For Paper, the information needed is the number of sheets per box and the size of the paper. For Ribbon, the size, color, and kind (Carbon or Cloth) are needed. For Labels, the size and number per box are needed. For each supply, the cost, number on hand, and the reorder point must also be stored. Use whatever data types are appropriate for each field.

3. Write the declaration for Vehicle. If the vehicle is a Truck, then BedSize and CabSize are needed. If the vehicle is a Wagon, then third seat or not is needed (Boolean). If the vehicle is a Sedan, then the information needed is TwoDoor or FourDoor. For all vehicles, we need to know whether the transmission is Manual or Automatic; if it has AirConditioning, PowerSteering, or PowerBrakes (all Boolean); and the gas mileage. Use whatever data types are appropriate for each field.

Programming Projects

1. Starting with the tic-tac-toe procedures from Section 11.1, develop an interactive program that allows two persons to play tic-tac-toe against each other.
2. Starting with the class-enrollment program segments in Section 11.2, develop an interactive program for the registrar to use.
3. Write a set of procedures to manipulate a pair of matrices. You should provide procedures for addition, subtraction, and multiplication. Each procedure should validate its input parameters (i.e., check all matrix dimensions) before performing the required data manipulation.
4. The results from the mayor's race have been reported by each precinct as follows:

Precinct	Candidate A	Candidate B	Candidate C	Candidate D
1	192	48	206	37
2	147	90	312	21
3	186	12	121	38
4	114	21	408	39
5	267	13	382	29

Write a program to do the following:
   a. Display the table with appropriate headings for the rows and columns.
   b. Compute and display the total number of votes received by each candidate and the percent of the total votes cast.
   c. If any one candidate received over 50% of the votes, the program should print a message declaring that candidate the winner.
   d. If no candidate received 50% of the votes, the program should print a message declaring a run-off between the two candidates receiving the highest number of votes; the two candidates should be identified by their letter names.
   e. Run the program once with the above data and once with candidate C receiving only 108 votes in precinct 4.
5. Write a program that reads the five cards representing a poker hand into a two-dimensional array (first dimension, suit; second dimension, rank). Evaluate the poker hand by using procedures to determine whether the hand is a flush (all one suit), a straight (five consecutive cards), a straight flush (five consecutive cards of one suit), four of a kind, a full house (three of one kind, two of another), three of a kind, two pair, or one pair.
6. Do Problem 5, but represent a card as a record with two fields representing the suit and the rank, and a poker hand as an array of these records.

Introduction to Unconstrained Array Types and Generics

12

12.1   Data Structures: Unconstrained Array Types
12.2   Case Study: A General Sorting Program
12.3   Case Study: Mathematical Vectors and Matrices
12.4   System Structures: Generic Units
12.5   Case Study: A Generic Sorting Program
12.6   Case Study: A Generic Vector Package
12.7   Tricks of the Trade: Common Programming Errors
       Chapter Review

This chapter introduces you to two features of Ada that make the language extremely useful for developing reusable software components: unconstrained array types and generics. An *unconstrained array type* is one declared in such a way that the bounds of the array are not specified in the type declaration; rather, they are supplied only when a variable of the type is declared. Many arrays of the same number of dimensions but differing sizes can be declared from the same type definition. Moreover, subprograms can be written that accept these arrays as parameters and work with them without knowing their sizes in advance. This is extremely helpful in writing general-purpose programs like sorts and numerical algorithms.

As it happens, we have been using an unconstrained array type all along in this book: Ada's String type is one of these, predefined in Standard. In this chapter you will learn how to define and use unconstrained array types of your own. Understanding unconstrained array types is an important part of understanding how to use generics well; that is why the two subjects are together in this chapter.

A *generic component* (package or subprogram) is one that is parametrized at the level of the types it works with. There are generic formal and actual parameters, just like the "normal" ones we use with subprograms and variant records. A generic component can be instantiated or "tailored" to work with a specific type. This means that a very general program or package can be written, whose code is independent of the type it manipulates. Versions of it can be created with a single statement in each case, to handle many different types.

You have been using several generic units from the start in this book—namely, the Integer_IO, Float_IO, and Enumeration_IO packages incorporated in Text_IO. At the very start of the book we created tailored instances called My_Int_IO and My_Flt_IO, and we have used them right along. Further, we tailored Enumeration_IO for different enumeration types, most recently Dates.Months in Chapter 10. This chapter shows you how to create your own generics and tailor them for many interesting purposes.

Through the careful design of generic units, an entire industry of reusable, tailorable, software components can be built up and used for a wide range of applications. Indeed, several small companies have been quite successful doing exactly that!

❖❖ 12.1 Data Structures: Unconstrained Array Types

The purpose of unconstrained array types is to allow writing subprograms that operate on arrays to be written without prior knowledge of the bounds of the arrays. Let us start with a type definition:

```
TYPE ListType IS ARRAY (Integer RANGE <>) OF Float;
```

The construct Integer RANGE <> means that the subscript range, or bounds, of any variable of type ListType must form an integer subrange; the symbol "<>" is read "box," and means "we'll fill in the missing values when we declare ListType variables."

The type ListType is said to be *unconstrained*. When variables are declared, the compiler must know how much storage to allocate, and so variable declaration *must* carry a range constraint, for example:

```
L1 : ListType(1..50);     -- 50 elements
L2 : ListType(-10..10);   -- 21 elements
L3 : ListType(0..20);     -- 21 elements
```

Operations on Unconstrained Array Types

The operations of assignment and equality testing are defined for unconstrained array types, but for either operation to proceed without raising Constraint_ Error, both operands must be variables of the same unconstrained array type and both operands must have the same number of elements. So

```
L1 := L2;
```

will raise Constraint_Error, but the following operations will all succeed:

```
L2 := L3;
L1 (20..40) := L2;
L2 (1..5) := L1 (6..10);
```

These slicing operations were introduced in Chapter 9 in the discussion of Ada strings. Ada's string type is actually defined in Standard as follows:

```
TYPE String IS ARRAY (Positive RANGE <>) OF Character;
```

making strings just a special case of unconstrained arrays. The slicing operations work for all one-dimensional arrays just as they do for strings.

Attribute Functions for Unconstrained Arrays

Ada defines a number of attribute functions that can be used to determine the bounds of array variables. Given the type ListType above and the variable L2,

L2'First returns the low bound of L2, or − 10 in this case;
L2'Last returns the high bound of L2, or 10;
L2'Length returns the number of elements in L2, or 21; and
L2'Range returns the range − 10..10.

The last attribute is useful in controlling loops, for instance,

```
FOR WhichElement IN L2'Range LOOP
   My_Flt_IO.Put(Item=>L2(WhichElement), Fore=>1, Aft=>2, Exp=>0);
   Text_IO.New_Line;
END LOOP;
```

The construct L2'Range is a short way of writing L2'First..L2'Last, so the same fragment could be written

```
FOR WhichElement IN L2'First..L2'Last LOOP
  My_Flt_IO.Put(Item=>L2(WhichElement), Fore=>1, Aft=>2, Exp=>0);
    Text_IO.New_Line;
END LOOP;
```

■ Example 12.1

To show the utility of unconstrained arrays, consider a function to find the maximum value stored in an array of floating point numbers. For this function to be generally useful and reusable, it needs to be able to work for all kinds of floating-point arrays, no matter what their bounds. Using the type ListType, Program 12.1 shows such a function contained in a test program. The program also contains a procedure DisplayList, which displays the contents of a ListType variable, whatever its bounds. The main program declares two lists of differing bounds, then displays the lists and tests the function MaxValue. From the output of the program, you can see that the maximum is found correctly even though the two lists have different sizes. ■

Program 12.1 A Demonstration of Unconstrained Arrays

```
WITH Text_IO;
WITH My_Flt_IO;
PROCEDURE TestMaxValue IS

  TYPE ListType IS ARRAY(Integer RANGE <>) of Float;

  L1 : ListType(1..5);     -- 5 elements
  L2 : ListType(-4..3);    -- 8 elements

  -- local procedure to display the contents of a list

  PROCEDURE DisplayList(L: ListType) IS

  -- display the contents of a list, represented as an unconstrained array
  -- Pre: L is defined
  -- Post: display all values in the list

  BEGIN -- DisplayList

    FOR Count IN L'Range LOOP
      My_Flt_IO.Put(Item=>L(Count), Fore=>3, Aft=>1, Exp=>0);
    END LOOP;
    Text_IO.New_Line;

  END DisplayList;


  FUNCTION MaxValue(L: ListType) RETURN Float IS

  -- return the largest value in an object of type ListType
  -- Pre: L is defined
  -- Post: returns the largest value stored in L

    CurrentMax : Float;

  BEGIN -- MaxValue

    CurrentMax := Float'First;-- minimum value of Float
```

```
FOR WhichElement IN L'Range LOOP
  IF L(WhichElement) > CurrentMax THEN
    CurrentMax := L(WhichElement);
  END IF;
END LOOP;
-- assert: CurrentMax contains the largest value in L

RETURN CurrentMax;

END MaxValue;


BEGIN -- TestMaxValue

  L1 := (0.0, -5.7, 2.3, 5.9, 1.6);
  L2 := (3.1, -2.4, 0.0, -5.7, 8.0, 2.3, 5.9, 1.6);

  Text_IO.Put(Item=> "Testing MaxValue for float lists");
  Text_IO.New_Line;
  Text_IO.New_Line;
  Text_IO.Put(Item=> "Here is the list L1");
  Text_IO.New_Line;
  DisplayList(L => L1);

  Text_IO.Put(Item=> "The maximum value in this list is ");
  My_Flt_IO.Put(Item => MaxValue(L=>L1),
                Fore=>1, Aft=>2, Exp=>0);
  Text_IO.New_Line;
  Text_IO.New_Line;

  Text_IO.Put(Item=> "Here is the list L2");
  Text_IO.New_Line;
  DisplayList(L => L2);

  Text_IO.Put(Item=> "The maximum value in this list is ");
  My_Flt_IO.Put(Item => MaxValue(L=>L2),
                Fore=>1, Aft=>2, Exp=>0);
  Text_IO.New_Line;

END TestMaxValue;
```

```
Testing MaxValue for float lists

Here is the list L1
  0.0 -5.7  2.3  5.9  1.6
The maximum value in this list is 5.90

Here is the list L2
  3.1 -2.4  0.0 -5.7  8.0  2.3  5.9  1.6
The maximum value in this list is 8.00
```

Slicing and Unconstrained Arrays

In Section 8.10 we studied array slicing in the context of strings. Slicing is actually more general: It is available for *all* one-dimensional unconstrained arrays in Ada. For example, given the function MaxValue from Program 12.1

Unconstrained Array Type

Form: TYPE *ArrayType* IS ARRAY (*IndexType* RANGE <>) OF *ValueType* ;

Example: SUBTYPE DaysInYear IS Positive RANGE 1..366;
           SUBTYPE Temperature IS Float RANGE −100.0 .. 200.0;
           TYPE TemperatureReadings IS
             ARRAY (DaysInYear RANGE <>) OF Temperature;

Interpretation: The array type is declared with minimum and maximum bounds given by *IndexType*. The actual bounds of an array variable must be supplied, as a subrange of *IndexType*, when that variable is declared. It is therefore illegal to declare

    Temps: TemperatureReadings;

Rather, the declaration must include bounds:

    Temps: TemperatureReadings (1..31);

---

and a float variable Y, it is permissible to call MaxValue with a slice as its parameter, as in

    Y := MaxValue(L => L2(0..2));

which would search only the given slice of the array for a maximum value. As an exercise, you can modify Program 12.1 to test this concept.

Exercises for Section 12.1

Programming

1. Modify Program 12.1 to call MaxValue with parameters L1(2..4), L2(0..2), and L2(−4..−1), and ascertain that the program correctly finds the given maximum values.

12.2 Case Study: A General Sorting Program

We have introduced the concept of sorting and sort procedures in earlier chapters. The utility of a sort procedure is greatly enhanced if it can be used with a wide variety of arguments. In this section we develop a sort that will work for arrays of the same unconstrained type but differing bounds; in Section 12.5 we will exploit the full generality of Ada's generics to create a sort that will work with any unconstrained array type at all, regardless of its index type or element type.

Problem

Develop a sort program that will work with arrays of positive numbers indexed by the six major colors: red, orange, yellow, green, blue, and violet. The program should handle correctly arrays of one through six elements.

Analysis and Design

Here is a good application of unconstrained array types. Let us define the two types

```
TYPE  Color IS (Red, Orange, Yellow, Green, Blue, Violet);
TYPE  CrayonVector IS ARRAY(Color RANGE <>) of Natural;
```

and write a procedure Exchange capable of exchanging two elements of type Natural. The procedure SwapSort will implement a very simple sorting algorithm called *exchange sort*.

Algorithm

For each position in the array, starting from the beginning of the array, fill that position with the smallest element in the subarray from that position to the end. This can be refined to

```
FOR each position in the array LOOP
    test each value from this position to the bottom; if the tested value is
    smaller than the value at the position to be filled, exchange the two
    values.
END LOOP;
```

This can be further refined to

```
FOR each position PositionToFill in the array LOOP
    FOR each position ItemToCompare from PositionToFill to the bottom
      of the array LOOP
      IF value at ItemToCompare < value at PositionToFill THEN
        exchange the two values
      END IF;
    END LOOP;
END LOOP;
```

This is not a very efficient sorting method, but its simplicity makes it useful for this example, which is designed to show the array structure without concentrating on the sort method.

Coding

Program 12.2 gives the sort procedure SwapSort, together with auxiliary procedures Exchange and DisplayCrayonVector. The main program declares three arrays of type CrayonVector with differing bounds, and illustrates the sort procedure operating on all three arrays in turn. Note how the attributes are used in SwapSort to make the procedure independent of the bounds of the parameter.

```
WITH Text_IO;
WITH My_Int_IO;
PROCEDURE TestSwapSort IS

    TYPE    Color IS (Red, Orange, Yellow, Green, Blue, Violet);
    TYPE    CrayonVector IS ARRAY(Color RANGE <>) of Natural;

    PACKAGE Color_IO IS NEW Text_IO.Enumeration_IO(Enum => Color);

    V1 : CrayonVector(Red..Green);
    V2 : CrayonVector(Yellow..Violet);
    V3 : CrayonVector(Red..Violet);

    -- local procedure to display the contents of a vector

    PROCEDURE DisplayCrayonVector (V: CrayonVector) IS

    -- display contents of a list represented as an unconstrained array
    -- Pre: V is defined
    -- Post: display all elements in the vector

    BEGIN -- DisplayCrayonVector

      FOR Count IN V'Range LOOP
        Color_IO.Put (Item=>Count,    Width=>6);
        My_Int_IO.Put(Item=>V(Count), Width=>4);
        Text_IO.New_Line;
      END LOOP;
      Text_IO.New_Line;

    END DisplayCrayonVector;

    PROCEDURE Exchange(Value1, Value2: IN OUT Natural) IS

    -- exchange two values
    -- Pre: Value1 and Value2 are defined
    -- Post: Value1 and Value2 are interchanged

      TempValue: Natural;

    BEGIN -- Exchange

      TempValue := Value1;
      Value1    := Value2;
      Value2    := TempValue;

    END Exchange;


    PROCEDURE SwapSort(List: IN OUT CrayonVector) IS

    -- sort elements of a list in ascending order
    -- Pre: List is defined
    -- Post: elements of List are arranged in ascending order

    BEGIN -- SwapSort

      FOR PositionToFill IN List'First..List'Last LOOP

        -- Store in List(PositionToFill) the smallest element remaining
```

```
        -- in the subarray List(PositionToFill..List'Last)

      FOR ItemToCompare IN PositionToFill..List'Last LOOP
        IF List(ItemToCompare) < List(PositionToFill) THEN
          Exchange(List(PositionToFill),List(ItemToCompare));
        END IF;
      END LOOP;
      -- assert: element at List(PositionToFill) is smallest in subarray

    END LOOP;

  END SwapSort;

BEGIN -- TestSwapSort

  V1 := (0, 100, 23, 27);
  V2 := (100, 23, 27, 15);
  V3 := (0, 100, 23, 27, 15, 94);
  Text_IO.New_Line;
  Text_IO.Put(Item=> "Testing SwapSort for crayon vectors");
  Text_IO.New_Line;
  Text_IO.Put(Item=> "Here is the vector V1 before sorting.");
  Text_IO.New_Line;
  DisplayCrayonVector(V => V1);
  Text_IO.New_Line;

  SwapSort(List => V1);
  Text_IO.Put(Item=> "Here is the vector after upward sorting.");
  Text_IO.New_Line;
  DisplayCrayonVector(V => V1);
  Text_IO.New_Line;

  Text_IO.Put(Item=> "Here is the vector V2 before sorting.");
  Text_IO.New_Line;
  DisplayCrayonVector(V => V2);
  Text_IO.New_Line;

  SwapSort(List => V2);
  Text_IO.Put(Item=> "Here is the vector after upward sorting.");
  Text_IO.New_Line;
  DisplayCrayonVector(V => V2);
  Text_IO.New_Line;

  Text_IO.Put(Item=> "Here is the vector V3 before sorting.");
  Text_IO.New_Line;
  DisplayCrayonVector(V => V3);
  Text_IO.New_Line;

  SwapSort(List => V3);
  Text_IO.Put(Item=> "Here is the vector after upward sorting.");
  Text_IO.New_Line;
  DisplayCrayonVector(V => V3);
  Text_IO.New_Line;

END TestSwapSort;


Testing SwapSort for crayon vectors
Here is the vector V1 before sorting.
RED        0
ORANGE 100
```

```
YELLOW   23
GREEN    27
```

```
Here is the vector after upward sorting.
RED       0
ORANGE 23
YELLOW 27
GREEN  100
```

```
Here is the vector V2 before sorting.
YELLOW 100
GREEN    23
BLUE     27
VIOLET   15
```

```
Here is the vector after upward sorting.
YELLOW   15
GREEN    23
BLUE     27
VIOLET 100
```

```
Here is the vector V3 before sorting.
RED        0
ORANGE 100
YELLOW   23
GREEN    27
BLUE     15
VIOLET   94
```

```
Here is the vector after upward sorting.
RED        0
ORANGE   15
YELLOW   23
GREEN    27
BLUE     94
VIOLET 100
```

Unconstrained arrays and slicing make it easier to write programs that deal with partially filled arrays. Look again at Program 8.18, in which an array of scores is sorted. If the score array type were defined as an unconstrained type similar to CrayonVector, and the variable Scores were declared as an array object similar to V1, then the procedure SelectSort would need only a single parameter—namely, the name of the actual array to be sorted. Once Scores was partially filled, the slice Scores(1..ClassSize) could be passed as the single actual parameter. You can make this change as an exercise.

Exercises for Section 12.2

Programming

1. Modify Program 8.18 so that ScoreArray is defined as an unconstrained array type and SelectSort requires only a single parameter.

12.3 Case Study: Mathematical Vectors and Matrices

A vector of N components is a set of N values which is ordered in the sense that each value is assigned a specific "position" in the set. For example, the vector $U = <3, 5, -1>$ is different from the vector $V = <5, -1, 3>$: They both have the same set of values, but they appear in different orders. Generally we implement vectors through the use of one-dimensional arrays.

It is important to realize that the type of a vector's elements need not be numerical, although integers and floats are the types seen most frequently in engineering problems. In Ada, we could of course also have vectors of rational numbers.

Problem
Develop a means of doing arithmetic on mathematical vectors.

Analysis
Mathematicians have defined a number of standard operations on vectors. Among these are several we will study here. In each case, we assume that U and V are vectors with the same element type and number of components; designate the element type as $ElementType$ and the index range, or bounds, of the vectors by the range $R_{min}..R_{max}$.

The *vector sum* of U and V, written $U + V$, is a vector T with bounds $R_{min}..R_{max}$ such that, for each r in the range $R_{min}..R_{max}$

$$T_r = U_r + V_r$$

That is, the components of the two vectors are added pairwise.

The *inner product* of U and V, written $U \cdot V$ and sometimes called the *scalar product* or *dot product*, is a value of type ElementType, whose value is the sum of all the pairwise products

$$U_r \times V_r$$

taken over all the components.

The *sum of V with a scalar K*, written $K + V$, is a vector T, with the same bounds as V, whose components have values

$$T_r = K + V_r$$

The *product of V by a scalar K*, written $K \times V$, is a vector T, with the same bounds as V, whose components have values

$$T_r = K \times V_r$$

Design of the Vector Package
We will develop Vectors as an ADT package, listing the operations above in the specification and implementing them in the package body. We can use an

unconstrained array type for the vectors, so that our vector operations can deal with vectors of differing sizes at different times.

```
TYPE Vector IS ARRAY (Integer RANGE <>) OF Float;
```

Now we can declare `Vector` variables like

```
V: Vector(1..5);
Q: Vector(-5..6);
```

and they'll have the proper dimensions.

Program 12.3 shows the package specification for `Vectors`. The `Vector` type is not defined as private because we wish to allow client programs access to the individual vector components in the usual array-referencing way, and if the type were private that access would be forbidden! The operations are specified as Ada operator symbols, which will allow a client program to write

```
V3 := V2 + V1;
```

for example, just as a mathematician would. An exception `Bounds_Error` is provided by the package, because the vector addition and inner product operations make no sense if their vector operands don't have the same bounds. This precondition will have to be checked in the bodies of these operations; if it is not met, `Bounds_Error` is raised to the client program.

Program 12.3 Specification of Vectors Package ADT

```
PACKAGE Vectors IS

  -- specification for vector arithmetic package

  TYPE Vector IS ARRAY(Integer RANGE <>) OF Integer;

  -- exported exception, raised if two vectors are not conformable
  -- (i.e., have different bounds)

  Bounds_Error : EXCEPTION;

  FUNCTION "+" (K : Integer; Right : Vector) RETURN Vector;
  -- adding a scalar to a vector
  -- Pre: K and Right are defined
  -- Post: returns the sum of the vector and the scalar
  --    Result(i) := K + Right(i)


  FUNCTION "*" (K : Integer; Right : Vector) RETURN Vector;
  -- multiplying a vector by a scalar
  -- Pre: K and Right are defined
  -- Post: returns the product of the vector and the scalar
  --    Result(i) := K * Right(i)
  FUNCTION "*" (Left, Right : Vector) RETURN Integer;
  -- finds the "inner" or "dot" product of two vectors
  -- Pre: Left and Right are defined and have the same bounds
  -- Post: returns the inner product of Left and Right
```

```
FUNCTION "+" (Left, Right : Vector) RETURN Vector;
-- finds the sum of two vectors
-- Pre: Left and Right are defined and have the same bounds
-- Post: returns the sum of Left and Right
--      result(i) := Left(i) + Right(i)


END Vectors;
```

Coding the Body of Vectors

The body of Vectors is shown in Program 12.4. Notice in the scalar addition operation how a vector is created to hold the result: The construct Right'Range is another way to write the longer form Right'First..Right'Last. When the result vector is returned to the calling program, there needs to be a vector there of the proper size to hold it; otherwise, Constraint_Error is raised as usual.

In the inner-product program, the vectors need to have the same bounds; note how the function checks the bounds of the two vector parameters before computing, raising Bounds_Error if the precondition is not met.

As an exercise, you can develop a test program to show that the package operations work as advertised. Be sure to send vectors with mismatched bounds to test the exception raising.

Program 12.4 Body of Vectors Package ADT

```
PACKAGE BODY Vectors IS

  -- body of Vectors package

  FUNCTION "+" (K : Integer; Right : Vector) RETURN Vector IS

  -- adding a scalar to a vector
  -- Pre: K and Right are defined
  -- Post: returns the sum of the vector and the scalar
  --    Result(i) := K + Right(i)

    Result : Vector(Right'Range);

  BEGIN -- "+"

    FOR R IN Right'Range LOOP
      Result(R) := K + Right(R);
    END LOOP;

    RETURN Result;

  END "+";
```

```
FUNCTION "*" (K : Integer; Right : Vector) RETURN Vector IS

-- multiplying a vector by a scalar
-- Pre: K and Right are defined
-- Post: returns the product of the vector and the scalar
--    Result(i) := K * Right(i)

   Result : Vector(Right'Range);

BEGIN -- "*"

   FOR R IN Right'Range LOOP
     Result(R) := K * Right(R);
   END LOOP;

   RETURN Result;

END "*";


FUNCTION "*" (Left, Right : Vector) RETURN Integer IS

-- finds the "inner" or "dot" product of two vectors
-- Pre: Left and Right are defined and have the same bounds
-- Post: returns the inner product of Left and Right

   Sum : Integer;

BEGIN -- "*"

-- First check for conformability
   IF Left'First = Right'First AND
      Left'Last  = Right'Last THEN

     -- if conformable, go on to compute
     Sum := 0;
     FOR R IN Left'Range LOOP
       Sum := Sum + Left(R) * Right(R);
     END LOOP;

     RETURN Sum;
   ELSE
     RAISE Bounds_Error;
   END IF;

END "*";

FUNCTION "+" (Left, Right : Vector) RETURN Vector IS

-- finds the sum of two vectors
-- Pre: Left and Right are defined and have the same bounds
-- Post: returns the sum of Left and Right
--      result(i) := Left(i) + Right(i)

   Result : Vector(Left'Range);

BEGIN -- "+"

-- First check for conformability
   IF Left'First = Right'First AND
      Left'Last  = Right'Last THEN
```

```
        -- if conformable, go on to compute
        FOR R IN Left'Range LOOP
          Result(R) := Left(R) + Right(R);
        END LOOP;

        RETURN Result;

      ELSE
        RAISE Bounds_Error;
      END IF;

  END "+";

END Vectors;
```

Matrix Arithmetic

So far we have seen unconstrained array types with only one dimension. Now we will examine multidimensional unconstrained array types. These are useful in representing tables or mathematical matrices of varying size. As an example, we will consider matrices. Matrix operations can be written in a manner similar to vector ones, using a type definition like

```
TYPE Matrix IS ARRAY (Integer RANGE <>, Integer RANGE <>) OF Float;
```

The two occurrences of the "box" symbol allow (and require) both sets of bounds to be specified when variables are declared. The specification for a package Matrices is shown as Program 12.5.

Program 12.5 Specification for a Matrix Package

```
PACKAGE Matrices IS

  -- specification for package Matrices

  TYPE Matrix IS ARRAY(Integer RANGE <>, Integer RANGE <>) OF Float;

  -- exported exception, raised if two matrices are not conformable
  Bounds_Error : EXCEPTION;

  FUNCTION "+" (K : IN Float; M : IN Matrix) RETURN Matrix;
  -- adds a scalar to a matrix
  -- Pre: K and M are defined
  -- Post: returns the sum of the scalar and the matrix
  --    Result(i,j) := K + M(i,j)

  FUNCTION "*" (K : IN Float; M : IN Matrix) RETURN Matrix;
  -- multiplies a matrix by a scalar
  -- Pre: K and M are defined
  -- Post: returns the product of the scalar and the matrix
  --    Result(i,j) := K * M(i,j)

  FUNCTION "+" (Left, Right : IN Matrix) RETURN Matrix;
  -- finds the sum of two matrices
  -- Pre: Left and Right are defined and have the same bounds
  -- Post: returns the sum of Left and Right
  --    Result(i,j) := Left(i,j) + Right(i,j)
  --    Raises Bounds_Error if the matrices are not conformable
```

```
FUNCTION "*" (Left, Right : IN Matrix) RETURN Matrix;
-- finds the product of two matrices
-- Pre: Left and Right are defined
--    and Left's column bounds agree with Right's row bounds
-- Post: returns the product of Left and Right
--    Raises Bounds_Error if the matrices are not conformable

FUNCTION Transpose(M : IN Matrix) RETURN Matrix;
-- finds the transpose of a matrix
-- Pre: M is defined
-- Post: returns a matrix such that Result(i,j) = M(j,i)
--    Result has M's bounds, interchanged

END Matrices;
```

Assuming M and N are matrices with the same bounds and K is a scalar, the operators $M + N$, $K + M$, and $K \times M$ are similar to their counterparts in the vector case. In the case of matrix addition, the precondition that the matrices must have matching bounds must be checked by the operators.

Here is the code for the matrix sum operation:

```
FUNCTION "+" (K : ElementType; M : IN Matrix) RETURN Matrix IS

   Result : Matrix(M'Range(1), M'Range(2));

BEGIN

   FOR R IN M'Range(1) LOOP
     FOR C IN M'Range(2) LOOP
       Result(R, C) := K + M(R, C);
     END LOOP;
   END LOOP;

   RETURN Result;

END "+";
```

Notice the attributes used to establish the bounds of the parameter and the result: M'First(1) means "the low bound of the first dimension;" M'Last(2) means "the high bound of the second dimension." The construct M'Range(1) is another way to write M'First(1)..M'Last(1). For multidimensional arrays the "dimension number" must be given; for one-dimensional arrays no dimension number is required or permitted.

Mathematically, the *transpose* of a matrix, T, returns a matrix whose second dimension is the same as M's first dimension, and whose first dimension is the same as M's second dimension. For all row and column values r and c, $T_{rc} = M_{cr}$. Here is the corresponding Ada operation:

```
FUNCTION Transpose(M : IN Matrix) RETURN Matrix IS

   Result : Matrix(M'Range(2), M'Range(1));
```

```
BEGIN

    FOR R IN M'Range (2) LOOP
        FOR C IN M'Range (1) LOOP
            Result(R, C) := M(C, R);
        END LOOP;
    END LOOP;

    RETURN Result;

END Transpose;
```

Notice how the bounds are interchanged when the Result variable is declared.

Matrix multiplication $M \times N$, common in many applications, has a definition that is not as obvious as the others. The precondition for multiplication is that the second bounds of M must be the same as the first bounds of N (M must have as many columns as N has rows). The product is a matrix P, with M's row bounds and N's column bounds. So if M has bounds (1..5,–3..0) and N has bounds (−3..0,6..8) then $M \times N$ has bounds (1..5,6..8). Each element of P, designated P_{rc}, is given by the formula

$$P_{rc} = \sum_{k} M_{rk} \times N_{kc}$$

where the index k ranges over the columns of M. Writing and testing the package body for Matrices is left as an exercise.

Exercises for Section 12.3

Programming

1. Write a program to test the vector package. Be sure you test for cases where the vectors have different bounds, to be sure that Bounds_Error is correctly raised.

 # 12.4 System Structures: Generic Units

Ada's system of types and procedures requires that the type of a procedure's actual parameter always match that of the formal parameter. This means that a procedure or function that needs to do the same thing to values of two different types must be written twice—once for each type. Consider the procedure Exchange, used in Program 12.2:

```
PROCEDURE Exchange(Valuel, Value2: IN OUT Natural) IS

    TempValue: Natural;

BEGIN

    TempValue := Valuel;
    Valuel    := Value2;
    Value2    := TempValue;

END Exchange;
```

A procedure to exchange two `Float` values would have the same sequence of statements, but the type references would be different:

```
PROCEDURE Exchange(Value1, Value2: IN OUT Float) IS

   TempValue: Float;

BEGIN

   TempValue := Value1;
   Value1    := Value2;
   Value2    := TempValue;

END Exchange;
```

Obviously, we could modify the first version to give the second version by using an editor. Because we are likely to need the `Natural` version again, we modify a copy of it. This gives two versions of a procedure, which are almost the same; because of overloading, the two can both be called `Exchange`. Carrying this to its extreme, we could build up a large library of `Exchange` programs with our editor and be ready for any eventuality. `Exchange` could even be made to work with array or record structures, because Ada allows assignment for any type.

There is a problem with this approach: It clutters our file system with a large number of similar programs. Worse still, suppose that a bug turns up in the statements for `Exchange` or in another program with more complexity. The bug will have turned up in *one* of the versions; the same bug will probably be present in all of them, but we would probably forget to fix all the others!

It would be nice if we could create *one* version of `Exchange`, test it, then put it in the library. When we needed a version to work with a particular type, we could just tell the compiler to use our pretested `Exchange` but to change the type it accepts. The compiler would make the change automatically, and we would still be left with only a single copy of the procedure to maintain.

It happens that Ada allows us to do exactly this. The solution to this problem is *generics*. A generic unit is a *recipe* or *template* for a procedure, function, or package. Such a unit is declared with *formal parameters* that are *types*, and sometimes that are *procedure* or *function names*. An analogy can be drawn with an unusual recipe for a layer cake: All the elements are there *except* that the following items are left as variables to be plugged in by the baker:

- the number of layers,
- the kind of filling between the layers,
- the flavor of the cake itself, and
- the flavor of the icing.

This recipe was pretested by the cookbook author, but before we can use it for a three-layer yellow cake with marshmallow filling and chocolate icing, we need to (at least mentally) make all the changes necessary to the ingredients list. Only after this *instance* of the recipe has been created does it make sense to try to make a cake using it.

■ Example 12.2

Here is a specification for a generic exchange program:

```
GENERIC
   TYPE ValueType  IS PRIVATE;   -- any non-limited type will do
PROCEDURE GenericSwap(Value1, Value2: IN OUT ValueType);
```

This specification tells the compiler that we wish ValueType to be a formal parameter. The formal parameters are listed between the word GENERIC and the procedure heading. Writing

```
TYPE ValueType IS PRIVATE;
```

tells the compiler that *any* type, *including* a private one, can be plugged in as the kind of element to exchange. We will introduce more examples of type parameters below.   ■

Here is the body of GenericSwap:

```
PROCEDURE GenericSwap(Value1, Value2: IN OUT ValueType) IS

   TempValue: ValueType;

BEGIN

   TempValue := Value1;
   Value1    := Value2;
   Value2    := TempValue;

END GenericSwap;
```

Notice that GenericSwap looks essentially the same as the integer and float versions, except for the use of ValueType wherever a type is required. ValueType is a *formal type parameter*.

Creating a file containing the specification and the body (many Ada compilers require both to be in the same file), then compiling this file, creates a version of the generic that is ready to be *instantiated*, or tailored by plugging in the desired type. This is shown as Program 12.6. Here are two instances:

```
PROCEDURE IntegerSwap IS NEW GenericSwap (ValueType => Integer);
PROCEDURE CharSwap    IS NEW GenericSwap (ValueType => Character);
```

The notation is familiar; we have used it in creating instances of Text_IO. Enumeration_IO. Program 12.7 shows how GenericSwap could be tested and used. The two instantiations above appear in the program.

Program 12.6 Generic Exchange Procedure

```
-- specification for procedure GenericSwap
GENERIC
  TYPE ValueType IS PRIVATE;  -- any type except a LIMITED PRIVATE is OK
PROCEDURE GenericSwap(Value1, Value2: IN OUT ValueType);
```

```
-- body for procedure GenericSwap
PROCEDURE GenericSwap(Value1, Value2: IN OUT ValueType) IS

    -- generic exchange procedure, must be instantiated
    -- Pre: Value1 and Value2 are defined
    -- Post: Value1 and Value2 are interchanged

    TempValue: ValueType;

BEGIN -- GenericSwap

    TempValue := Value1;
    Value1    := Value2;
    Value2    := TempValue;

END GenericSwap;
```

Program 12.7 A Test of the Generic Swap Program

```
WITH GenericSwap;
WITH Text_IO;
WITH My_Int_IO;
PROCEDURE TestGenericSwap IS

    -- Test program for GenericSwap

    X : Integer;
    Y : Integer;

    A : Character;
    B : Character;

    PROCEDURE IntegerSwap IS NEW GenericSwap (ValueType => Integer);
    PROCEDURE CharSwap IS NEW GenericSwap (ValueType => Character);

BEGIN -- TestGenericSwap

    X := 3;
    Y := -5;
    A := 'x';
    B := 'q';

    Text_IO.Put("Before swapping, X and Y are, respectively ");
    My_Int_IO.Put(Item => X, Width => 4);
    My_Int_IO.Put(Item => Y, Width => 4);
    Text_IO.New_Line;

    IntegerSwap(Value1 => X, Value2 => Y);

    Text_IO.Put("After swapping, X and Y are, respectively ");
    My_Int_IO.Put(Item => X, Width => 4);
    My_Int_IO.Put(Item => Y, Width => 4);
    Text_IO.New_Line;
    Text_IO.New_Line;

    Text_IO.Put("Before swapping, A and B are, respectively ");
    Text_IO.Put(Item => A);
    Text_IO.Put(Item => B);
    Text_IO.New_Line;
```

```
    CharSwap(Valuel => A,Value2 => B);

    Text_IO.Put("After swapping, A and B are, respectively ");
    Text_IO.Put(Item => A);
    Text_IO.Put(Item => B);
    Text_IO.New_Line;

END TestGenericSwap;
```

```
Before swapping, X and Y are, respectively    3  -5
After  swapping, X and Y are, respectively   -5   3

Before swapping, A and B are, respectively xq
After  swapping, A and B are, respectively qx
```

Generic Subprogram Parameters

Sometimes, a generic recipe needs to be instantiated with the names of functions
or procedures. To continue the food analogy, a certain fish recipe can be
prepared by either baking or broiling; the rest of the recipe is independent. So
the action "desired cooking method" would be a parameter of that recipe.

■ Example 12.3

Back in Program 4.7, we developed a function called Maximum, which returned
the larger of its two Integer operands:

```
FUNCTION Maximum (Valuel, Value2: Integer) RETURN Integer IS

    Result: Integer;

BEGIN

    IF Valuel > Value2 THEN
      Result := Valuel;
    ELSE
      Result := Value2;
    END IF;

    RETURN Result;

END Maximum;
```

We would like to make a function that returns the larger of its two operands,
regardless of the types of these operands. As in the case of GenericSwap, we can use
a generic type parameter to indicate that an instance can be created for any
type. This is not enough, however. The IF statement compares the two input
values: Suppose the type we use to instantiate does not have an obvious, predefined, "greater than" operation? Suppose the type is a user-defined record
with a key field, for example? "Greater than" is not predefined for records! We
can surely write such an operation, but we need to inform the compiler to use
it; when writing a generic, we need to reassure the compiler that all the operations used in the body of the generic will exist at instantiation time. Let us tell

the compiler in the generic specification that a comparison function will exist. Here is the desired generic specification:

```
GENERIC

  TYPE ValueType IS PRIVATE;
  WITH FUNCTION Compare(Value1,Value2: ValueType) RETURN Boolean;

FUNCTION GenericMaximum(Value1, Value2: ValueType) RETURN ValueType;
```

The WITH syntax here is strange and takes getting used to, but it works. The body of the generic function looks similar to the one just given for Maximum.

```
FUNCTION GenericMaximum(Value1,Value2: ValueType) RETURN ValueType IS

  Result: ValueType;

BEGIN

  IF Compare(Value1 , Value2) THEN
    Result := Value1;
  ELSE
    Result := Value2;
  END IF;

  RETURN Result;

END GenericMaximum;
```

An instantiation for Float values might be

```
FUNCTION FloatMax IS
  NEW GenericMaximum (ValueType=>Float, Compare=> ">");
```

Notice how the "greater than" operator is supplied. It makes no difference that the generic expected a function and we gave it an operator; after all, an operator *is* a function. What is important is that the *structure* of the actual parameter matches the structure of the formal parameter. As long as there is a ">" available for Float (of course there is, in Standard), the instantiation will succeed.

The Ada compiler has no idea what the function Compare will do when the generic is instantiated. It turns out, then, that if we just supply "<" as an actual parameter for Compare, the instantiation finds the minimum instead of the maximum!

In Section 5.7 we developed a package UsefulFunctions (Programs 5.15 and 5.16) which contains maximum and minimum operations for both Integer and Float. There are four almost identical functions bodies there. With our knowledge of generics, we could rewrite those four bodies using four instances of the single generic above:

```
FUNCTION Maximum IS
  NEW GenericMaximum (ValueType=>Float,    Compare=> ">");

FUNCTION Maximum IS
  NEW GenericMaximum (ValueType=>Integer, Compare=> ">");

FUNCTION Minimum IS
  NEW GenericMaximum (ValueType=>Float,    Compare=> "<");
```

```
FUNCTION Minimum IS
  NEW GenericMaximum (ValueType=>Integer, Compare=> "<");
```

GenericMaximum is shown as Program 12.8. To show that it works, Program 12.9 tests these four instantiations. ∎

Program 12.8 Generic Maximum Function

```
-- specification for GenericMaximum
GENERIC
  TYPE ValueType IS PRIVATE;
  WITH FUNCTION Compare(L, R : ValueType) RETURN Boolean;
FUNCTION GenericMaximum(L, R : ValueType) RETURN ValueType;

-- body of Generic Maximum
FUNCTION GenericMaximum(L, R : ValueType) RETURN ValueType IS

  -- generic version of maximum finder.
  -- Pre: L and R are defined
  -- Post: returns the "larger" of L and R, that is, L if the comparison
  --   is true and R otherwise.

BEGIN -- GenericMaximum

  IF Compare(L, R) THEN
    RETURN L;
  ELSE
    RETURN R;
  END IF;

END GenericMaximum;
```

Program 12.9 A Test of the Generic Maximum Program

```
WITH Text_IO;
WITH My_Flt_IO;
WITH My_Int_IO;
WITH GenericMaximum;
PROCEDURE TestGenericMaximum IS

  -- test program for Generic Maximum, using four instances

  FUNCTION Maximum IS NEW GenericMaximum (ValueType=>Float,   Compare=> ">");
  FUNCTION Maximum IS NEW GenericMaximum (ValueType=>Integer, Compare=> ">");
  FUNCTION Minimum IS NEW GenericMaximum (ValueType=>Float,   Compare=> "<");
  FUNCTION Minimum IS NEW GenericMaximum (ValueType=>Integer, Compare=> "<");

BEGIN -- TestGenericMaximum

  Text_IO.Put("Maximum of -3 and 7 is ");
  My_Int_IO.Put(Item => Maximum(-3, 7), Width=>1);
  Text_IO.New_Line;
  Text_IO.Put("Minimum of -3 and 7 is ");
  My_Int_IO.Put(Item => Minimum(-3, 7), Width=>1);
  Text_IO.New_Line;
  Text_IO.Put("Maximum of -3.29 and 7.84 is ");
  My_Flt_IO.Put(Item => Maximum(-3.29, 7.84), Fore=>1, Aft=>2, Exp=>0);
```

```
    Text_IO.New_Line;
    Text_IO.Put("Minimum of -3.29 and 7.84 is ");
    My_Flt_IO.Put(Item => Minimum(-3.29, 7.84), Fore=>1, Aft=>2, Exp=>0);
    Text_IO.New_Line;

END TestGenericMaximum;
```

```
Maximum of -3 and 7 is 7
Minimum of -3 and 7 is -3
Maximum of -3.29 and 7.84 is 7.84
Minimum of -3.29 and 7.84 is -3.29
```

Generic Array Parameters

An important use for generics, combined with unconstrained array types, is building very general subprograms to deal with arrays. For a generic to be instantiated for many different array types, we need to specify formal parameters for the index and array types.

■ Example 12.4

Here is a specification for a function `GenericArrayMaximum` that returns the "largest" of all the elements in an array, regardless of the index or element type. "Largest" is in quotes because we know already that we can make it work as a minimum-finder as well.

```
GENERIC

    TYPE ValueType IS PRIVATE;
    TYPE IndexType IS (<>);
    TYPE ArrayType IS ARRAY(IndexType RANGE <>) OF ValueType;
    WITH FUNCTION Compare (Value1, Value2 : ValueType) RETURN Boolean;

FUNCTION GenericArrayMaximum (List: IN ArrayType) RETURN ValueType;
```

The syntax of the specification for `IndexType` is again strange; it means "any discrete type is OK as an actual parameter." Recalling that discrete types are the integer and enumeration types and subtypes, this is exactly what we need for the index type of the array. The specification for `ArrayType` looks like a type declaration, but *it is not*. Rather, it is a description to the compiler of the *kind* of array type acceptable as an actual parameter. In this case, the array type must be indexed by `IndexType` (or a subtype thereof) and have elements of type `Valuetype` (or a subtype thereof).

Here is the body:

```
FUNCTION GenericArrayMaximum (List: IN ArrayType) RETURN ValueType IS

    Result : ValueType;

BEGIN
```

```
        Result := List(List'First);
        FOR WhichElement IN List'Range LOOP
          IF Compare(List(WhichElement), Result) THEN
            Result := List(WhichElement);
          END IF;
        END LOOP;
        RETURN Result;

      END GenericArrayMaximum;
```

You can write a test program for this as an exercise. As a hint, consider the declarations from Program 12.2:

```
    TYPE    Color IS (Red, Orange, Yellow, Green, Blue, Violet);
    TYPE    CrayonVector IS ARRAY(Color RANGE <>) of Natural;
```

and instantiate the generic as follows:

```
    FUNCTION Maximum IS
      NEW GenericArrayMaximum(ValueType=>Natural, IndexType=>Color,
                              ArrayType=>CrayonVector, Compare=>">");   ■
```

Exercises for Section 12.4

Self-Check

1. Review the ADTs we developed in Chapters 10 and 11. For which ones could GenericSwap *not* be instantiated? How about GenericMaximum?

Programming

1. Modify the test program for GenericSwap to instantiate for some other types. Try it for Rational and VString; don't forget the context clauses for those packages.
2. Repeat Problem 1 for GenericMaximum.
3. Write a test program for GenericArrayMaximum as suggested in the section. Use combinations of Float, Integer, and Color as index and value types.

 # 12.5 Case Study: A Generic Sorting Program

Let us continue our study of generics with the development of a generic sort procedure that uses much of what we have done in the chapter.

Problem

Develop a sort procedure that will work correctly for *any* variable of *any* unconstrained array type, regardless of its bounds, index type, or element type.

Analysis and Design

In Program 12.2 we developed SwapSort, which works for any array of a *particular* unconstrained array type. We just need to modify it to make it generic. We also have a procedure GenericSwap, which we can use to handle exchanges.

Coding

Here is the specification for the generic sort routine:

```
GENERIC -- procedure specification for GenericSwapSort

   -- here are all the generic formal parameters
   TYPE ElementType IS PRIVATE;   -- any non-limited type will do
   TYPE IndexType   IS (<>);      -- any discrete type for index
   TYPE ListType    IS ARRAY (IndexType RANGE <>) OF ElementType;
   WITH FUNCTION Compare (Left, Right : ElementType) RETURN Boolean;

   PROCEDURE GenericSwapSort(List: IN OUT ListType);
```

This is similar to `GenericArrayMaximum` from Section 12.4. With your current knowledge of generics, you can understand this specification easily. The entire generic can be found in Program 12.10. Notice that there the body begins with the context clause

```
WITH GenericSwap;
```

and instantiates this procedure for whatever the element type turns out to be. We have here a case of one generic instantiating another; this is the kind of situation that demonstrates the power of generics to help write very general programs. The rest of the procedure body is very similar to `SwapSort` (Program 12.2), with the necessary modifications. Program 12.11 demonstrates the sort for two entirely different array types.

Program 12.10 Generic Sort Procedure

```
-- procedure specification for GenericSwapSort
GENERIC

   -- here are all the generic formal parameters
   TYPE ElementType IS PRIVATE;   -- any nonlimited type will do
   TYPE IndexType   IS (<>);      -- any discrete type for index
   TYPE ListType    IS ARRAY (IndexType RANGE <>) OF ElementType;
   WITH FUNCTION Compare (Left, Right : ElementType) RETURN Boolean;

PROCEDURE GenericSwapSort(List: IN OUT ListType);


-- procedure body for GenericSwapSort
WITH GenericSwap;                 -- context clause
PROCEDURE GenericSwapSort(List: IN OUT ListType) IS

   -- we need to make an instance of GenericSwap for this case
   PROCEDURE Exchange IS NEW GenericSwap (ValueType => ElementType);

BEGIN -- GenericSwapSort

   FOR PositionToFill IN List'First..List'Last LOOP

      -- Store in List(PositionToFill) the "largest" element remaining
      -- in the subarray List(PositionToFill..List'Last)

      FOR ItemToCompare IN PositionToFill..List'Last LOOP
         IF Compare(List(ItemToCompare),  List(PositionToFill)) THEN
            Exchange(List(PositionToFill), List(ItemToCompare));
```

```
      END IF;
    END LOOP;
    -- assert: element at List(PositionToFill) is "largest" in subarray

  END LOOP;

END GenericSwapSort;
```

Program 12.11   A Test of the Generic Sort Program

```
WITH Text_IO;
WITH My_Int_IO;
WITH My_Flt_IO;
WITH GenericSwapSort;
PROCEDURE TestGenericSort IS

   TYPE    Color IS (Red, Orange, Yellow, Green, Blue, Violet);
   TYPE    CrayonVector IS ARRAY(Color RANGE <>) of Natural;

   PACKAGE Color_IO IS NEW Text_IO.Enumeration_IO(Enum => Color);

   SUBTYPE Index IS Integer RANGE 1..10;
   TYPE    FloatVector IS ARRAY(Index RANGE <>) OF Float;

   V1 : FloatVector(1..10);
   V2 : CrayonVector(Red..Violet);

   -- local procedures to display the contents of a vector

   PROCEDURE DisplayCrayonVector (V: CrayonVector) IS
   BEGIN
     FOR Count IN V'First..V'Last LOOP
       Color_IO.Put (Item=>Count,    Width=>6);
       My_Int_IO.Put(Item=>V(Count), Width=>4);
       Text_IO.New_Line;
     END LOOP;
     Text_IO.New_Line;
   END DisplayCrayonVector;

   PROCEDURE DisplayFloatVector (V: FloatVector) IS
   BEGIN
     FOR Count IN V'First..V'Last LOOP
       My_Flt_IO.Put(Item=>V(Count), Fore=>4, Aft=>2, Exp=>0);
     END LOOP;
     Text_IO.New_Line;
   END DisplayFloatVector;

   -- two instances of GenericSwapSort for Float vectors;
   -- the first sorts in increasing order, the second in decreasing order

   PROCEDURE SortUpFloat IS NEW GenericSwapSort
     (ElementType => Float,
      IndexType   => Index,
      ListType    => FloatVector,
      Compare     => "<");

   PROCEDURE SortDownFloat IS NEW GenericSwapSort
     (ElementType => Float,
      IndexType   => Index,
```

```
      ListType    => FloatVector,
      Compare     => ">");

   -- two instances of GenericSwapSort for Float vectors;
   -- the first sorts in increasing order, the second in decreasing order

   PROCEDURE SortUpCrayon IS NEW GenericSwapSort
     (ElementType => Natural,
      IndexType   => Color,
      ListType    => CrayonVector,
      Compare     => "<");

   PROCEDURE SortDownCrayon IS NEW GenericSwapSort
     (ElementType => Natural,
      IndexType   => Color,
      ListType    => CrayonVector,
      Compare     => ">");

BEGIN -- TestGenericSort

   V1 := (0.7, 1.5, 6.9, -3.2, 0.0, 5.1, 2.0, 7.3, 2.2, -5.9);
   Text_IO.New_Line;
   Text_IO.Put(Item=> "Testing GenericSwapSort for float vectors");
   Text_IO.New_Line;
   Text_IO.Put(Item=> "Here is the vector before sorting.");
   Text_IO.New_Line;
   DisplayFloatVector(V => V1);
   Text_IO.New_Line;

   SortUpFloat(List => V1);
   Text_IO.Put(Item=> "Here is the vector after upward sorting.");
   Text_IO.New_Line;
   DisplayFloatVector(V => V1);
   Text_IO.New_Line;

   SortDownFloat(List => V1);
   Text_IO.Put(Item=> "Here is the vector after downward sorting.");
   Text_IO.New_Line;
   DisplayFloatVector(V => V1);
   Text_IO.New_Line;

   V2 := (0, 100, 23, 27, 15, 94);
   Text_IO.New_Line;
   Text_IO.Put(Item=> "Testing GenericSwapSort for crayon vectors");
   Text_IO.New_Line;
   Text_IO.Put(Item=> "Here is the vector before sorting.");
   Text_IO.New_Line;
   DisplayCrayonVector(V => V2);
   Text_IO.New_Line;

   SortUpCrayon(List => V2);
   Text_IO.Put(Item=> "Here is the vector after upward sorting.");
   Text_IO.New_Line;
   DisplayCrayonVector(V => V2);
   Text_IO.New_Line;

   SortDownCrayon(List => V2);
   Text_IO.Put(Item=> "Here is the vector after downward sorting.");
   Text_IO.New_Line;
   DisplayCrayonVector(V => V2);

END TestGenericSort;
```

```
Testing GenericSwapSort for float vectors
Here is the vector before sorting.
    0.70    1.50    6.90   -3.20    0.00    5.10    2.00    7.30    2.20   -5.90

Here is the vector after upward sorting.
   -5.90   -3.20    0.00    0.70    1.50    2.00    2.20    5.10    6.90    7.30

Here is the vector after downward sorting.
    7.30    6.90    5.10    2.20    2.00    1.50    0.70    0.00   -3.20   -5.90


Testing GenericSwapSort for crayon vectors
Here is the vector before sorting.
RED      0
ORANGE 100
YELLOW  23
GREEN   27
BLUE    15
VIOLET  94


Here is the vector after upward sorting.
RED      0
ORANGE  15
YELLOW  23
GREEN   27
BLUE    94
VIOLET 100


Here is the vector after downward sorting.
RED    100
ORANGE  94
YELLOW  27
GREEN   23
BLUE    15
VIOLET   0
```

Using the Generic Sort to Order an Array of Records

GenericSwapSort can be especially useful in sorting arrays of records. Recall
the student grade record we used in Section 8.12:

```
MaxSize : CONSTANT Positive := 250;
MaxScore : CONSTANT Positive := 100;

SUBTYPE StudentName IS String(1..20);
SUBTYPE ClassIndex  IS Positive RANGE 1..MaxSize;
SUBTYPE ClassRange  IS Natural RANGE 0..MaxSize;
SUBTYPE ScoreRange  IS Natural RANGE 0..MaxScore;

TYPE ScoreRecord IS RECORD
   Name:  StudentName;
   Score: ScoreRange;
END RECORD;
```

Let us modify the definition of a score array to make it an unconstrained type:

```
TYPE ScoreArray IS ARRAY (ClassIndex RANGE <>) OF ScoreRecord;
```

Here is a "compare" function that tells us whether one record is "less than" another (in the sense that one score is lower than the other):

```
FUNCTION ScoreLess(Score1, Score2 : ScoreRecord) RETURN Boolean IS
BEGIN
  RETURN Score1.Score < Score2.Score;
END ScoreLess;
```

This function compares the score fields of the two records, returning `True` if the first record is "less than" the second and `False` otherwise. We could have named this function "<", of course, but chose not to do so in the interest of clarity. Given `GenericSwapSort`, it takes only a single instantiation statement to create a sort that will order an array of score records in ascending order:

```
PROCEDURE SortUpScores IS NEW GenericSwapSort
  (ElementType => ScoreRecord,
   IndexType   => ClassIndex,
   ListType    => ScoreArray,
   Compare     => ScoreLess);
```

Given variables `Scores` and `ClassSize` as follows:

```
Scores: ScoreArray(ClassIndex'First..ClassIndex'Last);
ClassSize: ClassRange;
```

we see that `Scores` can hold up to 250 records (as in Section 8.12), and `ClassSize` can be used to determine the actual number of records read from a file into the array. The array can easily be put in ascending order by score, just by calling `SortUpScores` with the appropriate array slice:

```
SortUpScores(List => Scores(1..ClassSize));
```

Exercises for Section 12.5

Self-Check

1. Explain how `GenericSwapSort` could be instantiated to order an array of score records in alphabetical order by the name of the student.
2. Explain how `GenericSwapSort` could be instantiated to order an array of score records in descending order by score.

Programming

1. Modify `TestGenericSort` so that the element type is a type we have defined in this book. Try it for `Rational`, for example.

 ## 12.6 Case Study: A Generic Vector Package

The generics written in the previous sections are all single procedures or functions. Generics can, and often are, used to build *packages* also. We conclude our study of generics by showing how to build a generic version of the Vectors package introduced in Section 12.3. Program 12.12 gives the specification of the package. The specification promises that we will provide actual parameters for the index type and value type; the package itself will create the vector type

Program 12.12   Specification for Generic Vector Package

```
GENERIC

    TYPE ValueType IS PRIVATE;
    TYPE IndexType IS (<>);

    WITH FUNCTION "+"(L,R: ValueType) RETURN ValueType;
    WITH FUNCTION "*"(L,R: ValueType) RETURN ValueType;

    Zero: ValueType;

PACKAGE GenericVectors IS

    -- generic specification for vector arithmetic package

    TYPE Vector IS ARRAY(IndexType RANGE <>) OF ValueType;

    -- exported exception, raised if two vectors are not conformable
    -- (i.e., have different bounds)

    Bounds_Error : EXCEPTION;

    FUNCTION "+" (K : ValueType; Right : Vector) RETURN Vector;

    -- adding a scalar to a vector
    -- Pre: K and Right are defined
    -- Post: returns the sum of the vector and the scalar
    --    Result(i) := K + Right(i)


    FUNCTION "*" (K : ValueType; Right : Vector) RETURN Vector;

    -- multiplying a vector by a scalar
    -- Pre: K and Right are defined
    -- Post: returns the product of the vector and the scalar
    --    Result(i) := K * Right(i)


    FUNCTION "*" (Left, Right : Vector) RETURN ValueType;

    -- finds the "inner" or "dot" product of two vectors
    -- Pre: Left and Right are defined and have the same bounds
    -- Post: returns the inner product of Left and Right


    FUNCTION "+" (Left, Right : Vector) RETURN Vector;

    -- finds the sum of two vectors
    -- Pre: Left and Right are defined and have the same bounds
    -- Post: returns the sum of Left and Right
    --    Result(i) := Left(i) + Right(i)


END GenericVectors;
```

so that a client program can use it, just like any other type provided by a package. The two WITH FUNCTION lines are necessary because the body of the package adds and multiplies elements—for example, in the dot product function. Finally, the line

```
Zero: ValueType;
```

promises that we will supply a "zero" value for the element type. Because in the inner product routine the Sum variable needs to be set to zero, this parameter is necessary. We cannot simply write

```
Sum := 0.0;
```

as in the nongeneric version; suppose ValueType is not Float? Then 0.0 does not exist! Instead, we need to write

```
Sum := Zero;
```

and pass the value of Zero as a generic parameter. You can write the package body as an exercise; it will be similar to the one shown in Program 12.4. A sample compilable instantiation, which will provide vectors of Float values, indexed by Integer ranges, is

```
WITH GenericVectors;
PACKAGE FloatVectors IS NEW GenericVectors
  (ValueType => Float,
   IndexType => Integer,
   "+" => "+",
   "*" => "*",
   Zero => 0.0);
```

A client program could use this instance by writing the context clause

```
WITH FloatVectors;
```

just as we have done many times for My_Int_IO, My_Flt_IO, Months_IO, and others.

Generic Specification

Form:
GENERIC
    list of generic formal parameters
PROCEDURE *pname* (*list of procedure parameters*);

GENERIC
    list of generic formal parameters
FUNCTION *fname* (*list of function parameters*) RETURN *resulttype*;

GENERIC
    list of generic formal parameters
PACKAGE *pname* IS
    specifications of resources provided by the package
END *pname* ;

Example: GENERIC

```
        TYPE ValueType IS PRIVATE;
        TYPE IndexType IS ( <> );

        WITH FUNCTION "+"(L,R: ValueType) RETURN ValueType;
        WITH FUNCTION "*"(L,R: ValueType) RETURN ValueType;

        Zero: ValueType;

    PACKAGE Matrices IS

        TYPE Matrix IS
            ARRAY(IndexType RANGE <>, IndexType RANGE <>) OF ValueType;

        Bounds_Error: EXCEPTION;

        FUNCTION "+"(L, R: Matrix) RETURN Matrix;
        FUNCTION "*"(L, R: Matrix) RETURN Matrix;
        FUNCTION Transpose(M: Matrix) RETURN Matrix;

    END Matrices;
```

Interpretation: The generic specification defines a generic procedure, function, or package, for which a corresponding body must also be provided. The list of generic formal type, procedure or function, and object parameters indicates the structure of the parameters to be supplied at instantiation of the generic.

Here are the forms of the generic type parameters we have seen here, and their interpretation. There are other generic type parameters, but their discussion is beyond the scope of this book. This form:

```
    TYPE ValueParameterName IS PRIVATE;
```

most commonly used as a value parameter, indicates that any type can be matched at instantiation, including a private type, as long as it is not LIMITED PRIVATE. That is, the operations of assignment and equality testing must be defined for the type. This form:

```
    TYPE IndexParameterName IS ( <> );
```

indicates that any discrete type—that is, an integer or enumeration type or subtype—can be matched at instantiation. This form is commonly used to specify the index type of an array type. This form:

```
    TYPE ArrayParameterName IS
        ARRAY(IndexParameterName RANGE <>) OF ValueParameterName;
```

indicates that any unconstrained array type with the given index and value types can be matched at instantiation.

12.7 Tricks of the Trade: Common Programming Errors

When dealing with unconstrained array types, a common error is neglecting to supply bounds when a variable is declared, which leads to a compilation error. Keep in mind that bounds are generally not supplied when declaring a procedure or function parameter whose type is an unconstrained array type.

When writing generic specifications, it is sometimes difficult to figure out exactly which formal parameters to write. We have studied generic type parameters only briefly, and you are wise to keep your generic specifications simple, following the examples in the chapter. Neglecting to supply a generic procedure or function parameter (such as "+" in the vectors package) will result in a compilation error if the compiler encounters that procedure or function in the body. We always need to reassure the compiler that an appropriate operation will be supplied at instantiation, and the way to do this is by defining appropriate formal parameters.

Chapter Review

In this chapter we studied two important concepts in building reusable software components. Unconstrained array types allow us to define array types such that the bounds of a given array are left unspecified until the array variable is declared. Unconstrained array types facilitate writing general-purpose subprograms that deal with arrays, such as vector operations and sort procedures.

Generic definition allows us to create templates, or recipes, for subprograms and packages. These templates allow us to leave such things as parameter types, sizes, and operations unspecified until instantiation time. Once a generic template is compiled, multiple versions of it, called instances, can then be created, each with a single statement. The availability of generic definition and instantiation gives us the potential for building large and powerful libraries of reusable software components with much less effort and with much greater maintainability. In this chapter we saw a number of useful generic components for exchanging values, finding the maximum, sorting, and vector handling.

New Ada Constructs in Chapter 12

The new Ada constructs introduced in this chapter are described in Table 12.1.

Table 12.1   Summary of New Ada Constructs

Unconstrained Array Types

`SUBTYPE Weeks IS Positive RANGE 1..52;` `SUBTYPE Rainfall IS Float RANGE 0.0..500.0;`	Declares an array type whose variables can

Table 12.1 *continued*

Unconstrained Array Types

| ```
TYPE RainTable IS
  ARRAY (Weeks RANGE <>) OF Rainfall;
``` | be indexed by any subrange of Weeks |
| ```
SecondQuarter: RainTable(14..26)
``` | and a variable with 13 elements. |

Generic Specification

| ```
GENERIC

  TYPE ValueType IS PRIVATE;
  TYPE IndexType IS (<>);
  TYPE ArrayType IS
    ARRAY(IndexType RANGE <>) OF ValueType;
  WITH FUNCTION Compare(L,R: ValueType)
    RETURN Boolean;

FUNCTION IndexOfMax(A: ArrayType) RETURN IndexType;
``` | Specifies a function to find the location of the "largest" value in an array. |

✓ *Quick-Check Exercises*

1. Define an unconstrained array type.
2. How many dimensions can an unconstrained array type have?
3. Explain what is meant by a generic template.
4. What is a generic type parameter? Give examples.
5. What is a generic procedure or function parameter? Give examples.
6. Given a generic parameter

       WITH FUNCTION Compare(L,R: ValueType) RETURN Boolean;

   explain why it is legal to match this with an operator "<" or ">" at instantiation.

Answers to Quick-Check Exercises

1. An unconstrained array type is one in which the bounds of array variables are not fixed until the variables are declared.
2. There is no language-defined limit on the number of dimensions; unconstrained array types are no different from other array types in this regard.
3. A specification of a procedure, function, or package that must be instantiated before it can be used.
4. A generic type parameter specifies which class of types is acceptable as a match in creating an instance. Examples are: any type that is not limited private, any discrete type, any unconstrained array type with given index and element types.
5. A generic procedure or function parameter indicates to the compiler that the name of a procedure or function with a matching parameter list will be supplied at instantiation.
6. An operator is just a certain kind of function. Ada does not care whether the name of such a function is an operator symbol or an identifier, as long as there is a correct match of the parameters and result type of the function.
```

Review Questions for Chapter 12

1. Explain how unconstrained array types, and array attributes, facilitate creating general-purpose array-handling programs.
2. One generic parameter form we did not discuss in the chapter is

   ```
   TYPE SomeParameterName IS LIMITED PRIVATE;
   ```

   which allows *any* type, even a LIMITED PRIVATE one, to be supplied as a match at instantiation. Suppose we used one of these type forms in a generic package specification. What limitations would this place on the kinds of statements that could appear in the body of the package?

Programming Projects

1. Suppose that *V* is a vector and *X* is a scalar. Mathematically, the operations on a vector and a scalar are commutative; that is, $V + X$ and $X + V$ give the same result, as do $V \times X$ and $X \times V$. The vectors package would be more useful if the corresponding operators were made commutative. This can be done in Ada using additional overloaded operators. Revise the vectors package to allow these commutatve operators. See Section 10.5 on VStrings for an example of how to do this; look specifically at the concatenation operators.
2. Complete the Matrices package by writing and testing the package body. As in Programming Project 1, make the operations combining a matrix and a scalar commutative.
3. In Section 8.11 we developed a function Search (Program 8.17) that looks through an array for a particular value. Revise Search to make it generic, and write a test program for several instances.
4. Modify the vectors package to make it generic. Test for some interesting index and element types.
5. Develop and test a generic package for matrices.
6. Revise the case study of Section 8.12, in which an array of score records is read from a file, then sorted. Use the generic sort procedure from Section 12.5, instantiating it as suggested there.
7. A useful function similar to GenericArrayMaximum is one that finds the *location* of the "maximum" value in an array or slice, rather than the value itself. Write such a function as a generic, then write a generic sort program that uses it. (*Hint:* Recall that in writing SelectSort in Section 8.12, part of the algorithm was to exchange the value at PositionToFill with the maximum value in the subarray ranging from PositionToFill to the end of the array.)

Recursion

13

13.1 Problem Solving: The Nature of Recursion
13.2 Tricks of the Trade: Tracing a Recursive Function
13.3 Problem Solving: Recursive Mathematical Functions
13.4 Problem Solving: More Recursive Programs
13.5 Case Study: Towers of Hanoi
13.6 Case Study: Picture Processing with Recursion
13.7 Problem Solving: Recursive Searching and Sorting
13.8 Tricks of the Trade: Common Programming Errors
       Chapter Review

T his book has shown many examples of procedures and functions, as well as programs that call them. You know that a function can call another function; that is, a statement in the body of a function F contains a call of another function G. What would happen if a statement in F contained a call of F? This situation—a function or procedure calling itself—is not only permitted but in fact is very interesting and useful. The concept of a subprogram—a function or a procedure—calling itself is a mathematical concept called *recursion,* and a subprogram that contains a call to itself is called a *recursive* subprogram.

You can use recursion as an alternative to iteration (looping). Often, a recursive solution to a given problem uses somewhat more computer time and space than an iterative solution to the same problem; this is due to the overhead for the extra procedure calls. However, in many instances the use of recursion enables us to specify a natural, simple solution to a problem that would otherwise be difficult to solve. For this reason, recursion is an important and powerful tool in problem solving and programming.

13.1 Problem Solving: The Nature of Recursion

Problems that lend themselves to a recursive solution have the following characteristics.

- One or more simple cases of the problem (called *stopping cases*) have a simple, nonrecursive solution.
- For the other cases, there is a process (using recursion) for substituting one or more reduced cases of the problem that are closer to a stopping case.
- Eventually the problem can be reduced to stopping cases only, all of which are relatively easy to solve.

The recursive algorithms that we write will generally consist of an IF statement with the form shown below.

```
IF  the stopping case is reached  THEN
    Solve it
ELSE
    Reduce the problem using recursion
END IF;
```

Figure 13.1 illustrates what we mean by this. Let's assume that for a particular problem of size N, we can split this problem into one involving a problem of size 1, which we can solve (a stopping case), and a problem of size $N - 1$, which we can split further. If we split the problem N times, we will end up with N problems of size 1, all of which we can solve.

■ Example 13.1

Consider how we might solve the problem of multiplying 6 by 3, assuming that we know the addition tables but not the multiplication tables. The problem of multiplying 6 by 3 can be split into the two problems:

Figure 13.1 Splitting a Problem into Smaller Problems $\qquad$ **627**

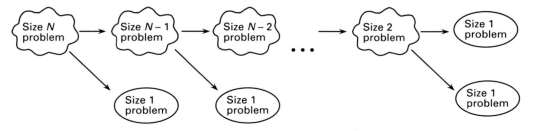

1. Multiply 6 by 2.
2. Add 6 to the result of problem 1.

Because we know the addition tables, we can solve problem 2 but not problem 1. However, problem 1 is simpler than the original problem. We can split it into the two problems 1.1 and 1.2, leaving us three problems to solve, two of which are additions.

    1. Multiply 6 by 2.
        1.1. Multiply 6 by 1.
        1.2. Add 6 to the result.
    2. Add 6 to the result of problem 1.

Even though we don't know the multiplication tables, we are familiar with the simple rule that, for any M, $M \times 1$ is M. By solving problem 1.1 (the answer is 6) and problem 1.2, we get the solution to problem 1 (the answer is 12). Solving problem 2 gives us the final answer, 18.

Program 13.1 implements this approach to doing multiplication as the recursive Ada function `Multiply`, which returns the product, $M \times N$, of its two arguments. The stopping case is reached when the condition N = 1 is true. In this case, the answer is M ($M \times 1$ is M). If N is greater than 1, the statement

```
Result := M + Multiply(M, N-1) -- recursive step
```

executes, splitting the original problem into the two simpler problems:

1. Multiply M by $N - 1$.
2. Add M to the result.

Program 13.1 A Recursive Multiplication Function

```
FUNCTION Multiply (M : IN Integer; N : IN Positive) RETURN Integer IS

-- Performs multiplication recursively using the + operator
-- Pre : M and N are defined and N > 0
-- Post: returns M * N

  Result: Integer;

BEGIN -- Multiply
```

```
                IF N = 1 THEN
                   Result := M;                          -- stopping case
                ELSE
                   Result := M + Multiply(M, N-1);   -- recursion
                END IF;

                RETURN Result;

             END Multiply;
```

The first of these problems is solved by calling `Multiply` again with `N-1` as its second argument. If the new second argument is greater than 1, there will be additional calls to function `Multiply`. The recursive step in function `Multiply` splits the problem of multiplication by N into an addition problem and a problem of multiplication by $N - 1$.

To demonstrate how this function works, Program 13.2 shows `Multiply` modified to display the values of its parameters each time it is called, and the return value before it returns. The test program prompts the user for two numbers, then calls `Multiply`. ∎

Program 13.2 A Test of the Recursive Multiply Function

```
WITH Text_IO;
WITH My_Int_IO;
PROCEDURE TestMultiply IS

   FirstInt   : Integer;
   SecondInt  : Positive;
   Answer     : Integer;

   FUNCTION Multiply (M : IN Integer; N : IN Positive) RETURN Integer IS

   -- Performs multiplication recursively using the + operator
   -- Pre : M and N are defined and N > 0
   -- Post: returns M * N

      Result: Integer;

   BEGIN -- Multiply

      Text_IO.Put(Item => "Multiply called with parameters");
      My_Int_IO.Put(Item => M);
      My_Int_IO.Put(Item => N);
      Text_IO.New_Line;

      IF N = 1 THEN
         Result := M;                              -- stopping case
      ELSE
         Result := M + Multiply(M, N-1);   -- recursion
      END IF;

      Text_IO.Put(Item => "Returning from Multiply with result");
      My_Int_IO.Put(Item => Result);
      Text_IO.New_Line;

      RETURN Result;
```

```
    END Multiply;

BEGIN -- TestMultiply

   Text_IO.Put(Item => "Please enter a integer > ");
   My_Int_IO.Get(Item => FirstInt);
   Text_IO.Put(Item => "Please enter a positive integer > ");
   My_Int_IO.Get(Item => SecondInt);

   Answer := Multiply(M => FirstInt, N => SecondInt);

   Text_IO.Put(Item => "The product of the two integers is ");
   My_Int_IO.Put(Item => Answer, Width => 1);
   Text_IO.New_Line;

END TestMultiply;
```

```
Please enter an integer > 6
Please enter a positive integer > 3
Multiply called with parameters          6          3
Multiply called with parameters          6          2
Multiply called with parameters          6          1
Returning from Multiply with result          6
Returning from Multiply with result         12
Returning from Multiply with result         18
The product of the two integers is 18
```

The next example is too difficult to solve right now, but we will examine it to illustrate how we might solve a difficult problem just by splitting it into smaller problems. We will solve this problem after we have more experience using recursion.

■ Example 13.2

The Towers of Hanoi problem is a representation of an old Asian puzzle. It involves moving a specified number of disks that are all different sizes from one tower (or peg) to another. Legend has it that the world will come to an end when the problem is solved for 64 disks. In the version of the problem shown in Fig. 13.2 there are 5 disks (numbered 1 through 5) and three towers or pegs (lettered A, B, C). The goal is to move the 5 disks from peg A to peg C subject to the following rules:

Figure 13.2   Towers of Hanoi

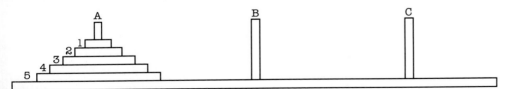

1. Only one disk may be moved at a time, and this disk must be the top disk on a peg.
2. A larger disk can never be placed on top of a smaller disk.

The stopping cases of the problem involve moving one disk only (e.g., "move disk 2 from peg A to peg C"). A simpler problem than the original would be to move four disks subject to the conditions above, or three disks, and so on. Therefore, we want to split the original five-disk problem into one or more problems involving fewer disks. Let's consider splitting the original problem into the three problems below.

1. Move four disks from peg A to peg B.
2. Move disk 5 from peg A to peg C.
3. Move four disks from peg B to peg C.

Step 1 moves all disks but the largest to tower B, an auxiliary tower not mentioned in the original problem. Step 2 moves the largest disk to the goal tower, tower C. Then step 3 moves the remaining disks from B to the goal tower where they will be placed on top of the largest disk. Let's assume that we will be able to perform step 1 and step 2 (a stopping case); Fig. 13.3 shows the status of the three towers after completing these steps. At this point, it should be clear that we can solve the original five-disk problem if we can complete step 3.

Unfortunately, we still don't know how to perform step 1 or step 3. However, both these steps involve four disks instead of five, so they are simpler than the original problem. We should be able to split *them* into even simpler problems. Step 3 involves moving four disks from tower B to tower C, so we can split it into two three-disk problems and a one-disk problem:

3.1. Move three disks from peg B to peg A.
3.2. Move disk 4 from peg B to peg C.
3.3. Move three disks from peg A to peg C.

Figure 13.4 shows the status of the towers after completing steps 3.1 and 3.2. We now have the two largest disks on peg C. Once we complete step 3.3 all five disks will be on peg C as required.

By splitting each n-disk problem into two problems involving $n - 1$ disks and a one-disk problem, we will eventually reach all cases of one disk, which we know how to solve. Later, we will write an Ada program that solves the Towers of Hanoi problem. ■

Figure 13.3 Towers of Hanoi after Steps 1 and 2

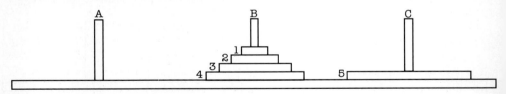

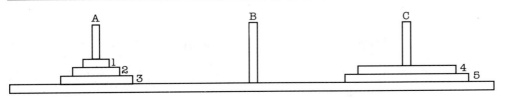

Exercises for Section 13.1

Self-Check

1. Show the problems that are generated by the procedure call statement Mul-tiply (5, 4). Use a diagram similar to Fig. 13.1.
2. Show the problems that are generated by attempting to solve the problem "Move two disks from peg A to peg C." Answer the same question for the problem "Move three disks from peg A to peg C." Draw a diagram similar to Fig. 13.1.

13.2 Tricks of the Trade: Tracing a Recursive Function

Hand-tracing an algorithm's execution provides us with valuable insight as to how that algorithm works. We can also trace the execution of a recursive procedure or function. We will illustrate how to do this by studying a recursive function next.

In the last section, we wrote the recursive function Multiply (see Program 13.1). We can trace the execution of the function call Multiply(6,3) by drawing an *activation frame* corresponding to each call of the function. An activation frame shows the parameter values for each call and summarizes its execution.

The three activation frames generated to solve the problem of multiplying 6 by 3 are shown in Fig. 13.5. Each downward arrow indicates a recursive call of the function; the arrow is drawn starting from the line of the activation frame in which the recursive call is made. The value returned from each call is shown alongside each upward arrow. The upward arrow from each function call points to the operator + because the addition is performed just after the return.

Figure 13.5 shows that there are three calls to function Multiply. Param-eter M has the value 6 for all three calls; parameter N has the values 3, 2, and finally 1. Because N is 1 in the third call, the value of M (i.e., 6) is returned as the result of the third and last call. After returning to the second activation frame, the value of M is added to this result and the sum (i.e., 12) is returned as the result of the second call. After returning to the first activation frame, the value of M is added to this result and the sum (i.e., 18) is returned as the result of the original call to function Multiply.

Figure 13.5 Trace of Function Answer := Multiply(6, 3)

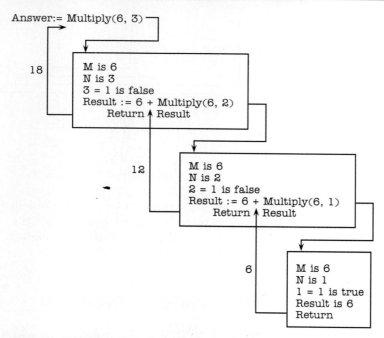

Parameter and Local Variable Stacks

You may be wondering how Ada keeps track of the values of M, N, and Result at any given point. Ada uses a special data structure, called a *stack*, that is analogous to a stack of dishes or trays. Think of the countless times you have stood in line in a cafeteria. Recall that clean dishes are always placed on top of a stack of dishes. When we need a dish, we always remove the one most recently placed on the stack. This causes the next to last dish placed on the stack to move to the top of the stack.

Similarly, whenever a new function call occurs, the parameter values associated with that call are placed ("pushed") on the top of the parameter stack. Also, a new cell whose value is initially undefined is placed on top of the stack that is maintained for the local variable Result. Whenever M, N, or Result is referenced, the value at the top of the corresponding stack is always used. When a procedure return occurs, the value currently at the top of each stack is removed ("popped"), and the value just below it moves to the top, just as in the cafeteria stack.

As an example, let's look at the three stacks right after the first call to Multiply (but before Multiply does any work). There is one cell on each stack, as shown below. Result has no value yet, because Multiply computes it.

After first call to Multiply:

M	N	Result
|6|	|3|	|?|

Just after the second call to `Multiply`, the number 2 is placed on top of the stack for N, and the top of the stack for `Result` becomes undefined again as shown below. The top cells represent the top of each stack.

After second call to `Multiply`*:*

```
M        N        Result

| 6|     | 2|     | ?|
| 6|     | 3|     | ?|
```

`Multiply` is called again, and this time the number 1 is placed on top of the stack.

After third call to `Multiply`*:*

```
M        N        Result

| 6|     | 1|     | ?|
| 6|     | 2|     | ?|
| 6|     | 3|     | ?|
```

Because 1 is the stopping case, `Result` can be computed.

After first computation of `Result`*:*

```
M        N        Result

| 6|     | 1|     | 6|
| 6|     | 2|     | ?|
| 6|     | 3|     | ?|
```

The function can now return, which causes the values at the top of the stack to be removed. Because `Multiply` was called in a statement that computes `Result`, a new value of `Result` is placed on top of the stack:

After first return and second computation of `Result`*:*

```
M        N        Result

| 6|     | 2|     | 12|
| 6|     | 3|     | ?|
```

The function can now return yet again and compute a new value of `Result`:

After second return and third computation of `Result`*:*

```
M        N        Result

| 6|     | 2|     | 18|
```

Finally, we return to the main program; the final value of `Result` is left on top of the stack, where it can be picked up and copied into `Answer`.

After third return:

```
M        N        Result

| ?|     | ?|     | 18|
```

Because these steps are all done automatically by Ada, we can write recursive subprograms without needing to worry about the stacks.

Implementation of Parameter Stacks in Ada

For illustrative purposes, we have used separate stacks for each parameter in our discussion; however, the compiler actually maintains a single stack. Each time a call to a subprogram occurs (even a nonrecursive one), all its parameters and local variables are pushed onto the stack along with the memory address of the calling statement. The latter gives the computer the return point after execution of the procedure or function. Although there may be multiple copies of a procedure's parameters saved on the stack, there is only one copy of the procedure body in memory.

We have introduced the stack here as a way to explain how recursive calls can be implemented. However, stacks are used by most programming languages to implement *all* subprogram calls, not just recursive ones. Indeed, recursive calls are really just a special case.

Exercises for Section 13.2

Self-Check

1. Trace the execution of `Multiply(5,4)` and show the stacks after each recursive call.

 ## 13.3 Problem Solving: Recursive Mathematical Functions

Many mathematical functions are defined recursively. An example is the factorial of a number n ($n!$).

- 0! is 1.
- $n!$ is $n \times (n - 1)!$, for $n > 0$.

Thus, 4! is $4 \times 3 \times 2 \times 1$, or 24. It is quite easy to implement this definition as a recursive function in Ada.

■ Example 13.3

Function `Factorial` in Program 13.3 computes the factorial of its argument N. The recursive step

```
Result := N * Factorial(N-1);
```

implements the second line of the factorial definition above. This means that the result of the current call (argument N) is determined by multiplying the result of the next call (argument N–1) by N.

A trace of

```
Answer := Factorial(N => 3);
```

is shown in Fig. 13.6. The value returned from the original call, `Factorial` (N => 3), is 6, and this value is assigned to `Answer`. Be careful when using the

Program 13.3 Factorial, Recursive Version

635

13.3 Problem
Solving: Recursive
Mathematical
Functions

```
FUNCTION Factorial (N : IN Natural) RETURN Positive IS

-- Computes the factorial of N (N!) recursively
-- Pre : N is defined and N >= 0
-- Post: returns N!

BEGIN -- Factorial

  IF N = 0 THEN
    RETURN 1;                   -- stopping case
  ELSE
    RETURN N * Factorial(N-1);  -- recursion
  END IF;

END Factorial;
```

Figure 13.6 Trace of Answer : = Factorial(3)

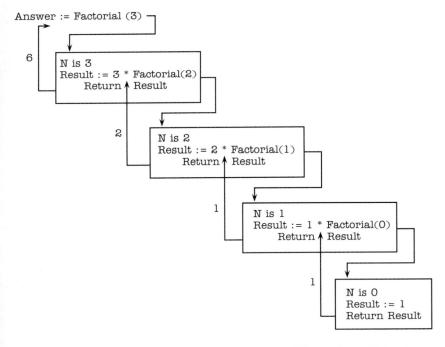

factorial function; its value increases very rapidly and could lead to an integer overflow exception (e.g., 10! is 24320 and 11! is 267520).

Although the recursive implementation of function Factorial follows naturally from its definition, this function can be implemented easily using iteration. The iterative version is shown in Program 13.4; it is in fact the same function that appeared back in Program 5.16, as one of the useful functions there. Note that the iterative version contains a loop as its major control structure, whereas the recursive version contains an IF statement. ∎

Program 13.4 Factorial, Iterative Version

```
FUNCTION Factorial (N : IN Natural) RETURN Positive IS

-- Computes the factorial of N (N!) iteratively
-- Pre : N is defined and N >= 0
-- Post: returns N!

  Result : Positive;                    -- holds the product

BEGIN -- Factorial

  Result := 1;
  FOR Count IN 2 .. N LOOP
    Result := Result * Count;
  END LOOP;

  RETURN Result;

END Factorial;
```

■ Example 13.4

The Fibonacci numbers are a sequence of numbers that have many varied uses. They were originally intended to model the growth of a rabbit colony. Although we will not go into details of the model here, the Fibonacci sequence 1, 1, 2, 3, 5, 8, 13, 21, 34,... increases rapidly. The fifteenth number in the sequence is 610 (that's a lot of rabbits!). The Fibonacci sequence is defined below.

- Fib_1 is 1.
- Fib_2 is 1.
- Fib_n is $Fib_{n-2} + Fib_{n-1}$, for $n > 2$.

Verify for yourself that the sequence of numbers shown above is correct. A recursive function that computes the Nth Fibonacci number is shown as Program 13.5.

Although easy to write, the Fibonacci function can run rather slowly because each recursive step generates two recursive calls to function `Fibonacci`. This is similar to procedure `Tower`, so the execution time grows exponentially as N increases.   ■

Program 13.5 Compute the Nth Fibonacci Number

```
FUNCTION Fibonacci (N : IN Natural) RETURN Positive IS

-- Returns the Nth Fibonacci number, computed recursively
-- Pre : N is defined and N >= 0
-- Post: returns N!

BEGIN  -- Fibonacci

  IF (N = 1) OR (N = 2) THEN
    RETURN 1;
```

```
ELSE
   RETURN Fibonacci(N-2) + Fibonacci(N-1);
END IF;

END Fibonacci;
```

■ Example 13.5

In Section 10.4 we introduced Euclid's algorithm for finding the greatest common divisor (GCD) of two positive integers, M and N. There we showed an iterative solution. GCD is defined recursively as follows. Recall that the *greatest common divisor* of two integers is the largest integer that divides them both.

- $GCD(M, N)$ is N if $N <= M$ and N divides M.
- $GCD(M, N)$ is $GCD(N, M)$ if $M < N$.
- $GCD(M, N)$ is $GCD(N,$ remainder of M divided by $N)$ otherwise.

This algorithm states that the GCD is N if N is the smaller number and N divides M. If M is the smaller number, then the GCD determination should be performed with the arguments transposed. If N does not divide M, the answer is obtained by finding the GCD of N and the remainder of M divided by N. The declaration and use of the Ada function GCD is shown as Program 13.6. ■

Program 13.6   Greatest Common Divisor, Recursive Version

```
FUNCTION GCD (M, N : IN Positive) RETURN Positive IS

-- Pre : M and N are defined.
-- Post: Returns the greatest common divisor of M and N.

  Result: Positive;

BEGIN -- GCD

  IF (N <= M) AND (M REM N = 0) THEN
    Result := N;
  ELSIF M < N THEN
    Result := GCD(N, M);
  ELSE
    Result := GCD(N, M REM N);
  END IF;

  RETURN Result;

END GCD;
```

Exercises for Section 13.3

Self-Check

1. If Ada did not have an exponentiation operation (**) we could write our own. Complete the following recursive function that calculates the value of a number (Base) raised to a power (Power).

```
FUNCTION PowerOf (Base: Integer; Power: Positive) RETURN Integer IS

   Result: Integer;

BEGIN -- PowerOf

   IF Power = _____ THEN
      Result := _____;
   ELSE
      Result := _____* _____;
   END IF;

END PowerOf;
```

2. What is the output of the following program? What does function Strange compute?

```
WITH Text_IO;
WITH My_Int_IO;
PROCEDURE TestStrange IS

   FUNCTION Strange (N : Integer) RETURN Integer IS
      Result: Integer;
   BEGIN
      IF N = 1 THEN
         Result := 0;
      ELSE
         Result := 1 + Strange (N / 2);
      END IF;
   END Strange;

BEGIN -- TestStrange

   My_Int_IO.Put(Item => Strange(8));
   Text_IO.New_Line;

END TestStrange;
```

3. Explain what would happen if the terminating condition for the Fibonacci function is just ($N = 1$).

Programming

1. Write a recursive function, FindSum, that calculates the sum of successive integers starting at 1 and ending at N (i.e., FindSum(N) = (1 + 2 + $\cdots$ + ($N - 1$) + N).

2. Write an iterative version of the Fibonacci function.

 # 13.4 Problem Solving: More Recursive Programs

This section examines three familiar problems and implements a recursive procedure or function to solve each.

◆ Case Study: Printing an Array Backward

Problem

Provide a recursive solution to the problem of displaying the elements of an array in reverse order.

Analysis

If the array X has elements with subscripts X'First..X'Last, then the element values should be displayed in the sequence X(X'Last), X(X'Last–1), X(X'Last–2), ..., X(X'First+1), X(X'First). The stopping case is displaying an array with one element; the solution is to display that element. For larger arrays, the recursive step is to display the last array element (X(X'Last)) and then display the subarray with subscripts X'First..X'last–1 backward.

Data Requirements

Problem Inputs
an array of integer values (X : IntArray)

Problem Outputs
the array values in reverse order (X(X'Last), X(X'Last–1), ... , X(X'First+1), X(X'First))

Design

Algorithm

1. IF X'First = X'Last (i.e., if the slice X has only one element) THEN
   2. Display X(X'Last)
   ELSE
   3. Display X(X'Last)
   4. Display the subarray with subscripts X'First..X'Last–1
   END IF;

Coding

Procedure PrintBackward in Program 13.7 implements the recursive algorithm and gives a test program. Given the following array type and variable:

```
TYPE IntArray IS ARRAY(Integer RANGE <>) OF Integer;
Test: IntArray(1..3);
```

the procedure call PrintBackward(Test(1..3)) results in the three Put statements being executed in the order indicated below, and the elements of Test will be printed backward as desired.

```
My_Int_IO.Put (Item => Test(3));
My_Int_IO.Put (Item => Test(2));
My_Int_IO.Put (Item => Test(1));
```

Program 13.7   Printing an Array Backward

```
WITH Text_IO;
WITH My_Int_IO;
PROCEDURE TestPrintBack IS

   TYPE IntArray IS ARRAY(Integer RANGE <>) OF Integer;
   Test: IntArray(1..10);

   PROCEDURE PrintBackward (X : IntArray) IS

      -- Prints a slice of an integer array X with bounds X'First..X'Last.
      -- Pre : Array X is defined and X'First <= X'Last.
      -- Post: Displays X(X'Last), X(X'Last-1), ... , X(X'First)

   BEGIN -- PrintBackward

      IF X'First = X'Last THEN -- stopping case - slice has only one element
         My_Int_IO.Put(Item => X(X'Last), Width => 3);
      ELSIF X'First > X'Last THEN     -- error in specifying slice bounds
         Text_IO.Put(Item => "Error in bounds of array slice");
         Text_IO.New_Line;
      ELSE
         -- recursive step
         My_Int_IO.Put(Item => X(X'Last), Width => 3);
         PrintBackward (X => X(X'First..X'Last-1));
      END IF;

   END PrintBackward;

BEGIN

   Test := (1,3,5,7,9,11,13,15,17,19);
   PrintBackward(X => Test(1..3));
   Text_IO.New_Line;

END TestPrintBack;



   5  3  1
```

To verify this we trace the execution of the procedure call statement above in Fig. 13.7. Each rightward arrow indicates a recursive procedure call; each leftward arrow indicates a return to the previous level.

Call PrintBackward with parameter Test(1..3).
   Display Test(3).
   Call PrintBackward with parameter Test(1..2).
      Display Test(2).
      Call PrintBackward with parameter Test(1..1).
         Display Test(1).
         Return from third call.
      Return from second call.
   Return from original call.

Figure 13.7   Trace of PrintBackward(Test(1..3))

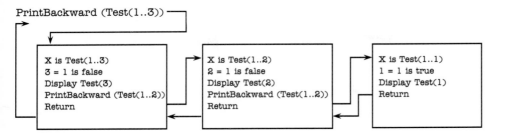

As shown, there are three calls to procedure `PrintBackward`, each with different parameters. The procedure returns always occur in the reverse order of the procedure calls; in other words, we return from the last call first, then we return from the next to last call, and so on. This time there are no statements left to execute after the returns, because the recursive call

```
PrintBackward (X(X'First..X'Last-1));
```

occurs at the end of the recursive step.

◆ Case Study: Displaying an Array in Normal Order

Problem
Provide a recursive procedure that displays the elements of an array in normal order.

Analysis
We can use the approach just followed to display the elements of an array in normal order. Again the stopping case is an array with just one element.

Data Requirements

Problem Inputs
an array of integer values (`X : IntArray`)

Problem Outputs
the array values in normal order (`X(X'First)`, `X(X'First+1)`, ... , `X(X'Last-1)`, `X(X'Last)`)

Algorithm

1. IF `X'First = X'Last` (i.e., if the slice X has only one element) THEN
   2. Display `X(X'Last)`
   ELSE

Case Study: Displaying an Array in Normal Order, continued

3. Display the subarray with subscripts X'First..X'Last-1
4. Display X(X'Last)
END IF;

The only difference between this algorithm and the one shown earlier is that steps 3 and 4 are transposed.

Coding
Procedure PrintNormal is shown in Program 13.8.

Program 13.8 Displaying an Array Recursively

```
WITH Text_IO;
WITH My_Int_IO;
PROCEDURE TestPrintNorm IS

   TYPE IntArray IS ARRAY(Integer RANGE <>) OF Integer;
   Test: IntArray(1..10);

   PROCEDURE PrintNormal (X : IntArray) IS

     -- Displays a slice of an integer array X with bounds X'First..X'Last.
     -- Pre : Array X is defined and X'First <= X'Last.
     -- Post: Displays X(X'First), X(X'First+1), ... , X(X'Last)

   BEGIN -- PrintNormal

      IF X'First = X'Last THEN -- stopping case - slice has only one element
         My_Int_IO.Put(Item => X(X'Last), Width => 3);
      ELSIF X'First > X'Last THEN      -- error in specifying slice bounds
         Text_IO.Put(Item => "Error in bounds of array slice");
         Text_IO.New_Line;
      ELSE
         -- recursive step
         PrintNormal (X => X(X'First..X'Last-1));
         My_Int_IO.Put(Item => X(X'Last), Width => 3);
      END IF;

   END PrintNormal;

BEGIN

   Test := (1,3,5,7,9,11,13,15,17,19);
   PrintNormal(X => Test(4..6));
   Text_IO.New_Line;

END TestPrintNorm;



   7  9 11
```

Testing

The trace of `PrintNormal(Test(4..6))` is shown in Fig. 13.8. The leftward
return arrows to each activation frame point to the display operation (`My_Int_
IO.Put`); therefore, the display operation is performed after the return. Follow-
ing the rightward arrows and then the leftward arrows results in the sequence
of events listed below. This time there are no statements that precede the
recursive calls.

  Call `PrintNormal` with parameter `Test(4..6)`.
    Call `PrintNormal` with parameter `Test(4..5)`.
      Call `PrintNormal` with parameter `Test(4..4)`.
        Display `Test(4)`.
        Return from third call.
      Display `Test(5)`.
      Return from second call.
    Display `Test(6)`.
    Return from original call.

Figure 13.8 Trace of PrintNormal(Test(4..6))

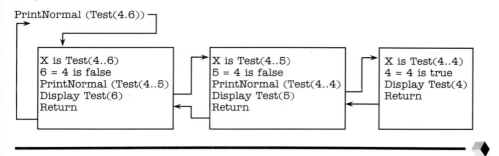

You might be wondering if there are any special performance problems
associated with passing arrays through a series of recursive calls. Recall that the
Ada standard does not specify whether an array is passed to a subprogram by
creating a local copy or by just passing its address. A compiler writer can choose
to do it either way.

If indeed the array is passed by copying, then hypothetically a large array
might be copied many times in a recursive call, leading to a huge consumption
of space for all the local copies and of time for the copying. In practice, however,
this is not a cause for concern, because in most Ada compilers, if the array to
be passed is longer than just a few elements, only its address is passed. Declaring
an array parameter with mode `IN` (or unspecified mode) guarantees that it
cannot be modified by the subprogram.

◆ Case Study: Discovering Whether a String Is a Palindrome

Problem

A *palindrome* is a string or sentence that reads the same backward and forward. RADAR is a palindrome. When the Biblical first man met the Biblical first woman, he might have said "Madam, I'm Adam," which is a palindrome if one neglects the punctuation. (Adam, in his first fit of anger, might also have said "Mad am I, Madam.") The problem is to write a program that discovers whether a string of 80 characters or less is a palindrome.

Analysis

Our program can discover whether a string is a palindrome by first finding the reverse of the string, then checking whether the string is the same as its reverse. We can use our package VStrings to make the string handling easy.

Data Requirements

> **Problem Inputs**
> the input string (S: VString)
>
> **Problem Outputs**
> a message to the user indicating whether S is a palindrome.

Design

Algorithm

1. Find the reverse R of the given string S
2. IF R is equal to S THEN
   > the original string is a palindrome
   > ELSE
   > the original string is not a palindrome
   > END IF;

   Step 1 can be refined into

1.1. IF S is empty or has only one character THEN
   > 1.2. R is equal to S
   > ELSE
   > 1.3. Remove the first character of S, and concatenate it to the reverse of the rest of S.
   > END IF;

   Step 1.3 contains the words "to the reverse of the rest of S". Because the purpose of the step is to find the reverse, this suggests a recursive algorithm. Step 1.1 tests for the stopping case; step 1.2 implements the stopping case. We can write this as a recursive code fragment:

```
IF Length(S) <= 1 THEN
  R := S;
ELSE
  R := StringReverse(Tail(S)) & Head(S);
END IF;
```

We call our recursive function StringReverse and not Reverse because the latter is a reserved word in Ada, which we cannot use for anything else.

Coding

Program 13.9 shows the program Palindrome which uses resources from package VStrings and the recursive function StringReverse just described. As you can see from the second and fourth test cases, this program treats blanks and punctuation marks as ordinary characters and so does not discover that "Madam, I'm Adam" is a palindrome. As an exercise, you can improve this program so that blanks and punctuation are ignored, and uppercase letters are treated the same as lowercase ones.

Program 13.9 A Palindrome-Finding Program

```
WITH Text_IO;
WITH VStrings; USE VStrings;
PROCEDURE Palindrome IS

  -- display the reverse of a string of 80 characters or less, and
  -- indicate whether the string is a palindrome

  S: VString;   -- the input string
  R: VString;   -- the reverse of the input string

  -- local function StringReverse

  FUNCTION StringReverse(S: VString) RETURN VString IS

    -- returns the reverse of a variable-length string
    -- Pre: S is defined
    -- Post: returns the reverse of S

    R: VString;   -- to hold the result

  BEGIN -- StringReverse

    IF Length(S) <= 1 THEN
      R := S;
    ELSE
      R := StringReverse(Tail(S)) & Head(S);
    END IF;

    RETURN R;

  END StringReverse;

BEGIN -- Palindrome
```

```
FOR Trial IN 1..5 LOOP

   Text_IO.Put(Item => "Please enter a string of 80 characters or less.");
   Text_IO.New_Line;
   VStrings.Get_Line(Item => S);

   R := StringReverse(S);
   Text_IO.Put("The reverse of the string is ");
   Text_IO.New_Line;
   VStrings.Put(Item => R);
   Text_IO.New_Line;

   IF R = S THEN
      Text_IO.Put(Item => "The string is a palindrome.");
      Text_IO.New_Line;
   ELSE
      Text_IO.Put(Item => "The string is not a palindrome.");
      Text_IO.New_Line;
   END IF;

   Text_IO.New_Line;

 END LOOP;

END Palindrome;


Please enter a string of 80 characters or less.
radar
The reverse of the string is
radar
The string is a palindrome.

Please enter a string of 80 characters or less.
Able was I ere I saw Elba
The reverse of the string is
ablE was I ere I saw elbA
The string is not a palindrome.

Please enter a string of 80 characters or less.
ablewasiereisawelba
The reverse of the string is
ablewasiereisawelba
The string is a palindrome.

Please enter a string of 80 characters or less.
Madam, I'm Adam
The reverse of the string is
madA m'I ,madaM
The string is not a palindrome.

Please enter a string of 80 characters or less.
madamimadam
The reverse of the string is
madamimadam
The string is a palindrome.
```

Exercises for Section 13.4

Self-Check

1. Trace the execution of `PrintNormal` and `PrintBackward` on an array that has the integers 5, 8, 10, 1 stored in consecutive elements.

Programming

1. Provide an iterative procedure that is equivalent to `PrintBackward`.
2. Write a recursive procedure that reverses the elements in an array `X(1..N)`. The recursive step should shift the slice `X(2..N)` down one element into the subarray `X(1..N-1)` (i.e., `X(1)` gets `X(2)`, `X(2)` gets `X(3)`, ... `X(N-1)` gets `X(N)`), store the old `X(1)` in `X(N)`, and then reverse the subarray `X(1..N-1)`.

 # 13.5 Case Study: Towers of Hanoi

This case study is a bit more complicated than the preceding ones. It leads to a recursive procedure that solves the Towers of Hanoi problem you encountered in Section 13.1.

Problem

Solve the Towers of Hanoi problem for *N* disks, where *N* is a parameter.

Design Overview

The solution to the Towers of Hanoi problem consists of a printed list of individual disk moves. We need a recursive procedure that can be used to move any number of disks from one peg to another, using the third peg as an auxiliary.

Data Requirements

Problem Inputs
the number of disks to be moved (`N : Integer`)
the *from* peg (`FromPeg : 'A'..'C'`)
the *to* peg (`ToPeg : 'A'..'C'`)
the *auxiliary* peg (`AuxPeg : 'A'..'C'`)

Problem Outputs
a list of individual disk moves

Initial Algorithm

1. IF `N` is 1 then
2. Move disk 1 from the *from* peg to the *to* peg
    ELSE
3. Move `N-1` disks from the *from* peg to the *auxiliary* peg using the *to* peg.
4. Move disk `N` from the *from* peg to the *to* peg.

5. Move N–1 disks from the *auxiliary* peg to the *to* peg using the *from* peg.
END IF;

If N is 1, a stopping case is reached. If N is greater than 1, the recursive step (following ELSE) splits the original problem into three smaller subproblems, one of which is a stopping case. Each stopping case displays a move instruction. Verify that the recursive step generates the three problems listed before Fig. 13.2 when N is 5, the *from* peg is A, and the *to* peg is C.

Coding

The implementation of this algorithm is shown as procedure Tower in Program 13.10. Procedure Tower has four parameters. The procedure call statement

```
Tower (FromPeg => 'A',ToPeg => 'C',AuxPeg => 'B',N => 5);
```

solves the problem posed earlier of moving five disks from tower A to tower C using B as an auxiliary.

In Program 13.10, the stopping case (Move disk 1) is implemented as a call

Program 13.10 A Test of Towers of Hanoi

```
WITH Text_IO;
WITH My_Int_IO;
PROCEDURE TestTower IS

   SUBTYPE Pegs IS Character RANGE 'A'..'C';

   PROCEDURE Tower (FromPeg : Pegs;
                    ToPeg   : Pegs;
                    AuxPeg  : Pegs;
                    N       : Natural) IS

   -- Moves N disks from FromPeg to ToPeg
   -- using AuxPeg as an auxiliary.

   BEGIN -- Tower

     IF N = 1 THEN
       -- stopping case
       Text_IO.Put(Item => "Move disk 1 from peg ");
       Text_IO.Put(Item => FromPeg);
       Text_IO.Put(Item => " to peg ");
       Text_IO.Put(Item => ToPeg);
       Text_IO.New_Line;
     ELSE
       -- recursive step
       Tower (FromPeg, AuxPeg, ToPeg, N-1);

       Text_IO.Put(Item => "Move disk ");
       My_Int_IO.Put(Item => N, Width => 1);
       Text_IO.Put(Item => " from peg ");
       Text_IO.Put(Item => FromPeg);
       Text_IO.Put(Item => " to peg ");
       Text_IO.Put(Item => ToPeg);
       Text_IO.New_Line;

       Tower (AuxPeg, ToPeg, FromPeg, N-1);
     END IF;
```

```
END Tower;

BEGIN -- TestTower

   Tower(FromPeg => 'A', ToPeg => 'B', AuxPeg => 'C', N => 5);

END TestTower;
```

```
Move disk 1 from peg A to peg B
Move disk 2 from peg A to peg C
Move disk 1 from peg B to peg C
Move disk 3 from peg A to peg B
Move disk 1 from peg C to peg A
Move disk 2 from peg C to peg B
Move disk 1 from peg A to peg B
Move disk 4 from peg A to peg C
Move disk 1 from peg B to peg C
Move disk 2 from peg B to peg A
Move disk 1 from peg C to peg A
Move disk 3 from peg B to peg C
Move disk 1 from peg A to peg B
Move disk 2 from peg A to peg C
Move disk 1 from peg B to peg C
Move disk 5 from peg A to peg B
Move disk 1 from peg C to peg A
Move disk 2 from peg C to peg B
Move disk 1 from peg A to peg B
Move disk 3 from peg C to peg A
Move disk 1 from peg B to peg C
Move disk 2 from peg B to peg A
Move disk 1 from peg C to peg A
Move disk 4 from peg C to peg B
Move disk 1 from peg A to peg B
Move disk 2 from peg A to peg C
Move disk 1 from peg B to peg C
Move disk 3 from peg A to peg B
Move disk 1 from peg C to peg A
Move disk 2 from peg C to peg B
Move disk 1 from peg A to peg B
```

to procedure Text_IO.Put. Each recursive step consists of two recursive calls to Tower with a call to Text_IO.Put sandwiched between them. The first recursive call solves the problem of moving N−1 disks to the *auxiliary* peg. The call to Text_IO.Put displays a message to move disk N to the *to* peg. The second recursive call solves the problem of moving the N−1 disks back from the *auxiliary* peg to the *to* peg.

Testing

The procedure call statement

```
      Tower (FromPeg => 'A',ToPeg => 'C',AuxPeg => 'B',N => 3);
```

solves a simpler three-disk problem: Move 3 disks from peg A to peg C. Its execution is traced in Fig. 13.9. Verify for yourself that this list of steps does indeed solve the three-disk problem.

Figure 13.9 Trace of Tower('A','B','C',3)

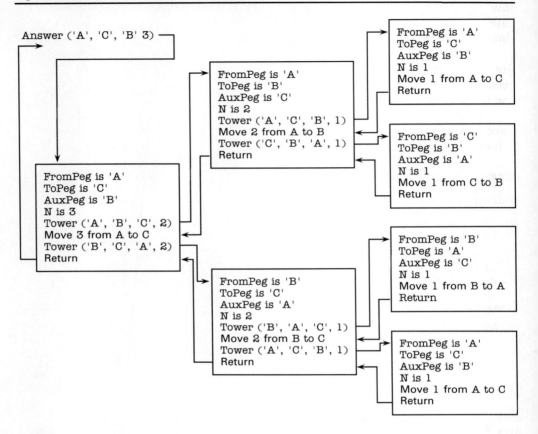

Comparison of Iteration and Recursive Procedures

It is interesting to consider that procedure Tower in Program 13.10 will solve the Tower of Hanoi problem for any number of disks. The three-disk problem results in a total of 7 calls to procedure Tower and is solved by 7 disk moves. The five-disk problem results in a total of 31 calls to procedure Tower and is solved in 31 moves. In general, the number of moves required to solve the n-disk problem is $2^n - 1$: We say that it is a $O(2^n)$ problem. Because each procedure call requires the allocation and initialization of a local data area in memory, the computer time increases exponentially with the problem size. For this reason, be careful about running this program with a value of N that is larger than 10.

The dramatic increase in processing time for larger towers is a function of this problem, not recursion. In general, however, if there are recursive and iterative solutions to the same problem, the recursive solution requires more time and space because of the extra procedure calls.

Although recursion was not really needed to solve the simpler problems in this section, it was extremely useful in formulating an algorithm for Towers of

Hanoi. For certain problems, recursion leads naturally to solutions that are much easier to read and understand than their iterative counterparts. In those cases, the benefits gained from increased clarity far outweigh the extra cost in time and memory of running a recursive program.

Many would argue that the recursive programs are esthetically more pleasing. They are indeed often more compact. Once you are accustomed to thinking recursively, the recursive form is somewhat easier to read and understand than the iterative form.

Some programmers like to use recursion as a conceptual tool. Once they have written the recursive form of a function or procedure, they can translate it into an iterative version if run-time efficiency is a major concern.

Exercises for Section 13.5

Self-Check

1. How many moves are needed to solve the six-disk problem?
2. Estimate the size of the largest Towers problem that could be solved in less than one day. Assume that one disk can be moved each second.
3. Estimate the size of the largest Towers problem that could be solved in less than one year. Assume that one disk can be moved each second.

Programming

1. Modify TestTower to read in a data value for N (the number of disks).

 # 13.6 Case Study: Picture Processing with Recursion

The next problem is a good illustration of the power of recursion. As for the Towers of Hanoi problem, its solution is relatively easy to write recursively; however, the problem would be much more difficult without using recursion. Unlike Towers of Hanoi, which is a cute and popular exercise, picture-processing algorithms have real application.

Problem

We have a two-dimensional grid G of cells, each of which may be empty or filled. The filled cells that are connected form a *blob*. There may be several blobs on the grid. We would like a function that accepts as input the coordinates of a particular cell and returns the size of the blob containing the cell.

There are three blobs in the sample grid in Fig. 13.10. If the function parameters represent the X and Y coordinates of a cell, the result of Blob-Count(G,3,4) is 5, the result of BlobCount(G,1,2) is 2, the result of Blob-Count(G,5,5) is 0, and the result of BlobCount(G,5,1) is 4.

Figure 13.10 Grid with Three Blobs

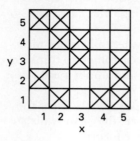

Analysis

Function `BlobCount` must test the cell specified by its arguments to see whether it is filled. There are two stopping cases: The cell (`X`, `Y`) is not on the grid or the cell (`X`, `Y`) is empty. In either case, the value returned by `BlobCount` is 0. If the cell is on the grid and filled, then the value returned is 1 plus the size of the blobs containing each of its eight neighbors. To avoid counting a filled cell more than once, we will mark it as empty once we have visited it.

Data Requirements

Problem Inputs
the grid (`Grid: BlobArray`)
the `X` and `Y` coordinates of the point being visited (`X`, `Y : Integer`)

Problem Outputs
the number of the cells in the blob containing point (*X, Y*)

Design

Intial Algorithm

1. IF cell (*X, Y*) is not in the array THEN
   2. Return a count of 0
ELSIF cell (*X, Y*) is empty then
   3. Return a count of 0
ELSE
   4. Mark cell (*X, Y*) as empty
   5. Add 1 and see whether the blob contains any of the eight neighbors of
      cell (*X, Y*)
END IF;

Function `BlobCount` is shown in Program 13.11, assuming the declarations below. The array type `BlobArray` has element values `Filled` or `Empty`. The array G has, as usual, bounds G'First(1) and G'Last(1) for the rows, and G'First(2) and G'Last(2) for the columns.

The auxiliary function `Blob` in Program 13.11, declared within `BlobCount`,

```
WITH Text_IO;
WITH My_Int_IO;
PROCEDURE TestBlobCount IS

   TYPE Fill IS (Empty, Filled);
   TYPE BlobArray IS ARRAY (Integer RANGE <>, Integer RANGE <>) OF Fill;

   Test: BlobArray(1..5,1..5);

   FUNCTION BlobCount(Grid : BlobArray; X, Y: Integer) RETURN Natural IS
   -- Counts the number of filled cells in the blob containing
   -- point (X, Y).
   -- Pre : Blob array Grid and point (X,Y) are defined.
   -- Post: Returns the size of the blob containing point (X, Y).
   --       Resets the status of each cell in the blob to Empty.

      CopyOfGrid : BlobArray(Grid'Range(1),Grid'Range(2));
                              -- because functions can't modify
                              -- their parameters, in Ada

      FUNCTION Blob (X, Y : Integer) RETURN Natural IS

      -- Inner function that performs the counting operation for BlobCount
      -- Pre : Global array CopyOfGrid and point (X,Y) are defined.
      -- Post: Returns the size of the blob containing point (X, Y).
      --       Resets the status of each cell in the blob to Empty.

      Result: Natural;

      BEGIN -- Blob

         IF (X NOT IN CopyOfGrid'Range(1)) OR
            (Y NOT IN CopyOfGrid'Range(2)) THEN
            Result := 0;                        -- cell not in grid
         ELSIF CopyOfGrid(X, Y) = Empty THEN
            Result := 0;                        -- cell is empty
         ELSE -- cell is filled
            -- recursive step
            CopyOfGrid(X, Y) := Empty;
            Result := 1 + Blob(X-1, Y+1) + Blob(X, Y+1) +
                          Blob(X+1, Y+1) + Blob(X+1, Y) +
                          Blob(X+1, Y-1) + Blob(X, Y-1) +
                          Blob(X-1, Y-1) + Blob(X-1, Y);
         END IF;

         RETURN Result;

      END Blob;

   BEGIN

      CopyOfGrid := Grid;
      RETURN Blob(X,Y);

   END BlobCount;

BEGIN -- TestBlobCount

   Test := ((Empty,  Filled, Empty,  Empty,  Filled),
```

```
              (Filled, Empty,  Empty,  Filled, Filled),
              (Empty,  Empty,  Filled, Filled, Empty ),
              (Filled, Empty,  Empty,  Empty,  Empty ),
              (Filled, Filled, Filled, Empty,  Empty ));

    Text_IO.Put(Item => "BlobCount(3,4) is ");
    My_Int_IO.Put(Item => BlobCount(Test,3,4), Width => 1);
    Text_IO.New_Line;

    Text_IO.Put(Item => "BlobCount(1,2) is ");
    My_Int_IO.Put(Item => BlobCount(Test,1,2), Width => 1);
    Text_IO.New_Line;

    Text_IO.Put(Item => "BlobCount(5,5) is ");
    My_Int_IO.Put(Item => BlobCount(Test,5,5), Width => 1);
    Text_IO.New_Line;

    Text_IO.Put(Item => "BlobCount(5,1) is ");
    My_Int_IO.Put(Item => BlobCount(Test,5,1), Width => 1);
    Text_IO.New_Line;

END TestBlobCount;



BlobCount(3,4) is 5
BlobCount(1,2) is 2
BlobCount(5,5) is 0
BlobCount(5,1) is 4
```

---

implements the counting algorithm; function `BlobCount` simply calls the recursive function `Blob`, passing on its arguments, and returns the count computed by function `Blob` as its own result. The purpose of the auxiliary function is to protect the actual array from being modified when filled cells are reset to empty by function `Blob`. We will come back to this point shortly.

If the cell being visited is off the grid or is empty, a value of zero is returned immediately. Otherwise, the recursive step executes, causing function `Blob` to call itself eight times; each time, a different neighbor of the current cell is visited. The cells are visited in a clockwise manner, starting with the neighbor above and to the left. The function result is defined as the sum of all values returned from these recursive calls plus 1 (for the current cell).

The sequence of operations performed in function `Blob` is important. The IF statement tests whether the cell (X, Y) is on the grid before testing whether (X, Y) is empty. If the order were reversed, `Constraint_Error` would be raised whenever (X, Y) was off the grid.

Also, the recursive step resets `Grid(X,Y)` to `Empty` before visiting the neighbors of cell (X, Y). If this were not done first, then cell (X, Y) would be counted more than once because it is a neighbor of all its neighbors. A worse problem is that the recursion would not terminate. When each neighbor of the current cell is visited, `Blob` is called again with the coordinates of the current cell as arguments. If the current cell is `Empty`, an immediate return occurs. If the current cell is still `Filled`, then the recursive step would be executed erroneously. Eventually the program will run out of time or memory space; the latter is signaled in Ada by the raising of `Storage_Error`.

A side effect of the execution of function `Blob` is that all cells that are part of the blob being processed are reset to `Empty`. This is the reason for using two functions. Because the array is passed as a parameter to function `BlobCount`, a local copy `CopyOfGrid` is saved when `BlobCount` is first called. Only this local array is changed by function `Blob`, not the actual array. If the counting operation were performed in function `BlobCount` instead of in function `Blob`, eight copies of this array would be made each time the recursive step was executed. Using the function `Blob` and the array that is global to all recursive calls of `Blob` (but still local to `BlobCount`) prevents the unnecessary copying.

Exercise for Section 13.6

Self-Check

1. Trace the execution of function `BlobCount` for the coordinate pairs (1, 1) and (1, 2) in the sample grid.
2. Is the order of the two tests performed in function `BlobCount` critical? What happens if we reverse them or combine them into a single condition?

 # 13.7 Problem Solving: Recursive Searching and Sorting

As we have seen in previous chapters, sorting and searching are important applications in computing for which a large number of techniques have been developed. In this section we examine two well-known and significant recursive algorithms, Binary Search and QuickSort.

Recursive Searching: Binary Search

We discussed one technique for searching an array in Section 8.11, and we wrote a function that returned the index of a target key in an array if the target was present. To do this, it was necessary to compare array element keys to the target key, starting with the first array element. The comparison process was terminated when the target key was found or the end of the array was reached. We must make N comparisons to determine that a target key is not in an array of N elements. On the average, we must make $N/2$ comparisons to locate a target key that is in the array. The number of comparisons is directly proportional to the number of elements in the array, so we say that this search method is $O(N)$.

Often we want to search an array whose elements are arranged in order by key field. We can take advantage of the fact that the array keys are in ascending order and terminate the search when an array key greater than or equal to the target key is reached. There is no need to look any further in the array; all other keys will also be larger than the target key.

Both these search techniques are called *sequential search* because we examine the array elements in sequence. The modified algorithm discussed above is a sequential search of an ordered array. On the average, a sequential search of an ordered array requires $N/2$ comparisons to locate the target key or determine that it is not in the array; so we still have an $O(N)$ process.

◆ Case Study: Binary Search

The array searches described above are considered *linear searches* because their execution time increases linearly (in direct proportion) with the number of array elements. This can be a problem when searching very large arrays (for example, $N > 1000$). Consequently, we often use the *binary search algorithm* described below for large sorted arrays.

Problem

Your employer has a directory of customers that she keeps in alphabetical order. Because business has been good, this list has become too large to search efficiently using a linear search. Write an improved search algorithm that takes advantage of the fact that the array is sorted.

Analysis

The binary search algorithm takes advantage of the fact that the array is ordered to eliminate half of the array elements with each probe into the array. Consequently, if the array has 1000 elements, it will either locate the target value or eliminate 500 elements with its first probe, 250 elements with its second probe, 125 elements with its third probe, and so on. Only 10 probes are necessary to completely search an array of 1000 elements. (Why?) You can use the binary search algorithm to find a name in a large metropolitan telephone directory using 30 or fewer probes, so this algorithm should be suitable for your employer.

The number of probes to completely search an N-element array obviously varies with the number of elements N. Can we find a formula for this variation? Because each probe eliminates half the elements, the maximum number of probes is determined by the number of times we can "cut the array in half" before we are left with only one element.

Let's consider some values of N corresponding to powers of 2. If N is 8 (2^3), for example, we first search an eight-element array, then a four-element array, then a two-element array, and finally a one-element array. We cut the array three times. If N is 32 (2^5), we cut the array five times; if N is 256 (2^8), we cut the array eight times; if N is 1024 (2^{10}), ten times. Indeed, we make a maximum of only 16 cuts even if N is 32768 (2^{16})! If N is not an exact power of two, the number of probes is determined by the next higher power of 2: If N is 1000, then 1024 (2^{10}) is the determining power of 2.

An equivalent way of saying "1024 is 2^{10}" is "10 is the logarithm, to the base 2, of 1024", or "$\log_2 1024 = 10$." The formula we are looking for is that the number of binary search probes into an array of N elements is $\log_2 N$.

Case Study: Binary Search, continued

657

13.7 Problem
Solving: Recursive
Searching and
Sorting

Another way of saying this is that binary search is an $O(\log_2 N)$ algorithm. This is much faster than sequential search, isn't it?

Now let's develop the binary search algorithm. Because the array is ordered, all we have to do is compare the target key with the middle element of the subarray we are searching. If their keys are the same, then we are done. If the middle value is larger than the target, then we should search the left half of the array next; otherwise, we should search the right half of the array.

The subarray to be searched, `Slice`, has subscripts `Slice'First..Slice'Last`. The variable `Middle` is the subscript of the middle element in this range. The right half of the array (subscripts `Middle..Slice'Last`) is eliminated by the first probe as shown in Fig. 13.11. The new subarray to be searched is `Slice(Slice'First..Middle-1)`, as shown in Fig. 13.12. The target value, 35, would be found on this probe.

Figure 13.11 First Probe of Binary Search

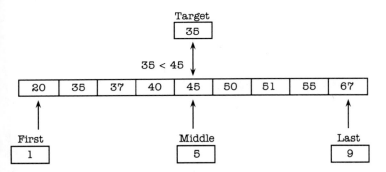

Figure 13.12 Second Probe of Binary Search

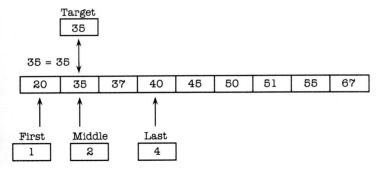

The binary search algorithm can be stated clearly using recursion. The stopping cases are:

- The array would have no elements (`Slice'First>Slice'Last` OR `Slice'Length=0`).
- The middle value is the target value.

In the first case, the function result is 0 (we'll require that arrays submitted to this algorithm have positive subscript ranges); in the second case, the function result is `Middle`. The recursive step is to search the appropriate subarray.

Data Requirements

Problem Inputs
array to be searched (`Slice : SearchArray`)
target being searched for (`Target : KeyType`)

Problem Outputs
the location of `Target` or 0 if not found

Design

Algorithm

1. Compute the subscript of the middle element
2. IF the slice has zero length then
       3. Return a result of 0
  ELSIF the target is the middle value THEN
       4. Return the subscript of the middle element
  ELSIF the target is less than the middle value THEN
       5. Search the subarray with subscripts `Slice'First..Middle-1`
  ELSE
       6. Search the subarray with subscripts `Middle+1..Slice'Last`
  END IF;

In each of the recursive steps (steps 5 and 6), the bounds of the slice are listed as a part of the actual table parameter in the recursive call. The actual parameters define the search limits for the next probe into the array.

Coding

In the initial call to the recursive procedure, the entire array is normally given. For example, given the following declarations:

```
SUBTYPE KeyType IS Integer;
TYPE SearchArray IS ARRAY(Positive RANGE <>) OF KeyType;

Test: SearchArray(1..9);
Location: Natural;
```

the procedure call statement

```
Location := BinarySearch (Test, 35);
```

could be used to search an array `Test` for the target key 35. Function `BinarySearch` is shown in Program 13.12.

The assignment statement

```
Middle := (Slice'First + Slice'Last) / 2;
```

Case Study: Binary Search, continued

659

13.7 Problem
Solving: Recursive
Searching and
Sorting

computes the subscript of the middle element by finding the average of
Slice'First and Slice'Last.

Program 13.12   A Test of Recursive Binary Search

```
WITH Text_IO;
WITH My_Int_IO;
PROCEDURE TestBinarySearch IS

   SUBTYPE KeyType IS Integer;
   TYPE SearchArray IS ARRAY(Positive RANGE <>) OF KeyType;
   Test: SearchArray(1..9);

   FUNCTION BinarySearch (Slice: SearchArray; Target: KeyType) RETURN Natural IS

   -- Performs a recursive binary search of an ordered array of
   -- keys with bounds Slice'First..Slice'Last.
   -- Pre : Target and Slice are defined.
   --     0 < Slice'First <= Slice'Last
   -- Post: Returns the subscript of Target if found in array Slice;
   --     otherwise, returns 0

     Middle : Integer;        -- the subscript of the middle element

   BEGIN -- BinarySearch

     Middle := (Slice'First + Slice'Last) / 2; -- define Middle

     -- Determine if Target is found or missing or redefine subarray.

     IF Slice'Length = 0 THEN
        RETURN 0;                           -- stopping case: Target missing
     ELSIF Slice(Middle) = Target THEN
        RETURN Middle;                      -- stopping case: Target found
     ELSIF Slice(Middle) > Target THEN      -- search lower subarray
        RETURN BinarySearch (Slice(Slice'First..Middle-1),Target);
     ELSE                                   -- search upper subarray
        RETURN BinarySearch (Slice(Middle+1..Slice'Last),Target);
     END IF;

   END BinarySearch;

BEGIN -- TestBinarySearch

   Test := (20,35,37,40,45,50,51,55,67);

   Text_IO.Put(Item => "BinarySearch(Test,35) is");
   My_Int_IO.Put(Item => BinarySearch(Test,35));
   Text_IO.New_Line;
   Text_IO.Put(Item => "BinarySearch(Test,19) is");
   My_Int_IO.Put(Item => BinarySearch(Test,19));
   Text_IO.New_Line;
   Text_IO.Put(Item => "BinarySearch(Test,75) is");
   My_Int_IO.Put(Item => BinarySearch(Test,75));
   Text_IO.New_Line;
   Text_IO.Put(Item => "BinarySearch(Test,20) is");
   My_Int_IO.Put(Item => BinarySearch(Test,20));
   Text_IO.New_Line;
   Text_IO.Put(Item => "BinarySearch(Test,67) is");
```

```
        My_Int_IO.Put(Item => BinarySearch(Test,67));
        Text_IO.New_Line;
        Text_IO.Put(Item => "BinarySearch(Test,54) is");
        My_Int_IO.Put(Item => BinarySearch(Test,54));
        Text_IO.New_Line;

END TestBinarySearch;
```

```
BinarySearch(Test,35) is          2
BinarySearch(Test,19) is          0
BinarySearch(Test,75) is          0
BinarySearch(Test,20) is          1
BinarySearch(Test,67) is          9
BinarySearch(Test,54) is          0
```

An iterative version of the binary search function is shown as Program 13.13. A Boolean flag, Found, is used to control repetition of a search loop. Found is set to False before the WHILE loop is reached. The WHILE loop executes until Target is found (Found is True) or the search array is reduced to an array of zero elements (a *null array*). The IF statement in the loop either sets Found to True (Target = Table(Middle)) or resets index Low or index High. The IF statement after the loop defines the function result.

Program 13.13   Iterative Binary Search Function

```
FUNCTION BinarySearch (Table: SearchArray; Target: KeyType) RETURN Natural I

-- Performs an iterative binary search of an ordered array of
-- keys with bounds Table'First..Slice'Last.
-- Pre : Target and Table are defined.
--      0 < Table'First <= Slice'Last
-- Post: Returns the subscript of Target if found in array Table;
--      otherwise, returns 0

   Middle : Natural;       -- the subscript of the middle element
   Found :  Boolean;       -- program flag
   Left :   Natural;
   Right :  Natural;

BEGIN -- BinarySearch

   Left := Table'First;
   Right := Table'Last;
   Found := False;

   WHILE (Left <= Right) AND (NOT Found) LOOP
      -- invariant:
      --     last subarray searched was not null and
      --     Target /= Table(Middle) for all prior values of Middle

      Middle := (Left + Right) / 2;    -- define Middle
```

Case Study: Binary Search, continued

661

13.7 Problem
Solving: Recursive
Searching and
Sorting

```
    IF Target = Table(Middle) THEN
      Found := True;
    ELSIF Target < Table(Middle) THEN
      Right := Middle - 1;                    -- search lower subarray
    ELSIF Target > Table(Middle) THEN
      Left := Middle + 1;                     -- search upper subarray
    END IF;

  END LOOP;

  -- Assertion: Target is found or search subarray is null.
  IF Found THEN
    RETURN Middle;                            -- Target is found
  ELSE
    RETURN 0;                                 -- Target not found
  END IF;

END BinarySearch;
```

Testing the Binary Search Functions

You should test both versions of the binary search function very carefully. Besides verifying that they locate target values that are present in the array, verify that they also determine when a target value is missing. Use target values that are within the range of values stored in the array, a target value that is less than the smallest value in the array, and a target value that is greater than the largest value in the array. Make sure that the binary search function terminates regardless of whether the target is missing or where it is located if it is not missing.

Subarrays with Subscript Zero

The binary search function is written to return 0 if the target is not found. This works only because we have required that the array bounds be positive, because otherwise 0 could be a valid subscript. Binary search would be more general if it could accept arrays with arbitrary integer bounds; in that case, it would be better to convert the binary search function to a procedure with two OUT parameters: the index of the target if found and a program flag indicating whether the target was found. This modification is left as an exercise.

Recursive Selection Sort

We have discussed selection sort and implemented an iterative selection sort procedure. Because the selection sort first finds the largest element in an array and places it where it belongs, and then finds and places the next largest element and so on, it is a good candidate for a recursive solution.

◆ Case Study: Recursive Selection Sort

Problem

Develop a recursive version of the selection sort algorithm.

Design Overview

The selection sort algorithm follows from the description above. The stopping case is an array of length 1, which is sorted by definition. Review Fig. 8.12 to see how the elements of an array are placed in their final positions by a selection sort.

Recursive Algorithm for Selection Sort

1. IF X'First = X'Last (i.e., if X has only one element) THEN
   2. The array is sorted.
   ELSE
   3. Place the largest array element in X(X'Last).
   4. Sort the subarray with subscripts X'First..X'Last-1.
   END IF;

Coding

This algorithm is implemented as a recursive procedure in Program 13.14. Procedure PlaceLargest performs step 3 of the algorithm. The recursive procedure SelectSort is simpler to understand than the one shown in Program 8.18 because it contains a single IF statement instead of nested FOR loops. This recursive procedure makes a nice example; however, it would not be used in practice because the total number of recursive calls is directly proportional to the square of the number of elements in the array. For large arrays, this would cause an unacceptably large number of calls.

Program 13.14   Selection Sort, Recursive Version

```
WITH Text_IO;
WITH My_Int_IO;
PROCEDURE TestSelectSort IS

  TYPE IntArray IS ARRAY(Integer RANGE <>) OF Integer;
  Test: IntArray(-4..5);


  PROCEDURE PlaceLargest (X : IN OUT IntArray) IS

    -- Finds the largest element in array slice X(X'First..X'Last)
    -- and exchanges it with the element at X(X'Last).
    -- Pre : Array X is defined and X'First <= X'Last.
    -- Post: X'Last contains the largest value.

    Temp :     Integer;  -- temporary copy for exchange
    MaxIndex : Integer;  -- index of largest so far

  BEGIN -- PlaceLargest
```

Case Study: Recursive Selection Sort, continued

663

13.7 Problem
Solving: Recursive
Searching and
Sorting

```
      MaxIndex := X'Last;   -- assume X(X'Last) is largest
      FOR j IN REVERSE X'First..X'Last-1 LOOP
        IF X(j) > X(MaxIndex) THEN
          MaxIndex := j;   -- X(j) is largest so far
        END IF;
      END LOOP;

      -- assertion: MaxIndex is subscript of largest element
      IF MaxIndex /= X'Last THEN -- exchange X(X'Last) and X(MaxIndex)
        Temp := X(X'Last);
        X(X'Last) := X(MaxIndex);
        X(MaxIndex) := Temp;
      END IF;

  END PlaceLargest;

  PROCEDURE SelectSort (X : IN OUT IntArray) IS

    -- Sorts an integer array slice X with bounds X'First and X'Last.
    -- Pre : Array X is defined and X'First <= X'Last.
    -- Post: The array elements are in numerical order.

  BEGIN -- SelectSort

    IF X'First = X'Last THEN
      RETURN;                  -- stopping case
    ELSIF X'First > X'Last THEN
      Text_IO.Put(Item => "Invalid slice bounds for SelectSort");
      Text_IO.New_Line;
    ELSE
      -- recursive step: place largest value in X(X'Last),
      -- then sort the slice X(X'First..X'Last-1)
      PlaceLargest (X => X);
      SelectSort (X => X(X'First..X'Last-1));
    END IF;

  END SelectSort;

BEGIN -- TestSelectSort

  Test := (1,19,3,17,5,15,7,13,9,11);
  Text_IO.Put(Item => "Before sorting: ");
  FOR Count IN Test'First .. Test'Last LOOP
    My_Int_IO.Put(Item => Test(Count), Width => 3);
  END LOOP;
  Text_IO.New_Line;

  SelectSort(X => Test);
  Text_IO.Put(Item => "After sorting: ");
  FOR Count IN Test'First .. Test'Last LOOP
    My_Int_IO.Put(Item => Test(Count), Width => 3);
  END LOOP;
  Text_IO.New_Line;

END TestSelectSort;


Before sorting:   1 19  3 17  5 15  7 13  9 11
After   sorting:  1  3  5  7  9 11 13 15 17 19
```

If the array has only one element, procedure SelectSort returns without doing anything. This behavior is correct because a one element array is always sorted.

Recursive Sorting: QuickSort

In the sorting methods we have seen so far, the running time is proportional to the square of the number of elements in the array being sorted. Many faster sorting methods have been developed; the last case study shows one such method, called QuickSort.

 ## Case Study: QuickSort

Problem
Develop a sorting algorithm that is faster than $O(N^2)$

Analysis
The data requirements follow.

> *Problem Inputs*
> the array (or array slice) being sorted (Table : IN OUT IntArray)
>
> *Procedure Outputs*
> the sorted array (or slice) (Table : IN OUT IntArray)

Design
Given an array Table with bound Table'First..Table'Last, QuickSort rearranges this array so that all element values smaller than a selected *pivot value* are first, followed by the pivot value, followed by all element values larger than the pivot value. After this rearrangement (called a *partition*), the pivot value is in its proper place. All element values smaller than the pivot value are closer to where they belong, because they precede the pivot value. All element values larger than the pivot value are closer to where they belong, because they follow the pivot value.

An example of this process is shown in Fig. 13.13. We will assume that the first array element is arbitrarily selected as the pivot. A possible result of the partitioning process is shown beneath the original array.

After the partitioning process, PivIndex is 5 and the fifth array element contains the pivot value, 44. All values less than 44 are in the left subarray; all values greater than 44 are in the right subarray, as desired.

We now have two unsorted subarrays; the pivot value is the boundary between the two. The next step would be to apply QuickSort recursively to the

Case Study: QuickSort, continued

665

13.7 Problem
Solving: Recursive
Searching and
Sorting

Figure 13.13   State of Array after First Partition

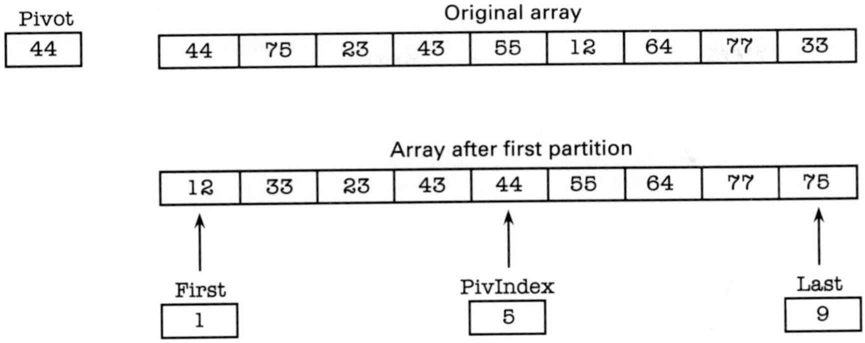

two subarrays on either side of the pivot value. The algorithm for QuickSort follows. We will describe how to do the partitioning later.

Local Variables
the subscript of the pivot value after partitioning (PivIndex : Integer)

Algorithm for QuickSort

1. IF Table'First < Table'Last THEN
    2. Partition the elements in the slice Table'First..Table'Last so that the pivot value is in place (subscript is PivIndex)
    3. Apply QuickSort to the slice Table'First..PivIndex−1
    4. Apply QuickSort to the slice PivIndex+1..Table'Last
    END IF;

A stopping case for QuickSort is an array of one element (Table'First = Table'Last), which is sorted by definition, so nothing is done. If Table'First > Table'Last, then the array bounds are improper (also a stopping case). If the array has more than one element, we partition it into two subarrays and sort the subarrays using QuickSort.

Coding

The implementation of procedure QuickSort is shown in Program 13.15. Use the procedure call statement

    QuickSort (Table);

to sort the array Table (type IntArray).

Program 13.15   Procedure QuickSort

```
PROCEDURE QuickSort (Table : IN OUT IntArray) IS

   -- Recursive procedure to sort the array slice Table with
   -- bounds Table'First and Table'Last.
```

Case Study: QuickSort, continued

```
-- Pre : array Table is defined and Table'First <= Table'Last
-- Post: Table is sorted.

PivIndex : Integer;          -- subscript of pivot value
                            -- returned by Partition
BEGIN -- QuickSort

   IF Table'First < Table'Last THEN
      -- Split into two subarrays separated by value at PivIndex
      Partition (Table, PivIndex);
      -- sort the two subarrays
      QuickSort (Table(Table'First..PivIndex-1));
      QuickSort (Table(PivIndex+1..Table'Last));
   END IF;

END QuickSort;
```

The two recursive calls to `QuickSort` in Program 13.15 cause the `QuickSort` procedure to be applied to the slices that are separated by the value at `PivIndex`. If any subarray contains just one (or zero) elements, an immediate return occurs.

Coding Procedure Partition

Procedure `Partition` selects the pivot and performs the partitioning operation. Because the arrays are randomly ordered to begin with, it does not really matter which element we choose to be the pivot value. For simplicity, we choose the element with subscript `Table'First`. We then search for the first value at the left end of the subarray that is greater than the pivot value. When we find it, we search for the first value at the right end of the subarray that is less than or equal to the pivot value. These two values are exchanged, and we repeat the search and exchange operations. This is illustrated in Fig. 13.14, with `Up` pointing to the first value greater than the pivot and `Down` pointing to the first value less than or equal to the pivot value.

Figure 13.14   Finding the First Pivot Value

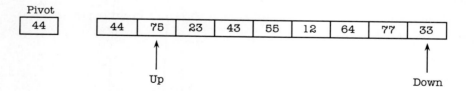

The first value at the left end of the array that is larger than 44 is 75; 33 is the first value at the right end that is less than or equal to 44. These two values are therefore exchanged. The pointers `Up` and `Down` are then advanced from their current positions to the positions in Fig. 13.15. The next value at the left end that is larger than 44 is 55; 12 is the next value at the right end

Case Study: QuickSort, continued

667

13.7 Problem
Solving: Recursive
Searching and
Sorting

Figure 13.15 State of Array after First Exchange

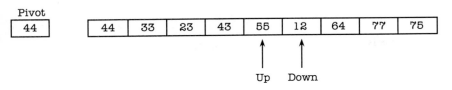

that is less than or equal to 44. These two values are therefore exchanged, and Up and Down are advanced again, as shown in Fig. 13.16.

After the second exchange, the first five array elements contain the pivot value and all values less than or equal to the pivot; the last four elements contain all values larger than the pivot. Up once again selects 55 as the next element larger than the pivot; 12 is selected by Down as the next element less than or equal to the pivot. Because Up has now "passed" Down, these values are not exchanged. Instead, the pivot value (subscript is Table'First) and the value at position Down are exchanged. This puts the pivot value in its proper position (new subscript is Down) as shown in Fig. 13.17.

Figure 13.16 State of Array after Second Exchange

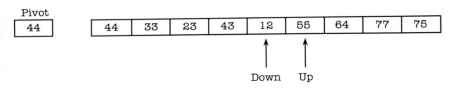

Figure 13.17 State of Array after Third Exchange

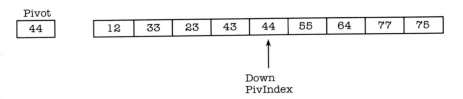

The partitioning process is now complete, and the value of Down is returned as the pivot index (PivIndex). QuickSort is called recursively to sort the left subarray and the right subarray. The algorithm for Partition follows; it is implemented as Program 13.16.

Local variables for Partition
the pivot value (Pivot : Integer)
index to array elements larger than Pivot (Up : Integer)
index to array elements less than or equal to Pivot (Down : Integer)

Case Study: QuickSort, continued

Program 13.16   Procedure Partition

```
PROCEDURE Partition (Table : IN OUT IntArray;
                          PivIndex : OUT Integer) IS

  -- Partitions the array slice Table with bounds Table'First and
  -- Table'Last into two subarrays.
  -- Pre : Table is defined and T'First <= T'Last.
  -- Post: PivIndex is defined such that all values less than or equal
  --     to Table(PivIndex) have subscripts < PivIndex; all values
  --     greater than Table(PivIndex) have subscripts > PivIndex.

  Pivot : Integer;              -- the pivot value
  Up    : Integer;              -- pointer to values > Pivot
  Down  : Integer;              -- pointer to values <= Pivot

BEGIN -- Partition

  Pivot := Table(Table'First);    -- define leftmost element as the pivot

  -- Find and exchange values that are out of place.
  Up :=Table'First;               -- set Up to point to leftmost element
  Down := Table'Last;         -- set Down to point to rightmost element

  LOOP
    -- Move Up to the next value larger than Pivot.
    WHILE (Table(Up) <= Pivot) AND (Up < Table'Last) LOOP
      Up := Up + 1;
    END LOOP;
    -- assertion: Table(Up) > Pivot or Up is equal to Table'Last

    -- Move Down to the next value less than or equal to Pivot.
    WHILE Table(Down) > Pivot LOOP
      Down := Down - 1;
    END LOOP;
    -- assertion: Table(Down) <= Pivot

    -- Exchange out of order values.
    IF Up < Down THEN
      Exchange (Table(Up), Table(Down));
    END IF;

    EXIT WHEN Up >= Down;        -- until Up meets or passes Down
  END LOOP;
  -- Assertion: values <= Pivot have subscripts <= Down and
  --   values > Pivot have subscripts > Down

  -- Put pivot value where it belongs and define PivIndex.
  Exchange (Table(Table'First), Table(Down));
  PivIndex := Down;

END Partition;
```

Algorithm for Partition

1. Define the pivot value as the contents of Table(Table'First).
2. Initialize Up to Table'First and Down to Table'Last.

Case Study: QuickSort, continued

669

13.7 Problem
Solving: Recursive
Searching and
Sorting

3. LOOP
    4. Increment Up until Up selects the first element greater than the pivot value.
    5. Decrement Down until Down selects the first element less than or equal to the pivot value.
    6. IF Up < Down THEN
        7. Exchange their values.
        END IF;
    EXIT WHEN Up meets or passes Down
    END LOOP;
8. Exchange Table(Table'First) and Table(Down).
9. Define PivIndex as Down.

The two WHILE loops in Program 13.16 advance pointers Up and Down to the left and right, respectively. Because Table(Table'First) is equal to Pivot, the second loop will stop if Down happens to reach the left end of the array (Down is Table'First). The extra condition (Up < Table'Last) is added to the first WHILE loop to ensure that it also stops if Up happens to reach the right end of the array.

Analysis of QuickSort

The QuickSort procedure works better for some arrays than it does for others. It works best when the partitioning process splits each subarray into two subarrays of almost the same size. The worst behavior results when one of the subarrays has zero elements and the other has all the rest except for the pivot value. Ironically, this worst-case behavior results when QuickSort is applied to an array that is already sorted. The pivot value remains in position Table'First, and the rest of the elements will be in the subarray with subscripts Table'First+1..Table'Last.

Procedure Partition compares each array element to the pivot value (an $O(N)$ process). If the array splits are relatively even, the number of calls to Partition is $O(\log_2 N)$ (this is similar to the analysis we did of BinarySearch). Therefore, QuickSort is an $O(N \times \log_2 N)$ process in the best case. In the worst case, there are N calls to Partition and QuickSort degenerates to an $O(N^2)$ process.

Because data values are usually distributed in random order in an array, QuickSort as presented will work quite well. A possible improvement is to use the average of two or more array elements as the pivot value. This requires more computation time and also requires a modification to the algorithm because the pivot value is no longer an array element value.

Exercises for Section 13.7

Self-Check

1. Trace the execution of SelectSort on an array that has the integers 5, 8, 10, 1 stored in consecutive elements.
2. Trace the search of the array Table shown in this section for a Target of 40. Specify the values of First, Middle, and Last during each recursive call.
3. Provide the algorithm for a recursive procedure that performs binary search and returns a flag as its second output parameter that indicates whether the search was successful.
4. Complete the trace of QuickSort for the subarrays remaining after the first partition.
5. In the event an array contains some values that are the same, in which subarray (left or right) will all values that are equal to the pivot value be placed?
6. Trace the execution of QuickSort on the array below. Show the values of First and Last for each recursive call and the array elements after returning from each call. Also, show the value of Pivot during each call and the value returned through PivIndex. How many times is QuickSort called and how many times is Partition called?

   55 50 10 40 80 90 60 100 70 80 20

   How do you think insertion sort would perform compared to QuickSort?

Programming

1. Write the procedure for Self-Check Exercise 2.

13.8 Tricks of the Trade: Common Programming Errors

The most common problem with a recursive procedure or function is that it may not terminate properly. For example, if the terminating condition is not correct or is incomplete, then the procedure may call itself indefinitely or until all available memory is used up. Normally, a "stack overflow" or Storage_Error exception is an indicator that a recursive procedure is not terminating. Make sure that you identify all stopping cases and provide a terminating condition for each one. Also be sure that each recursive step leads to a situation that is closer to a stopping case and that repeated recursive calls will eventually lead to stopping cases only.

Sometimes it is difficult to observe the result of a recursive procedure execution. If each recursive call generates a large number of output lines and there are many recursive calls, the output will scroll down the screen more quickly than it can be read. On most systems it is possible to stop the screen temporarily by pressing a control character sequence (e.g., Control-S). If this cannot be done, it is still possible to cause your output to stop temporarily by displaying a prompting message followed by a `Text_IO.Get(NextChar)` operation. Your program will resume execution when you enter a data character.

 # Chapter Review

This chapter provides many examples of recursive procedures and functions. Studying them should give you some appreciation of the power of recursion as a problem-solving and programming tool and should provide you with valuable insight regarding its use. It may take some time to feel comfortable thinking in this new way about programming, but it is certainly worth the effort.

✓ *Quick-Check Exercises*

1. Explain the use of a stack in recursion.
2. Which is generally more efficient (in terms of running time and space), recursion or iteration?
3. Which control statement do you always find in a recursive procedure or function?
4. Why would a programmer conceptualize the problem solution using recursion and implement it using iteration?
5. What causes a stack overflow error, indicated in Ada by `Storage_Error`?
6. What can you say about a recursive algorithm that has the following form?

```
IF condition THEN
    Perform recursive step
END IF;
```

Answers to Quick-Check Exercises
1. The stack is used to hold all parameter and local variable values and the return point for each execution of a recursive procedure.
2. Iteration is generally more efficient than recursion.
3. IF statement
4. When its solution is much easier to conceptualize using recursion but its implementation would be too inefficient
5. Too many recursive calls
6. Nothing is done when the stopping case is reached.

Review Questions for Chapter 13

1. Explain the nature of a recursive problem.
2. Discuss the efficiency of recursive procedures.
3. Differentiate between stopping cases and a terminating condition.
4. Convert the program below from an iterative process to a recursive function that calculates an approximate value for *e*, the base of the natural logarithms, by summing the series

$$1 + 1/1! + 1/2! + \cdots + 1/N!$$

until additional terms do not affect the approximation.

```
PROCEDURE ELog IS

   ENL:    Float;
   Delta:  Float;
   Fact:   Float;
   N:      Float;

BEGIN -- Elog

   ENL  := 1.0;
   N  := 1.0;
   Fact := 1.0;
   Delta := 1.0;

   LOOP
      ENL := ENL + Delta;
      N := N + 1.0;
      Fact := Fact * N;
      Delta := 1.0 / Fact;
      EXIT WHEN ENL = (ENL + Delta);
   END LOOP;

   Text_IO.Put(Item => "The value of e is ");
   My_Flt_IO.Put(Item => ENL, Fore => 3, Aft => 15, Exp => 0);

END Elog;
```

Programming Projects

1. Write a procedure that reads each row of an array as a string and converts it to a row of Grid (see Fig.13.10). The first character of row 1 corresponds to Grid(1,1), the second character to Grid(1,2), and so on. Set the element value to Empty if the character is blank; otherwise, set it to Filled. The number of rows in the array should be read first. Use this procedure in a program that reads in cell coordinates and prints the number of cells in the blob containing each coordinate pair.

2. The expression for computing $C(n, r)$, the number of combinations of n items taken r at a time is

$$C(n, r) = \frac{n!}{r!(n - r)!}$$

Write and test a function for computing $C(n, r)$ given that $n!$ is the factorial of n.

3. Write a recursive function that returns the value of the following recursive definition:

$F(X, Y) = X - Y$ if X or $Y < 0$
$F(X, Y) = F(X - 1, Y) + F(X, Y - 1)$ otherwise

4. Write a recursive procedure that lists all of the pairs of subsets for a given set of letters. For example:

```
('A','C','E','G') =>
   ('A','C'), ('A','E'),('A','G'), ('C','E'), ('C','G'), ('E','G')
```

5. Write a procedure that accepts an 8 × 8 array of characters that represents a maze. Each position can contain either an 'X' or a blank. Starting at position (1, 1), list

any path through the maze to get to location (8, 8). Only horizontal and vertical moves are allowed (no diagonal moves). If no path exists, write a message indicating this. Moves can be made only to locations that contain a blank. If an 'X' is encountered, that path is blocked and another must be chosen. Use recursion.

6. One method of solving a continuous numerical function for a root implements a technique called the *bisection method,* which is similar to the binary search. Given a numerical function, defined as $f(X)$, and two values of X that are known to bracket one of the roots, an approximation to this root can be determined through a method of repeated division of this bracket.

For a set of values of X to bracket a root the value of the function for one X must be negative and the other must be positive. This is illustrated in Fig. 13.18, which plots $f(X)$ for values of X between $X1$ and $X2$.

Figure 13.18 Diagram for Bisection Method

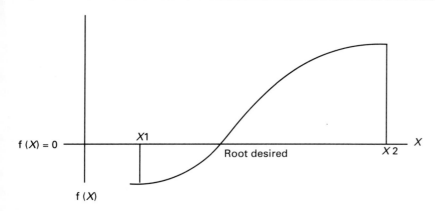

The algorithm requires that the midpoint between the left X and the right X be evaluated in the function. If the midpoint equals zero, the root is found; otherwise, the left X ($X1$) or right X ($X2$) is set to this midpoint. To determine whether to replace either $X1$ or $X2$, the sign of the midpoint is compared against the signs of the values of $f(X1)$ and $f(X2)$. The midpoint replaces the X ($X1$ or $X2$) whose function value has the same sign as the function value at the midpoint.

This routine can be written recursively. The terminating conditions are true when either the midpoint evaluated in the function is zero or the absolute value of the left minus the right X is less than some small predetermined value (e.g., 0.0005). If the second condition occurs, then the root is said to be approximately equal to the midpoint of the last set of left and right Xs.

7. We can use a merge technique to sort two arrays. The *mergesort* begins by taking adjacent pairs of array values and ordering the values in each pair. It then forms groups of four elements by merging adjacent pairs (first pair with second pair, third pair with fourth pair, etc.) into another array. It then takes adjacent groups of four elements from this new array and merges them back into the original array as groups of eight, and so on. The process terminates when a single group is formed that has the same number of elements as the array. Figure 13.19 shows a mergesort for an array with eight elements. Write a `MergeSort` procedure.

8. Improve the palindrome-finding program (Program 13.9) so that blanks and punctuation are ignored and the program is case-insensitive. (*Hint:* Use operations from

Figure 13.19 Merge Sort

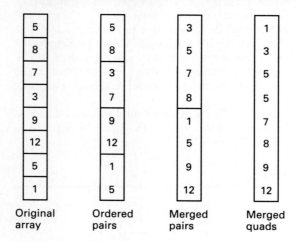

| Original array | Ordered pairs | Merged pairs | Merged quads |

VStrings to write a function that takes a VString S as parameter and returns S with all letters converted to uppercase, as well as blanks and punctuation removed. "Madam, I'm Adam" would be converted to "MADAMIMADAM". Use the result of calling this function as the input to StringReverse.)

9. Modify BinarySearch into a procedure with two output parameters: the location of the key if found, and a flag indicating whether or not the key was found.

10. Using the modified BinarySearch of Programming Project 9 as a starting point, write a generic binary search procedure that can handle any array with any non-limited element type and any index type.

11. Make QuickSort into a generic sorting procedure.

Dynamic Data Structures

14

14.1   Data Structures: Access Types and the NEW Operator
14.2   Data Structures: Linked Lists
14.3   Problem Solving: Specification of a Keyed-Table Abstract Data Type
14.4   Data Structures: Implementing the Keyed Table as a One-Way Linked List
14.5   Case Study: Airline Passenger List
14.6   Data Structures: Multiple-Linked Lists and Trees
14.7   Data Structures: Reimplementing the Keyed Table as a Search Tree
14.8   Tricks of the Trade: Common Programming Errors
        Chapter Review

In this chapter, we will see how Ada can be used to create *dynamic data structures*. Dynamic data structures are data structures that expand and contract as a program executes. A dynamic data structure is a collection of elements (called *nodes*) that are generally implemented as records. Whereas an array always contains storage for a fixed number of elements, a dynamic data structure can change its size as the program executes.

Dynamic data structures are extremely flexible. It is relatively easy to add new information by creating a new node and inserting it between two existing nodes. It is also relatively easy to delete a node.

Three examples of dynamic data structures are discussed in this chapter: ordered one-way lists, expression trees, and binary search trees. We will learn how to use these data structures for storing information and how to process information saved in them.

14.1 Data Structures: Access Types and the NEW Operator

Since Chapter 8 we have been using arrays to store collections of data. We know that it is possible for each array element to be a record, and we have seen a number of examples of such data structures. One characteristic of data collections is that they can vary in size considerably from one run of a program to the next, or even during a run. In such cases, an array is not the best structure in which to store the records, because the array size is fixed, and therefore must be estimated before the records are read in. If only a few records are present, much space is wasted. Worse, the array cannot expand to hold a number of records greater than its size.

There is a solution to this problem, called *dynamic data structures* or *linked data structures*. Using dynamic data structures, the data collection can expand and contract as necessary. In languages like Ada that provide built-in support for linked structures, the compiler associates with an executable program a special storage area, which it initially leaves unassigned to any program variable. The area is usually called the *heap* or *dynamic storage pool*. A system module, called the *heap manager* or *storage allocator,* is linked into the program and assumes responsibility for allocating blocks of storage from the heap, and returning extra blocks to the heap, *at execution time.* We can think of the heap as a "slush fund" from which a program can "borrow" storage to expand a structure, returning the storage when it is no longer needed. The heap manager can then use that storage to satisfy another storage request from the program.

A special kind of variable is provided for referencing space allocated dynamically from the heap. In Ada these are called *access variables;* in other languages, such as Pascal and C, they are referred to as *pointer variables.* Ada allows us to declare *access types,* and each access variable is an object of an access type. The values of each access type are called *access values,* or informally *pointers.* A pointer or access value is an abstraction for a hardware address.

Consider a record type called `RecType`, defined as

```
TYPE RecType IS RECORD

    ... fields ...

END RECORD;
```

The type definition

```
TYPE RecPointer IS ACCESS RecType;
```

gives us the ability to declare variables of type `RecPointer`, that is, variables that can hold pointers to things of type `RecType`. For example, a declaration

```
P1, P2, P3: RecPointer;
```

allocates storage for three such variables.

When an access variable is created in Ada, its value is always initialized to a special, unique internal value known as `NULL`. This indicates that the pointer doesn't point to anything (yet). It is important to realize that declaring such variables does not cause any records to be allocated; each variable is given just enough space to hold the address of a record.

How do the records themselves come into being? The Ada operator `NEW` exists to create them. An assignment statement such as

```
P1 := NEW RecType;
```

causes the heap manager to search the heap, looking for a block of space large enough to hold a record of type `RecType`. When such a block is found, its address is stored in the variable `P1`. Figure 14.1 shows diagrammatically how dynamic allocation works. The cloud-like shape represents the heap, arrows represent pointers, and diagonal lines represent `NULL`.

Access values can be copied using the assignment operator. For example,

```
P3 := P1;
```

causes P3 to point to the same record to which P1 points. *An assignment statement using an access variable copies only the pointer to (the address of) the structure involved, not the structure itself!*

If we write

```
P1 := NEW Rectype;
```

a second time, then space for another record is found in the heap, its address is stored in P1, and P3 is left pointing to the "old" record. If we write

```
P1 := NEW RecType;
```

a third time, the record previously pointed to by P1 is left with nothing pointing to it, thus making it *inaccessible*. This space, in general, remains allocated and unavailable for other use. This situation is often called a *storage leak* because the storage "leaks away" and can no longer be used. We will return to this subject later in the chapter.

Figure 14.1 Dynamic Allocation

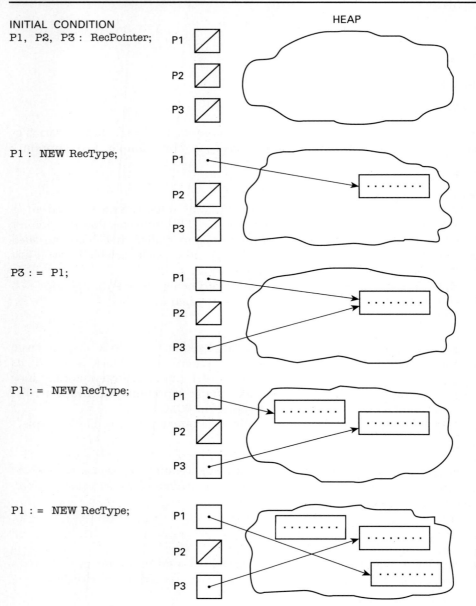

Creating a Linked Structure

Because we do not know beforehand how many nodes will be needed in a dynamic data structure, we cannot allocate storage for it in the conventional way, that is, through a variable declaration. Instead, we must allocate storage for each individual node as needed and somehow join this node to the rest of the structure.

We can connect two nodes if we include a pointer field in each node. The declarations

```
TYPE Node;

TYPE NodePointer IS ACCESS Node;

TYPE Node IS RECORD
    Current : String(1..2);
    Volts : Natural;
    Link : NodePointer;
END RECORD;
```

identify NodePointer as a pointer type. A pointer variable of type NodePointer points to a record of type Node with three fields: Current, Volts, and Link. The Link field is also of type NodePointer. We can use this field to point to the next node in a dynamic data structure.

Note that the first type definition is *incomplete;* it just mentions the name Node without filling in the details. This device is used to inform the compiler of the existence of the type Node so that the next type definition can use it. Using an incomplete type definition meets Ada's requirement that types must be defined before they can be used.

Now let us declare some pointer variables:

```
P : NodePointer;
Q : NodePointer;
R : NodePointer;
```

As in the previous example, P, Q, and R are automatically given initial NULL values. The assignment statements

```
P := NEW Node;
Q := NEW Node;
```

allocate storage for two records of type Node, storing their addresses in P and Q. Initially the Current and Volts fields of these records are undefined; the Link fields of both are initially NULL. Pointer initialization is one of the few cases in Ada where objects are given initial values at declaration.

In Ada terminology, a nonnull access object *designates* a value. The block of space pointed to by P is P's designated value. We can refer to the designated value of P using the expression P.ALL, and to the Current field of P.ALL by the expression P.ALL.Current. The assignment statements

```
P.ALL.Current := "AC";
P.ALL.Volts := 115;
Q.ALL.Current := "DC";
Q.ALL.Volts := 12;
```

define the nonlink fields of these nodes, as shown in Fig. 14.2. The Link fields are still NULL.

The .ALL construct is the way Ada represents a *dereferencing* operation, that is, an operation to find that value to which a pointer points. To simplify the syntax necessary to select a field of a designated value, Ada allows us to omit

Figure 14.2 Nodes P.ALL and Q.ALL

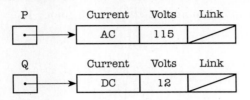

the .ALL part and just select the field directly. Therefore, the following four assignment statements are equivalent to the ones just given:

```
P.Current := "AC";
P.Volts := 115;
Q.Current := "DC";
Q.Volts := 12;
```

We will use the abbreviated form throughout this chapter. Because P is an access variable, we can read the expression P.Current as "find the value designated by P and select its Current field."

Let us do some more pointer manipulation. The assignment statement

```
R := P;
```

copies the value of pointer variable P into pointer variable R. This means that pointers P and R contain the same access value and, therefore, point to the same node, as shown in Fig. 14.3. Here and in later figures we have left out the cloud symbol for simplicity.

The pointer assignment statements

```
P := Q;
Q := R;
```

have the effect of exchanging the nodes pointed to by P and Q, as shown in Fig. 14.4.

Figure 14.3 Nodes R.ALL/P.ALL and Q.ALL

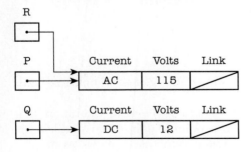

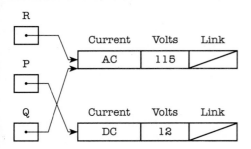

The statements

```
Text_IO.Put(Item => Q.Current);
Text_IO.Put(Item => P.Current);
```

display the Current fields of the records designated by Q and P. For the situation depicted in Fig 14.4, the line

```
ACDC
```

would be displayed.

The statement

```
Q := NEW Node;
```

changes the value of Q to designate a new node, thereby disconnecting Q from its previous node. The new values of pointer variables P, Q, and R are shown in Fig. 14.5. The data fields of the new node designated by Q are, of course, initially undefined.

It is important to understand the difference between P and P's designated value. P is an access variable (type NodePointer) and is used to store the address

Figure 14.5 Nodes R.ALL, P.ALL and Q.ALL

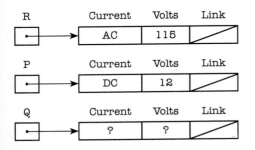

of a data structure of type `Node`. `P` can be assigned a new value either by calling `NEW` or by copying another access value of the same type. `P.ALL` is the name of the record designated by `P` and can be manipulated like any other Ada record. The field selectors `P.Current` and `P.Volts` may be used to reference data (a string and integer) stored in this record.

Connecting Nodes

One purpose in introducing dynamically allocated nodes is to be able to grow data structures of varying size. We can accomplish this by connecting individual nodes. If we look at the nodes allocated in the last section, we see that their `Link` fields are currently NULL. Since the link fields are type `NodePointer`, they can themselves be used to designate values. The assignment statement

```
R.Link := P;
```

copies the value stored in `P` (an access value) into the `Link` field of node `R.ALL`. In this way, nodes `R` and `P` become connected. Similarly, the assignment statement

```
P.Link := Q;
```

copies the access value stored in access variable `Q` into the link field of node `P.ALL`, thereby connecting nodes `P` and `Q`. The situation after execution of these two assignment statements is shown in Fig. 14.6.

The data structure pointed to by `R` has now grown to form a chain of all three nodes. The first node is referenced by `R.ALL`. The second node can be referenced by `P.ALL` or `R.Link.ALL` since they both have the same value. Finally, the third node may be referenced by `Q.ALL` or `P.Link.ALL` or even `R.Link.Link.ALL`.

Let us summarize the operations used in this section. The statement

```
P := NEW Node;
```

Figure 14.6 Connecting Nodes R.ALL, P.ALL, and Q.ALL

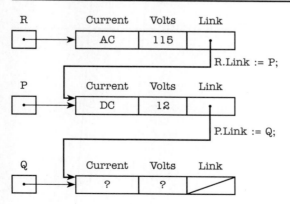

causes a node to be allocated and its address (an access value) to be stored in P. The expression

```
P.ALL
```

is the name of P's designated value (a Node); the expressions

```
P.ALL.Volts
P.Volts
```

are equivalent ways of selecting the Volts field of P.ALL.

Returning Dynamic Storage to the Heap

In Fig. 14.1 we allocated a block of storage from the heap but later caused its pointer to point elsewhere (see last two diagrams in Fig. 14.1). Because no other access value designated it, the block became inaccessible. What happens to a inaccessible block?

In theory, the Ada heap manager could include a module that automatically keeps track of inaccessible blocks and makes them available to be reallocated. Such a module is often called a *garbage collector,* because it keeps track of discarded memory blocks. Garbage collectors are provided in some languages, especially Lisp and Snobol, but are rarely included in Ada systems, primarily because this automatic operation requires too much CPU time.

An Ada program that continually allocates blocks, then discards them just by making them inaccessible, could well run out of heap storage at some point during operation. Because an Ada system is unlikely to provide an automatic garbage collector, the programmer is responsible for recycling the garbage. Luckily, Ada provides a standard operation, Unchecked_Deallocation, to return dynamically allocated storage to the heap. This is a generic procedure, with the specification

```
GENERIC
   TYPE Object IS LIMITED PRIVATE;
   TYPE Name IS ACCESS Object;
PROCEDURE Unchecked_Deallocation (X: IN OUT Name);
```

To use this procedure, it must be WITH-ed in a context clause, and instantiated using the access type and the designated type as actual parameters. For example,

```
PROCEDURE Dispose IS
   NEW Unchecked_Deallocation (Object => Node, Name => NodePointer);
```

creates an instance for the types used in this section, and the procedure call statement

```
Dispose (X => P);
```

will return P's designated value to the heap. Paraphrasing the Ada standard, we describe this operation as follows:

- After executing the Dispose call, the value of P is NULL.
- If P is already NULL, the call has no effect.
- If P is not NULL, then the call indicates that P.ALL is no longer needed and may be returned to the heap.

Because we can copy access values, the situation can arise in which more than one access value designates the same block of storage. For this reason, we must be careful when returning storage to the heap. Errors will result if the cells returned are later referenced by another access value that still designates them; indeed, the Ada standard says specifically that the effect of doing so is unpredictable. Suppose P designates a node. If we write

```
Q := P;
Dispose(X => P);
```

then the cells designated by P are returned to the heap and the meaning of Q.ALL or Q.Volts is unpredictable. In this situation, a variable like Q is usually called a *dangling pointer*. It is important to be sure that there is no need for a particular record before returning the storage occupied by it. Also, we must be careful when coding not to create dangling pointers; these lead to execution errors that will not always give rise to nice Ada exceptions.

Running Out of Heap Storage

It is possible to exhaust the supply of cells on the heap. If this happens in Ada, the heap manager will raise the predefined exception Storage_Error.

Normally we can assume that there are enough memory cells available in the heap. However, when writing large programs that create sizable dynamic data structures, it is advisable to code an exception handler for Storage_Error in the part of the program that does the allocation.

Exercises for Section 14.1

Self-Check

1. For Fig. 14.6, indicate whether each assignment statement is legal, and explain the effect of each legal one.

   a. R.Current := "CA";
   b. P.ALL := R.ALL;
   c. P.Current := "HT";
   d. P := 54;
   e. R.Link.Volts := 0;
   f. P := R;
   g. R.Link.Link.Current := "XY";
   h. Q.Volts := R.Volts;

2. The assignment statements

   ```
   R := P;
   P := Q;
   Q := R;
   ```

   are used to exchange the values of pointer variables R and Q (type Node-Pointer). What do the following assignment statements do?

   ```
   R.Current := P.Current;
   P.Current := Q.Current;
   Q.Current := R.Current;
   ```

♦ 14.2 Data Structures: Linked Lists

In this section, we will introduce an important data structure called a *linked list* (or simply a *list*). We will see how to build and manipulate lists in Ada.

Abstract Lists

An *abstract list* is a sequence of list elements or *nodes* in which each node is linked or connected to the node following it. An abstract list with three nodes follows.

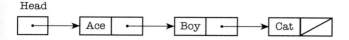

Each node in this list has two fields: the first field contains data, and the second field is a pointer to the next node. There is a pointer (Head) to the first node or *list head*. The last node always has a NULL pointer value, indicated as usual by a diagonal line.

Lists are an important data structure because they can be modified easily, regardless of how many elements may be in the list. For example, a new node containing the string "Bye" can be inserted between the strings "Boy" and "Cat" by changing only one pointer value (the one from "Boy") and setting the pointer from the new node to point to "Cat":

Similarly, it is easy to delete a list element. Only one pointer value has to be changed—the pointer that currently points to the element being deleted. For example, we can delete the string "Boy" from the previous linked list by changing the pointer from the node "Ace". The node containing string "Boy" is effectively disconnected from the list since there is no longer a pointer to it. The new list consists of the strings "Ace", "Bye", "Cat".

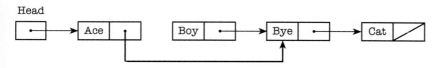

The abstract list above is relatively easy to create in Ada using access types and dynamic allocation. In Section 14.1, we saw how to connect three nodes with pointer fields. Although you did not know it at the time, the data structure shown in Fig. 14.6 could be considered a list of three nodes with pointer variable R as the pointer to its head.

The data structure in Fig. 14.6 implements the following linked list. Each node has two data fields (`Current` and `Volts`) and one pointer field (`Link`). The pointer value `NULL` is once again drawn as a diagonal line.

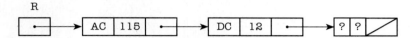

Building a List

This section and the ones that follow will treat some common list-processing operations and describe how they are implemented using access types and variables. We will assume that the structure of each list node corresponds to type `ListNode` declared as follows:

```
SUBTYPE String3 IS String (1..3);
TYPE ListNode;
TYPE ListPointer IS ACCESS ListNode;
TYPE ListNode IS RECORD
   Word : String3;
   Link : ListPointer
END RECORD;
```

Procedure `BuildList` in Program 14.1 creates a linked list by reading in a sequence of data strings ending with a sentinel ("***") and storing each string in a list. If the data lines

```
Hat
Boy
Cat
***
```

are entered, the following list will be created. Note that the sentinel string is not stored.

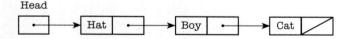

Procedure `BuildList` assumes the list is initially empty. (This is stated as a precondition.) The procedure first displays the user's instructions and then reads a data word into `NextWord`. If `NextWord` is the sentinel, then the list is empty and no further processing is done. If the first word is not the sentinel, then the statements

```
Head := NEW ListNode;    -- create the list head
Head.Word := NextWord;   -- store it in list head
```

allocate a new node `Head.ALL` into which `NextWord` is copied. The `WHILE` loop is then repeated until the sentinel is read. Each time the loop is repeated, the

```
PROCEDURE BuildList (Head : IN OUT ListPointer) IS
-- Builds a linked list of strings pointed to by Head.
-- Each new string is appended to the end of the list so
-- the strings will be stored in the order in which they were read.
-- Pre : None
-- Post: Head points to the first string entered. Head is
-- set to NULL if the sentinel string is the first string.

   Sentinel : CONSTANT String3 := "***";
   NextWord : String3;      -- data word
   Last     : ListPointer; -- always points to last node in list

BEGIN -- BuildList

   -- Display instructions to user.
   Text_IO.Put(Item => "Enter each data string on a line.");

   Text_IO.New_Line;
   Text_IO.Put(Item => "Enter ");
   Text_IO.Put(Item => Sentinel);
   Text_IO.Put(Item => " when done.");
   Text_IO.New_Line;

   -- Create and fill the list head.
   Text_IO.Get(Item => NextWord);     -- read first word
   IF NextWord = Sentinel THEN
      Head := NULL;                   -- empty list
   ELSE
      Head := NEW ListNode;           -- create the list head
      Head.Word := NextWord;          -- store it in list head
      Text_IO.Get(Item => NextWord);

      -- Now build the rest of the list
      Last := Head;
      WHILE NextWord /= Sentinel LOOP
      -- invariant:
      -- Last points to the last node in a list and
      -- the last string read is stored in node Last.ALL and
      -- no prior data string was the Sentinel.

         Last.Link := NEW ListNode;     -- attach a new node to Last.ALL
         Last      := Last.Link;        -- reset Last to new list end
         Last.Word := NextWord;         -- store last word read
         Text_IO.Get(Item => NextWord); -- read next word
      END LOOP;
      -- assert: The last string read was the Sentinel
   END IF;

END BuildList;
```

statements

```
(1)    Last.Link := NEW ListNode;     -- attach a new node to Last.ALL
(2)    Last := Last.Link;             -- reset Last to new list end
       Last.Word := NextWord;         -- store last word read
```

append a new node to the current end of the list, reset Last to point to the
new end of the list, and then store the data word in the node designated by

Figure 14.7 Partial List

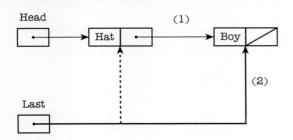

Last. Figure 14.7 shows the list after these statements have been executed one time.

Traversing a List

In many list-processing operations, we must process each node in the list in sequence; this is called *traversing* a list. In order to traverse a list, we must start at the list head and follow the list pointers.

Procedure `PrintList` in Program 14.2 displays the `Word` fields of each node in a list starting with the node pointed to by `Head`. Consequently, `PrintList` may be used to print the words stored in a list created by procedure `BuildList`. For the list

Head

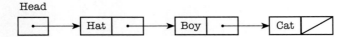

the output of `PrintList` would be

```
Hat
Boy
Cat
```

The temporary access variable `Current` is used in this procedure to indicate the node currently being processed. The statement

```
Current := Current.Link; -- advance to next node
```

advances `Current` to the next list element, which is designated by the `Link` field of the current list element. The `WHILE` loop is exited when `Current` becomes NULL.

Searching a List for a Target

List-processing operations can be formulated very naturally using recursion. As an example, we will consider the problem of searching a list to find a string

```
PROCEDURE PrintList (Head : IN ListPointer) IS
-- Displays the list pointed to by Head.
-- Pre : Head points to a list
-- Post: Displays the contents of the list pointed to by Head

  Current: ListPointer;         -- points to current node

BEGIN -- PrintList

  Current := Head;
  -- Traverse the list until the end is reached.
  WHILE Current /= NULL LOOP
    -- invariant:
    -- No prior value of Head was NULL.

    Text_IO.Put(Item => Current.Word);
    Text_IO.New_Line;
    Current := Current.Link;  -- advance to next node
  END LOOP;

END PrintList;
```

Target. The result will designate the list element containing Target; if Target
is not found, the result will be NULL. One stopping state would be an empty list;
in this case Target cannot be present. The other stopping state would be finding
Target at the head of the list. The recursion step is to search the rest of the
list (excluding the current list head) for Target. This algorithm is summarized
below; function Search is shown as Program 14.3.

Algorithm for List Search

1. IF the list is empty THEN

    2. Target is not present—the result is NULL.

    ELSIF Target is in the list head THEN

    3. Target is found—the result is a pointer to the list head.

    ELSE

    4. Search for Target in the rest of the list.

    END IF;

As indicated by the function header, a pointer value may be returned as a
function result. In the recursive step

```
RETURN Search(Head.Link, Target); -- search rest of list
```

the function Search is called recursively to search the rest of the list (pointed
to by Head.Link). Eventually a stopping state will be reached and a value will
be returned. The value returned from a lower-level call is not modified; it is
simply passed up as the function result.

```
FUNCTION Search (Head    : ListPointer;
                     Target : String3) RETURN ListPointer IS
-- Searches a list for a specified Target string.
-- Pre : Head points to a list and Target is defined.
-- Post: Returns a pointer to Target if found;
--   otherwise, returns NULL if Target is not found.

BEGIN -- Search

  IF Head = NULL THEN
     RETURN NULL;                       -- empty list; Target not found
  ELSIF Head.Word = Target THEN
     RETURN Head;                       -- Target is in Head
  ELSE
     RETURN Search(Head.Link, Target); -- search rest of list
  END IF;

END Search;
```

A trace of

```
P := Search(Head, "Boy");
```

is shown in Fig. 14.8 for our sample list "Hat", "Boy", "Cat". Since the Target string "Boy" is in the second list element, there is one recursive call to Search after the original function call. The result is a pointer to the node containing the string "Boy" as desired. The address of this node is saved in pointer variable P.

PROGRAM
STYLE

Testing for an Empty List

The order of evaluation of the terminating conditions in Program 14.3 is very important. The value of Head.Word is not defined if the list is empty (Head is NULL); consequently, the terminating condition Head = NULL must be evaluated before Head.Word = Target. In all list-processing operations, make sure that the program does not attempt to select a field designated by NULL. This illegal reference to a node that does not exist will cause Constraint_Error to be raised, and is a very common error.

Exercises for Section 14.2

Programming

1. Write procedure PrintList as a recursive procedure.
2. Write an iterative version of the function Search.
3. Write a recursive function that finds the length of a list.

Figure 14.8 Trace of P : = Search(Head, "Boy");

691

14.3 Problem
Solving: Specification
of a Keyed-Table
Abstract Data Type

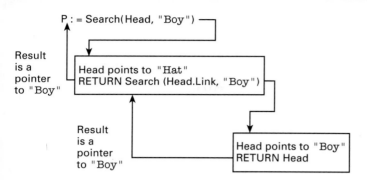

14.3 Problem Solving: Specification of a Keyed-Table Abstract Data Type

In this section, we will consider the problem of maintaining an ordered table of records. We would like to be able to insert a new record into the table automatically and know that the table will still be in order after the insertion. Similarly, after a record is deleted, the remaining elements should still be in order. As long as we maintain the order of list elements while performing each deletion or insertion, we will never have to sort the list. It will also be easier to search for a particular list element if the elements are in order. Such a table is called a *keyed table,* because each record in the table has a key field that is used to keep the table in order.

In this section, we develop an ADT for a keyed table, and then a generic package specification. In Sections 14.4 through 14.7, we will consider the implementation of the keyed table, first as a one-way linked list, and then as a search tree.

An abstract specification of the keyed table follows.

Specification of Keyed-Table Abstract Data Type

Data Structure: A keyed table consists of a collection of elements that are records (type `Element`). Each record has a key field (type `Key`) and a data field. For simplicity, we will assume that there are no duplicate keys. The elements of a keyed table are always ordered sequentially by key field.

Operators: For the following descriptions, assume these parameters: `Table` is the table; `El` is a record; `Target` is a key value; `Success` is a `Boolean` flag indicating success (`True`) or failure (`False`) of an operation. All parameters are `IN` unless otherwise indicated.

    `CreateTable(IN OUT Table)` creates an initialized table. `CreateTable` must be called before any other operators.

`SizeOfTable(Table)` returns the number of nodes currently in the ordered list.

`Search(Table, Target, OUT Success)` searches a table to find the key `Target`. If `Target` is found, `Success` is set to `True`; otherwise, `Success` is set to `False`.

`Insert(IN OUT Table, El, OUT Success)` inserts item `El` into the table, maintains the table order, and sets `Success` to `True`. If there is already an element with the same key value as `El`, `Success` is set to `False` and no insertion is performed.

`Delete(IN OUT Table, Target, OUT Success)` deletes the element whose key value is `Target`, maintains the order, and sets `Success` to `True`. If `Target` is not located, `Success` is set to `False`.

`Retrieve(IN OUT Table, Target, OUT El, OUT Success)` copies the record whose key is `Target` into `El` and sets `Success` to `True`. If there is no element with key `Target`, `El` is not defined and `Success` is set to `False`.

`Replace (IN OUT Table, El, OUT Success)` replaces the element whose key value is the same as the key value of `El` and sets `Success` to `True`. If there is no element whose key value matches the key value of `El`, `Success` is set to `False`.

`Traverse(Table)` traverses the elements in sequential order. Calls a procedure `Visit` to process each item.

The last operator requires some discussion. Traversing a table means processing all table elements in sequence. As each element is reached, procedure `Traverse` will call a procedure to perform a desired operation (e.g., display selected fields of that record). In our Ada implementation, `Visit` will be specified as a generic parameter.

The Generic Package Specification

We wish to specify the keyed table in a way that is, as far as is possible, independent of the record type, the key type, or indeed the data structures used for the implementation. In this manner, we give client programs the most flexibility in supplying keys and records, and we give ourselves the most flexibility in determining and changing implementations without affecting any of the statements of the client program.

To provide the desired flexibility to the client, we make the package generic, with the following list of generic formal parameters:

```
GENERIC

    TYPE Element IS PRIVATE;      -- assignment and equality predefined
    TYPE KeyType IS PRIVATE;      -- here too

    MinKey: KeyType;
    MaxKey: KeyType;

    -- These generic parameters specify how to insert a key in an
    -- element, retrieve the key from an element, compare elements
```

```
WITH PROCEDURE InsertKey  (El: IN OUT Element; Key: KeyType);
WITH PROCEDURE ExtractKey (El: Element;        Key: OUT KeyType);
WITH FUNCTION  Compare    (Key1, Key2: KeyType) RETURN Boolean;

-- This parameter specifies what to do with each element during
-- a traversal of a table;
WITH PROCEDURE Visit (El: Element);

PACKAGE GenericTables IS
   . . .
   TYPE TableType IS LIMITED PRIVATE;
   . . .
END GenericTables;
```

The types Element and KeyType are specified as PRIVATE to allow any types to be supplied as an actual parameters, as long as assignment and equality are defined for them. The parameters MinKey and MaxKey are necessary so that the table package can validate the range of incoming keys.

The generic procedure parameters InsertKey and ExtractKey are required to find the key field of a table record, because the table package does not have direct access to the record fields. Indeed, the record may itself be defined by the client as a PRIVATE type! The function Compare lets the client program indicate how two keys are compared. Finally the procedure Visit is required so that the client program can specify how each element is to be processed during a traversal of the table.

The definition of TableType as a LIMITED PRIVATE type warrants explanation. Recall from Section 9.6 that a LIMITED PRIVATE type not only excludes a client program from manipulating details of objects of the type, but removes the assignment and equality-testing operations as well. To give ourselves maximum flexibility in implementing the table package, we need to assure ourselves that a client program could not use the predefined symbols := or = in a meaningless or misleading way.

Suppose, for example, that the table is represented as a linked structure, and the type used by the client program is just a pointer to heap storage. We know already that copying a pointer value to a pointer variable copies only the pointer, not the designated value. The writer of a client program, writing an assignment operation on our table objects, might be misled into thinking that a copy of the entire table would be made. Since this is not the case, our best policy is simply to prevent the use of := by a client; the way to do this is by making the table type LIMITED PRIVATE. This gives us the most flexibility in choosing a table implementation while allowing us to guarantee (as ADT writers must) that client operations will always be meaningful ones.

Program 14.4 shows the full specification of the table package. Note the declaration of a package-defined exception UninitializedTable, which will be raised by several of the package operators if the client sends to them a table that was not initialized by a call to CreateTable. The operator specifications are taken directly from the abstract specification above; the PRIVATE section is discussed in Section 14.4.

```
GENERIC

  TYPE Element IS PRIVATE;      -- assignment and equality predefined
  TYPE KeyType IS PRIVATE;      -- here too

  MinKey: KeyType;
  MaxKey: KeyType;

  -- These generic parameters specify how to insert a key in an
  -- element, retrieve the key from an element, and compare elements.
  WITH PROCEDURE InsertKey  (El: IN OUT Element; Key: KeyType);
  WITH PROCEDURE ExtractKey (El: Element;        Key: OUT KeyType);
  WITH FUNCTION Compare      (Key1, Key2: KeyType) RETURN Boolean;

  -- This parameter specifies what to do with each element during
  -- a traversal of a table
  WITH PROCEDURE Visit (El: Element);

PACKAGE GenericTables IS

-- Specification of the abstract data type for an ordered table of
-- element records, each containing a key.
-- This version has type definitions to implement the table as a
-- one-way linked list. The client cannot see or use these types
-- because Table is LIMITED PRIVATE.

-- Data structure

  TYPE TableType IS LIMITED PRIVATE;

-- Exported exception

  UninitializedTable: EXCEPTION;
  -- UninitializedTable will be raised by an operator if its table
  -- parameter has not been initialized.

-- Operators

  PROCEDURE CreateTable (Table : IN OUT TableType);
  -- initializes a Table.
  -- Pre : None
  -- Post: Table is an initialized TableType.

  FUNCTION SizeOfTable (Table : TableType) RETURN Natural;
  -- Returns the number of elements in a Table.
  -- Pre : Table is an initialized TableType.
  -- Post: Returns the number of elements in Table.

  PROCEDURE Search (Table   : TableType;
                    Target  : KeyType;
                    Success : OUT Boolean);
  -- Searches a Table for Target.
  -- Pre : Table is an initialized TableType.
  -- Post: Success is True if Target is found; otherwise,
  --       Success is False.

  PROCEDURE Insert (Table   : IN OUT TableType;
                    El      : Element;
                    Success : OUT Boolean);
```

```
-- Inserts item El into a Table.
-- Pre : Table is an initialized TableType.
-- Post: Success is True if insertion is performed; Success is False.
--        if insertion is not performed because there is already
--        an element with the same key as El.

PROCEDURE Delete (Table   : IN OUT TableType;
                  Target  : KeyType;
                  Success : OUT Boolean);
-- Deletes the element with key Target from a Table.
-- Pre : Table is an initialized TableType.
-- Post: Success is True if deletion is performed; Success is False
--        if deletion is not performed because there is no element
--        whose key is Target.

PROCEDURE Replace (Table   : IN OUT TableType;
                   El      : Element;
                   Success : OUT Boolean);
-- Replaces the element of a Table with the same key as
-- El by the contents of El.
-- Pre : Table is an initialized TableType.
-- Post: Success is True if the replacement is performed; Success is
--        False if there is no element with the same key as El.

PROCEDURE Retrieve (Table   : TableType;
                    Target  : KeyType;
                    El      : OUT Element;
                    Success : OUT Boolean);
-- Copies the element whose key is Target into El.
-- Pre : Table is an initialized TableType.
-- Post: Success is True if the copy is performed; Success is False
--        if there is no element whose key is Target.


PROCEDURE Traverse (Table : TableType);
-- Repeatedly calls procedure Visit (a generic parameter) to
-- process each element of a Table.
-- Pre : Table is an initialized TableType.
-- Post: Each element is operated on in turn by procedure Visit.

PRIVATE

  TYPE ListNode;
  TYPE NodePointer IS ACCESS ListNode;
  TYPE ListNode IS RECORD
    Item: Element;
    Link: NodePointer;
  END RECORD;

  TYPE TableType IS RECORD
    Head     : NodePointer;
    NumItems: Natural;
  END RECORD;

END GenericTables;
```

14.4 Data Structures: Implementing the Keyed Table as a One-Way Linked List

So far in this chapter, we have seen many advantages to using pointer variables and dynamic allocation to implement linked lists. We have repeatedly emphasized the ease with which insertions and deletions can be performed on such a list. Let us therefore represent the keyed table as a linked list. Here are the type definitions as given in the PRIVATE part of the specification:

```
TYPE ListNode;
TYPE NodePointer IS ACCESS ListNode;
TYPE ListNode IS RECORD
  Item: Element;
  Link: NodePointer;
END RECORD;

TYPE TableType IS RECORD
  Head    : NodePointer;
  NumItems: Natural;
END RECORD;
```

The key field of each list node is part of field Item and is type KeyType; we can specify it no further because the structure of the record is provided by the client at instantiation time.

Each instance of a table will be represented by a record of type TableType containing a pointer field, Head, and a Natural field, NumItems. Head designates the first node in the linked list; NumItems is a count of the number of list nodes.

The Package Body; SEPARATE Subunits

Program 14.5 shows the package body of GenericTables. Note that Unchecked _Deallocation is instantiated to give us a Dispose operation. Note also the form of the operator body declarations, for example

```
PROCEDURE CreateTable (Table : IN OUT TableType) IS SEPARATE;
```

The reserved words IS SEPARATE indicate to the Ada compiler that the procedure's body is to be found in a compilation unit—usually in its own file—that is separate from the main package body. The separate compilation unit is called a *subunit,* and the declaration just given is often called a *subunit stub.* (This use of the term *stub,* different from the one used in Chapter 9, is unique to Ada.) Subunits are a convenience that allows large package bodies to be broken up into smaller files, and will help us in this section to discuss and illustrate the procedures individually. The main body must be compiled first, after which each subunit must be compiled.

Program 14.5   Package Body for GenericTables

697

14.4 Data Structures:
Implementing the
Keyed Table as a
One-Way Linked List

```
WITH Unchecked_Deallocation;
PACKAGE BODY GenericTables IS

-- Implementation of the abstract data type for a table of
-- element records, each containing a key.
-- This implementation uses one-way linked lists.

-- We need to instantiate Unchecked_Deallocation to get a Dispose
   PROCEDURE Dispose IS NEW Unchecked_Deallocation
      (Object => ListNode, Name => NodePointer);

-- Local procedure, not exported to client.
   PROCEDURE Locate(Target       : KeyType;
                    Previous     : IN OUT NodePointer;
                    Next         : OUT NodePointer;
                    SearchSuccess: OUT Boolean) IS SEPARATE;

-- Operators

   FUNCTION SizeOfTable (Table : TableType) RETURN Natural IS SEPARATE;

   PROCEDURE CreateTable (Table : IN OUT TableType) IS SEPARATE;

   PROCEDURE Search(Table   : TableType;
                    Target  : KeyType;
                    Success : OUT Boolean) IS SEPARATE;

   PROCEDURE Insert(Table   : IN OUT TableType;
                    El      : Element;
                    Success : OUT Boolean) IS SEPARATE;

   PROCEDURE Delete(Table   : IN OUT TableType;
                    Target  : KeyType;
                    Success : OUT Boolean) IS SEPARATE;

   PROCEDURE Replace (Table   : IN OUT TableType;
                      El      : Element;
                      Success : OUT Boolean) IS SEPARATE;

   PROCEDURE Retrieve (Table   : TableType;
                       Target  : KeyType;
                       El      : OUT Element;
                       Success : OUT Boolean) IS SEPARATE;

   PROCEDURE Traverse (Table : TableType) IS SEPARATE;

END GenericTables;
```

Program 14.6 shows the subunit CreateTable. Notice that it is preceded by the line

```
SEPARATE (GenericTables)
```

without a terminating semicolon.

Program 14.6   Procedure CreateTable

```
SEPARATE(GenericTables)
PROCEDURE CreateTable (Table : IN OUT TableType) IS
-- Creates an ordered one-way list containing two dummy nodes whose keys
-- are the constants MinKey and MaxKey.
-- Pre : None
-- Post: Table points to the header node for an ordered list.

BEGIN -- CreateTable

  Table.Head      := NEW ListNode;   -- allocate first dummy node
  Table.Head.Link := NEW ListNode;   -- allocate second dummy node
  InsertKey (Table.Head.Item, MinKey);
  InsertKey (Table.Head.Link.Item, MaxKey);
  Table.NumItems := 0;               -- dummy nodes don't count

END CreateTable;
```

Dummy Nodes in an Ordered List

It will simplify the list-processing operations if we assume that an ordered list always begins and ends with two dummy nodes. The dummy node at the head of the list should have a key value (MinKey) that is smaller than all the list keys; the dummy node at the end of the list should have a key value (MaxKey) that is larger than all the list keys.

The dummy nodes are analogous to sentinels. The presence of the first dummy node means that we never have to change the value of Head when a new node is inserted. The presence of the second dummy node keeps us from "falling off" the end of the list when searching for a target key. In this implementation, an "empty" list is not really empty; it always contains two dummy nodes, as shown in Fig. 14.9. The symbol "?" indicates that only the key fields of each node are defined. The procedure call statement

```
CreateTable (MyTable);
```

builds this list.

The two NEW statements in Program 14.6 allocate storage for two dummy list nodes that are connected. The pointer Table.Head designates the first dummy node in the empty list; Table.Head.Link designates the second dummy node. Procedure InsertKey stores MinKey and MaxKey as key values in the

Figure 14.9   An Empty List with Dummy Nodes

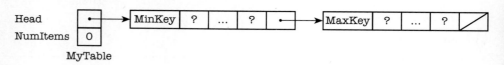

dummy nodes. The field NumItems in the node of type TableType is set to zero because the dummy nodes aren't counted with the actual list nodes.

Implementing the Remaining Operations

Procedure Search is used to determine whether a particular target key is present in the list; it returns a Boolean value to indicate the search result. Search calls procedure Locate—a procedure internal to the package body and not available to clients—to perform the actual search. Procedure Search is shown as Program 14.7, and procedure Locate as Program 14.8.

In writing procedure Locate, we can take advantage of the fact that the key values are in ascending sequence. Consequently, while searching for the target key, if we reach a list element whose key value is larger than the target key, then we know that the target key cannot be present in the list.

Procedure Locate advances pointer Current down the list until it reaches a node whose key value is greater than or equal to the target key. If the stopping key value is equal to the target key, then the OUT parameter Next is set to Current and SearchSuccess is set to True; otherwise, SearchSuccess is set to False.

Back in procedure Search, pointer Previous always points to the node just before the one pointed to by Next. Before Locate is called, Previous is initialized to the dummy node with key value MinKey. When Locate is entered, Current is initialized to the node following Previous. When Locate returns

Program 14.7 Searching an Ordered List

```
SEPARATE(GenericTables)
PROCEDURE Search (Table   : TableType;
                  Target  : KeyType;
                  Success : OUT Boolean) IS
--  Searches an ordered list for Target.
--  Pre : Table is an ordered list
--  Post: Success is True if Target is found; otherwise,
--        Success is False.

   Previous : NodePointer;  -- pointer to previous node
   Next     : NodePointer;  -- pointer to current node

BEGIN -- Search

   IF Table.Head = NULL THEN
     RAISE UninitializedTable;
   END IF;

   -- Start search at first dummy node.
   Previous := Table.Head;
   -- Perform search and define Success
   Locate (Target, Previous, Next, Success);

END Search;
```

Program 14.8   Locating an Item in an Ordered List

```
SEPARATE (GenericTables)
PROCEDURE Locate(Target       : KeyType;
                 Previous      : IN OUT NodePointer;
                 Next          : OUT NodePointer;
                 SearchSuccess: OUT Boolean) IS
-- Attempts to locate a node with key value Target in the
-- list whose first node is pointed to by Previous.
-- Pre : Target is defined; Previous points to the first dummy node.
-- Post: If Target is located, SearchSuccess is set to True;
--       otherwise, SearchSuccess is set to False.
--       Previous points to the last list node with key < Target;
--       Next points to the first list node with key >= Target.

  CurrentKey : KeyType;          -- key of node Next.ALL
  Current    : NodePointer;      -- keeps track of current node
                                 -- necessary because Next is OUT

BEGIN -- Locate

  -- Search for first node with key >= Target.
  -- Start with first actual node.
  Current := Previous.Link;
  ExtractKey (Current.Item, CurrentKey);    -- get first key
  WHILE Compare(Target, CurrentKey) LOOP
    -- invariant:
    --    Target > key of each node pointed to by Current so far.

    Previous := Current;                    -- advance Previous
    Current  := Current.Link;               -- advance Next
    ExtractKey (Current.Item, CurrentKey);  -- get next key
  END LOOP;
  -- assert: Target is located or CurrentKey is larger than Target.

  -- Set Next and flag to indicate search results.
  Next := Current;
  SearchSuccess := NOT Compare(CurrentKey, Target);

END Locate;
```

control to Search, Next points to the last node tested and Previous points to
its predecessor in the list.

Figure 14.10 shows the effect of calling Locate to search for the Target
key "ALPH" in a list of four-letter words. MinKey and MaxKey are "AAAA" and
"ZZZZ", respectively. Pointer Current has advanced down the list to the node
containing the key "BOYS", which is the first key greater than or equal to the
target "ALPH". Since the target was not found, the value False should be
returned as the search result.

The procedure call

```
ExtractKey (Current.Item, CurrentKey);
```

is used in Locate to get each key. In the WHILE loop header, the function call

```
Bigger(Target, CurrentKey)
```

Figure 14.10 Final Pointer Values in Search for "ALPH"

701

14.4 Data Structures:
Implementing the
Keyed Table as a
One-Way Linked List

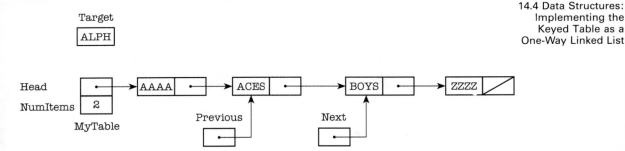

compares each key to Target and causes the WHILE loop to be exited when Current reaches a node whose key value, CurrentKey, is greater than or equal to Target. After loop exit, function Bigger compares CurrentKey to Target. If CurrentKey is greater than Target, SearchSuccess is set to False; otherwise, CurrentKey must be equal to Target, so SearchSuccess is set to True.

Procedure Insert is used to insert a node in the ordered list. It first calls Locate to search for the key value of the new record and, in this way, determines where the new record should be inserted. For example, a new record with key value "ALPH" should be inserted between nodes Previous.ALL and Next.ALL in the list shown in Fig. 14.11. If there is already a node with the same key value as the new record, Locate sets SearchSuccess to True and the insertion is not performed. Procedure Insert is shown in Program 14.9.

Procedure Insert begins by extracting ElKey from El and validating it. If Elkey is within the range MinKey to MaxKey, procedure Locate is called. If ElKey is in range and is a new key, record El is inserted. The statements

```
Previous.Link := NEW ListNode;     -- join new node to Previous.ALL
Previous.Link.Link := Next;        -- join new node to Next.ALL
Previous.Link.Item := El;          -- store El in new node
```

Figure 14.11 Inserting "ALPH" between Nodes Previous.ALL and Next.ALL

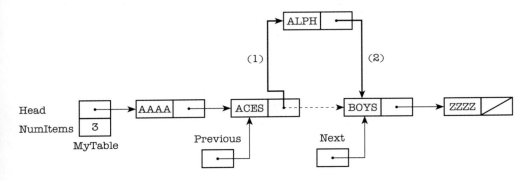

Program 14.9 Inserting an Item into an Ordered List

```
SEPARATE(GenericTables)
PROCEDURE Insert (Table   : IN OUT TableType;
                 El      : Element;
                 Success : OUT Boolean) IS
--  Inserts item El into an ordered list.
--  Pre : Table points to the header node for an ordered list.
--  Post: Success is True if insertion is performed; Success is False
--        if insertion is not performed because there is already
--        an element with the same key as El.

   Previous       : NodePointer;   -- pointer to node preceding El
   Next           : NodePointer;   -- pointer to node following El
   SearchSuccess  : Boolean;       -- search result
   ElKey          : KeyType;       -- key of record El

BEGIN -- Insert

   IF Table.Head = NULL THEN
     RAISE UninitializedTable;
   END IF;

   -- Validate ElKey and search for a valid key.
   ExtractKey (El, ElKey);
   IF Compare(MinKey, ElKey) OR Compare(ElKey, MaxKey) THEN
     Success := False;                -- ElKey is out of range
     RETURN;
   ELSE
     -- Search the list for ElKey.
     Previous := Table.Head;          -- start at first dummy node
     Locate (ElKey, Previous, Next, SearchSuccess);
   END IF;

   Success := NOT SearchSuccess;      -- ElKey is new if search fails

   -- Insert if ElKey is in range and is a new key
   IF NOT SearchSuccess THEN
     Previous.Link := NEW ListNode;   -- join new node to Previous.ALL
     Previous.Link.Link := Next;      -- join new node to Next.ALL
     Previous.Link.Item := El;        -- store El in new node
     Table.NumItems := Table.NumItems + 1;
   END IF;

END Insert;
```

---

perform the actual insertion. Figure 14.11 illustrates their effect in inserting a new node with key "ALPH". The new pointer values are shown as heavier lines; the disconnected pointer value is shown as a dashed line.

Let us now consider deletion, as shown in Program 14.10. Before we can delete a node containing a specified key (Target), we use procedure Locate to set Next to point to the node with that key. If the search succeeds, the statement

```
Previous.Link := Next.Link; -- disconnect node Next
```

redirects Previous.Link to point to the first node whose key is greater than Target, thereby disconnecting the node with key Target. Procedures Retrieve

Program 14.10   Deleting an Item from an Ordered List

703

14.4 Data Structures:
Implementing the
Keyed Table as a
One-Way Linked List

```
SEPARATE(GenericTables)
PROCEDURE Delete (Table   : IN OUT TableType;
                  Target  : KeyType;
                  Success : OUT Boolean) IS
  -- Deletes the element with key Target from an ordered list.
  -- Pre : Table points to the header node for an ordered list.
  -- Post: Success is True if deletion is performed; Success is False
  --       if deletion is not performed because there is no element
  --       whose key is Target.

  Previous : NodePointer;   -- pointer to last list key < ElKey
  Next     : NodePointer;   -- pointer to first list key >= ElKey
  Temp     : NodePointer;   -- temporary variable
  TempFlag : Boolean;       -- hold temporary success flag

BEGIN -- Delete

  IF Table.Head = NULL THEN
    RAISE UninitializedTable;
  END IF;

  -- Search the list for the key Target.
  Previous := Table.Head; -- Previous points to first dummy node
  Locate (Target, Previous, Next, TempFlag);
  Success := TempFlag;

  -- If Target is found, delete it.
  IF TempFlag THEN
    Temp := Next;                -- point Temp to the node being deleted
    Previous.Link := Next.Link;  -- disconnect node Next
    Dispose (Temp);              -- deallocate storage
    Table.NumItems := Table.NumItems - 1;
  END IF;

END Delete;
```

and `Replace` are quite similar and are left as an exercise along with function `SizeOfTable`.

Finally, procedure `Traverse` traverses the ordered list, visiting each actual node, but not the dummy nodes. Procedure `Traverse` is shown as Program 14.11.

Analysis of Operations on an Ordered List

We have gone through considerable effort to maintain our linked list in ascending order by key value; however, the improvement in search efficiency that results is relatively modest. If we assume that a target key is as likely to be at the front of a list as at the end of a list, then on the average we will have to examine half of the list elements. This is the same whether or not the target key is in the list. If a list is not ordered, then we will have to examine all of its elements to determine that a key is not in the list, but only half of its elements,

```
SEPARATE (GenericTables)
PROCEDURE Traverse (Table : TableType) IS
--  Repeatedly calls procedure Visit (a generic parameter) to
--  process each element of an ordered list.
--  Pre : List points to the header node of an ordered list.
--  Post: Each element is operated on in turn by procedure Visit.

  Next : NodePointer;       -- pointer to each list node
  NextKey : KeyType;        -- key of node Next.ALL

BEGIN -- Traverse

  IF Table.Head = NULL THEN
    RAISE UninitializedTable;
  END IF;

  Next := Table.Head.Link;                -- start after dummy
  ExtractKey (Next.Item, NextKey);        -- get node key
  WHILE Bigger(MaxKey, NextKey) LOOP
  -- invariant:
  --    MaxKey > key of each prior node pointed to by Next.
    Visit (Next.Item);                    -- visit node
    Next := Next.Link;                    -- advance Next
    ExtractKey (Next.Item, NextKey);
  END LOOP;

END Traverse;
```

on the average, to find a key that *is* in the list. Therefore, list search is an $O(N)$ process for both ordered and unordered lists.

It takes considerably longer to insert an item into an ordered list than into an unordered list. In an unordered list, we can arbitrarily insert a new element at the list head. In an ordered list, we must first search for the appropriate position of the new element before inserting it. The main advantage to using ordered lists occurs when displaying the list contents. An ordered list is always ready to be printed or displayed. If the list is unordered we must find some way to sort it before we can display it. We shall see later that using a different linked structure—a search tree—can reduce the time required for most table operations to $O(\log_2 N)$.

Exercises for Section 14.4

Self-Check

1. The two dummy records (see Fig. 14.9) were placed in the list to ensure that there would be no need to insert a record into an empty list or in front of the first list node (i.e., all valid keys follow the key MinKey in the first dummy node). Discuss what changes would be necessary for Locate, Insert, and Delete if these nodes were not present.

1. Write function SizeOfTable and procedures Retrieve and Replace.
2. In specifying the keyed-table ADT, we assumed there would be no insertion if the key of a new record was already present in the list. Modify procedure Insert (Program 14.9) to insert a record with a duplicate key before the first record with that key currently in the list. Discuss what changes would be required to insert the new record after the last record currently in the list with that key.

 # 14.5 Case Study: Airline Passenger List

Problem

Develop an interactive program for maintaining a list of airline reservations for a particular flight, given the name, class of travel, and number of seats reserved by each passenger. The classes of travel are First Class, Business, Economy, and Standby. We must provide the ability to add, change, and delete a reservation.

Analysis

We must first find a representation for a passenger record, and then build a table to hold the reservations and a "front end" program with which the user can interact.

Design

A detailed discussion of the design is left as a programming project; we choose now to specify a package implementing passenger records. Given such a package, we can use our generic table manager to maintain the passenger reservation list.

Program 14.12 gives a specification for Passengers. A passenger record is a straightforward record type, in which the passenger's name is stored as a VString. Minimum and maximum passenger names are provided. Four operations are listed in the specification: ReadPass, WritePass, StoreName, and RetrieveName, all of which have obvious meanings. The package body is given in Program 14.13; several of the operations are given as stubs only. We leave it as an exercise to modify this package to provide a full set of ADT operations on passenger records, with the record represented as a PRIVATE type.

Program 14.14 shows a simple and straightforward interactive client program, BuildFlightList; as a programming project, you can build a more elaborate and robust program for this case study. BuildFlightList uses the generic package `GenericTables` to create a flight list. Here is the statement that instantiates the generic package:

```
PACKAGE FlightLists IS NEW GenericTables(
   Element    => Passengers.Passenger,
   KeyType    => Passengers.NameType,
   MinKey     => Passengers.MinKey,
   MaxKey     => Passengers.MaxKey,
   InsertKey  => Passengers.StoreName,
   ExtractKey => Passengers.RetrieveName,
   Compare    => VStrings.">",
   Visit      => Passengers.WritePass);
```

Note that the actual parameters are all provided by the package `Passengers`, except for `Compare`, for which we can just substitute the `">"` operation from `VStrings`. Here is some sample output from a run of `BuildFlightList`.

```
Enter data for next passenger.
Passenger name > Jones
Class (F, B, E, S) > E
Number of Seats (1 to 30) > 3
Passenger inserted.

Enter data for next passenger.
Passenger name > Smith
Class (F, B, E, S) > B
Number of Seats (1 to 30) > 2
Passenger inserted.

Enter data for next passenger.
Passenger name > Jones
Class (F, B, E, S) > F
Number of Seats (1 to 30) > 1
Already booked - no insertion.

Enter data for next passenger.
Passenger name > Brown
Class (F, B, E, S) > B
Number of Seats (1 to 30) > 2
Passenger inserted.

Smith deleted.

The ordered passenger list follows.
Brown
Business Class
2 seats
Jones
Economy Class
3 seats

The number of passengers in the list is 2
```

Exercises for Section 14.5

Programming

1. Complete and test the Passengers package.

```
WITH VStrings; USE VStrings;
PACKAGE Passengers IS

-- Specification for package defining type Passenger.

  MaxSeats : CONSTANT Positive := 30;
  MinKey   : CONSTANT VString := MakeVString("AAAAAAA");
  MaxKey   : CONSTANT VString := MakeVString("zzzzzzz");

-- Data structure

  TYPE ClassType IS
     (FirstClass, Business, Economy, StandBy, Undesignated);
  SUBTYPE NameType IS VString;
  SUBTYPE SeatRange IS Positive RANGE 1..MaxSeats;
  TYPE Passenger IS RECORD
    Name     : NameType;
    Class    : ClassType;
    NumSeats : SeatRange;
  END RECORD;

-- Operators

  PROCEDURE ReadPass (OnePass : OUT Passenger);
  -- Reads one record of type Passenger.

  PROCEDURE WritePass (OnePass : Passenger);
  -- Displays one record of type Passenger.

  PROCEDURE StoreName (OnePass : IN OUT Passenger;
                       Name : NameType);
  -- Inserts the key value in record OnePass.

  PROCEDURE RetrieveName (OnePass : Passenger;
                          Name : OUT NameType);
  -- Extracts the key of record OnePass.

END Passengers;
```

Program 14.13   Package Body for Passengers

```
WITH Text_IO;
WITH My_Int_IO;
WITH VStrings; USE VStrings;
PACKAGE BODY Passengers IS

-- Package body for airline passenger abstract data type.

-- Operators

  PROCEDURE ReadPass (OnePass : OUT Passenger) IS
  -- Reads one record of type Passenger.
```

```
          ClassCh  : Character;              -- character for class type
          TempSeats: Positive;

          FUNCTION ClassConvert (ClassCh : Character) RETURN ClassType IS
          -- Converts a character to a class type.
          BEGIN -- ClassConvertStub
            RETURN Economy;
          END ClassConvert;

        BEGIN -- ReadPass

          Text_IO.Put(Item => "Passenger name > ");
          VStrings.Get_Line(Item => OnePass.Name);
          Text_IO.Put(Item => "Class (F, B, E, S) > ");
          Text_IO.Get(Item => ClassCh);
          OnePass.Class := ClassConvert(ClassCh);
          Text_IO.Put(Item => "Number of Seats (1 to 30) > ");
          My_Int_IO.Get(Item => TempSeats);
          Text_IO.Skip_Line;
          IF TempSeats > 30 THEN
            OnePass.NumSeats := 30;
            Text_IO.Put(Item => "Only 30 seats can be assigned now.");
          ELSE
            OnePass.NumSeats := TempSeats;
          END IF;

        END ReadPass;

        PROCEDURE WritePass (OnePass : Passenger) IS
        -- Displays one record of type Passenger.

        BEGIN -- WritePass stub

          Text_IO.Put(Item => "Procedure WritePass Entered.");
          Text_IO.New_Line;
          Text_IO.Put(Item => "Name: ");
          VStrings.Put(Item => OnePass.Name);
          Text_IO.New_Line;

        END WritePass;

        PROCEDURE StoreName (OnePass : IN OUT Passenger;
                             Name : NameType) IS
        -- Inserts the key value in record OnePass.

        BEGIN -- StoreName
          OnePass.Name := Name;
        END StoreName;

        PROCEDURE RetrieveName (OnePass : Passenger;
                                Name : OUT NameType) IS
        -- Extracts the key of record OnePass.

        BEGIN -- RetrieveName
          Name := OnePass.Name;
        END RetrieveName;

      END Passengers;
```

```
WITH Text_IO;
WITH My_Int_IO;
WITH Passengers;
WITH GenericTables;
WITH VStrings;
PROCEDURE BuildFlightList IS

-- Builds a flight list using abstract data type GenericTables

   PACKAGE FlightLists IS NEW GenericTables(
      Element    => Passengers.Passenger,
      KeyType    => Passengers.NameType,
      MinKey     => Passengers.MinKey,
      MaxKey     => Passengers.MaxKey,
      InsertKey  => Passengers.StoreName,
      ExtractKey => Passengers.RetrieveName,
      Bigger     => VStrings.">",
      Visit      => Passengers.WritePass);

   MaxPass : CONSTANT Positive := 4;        -- maximum table size

   Flight23 : FlightLists.TableType;        -- table of passengers
   OnePass  : Passengers.Passenger;         -- a passenger
   Success  : Boolean;                      -- program flag

BEGIN -- BuildFlightList

   -- Initialize the list
   FlightLists.CreateTable (Table => Flight23);

   -- Read and insert up to four passengers in Flight23
   FOR Count IN 1..MaxPass LOOP

      Text_IO.Put(Item => "Enter data for next passenger.");
      Text_IO.New_Line;
      Passengers.ReadPass (OnePass => OnePass);
      FlightLists.Insert (Table => Flight23,
                          El => OnePass, Success => Success);

      IF Success THEN
        Text_IO.Put(Item => "Passenger inserted.");
      ELSE
        Text_IO.Put(Item => "Already booked - no insertion.");
      END IF;
      Text_IO.New_Line;
      Text_IO.New_Line;

   END LOOP;

   -- Delete Smith
   FlightLists.Delete (Table => Flight23,
                       Target => VStrings.MakeVString("Smith"),
                       Success => Success);
   IF Success THEN
     Text_IO.Put(Item => "Smith deleted.");
     Text_IO.New_Line;
     Text_IO.New_Line;
   END IF;
```

```
-- Display the passenger list.
Text_IO.Put(Item => "The ordered passenger list follows.");
Text_IO.New_Line;
FlightLists.Traverse (Table => Flight23);
Text_IO.Put(Item => "The number of passengers in the list is ");
My_Int_IO.Put(Item =>
               FlightLists.SizeOfTable(Flight23), Width => 2);
Text_IO.New_Line;

END BuildFlightList;
```

 ## 14.6 Data Structures: Multiple-Linked Lists and Trees

All the examples seen so far have involved elements or nodes with a single pointer field. It is possible to have a list of elements with more than one link. For example, each element in the list below has a forward pointer that points to the next list element and a backward pointer that points to the previous list element. This allows us to traverse the list in either the left or right direction.

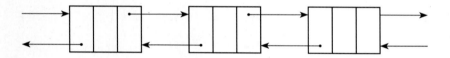

This structure is called a *doubly linked list*. The following declarations describe a general node of such a list.

```
TYPE MultiNode;
TYPE MultiLink IS ACCESS MultiNode;
TYPE MultiNode IS RECORD

   . . . Data Fields

   Left  : MultiLink;
   Right : MultiLink;
END RECORD;
```

Introduction to Trees

A special kind of multiple-linked list that has wide applicability in computer science is a data structure called a *tree*. A sample tree is drawn in Fig. 14.12.

Trees in computer science actually grow from the top down rather than the ground up. The topmost element is called the *root of the tree*. The pointer, Root, points to the root of the tree drawn in Fig. 14.12. Each tree node shown has a single data field and two pointer fields called the *left branch* and *right branch*, respectively.

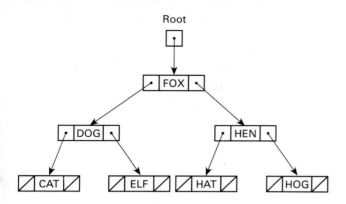

Family tree terminology is used to describe computer science trees. The node containing the string "HEN" is the *parent* of the nodes containing the strings "HAT" and "HOG". Similarly, the nodes "HAT" and "HOG" are *siblings* since they are both *children* of the same parent node. The root of the tree is an *ancestor* of all other nodes in the tree and they, in turn, are all *descendants* of the root node.

Each node in a tree can be thought of as the root node of its own *subtree*. Since each node has two branches, it spawns two more subtrees, a *left subtree* and a *right subtree*. Either one or both of these subtrees may be empty (denoted by a branch value of NULL). A node with two empty subtrees is called a *leaf node*. The *left (right) child* of a node is the root node of its left (right) subtree.

The following statements describe the form of a tree node in Fig. 14.12. Since each node can have at most two children, such a tree is called a *binary tree*.

```
TYPE TreeNode;
TYPE Branch IS ACCESS TreeNode;
TYPE TreeNode IS RECORD
   Info  : String(1..3);
   Left  : Branch;
   Right : Branch;
END RECORD;
```

Field Info contains the data associated with the tree node, a string of three characters.

Applications of Binary Trees

An important application for trees is in building the data structures used by compilers and other translators of expressions. In these programs, trees are commonly used for representing expressions in memory. For example, the expression

```
(X + Y) * (A - B)
```

Figure 14.13 Expression Stored in a Tree

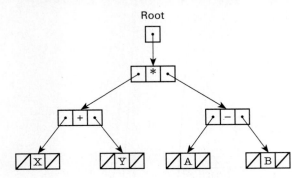

could be represented as the tree drawn in Fig. 14.13. This tree has the same shape as the one drawn in Fig. 14.12.

The root node contains the operator (*) that is evaluated last in the expression. Each subtree is also an expression and contains either the subexpression operator (+ or −) in its root or a variable (X, Y, A, or B). There are subtrees for the subexpressions (X + Y) and (A − B).

Trees are also used to organize related data items in order to facilitate efficient search and retrieval for a desired item. For example, the *binary search tree* shown in Fig. 14.12 is arranged so that the left child of each node precedes its parent alphabetically and the right child follows its parent alphabetically. Hence, in searching for a particular key at any level of this tree, the left subtree should be examined if the key value is "less than" the current node value and the right subtree should be examined if the key value is "greater than" the current node value. (What if the key value equals the current node value?) This can reduce the search space by a factor of 2 each time because all the descendants in the other subtree are ignored. Binary search trees will be discussed in detail later.

Traversing a Tree

In order to process the data stored in a tree, we need to be able to traverse the tree, that is, visit each node in a systematic way. Let us first consider an *LNR* (left-node-right) or *inorder traversal*. The algorithm for an LNR traversal is described as follows.

Algorithm for LNR Traversal

1. Traverse the left subtree.
2. Visit the root node.
3. Traverse the right subtree

You will recall that the left subtree of any node is the part of the tree whose root is the left child of that node. The inorder traversal for the tree shown in Fig. 14.12 would visit the nodes in the following sequence:

If we assume that each node's data are displayed when that node is visited, the strings would be displayed in this alphabetical order.

In Fig. 14.14, a numbered circle is drawn around each subtree. The subtrees are numbered in the order in which they are traversed. Subtree 1 is the left subtree of the root node. Its left subtree (numbered 2) has no left subtree (or right subtree); hence the string "CAT" is displayed first. The root node for subtree 1 is then visited and its contents, "DOG", displayed. Its right subtree consists of the leaf node containing the string "ELF" (number 3). After "ELF" is displayed, the root node for the complete tree is visited ("FOX" is displayed), and the right subtree of the root node (number 4) is traversed in like manner.

Procedure `Traverse` in Program 14.15 is a recursive procedure that performs an LNR traversal of a tree and displays each node's data. The parameter `Root` represents the pointer to the root node of the tree being traversed. If the tree is empty (`Root = NULL`), an immediate return occurs. Procedure `Traverse`, like most procedures that process trees, can be written much more simply with recursion than without it.

As we saw earlier, an LRN traversal of the tree shown in Fig. 14.12 would visit the nodes in alphabetical sequence. If we performed an inorder traversal of the expression tree in Fig. 14.13, the nodes would be visited in the sequence

    X + Y * A - B

Except for the absence of parentheses, this is the form in which we would normally write the expression. The expression above is called an *infix* expression because each operator is in-between its operands.

Figure 14.14 Subtrees of a Tree

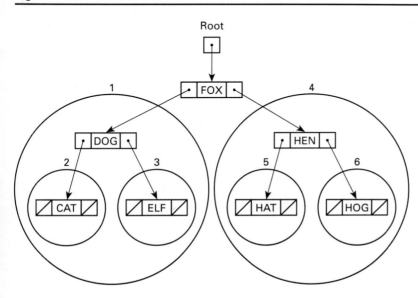

Program 14.15   Inorder Traversal of a Binary Tree

```
PROCEDURE Traverse (Root : Branch) IS
-- Performs an inorder traversal of a binary tree.
-- Pre : None.
-- Post: visits each node in left-node-right order

BEGIN -- Traverse

  IF Root /= NULL THEN
    -- recursive step
    Traverse (Root.Left);   -- traverse left subtree
    Visit    (Root.Item);   -- process the node element
    Traverse (Root.Right);  -- traverse right subtree
  END IF; -- recursive step

END Traverse;
```

An easy way to determine the order in which the nodes of a tree are visited is to outline the contour of the tree, following all indentations as shown in Fig. 14.15. Move your finger along the tree contour, starting to the left of the root node. As your finger passes under a node, that node is visited in an LRN traversal.

Switching the sequence of the three statements in the IF statement shown in Program 14.15 will produce rather different results. The sequence

```
Visit    (Root.Item);   -- process the node element
Traverse (Root.Left);   -- traverse left subtree
Traverse (Root.Right);  -- traverse right subtree
```

Figure 14.15   Outlining the Contour of a Tree

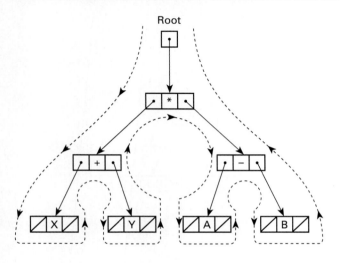

displays the root node before traversing its subtrees; consequently, the data field of the root node will be displayed before the data fields of its subtrees. This is called an *NLR* (node-left-right) or *preorder traversal*. The nodes in Fig. 14.12 would be visited in the sequence

```
FOX DOG CAT ELF HEN HAT HOG
```

The nodes in the expression tree in Fig. 14.13 are visited in the sequence shown below.

```
* + X Y − A B
```

This expression is called a *prefix* expression because each operator precedes its operands. The operands of + are X and Y; the operands of − are A and B; the operands of * are the two triples + X Y and − A B. To find the sequence in which the nodes are visited in a preorder or NLR traversal, trace the contour of the tree shown in Fig. 14.13. As your finger passes downward to the left of a node, that node is visited.

Finally, the sequence

```
Traverse (Root.Left);   −− traverse left subtree
Traverse (Root.Right);  −− traverse right subtree
Visit    (Root.Item);   −− process the node element
```

displays the root node after traversing each of its subtrees; consequently, each root value will be printed after all values in its subtrees. This is called an *LRN* (left-right-node) or *postorder traversal*. The nodes in Fig. 14.12 would be visited in the sequence

```
CAT ELF DOG HAT HOG HEN FOX
```

The nodes in the expression tree in Fig. 14.13 would be visited in the sequence

```
X Y + A B − *
```

This expression is called a *postfix* expression because each operator follows its operands. The operands of + are X and Y; the operands of − are A and B; the operands of * are the two triples X Y + and A B −.

To find the sequence in which the nodes are visited in a postorder or LRN traversal, trace the contour of the tree shown in Fig. 14.15. As your finger passes upward to the right of a node, that node is visited.

Note that in all three methods the left subtree is always traversed before the right subtree.

Exercises for Section 14.6

Self-Check

1. Draw the binary tree representation of the following expressions.

```
X * Y / (A + B) * C
X * Y / A + B * C
```

2. What would be displayed by the LNR (inorder), NLR (preorder), and LRN (postorder) traversals of the following tree?

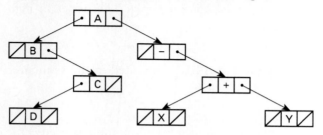

14.7 Data Structures: Reimplementing the Keyed Table as a Search Tree

You will recall that the table operations are all linear for the linked-list implementation. As we shall see, a binary search tree can provide faster operations—$O(\log_2 N)$—if the search tree is reasonably well balanced. Let us therefore reimplement the generic keyed table package using search trees to represent the table objects.

In developing the original specification for GenericTables (Program 4.4), we wrote general and fundamental operations on keyed tables, and we took care not to allow client programs to directly access details of our table representation. We argued there that making the table type LIMITED PRIVATE gave us the flexibility to choose our implementation. Here is where this careful design pays off: We can change to a search tree implementation with very little change to the package specification. More important, the identical client programs can be used, with no change at all!

In modifying Program 14.4, only the PRIVATE section requires change, as follows:

```
PRIVATE

   TYPE TreeNode;
   TYPE Branch IS ACCESS TreeNode;
   TYPE TreeNode IS RECORD
      Item : Element;
      Left : Branch;
      Right: Branch;
   END RECORD;

   TYPE TableType IS RECORD
      Root    : Branch;
      NumItems: Natural := 0;
   END RECORD;
```

We showed in Program 14.15 a simple Traverse procedure; we now develop the operations Search and Insert, leaving the remaining operations as an exercise.

An object of type `TableType` is a record, with `NumItems` and `Root` fields. The field `Root` (type `Branch`) points to the root of the tree. Each node (type `TreeNode`) of the tree consists of a field `Item` (type `Element`) containing a key (type `KeyType`) and two pointers, `Left` and `Right` (type `Branch`). Data types `Element` and `KeyType` are, as before, given as generic formal parameters.

Procedure `CreateTable` is shown in Program 14.16. It simply sets the `Root` field to `NULL` and the count field (`NumItems`) to zero.

Trying to locate an item in a binary search tree is analogous to performing a binary search on an array that has already been sorted. To find a particular item, we compare its key (the target key) to the key of the root node. If the target key is less than the root key, then we can eliminate the right subtree and search only the left subtree, thereby cutting the number of nodes to be searched in half. For this reason, the binary tree search is an $O(\log_2 N)$ algorithm. A recursive algorithm for searching a binary tree is shown below.

Recursive Algorithm for Binary Tree Search

1. IF the tree is empty THEN

　2. The target key is not in the tree.

　ELSIF the target key matches the root key THEN

　3. The target key is found in the root node.

　ELSIF the target key is larger than the root key THEN

　4. Search the right subtree.

　ELSE

　5. Search the left subtree.

　END IF;

Steps 2 and 3 are stopping steps; this algorithm is recursive.

Procedure `Search` is given in Program 14.17. It starts the search at the tree root by calling an inner procedure, also called `Search`, with the actual parameter `Table.Root`. By the overloading principle, it is possible to call both procedures `Search`, as long as they have different parameters, as these do. The inner `Search` implements our recursive search algorithm. We are assuming that the

Program 14.16 Initializing a Search Tree

```
SEPARATE (GenericTables)
PROCEDURE CreateTable (Table : IN OUT TableType) IS
-- Initializes a search tree.
-- Pre : None.
-- Post: Table is an initialized search tree.

BEGIN -- CreateTable
  Table.Root := NULL;
  Table.NumItems := 0;
END CreateTable;
```

```
SEPARATE (GenericTables)
PROCEDURE Search (Table   : TableType;
                  Target  : KeyType;
                  Success : OUT Boolean) IS
-- Searches a search tree for Target.
-- Pre : Target is defined.
-- Post: Success is True if Target is found; otherwise,
--          Success is False.

   PROCEDURE Search (Parent  : Branch;
                     Target  : KeyType;
                     Success : OUT Boolean) IS
   -- Searches the subtree pointed to by Parent
   -- Pre : Target is defined.
   -- Post: Success is True if Target is found; otherwise,
   --          Success is False.

      NextKey : KeyType;          -- key of node Parent.ALL

   BEGIN -- Inner Search
      IF Parent = NULL THEN
         Success := FALSE;          -- tree is empty
      ELSE
         ExtractKey (Parent.Item, NextKey);
         IF Bigger(Target, NextKey) THEN
            Search (Parent.Right, Target, Success);
         ELSIF Bigger(NextKey, Target) THEN
            Search (Parent.Left, Target, Success);
         ELSE -- Target = NextKey
            Success := TRUE;
         END IF;
      END IF;
   END Search;

BEGIN -- Outer Search
   Search (Table.Root, Target, Success);
END Search;
```

key field is of type KeyType and that procedures ExtractKey and Bigger are used to extract and compare keys.

Finally, Program 14.18 shows procedure Insert. It stores the key of El in ElKey and the tree root in Parent. Then it calls an inner Insert to perform a recursive search for ElKey, starting at the tree root. There are two stopping states for the recursion. If the inner Insert passes a leaf node without finding ElKey, it attaches a new node to the leaf node, stores El in the new node, and sets Success to True before returning. If Insert finds ElKey in the tree already, it sets Success to False and returns. Otherwise, Insert makes recursive calls to process the left subtree or right subtree of its current tree. After the return from the original call to the inner Insert, the outer Insert increments the count of tree nodes if the insertion was performed.

Program 14.18   Inserting an Element into a Binary Search Tree

719

14.7 Data Structures:
Reimplementing the
Keyed Table as a
Search Tree

```
SEPARATE (GenericTables)
PROCEDURE Insert (Table   : IN OUT TableType;
                  El      : Element;
                  Success : OUT Boolean) IS
-- Inserts item El into a search tree.
-- Pre : El is defined.
-- Post: Success is True if insertion is performed; Success is False
--       if insertion is not performed because there is already
--       an element with the same key as El.

   ElKey    : KeyType;              -- key of record El
   TempFlag : Boolean;              -- because Success is OUT

   PROCEDURE Insert (Parent : IN OUT Branch;
                     El      : Element;
                     ElKey   : KeyType;
                     Success: OUT Boolean) IS
   -- Inserts item El in the subtree with root Parent.

      NextKey : KeyType;           -- key of Parent.ALL

   BEGIN -- Inner Insert

      -- Check for empty tree.
      IF Parent = NULL THEN
         -- Attach new node containing El to Parent
         Parent := NEW TreeNode;
         Parent.Item := El;
         Success := True;
      ELSE -- search for correct insertion point
         ExtractKey (Parent.Item, NextKey);
         IF Bigger(ElKey, NextKey) THEN
           Insert (Parent.Right, El, ElKey, Success);
         ELSIF Bigger(NextKey, ElKey) THEN
           Insert (Parent.Left, El, ElKey, Success);
         ELSE -- ElKey is in tree
              Success := False;
         END IF;
      END IF;

   END Insert;

BEGIN -- Outer Insert

   ExtractKey (El, ElKey);                   -- get key
   Insert (Table.Root, El, ElKey, TempFlag);
   Success := TempFlag;
   IF TempFlag THEN
     Table.NumItems := Table.NumItems + 1;   -- new node in tree
   END IF;

END Insert;
```

The other procedures are left as an exercise; you can easily implement `Traverse` by using the procedure of Program 14.15 as the recursive inner procedure and writing the outer layer by analogy with `Search` and `Insert`.

Note that because the tree implementation does not use dummy nodes, there is no need to raise `UninitializedTable` in this package body. This creates no problems for a client program; even if it has handlers for this exception, they will simply never be executed because the exception will never be raised.

To use the new version of the package as the table implementation, it is necessary only to compile its specification and body. To test `BuildFlightList` with the new implementation, it is necessary to compile and link it, but because we were so careful in developing our table specification, not a single statement of the client needs to be changed. This is a very good example of the kind of careful generic, implementation-independent software development currently receiving much attention in industry.

Analysis of Binary Tree Search and Insert

The order in which data items are stored in a binary tree has a profound effect on the efficiency of the `search` and `insert` algorithms discussed in the last section. For example, if the data words arrive in the sequence "FOX", "DOG", "CAT", "HEN", "HOG", "HAT", "ELF", the result is the nicely balanced binary tree shown in Fig. 14.12. You should verify this yourself by tracing the trees that are formed as each word is inserted. This trace is shown in Fig. 14.16; note that after each element is inserted, the result is always a valid binary search tree. The pointers that are passed as parameters to the inner `Insert` procedure are shown as heavier lines in each tree diagram.

Since the tree is nicely balanced, `search` and `insert` operations are performed in time proportional to $O(\log_2 N)$. However, if the data words arrive in the sequence "CAT", "DOG", "ELF", "FOX", "HAT", "HEN", "HOG", the result is the very unbalanced tree shown in Fig. 14.17, which resembles an ordered linked list. In this case, `search` and `insert` operations are performed in time proportional to $O(N/2)$.

If we assume that the data to be inserted in a tree are random in nature, the actual situation will be somewhere between the best and worst cases illustrated above. There are algorithms that maintain tree balance by switching the positions of data items in tree nodes as the tree is formed; these algorithms are beyond the scope of this text.

Exercise for Section 14.7

Programming

1. Complete the search tree implementation of a keyed table by writing procedures `SizeOfTable`, `Traverse` (inorder traversal), `Retrieve`, and `Replace`.

Figure 14.16   Building a Binary Search Tree

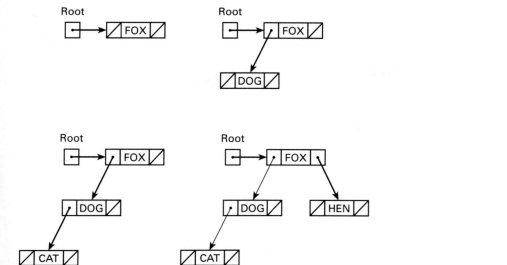

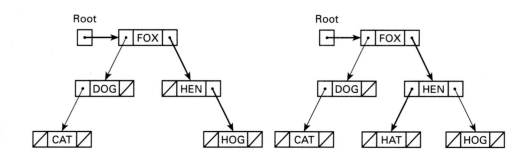

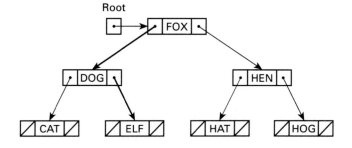

Figure 14.17 An Unbalanced Tree

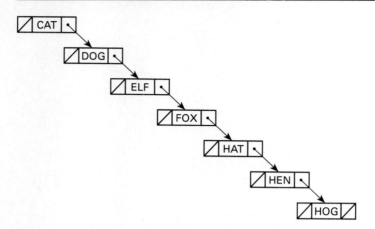

14.8 Tricks of the Trade: Common Programming Errors

The three most common errors in writing programs using dynamic structures are dereferencing a null pointer, infinite loops, infinite recursion, and off-by-one problems.

When processing linked data structures, make sure that the pointer to the next node is not NULL. If pointer Next has the value NULL, the record Next.ALL is undefined. Therefore, the condition

```
(Next.ID /= 9999) AND (Next /= NULL)
```

will cause Constraint_Error to be raised when Next is NULL. You can prevent this by writing the expression using the short-circuit operator AND THEN:

```
(Next /= NULL) AND THEN (Next.ID /= 9999)
```

This causes the left side to be evaluated first and evaluates the right side only if the left side is True.

If your program gets stuck in an infinite loop or infinite recursion while creating a dynamic data structure, it is possible to consume all memory cells on the storage heap. This situation will cause Storage_Error to be raised. Because linked-list problems often use WHILE loops, you must be especially careful in writing the WHILE condition and the loop incrementation statement. Be certain the loop is always initialized properly and incremented each time through. Also be careful that your recursive programs will eventually reach a stopping case.

Off-by-one errors are common in linked-list programs. In traversing a list with K elements, for example, sometimes only the first $K-1$ elements or the last $K-1$ are displayed. These logic errors will not raise exceptions but will give incorrect results. They are usually caused by careless loop initialization or termination conditions.

Some debugging tools allow you to display the value of a pointer variable, but such a value cannot normally be displayed with Text_IO procedures. It is therefore difficult to debug programs that manipulate pointers. You will have to trace the execution of such a program by printing an information field that uniquely identifies the list element being processed instead of the pointer value itself. In doing a trace, drawing a picture of the list as it is built and manipulated is enormously helpful.

When writing driver programs, it is often helpful to create a sample linked structure using the technique shown in Section 14.1. The data and pointer fields of the structure can be defined using assignment statements.

 Chapter Review

In this chapter, we introduced several dynamic data structures. We discussed the use of pointers to reference and connect elements of a dynamic data structure. The operator NEW was used to allocate additional elements or nodes of a dynamic data structure.

Many different aspects of manipulating linked lists were covered. We showed how to build or create a linked list, how to traverse a linked list, and how to insert and delete elements of a linked list.

We discussed techniques for maintaining a keyed table of records and studied two data structures, one-way linked lists and search trees, implementing these techniques.

Finally, we discussed binary trees in general and showed how they could be used to represent expressions in memory. We discussed the differences between inorder (LNR), preorder (NLR), and postorder (LRN) traversal, and related these three methods to infix, prefix, and postfix expressions.

New Ada Constructs in Chapter 14

The new Ada constructs introduced in this chapter are described in Table 14.1.

Table 14.1 Summary of New Ada Constructs

Statement	Effect
TYPE NodePointer IS ACCESS TreeNode;	Declares an access (pointer) type whose variables can point to values of type TreeNode any subrange of Weeks
P: NodePointer; Q: NodePointer;	and two variables of the access type.

Table 14.1 *continued*

Statement	Effect
PROCEDURE Dispose IS NEW Unchecked_Deallocation (Object => TreeNode, Name => NodePointer);	Instantiates a predefined generic procedure to give an operation to return tree nodes to the heap.
P := NEW TreeNode;	Allocates a tree node and stores a pointer to it in P.
Q := P;	Copies one pointer value to another
Q.ALL := P.ALL;	Copies one record's contents to the other.

Review Questions

1. Differentiate between dynamic and nondynamic data structures.
2. Define a simple linked list. Indicate how the pointers are utilized to establish a link between nodes. Also indicate any other variables that would be needed to reference the linked list.
3. Write a procedure that links a node into an existing list. Parameters are a pointer to the head of the linked list and a pointer to the node to be inserted. Assume dummy sentinel records exist at the beginning and end of the linked list and there are no duplicate records. Given the following type definitions, insert the new element preserving ID order:

```
TYPE Node;
TYPE Ptr IS ACCESS Node;
TYPE Node IS RECORD
   ID   : INTEGER;
   Name : String(1..10);
   GPA  : NonNegFloat;
   Link : Ptr;
END RECORD;
```

4. Write an algorithm to remove a node (identified by `TargetID`) from an ordered list that does not contain a dummy record at the beginning.
5. Write the necessary procedures to duplicate all elements with a GPA of 3.5 or above in one linked list in another linked list. The original list is ordered by ID number; the new list should be ordered by GPA. Do not remove nodes from the existing list. Assume the list nodes are type `Node` as described in question 3. Parameters will be a pointer to the head of the existing list and to the head of the new linked list (`GPAHead`).
6. Declare a node for a two-way or doubly linked list, and indicate how a traversal would be made in reverse order (from the last list element to the list head). Include any variables or fields that are necessary.

7. Discuss the differences between a simple one-way linked list and a binary tree. Consider such things as numbers of pointer fields per node, search technique, and insertion algorithm.

8. Write a procedure to delete all males over 25 from an existing linear linked list, given the following type declarations and assuming no dummy nodes:

```
TYPE Gender IS (Male, Female);
TYPE Node;
TYPE Ptr IS ACCESS Node;
TYPE Node IS RECORD
   ID   : INTEGER;
   Name : String(1..10);
   Age  : Positive;
   Sex  : Gender;
   Link : Ptr;
END RECORD;
```

The procedure parameter is a pointer to the head of the list.

9. How can you determine whether a tree node is a leaf?

10. Traverse the following tree in inorder, preorder, and postorder.

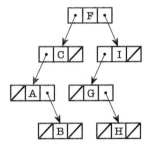

Provide one sequence that would create this ordered binary tree. Are there any letters that must occur before other letters?

11. Discuss how you might delete a node from a binary tree. Consider first nodes with zero or one child.

Programming Projects

1. Use the generic table package shown in Section 14.4 to maintain an airline passenger list. The main program should be menu-driven and should allow its user to display the data for a particular passenger, display the entire list, create a list, insert a node, delete a node, and replace the data for a particular passenger.

2. Redo project 1 using a binary search tree for storage of the airline passenger list. When deleting a node, simply change the number of seats assigned to zero and leave the passenger's node in the tree.

3. Develop a linked-list representation to store sets. Write the necessary routines needed to insert and delete integer values from a set. Also write the routines necessary to implement the set operations of difference, intersection, and union. To verify the results, display the contents of the sets before and after each operation.

4. In preparing mailing lists, it is often useful to be able to reference the information

by using either the person's name or zip code. This can be done if each list node has a pointer to the next node by name and a pointer to the next node by zip code. The nodes representing each person's data should be linked together in both name and zip-code order; there should only be one copy of the data for each person. Provide a header node that has pointers to the first element in each of the two lists.

Write a program that reads a record containing first name, last name, street address, city, state, and zip code, and connects each new record to the appropriate nodes of both lists. After all of the information has been entered, display a list of the information in name order and a second list in zip-code order.

5. A polynomial may be represented as a linked list where each node contains the co-efficient and exponent of a term of the polynomial. The polynomial $4x^3 + 3x^2 - 5$ would be represented as the following linked list:

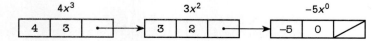

Write an abstract data type for polynomials that has operators for creating a polynomial, reading a polynomial, and adding and subtracting a pair of polynomials. (*Hint*: To add or subtract two polynomials, traverse both lists. If a particular exponent value is present in either one, then it should be present in the resulting polynomial unless its coefficient is zero.)

6. Because each student in the university takes a different number of courses, the registrar decided to use a linked list to store each student's class schedule and an array of records to represent the whole student body. A portion of this data structure follows.

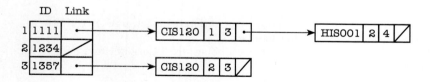

These records above show that the first student (ID 1111) is taking section 1 of CIS120 for 3 credits and section 2 of HIS001 for 4 credits; the second student (ID 1357) is not enrolled, and so on. Write an abstract data type for this data structure. Provide operators for creating the original array of student ID numbers, inserting a student's initial class schedule, adding a course, and dropping a course. Write a menu-driven program that uses this abstract data type.

Appendix A: The Ada Character Set, Delimiters, and Reserved Words

This appendix is adapted from the *Ada Language Reference Manual*, Sections 2.1, 2.2, and 2.9.

The Ada Character Set

The basic character set is sufficient for writing any program. The characters included in each of the categories of basic graphic characters are defined as follows:

1. upper case letters

   A B C D E F G H I J K L M N O P Q R S T U V W X Y Z

2. digits

   0 1 2 3 4 5 6 7 8 9

3. special characters

   " # & ' ( ) * + , – . / : ; < = > _ |

4. the space character

Format effectors are the ISO (and ASCII) characters called horizontal tabulation, vertical tabulation, carriage return, line feed, and form feed.

The characters included in each of the remaining categories of graphic characters are defined as follows:

5. lower case letters

   a b c d e f g h i j k l m n o p q r s t u v w x y z

6. other special characters

   ! $ % ? @ [\ ] ^ ` { } ~

The following names are used when referring to special characters and other special characters:

Symbol	Name	Symbol	Name
"	quotation	>	greater than
#	sharp	_	underline
&	ampersand	|	vertical bar
'	apostrophe	!	exclamation mark
(	left parenthesis	$	dollar
)	right parenthesis	%	percent
*	star, multiply	?	question mark
+	plus	@	commercial at
,	comma	[	left square bracket
–	hyphen, minus	\	back-slash
.	dot, point, period	]	right square bracket
/	slash, divide	^	circumflex
:	colon	`	grave accent
;	semicolon	{	left brace
<	less than	}	right brace
=	equal	~	tilde

Delimiters

A delimiter is either one of the following special characters (in the basic character set)

    & ' ( ) * + , – . / : ; < = > |

or one of the following compound delimiters each composed of two adjacent special characters

    => .. ** := /= >= <= << >> <>

The following names are used when referring to compound delimiters:

Delimiter	Name
=>	arrow
..	double dot
**	double star, exponentiate
:=	assignment (pronounced: "becomes")
/=	inequality (pronounced: "not equal")
>=	greater than or equal
<=	less than or equal
<<	left label bracket
>>	right label bracket
<>	box

Reserved Words

The identifiers listed below are called reserved words and are reserved for special significance in the language. In this book the reserved words always appear in uppercase.

ABORT	DECLARE	GENERIC	OF	SELECT
ABS	DELAY	GOTO	OR	SEPARATE

ACCEPT	DELTA		OTHERS	SUBTYPE
ACCESS	DIGITS	IF	OUT	
ALL	DO	IN		TASK
AND		IS	PACKAGE	TERMINATE
ARRAY			PRAGMA	THEN
AT	ELSE		PRIVATE	TYPE
	ELSIF	LIMITED	PROCEDURE	
	END	LOOP		
BEGIN	ENTRY		RAISE	USE
BODY	EXCEPTION		RANGE	
	EXIT	MOD	RECORD	WHEN
			REM	WHILE
		NEW	RENAMES	WITH
CASE	FOR	NOT	RETURN	
CONSTANT	FUNCTION	NULL	REVERSE	XOR

A reserved word must not be used as a declared identifier.

Appendix B*: The Ada Syntax Charts

There exist several ways to formally define the syntax of a programming language, with Backus–Naur Form (BNF) being the most popular due to its conciseness. However, BNF productions are not very readable to the uninitiated; so we instead present Ada's form with syntax charts, which are essentially graphic representations of the BNF.

Syntax charts are read from left to right, following the direction of the arrows. The directed lines may loop back on themselves, indicating that a construct may be repeated. A rectangle surrounds a construct that is defined in another syntax chart (a nonterminal). A circle or ellipse denotes a literal string that appears exactly as stated. For consistency with the Ada standard, we have left the reserve words in lower case. If a syntactic category is prefixed by an italicized word, it is equivalent to the unprefixed corresponding category name; the prefix simply conveys some semantic information.

We present the syntax charts in alphabetical order. Every construct is included, except for <upper_case_character>, <digit>, <lower_case_character>, and <graphic _character>, since their form is obvious. In addition, we have drawn the syntax charts in a style that indicates the recommended indentation style for each production.

In tracing a syntax error in a student program, the reader will most probably wish to begin with the nonterminal Compilation_Unit.

Abort_statement

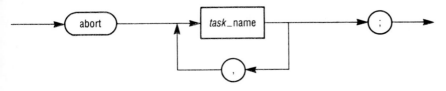

Accept_alternative

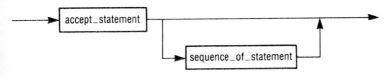

* Reprinted with permission of Benjamin/Cummings Publishing Company, Menlo Park, CA, from Grady Booch, *Software Engineering with Ada*, Second Edition, © 1987 by Benjamin/Cummings Publishing Company.

Accept_statement

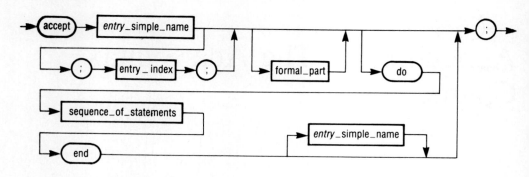

Access_type_definition

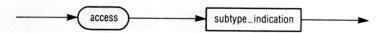

Actual_parameter

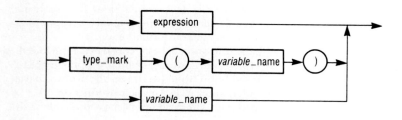

Actual_parameter_part

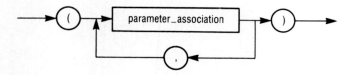

Address_clause

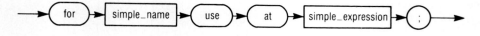

Aggregate

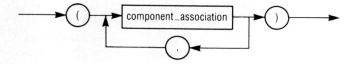

Alignment_clause

Allocator

Argument_association

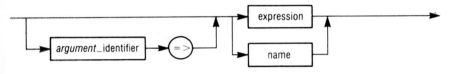

Array_type_definition

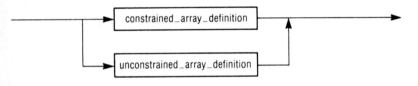

Assignment_statement

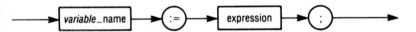

Attribute

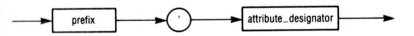

Attribute_designator

Base

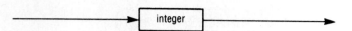

Based_integer

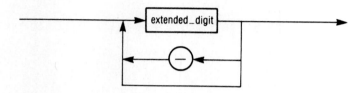

Based_literal

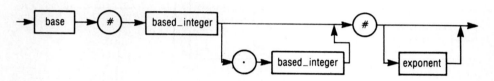

Basic_declaration

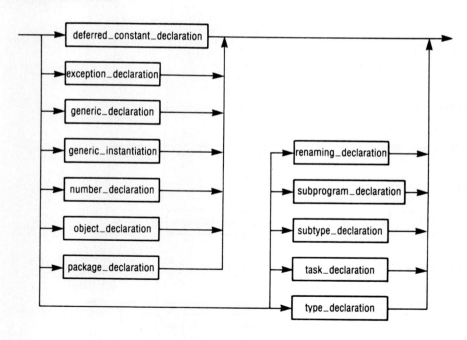

Basic_declarative_item

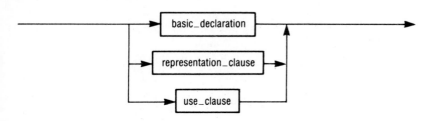

Binary_adding_operator

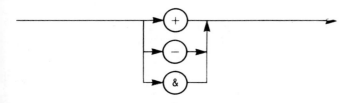

Block_statement

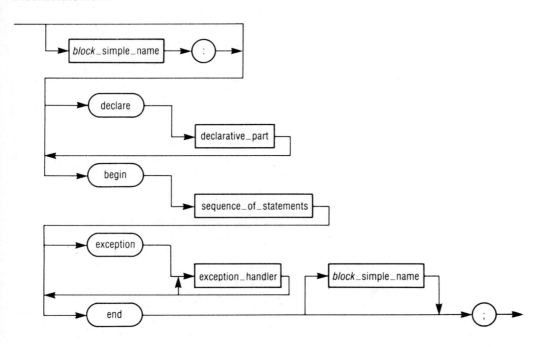

Body

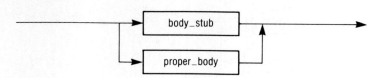

Body_stub

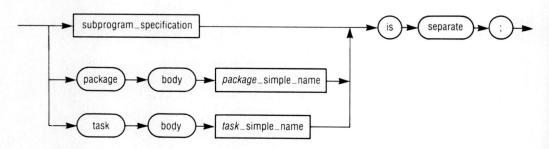

Case_statement

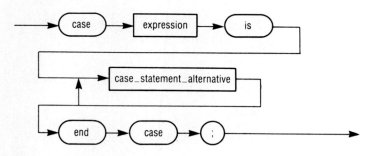

Case_statement_alternative

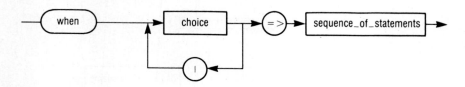

Character_literal

Choice

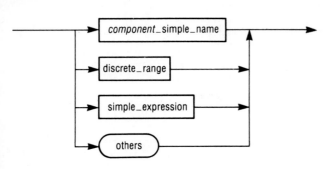

Code_statement

Compilation

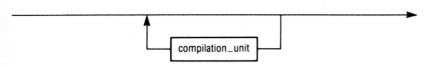

Compilation_unit

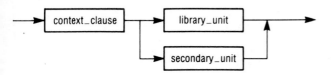

Component_association

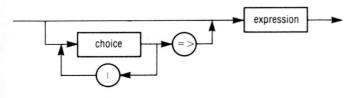

Component_clause

Component_declaration

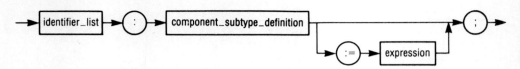

Component_list

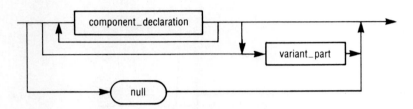

Component_subtype_definition

Compound_statement

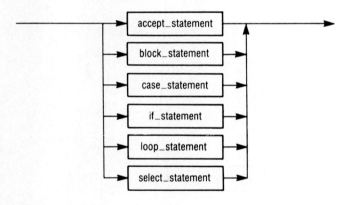

Condition

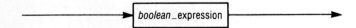

Conditional_entry_call

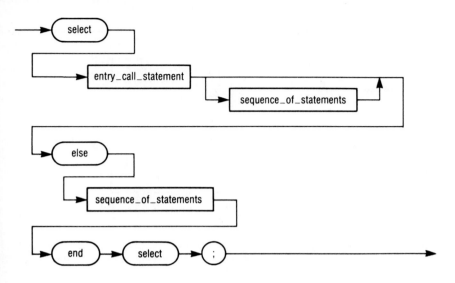

Constrained_array_definition

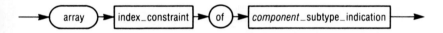

Constraint

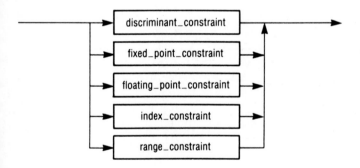

Context_clause

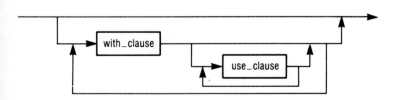

Decimal_literal

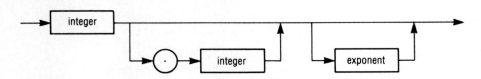

Declarative_part

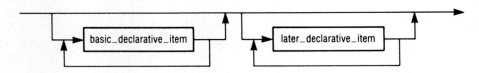

Deferred_constant_declaration

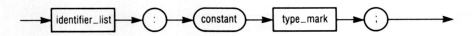

Delay_alternative

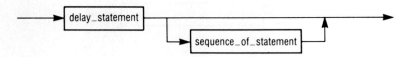

Delay_statement

Derived_type_definition

Designator

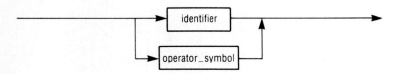

Discrete_range

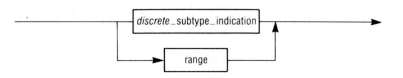

Discriminant_association

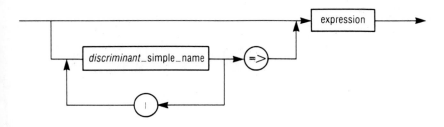

Discriminant_constraint

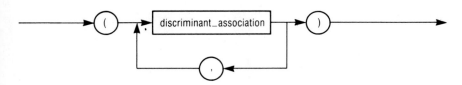

Discriminant_part

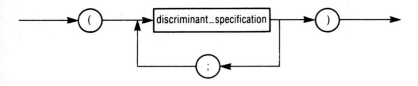

Discriminant_specification

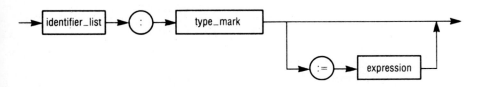

Entry_call_statement

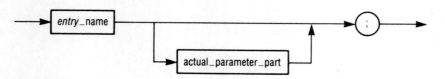

Entry_declaration

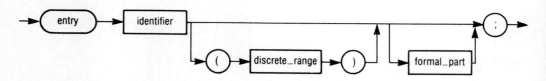

Entry_index

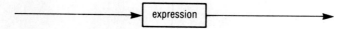

Enumeration_literal

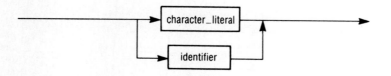

Enumeration_literal_specification

Enumeration_representation_clause

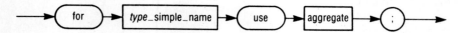

Enumeration_type_definition

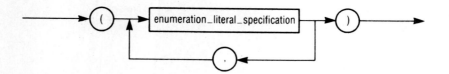

Exception_choice

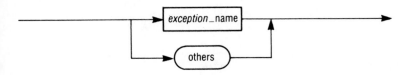

Exception_declaration

Exception_handler

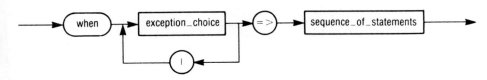

Exit_statement

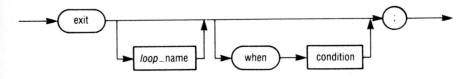

Exponent

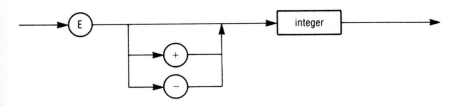

Expression

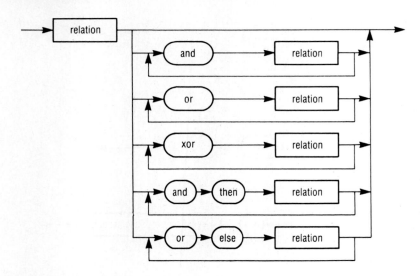

Extended_digit

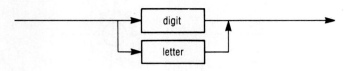

Factor

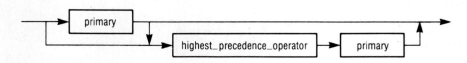

Fixed_accuracy_definition

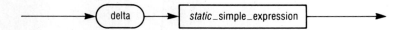

Fixed_point_constraint

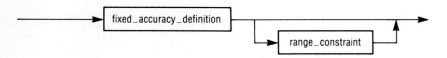

Floating_accuracy_definition

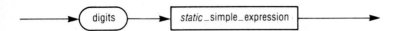

Floating_point_constraint

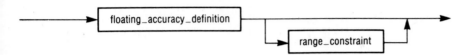

Formal_parameter

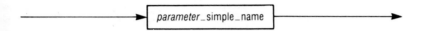

Formal_part

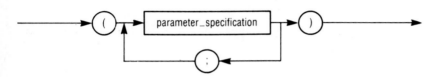

Full_type_declaration

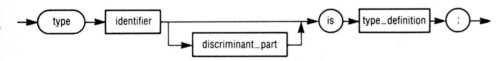

Function_call

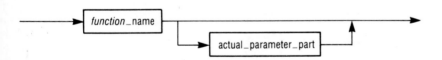

Generic_actual_parameter

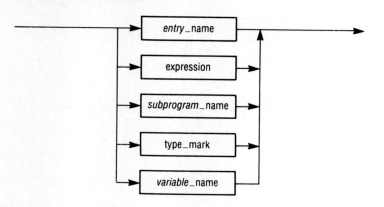

Generic_actual_part

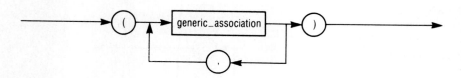

Generic_association

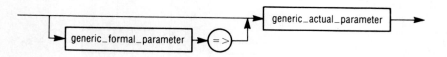

Generic_declaration

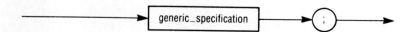

Generic_formal_parameter

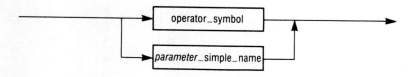

Generic_formal_part

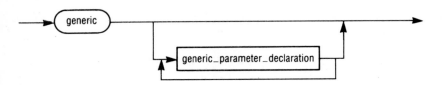

Generic_instantiation

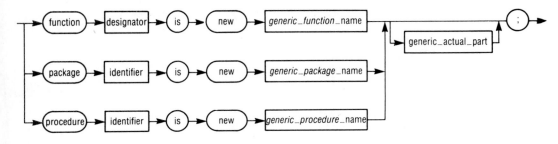

Generic_parameter_declaration

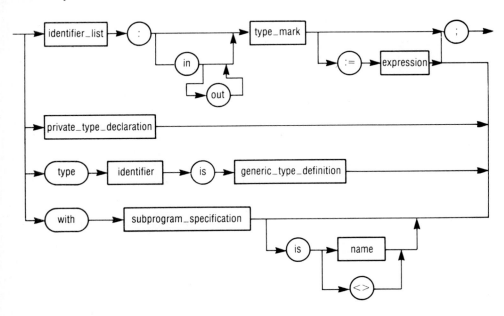

Generic_specification

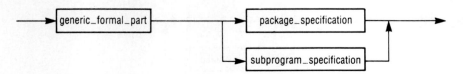

Generic_type_definition

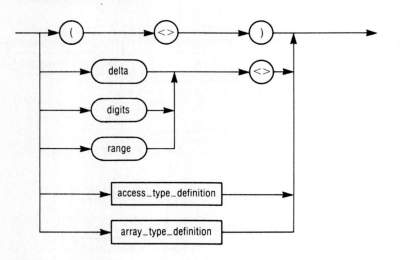

Goto_statement

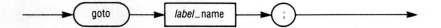

Highest_precedence_operator

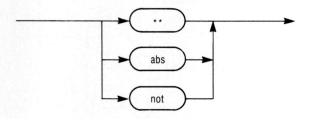

Identifier

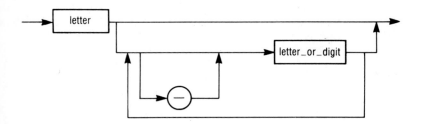

Identifier_list

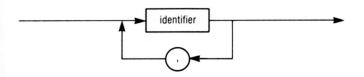

If_statement

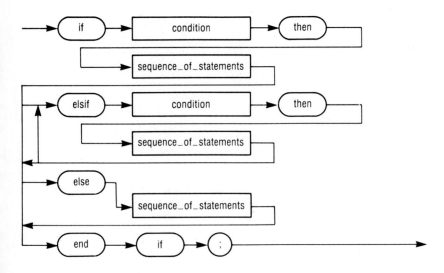

Incomplete_type_declaration

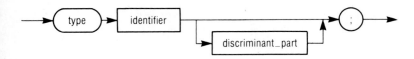

Index_constraint

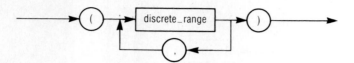

Index_subtype_definition

Indexed_component

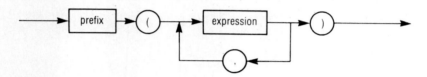

Integer

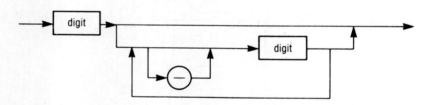

Integer_type_definition

Iteration_scheme

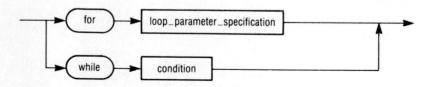

Label

Later_declarative_item

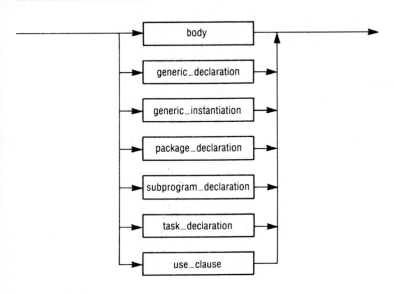

Length_clause

Letter

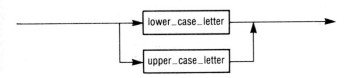

Letter_or_digit

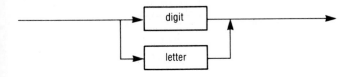

Library_unit

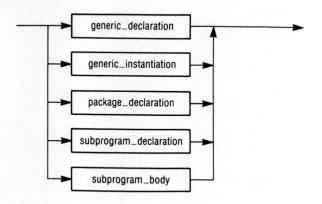

Library_unit_body

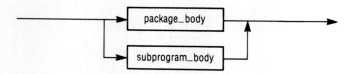

Logical_operator

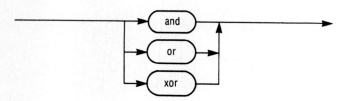

Loop_parameter_specification

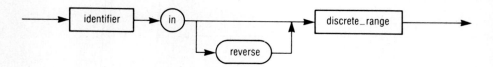

Loop_statement

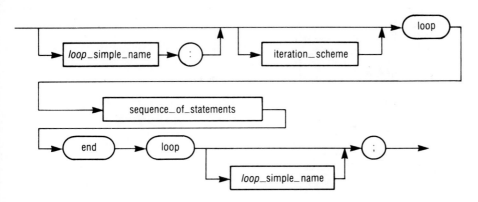

Mode

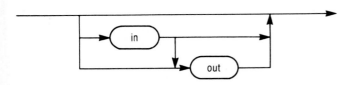

Multiplying_operator

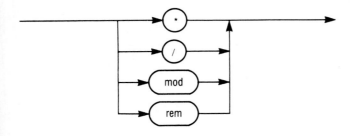

Name

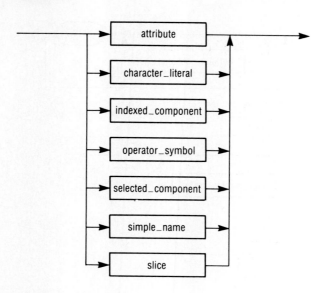

Null_statement

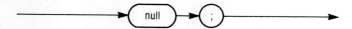

Number_declaration

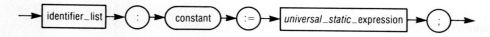

Numeric_literal

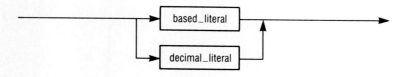

Object_declaration

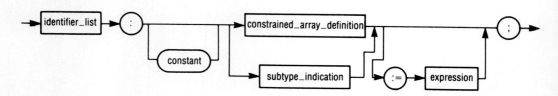

Operator_symbol

Package_body

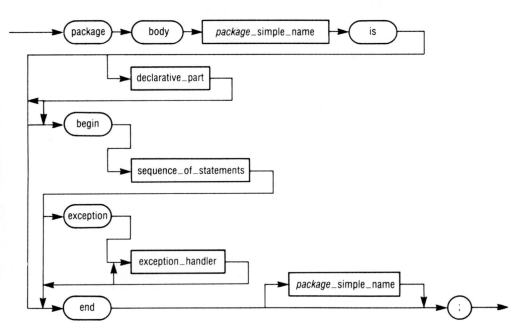

Package_declaration

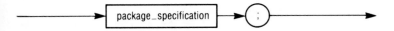

Package_specification

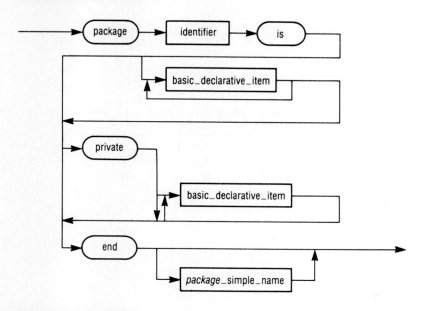

Parameter_association

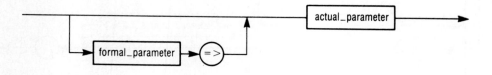

Parameter_specification

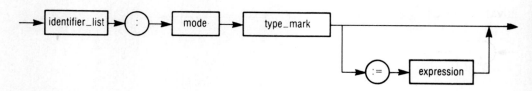

Pragma

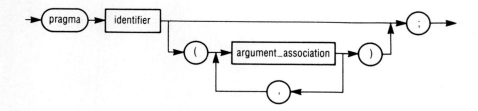

Prefix

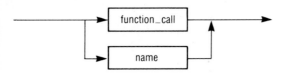

Primary

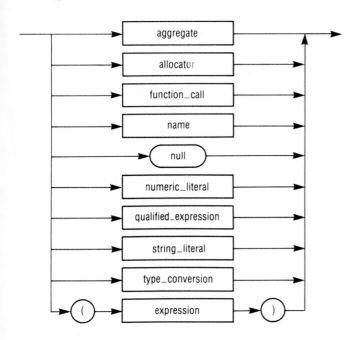

Private_type_declaration

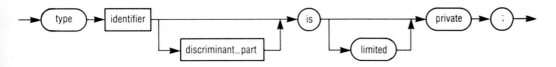

Procedure_call_statement

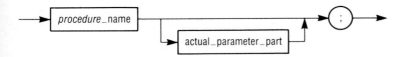

Proper_body

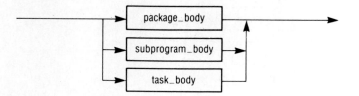

Qualified_expression

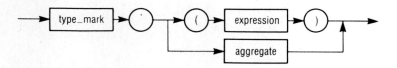

Raise_statement

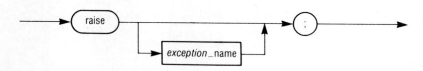

Range

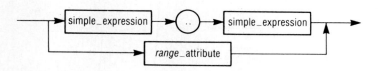

Range_constraint

Real_type_definition

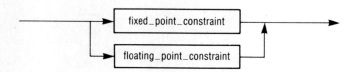

Record_representation_clause

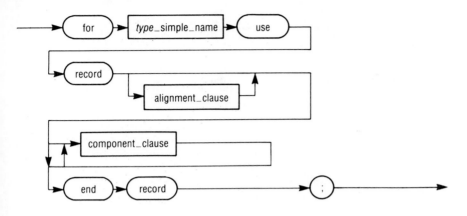

Record_type_definition

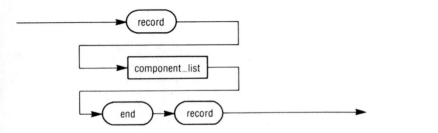

Relation

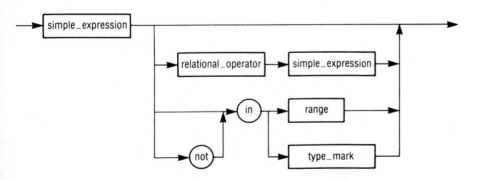

Relational_operator

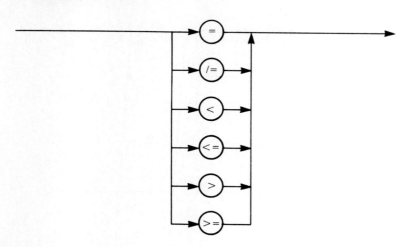

Renaming_declaration

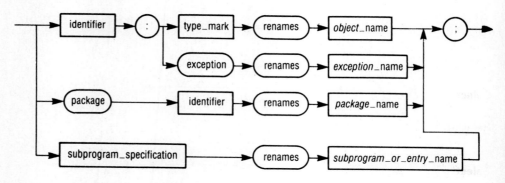

Representation_clause

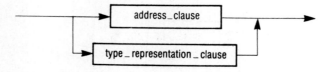

Return_statement

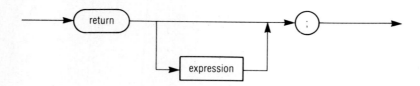

Secondary_unit

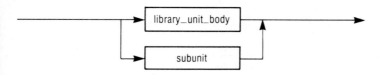

Select_alternative

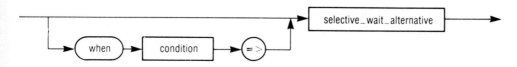

Select_statement

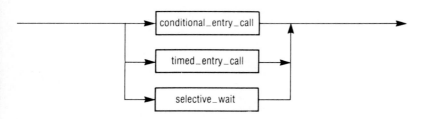

Selected_component

Selective_wait_alternative

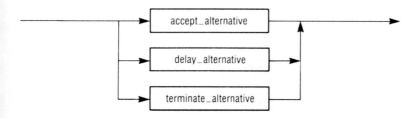

Selective_wait

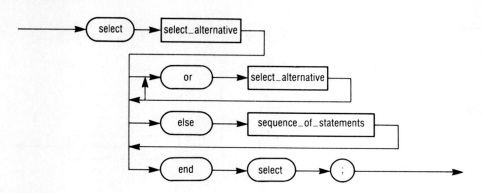

Selector

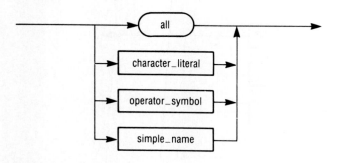

Sequence_of_statements

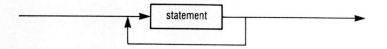

Simple_expression

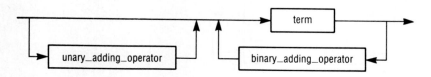

Simple_name

Simple_statement

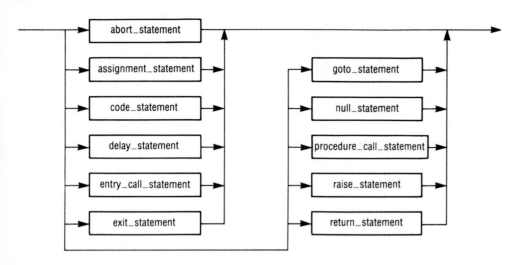

Slice

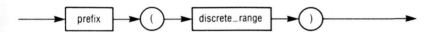

Statement

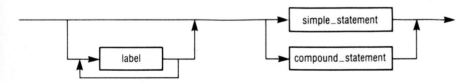

String_literal

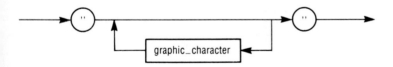

Subprogram_body

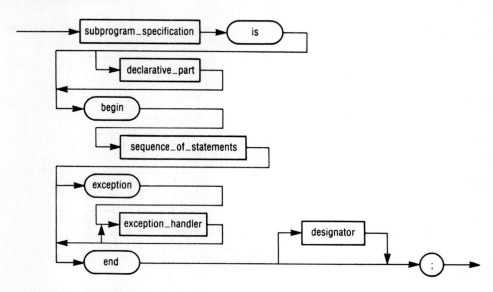

Subprogram_declaration

Subprogram_specification

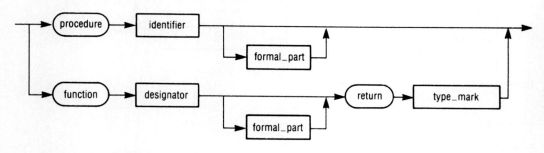

Subtype_declaration

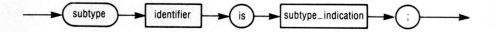

Subtype_indication

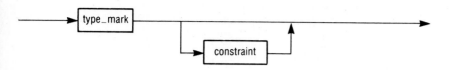

Subunit

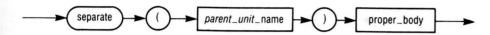

Task_body

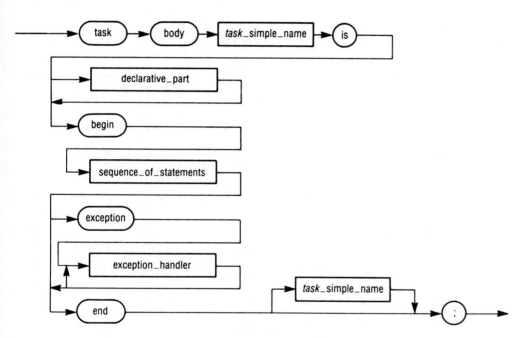

Task_declaration

Task_specification

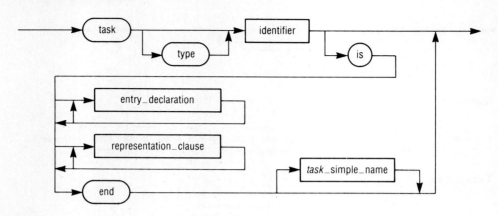

Term

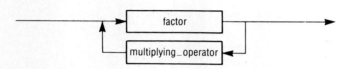

Terminate_alternative

Timed_entry_call

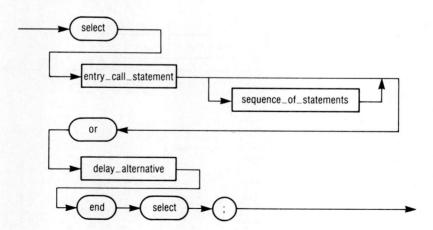

Type_conversion

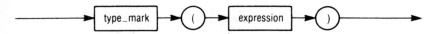

Type_declaration

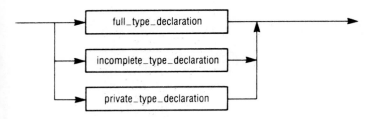

Type_definition

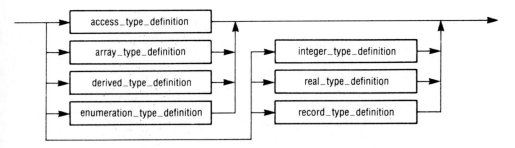

Type_mark

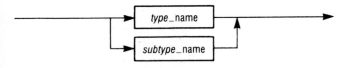

Type_representation_clause

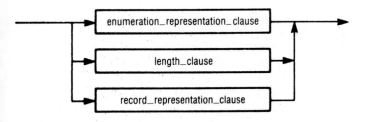

Unary_adding_operator

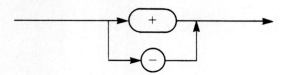

Unconstrained_array_definition

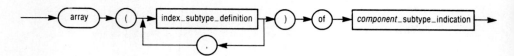

Use_clause

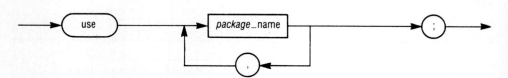

Variant

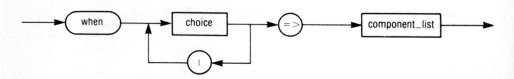

Variant_part

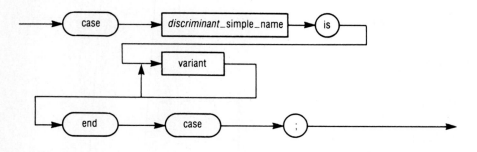

With_clause

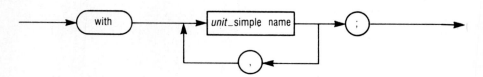

Appendix C: The Ada Predefined Language Environment

This appendix outlines the specification of the package Standard containing all prede-fined identifiers in the language. It is taken verbatim from the *Ada Language Reference Manual*, Appendix C; the only changes are to conform to the case convention used in this book. The corresponding package body is implementation-defined and is not shown.

The operators that are predefined for the types declared in the package Standard are given in comments since they are implicitly declared. Italics are used for pseudo-names of anonymous types (such as *Universal_Real*) and for undefined information (such as *Implementation_Defined* and *Any_Fixed_Point_Type*).

```
PACKAGE Standard IS

   TYPE Boolean IS (False, True);

   -- The predefined relational operators for this type are as follows:

   -- FUNCTION "="   (Left, Right : Boolean) RETURN Boolean;
   -- FUNCTION "/="  (Left, Right : Boolean) RETURN Boolean;
   -- FUNCTION "<"   (Left, Right : Boolean) RETURN Boolean;
   -- FUNCTION "<="  (Left, Right : Boolean) RETURN Boolean;
   -- FUNCTION ">"   (Left, Right : Boolean) RETURN Boolean;
   -- FUNCTION ">="  (Left, Right : Boolean) RETURN Boolean;

   -- The predefined logical operators and the predefined logical negation
   -- operator are as follows:

   -- FUNCTION "AND" (Left, Right : Boolean) RETURN Boolean;
   -- FUNCTION "OR"  (Left, Right : Boolean) RETURN Boolean;
   -- FUNCTION "XOR" (Left, Right : Boolean) RETURN Boolean;

   -- FUNCTION "NOT" (Right : Boolean) RETURN Boolean;

   -- The universal type Universal_Integer is predefined.

   TYPE Integer IS Implementation_Defined;

   -- The predefined operators for this type are as follows:

   -- FUNCTION "="   (Left, Right : Integer) RETURN Boolean;
   -- FUNCTION "/="  (Left, Right : Integer) RETURN Boolean;
   -- FUNCTION "<"   (Left, Right : Integer) RETURN Boolean;
   -- FUNCTION "<="  (Left, Right : Integer) RETURN Boolean;
```

```
--  FUNCTION ">"  (Left, Right : Integer) RETURN Boolean;
--  FUNCTION ">=" (Left, Right : Integer) RETURN Boolean;


--  FUNCTION "+"   (Right : Integer) RETURN Integer;
--  FUNCTION "-"   (Right : Integer) RETURN Integer;
--  FUNCTION "ABS" (Right : Integer) RETURN Integer;

--  FUNCTION "+"   (Left, Right : Integer) RETURN Integer;
--  FUNCTION "-"   (Left, Right : Integer) RETURN Integer;
--  FUNCTION "*"   (Left, Right : Integer) RETURN Integer;
--  FUNCTION "/"   (Left, Right : Integer) RETURN Integer;
--  FUNCTION "REM" (Left, Right : Integer) RETURN Integer;
--  FUNCTION "MOD" (Left, Right : Integer) RETURN Integer;

--  FUNCTION "**"  (Left : Integer; Right : Integer) RETURN Integer;
```

-- An implementation may provide additional predefined integer types.
-- It is recommended that the names of such additional types end with
-- Integer as in Short_Integer or Long_Integer. The specification of
-- each operator for the type *Universal_Integer*, or for any additional
-- predefined integer type, is obtained by replacing Integer by
-- the name of the type in the specification of the corresponding
-- operator of the type Integer, except for the right operand of the
-- exponentiating operator.

-- The universal type *Universal_Real* is predefined.

TYPE Float IS *Implementation_Defined*;

-- The predefined operators for this TYPE are as follows:

```
--  FUNCTION "="  (Left, Right : Float) RETURN Boolean;
--  FUNCTION "/=" (Left, Right : Float) RETURN Boolean;
--  FUNCTION "<"  (Left, Right : Float) RETURN Boolean;
--  FUNCTION "<=" (Left, Right : Float) RETURN Boolean;
--  FUNCTION ">"  (Left, Right : Float) RETURN Boolean;
--  FUNCTION ">=" (Left, Right : Float) RETURN Boolean;


--  FUNCTION "+"   (Right : Float) RETURN Float;
--  FUNCTION "-"   (Right : Float) RETURN Float;
--  FUNCTION "ABS" (Right : Float) RETURN Float;

--  FUNCTION "+"   (Left, Right : Float) RETURN Float;
--  FUNCTION "-"   (Left, Right : Float) RETURN Float;
--  FUNCTION "*"   (Left, Right : Float) RETURN Float;
--  FUNCTION "/"   (Left, Right : Float) RETURN Float;

--  FUNCTION "**"  (Left : Float; Right : Integer) RETURN Float;
```

-- An implementation may provide additional predefined floating point
-- point types. It is recommended that the names of such additional
-- types end with Float as in Short_Float or Long_Float. The
-- specification of each operator for the type *Universal_Real*, or for
-- any additional predefined floating point type, is obtained by
-- replacing Float by the name of the type in the specification of the
-- corresponding operator of the type Float.

-- In addition, the following operators are predefined for universal type

-- FUNCTION "*" (Left : *Universal_Integer*; Right : *Universal_Real*)
-- RETURN *Universal_Real*;

```
--- FUNCTION "*" (Left : Universal_Real;    Right : Universal_Integer)
--- RETURN Universal_Real;

--- FUNCTION "/" (Left : Universal_Real;    Right : Universal_Integer)
--- RETURN Universal_Real;

--- The type Universal_Fixed is predefined. The only operators declared
--- for this type are

--- FUNCTION "*" (Left : Any_Fixed_Point_Type; Right : Any_Fixed_Point_Type)
--- RETURN Universal_Fixed;

--- FUNCTION "/" (Left : Any_Fixed_Point_Type; Right : Any_Fixed_Point_Type)
--- RETURN Universal_Fixed;

---    The following characters form the standard ASCII character set.
---    Character literals corresponding to control characters are
---    not identifiers; they are indicated in italics in this
---    definition.


TYPE Character IS

( nul,   soh,   stx,   etx,        eot,   enq,   ack,   bel,
  bs,    ht,    lf,    vt,         ff,    cr,    so,    si,
  dle,   dc1,   dc2,   dc3,        dc4,   nak,   syn,   etb,
  can,   em,    sub,   esc,        fs,    gs,    rs,    us,

  ' ',   '!',   '"',   '#',        '$',   '%',   '&',   ''',
  '(',   ')',   '*',   '+',        ',',   '-',   '.',   '/',
  '0',   '1',   '2',   '3',        '4',   '5',   '6',   '7',
  '8',   '9',   ':',   ';',        '<',   '=',   '>',   '?',

  '@',   'A',   'B',   'C',        'D',   'E',   'F',   'G',
  'H',   'I',   'J',   'K',        'L',   'M',   'N',   'O',
  'P',   'Q',   'R',   'S',        'T',   'U',   'V',   'W',
  'X',   'Y',   'Z',   '[',        '"',   '"',   '~',   '_',

  ''',   'a',   'b',   'c',        'd',   'e',   'f',   'g',
  'h',   'i',   'j',   'k',        'l',   'm',   'n',   'o',
  'p',   'q',   'r',   's',        't',   'u',   'v',   'w',
  'x',   'y',   'z',   '{',        '|',   '}',   '~',   del );


FOR Character USE -- 128 ASCII character set without holes
     (0, 1, 2, 3, 4, 5, ..., 125, 126, 127);

--- The predefined operators for the type Character are the same as for
--- any enumeration type.


PACKAGE ASCII IS

-- Control characters:

   NUL   : CONSTANT Character := nul;   SOH: CONSTANT Character := soh:
   STX   : CONSTANT Character := stx;   ETX: CONSTANT Character := etx;
   EOT   : CONSTANT Character := eot;   ENQ: CONSTANT Character := enq:
   ACK   : CONSTANT Character := ack;   BEL: CONSTANT Character := bel;
   BS    : CONSTANT Character := bs;    HT : CONSTANT Character := ht;
   LF    : CONSTANT Character := lf;    VT : CONSTANT Character := vt;
   FF    : CONSTANT Character := ff;    CR : CONSTANT Character := cr;
```

```
SO      : CONSTANT Character := so;    SI : CONSTANT Character := si;
DLE     : CONSTANT Character := dle;   DC1: CONSTANT Character := dc1;
DC2     : CONSTANT Character := dc2;   DC3: CONSTANT Character := dc3;
DC4     : CONSTANT Character := dc4;   NAK: CONSTANT Character := nak;
SYN     : CONSTANT Character := syn;   ETB: CONSTANT Character := etb;
CAN     : CONSTANT Character := can;   EM : CONSTANT Character := em:
SUB     : CONSTANT Character := sub;   ESC: CONSTANT Character := esc;
FS      : CONSTANT Character := fs;    GS : CONSTANT Character := gs;
RS      : CONSTANT Character := rs;    US : CONSTANT Character := us;
DEL     : CONSTANT Character := del;

        -- Other characters:

Exclam   : CONSTANT Character := '!';   Quotation  : CONSTANT Character := '"';
Sharp    : CONSTANT Character := '#';   Dollar     : CONSTANT Character := '$';
Percent  : CONSTANT Character := '%';   Ampersand  : CONSTANT Character := '&';
Colon    : CONSTANT Character := ':';   Semicolon  : CONSTANT Character := ';';
Query    : CONSTANT Character := '?';   At_Sign    : CONSTANT Character := '@';
L_Bracket: CONSTANT Character := '[';   Back_Slash : CONSTANT Character := '\';
R_Bracket: CONSTANT Character := ']';   Circumflex : CONSTANT Character := '^';
Underline: CONSTANT Character := '_';   Grave      : CONSTANT Character := '`';
L_Brace  : CONSTANT Character := '{';   Bar        : CONSTANT Character := '|';
R_Brace  : CONSTANT Character := '}';   Tilde      : CONSTANT Character := '~';

        -- Lower case letters:

    LC_A : CONSTANT Character := 'a';
    ...
    LC_Z : CONSTANT Character := 'z';

END ASCII;

-- Predefined subtypes:

SUBTYPE Natural  IS Integer RANGE 0 .. Integer'Last;
SUBTYPE Positive IS Integer RANGE 1 .. Integer'Last;


-- Predefined string type:

TYPE String IS ARRAY(Positive RANGE <>) OF Character;

PRAGMA Pack(String);

-- The predefined operators for this type are as follows:

-- FUNCTION "="  (Left, Right : String) RETURN Boolean;
-- FUNCTION "/=" (Left, Right : String) RETURN Boolean;
-- FUNCTION "<"  (Left, Right : String) RETURN Boolean;
-- FUNCTION "<=" (Left, Right : String) RETURN Boolean;
-- FUNCTION ">"  (Left, Right : String) RETURN Boolean;
-- FUNCTION ">=" (Left, Right : String) RETURN Boolean;

-- FUNCTION "&" (Left : String;    Right : String)    RETURN String;
-- FUNCTION "&" (Left : Character; Right : String)    RETURN String;
-- FUNCTION "&" (Left : String;    Right : Character)  RETURN String;
-- FUNCTION "&" (Left : Character; Right : Character)  RETURN String;

TYPE Duration IS DELTA Implementation_Defined RANGE Implementation_Defined;

-- The predefined operators for the type Duration are the same as for
-- any fixed point type.
```

```
--  The predefined exceptions:

Constraint_Error : EXCEPTION;
Numeric_Error    : EXCEPTION;
Program_Error    : EXCEPTION;
Storage_Error    : EXCEPTION;
Tasking_Error    : EXCEPTION;

END Standard;
```

Appendix D: Specification of the Package Text_IO

This appendix is taken from the *Ada Language Reference Manual (LRM)*, Section 14.3.10. The only changes are to conform to the case convention used in this book.

```
WITH IO_Exceptions;
PACKAGE Text_IO IS

   TYPE File_Type IS LIMITED PRIVATE;

   TYPE File_Mode IS (In_File, Out_File);

   TYPE Count IS RANGE 0 .. implementation defined;
   SUBTYPE Positive_Count IS Count RANGE 1 .. Count'Last;
   Unbounded : CONSTANT Count := 0; -- line and page length

   SUBTYPE Field      IS Integer RANGE 0 .. implementation defined;
   SUBTYPE Number_Base IS Integer RANGE 2 .. 16;

   TYPE Type_Set IS (Lower_Case, Upper_Case);

   -- File Management

   PROCEDURE Create (File : IN OUT File_Type;
                     Mode : IN File_Mode := Out_File;
                     Name : IN String    := "";
                     Form : IN String    := "");

   PROCEDURE Open   (File : IN OUT File_Type;
                     Mode : IN File_Mode;
                     Name : IN String;
                     Form : IN String := "");

   PROCEDURE Close  (File : IN OUT File_Type);
   PROCEDURE Delete (File : IN OUT File_Type);
   PROCEDURE Reset  (File : IN OUT File_Type; Mode : IN File_Mode);
   PROCEDURE Reset  (File : IN OUT File_Type);

   FUNCTION Mode    (File : IN File_Type) RETURN File_Mode;
   FUNCTION Name    (File : IN File_Type) RETURN String;
   FUNCTION Form    (File : IN File_Type) RETURN String;

   FUNCTION Is_Open(File : IN File_Type) RETURN Boolean;
```

```
-- Control of default input and output files

PROCEDURE Set_Input (File : IN File_Type);
PROCEDURE Set_Output(File : IN File_Type);

FUNCTION Standard_Input  RETURN File_Type;
FUNCTION Standard_Output RETURN File_Type;

FUNCTION Current_Input   RETURN File_Type;
FUNCTION Current_Output  RETURN File_Type;


-- Specification of line and page lengths

PROCEDURE Set_Line_Length(File : IN File_Type; To : IN Count);
PROCEDURE Set_Line_Length(To : IN Count);

PROCEDURE Set_Page_Length(File : IN File_Type; To : IN Count);
PROCEDURE Set_Page_Length(To : IN Count);

FUNCTION Line_Length(File : IN File_Type) RETURN Count;
FUNCTION Line_Length RETURN Count;

FUNCTION Page_Length(File : IN File_Type) RETURN Count;
FUNCTION Page_Length RETURN Count;




-- Column, Line, and Page Control

PROCEDURE New_Line  (File : IN File_Type; Spacing : IN Positive_Count := 1);
PROCEDURE New_Line  (Spacing : IN Positive_Count := 1);

PROCEDURE Skip_Line  (File : IN File_Type; Spacing : IN Positive_Count := 1);
PROCEDURE Skip_Line  (Spacing : IN Positive_Count := 1);

FUNCTION End_Of_Line(File : IN File_Type) RETURN Boolean;
FUNCTION End_Of_Line RETURN Boolean;

PROCEDURE New_Page   (File : IN File_Type);
PROCEDURE New_Page;

PROCEDURE Skip_Page  (File : IN File_Type);
PROCEDURE Skip_Page;

FUNCTION End_Of_Page(File : IN File_Type) RETURN Boolean;
FUNCTION End_Of_Page RETURN Boolean;

FUNCTION End_Of_File(File : IN File_Type) RETURN Boolean;
FUNCTION End_Of_File RETURN Boolean;

PROCEDURE Set_Col (File : IN File_Type; To : IN Positive_Count);
PROCEDURE Set_Col (To   : IN Positive_Count);

PROCEDURE Set_Line(File : IN File_Type; To : IN Positive_Count);
PROCEDURE Set_Line(To   : IN Positive_Count);

FUNCTION Col (File : IN File_Type) RETURN Positive_Count;
FUNCTION Col  RETURN Positive_Count;

FUNCTION Line(File : IN File_Type) RETURN Positive_Count;
FUNCTION Line RETURN Positive_Count;
```

```
FUNCTION Page(File : IN File_Type) RETURN Positive_Count;
FUNCTION Page RETURN Positive_Count;


-- Character Input-Output

PROCEDURE Get(File : IN File_Type; Item : OUT CHARACTER);
PROCEDURE Get(Item : OUT CHARACTER);
PROCEDURE Put(File : IN File_Type; Item : IN CHARACTER);
PROCEDURE Put(Item : IN CHARACTER);


-- String Input-Output

PROCEDURE Get(File : IN File_Type; Item : OUT String);
PROCEDURE Get(Item : OUT String);
PROCEDURE Put(File : IN File_Type; Item : IN String);
PROCEDURE Put(Item : IN String);

PROCEDURE Get_Line(File : IN File_Type;
                   Item : OUT String;
                   Last : OUT Natural);
PROCEDURE Get_Line(Item : OUT String; Last : OUT Natural);
PROCEDURE Put_Line(File : IN File_Type; Item : IN String);
PROCEDURE Put_Line(Item : IN String);

-- Generic PACKAGE for Input-Output of Integer Types

GENERIC
  TYPE Num IS RANGE <>;
PACKAGE Integer_IO IS

  Default_Width : Field := Num'Width;
  Default_Base :  Number_Base := 10;

  PROCEDURE Get(File : IN File_Type;
               Item : OUT Num;
               Width : IN Field := 0);
  PROCEDURE Get(Item : OUT Num; Width : IN Field := 0);

  PROCEDURE Put(File : IN File_Type;
               Item  : IN Num;
               Width : IN Field := Default_Width;
               Base  : IN Number_Base := Default_Base);
  PROCEDURE Put(Item  : IN Num;
               Width : IN Field := Default_Width;
               Base  : IN Number_Base := Default_Base);
  PROCEDURE Get(From : IN String; Item : OUT Num; Last : OUT Positive);
  PROCEDURE Put(To   : OUT String;
               Item : IN Num;
               Base : IN Number_Base := Default_Base);

END Integer_IO;


-- Generic Packages for Input-Output of Real Types

GENERIC
  TYPE Num IS DIGITS <>;
PACKAGE Float_IO IS

  Default_Fore : Field := 2;
  Default_Aft  : Field := Num'Digits-1;
  Default_Exp  : Field := 3;
```

```
        PROCEDURE Get(File : IN File_Type; Item : OUT Num; Width : IN Field := 0
        PROCEDURE Get(Item : OUT Num; Width : IN Field := 0);

        PROCEDURE Put(File : IN File_Type;
                      Item : IN Num;
                      Fore : IN Field := Default_Fore;
                      Aft  : IN Field := Default_Aft;
                      Exp  : IN Field := Default_Exp);
        PROCEDURE Put(Item : IN Num;
                      Fore : IN Field := Default_Fore;
                      Aft  : IN Field := Default_Aft;
                      Exp  : IN Field := Default_Exp);

        PROCEDURE Get(From : IN String; Item : OUT Num; Last : OUT Positive);
        PROCEDURE Put(To   : OUT String;
                      Item : IN Num;
                      Aft  : IN Field := Default_Aft;
                      Exp  : IN Field := Default_Exp);
      END Float_IO;

      GENERIC
        TYPE Num IS DELTA <>;
      PACKAGE Fixed_IO IS

        Default_Fore : Field := Num'Fore;
        Default_Aft  : Field := Num'Aft;
        Default_Exp  : Field := 0;

        PROCEDURE Get(File : IN File_Type; Item : OUT Num; Width : IN Field := 0);
        PROCEDURE Get(Item : OUT Num; Width : IN Field := 0);

        PROCEDURE Put(File : IN File_Type;
                      Item : IN Num;
                      Fore : IN Field := Default_Fore;
                      Aft  : IN Field := Default_Aft;
                      Exp  : IN Field := Default_Exp);
        PROCEDURE Put(Item : IN Num;
                      Fore : IN Field := Default_Fore;
                      Aft  : IN Field := Default_Aft;
                      Exp  : IN Field := Default_Exp);

        PROCEDURE Get(From : IN String; Item : OUT Num; Last : OUT Positive);
        PROCEDURE Put(To   : OUT String;
                      Item : IN Num;
                      Aft  : IN Field := Default_Aft;
                      Exp  : IN Field := Default_Exp);
      END Fixed_IO;

      -- Generic Package for Input-Output of Enumeration Types

      GENERIC
        TYPE Enum IS (<>);
      PACKAGE Enumeration_IO IS

        Default_Width   : Field := 0;
        Default_Setting : Type_Set := Upper_Case;

        PROCEDURE Get(File : IN File_Type; Item : OUT Enum);

        PROCEDURE Get(Item  : OUT Enum);

        PROCEDURE Put(File  : IN File_Type;
                      Item  : IN Enum;
```

```
                 Width  :  IN Field:       = Default_Width;
                 Set    :  IN Type_Set  := Default_Setting);
    PROCEDURE Put(Item   :  IN Enum;
                 Width  :  IN Field      := Default_Width;
                 Set    :  IN Type_Set  := Default_Setting);

    PROCEDURE Get(From   :  IN   String; Item : OUT Enum; Last : OUT Positive);
    PROCEDURE Put(To     :  OUT String;
                 Item   :  IN Enum;
                 Set    :  IN Type_Set := Default_Setting);
  END Enumeration_IO;

-- Exceptions

  Status_Error : EXCEPTION RENAMES IO_Exceptions.Status_Error;
  Mode_Error   : EXCEPTION RENAMES IO_Exceptions.Mode_Error;
  Name_Error   : EXCEPTION RENAMES IO_Exceptions.Name_Error;
  Use_Error    : EXCEPTION RENAMES IO_Exceptions.Use_Error;
  Device_Error : EXCEPTION RENAMES IO_Exceptions.Device_Error;
  End_Error    : EXCEPTION RENAMES IO_Exceptions.End_Error;
  Data_Error   : EXCEPTION RENAMES IO_Exceptions.Data_Error;
  Layout_Error : EXCEPTION RENAMES IO_Exceptions.Layout_Error;

PRIVATE
  -- implementation-dependent
END Text_IO;
```

Appendix E: Ada Hints for Pascal Users

Ada is a language that is, in many respects, similar to Pascal. However, it is not a "superset" of Pascal. The statement syntax is slightly different (simpler, in the opinion of many), and many familiar Pascal features are implemented somewhat differently. As a learning aid to those experienced in Pascal but new to Ada, this appendix summarizes areas in which the languages differ enough to cause some difficulty in the form of compilation errors.

Declarations and Declaration Order

The Pascal standard requires a rigid declaration order (constants, types, variables, subprograms) that is relaxed by some implementations. Ada declaration order is somewhat more flexible. The Ada standard refers to "basic declarative items" and "later declarative items." Among the former are declarations of constants, types, and variables; among the latter are functions and procedures. (Other declarations are beyond the scope of this book.) In the declarative part of a program or subprogram, basic declarative items can be freely intermixed—with the understanding, of course, that everything must be declared before it is referenced. All basic items must precede all later items; put simply, subprogram declarations must follow the others.

In Pascal, the words TYPE, CONST, and VAR appear only once in a declarative section. In Ada, each type or subtype declaration must be opened by TYPE or SUBTYPE, respectively. A constant is declared as, for example,

```
FirstLetter: CONSTANT Character := 'A';
```

and the reserved word VAR is not used at all; a variable is simply declared as, for example,

```
Sum : Integer;
```

A record type declaration must be closed by END RECORD.

Control Structures

All control structures are fully bracketed in Ada, including IF–END IF, LOOP–END LOOP, CASE–END CASE. Further, a semicolon terminates a statement—it does not separate statements, as in Pascal. This yields a syntax that is easier to use correctly than Pascal's. For example, the Pascal statement

```
IF X < Y THEN
   A := B;
```

is written in Ada as

```
IF X < Y THEN
   A := B;
END IF;
```

and the Pascal statement

```
IF X < Y THEN
   BEGIN
      A := B;
      Z := X
   END
ELSE
   BEGIN
      A := X;
      Z := B
   END;
```

is written in Ada as

```
IF X < Y THEN
   A := B;
   Z := X;
ELSE
   A := X;
   Z := B;
END IF;
```

The fully bracketed syntax ensures that a "dangling ELSE" cannot be written.

FOR loop control variables are declared implicitly; this is the only exception to the rule that everything must be explicitly declared. A FOR counter is local to the loop body. Declaring the loop counter as a variable, as in Pascal, does no real harm, but it declares a different variable, which is then hidden by the actual loop counter and therefore not visible in the loop body.

FOR loop ranges are often stated as type or subtype names, as in

```
FOR Count IN IndexRange LOOP
```

Ada has no REPEAT loop structure; instead, use LOOP–END LOOP with an EXIT WHEN clause at the bottom of the loop.

Types and Data Structures

Two-dimensional arrays are *not* arrays of arrays. Therefore, A(J)(K) is *not* the same as A(J,K): The former indeed refers to an array of arrays, the latter to a two-dimensional array. One reason these are different structures in Ada is that the standard does *not* specify the storage mapping (row- or column-major) for multidimensional arrays. This allows a clever implementer to use a nonlinear mapping, for example. In practice, most current Ada compilers use a row-major mapping, in keeping with Pascal and C rules.

The type of a record field must always be a type name; it cannot be an anonymous type such as ARRAY or RECORD. To build hierarchical record types, build the lower-level ones first, then use their names as fields in the higher-level ones.

There is nothing in Ada that corresponds to Pascal's WITH. All record and array references must always be fully qualified.

Variant records are much more tightly controlled in Ada than in Pascal. It is not possible to write a "free union," or variant record without a discriminant (tag field). In Pascal and C, free unions are frequently used to evade type checking, but cannot be used for this purpose in Ada. (Ada has a generic function called Unchecked_Conversion that indeed is used to evade type checking, but use of this is beyond the scope of this book.)

There is no SET type in Ada. One must write a package for this; a sketch of such a package is given in the *Reference Guide to Ada Constructs* in Appendix F.

Type and Subtype Compatibility

This matter is discussed at length throughout the book. The most important thing to remember is that Ada uses named type equivalence, not structural equivalence. For example, given the declarations

```
A, B: ARRAY(1..10) OF Float;
C   : ARRAY(1..10) OF Float;
```

the array assignment statements

```
A := B;
C := B;
```

are both invalid, because each of the three arrays has a different anonymous type, assigned by the compiler. (Some Pascal compilers would allow the first assignment.) To allow the array assignments, one must give a type name:

```
TYPE List IS ARRAY(1..10) OF Float;
A, B: List;
C: List;
```

Both assignments are now valid.

Subprogram Parameters

Ada's parameter modes IN, OUT, and IN OUT are only roughly equivalent to the value and VAR parameters of Pascal.

Within the body of a subprogram, IN parameters can only be read, never written, and OUT parameters can only be written, never read. Functions cannot have OUT or IN OUT parameters.

There is no efficiency to be gained by passing as IN OUT an array to be used as an IN parameter. This is common in Pascal, where large arrays are usually passed as VAR parameters. Pascal requires VAR parameters to be passed by reference and value parameters to be copied. The rules in Ada are different: Scalar parameters are always passed by value/result, whatever their mode. Ada permits array and record parameters to be passed by value/result, but compilers almost never do this, especially if the composites are large. Most compilers pass arrays and large records by reference even if they are IN; since IN parameters cannot be written, there is no danger of changing their value in the calling program.

The input/output statements in Ada are ordinary procedure calls, which means that only a single integer, float, character, string, or enumeration value can be read or displayed with each call of Get or Put. One cannot supply an arbitrary number of parameters to input/output statements, as one would do in Pascal. Doing so will surely result in compilation errors of the form "unmatched procedure call," when the compiler searches for a Get or Put whose expected parameters match the supplied ones.

The Use of IS and the Semicolon

Endless grief awaits Ada users who confuse the use of the semicolon with the use of IS. The worst offense is using a semicolon instead of IS in a subprogram declaration, as one would do in Pascal.

```
PROCEDURE DoSomething(X : Integer); ---- <---- this means TROUBLE!

   -- declarations

BEGIN

   -- statements

END DoSomething;
```

The problem is that it is *legal* to use the semicolon, but the meaning is not what you expect. The line

```
PROCEDURE DoSomething(X : Integer);
```

is not a declaration, but a procedure *specification*, similar to a Pascal FORWARD specification. Confusing the semicolon with the IS is therefore almost guaranteed to lead to a large number of propagation errors from the compiler: Since the Ada parser treats the statement as a specification, it is confused by the declarations and BEGIN–END block that follow, which seem to be out of context and not well-formed. IS is precisely the way that Ada knows a procedure *body* is expected next; the user forgets this at his or her peril.

Subprogram specifications appear as a part of package specifications, and can also be useful in contexts where a Pascal FORWARD would be written. In the latter case, the first line of the body must be identical to the specification, except for replacing the semicolon by IS. This is different from Pascal, where the parameter list is not repeated.

Appendix F: Summary of Ada Execution-Time Exceptions

This appendix summarizes the predefined Ada exceptions. Ada distinguishes exceptions defined in the language from those defined in standard packages. The summary should help students to write exception handlers and to interpret run-time messages that report unhandled exceptions propagated out of a main program.

Exceptions Defined in the Language

The following exceptions are predefined in the Ada language:

- Constraint_Error is raised if an attempt is made to store a value in a variable that is out of range for that variable, that is, out of the range of the variable's type or subtype. It will also be raised if an attempt is made to dereference a null access value (pointer), or to copy a string or similar array into another of a different size, or to copy a variant record object into another that is constrained to a different value of the discriminant.
- Numeric_Error is raised if an attempt is made to carry out an operation that violates the arithmetic system of the computer, usually an overflow or a division by zero. Because not all computers can reliably raise Numeric_Error (some computers cannot test for overflow), some compilers may cause Constraint_Error to be raised instead. Therefore, it is advisable to write a handler for Numeric_Error as

  ```
  WHEN Numeric_Error | Constraint_Error => . . .
  ```

- Program_Error is raised in a number of situations unlikely to arise in courses that use this book. For example, WITH-ing a number of packages may cause an attempted call of a subprogram whose body has not yet been elaborated. This occurrence is rare in student projects with simple package dependencies, but arises occasionally in industry.
- Storage_Error is raised if the heap is exhausted by dynamic allocation, typically in an infinite loop in whose body a NEW call is executed. The exception is also raised if the run-time stack is exhausted by subprogram calls, for example, by an infinite recursion.
- Tasking_Error is raised if two concurrent Ada tasks are unable to communicate. This exception should never be raised in programs based on material in this book, which does not use tasking at all.

Exceptions Defined in Calendar

One exception is defined in package `Calendar`:

- `Calendar.Time_Error` is raised if the actual parameters in a call of `Calendar.Time_Of` do not form a valid date, or if subtracting two values of type `Calendar.Time` results in a value that lies outside the range of the predefined type Duration.

Exceptions Defined in Text_IO

The following exceptions can be raised by `Text_IO` operations:

- `Text_IO.Status_Error` is raised by an attempt to operate upon a file that is not open, and by an attempt to open a file that is already open.
- `Text_IO.Mode_Error` is raised by an attempt to read from, or test for the end of, a file whose current mode is `Out_File`, and also by an attempt to write to a file whose current mode is `In_File`. This exception is also raised by specifying a file whose current mode is `Out_File` in a call of `Set_Input`, `Skip_Line`, `End_Of_Line`, `Skip_Page`, or `End_Of_Page`; or by specifying a file whose current mode is `In_File` in a call of `Set_Output`, `Set_Line_Length`, `Set_Page_Length`, `Line_Length`, `Page_Length`, `New_Line`, or `New_Page`.
- `Text_IO.Name_Error` is raised by a call of `Create` or `Open` if the string given for the parameter Name does not allow the identification of an external file. For example, this exception is raised if the string is improper, or, alternatively, if either none or more than one external file corresponds to the string. In student programs, this exception is often raised if the *case* of the file name given in the procedure call does not agree with the case of the name in the student's directory. This is especially common in Unix, in which file names are case-sensitive.
- `Text_IO.Use_Error` is raised if an operation is attempted that is not possible for reasons that depend on characteristics of the external file. For example, this exception is raised by the procedure `Create`, among other circumstances, if the given mode is `Out_File` but the form specifies an input only device, if the parameter Form specifies invalid access rights, or if an external file with the given name already exists and overwriting is not allowed.
- `Text_IO.Device_Error` is raised if an input-output operation cannot be completed because of a malfunction of the underlying system. This should rarely occur in a student program.
- `Text_IO.End_Error` is raised by an attempt to skip (read past) the end of a file. In student programs, this may happen if the file terminator is immediately preceded by a line terminator. In this case a solution is to include a handler for this exception in the file input section of the program. Sometimes inserting a `Text_IO.Skip_Line` call in the file input loop will work as well.
- `Text_IO.Data_Error` is raised by a procedure `Get` if the input character sequence fails to satisfy the required syntax, or if the value input does not belong to the range of the required type or subtype. Common causes are entering an integer or character literal where a `Float` literal is required, or entering an invalid enumeration literal.
- `Text_IO.Layout_Error` is raised by `Col`, `Line`, or `Page` if the value returned exceeds `Count'Last`. The exception `Layout_Error` is also raised on output by an attempt to set column or line numbers in excess of specified maximum line or page lengths, respectively (excluding the unbounded cases). It is also raised by an attempt to `Put` too many characters to a string.

Index

A

Abstract
  array, 348–49
  records, 330
Abstract data types, 468–525
Abstract list, 685
Access Type, 676, 724
Activation frame, 631
Actual parameter, 145, 239
  named association, 247
Ada, 16, 17, 18
  character set, 675
  delimiters, 676
  library set up, 21–22
  programs and packages, 32–33
  reserved words, 676–77
  strings in, 375–85
  systems structures, 33–36
Ada Compiler Validation Capability, 27
Ada features, 472
  package calendar as, 473–80
  package standard, 469
AddArray, 355
Address, 9
AddTable, 188–89
AdjustTime, 480
ADT. *See* Abstract data types
Aft, 54
Aggregate, 335–36
Aggregate array, 349–50
Algorithm, 15–16
  decision steps in, 120–26
  development. *See* Top-down design
  in everyday life, 88
  tracing, 126–28
ALL, 679, 724
AlphaFirst, 123–25

American National Standards Institute (ANSI), 299
American Standard Code for Information Interchange. *See* ASCII
Analogy solution, 130
Analysis, 15
AND THEN, 287
AnnualTotals (body), 548–50
AnnualTotals (spec), 544–45
Anonymous type identifier, 347, 365
ANSI control sequences, 110
Area, 568
AreaAndCircum (complete), 82
AreaAndCircum (outline), 81
Arithmetic overflow, 282
Arithmetic underflow, 282
Array, 26, 326, 344–51
  access, 363–64
  backward, 639
  copying and comparing, 364–65
  declaration, 344–45, 347
  expansion, 363
  FOR loop use with, 352–53
  generic parameters, 612
  multidimensional, 530–38
  with noninteger subscripts, 371–75
  in normal order, 641
  as parameters, 365, 367
  of records, 393–97, 617–18
  reference, 345
  search, 385–87, 390–92
  selecting elements for processing, 351–57
  sorting, 387, 390–92
  two-dimensional, 532
ASCII, 294, 297, 506

Assertions, 225–30
Assignment compatibility, 269
Assignment statements, 46–48, 60, 74
Assignment symbol, 47
Atanasoff, Dr. John, 2
Attribute, 93–94, 473

B

Babbage, Charles, 28
Backward array case study, 639–41
Bar graph, 456
Base type, 183
BASIC, 16–17
Beep procedure, 107–8
BEGIN, 29, 45, 146
Big-O Notation, 390–91
BinarySearch (iterative), 660–61
Binary search algorithm, 656
Binary Search Tree, 710
Binary string, 17
Binary tree, 710
Binder program, 18
Bisection method, 673
Bit, 10
BlankCount, 293–94
Blank space, 46
BlobCount, 653–55
Block, 232, 234, 425
Body, 29
Body file, 107, 148
Boolean data type, 114–16, 284–92, 562
"Boot up", 21
Bottom-up testing, 423
Boundary values, 279–80
Breakpoints, 194
Bugs, 68

BuildFlightList, 708–9
BuildList, 687
Byron, Augusta Ada, 28
Bytes, 10

C

C, 16, 17
Calendar, 98–106, 473–74
Calendar.Clock, 480
Calendar dates package, 336–40
Calendar.Time, 271
Call by reference, 367
Cancellation error, 282
Case-sensitive file names, 175
CASE statement, 305–10
  IF statement compared, 309
Central processor unit (CPU), 8, 10
ChangeTime, 333
Character, 59
  enumeration type, 116
  strings, 375, 376
Character Get procedure, 51, 379
Character Put procedure, 54
Character type, 292–300
Checkbook, 429–33
Check printing case study, 315–18
Circle, finding area and circumference of, 79–81
ClearScreen procedure, 107–8
COBOL, 16
Coded design, 408
Coding, 15
Coin Collection, 64–66
Collate, 298
Collating sequence, 298
Colors, 96–97
Comment(s), 39, 43, 86–87
  preconditions and postconditions as, 242–43
Common programming errors. See Programming errors
Compatibility rules, types and subtypes, 186–87
CompDividend, 132–33
Compilation errors, 68–72, 241, 428
Compiler listing, 69
Compiler program, 18–20
Composite types, 326–401
  arrays, 344–75, 385–97
  calendar dates package, 336–40
  hierarchical records, 340–44
  records as operands and parameters, 331–36

record types, 326–31
  strings in Ada, 375–85
ComputeArea, 568
ComputePerimeter, 568
Computer(s)
  categories of, 6–7
  components of, 8–13
  definition, 2
  history of, 2–6
  using, 20–22
Computing overtime case study, 128–30
Concordance, 373–74
Concurrent programs, 27
Condition, 231
Constant declaration, 41, 43, 74, 260–61
Constants, 41, 122–23
Constrained record variable, 563
Constraint_Error, 72, 93, 233
Constraints, 14
Constructor, 495
Constructor operation, 476
Contents, 9
Context clause, 32, 40, 43, 44, 74
Control characters, 107
Control structures, 26, 89
  assignment statements, 46–48
  CASE statement, 305–10
  general LOOP and EXIT statements, 230
  IF statement, 133–44
  input/output statements, 49–56
  nested loops, 179–83
  selection and repetition, 89–90
  WHILE statement, 208–16
Conversions, 269–70
CopyFile, 453
Count, 161
Counter, 192
Counting loops, 161, 164, 192
CreateTable, 698, 717
Cryptogram, 381–83
Cryptography, 456
Cursor, 29

D

Dangling pointer, 684
Data abstraction, 411, 468
Data base, 326
Data_Error, 488
Data file, creating, 21–22
Data structures, 26
  array types, 344–51, 371–75, 590–94

character type, 292–300
constant declarations, 260–61
data types and expressions, 59–68
declaring constants and variables, 40–45
enumeration type introduction, 91–97
hierarchical records, 340–44
multidimensional arrays, 530–36
numeric data types, 261–74
scalar type subtypes, 183–93
strings in Ada, 375–85
unconstrained array types, 590–94
variant records, 558–65
Data type, 41, 59, 540–43
Date_Error, 482
Dates (body), 484–88
Dates (spec), 481–82
Dates.Get, 488
Dates.Put, 488
Dates (SimpleDates), 336–40
Day, 476
Debugging programs, 68, 73, 193–94, 460–61
  global Boolean constant, 291–92
Decision statements, 114–55
  Boolean expressions, 114–16
  decision steps in algorithms, 120–26
  IF statement, 116–19, 133–44
  problem solution, extending, 128–33
  simple functions, 144–48
  simple package, 148–54
  tracing program or algorithm, 126–28
Decision table, 140
Declarations, 29, 44, 46, 183
Declarative section, 29
Default value, 54
DELAY statement, 109, 236
Delete, 703
Delimiters, 676
Denom, 495
Department of Defense, 26
Dereferencing operation, 679
Design, 15
Designated value, 679
Desk check, 126
Dialects, 19
Discrete range, 208
Discriminant field, 530, 559, 562
Disk drive, 11
Diskettes, 11
DisplayBoards, 533

DisplayCheck, 317–18
DisplayDays, 189–90
DisplayDigits, 264–65
DisplayEmployee, 521
DisplayList, 592
DisplaySales, 542
Display screen, 10
DisplayTime, 478
Dispose, 683, 724
Distance, 36
DistOrigin, 329–30
DistPoints, 334–35
Divide and conquer, 16
DoScores, 443
Dumb terminal, 11
Dummy node, 698
Duration, 271, 473
Dyadic operator, 262–63
Dynamic data structure, 676

E

Editor program, 18
Elapsed time, 271
Element-type, 347, 531
ELSE, 116
Embedded computer, 2, 6
Employees (body), 521–22
Employees (spec), 519–20
Employee inquiry system case
    study, 523–24
EmptyString, 508
END, 29, 45, 146
End-of-file character, 448–50
END IF, 118
End-of-line character, 448–50
END pname, 45
Engineering and scientific method,
    14
English to French color case study,
    95–97
Enhancement, 409
ENIAC, 2–3, 4
EnterMove, 535
EnterSales, 542, 551
Enumeration Get procedure, 94
Enumeration literals, 91
Enumeration Put procedure, 95
Enumeration types, 91–97
    attributes and operations, 92–
        94
    and Boolean value, 115, 289–90
    defining, 91
    input/output operations for, 94
eSeries, 281–82
Euclid's algorithm, 492

Exam grade summary case study,
    437–45
Exception, 68, 72, 785–6
Exception declaration, 483
Exception handlers, 202
Exception handling, 26, 202–4,
    232–37
    testing with, 252
ExceptionLoop, 235–36
Exception report, 36
Exchange, 368
Executable image, 18
Executable statements section, 29,
    45, 46
EXIT statements, 230–32
Exp, 54
Explicit conversion, 270, 271
Exponentiation, 61–62
Expression(s), 62–63, 213
    rules for evaluation, 266
    type of, 262
External file
    for input data, 174–76
    reading records from, 393–94
External math library, 274–75

F

Factorial, 195
Factorial (iterative), 636
Factorial (recursive), 634–36
False, 114
Federal Aviation Administration, 27
Fibonacci, 636–37
Field-list, 562
Fields, 326
Field selector, 328
File, 12
    directory name, 451
    preparing for input or output,
        451–52
    records, 397–98
File terminator, 448
First, 93
First generation computers, 3
FirstLetter, 125
First–Name, 30
FirstYear, 541
Fixed-point type, 271
Fixed set of values, representing,
    91
Flag, 218
Flag-controlled loop, 218–19
Flat tire case study, 88–89
Float data type, 60–61
    and Boolean condition, 115

Floating-point Get procedure, 52
Floating-point number, 50
Floating-point Put procedures, 53–
    54, 55
Floating-point values, 33
Float_IO, 33
Float literal, 66
Floppy disks, 11–13
Flow chart, 116
FOR statement, 160–67, 213
    limitations of, 193
Fore, 54
Formal parameter(s), 145, 148, 239,
    606
Formatting
    IF statement, 119
    output values, 53–56
FormLetter, 514–16
FORTRAN, 16, 532
FourPieces, 191–92
Fourth generation computers, 3
Fractions case study, 492–94
Frame, 232
FreeFall, 214–15
Function body, 145
Function call, 101–2
    syntax, 270
Function keys, 10
Functions, 26, 144–48

G

Garbage collector, 683
GCD (recursive), 637
General LOOP, 208, 230–32
General sorting case study, 594–98
General sum problem case study,
    168–70
Generic component, 590
Generic definition, 473
GenericMaximum, 611
Generic package, 33, 619–22
GenericSwap, 607–8
GenericSwapSort, 613–15
GenericTables (body), 697
GenericTables (spec), 694–5
Generic units, 605–13
GenericVectors, 619
Geometry (body), 565–73
Geometry (spec), 566–67
Get (robust), 289
GetNaturalToken, 296
Get operations, 174
    behavior in Text_IO, 454–55
Get statement, 35
Global Boolean constant, 291–92

Global variables, 427
Grader, 439–41
GraphYear, 550
Greatest common divisor, 492, 637
Gross, 114
GrowMoney, 228–30

H

Hand trace, 126
Hard-copy output, 11
Hard disks, 11–12
Hardware, 14
Heap, 676–8
Hello, 22, 28
HelloInitials, 30
HelloName, 31
Heterogeneous composite type, 344
Hierarchical records, 340–44
High-level (high order) languages, 16, 17
    processing a program, 18–20
HiMom, 415–19
Histogram, 456–59
HomeBudget, 357–62
Homogeneous composite type, 344

I

Identifier-list, 92
Identifiers, 30–31, 32
    multiple declarations of, 427–28
    scope of, 426–27
    selecting, 41–42, 44
IF statement, 116–19, 133–44
    and CASE statement compared, 309
    nested IF statements, 142–43
    writing multiple-alternative, 139
Implementation, 15
Improper rational, 491
IN, 187
"IN", 496
IN parameters, 238
InchToCM, 35
Incomplete type definition, 679
Indentation style, 143
Index, 351
IndexType, 594
InitializeLetter, 514, 517
Input data, and external file, 174–76
Input devices, 8, 10–11
Input operation, 49, 50–52
    for enumeration types, 94
Input statement, 49, 74

IN REVERSE, 163
Insert, 702, 719
Instances, 33, 94–95
Instantiated package, 33
Insurance dividends case study, 130–33
Integer, 51
    Boolean variables, 115
    and output formatting, 53
    using integer objects, 63–66
Integer data type, 60–62
Integer'First, 171
Integer Get procedure, 51
Integer Put procedure, 55
Integer_IO, 33
Integer values, 33, 171
Interactive programming, 449
Interpretation, 44
InvalidArguments, 508
IS, 29, 71, 146
IsFilled, 534
Iteration. *See* Repetitions
Iteration versus recursion, 650–51

J

"Julian," 482

K

Keyboard, 8, 10, 11, 449
Keyed table, 691

L

Language Reference Manual, 27, 197
Last, 93
LastYear, 541
Library packages, 49
Library of procedures, 412
Linear search, 656
Line terminator, 448
Linked list, 685
Linker program, 18
List of numbers case study, 170–74
ListType, 592
Literal, 66
    position in type, 92
Loader program, 18
Load file, 18
Local declaration section, 148
Local variable, 146
Locate, 700
"Log on," 21

Loop, 160
    design, 216–25
    determining initialization, 217
    previous data value, 221–23
    removing unnecessary computation, 304
Loop body, 160
Loop control variable, 161
Looping, 26
Loop invariants, 225–30
Lovelace, Ada, 17, 28
Lowercase, 32
LRM, 27

M

Mail merge, 513–19
Mainframes, 7
Main memory, 9
    and secondary memory compared, 12–13
Maintenance, 409
MakeCircle, 568
MakeEmployee, 521
MakeRect, 568
MakeSquare, 568
Mathematical formulas, 268
Mathematical functions, recursive, 634–38
Mathematical vectors and matrices, 599–605
Matrices (spec), 603–5
Matrix arithmetic, 603
MaxByYear, 550
Maximum, 146, 149–50
MaxIntFlt, 199–200
MaxTwo, 146–7
Measurement units, converting, 37–40
Memory, 8
    programs in, 57–59
Memory buffer register, 10
Memory cells, 9
Menu-driven program, 540
MenuHandler, 23–37
Mergesort, 673
MetricConversion, 39
MetricSystem (body), 574–80
MetricSystem (spec), 576–77
Microcomputers, 6
Minicomputers, 7
Minimum function, 149–50
MinMax (body), 150
MinMax (spec), 150
MinMaxAverage, 172–74
MinMaxAvgFile, 175–76

MinMaxThree, 153
Minus signs, 39
Mode, 174
    parameters, 238
Modified payroll problem case
    study, 120–23
ModPay, 121–22
Modules, 26
MomOrDad, 118
Monadic operator, 262–63
Money in bank case study, 226–30
Monitor, 8, 10
Monotonically increasing, 476
Month, 476
MonthlyTotals (spec), 545–46
Mother's Day greeting, 413–19
Mouse, 11
MoveColumn, 535
MoveCursor, 299
MoveRow, 535
MS-DOS, 455
Multidim, 531
Multidimensional arrays, 530–38
MultiPay, 178–79
Multiple-alternative decisions, 137–
    39
Multiple declarations of identifiers,
    427–28
Multiple-employee case study, 177–
    79
Multiple-operator expressions, 265–
    66
Multiply, 223–24
Multiply (recursive), 627–28
My_Flt_IO, 33, 34, 75
My_Int_IO, 33, 34, 36, 75

N

Named association, 247
NASA Space Station, 27
Natural, 41, 61, 92
Natural languages, 16
Nested IF statements, 142–43
Nested loops, 179–83
NestLoop, 180–81
NEW, 677, 724
New-Line procedure, 56
NextLetter, 293
Node, 685–6
NonNegFloat, 61
Nonvolatile data, 12
Normal-sequence-of-statements,
    234
"NOT IN", 496
NULL, 80, 81

Null array, 660
Numer, 495
Numerical inaccuracies, 282
Numerical values, tailoring
    Text_IO packages for, 33–36
Numeric data types, 261–74
    differences, 261–62
Numeric_Error, 233
Numeric literals, 262
Numeric operators, 262–63
NumToWord (body), 312–14
NumToWord (spec), 310

O

Object file, 18
Objects, 29
OddNumbers, 209
Offsets, 480
One-way list, 696
Operands
    compatibility of, 186
    records as, 331–36
Operator **, 61
Operator overloading, 472, 495,
    501–2
Operator precedence, 285
Order of conditions, 139–42
Order of magnitude, 391
OR ELSE, 287
OUT parameters, 238
Output devices, 8, 10–11
Output operations, 49
    for enumeration types, 94
    performing, 52–53
Output statement, 49, 74
Output values, formatting, 53–56
Overloading principle, 195–97,
    199–200

P

Package(s), 26, 29, 472
    importance of, 97–98
    rationals, 495–96
    standard, 469
    writing a simple, 148–54
Package bodies, 107, 148, 151
    extra subprograms in, 315
Package specification, 98, 107, 148,
    151, 469
PACKAGE Standard, 197
Palindrome, 644–45
Parameter(s), 53, 148
    arrays as, 365, 367

choosing formal parameter
    names, 423
executing procedure with, 243–
    44
generic array, 612
mode, 175
profiles, 196–97
records as, 332–333, 367
stacks, 634
structured, 367
Parameter lists, 245–47
    correspondence rules for, 247
    syntax rules for, 245–47
Parameterized record, 559
Parentheses
    for expression writing, 63
    for formal parameters, 148
Partition, 664, 666–69
Pascal, 16, 17, 18
Pascal, Blaise, 17
Passengers (body), 706–7
Passengers (spec), 706
PayRecord, 559
Payroll, 57
    modified program, 120–23, 128–
    30
Payroll (with errors), 69
PayStatus, 559
Perimeter, 568
Personal computer, 21
Picture processing case study, 651
Pivot value, 664
Pizzeria (complete), 85–86
Pizzeria (outline), 85
Pointer, 676
Portability, 18–20
Pos, 93
Positive data type, 61
Postconditions, 242–43
Preamble, 514, 517
Precedence and association rules,
    63
Precompiled input/output libraries,
    33
Preconditions, 242–43
Pred, 93
Predefined data type, 59, 61
Predefined identifiers, 30–31
Predefined scalar types, subtypes
    of, 183–85
PrimeNumber, 300–304
Priming read, 220
Printer, 11
PrintList, 689
PrintStat, 332
Private type, 99, 472–476, 502–3
Problem inputs, 14, 15

Problem outputs, 14, 15
Problem solving, 13–14
  array element selection, 351–57
  array use, 357–69
  assertions and loop invariants, 225–30
  decision steps in algorithms, 120–26
  extending a problem solution, 83–87, 128
  generalizing a solution, 168–76
  loop design, 216–25
  multidimensional arrays, 536–39
  reading partial arrays, 369–70
  recursion, 626–31
  recursive programs, 634, 638
  repeating a program body, 176–79
  software development, 37–40
  structured programming, 87–91
  top-down design, 78–83
Problem specification, 14
Procedural abstraction, 408–62
  complexity management, 410–12
  nested procedures, 424–26
  and refinement, 412–24
  scope of identifiers, 426–27
  software life cycle, 408–10
Procedure(s), 26, 49
  call statement, 49–50, 97
  data area, 245
  executing with parameters, 243–44
  writing, 237–47
Process, 435–35
Product, 117
Program(s)
  comment, 39, 43
  creating, 21–22
  developing from documentation, 79
  in memory, 57–59
  reexecuting a file, 22
  repeating a program body, 176–79
  tracing, 126–28
Program flags, 288
Program heading, 43, 74
Programmers, 16
Programming
  See Abstract data types; Procedural abstraction
Programming errors
  compilation, 68–72, 398, 428, 622
  END IF; requirement, 154
  enumeration types, 110–11

FOR loop, 204, 583
  incorrect record field, 398
  IF statements, 154, 252–53
  multidimensional arrays, 583
  parameter/procedure match, 154, 461
  parenthesis elimination, 318
  quotation marks, 524
  recompiling body, 154
  recursive procedures, 670–71
  run-time, 72–73, 398
  specification excess, 524
  supplying bounds, 622
  type inconsistencies, 398
  variant records, 583
  WHILE statements, 252
Programming languages, 4–5, 16–17
Prompting message, 51, 53
Prompts, 53
Propagation errors, 71
Put, 29
  diagnostic Put statements, 193–94
Put1 and Put2Digits, 310

Q

Qualification, 276
QuickSort, 664–69
Quotation marks, 71, 524

R

Random access to arrays, 363–64
Range error, 72
Rational number, 491
  package, 495–96
Rationals (body), 496–99
Rationals (spec), 493–94
ReadEmployee, 343, 521
ReadNewEmp, 343–44
ReadScores, 369–70
Record(s), 26, 326
  aggregate assignment, 335
  as operands and parameters, 331–36
  reading, 334
Record field initialization, 472, 541
Record types, 326–31
  abstract, 330
  declaration, 326–28
  field selector, 328
  with variant part, 562–63

Recursion, 626–68
  recursive function trace, 631–32
Recursive procedure call, 428
Recursive search and sort, 655–61
  case study, 662–64
Refinement, 412
Refining the algorithm, 16
Relational operators, 115, 294
REM, 61
Repetitions, 87, 89, 91, 160–205
  debugging and testing programs, 193–94
  exception handling, 202–4
  generalizing a solution, 168–76
  loops and FOR statement, 160–67
  nested loops, 179–83
  of program body, 176–79
  subtypes of scalar types, 183–93
  type and subtype compatibility, 186
  useful functions and overloading, 195–201
Representational error, 282
Representation specifications, 27
Requirements specification, 15, 408
Reserved words, 30–31, 32
Result type, 148
RetrieveGender, 521
RetrieveName, 521
RetrieveNumDepend, 521
RetrieveRate, 521
RetrieveTaxSal, 521
RETURN statements, 148
REVERSE, 163
ReverseDisplayDays, 190–91
ReverseLetters, 60
ReverseSquares, 163
Right-adjust, 54
Robust exception handling, 232–37
RobustInput (body), 249–50
RobustInput (spec), 248
Robust_Input.Get, 535
Robust numeric input, 235–36
RobustSumFact, 203–4
Row-major order, 531
Run-time errors, 68, 72–73, 202

S

SalesAnalysis, 544
  main program, 556–57
SalesRecord, 541
SalesTable (body), 551–54
SalesTable (spec), 546–47
Sales trend analysis case study, 539–58

Scalar types, 26, 259–319
  Boolean type, 284–92
  CASE statement, 305–10
  character type, 292–300
  constant declarations, 260–61
  displaying number in words, 310–15
  external math library, 274–76
  numeric data types, 261–74
  prime numbers, testing for, 300–305
  subtypes of, 183–93
  USE clause, 276–77
Scalar variables, 326
Scale factor, 66
Scientific notation, 52
Scope of an identifier, 426–27
Screen (body), 108, 298–99
Screen (spec), 107
Screen.MoveCursor, 236
Search, 386–87, 690, 699, 718
Secondary memory, 11–13
Secondary storage device, 8
Second generation computers, 3
Seconds, 476
Selection, 87, 89, 91
Selection sort, 387
Selector function, 495
Selector operation, 476
Semantic error, 71
Sentinel, 218
Sentinel-controlled loops, 219–21, 253
  problem with, 224
Sentinel value, 219
SEPARATE, 696
Sequence, 87, 89
Sequence of executable statements, 45
Sequential access to arrays, 363–64
Sequential execution, 89
Sequential search, 656
Short-circuit Boolean operators, 287
ShowDeMorgan, 290–91
ShowDiff, 353–54
Side effect, 427
SimpleDates (body), 338–39
SimpleDates (spec), 337–38
Simple functions, writing, 144–48
Simple procedures, writing, 237–47
Simplifying assumptions, 14
SineCurve, 278–79
Single character literal, 71
Slicing, 379, 593
Smiley, 109–10
Software, 14

Software developer ("engineer"), 14–15
Software development
  illustrated, 37–40
  life cycle, 408–10
  method, 14–16, 78
Solution by analogy, 130
SortScoreFile, 394–97
SortScores, 388–90
Sort3Numbers, 239–40
Source file, 18
Special symbols, 30–31
Specification file, 107, 148
Split, 476
SquareRoots, 274–75
Squares, 162
Stacks, 632–34
Standard, 18, 27, 469
Statement, 29
Statement sequences, 118, 192, 231
Stopping cases, 626
Storage allocator, 676
Storage pool, 676
Storage_Error, 684, 785
Stored program computer, 3
String(s), 375–85
  assigning, comparing, displaying, 377
  concatenation, 380
  reading, 377–78
  variable-length, 503–13
String Get_Line procedure, 379
String Get procedure, 51, 379
String literal, 71
StringOverflow, 508
String Put procedure, 54
String slicing, 379
String variable, 375
Structured programming, 87–91
Stubs, 411, 421, 696
Style conventions, 32
Subarrays with subscript zero, 661
Subproblems, 15
Subprograms, 238
Subscripted variable, 345
Subscript-type, 347, 348
  using as array index, 351
Subscript zero, 661
Subtype declaration, 58, 183–93
Subtype definition, 61, 183
Subtypes
  and abstract data types, 472
  compatibility rules for, 186
  of enumeration types, 185–86
  motivation for using, 186
  of predefined scalar types, 183–85

Subunits, 412, 696
Succ, 93, 208
SumByYear, 541
SumFact, 200–201
SumIntegers, 165–67
SumItems, 169–70, 420–22
Supercomputers, 7
Syntax
  errors, 18, 22, 71
  rules for parameter lists, 245–46
Syntax display
  abstract array, 348
  abstract record, 330
  array reference, 352
  array type declaration (1-dimensional), 347
  array type declaration (multidimensional), 531
  array type declaration (unconstrained), 594
  assignment, 47
  attribute query, 93
  block with exception handler, 234
  CASE statement, 308
  comment, 43
  constant declaration, 43
  context clause, 43
  enumeration type declaration, 92
  exception declaration, 483
  exception handler, 233
  FOR statement (simple), 164
  FOR statement (with type), 192
  function body, 147
  function call, simple, 101
  function specification, 147
  general LOOP, 231
  genetic specification, 620
  Get, character, 51
  Get, enumeration, 94
  Get, floating point, 52
  Get, integer, 51
  Get, string, 51
  Get_Line, string, 379
  IF statement (1 alternative), 118
  IF statement (2 alternatives), 118
  IF statement (multialternative), 138
  New_Line, 56
  NULL statement, 81
  operator overloading, 501
  package body, 151
  package specification, 151
  private type definition, 482
  procedure body, 246
  procedure call (with parameters), 246
  procedure call (simple), 49

Syntax display *(continued)*
    procedure specification, 245
    program heading, 43
    Put, character, 54
    Put, enumeration, 95
    Put, floating point, 55
    Put, integer, 55
    Put, string, 54
    record type declaration (simple), 328
    record type declaration (variant), 562
    subtype declaration, 185
    variable declaration, 43
    WHILE statement, 212
Systems analysts, 408
Systems approach, 14
System structures, 26
    abstract data type, 468–73, 491–503
    Ada program, 45–46
    ADT for calendar dates, 480–91
    ADT for employee records, 519–23
    ADT for variable-length strings, 503–13
    calendar package, 98–106, 336–40
    exception handling, 202–4
    generic units, 605–13
    importance of packages, 97–98
    nested procedures, 424–26
    number in words display, 310–15
    overloading principle, 195–97
    robust exception handling, 232–37
    robust input package, 247–51
    scope of identifiers, 426–27
    screen-control package, using, 107–110
    tailoring Text_IO packages, 33–36
    text files, 445–60
    useful functions, 195–201
    writing simple functions, 144–48
    writing simple package, 148–54
    writing simple procedures, 237–47

T

Table display, 201
TabMonth, 542
TabYear, 542
Tasking, 27

Temp, 239
Templates, 216, 606
    flag-controlled loop, 219
    processing text file, 449–50
    robust input loop, 232–33
    sentinel-controlled loop, 221
TempTable, 210
Terminal emulator, 11
TestAnnualSums, 550–51
TestBinarySearch, 658–60
TestBlobCount, 652–55
Test cases, selecting adequate, 304–5
TestDates, 489–90
TestGenericMaximum, 611–12
TestGenericSort, 615–17
TestGenericSwap, 608–9
TestGeometry, 573
Testing, 15, 193–94
    with exception handling, 252
    top-down and bottom-up, 423–24
TestMaxValue, 592–93
TestMetric, 581–82
TestMultiply, 628–29
TestNumToWord, 314–15
TestPrintBack, 639–41
TestPrintNorm, 642–43
TestRational1, 499–500
TestRational2, 501
TestRobustInput, 250–51
TestRunTimeError, 72
TestSalesTable, 555
TestSelectSort, 662–64
TestSimpleDates, 339–40
TestSwapSort, 596–98
TestTower, 648–50
TestTriangle, 424–25
TestVStrings, 512
Text files
    Ada's package specification, 446
    declaring, 451
    reading and writing, 452
    systematic view of, 445–60
Text_IO, 29, 98
    and control characters, 107
    data errors, 233, 234
    Get operations, 454–55
    reading and writing files with, 448–49
    tailoring for numerical values, 33–36
Text_IO.Enumeration_IO, 547
THEN, 116
Third generation computers, 3
ThreeDays, 136–37
Three numbers case study, 152–53
TicTacToe, 531

Time, 99, 473
    private type, 476
    values, 476
Time_Error, 477
TimeOfDay, 272–73
Timeshared computer, 21
Time zones case study, 477
TodayDate, 102–5
TodayDate2, 105–6
Token, 50–51, 66
Top-down design, 78–83
Top-down development case study, 429–45
Totally ordered, 476
Towers of Hanoi, 629, 647–50
Tracing a program or algorithm, 126–28
Traverse, 704, 714
Tree, 710
Tree traversals, 712–14
Triangle, 181
True, 114
Type constructors, 326
Type mismatch syntax error, 352
Type-name, 192
Types, 29

U

Unchecked_Deallocation, 683
Unconstrained array types, 590–94
    attribute functions for, 591–92
Unconstrained record variable, 563
Undefined identifier, 44
Undefined variable, 59
United States Department of Defense, 26
UNIX, 110, 455
UpdateSales, 542, 554
Uppercase, use of, 32
USE clause, 276–77, 502
UsefulFunctions (body), 197–99
UsefulFunctions (spec), 195
User-defined exceptions, 472–73
User-defined identifiers, 42, 46

V

Val, 93
Validated compilers, 27
Validating value of variables, 142
Validation tests, 20
Variable, 41
    and enumeration procedures, 94–95

validating value of, 142
Variable declarations, 41, 43, 74
Variable-length strings, 503–13
Variant records, 558–65
    constrained and unconstrained,
        563–64
    operations on, 564–65
    storing values, 564
VAX-11, 469
Vectors (body), 601–3
Vectors (spec), 600–1
VMS terminal, 110
Vocabularies, 16
Volatile data, 12
Von Neumann, Dr. John, 3
VStrings (body), 508–11
VStrings (spec), 504–5

W

Wall clock time, 473
What if? questions, 168
WHEN, 202
WHEN OTHERS, 306–8
WHILE loop, 193, 208–16
    entering unspecified number of
        values, 218
    with zero iterations, 217–18
Width, 53–54
WITH clause, 32–33
WITH My_Flt_IO, 34
WITH My_Int_IO, 34
WorkDays, 187–88
Workstations, 6
WorldTime, 478–80

WormAndApple, 211
WriteBody, 514
WriteFull, 488
WriteJulian, 488
WriteNumeric, 488
WriteShort, 488
Writing
    simple functions, 144–48
    simple packages, 148–54
    simple procedures, 237–47

Y

Year, 476
YearRange, 541
Yesterday and tomorrow case study,
    135–37

PINTURA ACTUAL MEXICO 1966

introducción de JUSTINO FERNANDEZ

por ALFONSO DE NEUVILLATE

Edición de ARTES DE MEXICO Y DEL MUNDO S.A.

Tanto los Editores como los Autores agradecen la valiosa colaboración y ayuda que prestaron en la realización de este libro las siguientes personas: Sra. Lourdes Chumacero, Directora del Salón de la Plástica Mexicana; Sra. Inés Amor, Directora de la Galería de Arte Mexicano; Sra. Olga Dondé, Directora de la Galería Mexicana de Arte; Sra. Merle P. de Kuper, Directora de la Galería Mer-Kup; Sr. Juan Martín y Sr. Antonio Souza.

Todas las fotografías que ilustran al texto son del Sr. Enrique Bordes.

The editors as well as the authors are grateful for the valuable collaboration and help that the following people gave in the preparation of this book: Sra. Lourdes Chumacero, director of the Salón de la Plástica Mexicana; Sra. Inés Amor, director of the Galeria de Arte Mexicano; Sra. Olga Dondé, director of the Galeria Mexicana de Arte; Sra. Merle P. de Kuper, director of the Galeria Mer-kup; Sres. Juan Martin and Antonio Souza.

All photographs illustrating the text are by Sr. Enrique Bordes.

INTRODUCCION   Pág. 1

PINTURA CONTEMPORANEA: MEXICO 1966   Pág. 9

NOTAS BIOGRAFICAS   Pág. 21

ILUSTRACIONES   Pág. 68

ENGLISH TEXT   Pág. 35

ILLUSTRATIONS   Pág. 68

por JUSTINO FERNANDEZ

La vida humana y el arte —es decir, la historia— no se detienen, puesto que son energías espirituales que por necesidad deben desenvolverse y encontrar salidas de una manera u otra. El hombre, para ser tal, necesariamente ha de humanizar el mundo, y una de las maneras de hacerlo en el más alto nivel es la poesía. Pero entendamos lo que quiere decir este clásico término, usado vagamente por lo general. Poesía viene del griego, *poiesis,* y significa creación, algo distinto de la *praxis* o práctica, que es otra manera de hacer humano el mundo de la realidad bruta.

El poeta, el artista, crea o recrea el mundo a su modo; y de acuerdo con las posibilidades de su sensibilidad, su intelecto y su imaginación, expresa bellamente sus visiones, sus anhelos, sus ideales y creencias. Si no hubiera artistas el mundo sería ciego, sordo y mudo; no existiría como *mundo,* como habitáculo propio del hombre.

Al expresarse, el artista nos hace ver, a través de sus obras, aspectos nuevos y bellos de la realidad, que se descubren por la emoción que aquéllas provocan. Al mostrar su propio ser conduce a la visión especial que quiere comunicar. Nos toca a nosotros, al público, escuchar a los artistas y comprenderlos, si tenemos la capacidad de ponernos en relación con ellos, o dicho de otro modo, si entre ellos y nosotros se da el milagro de la coincidencia.

La historia es cambiante, bien lo sabemos, y ésta es su mayor cualidad. Lo absolutamente estático no es de este mundo. Las circunstancias, los intereses, las actitudes, los modos de sentir, entender e imaginar la realidad y la manera de expresarse son varios y distintos, según los tiempos y los temperamentos. En las cuestiones humanas no hay atrasos ni adelantos, y en el arte se hace objetivo el presente y las visiones de los artistas por medio de sus obras. Estos deben tender la vista al pasado para saber dónde se encuentran situados y, así, inevitablemente, empujan desde el presente al porvenir, porque la existencia humana es proyección al futuro.

Es natural que las nuevas generaciones se rebelen contra sus antecesores. Pero si los niegan están perdidas. Abominar de ellos y además construir sus propias visiones poéticas es salvarse, porque entonces existen por sí mismas. Toda revolución tiene que recoger, reinterpretar el pasado cercano y remoto, de una manera u otra, desde sus nuevos puntos de vista, porque si no lo hace se queda sin historia y aun sin razón de ser, sin conciencia de lo que ha sido, que es lo peor que le puede pasar, porque las vuelve infecundas. En cambio, cargar la historia a cuestas y renovarla, enriquecerla con las propias visiones y obras, es fecundarla y abrirle caminos al porvenir.

Así, en un orden ideal, es obligación de todos intentar comprender a los nuevos creadores de arte, lo que puede conducir al goce de sus obras y al enriquecimiento propio con las bellas visiones que aquéllos nos presentan. Pero también es obligación de los nuevos artistas conocer y comprender nuestros pasados comunes, por su propio bien, porque negarlos es negarse a sí mismos, empobrecerse. La solidaridad humana debe existir y funcionar de atrás hacia adelante y viceversa, ya que cualquier otra actitud no es sino una forma de autolimitación esclerótica. Todo gran artista absorbe la historia entera y toma posición frente a ella y en ella misma.

Parece conveniente considerar dos cuestiones más. La primera es que, por lo general, resulta difícil comprender que las expresiones artísticas de

1

una visión dramática o trágica del mundo puedan ser estéticas. Es un error, porque se confunde el "qué" se expresa con el "cómo" se expresa. El artista puede expresar lo que le venga en gana, siempre que sea dentro de los límites del arte, porque éste es el juego y en él existe aquella libertad. Por muy negra que sea la visión del mundo que tenga un artista, si la convierte en arte, la transfigura en goce y deleite para sí y para los demás, por la emoción estética que provoca, sin que por eso pierda su carácter dramático o trágico. Hay obras que nos atraen haciéndonos gozar, por el modo *como* están hechas, y que terminan por hacernos llorar por lo *que* expresan.

La segunda cuestión consiste en saber las posibilidades de comunicación del arte abstracto, o el "no objetivo". Porque ciertamente si se crean obras de arte es por propia necesidad de expresión, de comunicación, de comunicar algo a otros. Y sin duda el llamado genéricamente "arte abstracto", tiene las posibilidades de comunicación de sentimientos, de estados de ánimo, ideas de mundos reales o imaginados. Mas sucede que tales expresiones tienen carácter de universales; así, si se expresan el amor, el odio, la tristeza o la jocundia, tales conceptos se localizan sólo en el artista, pero sin otros contextos históricos o particulares. El poeta ha elevado su estado de ánimo, sus ideas o su imaginación a conceptos abstractos expresados en imágenes no objetivas —cuando no se trata de meros juegos formales, que también son significativos de la personalidad— y de ahí proviene la dificultad de la comunicación para un espectador no avisado ni acostumbrado a abstraer conceptos e imágenes de la realidad. El arte abstracto se remonta a la estratósfera de los sentimientos del intelecto y del espíritu, mas sin embargo, en él están las líneas, los colores, las texturas, los materiales... y el artista que los maneja, que al expresarse se desnuda o se confiesa.

En suma, todo arte auténtico, del tipo que sea, suscita nuestra emoción y nuestras reflexiones, y acaba por encontrar su sitio en la historia. A la confusión contribuyen con eficacia aquellos cuya actitud es falsa, consciente o inconscientemente, o tan superficial que pronto se convierten en paja, si bien un ojo experto y una intuición certera sabrán descubrir donde está el grano. Se habla mucho hoy día de los problemas del arte actual, pero son los artistas los que han de irlos resolviendo de acuerdo consigo mismo y cada cual tomando la dirección que le sea más afín. Posteriormente los problemas serán de la crítica y, al final, de la historia. Tan sólo vociferan antes de tiempo los aspirantes a dirigir el arte, lo que es un contrasentido. Los problemas del arte maduran en el silencio.

México tiene una larga tradición de, a lo menos, veinte siglos en el campo de la creación artística, y con sus grandes obras ha contribuido a la historia universal. Prueba de ello es cuanto ha llegado a nosotros del antiguo mundo indígena. Los monumentos de las culturas Olmeca, Maya de los períodos clásicos y postclásicos, Mixteca, Zapoteca, Teotihuacana, Tolteca y Nahua, son muestras elocuentes de la grandeza y capacidad creadora de los hombres de aquel pasado remoto. Mas aún deben recordarse las finísimas obras de cerámica del Occidente de México, las pinturas murales de Bonampak y de otros sitios, los códices mixtecas, mayas y nahuas; las joyas de jade, de cristal de roca y de oro; los relieves de los mayas clásicos, unos naturalistas y los más abstractos; la formidable y sin par escultura azteca. No faltan, pues, ni las formas abstractas de rigor geométrico, como en Uxmal, en Mitla y en Teotihuacán, ni las libremente expresivas, como se puede ver en ejemplos innumerables, hasta la belleza refinadamente naturalista de los relieves de Palenque; y en cuanto a dramatismo y sentido trágico de la existencia nada excede a los cráneos aztecas y a otras esculturas monumentales del mundo mexica, entre las que no tiene rival la gran *Coatlicue*.

No menos magnífico es el legado de la Nueva España. Desde el siglo XVI, con el advenimiento del arte occidental, comenzó una actividad creadora que levantó con originalidad los grandes monasterios de las Ordenes mendicantes en todos los rumbos del país. Las capillas abiertas, las iglesias y claustros fueron ornamentados con pinturas murales al fresco. Los retablos dorados en que se acumulan pinturas, esculturas y tallas de mil formas, son maravillosos y están al nivel de los mejores de España. Después se construyeron las catedrales, las iglesias parroquiales, las capillas, los palacios de gobierno y particulares, los hospitales, las escuelas, y se fundó la Universidad. Todavía guarda muchas sorpresas el estudio de la escultura de Nueva España, la de piedra y la de madera dorada y estofada. La pintura tuvo su apogeo en el siglo XVII; hoy día sabemos que las mejores obras tienen calidad suficiente para ponerse al lado, sin desdoro, de otras europeas, y aun la pintura más suave y decorativa del siglo XVIII es atractiva y llena de recursos muy estimables.

Mas si todo lo evocado tiene gran valor e interés, el arte barroco y el ultrabarroco de los siglos XVII y XVIII significa una de las mayores contribuciones de México al arte universal. Nada iguala la riqueza y el esplendor de monumentos originales como el Sagrario Metropolitano, la iglesia de la Enseñanza, la de Tepotzotlán, la Parroquia de Santa Prisca en Taxco, las iglesias de Ocotlán, en Tlaxcala, de Acatepec y Santa María Tonantzintla en Puebla, y en la capital de ese Estado, la Capilla del Rosario, la Catedral y tantos otros palacios y monumentos. Pero sin ir muy lejos, la Catedral de México resume en su arquitectura y en lo que guarda su interior toda la historia del arte de la Nueva España. Primero entre todos es el retablo de la Capilla de los Reyes, maravilla, gruta de oro, punto de partida de cuanto creó el espléndido arte ultrabarroco, cuyas muestras están en casi todas las ciudades y pueblos del país.

Aún deben recordarse las obras del arte neoclásico, algunas de ellas de primer orden, como las torres y cúpula de la Catedral Metropolitana, el Palacio de Minería y la estatua ecuestre de Carlos IV.

En el arte de Nueva España hay formas de abstraccionismo geométrico, como todo el arte mudéjar y todas las formas clásicas, y hay también libertades extremas de tipo expresionista en el arte ultrabarroco y en el barroco popular.

Cuando México se constituyó en nación independiente floreció el arte romántico académico, que dio sus mejores frutos en el retrato y, sobre todo, en la pintura de paisaje en la que Velasco creó una visión histórica monumental de nuestro país. La pintura independiente de la académica dejó una producción llena de encanto y de sabiduría. Aun debe ser estimado con justicia el arte del siglo XIX, que con todo y sus valores ha sido menospreciado, simplemente por tratarse del pasado inmediato contra el que se rebelaron oportunamente los artistas de la primera mitad de nuestro siglo; pero salvaron a un artista singular, Posada, quien con su obra de sentido moderno, expresionista y crítico inspiró a los mejores que habían de venir después.

Parece imposible, si bien todo es posible, negar la significación y los valores de la pintura mural de nuestro tiempo, una de las grandes contribuciones de México al arte universal. Las obras monumentales de Orozco, entre otras los frescos del Hospicio Cabañas, en Guadalajara; las de Rivera en la Escuela Nacional de Agricultura, en Chapingo; las de Siqueiros y de algunos otros pintores, constituyen los ejemplos de mayor categoría en su género del siglo XX. Su estudio cuidadoso fecundará a cualquier artista que se acerque a ellas con el espíritu abierto a la comprensión y sensible a la belleza.

Ya se ha dicho, y es verdad, que el primer artista mexicano de calidad superior que renegó del arte que se hacía en la tercera década de nuestro siglo, fue Tamayo. Y era natural que así fuera, pues su visión y temperamento eran distintos y se lanzó por nuevos caminos para reafirmar su original personalidad. Su arte, si bien abstracto propiamente dicho, por serlo no ha perdido nunca el punto de partida de la realidad; por eso y por sus cualidades inigualables se ha colocado en el nivel de los grandes artistas contemporáneos. Con Tamayo coinciden algunos de los nuevos conceptos de la pintura que alcanzan a la más reciente generación, pero en las obras de ésta también se encontrarán huellas de otros maestros.

□

He procurado evocar en breves rasgos la historia del arte mexicano para que la conciencia de sus valores se tenga por antecedente de la pintura de hoy y como horizonte estético de referencia para la misma. Todo ese formidable pasado gravita, creo, sobre los jóvenes artistas, pues de un modo u otro lo llevan en el espíritu y debe ser en ellos un acicate de superación y no un dato depresivo. La historia del arte mexicano no puede verse aislada y hay que ponerla en relación con las corrientes universales de todos los tiempos. Dicho de otro modo, los artistas deben estar empapados en la historia hasta donde ello sea posible.

Ha llegado el momento de considerar el contenido del libro que tenemos entre las manos. Espectáculo magnífico, emocionante hasta el grado de tocarnos las fibras más sensibles, es el acervo de obras aquí reunidas y presentadas por el espíritu seleccionador de Alfonso de Neuvillate. Espectáculo único, porque a más de que los artistas son representativos de las nuevas corrientes de la pintura mexicana actual, a la reproducción de sus obras se unen los textos de un joven crítico que pertenece a los gustos e intereses también más actuales. Así, el libro tiene unidad completa y un valor histórico cabal. Como toda antología será, quizá, decepcionante para algunos, mas hay que recordar que no se trata de un "diccionario" de pintores —y aun los "diccionarios" nunca son completos— sino de una selección hecha por un crítico sensible al arte de su tiempo. De su acierto se puede juzgar con sólo recorrer la lista de nombres y el catálogo de las obras reproducidas. No están incluidos todos los que son, pero todos los que están son artistas representativos de este momento.

En un acervo de obras como el reunido aquí, la presencia de un pin-

4

tor de la categoría de Pedro Coronel y de un artista extraordinario, José Luis Cuevas, da realce a la colección, cuya calidad está refrendada por otros como Cordelia Urueta, José Hernández Delgadillo, Ricardo Martínez, Benito Messeguer, Juan Soriano, Francisco Moreno Capdevila, Lilia Carrillo, Manuel Felguérez, Fernando García Ponce, Alberto Gironella, Antonio Peláez, Vicente Rojo, Francisco Corzas, y Vlady. Todos ellos y los que completan los treinta y cinco números del catálogo tienen obras de varia importancia y, de hecho, como en toda exposición colectiva, no son suficientes dos pinturas para tener cabal idea de sus capacidades poéticas. Sin embargo, hay que atenerse objetivamente a lo que es la exposición presentada, que honraría a cualquier museo.

Bien sabemos que las actuales generaciones se interesan en la posición universalista y que han renegado de todo pintoresquismo regional y de los grandes asuntos históricos, religiosos y filosóficos. Es una circunstancia semejante al cambio operado hace un siglo, cuando surgió el impresionismo, sólo que ahora las corrientes se han multiplicado.

Hay en la presente exposición un grupo de obras en las que de una manera u otra aparecen imágenes humanas. El primero en hacer de ellas la médula de su expresionismo es José Luis Cuevas. Por contraste Ricardo Martínez se atiene a las líneas puras, de sentido clásico. En forma dramática se expresan Francisco Corzas y Rafael Coronel, y más acentuadamente, hasta la tragedia, Francisco Moreno Capdevila. Pero con sentido distinto, de alegre farsa o de dramática nostalgia que evoca el mundo antiguo occidental, están las obras de José García Ocejo. Cierta anécdota recoge y expresa Pilar Sánchez Castañeda. La robusta técnica y el concepto preciso están manejados con maestría por Vlady.

En otro grupo de obras las imágenes provenientes del mundo objetivo se diluyen, se fragmentan o se vuelven tan espectrales que a duras penas son reconocibles. Así sucede en las obras de Pedro Coronel, en las que el gran colorista se sirve de este medio para hacer más intensas las significaciones. En las pinturas de Juan Soriano formas y colores se funden en unidad para comunicar un carácter o un concepto. Lilia Carrillo ha introducido, con la magia de su arte exquisito, referencias o imágenes humanas que se conforman momentáneamente o se diluyen, como en el sueño. El genio zumbón de Alberto Gironella se inspira en Velázquez para hacer lo diametralmente opuesto, y al renegar del Maestro logra sus propias creaciones. José Hernández Delgadillo ha depurado tanto su arte y las imágenes que presenta que se ha quedado con unos cuantos elementos, manejados con sabiduría, a los que da proporciones monumentales. Las dos obras de Pedro Cervantes son dispares, ambas bien ejecutadas, una evoca a un tipo de expresión y la segunda a otra. Ateniéndose a imágenes de formas esenciales Arnaldo Coen crea armonías de color en las que realidad y fantasía se confunden. Rodolfo Nieto logra inusitados efectos con unas cuantas manchas de color bien graduadas. Con gracia espontánea y sabiduría Rodolfo Hurtado casi convence del infantilismo de sus imágenes, por lo demás, bien concebidas. En las obras de Maka la simplificación llega al esquema, pero es suficiente para evocar la realidad del mundo poético del que parte para hacer su pintura. Lucinda Urrusti se atiene a las imágenes reales, pero las transfigura en poesía de ricas texturas y ya son algo distinto, se convierten en pintura.

Aunque de visiones muy diferentes hay un "no sé qué" de común en las expresiones de Francisco Toledo y de Luis López Loza, las formas planas y recortadas, de color imaginativo; pero, en el mundo del primero domina la fantasía onírica y lo absurdo, mientras que en el segundo aparecen elementos del mundo orgánico convertidos en metáforas.

En un tercer grupo de obras triunfa la pintura abstracta, o la "no objetiva", ya sin miramientos, aunque algunos de los artistas tengan en su haber obras, digamos, figurativas. Fernando García Ponce tiene el secreto del equilibrio constructivo, no sólo de las formas, sino del color, ambos en armoniosa unidad que produce obras rotundas. No por tener gracia y ligereza las pinturas de Cordelia Urueta carecen de fuerza, que proviene de la seguridad con que compone y de sus aciertos en el color. Otro sabio en la composición es Manuel Felguérez, pero disfraza las estructuras con la violencia de su pincel y los grafismos. Antonio Peláez, quien a veces evoca mundos siderales, ha logrado ser un maestro en las texturas y en el color, todo en un límite preciso y dentro de él lo fino y lo áspero. Las incursiones de Benito Messeguer en la pintura abstracta no hacen olvidar sus cualidades cuando incluye imágenes humanas, pero tan simplificadas que resultan formas en aquella dirección. Texturas gruesas o finas se encuentran en las obras de Gilberto Aceves Navarro, equilibradas y sugerentes. Carlos Belaunzarán maneja el color, las formas y los grafismos con positivo y controlado talento como lo muestran sus obras incluidas aquí. Amplias manchas y un pincel que se mueve con desenfado hacen las obras de Enrique Echeverría, mas la aparente espontaneidad tiene por guía el intelecto. Los grafismos supuestamente ingenuos de Fernando Ramos Prida, las incisiones sobre manchas de color, tienen gracia inefable y compone con positiva sensibilidad. De sentido violento, nervioso, es la expresión de Gabriel Ramírez, pero el refinamiento de sus líneas y manchas nos dicen que no se trata de un desesperado sino de un artista cabal. Roberto Donís es el polo opuesto, domina el equilibrio, la mesura, y con pocos elementos sugiere cuanto le place.

En un cuarto y último grupo de obras encontramos las más atrevidas, que son las de Vicente Rojo; este artista se ha decidido a romper con todas las tradiciones, inclusive con las de sí mismo, y a sugerir algo con la mayor economía de elementos; sus obras colindan con el "op art", ya en efectos violentos o en otros finísimos. El mundo fantástico de Pedro Friedeberg se expresa por medio de su geometría laberíntica, que construye pacientemente sin permitir que el azar se la descomponga; también el arte de Friedeberg, como el de Rojo, tiene de cerca el "op art". Y el último artista que hemos de considerar, Xavier Esqueda, combina, no sabemos cómo pudo ocurrírsele, el "opt art", tan intelectual, con imágenes del mundo objetivo, causando desazón; por lo demás, cuando pinta la nuda realidad lo hace con perfección y fuerte acento dramático.

El espectáculo se ha terminado, pero nos queda el gusto y la euforia de haber cobrado una experiencia al acercarnos a la pintura mexicana más actual. En ella reinan la ponderación, el equilibrio, la sinceridad, el afán de crear con novedad y calidad, por eso debe prestársele seria atención. Es arte auténtico, de varias direcciones, de creadores con personalidad. ¿Influencias? ¿Relaciones con otras corrientes de nuestros días, con otros artistas? Bien, podrían descubrirse y localizarse, con lo cual brillarían más las diferencias, las originalidades. Hoy por hoy México tiene una nueva pintura, lozana, realizada con responsabilidad y llena de interés. Como toda pintura tiene dos vistas —según el dicho de un ranchero—, "una para el que le guste y otra para el que no le guste". La decisión se deja a la historia.

PINTURA ACTUAL: MEXICO 1966.

por ALFONSO DE NEUVILLATE

Es difícil presentar el panorama de la nueva estética, de las nuevas consideraciones del lenguaje pictórico, dado que, existen tantas aventuras singulares como artistas capaces de intentarlas. En estos caóticos caminos hacia lo desconocido, hay varios factores que, inmersos en los valores formales, nos envuelven en un congelado desierto de pensamientos. El nuevo arte tiene un poder específico para aterrarnos, para sugerirnos, para determinarnos y concluirnos en procesos ontológicos, en instantes en los que, las interpretaciones, sean de cualquier índole, son pretextos para comprender esa serie de vivencias intelectuales o sentimentales y aún románticas, que es la obra producto de un artista. Sin embargo, en la interpretación crítica está la unión o comunión del crítico con la obra misma. En estos encuentros, apresurados de emoción, hay que compenetrarse en las profundidades silenciosas, purísimas de referencias a una realidad mágica o cotidiana, que hacen sublimar el razonamiento y a su vez, nos proponen una creación. Lógicamente se trata de un fenómeno que plasma esas situaciones anímicas que motivan los artistas.

Las tres últimas décadas de este siglo han deparado para las artes, en especial la pintura, una serie de cambios, modificaciones y transformaciones radicales en el concepto estético tradicional, de una manera tan acelerada e inesperada, que la han conducido a un momento de tensión en el que es difícil prever el incierto porvenir o las nuevas rutas, los nuevos senderos que habrán de seguir después de esta larga, afanosa, despiadada, apresurada búsqueda de una verdad; ya que el arte siempre ofrece soluciones tentativas, dejando sensaciones en el umbral de la inquietud y del desconcierto.

En ese anhelo por investigar lo que el artista es capaz de resumir en su obra, se ha creado un proceso intelectual en donde la casualidad, que mezcla el hallazgo con la mentalidad constructiva, ha jugado un papel importante dentro del concepto estético.

Se han concebido, un sin fin de movimientos o tentativas estetizantes que de una u otra manera, han recabado infinitas inquietudes y lecciones del arte y del artista en su constante experimentación para hallar la síntesis que es el epílogo de todos los caminos de manifestación plástica. Así, con esa increíble vitalidad, se ha visto nacer, evolucionar y fenecer a tendencias con sus aportaciones, soluciones, márgenes de especulación, individualismos, experimentos ópticos, estilos redundantes en conceptos y en ideas; pero también se ha visto que determinados sucesos del devenir plástico, han fracasado en su tentativa de originalidad, por la misma angustia creativa que los hizo surgir a la luz del paisaje terrible del marco histórico.

Todos los movimientos obedecían y obedecen a la imperiosa necesidad que el artista posee y que tiende a una reproducción sutil de su mundo, de su arcano, y al acierto de lo desprendido de la obra en sí.

El arte de la abstracción introduce todos aquellos elementos y sucesos exclusivos de la mentalidad que ordena un caos. Nunca es un juego pirotécnico; introduce, también, las efímeras vivencias cromáticas que consolidan formas, una renovación del espacio y la ruptura en la metáfora y el axioma de la creación.

En esa concreción de tema, idea, forma y situaciones, se encuentra la variedad expresiva de una aparente facilidad constructiva; así, el expresionismo abstracto, el tachismo, el manchismo, el microbismo, el informalismo, el sintetismo, la pintura de acción, y por último, dentro de este resumen de elementos fabricantes de mundos e imágenes de la pintura más pura, se llega a la anarquía libérrima, al momento en que la pintura deja de expresar algo concreto y se queda en las implicaciones fantasmales de un universo cuajado de color, en el que principia y finaliza toda una actitud frente a la vida y frente, asimismo, a las ideas que dan el factor de individualidad. Es el momento cero del que se debe partir nuevamente, para iniciar, otra vez, una trayectoria hacia el desciframiento de la verdad y la razón, coherente con un mundo que tiende a eliminar al individuo para hacerlo partícipe de una maquinización dolorosa. Se debe iniciar un arte a partir de la nada estética que, celosamente, presenta a la pintura en cuanto tal, sin que para ello se necesite ya hablar de un lenguaje ni de un vocabulario.

En ese terreno de la destrucción del arte, de la negación de las formas que, tradicionalmente, son la imagen de algo conocido; adquieren el poder de seducción o sugestión en esta antipintura. Salen la riqueza de la imaginería, las vetas inagotables del artepurismo, cuya consecuencia o finalidad es el reducto de la soledad angustiosa conseguida por el artista.

Por otra parte, la especulación con los diversos motivos de la pintura ha dado como consecuencia la fusión de muchos elementos y conceptos. Las artes combinadas son las más vivas introducciones a la realidad cotidiana.

Las artes del ensamblado y del collage, respectivamente, llevan a la escultura, o a los objetos perdidos, al orden de una pintura viva. Los objetos adquieren otro cariz, se van revalorizando de su esencia primaria para transformarse en radical elemento viviente de la obra de arte. En las artes de la basura, del desperdicio o de los pegostes, se redimen los objetos olvidados y se observan las relaciones, las implicaciones que éstos cobran en la actualidad. Victoria de la realidad sorpresiva, cruel y desdeñada sobre la belleza tradicional. En los artistas del collage y el ensamblado existe una verdadera crueldad constructiva; con ellos se inicia un diálogo vital entre el receptor o espectador y el artista a partir de los elementos materiales más disímbolos.

Una lección que los futuristas y los cubistas proporcionaron al mundo y que los pintores de hoy emplean con un fin definido: dar sus visiones caóticas de su mundo caótico, darles valor estético a esos objetos rechazados por la colectividad.

En sus cuadros, los cubistas introdujeron la realidad directa. Pegaron en los lienzos, rectores de periódicos, fragmentos reconocibles de papeles pautados; efectos que le dieron a la obra el poder de sugerencia, la dimensión del realismo y la atmósfera evocativa por los placeres de la *joie de vivre*. Precisamente por haber introducido en sus pinturas lo que los rodeaba, esa escuela quedó como un período de búsqueda y de análisis por y del objeto cotidiano. *Apollinaire,* crítico del cubismo expresó: "Las obras de arte son lo más enérgico que produce una época desde el punto de vista de la plástica. Esa energía se impone a los hombres y es para ellos la medida plástica de una nueva época. Así, aquellos que se burlan de los pintores nuevos, se burlan de su propia apariencia, porque la humanidad de lo porvenir se imaginará a la humanidad de hoy según las representaciones que los artistas del arte más vigente, es decir, los más nuevos, le habrán dejado" . . .

En el futurismo, en cambio, "la liberación de formas tipográficas, la introducción de novedosos estilos de impresión, las letras aisladas y solitariamente engarzadas por ritmos sugerentes, la arquitectura de las ciudades del futuro; la integración del mundo plástico a la poesía; la creación de obras escultóricas por los poetas; la idea de una nueva religión del hombre moderno con su fe en un futuro distinto, fueron los aportes de la ética futurista"... (*Ida Rodríguez*).

Estos son, en síntesis, los gérmenes para las posteriores manifestaciones Dadaístas y Surrealistas. Artistas como *Kurt Schwitters* y *Marcel Duchamp,* realizaron, obras escultóricas en las que el objeto valía por él mismo; objetos encontrados, recobrados y elevados a una dimensión y categoría estética. Por ejemplo, El Homenaje a la Humanidad (que era un conjunto de basura) del primero y las Esculturas Prefabricadas del segundo.

Otras artes se integran o se desintegran a la pluralidad de conceptos emotivos. La pintura y la escultura, por lo general, se conciben con respecto a la arquitectura, así como algunas otras manifestaciones individuales irán a exornar otros medios y otras expresiones.

La reacción en contra de los valores establecidos, sean de cualquier tipo; la negación de las formas aceptadas como de belleza, y el afán, ya no de perennidad, sino lo opuesto, de lo efímero de los valores humanos, ha conducido a los más extraordinarios y descabellados experimentos: como las sobrenaturales y diabólicamente bellas máquinas esculto-pictóricas-musicales de artistas como *Schaffer* y *Tinguely.*

También se ha llegado a crear un tipo de arte popular, cuyo mérito, a diferencia del movimiento Dadá (1916), es el de tratar de concebir un lenguaje artístico que principia con el uso de las cosas y los objetos de auténtica idiosincrasia. Si bien el movimiento Dadá poseía aspectos totalmente negativos, dio origen al Surrealismo; superándolo, el arte Pop, lleva aspectos de absoluta trascendencia positiva, puesto que comprende todo lo que nos rodea, o bien todo aquello que nos proporciona algo, elevado a un rango artístico en su dura, fría, elemental y desconcertante belleza. Ahora no puede olvidarse que existe belleza hasta en los hechos y en las cosas más incoherentes o comunes: como las hamburguesas, las tiras cómicas, los muebles modernos, etcétera.

Artistas como *Roy Lichtenstein; Claes Oldenburg; Tom Wesselmann; James Rosenquist; Andy Warhol; Jasper Johnes* y *Rauschenberg* han presentado su concepto del arte, sarcástica, cáusticamente; brindándonos la belleza helada del mundo que nos rodea, siempre con un humor negro que guarda la poderosa angustia del creador frente a los valores morales.

Aún más lejos ha ido el arte óptico, puesto que el uso y el abuso de las detalladas formas geométricas y sus juegos de mareante ebriedad de formas, de minucia detallista, son la mejor muestra de que los valores estéticos se encuentran en un momento crítico, y de que existe un caos dramático en las psiquis de los creadores. En todas estas negaciones de un arte que cumple fines sociológicos, históricos y estéticos se encuentra la pregunta básica con respecto al futuro de las manifestaciones del individualismo que concibe un arte, primero para satisfacer una necesidad de expresión; y segundo, para enfrentar su desplazamiento del yo, que es la obra, al determinante juicio de la estética y al devenir histórico.

Yo no creo que el arte se encuentre en un callejón sin salida, por lo contrario, considero que todas las últimas manifestaciones son aquella lucha enconada que sostiene el artista para comunicar, en formas no siempre explí-

11

citas, esa llama volcánica llamada necesidad de expresión, ese sendero de lenguajes que es soporte de la angustia del hombre, cuya única finalidad obedece y se encuentra, en la búsqueda de nuevas formas, de nuevos acentos artísticos, y cuya problemática es ser la imagen del, para y por el hombre de nuestro tiempo.

No puedo dejar de mencionar, aunque sea someramente, a ese movimiento, tan antiguo como el mundo mismo, que lleva a la expresión humana a un punto de climax y catarsis. El neo-expresionismo o neo-humanismo posee una dinámica y un proceso inteligente en el que se asimilan las fuerzas espirituales, concomitantes con ideologías o acontecimientos del vivir dramático. En esta expresión se da cabida a la riqueza de alusiones del hombre desde una profundidad esencial, y se va hacia el ensimismamiento. Sus temas, sus ideas, sus sugestiones y críticas sociales, políticas e históricas, y el testimonio trágico que encierra en su axioma, son aquellos instantes solitarios de la enajenación de hoy.

Sin embargo, la historia de la pintura no existiría sin los acentos peculiares y dinámicos de los artistas individuales. Los pintores de hoy, 1966, si bien, en precisos momentos se han reunido en grupos, con semejanzas en ideas y en ideales, han creado intimidad, movidos única y exclusivamente por su interiorismo estético. Yo no creo en las escuelas o en los academismos que tratan de hacer surgir pintores; odio las escuelas pictóricas puesto que si bien dan bases para la expresión, prostituyen las conciencias libres.

Busco, descubro y trato de interpretar los valores escondidos en la intimidad de los cuadros. Veo los aciertos y quiero introducirme hasta la profundidad de la idea del propio creador, para así ver el drama, el sentido pánico, lo poético, el purismo, el afán de sintetismo de los valores ocultos o semidescubiertos en las superficies de trabajo. Mis afinidades poéticas se desdoblan cuando encuentran, cuando se encuentran con obras ensimismadas productos vigorosos de procesos de libertad, en esa condensación de la vivencia emocional.

En fin, trato de complementar a la obra de arte, con otra obra interpretativa, cuyas voces y cuyos ecos, hablen de esa individualidad que sabe concebir un mundo metafórico, lleno de paradojas y enigmas tácitos en la fenomenología de la creación.

México no ha quedado a la zaga en lo que respecta al fenómeno de los cambios en las maneras o formas estéticas. Si bien es cierto que, después de los tres grandes de nuestra pintura: *Orozco, Rivera* y *Siqueiros,* sus inefables seguidores, creyeron ingenuamente que la única ruta que existía de expresión artística era la del realismo naturalista, superficial y hasta folklórico; y si bien es cierto también que anquilosaron todo un movimiento trascendente y respetable, ya que trataron de seguir, escasos de talento, a sus predecesores, pero con la diferencia de que los "grandes" fueron hombres de genio y sus seguidores, tal vez se quedaron en artesanos o segundas malas partes.

El primer gran desertor de las normas establecidas por toda esa escuela de pintura, es *Rufino Tamayo,* quien, profundizando ya no sólo en lo aparente de lo mexicano, sino ahondando y canalizando su manera de ver y decir las cosas, llegó a la esencia pictórica de una raíz ancestral; raíz cósmica, cuyos antecedentes, estaban en el arte antiguo de México.

Con ese gran ejemplo dado por *Tamayo,* otros artistas desertarían también de los cánones impuestos que los obligaban a plasmar en sus telas una realidad de tan superficial, efímera y hasta grotesca, cuyas concesiones y consecuencias nefastas, aún hoy, algunos pintores no ven y tratan de seguir, no contentos con la pavorosa lección de anonadamiento a la que llegó la pintura nacional.

Todos los jóvenes rebeldes de la pintura (*Mérida, Gerzso, Martínez, Urueta, Soriano, Michel, Cuevas,* etcétera), que tomaban nuevos senderos y se inquietaban por lo que pasaba en el resto del mundo, supieron ampliar sus horizontes con las lecciones de los maestros europeos y americanos, quienes, en varias décadas, habían producido obras nuevas, de novísimo acento dinámico. Esos jóvenes de ayer y de hoy no trataron ni tratan de copiar ni de ponerse a la moda, sino que en su impulso de rechazo contra normas preestablecidas, y al abrir sus miras al exterior, portaban el germen para la manifestación mucho más universalista, tratando no sólo de ser artistas reflejos de época, sino aún más, en esa ampliación de sus horizontes, dar climax a sus aventuras y crear lenguajes simbólicos convencidos de la vitalidad y las soluciones esencialmente sintéticas que también el arte prehispánico les había brindado.

En todas las manifestaciones artísticas del México contemporáneo la influencia que han ejercido las culturas ancestrales (entre otras, la azteca, la tolteca y la maya) sobre la conciencia creadora, ha sido definitiva, trascendente, demoledora y exhaustiva.

En su afán por adquirir, por devenir una fisonomía, un lenguaje y un carácter propios, los artistas han observado que la expresión genuina debe partir de una concepción trágica, patética, desgarradora, sangrienta y a la vez catártica que afirma las voces y los acentos de lo dinámico personal de este arte con el de otros países; y, precisamente, esos conceptos, además de la admirable solución sintética de los valores espaciales cuanto temáticos a los que llegó el arte prehispánico, se han convertido en antecedentes y puntos de arranque para señalar la verdadera expresión nacional.

Artistas como *Orozco,* como *Tamayo,* como *Siqueiros, Cuevas* y *Martínez,* están más cerca del terror expresivo de *Coatlicue, Huehuetéotl* y *Xiuhcóatl* que de las venus renacentistas.

Todo ese horror, toda la simbología y todo el potente dramatismo de la escultórica antigua son parte de un mismo espíritu: la predilección por la tragedia del ente nacional. También es prudente y obligado señalar que otros artistas, como el inglés *Henry Moore,* confiesan que deben su obra a la lección del arte antiguo mexicano, por esa admirable sugerencia expresiva, por el juego de volúmenes y por la gran masa, parte básica de la expresión sintética.

En esas búsquedas por penetrar conscientemente a otros mundos, a otros ámbitos, por buscar los espacios, la luz y las características diferenciales en la creación individual, ésta fue la que los llevó a terrenos de asombrosas calidades; a los momentos poéticos del verdadero dramatismo, a la evocación por atmósferas escondidas e irredentas del arte secular, y asimismo, a la espiritualidad de las imágenes conseguidas. Se dio un nuevo acento a una plástica que si bien, como he anotado, dio frutos óptimos, que son las obras murales de los llamados "grandes", también dio el lado negativo, de los segundones de un todo realizado con esplendor y brillantez.

Los treintaicinco pintores seleccionados en el presente texto, son un magnífico ejemplo de la diversidad, de la gran variedad de manifestaciones a la que ha llegado la pintura mexicana. Estos artistas obedecen en sus creaciones a la necesidad de plasmar sus mundos, diferentes todos en cuanto a las formas y a la temática y aún a la manera de resolver los problemas a los que se enfrentan en el momento de la concepción.

Todos estos pintores en su desigualdad estética, en su múltiple y varia invención, en su modo de aceptar o rechazar determinadas verdades del concierto estético, son la muestra que confirma el aserto, en el sentido de que la pluralidad, en la multitud de individualidades, es donde en verdad se encuentra el signo de una escuela viva, y no en la repetición temática impuesta por anteriores maestros.

Las búsquedas de *Ricardo Martínez* por encontrar la síntesis luminosa del hombre que se debate en la duda y la angustia de la vida y la muerte; su consciente trabajo que lo ha llevado a depurar las formas hasta el esquema sintético de la emoción profunda, y principalmente, por la idea que lo conduce a un páramo de soledad y por su colorido, refinado en extremo hasta ser refulgente, monocromo, diáfano, interno, apocalíptico, cósmico; y cuya visión del pasado monumental, de la escultórica prehispánica que él ve como una raíz de la cual hay que partir para luego retornar, enriquecido por la experiencia; han hecho de este artista y de su obra monolíticas acepciones en las que la duda del sentimiento que confronta y combina un pasado con un futuro incierto, de expresiones dramáticas, una de las pinturas que con mayor validez, ternura y valentía han surgido en los últimos años. Sin embargo, *Ricardo Martínez* no llegó a lo que ha llegado por hábil facilidad, sino que fue una depuración de ámbitos, de búsquedas lumínicas en donde en el espacio, sorpresivamente, aparecen sus hombres y mujeres-esculturas con la soledad melancólica de sus símbolos respecto a la fertilidad y la reproducción sensual; repentinamente el mundo se convierte en haz de luz y en conjunción de atmósferas que lo significan todo.

Cordelia Urueta es el otro polo de luces positivas de nuestra plástica. Es el suyo un arte imaginario, de imaginería constante; arte en donde el poder de la fantasía subvenciona a los valores para un fin que ella misma establece; finalidad de lograr lo inmanente a la poesía y a su emoción despegada, desprendida, de las situaciones vitales que se dan cita en sus lienzos. Paralelamente a una idea que la guía como faro con luz propia, *Cordelia Urueta* ha incursionado en el terreno del mito, con soluciones admirables que la introducen en los senderos de la pintura no-objetiva, partiendo de sólidas bases de una figuración que buscaba, que se internaba hasta las profundidades desdibujadas de un espacio onírico, y reproducía solamente aquellas imágenes de una realidad distante. La actual pintura de *Cordelia Urueta*, incapaz de quedarse en una sola manera de expresión, en una única tendencia, ha ido por otros caminos, llevando a su abstracción hasta los linderos de otra figuración sui-géneris, consecuente con un espíritu que ve el espacio, a la luz sideral y a la poesía, como factores nunca anecdóticos, con los cuales va a construir su inclemente mundo diferencial, en el que existe un cierto apunte de una vitalidad renovada, recreada, vuelta a hacer. El onirismo y la magia más intensa, junto con el elemento alucinante del absurdo y la alusión velada, son algunas de las cifras rectoras de esta obra, una de las más bellas en intensidad y en emoción apasionada de las muchas que se hacen en México. Es, además, pintura totalmente joven, con todos los problemas y las dificultades que se presentan en la juventud.

14

Pedro Coronel representa, asimismo, una fuente de inagotable inspiración por los temas o las ideas que provienen de un mundo que es mezcla de imaginación con lo popular, con un sentido de fecundidad, con las vibraciones que se desprenden del color y con un sentido hacia lo monumental, obviamente extraído a la conciencia de un arte de raíz antigua; más una capacidad asombrosa por descubrirnos, con crueldad en fuerte dosis, los remotos parajes de la catarsis. Esto último provocado por la composición, sugestiva y dinámica y por las formas originales, a veces bestiales, volcánicas, que llevan al espectador a la subjetividad espiritual. *Coronel* es, además, un escultor monumental, que alternando la pintura con la escultura ha logrado la armonía a partir de la lucha de fuerzas antagónicas, que en sus cuadros y en sus modelos tetradimensionales, adquieren caracteres simbólicos. Evolucionando desde una expresión poética simplificada, este pintor ha llegado al punto crítico en el que el dominio del color, el dominio de su temática y el rigor en la descripción de sus vivencias, aunado con su coherente armonía en la regia variedad de texturas, y a veces, por la intensidad dramática que absorbe prácticamente al espectador en el mundo de la emoción intensa, ha hecho de su expresión un mar de sensaciones audaces, de extraña pasión desbordada: la obra maestra.

José Luis Cuevas es un caso único y excepcional en la pintura mundial. Talento precoz, ya que desde su adolescencia logró captar y plasmar un mundo teratológico de atroz expresionismo, y que ha ido consumando, paso a paso, con una vitalidad avasalladora, todos aquellos caminos que su temática le ha impuesto. Uno de los mejores dibujantes jamás dotados, *Cuevas* ha hecho de esta técnica difícil un modo de decir, con rapidez, sus visiones que son parte de su mundo y de una realidad trágica. Visiones aterrantes, llenas de la angustia del vivir en un mundo absurdo, incoherente, negativo, cuya sola presentación, con un sadismo y un horror pocas veces concebido, hace pensar en todas las miserias y en los vicios en los que la humanidad está sepultada. Temas de su predilección lo han sido y lo siguen siendo la vida patológica, los enfermos y los mutilados, la vida misma tomada como una nueva comedia humana, los dictadores, las prostitutas, los enanos de Coney-Island, los seres monstruosos que se mueven y reptan alrededor de nosotros. Todos estos temas de una acongojante realidad y verismo, nos los presenta tal cual son, es decir, como la reproducción de un mundo cotidiano; como una lección ante nuestros ojos, como una amonestación trágica de la vida de los hombres.

Cuevas, con su obra, ha consolidado un expresionismo tan singular, que lo hermana, por tener el mismo espíritu de severidad crítica, con las obras de *Goya,* de *Toulouse-Lautrec* y de *Orozco.* A *Cuevas* se ha tratado de ligarlo, de buscarle antecedentes con los artistas que he mencionado, pero creo que, si existen coincidencias en los temas y aún en las ideas, es debido a la afinidad espiritual en todos ellos; afinidad que lleva al artista a enjuiciar su tiempo con una mirada aterradora, cuya angustia está precisamente en la fuerza de sus descripciones cotidianas. *Cuevas* es un moralista que se burla de lo moral; *Cuevas* es un testigo que niega su presencia en los mundos infrahumanos; *Cuevas* se expresa repentinamente, con líneas nerviosas, de calidades extraordinarias, como si estuviera escribiendo su diario íntimo de las situaciones agobiantes por las que pasa el hombre de todos los días.

También agrupa sus obras en temas genéricos puesto que así, desarrolla una idea, una vivencia, en varias pinturas, cuyo numen está encaminado a dar por hecho, todos los ritos absurdos en los que nos movemos. Por eso, la obra de *Cuevas* tiende a las fuentes literarias, más que a las pictóricas. El cine de horror, las vertiginosas secuencias de las comedias silentes de *Mack Sennett* y el teatro del absurdo (*Ionesco, Arrabal, Becket*) son las afinidades de la obra de este expresionista. Así como los cuentos de *Poe,* las narraciones de *Dickens,* los textos de *Dostoyewski* y *Kafka.*

La gran lección humana que encierran todas las obras de *Cuevas,* son el ejemplo de que este pintor, está más próximo a los linderos del genio que con las manifestaciones de un ego atormentado por la angustia de vivir; aunque también eso último tenga un papel de importancia en el desarrollo de su maquiavélica obra. Su atormentada y atormentante psiquis lo hace plasmar una infinidad de autorretratos en los que él mismo, como artista y como hombre, es el agonista básico del drama de la humanidad.

Dentro de la corriente expresionista mexicana, existen varios, importantes pintores, que conjugan la grandeza de sus sentimientos, con formas tradicionales. Cada uno de ellos, en escala de sus posibilidades presentan sus propias inquietudes fenoménicas, y brindan su personal interpretación del mundo de la vigilia. Pero todos ellos, poseen una conciencia profunda de los valores morales del humanismo rector. Por eso, la obra de *Rafael Coronel,* con tentativas de evocación a mundos lejanos, de retratos imaginarios que nos traen de inmediato recuerdos de sucesos lejanos y sus prístinas calidades en el uso del color, del óleo trabajado a la perfección, y por su demoledor sentido de profundidad psicológica, de enajenación histórica, que diseca a sus caracteres expuestos, lo diferencian de las obras expresionistas de *Benito Messeguer,* de *Francisco Moreno Capdevila,* de *Hernández Delgadillo,* de *Francisco Corzas* y de *Pilar Sánchez Castañeda.*

Messeguer y *Capdevila* han realizado, en el terreno del mural, sus más ambiciosas creaciones. Uno y otro tienen por base de su manifestación artística, los sufrimientos del hombre acosado por el hombre y destruido por la guerra y las consecuencias que se desprenden de ella. El hombre contra el hombre mismo y su negatividad. Ambos artistas, cuya afinidad es comprensiva, son de una modernidad absoluta. Sus obras siempre en proceso de evolución llaman la atención; obras de dos pintores de honradez profesional.

En tanto, *José Hernández Delgadillo* ve al hombre como arquetipo, como espíritu de una mitología, como el redivivo Prometeo. Por eso, los hombres y las mujeres que él pinta, son gigantes dentro de un universo titánico, imposibles de aprehender.

Francisco Corzas hace una pintura de sugestión hipnótica. Una obra de convicciones que hacen patente, las alegrías de un mundo esencialmente trágico. Por ello, todos sus personajes concebidos, están rodeados o ataviados con vestuarios de la antigüedad; en momentos, o en presencias, de un constante, un perenne carnaval. El carnaval, la mascarada, el juego de antifaces que es la vida misma. Su técnica es finísima, hasta en el último trazo se ve al pintor buscador de una belleza ideal; perfeccionador de las emociones sutiles del alma pánica. En su integridad, se reconocen las intenciones que proponen el establecimiento de un mundo rodeado de fantasmas que hacen presentes las preguntas acerca de la vida y acerca de los gozos trágicos de ésta. ¿Quiénes somos, qué somos y cómo somos? continuamente surgen en sus cuadros.

Mundo de sueño, distante y cercano; amplios horizontes que recrean y desnudan la realidad circundante. Búsqueda de la esencia del vivir. Patetismo revestido con máscaras de soledad; todo esto y más es la obra de *Corzas,* uno de los grandes figurativos de la pintura mexicana.

De expresionismo tibio, a veces ingenuo, puede clasificarse la plástica de *Pilar Sánchez Castañeda.* Sus temas favoritos son aquellos en donde grupos de hombres y mujeres están en situaciones cotidianas, comunes; con una fría aceptación de lo cotidiano. En sus naturalezas muertas se encuentra la alegría del vivir, pero siempre con un patetismo en medio tono, logrado en silencio, perdiéndose en la misma idea.

Dentro de los pintores que jamás podrán etiquetarse o clasificarse en determinadas tendencias o ismos plásticos se encuentran *Juan Soriano, Enrique Echeverría, Pedro Friedeberg, Xavier Esqueda, José García Ocejo* y *Pedro Cervantes.*

Soriano pasa de la figuración la no-figuración con pasmosa rapidez, desdeñando a un público ávido de "niños de tierna mirada" para complicarse en las dificultades de la expresión de sugerencias y evocaciones.

Su pintura es un reflejo de actividad, de inquietud, de problemas que lo obligan a retener los momentos precisos de una gravedad expresiva.

Más que emplear la pintura como un medio de comunicar sus emociones, es la pintura la que lo emplea a él; es decir, es su medio y es su fin, es su principio y es su unión con lo alucinante, es su deber y su haber en la rica variedad de exaltaciones que hacen esquema todo lo conocido, a lo que ha limitado sus luces, de una paleta de inagotable riqueza.

Su pintura es poesía pura y ésta es la sensación humana concomitante a un inteligente resumen de las formas y de los espacios. Su serie de retratos de *Lupe Marín,* vinieron a enriquecer este género de la pintura por la audacia de la composición, del color y del ambiente mágico que poseían estas dramáticas biografías.

Echeverría, paulatinamente, se fue alejando de la figura humana y de las representaciones conocidas. Se fue quedando con una paleta oscura, de oscuras pero a la vez elocuentes tonalidades. Se fue haciendo más grave su pintura cada vez y encontró los planos; planos de color que en la sugerencia intelectual está la emoción controlada, ceñida a los juegos serenos de su constructividad. A veces, por una fuerza interior y misteriosa, vuelven a aparecer las esencias de, por ejemplo, una naturaleza muerta, un bodegón, unas flores o bien el asomo de una o varias figuras humanas. Pero son sólo instantes de espontaneidad de una profundidad simbólica. Los bosquejos de su figuración, de transparencias sentimentales, de gozos de la vida, llenos de nostalgia, llevan el sello de los pintores en plena madurez.

José García Ocejo, curiosa, deliberadamente, profundiza en lo bucólico y en los linderos del romanticismo. Nunca emplea una gama rica en colores puesto que no la necesita. Sus expresiones se encaminan al monocromatismo para subrayar los matices espectrales de las vivencias de tipo mágico. Y, sentimentalmente, con un espíritu que colinda con el arte fantástico, concibe un mundo de extrañas figuras mitológicas: faunos, ninfas, minotauros, etcétera; que viven y se encierran en momentos intimistas propicios para el erotismo refinado. Y en su romanticismo son válidas todas las alusiones que emplea, puesto que, como claramente lo sentenció *Baudelaire* "Quien dice romanticismo dice arte moderno, es decir, intimidad, espiritualismo, color, aspiración hacia lo infinito, expresadas mediante todos los recursos que contienen las artes".

Un arte fantástico, del más puro surrealismo, enajenado, cruel, hiriente hasta llegar a lo sardónico; nihilista, de intención destructiva y burla sanguinaria, es el que hace *Pedro Friedeberg*. Dibujante de excepción, concibe cada cuadro, como la reproducción de millares de pequeñas figuras geométricas, cada una con distintos motivos, en cuyo eje, centro de atención, surgen los dictados fantásticos de una mente que va más allá de la simple especulación con los factores de la vigilia.

Su pensamiento constructivista de edificios plásticos, irreales, supranaturales, son las imágenes poseídas de punzante ironía. Cada cuadro de *Friedeberg* es una síntesis del pensamiento existencial en el que expresa, en su afán de concebir los momentos del absurdo, aquel caos del desconcierto, los datos contemporáneos de un arte ensimismado y reiterativo que se encuentra en un punto crítico, climático y lleno de dudas acerca de la verdad pictórica.

Xavier Esqueda es de los más jóvenes pintores mexicanos. Su sentido, creador del símbolo y del mito, lo ha hecho realizar sus obras mediante el uso del collage, revalorando así, los objetos elementales del caos material. Obviamente, su misma inquietud, lo conduce a crear juegos ópticos en donde los objetos y las cosas cotidianas en sí adquieren un cariz emocional diferente, y por eso, puede considerársele junto a las expresiones POP y OP de la actualidad. Otra faceta de su obra, es aquella dramática que identifica las naturalezas muertas con los ambientes de una tristeza infinita, de duda y de perfecto equilibrio temático.

Por último, *Pedro Cervantes*, escultor y pintor, da en su obra, un horizonte monocromo, de blancura espacial, en el que existe un plano logrado merced a los esgrafiados y a una caligrafía dibujística elemental. En sus laberintos espectrales, de blancura irreal, *Cervantes* acepta aquella visión erosionada y antigua del mundo de las formas.

En la tendencia abstraccionista, han destacado, por sus obras de primerísimo orden, los siguientes pintores: *Lilia Carrillo, Fernando García Ponce* y *Roberto Donís,* cuya evolución a la síntesis ha sido lograda después de largas experiencias con los matices de la pintura, en cuanto tal. *Vlady,* que pretende un aire violento de expresión poética, en especial, en sus imágenes acuáticas, aunque también lo haga con la figura humana con reminiscencias de antiguos maestros flamencos, posee una fuerte voz dentro de un expresionismo combinado con elementos de otros ismos estéticos. En ese expresionismo hay un fuerte contraste por los claroscuros y por la mezcla de colores, paciente, apasionadamente, terriblemente trabajados con finísima sensibilidad.

Gabriel Ramírez, en su abigarrado barroquismo de líneas y colores, que une las expresiones de libertad de acción, da, como consecuencia plausible, obras de tierna musicalidad; en tanto que *Lucinda Urrusti,* siempre en deliberado tono menor, de cualidades y calidades pictóricas riquísimas, deviene un mundo subjetivo en el que se alude a una rica naturaleza transformada por el placer de transformarla y hacerla parte del gozo diario.

Carlos Belaunzarán, otro de los nuevos valores de la pintura nacional, consolida en su pintura, un axioma y una metáfora alada; partes de una mente que va a reducir a las formas y a los colores a una nada motriz;

de la cual, va construyendo un edificio dinámico de certera belleza objetiva con los elementos puramente subjetivos.

Manuel Felguérez, en su pintura, refleja siempre un equivalente al drama de las fuerzas dinámicas que solucionan magistralmente, la unidad y el ritmo, el movimiento y el estatismo de una plástica constructiva. En esta organización de elementos constituidos por orgánicos acentos, es donde se van a encontrar las diferenciaciones de su pintura con el resto de los artistas no-objetivos. *Felguérez,* también escultor, emotivo y monumental, ha creado una de las máximas realizaciones artísticas de este siglo, que es su mural escultórico en hierro del cine Diana de la ciudad de México.

Si en alguna ocasión, en el futuro, se quisiera ver y analizar esta década artística del país y ejemplificarla, forzosamente deberá uno remitirse, tanto a las obras de *Cuevas* como a éste mural, que es, la obra más drástica, emocionante, subjetiva, telúrica de la explosión de fuerzas del siglo XX; al igual que las alucinantes torres de *Matías Goeritz.*

En un primitivismo que alude al sentimiento sensual refinado y sexual del hombre contemporáneo, deben de resaltarse las creaciones tanto de *Toledo* como de *Arnaldo Coen,* así como ciertos sintetismos eróticos de *Rodolfo Nieto* y las caligrafías, mezcla de humor infantil e intención adulta, de *Fernando Ramos Prida. Luis López Loza* se acerca, a veces, a esta preocupación erótica y pánica, aunque le interesen también, las reconstrucciones intimistas del mundo extranatural.

Coen en su pintura, da rienda suelta a las emociones a partir de una alegre manera de ver la vida, la subjetividad onírica da pauta para que se planteen todas aquellas posibilidades que tocan temas del erotismo que subyugan por el uso del color, por las formas de una aparente calma anímica y por las sensaciones de una intimidad de diáfanas y claras intenciones.

En este panorama, de tan vital, riquísimo en singularidades, que sintetiza a la forma para el servicio de las individualidades espirituales; que desconcierta por la cada vez más vertiginosa evolución en las maneras estéticas, que hacen resaltar las posibilidades de la soledad, en un deslinde de fuerzas creativas, están las producciones de *Aceves Navarro,* de *Maka,* las finuras evocativas de *Antonio Peláez,* el esquematismo, a la manera de *Klee* de *Rodolfo Hurtado* y las subjetivizaciones, terribles en conceptos, de *Alberto Gironella.*

Peláez con su pintura, elegante, de apagados tonos; en sus prismas, rombos, esferas, picos, y otras geometrizantes figuras, da su mundo infinito, de silenciosa voz, de angustia evocadora. El ámbito ocre, las llamaradas amarillas y azules tibias, atrapan la conciencia plástica capaz de albergar la emoción disimulada. Pintura de pantanos olvidados, con una grandeza confundida en horizonte arcaico. En síntesis, un verdadero creador, recio y poético.

En sus verdades o misterios historicistas, ya que en su obra la historia desempeña un papel fundamental, *Alberto Gironella* lleva una angustia que desintegra, que tiende a romper hasta a la misma esencia del dramatismo de sus protagonistas, creados para satisfacer un afán investigador de los motivos crueles que la misma historia depara y que satisface un pensamiento surrealista y que cobra, asimismo, una grandilocuencia esquemática.

Gironella, en su obra, destruye las visiones características del devenir contemporáneo; en sus collages y en sus ensambles posee la peculiaridad de reconstituir, de recabar, los datos del acaecer anterior, en donde la belleza del objeto en sí es un hecho de perversidad hacia las maneras plásticas de nuestro tiempo, el leit-motiv de su recreación.

Vicente Rojo cubre en sus lienzos, aquella destrucción de los órdenes conocidos y establece uno nuevo, coherente y afín con las descripciones temáticas de lo contemporáneo. Es la suya, una obra honrada que da, a partir de la nada estética, una nueva ordenación de la materia y de nuestras angustias inmediatas.

El arte en México cumple, satisface la función de ser un acto necesario en, y por la conducta del hombre, porque construye un mundo ejemplar que es parte íntima de su ser. Imposible concebir al hombre sin un arte que vaya aparejado con su vida y que satisfaga su necesidad de comunión entre los valores plásticos y la verdad, que tiene que ser poética, por ser creación dramática o de otro tipo; puesto que es el arte esa necesidad que ayuda al hombre a entender la vida tal cual es: un sostén de su actividad moral.

Por eso, por esa necesidad cambiante, según es el marco histórico, han surgido multitud de estilos individualistas; diferentes maneras de ser del arte que responden a esa necesidad de comunicación entre los hombres, ese impulso de crear, ya no sólo actos de belleza tradicional sino lo opuesto, obras en donde se reflejen las situaciones y las vivencias de nuestro trágico acontecer.

Entrar de lleno al mundo del arte, entender sus problemas, su trascendencia y su alcance es, en síntesis, la más pura de las sensaciones humanas, o bien, como definió *André Malraux*: "Nada da una idea más corrosiva a la idea del destino que los grandes estilos, cuya evolución y metamorfosis parecen las anchas cicatrices del pasaje de la fatalidad sobre la tierra".

ACEVES NAVARRO GILBERTO

Nació en la ciudad de México en 1931. En 1950 ingresó en la Escuela de Pintura y Escultura "La Esmeralda", en la cual estudió bajo la dirección del maestro Carlos Orozco Romero. En 1953 fue ayudante de Luis Arenal en los murales que éste realizó en el Palacio de Gobierno de Chilpancingo, Guerrero. Posteriormente colaboró en el equipo de David Alfaro Siqueiros en sus trabajos murales de la Ciudad Universitaria. En 1954 expuso individualmente en las Galerías de las Nuevas Generaciones de la Biblioteca Cervantes, anexa a la mencionada escuela. Ha efectuado siete exposiciones individuales en la ciudad de México: en las Galerías de Antonio Souza, Salón de la Plástica Mexicana y Plástica de México, más numerosas colectivas. En 1958 expuso sus óleos y dibujos en la Unión Panamericana de Washington, D. C. En 1959 y en 1960 realizó exposiciones individuales en varias ciudades de los Estados Unidos. Su obra ha sido seleccionada para las Bienales de París (1961, 1963 y 1965), de Tokio (1962), y de México (1960 y 1962). Aceves Navarro ha ejecutado tres murales de gran interés. En 1960 un muro denominado "Canto a la Raza" en la sucursal 14 del Banco de Londres y México. En 1961 el mural "Danzas de la vida y de la muerte" en la sucursal 17 de la misma institución bancaria y en 1962 un muro alegórico para el mismo Banco en su sucursal de Querétaro, Querétaro. Ha obtenido varios Premios-Adquisición en los Salones Anuales de Pintura del Salón de la Plástica Mexicana.

BELAUNZARAN CARLOS

Nació en Guanajuato, Guanajuato, en 1940. A los doce años, residiendo en Jalapa, Veracruz, inició sus estudios de dibujo y pintura bajo la dirección de los maestros Daniel Aguilar y Ramón Alva de la Canal. Desde los dieciséis años vive en la ciudad de México. En 1958 ingresó en la Academia de San Carlos, en la cual, asistió a las clases de Benjamín Coria, Gabriel Fernández Ledesma, Antonio Rodríguez Luna, Luis Nishizawa e Ignacio Asúnsolo. Sus primeros trabajos tenían la influencia de artistas como Afro, Karl Dahmen, Millares y John Leveé. Mas, pronto, las abandonó e inició el desarrollo de su propio lenguaje en los terrenos de la abstracción. Ha participado en varias exposiciones colectivas y ha recibido algunos premios, como el "Accesit Ier Premio Concurso Pictórico de la Reseña Cinematográfica de Acapulco, 1962". En 1965 fue uno de los seleccionados en el Salón ESSO de artistas jóvenes celebrado en el Museo de Arte Moderno de México. Sus cuadros se encuentran en importantes colecciones de los Estados Unidos y de Europa y en el Museo de Arte Moderno de México. En 1965 presentó su primera exposición individual, con gran éxito crítico, en la Galería Mexicana de Arte "Tianquiztli".

CARRILLO LILIA

Nació en la ciudad de México en 1930. Estudió pintura en México y más tarde en París en la Academia de La Grande Chaumiere. Es maestra en Artes Plásticas. Ha presentado exposiciones individuales en París (1955); México (1956, 1957, 1958, 1961 y 1964); y en Washington, D. C. (1959). Ha participado en muestras colectivas en Francia, Estados Unidos, Perú, Israel, Brasil, Chile y Japón. Sus cuadros tuvieron una magnífica acogida por parte de la crítica especializada en la Bienal de Jóvenes de París (1959); en la Bienal Interamericana de Pintura de México (1960) y en la Bienal de Tokio (1961). En 1965, en el Salón ESSO celebrado en el Museo de Arte Moderno de México obtuvo el Segundo Premio de Pintura.

CERVANTES PEDRO

Nació en la ciudad de México en 1933. Estudió dos años en la Academia de San Carlos. En 1958 efectuó su primera exposición en la Galería Excélsior. En 1960 comenzó a trabajar en esculturas de metal soldado. En 1961 participó en una exposición de carácter internacional celebrada en San Angel. En 1962, en el Salón de la Plástica Mexicana concursó en la muestra denominada de "Nuevos Valores". En 1962, en las Galerías del periódico "Novedades", en colaboración con el fotógrafo Nacho López hizo una exposición de dibujos sobre el Jazz. Desde 1963 alterna la escultura con la pintura, produciendo obras de alto mérito, como el mural de hierro y cerámica para el Banco de Fomento Cooperativo. En 1964 realizó una escultura monumental, de ocho metros de altura, en bronce, para el Puerto Piloto de Alvarado, Veracruz. El tema de esa escultura lo fue un moderno "Prometeo". En 1965 participó en el Salón ESSO de artistas jóvenes celebrado en el Museo de Arte Moderno de México. Ese mismo año, dos pinturas suyas fueron seleccionadas para la muestra de Pintura Contemporánea de México, celebrada en la Casa de las Américas, de La Habana, Cuba.

COEN ARNALDO

Nació en la ciudad de México en 1940. Estudió durante algún tiempo en el Instituto de Artes Publicitarias y en el taller de Lawrence Calcagno, sin embargo, se le puede considerar un pintor autodidacta. En 1962 participó en una exposición colectiva de las nuevas tendencias del arte mexicano en la Galería del Centro Deportivo Israelita de México. Ese mismo año realizó su primera exposición individual, compuesta de numerosos temples sobre papel, con el tema de "Las Figuras de la Opera" en la Galería Mer-Kup. En 1963 celebró otra muestra individual, esta vez de óleos en la Galería del periódico "Novedades". En 1964 efectuó su tercera exposición individual en la Galería de Juan Martín. En 1965 realizó otra muestra, de acuarelas y óleos en esa misma galería de arte. Ha participado en exposiciones colectivas del Centro Deportivo Israelita (1964), en el Salón ESSO del Museo de Arte Moderno de México (1965) y en la Bienal de Jóvenes de París (1965). Su obra ha llamado poderosamente la atención de la crítica desde sus primeros trabajos, que colindaban con la manifestación expresionista. Sus creaciones recientes, de absoluta libertad, lo califican como uno de los auténticos valores con que cuenta la pintura de vanguardia del país. Este año expondrá en la Unión Panamericana de Washington, D. C.

CORONEL PEDRO

Nació en Zacatecas, Zacatecas, en 1923. En 1940 se trasladó a la ciudad de México y estudió en la Escuela de Pintura y Escultura "La Esmeralda". De 1945 a 1946 fue profesor de esa escuela, impartiendo la clase de Escultura. A fines de 1946 viajó por Europa en donde asistió al taller del pintor Brauner y del escultor Brancusi. En 1952 se reincorporó a la vida artística de México y realizó exposiciones en la Galería Proteo (1954, 1956); y desde 1958 ha expuesto con cierta regularidad en la Galería de Arte Mexicano. Ha realizado dos obras públicas en las que ha combinado la pintura con la escultura; mosaicos de cerámica vidriada, con esculturas exteriores tanto en la Unidad Comercial "Servicentro" como en el edificio del Sindicato del Seguro Social. A Octavio Paz se le debe el descubrimiento de este artista, ya que fue él quien lo presentó en su exposición de 1954. En 1959, obtuvo el Primer Premio Nacional de Pintura y en 1960, en la II Bienal Interamericana de Pintura celebrada en México, obtuvo el Premio José Clemente Orozco para un pintor mexicano. En 1960, el Museo de Arte Moderno de México presentó una extraordinaria exposición retrospectiva del artista en el Palacio de Bellas Artes. En 1961 presentó una muestra de pintura y escultura en la Galería Le Point Cardinal de París. En 1962 efectuó una exposición de pintura en Tokio, con magnífico éxito crítico. En 1965, la Galería de Arte Mexicano presentó las obras últimas de Coronel, para celebrar así, sus veinticinco años de pintor.

CORONEL RAFAEL

Nació en Zacatecas, Zacatecas, en 1932. Estudió en su estado natal tanto la secundaria como la preparatoria. Ingresó en la Universidad de Zacatecas con el propósito de estudiar Arquitectura, pero como su familia se trasladó a la ciudad de México en 1952, no pudo terminar la carrera que había escogido. Ese año comenzó a estudiar arte en la Escuela de Pintura y Escultura "La Esmeralda", en las clases que impartía el maestro Carlos Orozco Romero. Dadas sus dotes excepcionales para el dibujo, ganó un concurso estudiantil que le valió una beca para continuar sus estudios. Desde 1954 participa en exposiciones colectivas. Por esas fechas efectuó su primera exposición individual en la Galería de las Nuevas Generaciones, anexa a la Escuela. En 1960 realizó una exposición de carácter retrospectivo, con infinidad de obras, en el Museo de Arte Moderno del Palacio de Bellas Artes y sus pinturas despertaron la curiosidad de la crítica, por tratarse de un artista de singular personalidad. En 1961 expuso en los Estados Unidos, en la Galería Forsythe, en Ann Arbor, Michigan. En 1964 hizo una obra mural para el nuevo edificio del Museo de Antropología e Historia de Chapultepec. En 1965 exhibió cincuenta obras en la Galería de Arte Mexicano. Ese año, sus obras fueron seleccionadas para la Bienal de Sao Paulo, Brasil, en donde obtuvo el Primer Premio Internacional de Pintura. También en ese año, presentó una selecta colección de pinturas y óleos en la sede de la Unión Panamericana de Washington, D. C. Este año presentará sus obras en una prestigiada Galería de Nueva York. Su obra ha sido estudiada en el Libro de Alfonso de Neuvillate titulado *cuatro actitudes ensimismadas*.

CORZAS FRANCISCO

Nació en la ciudad de México en 1936. En 1952 estudió en la Escuela de Pintura y Escultura "La Esmeralda", estudios que terminó en 1955.

En 1953 y 1954 participó en las exposiciones colectivas de la Galería Nuevas Generaciones, anexa a la Escuela. En 1955 y 1956 participa en los concursos de los Nuevos Valores del Salón de la Plástica Mexicana. A fines de 1956 viaja a Europa y reside en Roma. En 1958 ingresó en la Academia de San Giacomo y en la Academia Di Belle Arti; ambas de Roma. En junio de 1958 participó en la exposición "Vía Margutta" y obtuvo la Medalla de Plata y Diploma para Artistas Extranjeros. Ese mismo año celebra su primera exposición individual y participa, asimismo, en la muestra colectiva de los "Artistas Latinoamericanos en Roma". En 1959 retorna a México. Ese año participa en el Primer Salón organizado en el Museo de Arte Moderno del Palacio de Bellas Artes y su obra es seleccionada para la Primera Bienal de Jóvenes de París. En 1960 efectuó una exposición individual en la Galería de Antonio Souza. En 1961 sus obras componen la exposición de los "Interioristas", celebrada en las Galerías del Centro Deportivo Israelita de México. En 1963 presenta un conjunto considerable de óleos y dibujos en la Galería Misrachi. En 1965, su obra es seleccionada para la exposición de artistas jóvenes, convocada por la compañía ESSO y efectuada en el Museo de Arte Moderno. Ese año obtiene el Premio-Adquisición en el Salón Anual de Pintura del Salón de la Plástica Mexicana.

CUEVAS JOSE LUIS

Nació en la ciudad de México en 1934. Ingresó a los diez años en la Escuela de Pintura y Escultura "La Esmeralda", en la cual permaneció escasamente unos meses. En 1947, en un local de la calle de Donceles, de la ciudad de México, hizo su primera exposición individual de dibujos y óleos, en los cuales, apuntaba ya, su temática preferida; la de exaltar en forma expresionista los valores humanos. En 1953 realizó tres exposiciones; dos en la capital de la República y otra en Mérida, Yucatán. En 1954 exhibió en la Unión Panamericana de Washington, D. C., y un año más tarde, en la Galería Edouard Loeb, de París. Desde esa fecha, ha realizado más de treinta exposiciones individuales en los siguientes lugares: La Habana, Nueva York, Washington, París, Lima, Caracas, Buenos Aires, Sao Paulo, Filadelfia, Los Angeles, Fort Worth, Roma, Austin, Santa Bárbara, Toronto, Milán, St. Louis, Bogotá y México. Ha participado en más de trescientas exposiciones colectivas tanto en México como en el extranjero. En 1959 obtuvo el Primer Premio Internacional de Dibujo en la V Bienal de Sao Paulo. En 1960 le fue otorgado el Segundo Premio en la II Anual Interamericana de Pintura, en Barranquilla, Colombia. En 1962 obtuvo el Primer Premio en la VII Mostra Internazionale di Bianco e Nero, celebrada en Lugano, Suiza. Ha ilustrado numerosos libros, entre los que destacan: *El mundo de Kafka y Cuevas,* publicado por Falcon Press (Filadelfia, 1959), y *Las citas,* de Manuel Moreno Jimeno. Ha escrito dos libros autobiográficos: *Recollections of Childhood* (Kanthos Press, Los Angeles, 1962) y *Cuevas por Cuevas* (Ed. Era. México, 1964). En 1966 fue invitado por el centro litográfico "Tamarrild" de Los Angeles, para desarrollar una serie de obras gráficas. Su pintura ha sido estudiada en las mejores monografías de arte, principalmente en los libros de Justino Fernández, Luis Cardoza y Aragón e Ida Rodríguez, de México; *Artistes de ce temps,* con textos de Jean Cassou y Philippe Soupault, editado en Francia y en *Los cuatro monstruos cardinales,* de la crítica Marta Traba (Ed. Era. México, 1965).

DONIS ROBERTO

Nació en San Luis Potosí en 1934. Durante tres años estudió en la Escuela de Pintura y Escultura "La Esmeralda" dependiente de la Secretaría de Educación Pública. Su pintura, de fuerte vigor expresivo, en la tendencia realista, fue modificándose, hasta alcanzar una síntesis temática, cuanto formal, que lo condujo, a una abstracción expresiva e inmanente de los estados de ánimo. Su obra obedece a una rígida construcción en la que abundan los conceptos subjetivos que hacen patente, a la materia con sus calidades y texturas como mundos desconocidos en los que hay riqueza de imágenes poéticas. Donis ha realizado nueve exposiciones individuales: siete en México, una en Nueva York, y una en París. Ha participado en multitud de exposiciones colectivas, de las que sobresalen, las siguientes: III Bienal de Barcelona, I, II, III y IV Bienales de Artistas Jóvenes de París; y otras celebradas en Japón, Rusia, Estados Unidos, Cuba y Francia. En 1965, en el Concurso Latinoamericano de Grabado, que se efectuó en la Casa de las Américas de La Habana, Cuba, obtuvo una Mención Honorífica.

ECHEVERRIA ENRIQUE

Nació en la ciudad de México en 1923. Estudió dibujo y pintura en el taller del pintor español Arturo Souto. A esa clase asistió de 1943 a 1946, alternándola con las lecciones que recibía en la Escuela de Pintura y Escultura "La Esmeralda". Obtuvo una beca del Gobierno de España para estudiar un año en Madrid. Viajó extensamente por el resto de Europa y el norte de Africa. Desde 1952 participa en exposiciones colectivas y realizó, además, varias individuales de importancia y éxitos críticos. En 1955 presentó una muestra personal de su obra en la Unión Panamericana de Washington, D. C. A partir de esa fecha, dueño de una técnica segura y con su voz perfectamente definida, ha exhibido sus creaciones en: Houston, Chicago, Washington, Bruselas, Caracas, Fort Worth, Dallas, Nueva Orleans, París y México. En 1964, en la Galería de Arte Mexicano, presentó un numeroso conjunto de óleos que lo pusieron en un sitio de relieve dentro de la plástica joven del país.

ESQUEDA XAVIER

Nació en la ciudad de México en 1943. Ha pintado desde niño en forma autodidacta. Expuso por primera vez a los catorce años de edad en el Seminario del Arte, del Distrito Federal. Hizo estudios irregulares en el Taller Libre de Cerámica del maestro Juan Soriano. Ha participado en exposiciones colectivas, tanto en México como en los Estados Unidos. En ese país, pertenece a los artistas de la Byron Gallery y a The Contemporaries Gallery; ambas de Nueva York. En una de las exposiciones efectuadas en la última galería anotada, sus obras fueron colgadas junto a las de Raushenberg, Marisol Escobar, Jasper Johnes y Joseph Cornell. En México lo representa la Galería de Antonio Souza en donde expone anualmente. En esa Galería, en 1965, montó una muestra de óleos, collages y cajas cinéticas; esta exposición fue presentada por Alfonso de Neuvillate. En el otoño de 1965 fue invitado por Darmouth College en calidad de artista en residencia; ahí exhibió sus obras y, además, dictó conferencias sobre el arte mexicano de vanguardia.

FELGUEREZ MANUEL

Nació en Zacatecas, Zacatecas, en 1928. Realizó sus estudios en París con el escultor Ossip Zadkine. Alterna la escultura mural con la pintura.

Ha realizado diez exposiciones individuales en México (Instituto Francés de la América Latina, Galería de Antonio Souza, Galería de Juan Martín y Galería de la Casa del Lago); en los Estados Unidos (Unión Panamericana de Washington, D. C.); en París y en Lima. Dentro de las exposiciones colectivas en las que ha participado, deben mencionarse especialmente, la I Bienal de Jóvenes de París (1959); Bienal de Tokio (1961); VI Bienal de Sao Paulo (1961); III Bienal de Jóvenes de París (1963); ese año obtiene el Primer Premio en la Casa de México; II Salón Interamericano, Bogotá, Colombia (1961) en donde obtiene una Mención Especial. Ha realizado los siguientes murales en hierro forjado: "Mural de Hierro" en el Cine Diana, en 1962; en el Banco de Fomento Cooperativo en 1962; en el Club Deportivo Bahía, el mural titulado "Canto al Océano", en 1963; en la Cámara de Industriales (CONCAMIN) un biombo de hierro para las oficinas en 1964; además de otros para casas particulares de la ciudad de México. También en 1964 realizó dos celosías para el nuevo Museo de Antrología e Historia de Chapultepec. En las dos Bienales de Escultura celebradas en México, en 1962 y en 1964, ha obtenido importantes premios. Durante este año expondrá un número elevado de óleos en la nueva Galería de Juan Martín.

FRIEDEBERG PEDRO

Nació en Florencia, Italia, en 1937. Es mexicano desde su residencia en 1940. Hizo estudios de Arquitectura en la Universidad Iberoamericana de México. Es un pintor autodidacta. Ultimamente se ha dedicado también a la escultura fantástica, concibiendo objetos útiles e inútiles, esculturas funcionales y muebles escultóricos. En 1959 realizó su primera exposición individual en la Galería Diana. En 1960 exhibe sus obras en la Galería Proteo. En 1961 es representado por Antonio Souza y es en esa Galería en donde ha exhibido en cuatro ocasiones. También ha efectuado exposiciones individuales en Nueva York, en París, en Lisboa, en Munich, en Washington, D. C., en Chicago, en Baltimore, en Dusseldorf, en Hannover y en Berlín. Artículos sobre su obra, críticas y reproducciones han aparecido en las siguientes revistas y periódicos: Time, Horizon, Motive, Esquire, Art News, Show, Life, Architecture Fantastique, Die Kunst und das Schone Heim, El Rehilete, México en la Cultura y El Corno Emplumado. Su obra ha sido estudiada y analizada en los siguientes libros: *Arte contemporáneo*, de Ida Rodríguez; *Art and architecture in Latin America*, de Paul Damaz; *Kindler malerei lexicon* y en *cuatro actitudes ensimismadas*, de Alfonso de Neuvillate.

GARCIA OCEJO JOSE

Nació en Córdoba, Veracruz, en 1928. De 1946 a 1950 estudió en la Escuela de Arquitectura de la Universidad Nacional Autónoma de México. En 1948 realizó sus primeros retratos e hizo intentos en la pintura mural. Frecuentó el estudio de Diego Rivera, quien lo encomió como dibujante. En 1950 abandonó la carrera de arquitectura y obtuvo una beca del Instituto de Cultura Hispánica. Residió en Madrid. Ahí pintó murales en la Ciudad Universitaria. Obtuvo del Instituto mencionado un Diploma y Beca Ad-Honorem. Ha realizado siete exposiciones individuales en los siguientes lugares: Sociedad de Arquitectos; Galería Diana; Galería Proteo; Instituto Hispánico de México; Galería de Bellas Artes de Tenerife (Africa Española); Instituto Mexicano-Norteamericano de Monterrey y Guadalajara. En

1964 estudió en Salzburgo, Austria, en la "Sommer Academie", fundada y dirigida por Oscar Kokoschka; obtiene diploma. En marzo de este año expuso sus óleos y dibujos en el Museo del Palacio de Bellas Artes de México.

GARCIA PONCE FERNANDO

Nació en Mérida, Yucatán, en 1933. Estudió arquitectura en la Escuela dependiente de la Universidad Nacional Autónoma de México y pintura en el taller del maestro Enrique Climent. Desde 1956 hasta la fecha realiza, periódicamente, viajes de estudio a Europa. Ha efectuado dos exposiciones individuales en la Galería de Arte Mexicano (1959 y 1961), una en la Galería de Juan Martín (1964) y otra más en la Galería de la Casa del Lago (1964). Ha participado en numerosas colectivas, siendo las de mayor importancia, las siguientes: 1959, Salón Nacional de Pintura, en el que obtuvo Mención Honorífica. 1960, Pintores y Grabadores de Yucatán. 1961 y 1965, Bienal de Jóvenes de París. 1965, exposición para artistas jóvenes celebrada en el Museo de Arte Moderno de México (Salón ESSO), en esta muestra ganó el Primer Premio de Pintura.

GIRONELLA ALBERTO

Nació en la ciudad de México en 1929. Hizo sus estudios en la Facultad de Filosofía y Letras de la Universidad Nacional Autónoma de México. Es un pintor autodidacta. Fundó con otros artistas la ya desaparecida Galería Prisse, en la cual expuso en 1952 y en 1953. Ese año exhibió también en la Galería "El Gallo Pitagórico" de la ciudad de Guanajuato. Ha realizado ocho exposiciones personales en México, Washington y París. Además, sus obras han participado en multitud de exposiciones colectivas celebradas en México, Estados Unidos, Francia, Japón, Italia, Brasil, Venezuela y Argentina. En 1959 obtuvo uno de los Primeros Premios en la I Bienal de Jóvenes de París. En 1963 y en 1964 expuso en la Galería de Juan Martín dos muestras de sus pinturas-collages-ensambles, de temas específicos: "Festín en Palacio" y "El Obrador de Francisco Lezcano", respectivamente. En 1964 apareció la monografía titulada *Gironella,* por Edouard Jaguer (Editorial Era). Actualmente reside en París, en donde tiene compromisos para exponer sus obras en varias muestras individuales.

HERNANDEZ DELGADILLO JOSE

Nació en Tepeapulco, Estado de Hidalgo, en 1927. Se radicó en México desde 1945 y realizó estudios de pintura y dibujo con el maestro Antonio Navarrete Tejero. En 1945 hizo su primera exposición individual que comprendía cuarenta y cinco obras, entre óleos y dibujos. En 1955 estudió en un taller de arquitectura y en 1957 estudió la técnica de la pintura mural en la Escuela de Pintura y Escultura "La Esmeralda". Producto de estos estudios lo es el mural que pintó en la Escuela Belisario Domínguez con el tema de la Educación Indígena; es un mural de 8.00 x 3.50 metros. En 1958 hizo una serie de relieves para la Ciudad Deportiva de México. En 1960 fue uno de los colaboradores en el proyecto y la ejecución de la VIII Feria Mexicana del Libro. En 1960 resultó premiado con una Mención Honorífica, por su cuadro titulado "Mi Tiempo", en la II Bienal Interamericana de Pintura y Escultura, celebrada en el Palacio de Bellas Artes de México. En 1961, fue uno de los artistas mexicanos seleccionados para la Bienal de Jóvenes de París y ahí obtuvo un Primer Premio por su cuadro denominado "Hombres". En 1964 obtuvo, asimismo, un Premio-Adquisición en el Salón Anual de Pintura efectuado en el Salón de la Plástica Mexicana.

HURTADO RODOLFO

Nació en la ciudad de Méxicoen 1940. Empezó a pintar desde su infancia en forma autodidacta y en 1962 obtuvo el Primer Premio de Pintura en el Tercer Salón Estudiantil de la Universidad Nacional Autónoma de México, en donde fueron jurados, entre otros, Rufino Tamayo y Matías Goeritz. En 1963 participó en una exposición colectiva celebrada en la ciudad de Bruselas y ahí llegó a obtener una importante Mención Honorífica. Actualmente es maestro de pintura en varias Instituciones. En 1965 realizó su primera exposición individual en la prestigiada Galería de Antonio Souza, exposición que fue presentada por el pintor José Luis Cuevas. Hurtado expondrá en la Galería de la Unión Panamericana de Washington, D. C., en 1966.

LOPEZ LOZA LUIS

Nació en la ciudad de México en 1939. Estudió pintura, grabado y escultura en el Centro Superior de Artes Aplicadas del Distrito Federal, y en el Pratt Graffic Center de los Estados Unidos. También acudió durante algún tiempo al Taller de Cerámica del maestro Juan Soriano y, asimismo, estudió grabado con Carlos Alvarado Lang e Isidoro Ocampo. Ha realizado diez exposiciones individuales en la Galería de Artes Visuales, en la Galería México, en la Galería Proteo, en la Galería de la Universidad y en la Galería de Antonio Souza de México, D. F. Ha efectuado exposiciones también personales en Southampton University, Jewish Museum (Nueva York); Chicago Art Center, Pan American Gallery de Washington, D. C., Phoenix Museum, Martha Jackson Gallery (Nueva York) de los Estados Unidos; en Sao Paulo y en el Museo de Arte Moderno de Colombia.

MARTINEZ RICARDO

Nació en la ciudad de México en 1918. En 1927 se trasladó con su familia a los Estados Unidos. En 1930 retornó a México y estudió en el taller de su hermano Oliverio Martínez de Hoyos. Sin embargo, puede considerársele un artista autodidacta, que ha dibujado desde su más temprana infancia. En 1942 participó en una exposición colectiva, de pintores mexicanos, que se instaló en Guadalajara, Jalisco; alternando sus obras junto con las de Orozco y Rivera. Ha realizado a partir de esa fecha, ocho exposiciones personales en la Galería de Arte Mexicano (la última en 1964). En 1958 fue, como artista huésped, a la Bienal de Venecia. En 1960 la Galería de los Contemporáneos de Nueva York presentó una exposición personal del artista. En 1952 exhibió sus obras en el Carnegie International de Pittsburgh así como en las exposiciones internacionales de Mainichi, Japón. Actualmente sus obras se encuentran en las muestras siguientes: "Moods of Ligths" y

"Mother and Child in Modern Art" que recorren los Estados Unidos. En 1961 y en 1964 fueron expuestas las obras de este gran artista en la Galería de Los Contemporáneos con un creciente éxito de la crítica especializada. En 1963 fue el único pintor mexicano invitado a la Bienal de Sao Paulo; ahí obtuvo el Premio Mohino Santista. En los más importantes Museos y colecciones particulares de los Estados Unidos, de Europa y de México se encuentran las obras del pintor. Ha participado en más de doscientas exposiciones colectivas, tanto en México como en el extranjero. También ha ilustrado libros, entre los que deben mencionarse *Muerte sin fin,* de José Gorostiza y *Junta de sombras,* de Alfonso Reyes. En 1965, en la Colección de Arte, N° 16, de la Universidad Nacional Autónoma de México apareció la monografía *Ricardo Martínez* escrita por el poeta Rubén Bonifaz Nuño.

MAKA

Nació en París, en 1925. Hija de padre ruso-francés y madre mexicana. Realizó algunos estudios con el maestro Manuel Rodríguez Lozano pero puede considerársele una pintora autodidacta. Ha efectuado trece exposiciones individuales; la primera en 1955 en la Galería Excélsior y la última en 1965 en el Salón de la Plástica Mexicana. Destacan, dentro de ese conjunto de exhibiciones individuales, las efectuadas en Caracas, Venezuela, en 1958; en Forth Worth, E. U. A., en 1960; en Nueva York, también en 1960 y las que celebró en la Galería Souza en 1962; y en la Galería Juan Martín en 1963 y 1964. Su obra ha sido seleccionada para las muestras de pintura mexicana que se han presentado en Tel-Aviv, Arizona, St. Louis, Los Angeles, Nueva York y París. Su pintura, asimismo, ha sido estudiada en los siguientes libros: *El arte contemporáneo,* de Ida Rodríguez y en *El expresionismo mexicano,* de Margarita Nelken.

MESSEGUER BENITO

Nació en Tarragona, España, en 1930. Es mexicano desde 1950. De 1946 a 1951 estudió en la Escuela de Pintura y Escultura "La Esmeralda", dependiente de la Secretaría de Educación Pública. Durante sus estudios mereció una de las becas concedidas por la escuela. También se le otorgó una beca en el taller de integración plástica. Se dio a conocer en 1956 en la Exposición de Nuevos Valores del Salón de la Plástica Mexicana en donde ganó el Primer Premio. En 1957 vuelve a obtener el Primer Premio en ese concurso. A partir de esa fecha, exhibe colectivamente en exposiciones como El Primer Salón Nacional de Pintura (1959); la Segunda Bienal Interamericana de México (1960); la Bienal de Tokio (1961); y en la Bienal de Jóvenes de París (1965). Ha obtenido importantes premios como la Mención Honorífica en el Certamen de Honor a la Madre en la Casa del Arquitecto (1959); Mención Honorífica en el Primer Salón Nacional de Pintura (1959); Medalla de Oro en la exposición de maestros de Artes Plásticas (1961); y Segundo Premio y Medalla de Plata en el II Salón Nacional del Paisaje (1961). Ha realizado murales en el Hotel Casino de la Selva, de Cuernavaca, Morelos; en el Auditorio Narciso Bassols de la Escuela de Economía de la Ciudad Universitaria y tiene en proceso un mural en el cubo de la escalera del Instituto Mexicano de la Audición y el Lenguaje. Es profesor en la Escuela de Pintura "La Esmeralda" y en la Escuela para Estudiantes Extranjeros de la Universidad Nacional.

MORENO CAPDEVILA FRANCISCO

Nació en Barcelona, España, en 1926. Reside en México desde 1939. Estudió pintura en la Escuela de Iniciación Artística Nº 1 y grabado en la Escuela Artes del Libro; ambas de México. Ha participado en las exposiciones siguientes de grabado: "Biblioteca del Congreso de Washington" (1953-1954-1955); la "Xylon", en Yugoslavia (1956); en la Bienal de Tokio (1957); en el Museo Galliera (1958); en la Bienal Interamericana de México (1958-1960); en la Muestra Internacional de Lugano, Suiza (1960) y en muchas exhibiciones representativas del grabado mexicano en Japón, Francia, Italia, Polonia y Latinoamérica. Ha sido premiado en los Salones de Grabado en 1957 y 1959. Obtuvo una Mención Honorífica en la Bienal Interamericana de México en 1960. En 1962 presentó sus primeros trabajos pictóricos en el concurso anual de pintura del Salón de la Plástica Mexicana. Ahí obtuvo el Premio de Adquisición por su obra titulada "La Víctima". En 1963 expuso individualmente un numeroso conjunto de óleos, en el Salón de la Plástica Mexicana y en 1964 volvió a exponer sus trabajos en la Galería Mer-Kup. Ese año realizó un mural sobre "La Destrucción de Tenochtitlán" en el Museo de la ciudad de México.

NIETO RODOLFO

Nació en Oaxaca, Oaxaca, en 1937. De los diecisiete a los diecinueve años de edad estudió en la Escuela de Pintura y Escultura "La Esmeralda". En 1961 se trasladó a Francia. Desde esa fecha reside en París. En 1961 efectuó una muestra individual de sus obras en la famosa Galería de Francia (que es la misma Galería que representa a Rufino Tamayo). En 1962 exhibe personalmente en Oslo. Ese año participa en el Salón de Mayo en París. En 1963 participa en la III Bienal de Jóvenes de París y ahí obtiene uno de los Primeros Premios. En 1964 y 1965 vuelve a exponer en la Galería de Francia. En 1965 exhibe un conjunto de acuarelas y gouaches en la Galería de Juan Martín, de México. Ha participado en varias colectivas celebradas en Europa. Ha ilustrado la *Zoología fantástica,* de Borges, editada por Gallimard.

PELAEZ ANTONIO

Nació en Llanes, Asturias, España, en 1921. Estudió en el Instituto Pérez Galdós de Madrid. Llegó a México en 1936 en donde vivía su padre como residente. En 1937 adoptó la nacionalidad mexicana. Estudió en la Escuela de Pintura y Escultura "La Esmeralda". En 1949 hizo un largo viaje por Italia, Grecia y Egipto. En 1952, a su regreso a México, hizo su primera exposición individual en la Galería de "Arte Contemporáneo", exhibición que presentó Frida Kalho. Ha expuesto individualmente en la Galería de Arte Mexicana en 1956 y 1960; en el Instituto Francés de América Latina en 1960; en la Universidad de Veracruz en 1961. En París ha expuesto individualmente en la Galería de Edouard Loeb en 1959 y 1964. En España expuso una muestra de sus pinturas en la Sala de Santa Catalina del Ateneo de Madrid. Su obra ha estado en exposiciones colectivas celebradas en los Estados Unidos, Europa y México. En 1966 presentará sus trabajos en la Byron Gallery de Nueva York. En 1956 apareció el libro titulado *21 mujeres de México* con textos de Alfonso Reyes, Carlos Chávez, Diego Rivera, Rodolfo Usigli, Octavio Paz y Carlos Pellicer; ilustrado por el artista. Artículos así como reproducciones de su obra han aparecido en las siguientes revistas y en periódicos: México en la Cultura, Bellas Artes, Hoy (México); Cuadernos Americanos (Argentina); Time, Pictures on Exhibit (Estados Unidos); ABC (España); Cahiers du Musée de Poche, Prisme des Arts, Chef d'Oeuvre de l'Art (Francia); The Arts Review (Londres).

RAMIREZ GABRIEL

Nació en Mérida, Yucatán, en 1938. Es autodidacta. Empezó a pintar profesionalmente en 1959. En 1965 expuso individualmente en la Galería de Juan Martín. Ese mismo año, fue seleccionado para participar en la Bienal de Jóvenes de París. Su forma de expresión lo liga espiritualmente con el grupo COBRA, aunque él, introduzca en sus realizaciones, un espíritu de un barroquismo exacerbado. Sus obras son casi musicales por la gama cromática que emplea. En su exposición recibió una crítica elogiosa puesto que ahí se apuntaban las bases de un futuro prometedor.

RAMOS PRIDA FERNANDO

Nació en la ciudad de México en 1937. Estudió en la Escuela de Pintura y Escultura "La Esmeralda" y en la Academia de San Carlos. A los dos años abandonó las disciplinas académicas para buscar medios de expresión que armonizaran más con su personalidad inquieta. En 1958 expone en la Galería de Artes Visuales. Ese mismo año participa en la Bienal de Acuarela de la ciudad de Filadelfia, Estados Unidos. En 1965 expone individualmente en la Galería de Arte Mexicano un numeroso conjunto de óleos, acuarelas y dibujos con gran éxito crítico. En 1965, su obra es seleccionada para la Bienal de Jóvenes de París.

ROJO VICENTE

Nació en Barcelona, España, en 1932. Vive en México desde 1949. Estudió pintura con Arturo Souto y tipografía con Miguel Prieto. Ha realizado viajes de estudio por Europa en 1953, 1955, 1960 y 1964. Ha expuesto individualmente en México en 1958, 1959 y 1961; en Miami en 1961; nuevamente en la ciudad de México en 1962 y 1964; en Madrid y en Barcelona, España, en 1964. En 1965 realizó simultáneamente, dos exposiciones, una en la Galería de Juan Martín y otra, de Iconos, Mitos y Geometrías en la Galería de la Casa del Lago de la Universidad Nacional Autónoma de México. Ha participado en multitud de muestras colectivas, de las que sobresalen, las siguientes: 1958, Musée d'Art Moderne de la Ville de París; 1959, Primer Salón Nacional de Pintura en el Palacio de Bellas Artes de México; 1961, Bienal de Sao Paulo; 1961, Bienal de Tokio; 1964, Exposición del Dibujo Mexicano en Bellas Artes, México; 1965, Contemporary Mexican Art, Phoenix Art Museum, Estados Unidos; 1965, Bienal de Jóvenes de París. Fue director artístico del Suplemento "México en la Cultura" y actualmente es Director artístico del suplemento cultural de la revista Siempre: "La Cultura en México".

SANCHEZ CASTAÑEDA PILAR

Nació en la ciudad de México en 1941. Tomó clases de pintura con profesores particulares de 1958 a 1960. Desde 1961 a la fecha es alumna en la Escuela de Artes Plásticas del maestro Antonio Rodríguez Luna. Ha participado en colectivas, tanto en México como en el extranjero. En 1962 obtiene el Premio Exposición del Concurso de Nuevos Valores del Salón de la Plástica Mexicana. En 1963 gana el Premio-Adquisición del Instituto Nacional de Bellas Artes para el Museo de Arte Moderno en la muestra realizada como consecuencia del premio anteriormente mencionado. Es aceptada como miembro del Salón de la Plástica Mexicana. En 1964 obtiene el Primer Premio de Pintura en la exposición de la Escuela Nacional de Artes Plásticas. Ese año obtiene también el Primer Premio de Pintura en una exposición colectiva efectuada en Guadalajara, Jalisco. Recibe el Premio de la Prensa en el Salón de Pintura 1964 que se efectuó en Chihuahua, Chihuahua. Es maestra de Pintura del tercer año de Artes Plásticas de la Universidad Iberoamericana. En 1966 realizó una muestra de pintura en el Salón de la Plástica Mexicana.

SORIANO JUAN

Nació en Guadalajara, Jalisco, en 1920. A la edad de catorce años realizó su primera exposición en el Museo de Guadalajara, Jalisco. Influyó en la orientación pictórica del artista, el singular pintor Jesús Reyes Ferreira. En 1935 se traslada a la ciudad de México y un año después, participa en la exposición organizada por la Liga de Artistas y Escritores Revolucionarios (LEAR). Posteriormente, expone sus obras en la Galería de la Universidad (1941); en la Galería de Arte Mexicano (1945); y en el Salón de la Plástica Mexicana, una colección de retratos (1948). En 1951 vuelve a exhibir en la Galería de Arte Mexicano, esta vez un numeroso conjunto de óleos, acuarelas y dibujos, que lo situaron como uno de los más vigorosos creadores de México. En 1951 hace un viaje de estudios por Italia. En 1954 expone en Roma y al año siguiente, presenta una muestra de sus trabajos en la Galería de Arte Mexicano. En la Galería de Antonio Souza expone en 1957 un conjunto de óleos y cerámicas, modalidad ésta, que siempre le había atraído. Ha participado en colectivas, como la Exposición Internacional de San Francisco (1938); y otras de interés que se han celebrado en el Museo de Arte Moderno de Nueva York, en el Museo de Filadelfia, en La Habana, en París, en Londres, en Estocolmo, en Toronto y en Tokio. En 1959, el Museo de Arte Moderno del Palacio de Bellas Artes de México presentó una muestra retrospectiva de Soriano que abarcaba sus veinticinco años de pintor; exposición organizada en conmemoración del XXV Aniversario del Palacio de Bellas Artes. Es maestro de cerámica, grabador y escenógrafo. Sus trabajos para el teatro fueron para el grupo denominado "Poesía en Voz Alta", y demostraron las ambiciosas y sugerentes combinaciones plásticas que este pintor logró para la escena nacional.

TOLEDO FRANCISCO

Nació en Juchitán, Oaxaca, en 1937. Es un pintor autodidacta. Se dio a conocer con una exposición que celebró en la Galería de Antonio Souza en 1959. En 1960 expuso en el Fort Worth Art Center. Ese año viajó a Europa y exhibió en París en la Galería Flinker; en el Museo Nacional de

Oslo; en la Galería Hamilton de Londres y después mostró sus trabajos en Nueva York, en la Galería Saidenberg. A partir de esa fecha exhibe con frecuencia en París, Berna, Suiza, Hamburgo, Londres y Nueva York. Ha efectuado un total de veinte exposiciones individuales, incluso en la India y en Japón. En 1963, a raíz de la exposición que tuvo en la Galería Flinker de París, André Pierre de Mandiargues, escribió en la revista Siglo XX un largo poema a propósito de su obra. El Ministro de Cultura de Francia, André Malraux se cuenta entre los coleccionistas de Toledo. Sus pinturas se encuentran en el Museo de Arte Moderno de París, en el Museo de Arte Moderno de Nueva York y en colecciones particulares de los Estados Unidos, Europa, Asia y México. En 1965 exhibió una extensa muestra de sus creaciones recientes (óleos, gouaches, acuarelas) en la Galería de Antonio Souza; en donde volverá a exponer en noviembre de 1966.

URUETA CORDELIA

Nació en Coyoacán, México, en 1908. Hija del distinguido revolucionario, orador y hombre de letras, Lic. Jesús Urueta. El Dr. Atl, al ver sus dibujos infantiles la alentó para que siguiera por el camino del arte. En 1925 asistió durante algún tiempo a la Escuela de Pintura al Aire Libre de Churubusco, dirigida por Alfredo Ramos Martínez. En 1930, en su estadía en Nueva York, en la Galería de Alma Reed llamada "Delphics Studios", conoció a Orozco y a Tamayo. Sus dibujos fueron colgados en una muestra colectiva de pintores mexicanos que celebró dicha galería. En 1932 fue profesora de dibujo en Escuelas Primarias de la ciudad de México. De 1938 hasta 1943 viajó por Europa, comisionada por la Secretaría de Relaciones Exteriores. Al regreso a su patria, se decidió a pintar profesionalmente. Su primera exposición individual la realizó en 1950 en el Salón de la Plástica Mexicana auspiciada por Margarita Nelken. En 1952 expuso sus obras en París en la Galería André Weill. Desde esa fecha su obra ha sido enviada en las exposiciones mexicanas que se han presentado en Londres, París, Tokio, América del Sur, etcétera. En 1955 fue nombrada Productora de Arte para el Instituto Nacional de Bellas Artes. En 1957 volvió a exhibir en el Salón de la Plástica Mexicana. En 1960 presentó una muestra en la Galería Proteo. En la Bienal de México, celebrada en 1960, obtuvo una Mención de Honor. En 1961 expuso individualmente en la Galería de Jacobo Glantz. En 1962 obtuvo una Mención Honorífica en la VI Bienal Internacional de Sao Paulo. En 1965 exhibió en el Salón de la Plástica Mexicana. Su obra ha sido estudiada en el libro *cuatro actitudes ensimismadas*, de Alfonso de Neuvillate.

URRUSTI LUCINDA

Nació en Melilla, Marruecos Español, en 1929. En México estudió en la Escuela de Pintura y Escultura "La Esmeralda". También recibió lecciones del maestro Ricardo Martínez. En 1957 obtuvo el Primer Premio en el Salón Anual denominado de Nuevos Valores del Salón de la Plástica Mexicana, premio que le dio el derecho de exponer individualmente al año siguiente. En 1959 exhibió por segunda vez, individualmente, en la Galería Diana. En 1960 participó en la Segunda Bienal Interamericana de Pintura y Escultura de México y en la cual, ganó una Mención Honorífica. Ha participado en multitud de muestras colectivas de la pintura mexicana, celebradas, tanto en la República como en el extranjero. La pintura de Lucinda Urrusti siempre ha llamado la atención por la finura de sus texturas y por su rico color que crea situaciones de belleza insólita. Es, en verdad, una de las más sutiles artistas de la pintura de hoy.

VLADY

Nació en Leningrado, Rusia, en 1920. De 1936 a 1939 vivió en París. Posteriormente se trasladó a La Martinica, Santo Domingo, en donde vivió dos años. En 1941 llegó a México y aquí adquirió la nacionalidad mexicana. Es un pintor autodidacta. Su primera exposición individual la efectuó en 1947 en la Galería del Instituto Francés de la América Latina; después realizó exposiciones personales en la Librería Juárez (1951), en la Galería Prisse (1953) y en la Galería Proteo (1956 y 1958). Ha realizado varios murales, en la ciudad de México y uno de mosaicos en el Hotel Cassino Hornos de Acapulco, Guerrero. En 1963 presentó un buen conjunto de óleos y dibujos en la Galería Misrachi. En 1965 expuso litografías en el Salón de la Plástica Mexicana.

Human life and art —that is, history— never stand still, since they are spiritual forces which of necessity must develop and find expression in one way or another. Man, in order to be man, must necessarily humanize the world, and one of the ways to do so on the highest level is through poetry. But let us understand what this classic term means, a term that is generally used very vaguely. Poetry comes from the Greek *poiesis,* which signifies creation, something quite different from *praxis,* or practice, which is another way of making human the world of brutal reality.

The poet, the artist, creates or recreates the world in his fashion; and in accordance with the possibilities of his sensibility, his intellect, and his imagination, he expresses in beauty his visions, his desires, his ideals and beliefs. If there were no artists the world would be blind, deaf and dumb; it would not exist as *world,* as the native habitation of man.

In expressing himself, the artist makes us see, through his works, new and beautiful aspects of reality, which are uncovered by the emotion that these provoke. By revealing his own being he leads to the special vision he wishes to communicate. It falls to us, the public, to listen to the artists and understand them, if we have the capacity to place ourselves in relation to them; or, to say it another way, if by some miracle there is concurrence between them and us.

History is ever-changing, as we well know, and this is its greatest quality. Absolutely static things are not of this world. Circumstances, interests, attitudes, ways of feeling, understanding and imagining reality and the manner of expressing oneself are several and different, according to the times and to one's temperament. In human matters there are no regressions or advances, and in art the present and the artists' visions become objective through their work. The artists must look back into the past so as to know where they are today and, thus, inevitably strain toward the future from the present; because human existence is a projection into the future.

It is natural that new generations should rebel against their predecessors. But if they deny them they are lost. To hate them and yet to build their own poetic visions is to save themselves, since then they exist by their own efforts. Every revolution must, in one way or another, absorb, reinterpret from its new points of view, both the near and the remote past, because otherwise it remains without history and without even a *raison d'etre,* without knowledge of what it has been, which is the worst thing that could happen to it since this makes revolutions sterile. On the other hand, to carry history on one's shoulder and to renew it, to enrich it with one's own visions and work is to make it fertile and to open new roads into the future.

Thus, in an ideal society, it is everyone's duty to try to understand the new creators of art, which can lead to an enjoyment of their work and to one's own enrichment with the beauty of vision that these artist set before us. But, for their own good, it is also the duty of new artists to know and understand our common pasts, because to deny them is to deny themselves, to impoverish themselves. Human solidarity must exist and function from past to present and vice versa, since any other attitude is only a form of sclerotic self-limitation. Every great artist absorbs history in its entirety and takes a position before it and in it.

It seems fitting to consider two further questions. The first is that, in general, it is difficult to understand how the artistic expression of a dramatic, or tragic, vision of the world can be aesthetic. The difficulty here is that "what" is expressed is confused with "how" it is expressed. The artist may express whatever he wishes, as long as it is within the limits of art, because art is the game and this liberty is an inherent part of it. However black may be the vision of the world that an artist has, if he converts it into art, he transforms it —by the aesthetic emotion that it provokes— into pleasure and delight for himself and for others, without in doing so losing its dramatic and tragic character. There are works that appeal to us because we find pleasure in the *way* in which they are made, and which end by making us cry because of *what* they express.

The second question consists of understanding the possibilities of communication in abstract, or "non-objective", art. Because surely if works of art are created it is because of a personal need of expression, of communication, a need to communicate something to others. And undoubtedly the generically-named "abstract art" has possibilities of communicating emotions, states of mind, ideas of real or imagined worlds. But such expressions have a universal character; thus, if the expressions are of love, hate, sadness or joy, these concepts are localized only in t h e artist, without other historical or special contexts. The poet has elevated his state of mind, his ideas or his imagination to abstract concepts expressed in non-objective images —when not playing mere word-games, which are also indicative of personality— and from this a certain difficulty of communication arises for a spectator who is not forewarned or accustomed to drawing abstract concepts and images from reality. Abstract art ascends into the stratosphere of intellectual and spiritual perceptions, but within it, nevertheless, are lines, colors, textures, materials. . . and the artist who manipulates them, who on expressing himself lays his soul bare or makes his confession.

In short, all authentic art, whatever its nature may be, excites our emotion and our reflections, and ends by finding its place in history. The confusion is increased effectively by those whose attitude is consciously or unconsciously false, or so superficial that soon enough they become mere straw figures; but an expert eye and a sure intuition will know how to find where the grain is. A great deal is said today about the problems of current art, but it is the artists themselves who must find solutions for them in accordance with their individual natures, and separately take directions that are most suitable for each of them. Later, these will be problems of criticism and, in the end, of history. Those who aspire to direct art are only being prematurely vociferous, which is a contradiction. The problems of art are resolved in silence.

* * *

Mexico has a long tradition —at least twenty centuries— in the field of artistic creation and, with her great works, has contributed to universal history. Proof of this can be seen in the amount of these works that has reached us from the old indigenous world. The monuments of many cultures —Olmec, Mayan classic and post-classic periods, Mixtec, Zapotec, Teotihuacan, Toltec and Aztec— are eloquent indications of the greatness and creative capacity of the men in that remote past. In addition, we should not forget the exquisite ceramic work of Western Mexico; the mural paintings at Bonampak and at many other sites; the Mixtec, Mayan and Aztec codices; the jade, rock crystal and gold jewelry; the reliefs of the classic Mayas, some naturalistic, others completely abstract; the huge unequalled Aztec sculpture. There is no absence of even the most strictly geometrical abstract froms, as evidenced at Uxmal, Mitla and Teotihuacan; or of those freely expressive, as can be seen in numerous examples, even to the refined naturalistic beauty of the reliefs at Palenque. And as for a dramatic and tragic sense of existence, nothing surpasses the Aztec heads and other monumental sculptures of the Mexica world, among which the great *Coatlicue* is unrivalled.

No less magnificent is the legacy of New Spain. With the advent of Western art in the sixteenth century, there began a creative activity which built, with striking originality, the great monasteries of the mendicant orders in every corner of the country. The open chapels, the churches and cloisters were decorated with frescoes. The gilt altarpieces, with their accumulation of paintings, sculptures and carvings in a thousand forms, are marvels to behold, equal in every way to the best in Spain. Later, the cathedrals, the parish churches, chapels, private and government palaces, hospitals and schools were built, and the University was founded. The study of the sculpture of New Spain —in stone and in ornamented and gilded wood— still holds many surprises. Painting had its apogee in the seventeenth century; today we know that its best works are of high enough standard to be placed, without shame, alongside those of Europe, and that even the mildest and most decorative painting of the eighteenth century is attractive and full of very admirable qualities.

But if all this is of great interest and value, the Baroque and ultra-Baroque art of the XVII and XVIII centuries represent one of Mexico's greatest contributions to universal art. Nothing equals the richness a n d splendor of original monuments like the Mexico City Cathedral (sanctuary, tabernacle, ciborium); the churches of La Enseñanza and Tepotzotlan; the parish church of Santa Prisca in Taxco; the churches of Ocotlan in Tlaxcala, of Acatepec and Santa Maria Tonantzintla in Puebla, and in the capital of that state, the Rosary Chapel, the Cathedral and m a n y other palaces and monuments. But without searching afield, one can find in the Mexico City Cathedral —in its architecture and in the totality of its interior— a summarization of the history of the art of New Spain. Especially outstanding is the altarpiece of the Kings' Chapel, a marvel, a golden grotto, the starting point for all the splendid art of the ultra-Baroque, examples of which can be found in almost every city and town throughout the country.

We must also not forget the works of neoclassic art —some of which are truly first-class— such as the towers and dome of the Mexico City

Cathedral, the Palace of Mining, and the equestrian statue of Charles IV.

In the art of New Spain there are forms of geometric abstraction, such as all *mudejar* art and all classic figures; and there also appear the most extreme liberties of an expressionist nature in both ultra-Baroque art and popular Baroque.

Once Mexico had become an independent nation, academic Romantic art flourished. Its best achievements were in portraiture and, above all, in landscape painting, in which Velasco created a monumental historic vision of our country. Independent academic painting left a production full of enchantment and human knowledge. One must still appraise more justly the art of the XIX century, which, with all its obvious merits, has been undervalued simply because it dealt with the immediate past against which artists of the first half of our century have opportunely rebelled. But one of its exceptional artists has been salvaged —Posada— whose modern-feeling, expressionistic and critical work inspired the best of those who would come later.

It seems impossible —although perhaps everything is possible— to deny the significance and values of mural painting in o u r time, one of Mexico's greatest contributions to international art. The monumental works of Orozco, of which the frescoes in the Cabañas Institute at Guadalajara stand out among many; those of Rivera in the National School of Agriculture at Chapingo; those of Siqueiros and a few other painters, are examples of the best work of their genre in the XX century. A careful study of these works will enrich any artist who approaches them with a spirit open to understanding and sensitive of beauty.

It has been said before, and with obvious truth, that the first top-rank Mexican artist who rejected the art being created during the third decade of our century was Tamayo. And it was natural that this should occur, since his vision and temperament were distinct, and he directed his efforts along new roads to reaffirm his very unique personality. Although his art is, strictly speaking, abstract, it has never ceased to sink its roots in reality. For this reason, and because of his unmatchable qualities, he has placed himself on a level with the great contemporary artists. With Tamayo coincide some of the new concepts of painting that have reached the most recent generation; but in the works of this generation traces of other masters will also be found.

* * *

In swift sketches I have tried to evoke the history of Mexican art in order that an awareness of its values may serve as the antecedent of painting today and as an aesthetic field of reference of the same. All that formidable past gravitates, I believe, around the young artists, since in one way or another they carry it in spirit, and in them it should be an inducement to excel and not a depressing document of facts. T h e history of Mexican art cannot be viewed in isolation; it must be placed in relation to the universal currents of all epochs. In other words, artists must be steeped in history as far as possible.

The moment has now come to consider the content of the book that we have in our hands. The mass of works collected and presented here by the selective spirit of Alfonso de Neuvillate is a truly magnificent spectacle, thrilling to the point of touching our most sensitive fibres. A unique spectacle because, besides the artists being representative of the new currents in present-day Mexican painting, the reproductions of their work is accompanied by the text of a young critic who also belongs to the most up-to-date tastes and interests. Thus the book has overall unity and full historical value. Although every anthology is, perhaps, disappointing for some, one must remember that this is not a "dictionary" of painters —and even "dictionaries" are never complete— but a selection made by a critic sensitive of the art of his time. His success can be judged by merely glancing at the list of names and the catalogue of works reproduced. Not all who are artists have been included, but all who have been included are artists representative of the current moment.

In an assemblage of works like the one here presented, the presence of a painter of the category of Pedro Coronel and of an extraordinarily talented artist, José Luis Cuevas, gives high light to the collection, whose quality is authenticated by others like Cordelia Urueta, José Hernández Delgadillo, Ricardo Martínez, Benito Messeguer, Juan Soriano, Francisco Moreno Capdevila, Lilia Carrillo, Manuel Felguérrez, Fernando García Ponce, Alberto Gironella, Antonio Peláez, Vicente Rojo, Francisco Corzas, and Vlady. All of them, as well as those others who make up the thirty-three numbers in the catalogue, have produced works of widely varying importance and, in fact, as in any collective exhibition, two paintings are not sufficient to give a complete idea of an artist's poetic capacities. Nevertheless, one should accept objectively what the presented exhibition is —a collection that would do honor to any museum.

We are all well aware that present generations are interested in the universal position, and that they have rejected all regional picturesqueness as well as the great historical, religious and philosophical themes. It is a condition similar to the one that developed a century ago when Impressionism first sprang up, only that now the currents have multiplied.

In the present collection there is a group of works in which, in one way or another, human figures appear. The first to use them as the marrow of his expression was José Luis Cuevas. By contrast, Ricardo Martínez sticks to pure lines, in the classic sense. Francisco Corzas, Rafael Coronel and —in a more accentuated way that approaches tragedy— Francisco Moreno Capdevila express themselves in a dramatic form. But the works of José García Ocejo show a very different feeling, that of happy farce or dramatic nostalgia evoking the ancient western world. Pilar Sánchez Castañeda captures and expresses a certain sense of anecdote, while vigorous technique and the precise idea are masterfully handled by Vlady.

In another group of works, images taken from the objective world are diluted, fragmented or have become so spectral that only with great difficulty are they recognizable. In such a category belong the works of Pedro Coronel, in which a master of color has made use of this technique to intensify his meaning. In the paintings of Juan Soriano, forms and colors are fused into a unity to express character or concept. By the magic of her exquisite art, Lilia Carrillo has introduced human images or references which come together momentarily or drift apart as in a dream. The waggish genius of Alberto Gironella is rooted in Velázquez in order to produce the diametrical opposite, and in thus rejecting the master he achieves his own creations. José Hernández Delgadillo has polished his art and the images that he presents to such a degree that he is left with only a minimum of skillfully-manipulated elements, to which he gives monumental proportions. The two works of Pedro Cervantes presented here are dissimilar, both well executed, evoking distinct kinds of expression. Keeping to images of essential forms, Arnaldo Coen creates harmonies of color in which reality and fantasy become confused. Rodolfo Nieto achieves unusual effects with a few dabs of well-graduated color. With spontaneous grace and skill, Rodolfo Hurtado almost convinces with the childlike simplicity of his images, on the whole well conceived. In the works of Maka simplification becomes outline, but it is sufficient to evoke a reality of the poetic world from which her painting springs. Lucinda Urrusti relies on real images, but transforms them into richly textured poetry; and now they are changed into something else —they have become painting. Although their visions are quite different, Francisco Toledo and Luis López Loza show a similar "something" in t h e i r paintings— flat, delineated forms; imaginative color —but in the world of the former a dreamlike fantasy and absurdity prevail, while in the latter elements of the organic world converted into metaphors appear.

In a third group of works, abstract —or "non-objective"— painting triumphs now without circumspection, although some of the artists have, at one time or another, produced figurative art. Fernando García Ponce has the secret of constructive equilibrium not only in forms but in color, which appear together in harmonious unity producing well-rounded works. Not for having grace and lightness do t h e paintings of Cordelia Urueta lack strength, which comes from the surety with which she composes and from her skillful use of color. Manuel Felguérez is another master of composition, but he disguises forms with the violence of his brush and line. Antonio Peláez, who sometimes evokes astral worlds, has become a master in texture and color within a very precise limit, and within this limit appears the rough as well as the refined. Benito Messeguer's incursions into abstract painting fail to make one forget his inherent qualities when he includes human images, but these are so simplified that they become little more than abstract forms. Balanced and suggesting, the works of Gilberto Aceves Navarro present both coarse a n d delicate textures. Carlos Belaunzarán handles color, form and line with a sure and controlled talent, as attested by his works included here. Large masses and an easily-moving brush combine in the paintings of Enrique Echeverría, b u t the apparent spontaneity is guided by the intellect. The deceptively ingenuous lines of Fernando Ramos Prida —incisions upon blotches of color— have an ineffable grace, and he composes with a sure sensitivity. Gabriel Ramírez' art is violent and nervous, but the refinement of his lines and masses tell us that it is not a question of a desperate man but of an accomplished painter. At the opposite pole is Roberto Donis, a master of balance and moderation, who, with few elements, suggests whatever he pleases.

In a fourth and final group of works we find the most daring, which include those of Vicente Rojo. This artist has decided to break with all tradition, including his own, and to suggest something with the greatest economy of elements. His works border on "op art," either in their violent or other very delicate effects. The fantastic world of Pedro Friedeberg is expressed by means of his labyrinthine geometry which he builds patiently without allowing chance to ruin it. Like the art of Rojo, that of Friedeberg is close to "op art". And the last artist that we are to consider, Xavier Esqueda, combines —one is at a loss to understand how it ocurred to him— "op art," which is so intellectual, with images of the real world, causing a certain uneasiness; otherwise, when he paints stark reality he does so with perfection and strong dramatic accent.

The show has come to an end, but we are left with the pleasure and the euphoria of having gained an experience by drawing near to the most modern Mexican painting. Deliberation, balance, sincerity, the desire to create with newness and quality are all present in it, which is why it demands our serious attention. Headed in several directions, produced by men with personality, it is authentic art. Influences? Relationships with other current trends, with other artists? They could quite probably be discovered and localized, which would only tend to make the differences, the originalities shine more brilliantly. Today, Mexico has a new art —lusty, executed with responsibility and full of interest. According to a backwoods saying there are two ways of looking at painting— "one for those who like it and one for those who don't". The decision is left to history.

ACTUAL PAINTING: MEXICO 1966

It is difficult to present a panorama of the new aesthetics, of the new considerations in pictoric language, since there exist as many singular adventures as there are artists capable of embarking on them. On these chaotic roads into the unknown there are several factors which, immersed in formal values, envelope us in a frozen desert of thoughts. The new art has a specific power to fill us with terror, to suggest to us, to define us and to complete us in ontological processes in moments in which interpretations, of whatever kind they may be, are pretexts for understanding that series of intellectual or sentimental and even romantic worlds, which make up the work output of an artist. The union or communion of the critic with the work itself lies, however, in critical interpretation. In these encounters, pressured by emotion, one must penetrate into the silent, uncharted depths to a magical or everyday reality, which sublimates reason and at the same time offers us a creation. Logically it is a question of a phenomenon which molds those psychic situations that motivate artists.

The last three decades of this century have afforded the arts, especially painting, a series of radical changes, modifications and transformations in the traditional aesthetic concepts, in such an accelerated and unexpected way that art has been driven to a moment of tension in which it is difficult to foresee the uncertain future or the new directions, the new paths that will have to be followed after this long, eager, godless, hurried search for truth —since art always offers tentative solutions, abandoning sensations on the threshold of restlessness and disagreement.

In this thirst to investigate what the artist is capable of condensing in his work, an intellectual process has been created in which accident, which mixes discovery with the constructive mind, has played an important role within the aesthetic concept.

An endless number of movements, or attempts at movements, based on aesthetics have been conceived. These, in one way or another, have borrowed myriad anxieties and lessons from art and from the artist in their constant experimenting to find the one synthesis that could be the epilogue of all the roads of plastic expression. Thus, with an incredible vitality, there have appeared, evolved and died various tendencies with their contributions, solutions, margins of speculation, individualities, optical experiments, and styles redundant in concept and idea. But it has also been evident that certain results of this experimenting have failed in their attempts at originality because of the same creative anguish that made them appear on the terrible landscape of the historic frame.

All movements obeyed and still obey the imperious necessity that the artist possesses, forcing a subtle reproduction of his world, of his secret vision, and successfully catching what issues from the work itself.

The art of abstraction introduces all these elements and events, with the exception of the mentality that brings order out of chaos. It is never a game of fireworks; it introduces also the ephemeral chromatic worlds that consolidate forms, spatial rearrangement, and the breakdown of maxim and metaphor in creating.

In this concrete coming-together of theme, idea, form and situation is found the expressive variety of an apparent constructive facility; thus, abstract expressionism, blotch painting, smear painting, dripping, informalism, synthesism, action painting; and, lastly, within this compendium of elements making up worlds and images of the purest painting, it arrives at unrestrained anarchy, at the moment when painting ceases to express something concrete and lingers in the phantasmal implications of a universe caked with color, in which it begins and ends a whole attitude face to face with life, and, at the same time, with the ideas that give it its factor of individuality. It is the zero-hour of having to start anew, of setting out once again upon a path that leads to unravelling truth and reason, consistent with a world that is tending to eliminate the individual in order to make him partner to a miserable mechanization. One must take up an art stemming from the aesthetic of nothing, which zealously presents painting in such a manner, without it now having to mention either a language or a vocabulary.

In this terrain of the breakdown of art, of the denial of forms that traditionally have been the images of known things, in this anti-painting forms acquire a seductive or suggestive power. There bursts forth a richness of imagery —the inexhaustible veins of pure-art— the consequence, or result, of which is the redoubt of agonizing loneliness attained by the artist.

On the other hand, speculation on the various themes in painting has resulted in a fusion of many elements and concepts. The composite arts are the most vital introductions to everyday life.

The arts of assemblage and collage respectively lead one to sculpture —or to lost objets— and to a kind of living painting. Objects take on a new look, become revaluated on a basis of their primary essence, changing into radical, living elements of works of art. In junkyard, cast-off and paste-up art, forgotten objects are redeemed and one sees the relationships, the implications that these take on in the present. Victory for cruel, surprising and despicable reality over traditional beauty. Within artists who work in assemblage and collage there exists a truly cruel constructiveness, with them there begins a vital dialogue between the receiver —or viewer— and the artist; a dialogue that arises from the most generically dissimilar material elements.

A lesson that the futurists and cubists left the world, and which present-day painters employ to a definite end is: express your chaotic visions of a chaotic world, give aesthetic value to those objects rejected by the majority.

The cubists put stark reality into their paintings. On their canvases they pasted cut-outs from newspapers, familiar fragments of musical scores; effects that gave their works a power of suggestion, a realistic dimension and an atmosphere evocative of the pleasure of *joie de vivre*. Precisely because it had put in its paintings things that surrounded it, that school remained merely a searching for, an analyzing of, everyday objects. Apollinaire, a critic of cubism, noted: "From a visual point of view, works of art are the most vital product of any age. This energy imposes itself upon men, and for them it becomes the visual media of a new epoch. Thus, those men who mock the new painters are in fact mocking their own likeness, since future humanity will visualize present-day humanity according to the representations that the artists of the prevailing trend —that is to say, today's artists —will have left behind..."

On the other hand, in futurism, "The freedom of typographical forms, the introduction of new styles of printing, letters isolated and solitarily linked by suggestive rhythms, the architicture of the cities of the future; the integration of the visual and poetical worlds; creation of sculptural works by the poets; the idea of a new religion for modern man with his faith in a different future; these were the contribution of futurism's ethics..." (Ida Rodríguez).

These are, in synthesis, the sources of the later Dadaism and Surrealism. Artists like Kurt Schwitters and Marcel Duchamp produced works of sculpture in which the object had an importance of its own; found, recovered objects raised to an aesthetic category and dimension. For example, Schwitters' "Homage to Humanity" (which was a collection of trash) and Duchamp's "Prefabricated Sculptures."

Other arts hold together or disintegrate before a variety of emotional concepts. Generally, painting and sculpture are conceived in relation to architecture, in the same way that individuality will embellish other fields and other expressions.

The reaction against established values, irrespective of their type; the denial of forms accepted as beautiful; and the desire for ephemeral rather than lasting human values, have lead to the most extraordinary and reckless experiments: for example, the supernaturally and diabolically beautiful pictorial-musical-sculptural machines of artists like Schaffer and Tinguely.

There has also been created a type of popular art, whose merit —distinct from that of Dadaism (1916)— lies in attempting to introduce an artistic language that begins by using things and objects of a genuine idiosyncracy. Although Dadaism contained totally negative aspects, it did father Surrealism; surpassing the latter, pop art brings with it aspects of absolute, indubitable transcendence, since it includes everything that surrounds us —or everything that means something to us— now raised to an artistic level in its hard, cold, elemental and distracting beauty. Now one cannot forget that beauty exists in even those acts and things most disparate and common: things such as hamburgers, comic strips, modern furniture, etc.

Artists like Roy Lichtenstein; Claes Oldenburg; Tom Wesselman; James Rosenquist; Andy Warhol; Jasper Johnes and Rauschenberg have presented, sarcastically and bitingly, their concepts of art; they cheerfully offer the frozen beauty of the world that surrounds us, always with a black humor that covers the overwhelming anguish of the artist faced by moral values.

Optical art has gone ever further, since the use and abuse of highly complicated geometrical forms and its play of dizzily intoxicating designs of minute detail are the best proof that aesthetic values have reached a critical moment, and that a dramatic chaos is present in the psyche of these artists. In all of these negations of an art that fulfills sociological, historical and aesthetical ends, one encounters the basic question of the future of individualism, which creates an art —first, in order to satisfy a need for expression; and second, to confront its displacement of the ego —which is the work itself— with the determinate judgment of aesthetics and, finally, history.

I do not believe that art is in a dead-end street; just the opposite, I consider all the latest manifestations are part of the angry fight the artist wages in order to communicate, in forms not always clear, that volcanic flame called the need for expression, that path of languages which is a support for man's anguish, whose sole end he pursues and obtains in the search for new forms, for new artistic accents, and whose problem is to be the image of, for, and by man in our time.

I should not fail to mention, even though superficially, that movement as old as the world itself which carries human expression to a point of climax and catharsis. Neo-expressionism, or neo-humanism, possesses dynamics and intelligent progression in which spiritual forces, along with ideologies or events of dramatic life, are assimilated. This expression allows room for the richness of man's allusions in his deepest essence, and it leads toward subjectivity. Its themes, its ideas, its suggestions and its social, political and historical cristicisms —as well as the tragic testimony it encloses in its axiom— are those lonely moments of present-day alienation.

The history of painting would not exist, however, without the peculiar and dynamic accents of individual artists. Today's painters —those of 1966— although at certain moments they have been grouped together because of a similarity of ideas and ideals, have —motivated wholly and exclusively by their inner aesthetics— created intimacy. I have no faith in schools or academic systems that try to fabricate painters. I despise schools of painting because, although they provide a basis for expression, they prostitute free thought and intention.

I search for, discover, and try to interpret the hidden values within the intimacy of paintings. I look at the successful canvases, and I want to place myself at the very depth of the painter's idea, in order thus to see the drama, to feel the panic, the poetry, the purity, the need to bring together secret or half-discovered values on the work's surfaces. My poetic affinities unfold when they meet, are met by, subjective works, vigorous products of free processes in that concentration of an emotional world.

In short, I try to complement a work of art with a work of interpretation, whose voices and echoes speak of an individuality that knows how to bring to life a metaphorical world, one full of paradoxes and tacit enigmas in the phenomenon of creation.

Mexico has not remained behind with respect to startling changes in aesthetic styles and forms. Although it is quite true that those who followed Mexico's three great contemporary painters —Orozco, Rivera, and Siqueiros— believed rather naively that the only artistic expression remaining was a naturalist, superficial, and even folkloric realism; although it is also true that they destroyed an important, valuable movement by attempting —without talent— to follow their predecessors, but with this difference: that the "greats" were men of genius and their followers no more than artisans or second-rate workmen.

The first important artist who rejected the norms established by this whole school of painting was Rufino Tamayo who, not only exploring the conspicuous surface of what was Mexican but immersing and chanelling his manner of seeing and expressing things, arrived at the pictorial essence of an ancestral source; a cosmic source whose antecedents were in the ancient art of Mexico.

Once Tamayo had set this important example, other artists also rejected the imposed canons that had obligated them to shape on their canvases a highly superficial, ephemeral and even grotesque reality, whose fatal concessions and consequences are still today unseen by certain painters, who continue in their attempt to follow them, not satisfied by the dreadful lesson of annihilation, which Mexican painting had received.

All of painting's young rebels —Merida, Gerzso, Martinez, Urueta, Soriano, Michel, Cuevas, etc.— who had taken new paths and were preoccupied with what was happening in the rest of the world, knew how to widen their horizons with lessons learned from European and American painters, who, during several decades, had produced new works expressing the latest dynamic tone. Those young men of the recent past and of today neither attempted nor attempt to copy or keep up with the latest fashion; in their reaction against pre-established norms, and in observing the foreign scene, they carried the seed of a much greater universal expression, trying —by this enlargement of their horizons— not only to reflect the times, but to reach a climax in their experiences and, convinced of the vitality and the essentially composite solutions that pre-Columbian art also has offered them, to create new symbolic languages.

Within all of the many artistic expressions found in contemporary Mexico, the influence of its ancient cultures —especially Aztec, Toltec and Maya— on the creative consciousness has been definitive, transcedent, overwhelming and exhaustive.

In their eagerness to acquire, to create features, idioms, and characteristics of their own, artists have noticed that genuine expression must stem from a tragic, pathetic, heart-rending, bloody conception —cathartic in its effect —that asserts the dynamically personal voices and accents of this art with that of other countries; and, in effect, these concepts— in addition to the admirable composite solution of spatial and thematic values that pre-Columbian art reached —have become antecedents and starting points of a truly national expression.

Artists like Orozco Tamayo, Siqueiros, Cuevas and Martinez are closer to the expressive terror of Coatlique, Huehueteotl, and Xiuhcoatl than to the Renaissance Venuses.

All of the horror, symbolism and powerful drama found in ancient sculpture are part of a single spirit: the national character's preference for tragedy. It is also judicious and necessary to point out that other artists, such as the Englishman Henry Moore, admit that they owe much to lessons learned from ancient Mexican art —for its admirable expressive suggestiveness, its handling of volumes, and its great massiveness, a basic part of a synthesized expression.

This probing to enter consciously into other worlds, other confines —in the search for space, light and differentiating individual creation— was what brought them to lands of astonishing features, to poetical moments of true drama, to the evocation— by means of hidden and unredeemed worlds— of secular art, and, moreover, to the spiritual essence of images achieved. It gave a new accent to an art that, as I have already mentioned, not only brought forth the finest of products —the murals of the so-called "three greats"— but also generated a negative side, the second-rate works in the brilliantly and splendidly realized total output.

The thirty-five painters included in the present volume are oustanding examples of the diversity, the great variety of expression that Mexican painting has reached. In their creations, these artists obey the need to mold personal worlds, each of them different —with respect to forms, themes, and even ways of resolving problems with which they are confronted at the moment of conception.

In their aesthetic dissimilarities, in their many and widely-varying inventions, in their ways of accepting or rejecting certain truths of aesthetic order, all of these painters are proof that verifies affirmation, in the sense that the majority —in a great body of individual styles— is where one will really find indications of a living school, and not in the repetition of themes already laid down by earlier masters.

Ricardo Martinez's search for the luminous synthesis of man, whose spirit fights amidst doubt and the anguish of life and death; his conscientious work that led him to reduce forms to the synthetic outline of profound emotion and, mainly, for the thought that leads him to a lonely plateau; and for his color —refined to the extreme degree of becoming radiant, monochrome, diaphanous, inward, apocalyptic, cosmic; and whose vision of the monumental past, of pre-Columbian sculpture, which he sees as a source from which one must start in order to return, enriched by the experience; all of these have made this artist and his work —monolithic meanings of dramatic expression in which inner doubt confronts and combines the past with the uncertain future —one of the most valid, sensitive and courageous painters that have come to the fore in recent years. Ricardo Martinez did not, however, reach where he has by agile facility; on the contrary, it was a ceaseless cleansing of atmosphere, luminous searches in which, suddenly in space, there appeared his sculptural men and women, with the melancholic loneliness of their symbols representing fertility and sensual reproductivity; all at once the world is changed into flaming sheaves and into a conjunction of atmospheres that holds in it all meaning.

Cordelia Urueta is at the other pole of our painting's positively shining lights. Hers is an imagined art of constant imagery; an art in which the power of fantasy helps certain values attain an end that she herself establishes; the aim of catching what is inherent in poetry, and her emotion, detached, unconnected to the vital situations that are called forth in her canvases. Parallel to the idea that guides her like a beacon shining with her own light, Cordelia Urueta has invaded the terrain of myth with admirable solutions that put her onto the path of non-objective art. Beginning from the solid basis of a form she had been searching for, she has entered to the undrawn depths of a dreamed space, and reproduced only those images of a distant reality. The most recent painting of Cordelia Urueta —she seems incapable of expressing herself in merely one manner, in a single trend —has struck out along new roads, carrying her abstraction to the limits of another form in a class by itself, consistent with a spirit that sees space, starlight and poetry as factors other than anecdotal, and with which she sets about building her severe, differential world in which a definite mark of renewed, recreated, remade vitality exists. Fantasy and the most intense sort of magic —together with the hallucinatory element of the absurd and veiled allusion —are some of the principal characteristics of her work, certainly one of the most beautiful in its intensity and passionate feeling of all those now being produced in Mexico. Moreover, it is a wholly youthful painting, with all the problems and difficulties that present themselves during youth.

Similarly, Pedro Coronel represents a fountain of inexhaustible inspiration in his themes, or ideas, which come from a world that is a mixture of imagination, an everyday popular spirit, a sense of rich invention, vibrations that emanate from color and a feeling for the monumental, obviously taken outright from an art of ancient sources. Moreover, his

48

work has an astonishing capacity to uncover for us —with a strong sense of cruelty —the far-flung reaches of catharsis. This is provoked by suggestive and dynamic composition and by original forms —at times beastial, volcanic— that lift the viewer to a spiritual subjectivity. Furthermore, Coronel is a monumental sculptor who, by alternating painting with sculpture, has attained a certain balance from the fight between antagonistic forces which, in his canvases and his four-dimensional models, take on symbolic characteristics. Evolving from a simplified poetic expression, this painter has reached a critical point in which his mastery of color, his mastery of theme, and the discipline in the description of his world —plus his tightly-held harmony in the regal variety of textures and, at times, a dramatic intensity that almost completely absorbs the spectator in a world of intense emotion —has made his expression a sea of bold sensations, of strange overflowing emotion: the masterpiece.

Jose Luis Cuevas is a unique and exceptional case in international painting. A precocious talent —since even in his early youth he succeeded in capturing and molding a four-dimensional world of cruel expressionism— that has continued, step by step, and with an enslaving vitality, to take and exhaust all the roads that his thematic limits have driven him to. One of the world's finest draftsmen, Cuevas has fashioned from this difficult technique a way of expressing —with extreme rapidity— his visions which are part of his world and his tragic reality. Terrifying visions full of anguish for having to live in an absurd, incoherent, negative world, whose presentation alone —here with horror and sadism seldom imagined— makes one think of all the misery and vice in which humanity is sunk. His favorite themes have been, and undoubtedly will continue to be: pathological life, the sick and mutilated, all the realities of life taken as a new human comedy —dictators, prostitutes, Coney Island dwarfs, monstruous beings who move and slither about us. All of these themes of an anguished, verisimilar reality are presented to us exactly as they are; that is, as the reproduction of an everyday world, as a lesson before our eyes, as a tragic admonition of the life of men.

In his work, Cuevas has consolidated an expression so singular that, because of having the same critical spirit, is strongly related to the work of Goya, Toulouse-Lautrec, and Orozco. Attempts have been made to link Cuevas's work with, or find direct antecedents in, these artists, but I believe if similarities of theme and idea exist, this is due to a spiritual affinity among all of them —an affinity that leads an artist to judge his times with a terrible gaze, and whose anguish is precisely in the force of its everyday descriptions. Cuevas is a moralist who mocks morality; Cuevas is a witness who refuses to be present in sub-human worlds. Cuevas creates in a rush —with nervous lines of extraordinary quality— as if he were writing an intimate diary of oppressing situations through which the common man passes daily.

He also groups his works under generic themes, thereby developing in several paintings an idea, a world, whose inspiration is oriented toward putting an end to all the absurd rituals through which we move. For this reason, Cuevas's work tends toward literary sources rather than visual ones. The horror movie, the cliff-hanging sequence of the Mack Sennett silent comedies and the theatre of the absurd (Ionesco, Arrabal, Becket) are the spiritual relations of this expressionist's works. One should also include the short stories of Poe and the novels of Dickens, Dostoevski and Kafka.

The great human lesson that surrounds all of Cuevas's work is proof that this painter is closer to the limits of genius that to mere expressions of an ego tormented by the anguish of life —although the latter also played an important role in the development of his Machiavellian work. His tormented and tormenting psyche allows him to mold an infinite number of self-portraits in which he himself —as artist and man— plays the basic role of agony in humanity's drama.

Within the Mexican expressionist movement, there exist several important painters who combine the wide scope of their emotions with traditional forms. Each one, according to his possibilities, presents his own particular restlessness, offering his personal interpretation of the observed world. But they all possess a deep consciousness of the moral values of prevailing humanism. This is why the works of Rafael Coronel —with their attempts at evoking distant worlds, imaginary portraits which immediately remind us of far-off events; and his pristine use of color, of oils perfectly executed; and through his overwhelming sense of psychological depth, of historical alienation, which cut across his patent characteristics— set him apart from the expressionist works of Benito Messeguer, Francisco Moreno Capdevila, Hernandez Delgadillo, Francisco Corzas and Pilar Sanchez Castañeda.

Messeguer and Capdevila have carried out their most ambitious creations in the field of mural painting. Both have as the basis of their artistic expression the sufferings of man confronted by man, destroyed by war and the consequences of war. Man against man himself and his negativity. Both artists —whose affinity is complete— are absolutely modern. Their works, in a constant process of evolution, attract attention; and are creations of two painters with professional integrity.

Meanwhile, Jose Hernandez Delgadillo sees man as an archetype, as a mythological spirit like the restored Prometheus. For this reason, the men and women he paints are giants —impossible for the mind to grasp— within a titanic universe.

Francisco Corzas paints with hypnotic suggestion. Works of conviction that express the joys of an essentially tragic world. Therefore, all his personages are surrounded by antiquity or dressed in ancient apparel; held in moments or the presence of a constant, a perennial carnival. The carnival, the fancy dress, the masquerade that is life itself. His technique is very fine, and even in the last brush-stroke one can see a painter who is searching for ideal beauty; a perfectionist in the subtle emotions of the panic-stricken soul. One can recognise in his integrity an attempt to propose a stablization of the world surrounded by phantoms which constantly bring to mind the questions of life and the tragic enjoyment of life: Who are we, what are we, and what are we like? These questions always appear in his painting.

A world of dreams, distant yet near; wide horizons that recreate and strip bare surrounding reality. A search for the essence of living. An emotional attitude masked in loneliness; all this and more is the work of Corzas, one of the great figure painters of Mexican art.

The art of Pilar Sanchez Castañeda can be classified as a warm, sometimes ingenuous, expressionism. Her favorite themes are those depicting groups of men and women in common, everyday situations —expressed with a cold acceptance of everyday reality. A joy of living is found in her still life painting, but always in an emotional under-tone, achieved in sillence and losing itself in the same idea.

Among the painters who will never be labelled or classified in set trends or "isms" of art, we find Juan Soriano, Enrique Echeverria, Pedro Friedeberg, Xavier Esqueda, Jose Garcia Ocejo and Pedro Cervantes.

Soriano goes from figurative to non-figurative with terrible rapidity, disdaining an avid public for his "Tender-eyed Children" to involve himself with the difficulties of suggestive and evocative expression.

His painting is a reflection of activity, of restlessness, of problems that force him to retain the precise moments of an expressive gravity.

Instead of his employing painting as a means of communicating his emotions, it is painting that makes use of him; that is to say, it is his means and his end, it is his beginning and his union with hallucination, it is his due and his credit in the richly varied exaltations sketching all that is known —to the limit of light— from an inexhaustibly rich palette.

His painting is a pure poetry of human feeling evoked by an intelligent résumé of form and space. His series of portraits of *Lupe Marin* enriched this genre of painting by the boldness of composition, color, and the magical atmosphere that these dramatic biographies possessed.

Echeverria, by degrees, moved away from the human figure and from recognisable representations. He limited himself to a dark palette, of dark, but at the same time, eloquent colors. He became increasingly serious in his painting and found the planes of color that, through mental suggestion, become controlled emotion bound to the serene play of his constructiveness. At times, through some inner mysterious force, there again appear indications of still lifes; for example, flowers, or even one or several human figures. But they are only moments of a profoundly symbolic spontaneity. The outlines of their forms —sentimental transparencies, joys of life, all of them full of nostalgia— carry the seal of a fully-developed painter.

Jose Garcia Ocejo curiously, and deliberately, explores the bucolic world and the boundaries of Romanticism. He never employs a rich range of color since he does not need to. His works are executed in monochrome to heighten the spectral shades of magical worlds. And, sentimentally, with a spirit that borders on fantastic art, he conceives a world of strange mythological figures: fauna, nymphs, minotaurs, etc. that live and move in intimate moments propitious for refined eroticism. And all the allusions that he uses in his romanticism are valid since, as Baudelaire clearly stated: "When one speaks of Romanticism, one is saying modern art; that is, intimacy, spirituality, color, aspiration toward the infinite, all expressed be every means possessed by the arts".

A fantastic art, of the purest surrealism, alienated, cruel, wounding to the point of being sardonic; nihilistic, of destructive intent and bloody mockery —this is the art of Pedro Friedeberg. An exceptional draftsman, he conceives each picture as the reproduction of thousands of small geometrical figures —each with a different motif— from whose axis, the center of attention, stems the fantastic dictates of a mind that goes further than simple speculation on the fruit of observance.

His structural conception of plastic buildings —unreal, supranatural —are images possessed of a biting irony. Each of Friedeberg's pictures is a synthesis of existential thought in which— in his desire to conceive moments of absurdity —he expresses the chaos of disharmony, the contemporary facts of an introverted and repetitive art that is now at a critical, climactic moment, and full of doubts about pictorial truth.

Xavier Esqueda is one of the youngest Mexican painters. His artistic sensibility, creator of symbol and myth, made him execute his works through the use of collage, thus giving new values to the elemental objects of material chaos. Obviously, his very restlessness leads him to create optical games where objects and things, everyday in themselves, acquire a different emotional aspect; and for this reason he can be grouped with present-day pop and op artists. Another facet of his work is that dramatic one in which he identifies still life with an infinite sadness, with doubt and perfect thematic balance.

Lastly, Pedro Cervantes, sculptor and painter, gives to his work a monochromatic horizon of spatial whiteness, in which the plane achieved is the result of line and an elementary draftsmanship. In his spectral labyrinths —of an unreal whiteness— Cervantes accepts that eroded and ancient vision of the world of form.

In the abstract trend, the following painters have distinguished themselves by works of the very first order: Lilia Carrillo, Fernando Garcia Ponce, and Robert Donis, whose evolution into fully-realized composition has been achieved after long experiments with color tones. Vlady, who aims at a violent mood of poetic expression —particularly in his watercolors, although he also does so with the human figure in a style reminiscent of the ancient Flemish masters— exerts effective influence in an expressionism combined with elements of other aesthetic "isms". In this expressionism, strong constrast results from the use of chiaroscuro and the mixing of colors, patiently, passionately, and terribly worked with extremely fine sensibility.

Gabriel Ramirez —with his baroque use of line and color that blends together expressions of liberty of action— presents, as a plausible consequence, works of tender musicality; while Lucinda Urrusti —always in a deliberate half-tone of very rich pictorial qualities and grades— evokes a subjective world in which allusion is made to a rich nature transformed by the pleasure of transforming it, and making it part of everyday enjoyment.

Carlos Belaunzaran, another of the new artists in Mexican painting, has consolidated in his painting axiom and winged metaphor —parts of a mind that is going to reduce forms and colors to a moving nothingness— from which he is building a dynamic structure of skillful objective beauty using purely subjective elements.

Manuel Felguerez always reflects in his painting an equivalent of the drama of dynamic forces that solve, in a masterly fashion, the problems of unity and rhythm, movement and static force in artistic structure. It is in this organization of elements composed of organic accents, that the differences between his painting and the other non-objective artists will be found. Felguerez —who is also an emotive, monumental sculptor— has realized one of the maximum artistic creations of this century, which is a sculptural mural in iron at the Diana Cinema in Mexico City.

If, on some occasion in the future, one were to try to see and analyze this artistic decade in Mexico, and then to select representative examples, one would of necessity have to recur not only to Cuevas's works but to this mural, which is the most drastic, emotional, subjective, and telluric work of the explosion of forces in the 20th century.

The creations of Toledo as well as of Arnaldo Coen must stand out in a primitiveness that makes allusion to the refined sensual and sexual sentiment of contemporary man; this is also true of certain erotic combinations of Rodolfo Nieto and the calligraphies —a mixture of infantile humor and adult intent— of Fernando Ramos Prida. Luis Lopez Loza sometimes approaches this erotic and panic-filled preoccupation, although he is also interested in the intimate reconstructions of the extramural world.

Coen in his painting gives rein to emotions stemming from a joyful way of looking at life. His dreamlike subjectivity serves as guide for presenting all those possibilities dealing with themes of eroticism which are dominated by the use of color, the forms of an apparent spiritual calm, and the sensations of an intimacy of diaphanous, clear intention.

In this highly vital panorama, so singularly rich, that puts synthetized form at the service of spiritual individualism; that creates disharmony by the increasingly dizzy evolution in aesthetic styles; that emphasizes the possibilities of solitude in an overflowing of creative forces—, these are the works of Aceves Navarro, Maka, the evocative fine art of Antonio Pelaez, the schematic work in Klee's style of Rodolfo Hurtado, and the subjectivity —terrible in concept— of Alberto Gironella.

Pelaez with his elegant painting in half-tones, in his prisms, rhombuses, spheres, angles, and other geometrical figures, presents his myriad worlds in a silent voice, with evocative anguish. The ochre contour, the blazing yellows, and warm blues overtake the artistic conscience capable of housing dissimulated emotion. A painting of forgotten screens, with a greatness blurred in archaic horizon. In brief, a true, vigorous, and poetic creator.

In his historical truths, or mysteries —since history plays a fundamental role in his works— Alberto Gironella expresses an anguish that disintegrates, that tends to break even the very essence of the dramatism of his protaginists who were created to satisfy an eager investigation of the cruel motives that history itself offers, and that satisfies a surrealist idea that takes on, at the same time, a schematic grandiloquence.

In his work, Gironella destroys the visions characteristic of contemporary happenings; in his collages and in his assemblages he possesses the peculiar talent of reconstituting, or recompiling, the facts of previous events, where the beauty of object in itself is a perverse act against artistic styles of our time —the leit-motif of his re-creation.

Vicente Rojo covers his canvases with the disintegration of recognized orders and establishes a new, coherent, and related one with thematic descriptions of the contemporary world. His is an honest work which —stemming from the aesthetics of nothingness— presents a new ordering of material and of our immediate anguishes.

Art in Mexico fulfils, satisfies the function of being a necessary act in and by means of man's life, because it constructs an exemplary world which is an intimate part of his being. It would be impossible to conceive of man without an art that parallels his life, and that satisfies his need for communion between artistic values and truth; an art that must be poetic,

53

since it is a dramatic —or other kind of— creation; and since art is that necessity that helps man to understand life as it is: a basis for his moral activity.

Thus it is, because of the ever-changing necessity of the historical frame, that a multitude of individualistic styles have emerged; different artistic ways of being that respond to that need for communication between men, that impulse to create not only acts of traditional beauty but also the opposite —works where the situations and worlds of our tragic life are reflected.

To enter fully into the world of art, to understand its problems, its transcendency and its scope is, in short, the purest of human sensations, or rather, as Andre Malraux said: "Nothing gives a more disturbing idea of the concept of destiny than the great styles, whose evolution and metamorphosis seem to be the wide scars of Fate's journey over the earth."

ACEVES NAVARRO GILBERTO

Born in Mexico City in 1931. In 1950 he entered "La Esmeralda" School of Painting and Sculpture, where he studied under Carlos Orozco Romero. In 1953 he worked as assistant to Luis Arenal on murals the latter painted in the Government Buildings at Chilpancingo, Guerrero. Later he worked on the team of David Alfaro Siqueiros on his murals at University City. In 1954 he held a one-man show at the Cervantes Library's Gallery of the New Generations, attached to the above-mentioned school. He has had seven one-man shows in Mexico City: at the galleries of Antonio Souza, the Salon of Mexican Plastic Arts, and the Plastic Arts of Mexico, in addition to several collective exhibitions. In 1958 he exhibited oils and drawings in the Pan-American Union in Washington, D. C. In 1959 and 1960 he held one-man shows in several cities of the United States. His work has been selected for the Biennials in Paris (1961, 1963 and 1965); in Tokyo (1962); and in Mexico (1960 and 1962). Aceves Navarro has painted three murals of great interest. In 1960, one entitled "Song to the Race" in the Fourteenth Branch of the Bank of London and Mexico. In 1961, the mural "Dances of Life and Death" in the Seventeenth Branch of the same banking institution, and in 1962 an allegorical mural for the same bank in Queretaro, Queretaro. He has won several prizes in the annual exhibitions held at the Salon of Mexican Plastic Arts.

BELAUNZARAN CARLOS

Born in Guanajuato, Guanajuato in 1940. At 12 years of age, living in Jalapa, Veracruz, he began his studies of drawing and painting under the direction of Daniel Aguilar and Ramon Alva de la Canal. He has lived in Mexico City since he was sixteen. In 1958 he entered San Carlos Academy, where he attended classes given by Benjamin Coria, Gabriel Fernandez Ledesma, Antonio Rodriguez Luna, Luis Nishizawa, and Ignacio Asunsolo. His first works showed the influence of artists like Afro, Karl Dahmer, Millares and John Levee. But he soon abandoned them and began to develop his own idiom in the field of abstraction. He has taken part in several collective shows and has received prizes such as the "Accesit First Prize, Pictorial Contest of the 1962 Acapulco Film Festival." In 1965 he was one of those selected to exhibit in the ESSO Salon of Young Artists held at the Museum of Modern Art in Mexico City. His pictures are found in important collections in the United States and Europe and in the Museum of Modern Art in Mexico City. In 1966 he held his first one-man show, with great critical acclaim, in the Mexican Gallery of "Tianquiztli" Art.

CARRILLO LILIA

Born in Mexico City in 1930. She studied painting in Mexico City and later in Paris at La Grande Chaumiere Academy. She is a teacher of drawing and painting. She has had one-man shows in Paris (1955); Mexico City (1956, 1957, 1958, 1961, and 1964); in Washington, D. C. (1959). She has taken part in collective shows in France, the United States, Peru, Israel, Brazil, Chile and Japan. Her paintings were very well received by critics at the Biennial of Young Artists in Paris (1959); at the Inter-American Biennial of Painting in Mexico City (1960) and at the Tokyo Biennial (1961). In 1965, in the ESSO Salon held at the Museum of Modern Art in Mexico City she won Second Prize in Painting.

CERVANTES PEDRO

Born in Mexico City in 1933. He studied for two years at San Carlos Academy. In 1958 he held his first show at the Excelsior Gallery. He began to work in soldered metal sculptures in 1960, and the following year he took part in an international exhibition held in San Angel, Mexico City. In 1962, he entered his work in the show called "New Values" held at the Salon of Mexican Plastic Arts. Also in 1962 he held a show, together with the photographer Nacho López, of drawings on "jazz" at the Novedades Gallery. Since 1963 he has been alternating painting with sculpture, producing works of great merit, such as the iron and ceramic mural for the Bank of Cooperative Development. In 1964 he completed a monumental sculpture, eight meters high, in bronze, for the port project in Alvarado, Veracruz. The theme of this sculpture was a modern "Prometheus". In 1965 he took part in the ESSO Salon of Young Artists held at the Museum of Modern Art in Mexico City. That same year, two of his paintings were selected for the Exhibition of Mexican Contemporary Painting held at the Casa de las Americas in Havana, Cuba.

COEN ARNALDO

Born in Mexico City in 1940. He studied for some time in the Institute of Publishing Arts and in the workshop of Lawrence Calcagno; nevertheless he can be considered a self-taught painter. In 1962 he took part in a collective exhibition of new trends in Mexican art at the Israeli Sports Club Gallery in Mexico City. That same year he held his first one-man show, composed of numerous paintings on the theme "Figures of the Opera" at the Mer-Kup Gallery. In 1963 he held another one-man show, this time of oils, in the Novedades Gallery. In 1964 he had his third one-man show, at the Juan Martin Gallery, and the following year he exhibited water-colors and oils in the same gallery. He has taken part in collective shows at the Israeli Sports Club (1964); in the ESSO Salon at the Museum of Modern Art in Mexico City (1965); and the Paris Biennial of Young Artists (1965). His work has attracted great attention from critics since his first exhibition of paintings, which showed close affinity to Expressionism. His recent creations, now completely free in expression, qualify him as one of the authentic forces in vanguard painting in Mexico. This year he will exhibit at the Pan-American Union in Washington, D. C.

CORONEL PEDRO

Born in Zacatecas, Zacatecas in 1923. In 1940 he moved to Mexico City and studied at the "La Esmeralda" School of Painting and Sculpture. From 1945 to 1946 he was an instructor at that school, teaching sculpture. At the end of 1946 he travelled in Europe where he attended the workshops of Brauner, the painter, and Brancusi, the sculptor. In 1952 he returned to the artistic life of Mexico City, and held exhibitions at the Proteo Gallery (1954, 1956); and since 1958 has exhibited with fair regularity at the Gallery of Mexican Art. He has executed two public works in which he combined painting with sculpture —glass-ceramic mosaics with exterior sculpture— one at the Commercial Centre "Servicentro" and the other in the Social Security Union Building. We owe the discovery of this artist to Octavio Paz, since it was he who introduced him in his 1954 exhibition. In 1959 Pedro Coronel won the José Clemente Orozco Prize for a Mexican painter. In 1960, the Museum of Modern Art in Mexico City presented a special exhibition of the artist's work in retrospect at the Palace of Fine Arts. In 1961 he held a show of painting and sculpture at Le Point Cardinal Gallery in Paris. In 1962 he held an exhibition of paintings in Tokyo, to great critical acclaim. In 1965 the Gallery of Mexican Art presented the latest works of Pedro Coronel, celebrating his twenty-five years as a painter.

CORONEL RAFAEL

Born in Zacatecas, Zacatecas in 1932. He received his secondary and high school education in his native state. He entered the University of Zacatecas with the purpose of studying architecture, but as his family moved to Mexico City he was unable to finish the course he had chosen. In that year he began to study art at "La Esmeralda" School of Painting and Sculpture, under the tutelage of Carlos Orozco Romero. Given his exceptional gift for drawing, he won a student competition which earned him a scholarship to continue his studies. Since 1954 he has been taking part in collective shows. At about this time he held his first one-man show at the New Generations Gallery attached to the School. In 1960 he held a retrospective show, which included a great number of works, at the Museum of Modern Art of the Palace of Fine Arts, and his paintings awakened the curiosity of the critics as being the work of an artist of singular personality. In 1961 he exhibited in the United States, at the Forsythe Museum, in Ann Arbor, Michigan. In 1964 he finished a mural for the new National Museum of Anthropology and History in Chapultepec Park. In 1965 he exhibited 50 works at the Gallery of Mexican Art. That year his works were selected for the Biennial of Sao Paolo, Brazil, where he won the International First Prize in Painting. Also in that year he presented a select collection of paintings and oils at the headquarters of the Pan-American Union in Washington, D. C. This year he will exhibit his works in a well-known New York gallery. His work has been studied in Alfonso de Neuvillate's book "Four Introverted Attitudes".

CORZAS FRANCISCO

Born in Mexico City in 1936. In 1952 he entered "La Esmeralda" School of Painting and Sculpture, where he finished his studies in 1955. In 1953 and 1954 he took part in collective exhibitions at the New Generations

Gallery attached to the school. In 1955 and 1956 he participated in New Values competitions at the Salon of Mexican Plastic Arts. At the end of 1956 he travelled to Europe and took up residence in Rome. In 1958 he entered the San Giacomo Academy and the Di Belle Arti Academy, both in Rome. In June, 1958, he took part in the "Via Margutta" exhibition and won the Silver Medal and Diploma for Foreign Artists. That same year he held his first one-man show, at the same time participating in the collective exhibition of "Latin American Artists in Rome". In 1959 he returned to Mexico. That year he took part in the First Salon organized at the Museum of Modern Art of the Palace of Fine Arts and his work was chosen for the First Paris Biennial of Young Artists. In 1960 he held a one-man show at the Antonio Souza Gallery. In 1961 his works were included in the exhibition of "Interiorists" held at the Israeli Sports Club Gallery in Mexico City. In 1963 he presented a large collection of oils and drawings at the Misrachi Gallery. In 1965 his work was selected for the exhibition of young artists, organized by the ESSO Company, which was held at the Museum of Modern Art. This year he won the Acquisition-Prize at the Annual Salon of Painting in the Salon of Mexican Plastic Arts.

CUEVAS JOSE LUIS

Born in Mexico City in 1934. At ten years of age he registered at "La Esmeralda" School of Painting and Sculpture, where he remained only a few months. In 1947, in a Donceles Street shop-room in Mexico City, he held his first one-man exhibition of drawings and oils, in which his favorite theme was already apparent: that of exalting human values in an expressionist form. In 1953 he presented three exhibitions: two in Mexico City and another in Merida, Yucatán. In 1954 he exhibited at the Pan-American Union in Washington, D. C., and a year later at the Edouard Loeb Gallery in Paris. Since that date he has held more than thirty one-man exhibitions in the following cities: Havana, New York, Washington, Paris, Lima, Caracas, Buenos Aires, Sao Paolo, Philadelphia, Los Angeles, Fort Worth, Rome, Austin, Santa Barbara, Toronto, Milan, St. Louis, Bogota, and Mexico City. He has taken part in more than 300 collective exhibitions both in Mexico and abroad. In 1959 he won the International First Prize for Drawing at the V Sao Paolo Biennial. In 1960 he was awarded Second Prize at the II Inter-American Annual of Painting, at Barranquilla, Colombia. In 1962 he won First Prize at the VII Mostra Internazionale Di Bianco e Nero, held at Lugano, Switzerland. He has illustrated numerous books, among which are prominent: "The World of Kafka and Cuevas", published by Falcon Press (Philadelphia, 1959), and "The Appointments" by Manuel Moreno Jimeno. He has written two autobiographical books: "Recollections of Childhood" (Kanthos Press, Los Angeles, 1962) and "Cuevas by Cuevas" (Editorial Era, Mexico, 1964). In 1966 he was invited by the "Tamarind" Lithographic Centre in Los Angeles to work on a series of lithographs. His painting has been reviewed in the best critical writings on art, principally in the books of Justino Fernandez, Luis Cardoza y Aragon and Ida Rodriguez, of Mexico; *Artistes de cc Temps* with text by Jean Cassou and Philippe Soupault, published in France, and in "The Four Cardinal Monsters" by the critic Marta Traba (Editorial Era, Mexico, 1965).

DONIS ROBERTO

Born in San Luis Potosi in 1934. He studied for three years at "La Esmeralda" School of Painting and Sculpture, a dependency of the Ministry of Public Education. His painting, of a strong expressive vigor in the realist trend, underwent changes until it reached a synthesis of theme and form which led him to an expressive, subjective abstraction of states of mind. His work obeys a rigid construction in which subjective concepts abound, making patent the material with its qualities and textures, like unknown worlds in which poetic images are everywhere present. Donis has held nine one-man exhibitions: seven in Mexico City, one in New York, and one in Paris. He has taken part in many collective exhibitions, the most outstanding of which are the following: III Barcelona Biennial; I, II, III, and IV Paris Biennials of Young Artists; and others held in Japan, Russia, the United States, Cuba, and France. In 1965, at the Latin-American Competition of Drawing which was held at the Casa de las Americas in Havana, Cuba, he won an Honorable Mention.

ECHEVERRIA ENRIQUE

Born in Mexico City in 1923. He studied drawing and painting in the workshop of the Spanish painter Arturo Souto. He attended this class from 1943 to 1946, at the same time taking lessons at "La Esmeralda" School of Painting and Sculpture. He won a scholarship from the Spanish Government to study in Madrid for a year. He travelled extensively through Europe and North Africa. Since 1952 he has taken part in collective exhibitions and, besides, held several important one-man shows that brought high critical praise. In 1955 his work was exhibited at the Pan-American Union in Washington, D. C. Since then —a master of sure technique with a perfectly defined voice— he has shown in: Houston, Chicago, Washington, Brussels, Caracas, Fort Worth, Dallas, New Orleans, Paris, and Mexico. In 1964, at the Gallery of Mexican Art, he presented a numerous collection of oils which placed him in a prominent position among Mexico's young artists.

ESQUEDA XAVIER

Born in Mexico City in 1943. He has painted since childhood in a self-taught manner. He exhibited for the first time at the age of fourteen, at the Art Seminary in Mexico City. He carried out irregular studies at Juan Soriano's Open Workshop of Ceramics. He has taken part in collective exhibitions in Mexico as well as in the United States. In the latter, he shows at the Byron and the Contemporaries Galleries, both in New York. In one of the exhibitions held at the latter gallery, his works were hung next to those of Raushenberg, Marisol Escobar, Jasper Johns and Joseph Cornell. In Mexico City he is represented by the Antonio Souza Gallery, where his works are exhibited annually. There, in 1965, he gave a show of oils, collages and kinetic boxes; this exhibition was presented by Alfonso de Neuvillate. In the autumn of 1965 he was invited by Dartmouth College to be the artist in residence; there he exhibited his works and, in addition, gave lectures on Mexican avant-garde art.

FELGUEREZ MANUEL

Born in Zacatecas, Zacatecas in 1928. He studied in Paris under the sculptor Ossip Zadkine. He alternates mural sculpture with painting. He has held ten one-man exhibitions in Mexico (French Institute of Latin America, Antonio Souza Gallery, Juan Martin Gallery and the Casa del Lago Gallery); in the United States (Pan-American Union of Washington, D. C.); in Paris and Lima. Among the collective exhibitions in which he has participated, the following merit special mention: I Paris Biennial of Young Artists (1959); Tokyo Biennial (1961); VI Sao Paolo Biennial (1961); III Paris Biennial of Young Artists (1963); that year he was awarded First Prize at the Casa de Mexico; and in 1961 he won Special Mention at the II Inter-American Salon, Bogota, Colombia. He has executed the following murals in wrought iron: "Iron Mural" in the Diana Cinema in 1962; in the Bank of Cooperative Development in 1962; in the Bahia Sports Club, the mural "Hymn to the Ocean" in 1963; in the Industrial Chamber, an iron screen in 1964; besides others for private homes in Mexico City. In 1964 he also executed two jalousies for the new Museum of Anthropology and History in Chapultepec Park. In the two Biennials of Sculpture held in Mexico City, in 1962 and 1964, he won important prizes. During 1966 he will exhibit a large number of oils at the new Juan Martin Gallery.

FRIEDEBERG PEDRO

Born in Florence, Italy in 1937. He became a Mexican on taking up residence in 1940. He studied architecture at the Ibero-American University in Mexico City. He is a self-taught painter. Lately he has devoted himself also to fantastic sculpture, inventing useful and useless objects, functional sculptures, and sculptural furniture. In 1959 he held his first one-man show at the Diana Gallery. In 1960 he exhibited his work at the Proteo Gallery. In 1961 he was represented by Antonio Souza, and since then has had four showings in this gallery. He has also held one-man exhibitions in New York, Paris, Lisbon, Munich, Washington, D. C., Chicago, Baltimore, Duesseldorf, Hannover, and Berlin. Articles on his work, criticisms, and reproductions have appeared in the following magazines and newspapers: Time, Horizon, Motive, Esquire, Art News, Show, Life, Architecture Fantastique, Die Kunst und das Schone Heim, El Rehilete, Mexico en la Cultura, and El Corno Emplumado. His work has been studied and analyzed in the following books: "Arte Contemporaneo" by Ida Rodriguez; "Art and Architecture in Latin America" by Paul Damaz; "Kindler Malere Lexicon" and "4 Actitudes Ensimismadas" by Alfonso de Nuevillate.

GARCIA OCEJO JOSE

Born in Cordoba, Veracruz in 1930. From 1946 to 1950 he studied at the School of Architecture of the National Autonomous University of Mexico. In 1948 he executed his first portaits and tried his hand at mural painting. He frequented the studio of Diego Rivera who praised his draftsmanship. In 1950 he abandoned his career in architecture and won a scholarship to the Institute of Hispanic Culture in Madrid There he painted murals at University City, and earned from the above-mentioned institute a Diploma and Scholarship Ad-Honorem. He has had seven one-man exhibitions at the following places: Society of Architects, Diana Gallery, Proteo Gallery, Hispanic Institute of Mexico, Gallery of Fine Arts in Tenerife (Canary Islands), Mexican-North American Institute in Monterrey and Guadalajara. In 1946 he studied in Salzburg, Austria, at the "Sommer

Academie", founded and directed by Oscar Kokoschka, where he received a diploma. In March, 1966, he exhibited oils and drawings at the Museum of the Palace of Fine Arts in Mexico City.

GARCIA PONCE FERNANDO

Born in Merida, Yucatan in 1933. He studied architecture at the school attached to the National Autonomous University of Mexico, and painting at Enrique Climent's workshop. From 1955 to the present he has made periodic study-trips to Europe. He has held two one-man exhibitions at the Gallery of Mexican Art (1959 and 1961), one at the Juan Martin Gallery (1964) and another at the Casa del Lago Gallery (1964). He has participated in numerous collective exhibitions, the most important being the following: 1959, National Salon of Painting, at which he won an Honorable Mention. In 1960, Painters and Engravers of Yucatan. 1961 and 1965, Paris Biennial of Young Artists. 1965, exhibition of young artists held at the Museum of Modern Art in Mexico City (ESSO Salon), in which show he won First Prize in Painting.

GIRONELLA ALBERTO

Born in Mexico City in 1929. He studied at the School of Philosophy and Letters at the National Autonomous University of Mexico. He is a self-taught painter. Together with other artists he founded the now defunct Prisse Gallery, where he exhibited in 1952 and 1953. That year he also exhibited at "El Gallo Pitagorico" Gallery in the city of Guanajuato. He has held eight one-man shows in Mexico, Washington and Paris. In addition, his works have been included in many collective exhibitions held in Mexico, the United States, France, Japan, Italy, Brazil, Venezuela, and Argentina. In 1959 he was awarded one of the First Prizes at the I Paris Biennial of Young Artists. In 1963 and 1964, at the Juan Martin Gallery, he presented two shows of his collage-ensamblage paintings on specific themes: "Palace Feast" and "The Workshop of Francisco Lezcano", respectively. In 1964 the monograph entitled "Gironella" by Edouard Jaguer (Editorial Era) appeared. He resides at present in Paris where he has engagements to exhibit his works in several one-man shows.

HERNANDEZ DELGADILLO JOSE

Born at Tepeapulco, Hidalgo in 1927, he has been living in Mexico City since 1945. He studied painting and drawing under Antonio Navarrete Tejero. In 1945, he held his first one-man exhibition which included 45 oils and drawings. In 1955, he attended an architecture workshop, and in 1957, he studied the technique of mural painting at "La Esmeralda" School of Painting and Sculpture. A result of these studies is the mural he painted at Belisario Dominguez School. Having the theme of indigenous education, it is a mural 8 by 3½ meters. In 1958 he completed a series of reliefs for the Sports City in Mexico City. In 1960 he collaborated in organizing the VIII Mexican Book Fair. In 1960 he was awarded Honorable Mention for his picture "My Times" at the II Inter-American Biennial of Painting and Sculpture held at the Palace of Fine Arts in Mexico City. In 1961 he was one of the Mexican artists selected for the Paris Biennial of Young Artists, where he won a First Prize for his picture called "Men". In

1964 he also won a Prize-Acquisition at the Annual Salon of Painting held at the Salon of Mexican Plastic Arts.

HURTADO RODOLFO

Born in Mexico City in 1940. He has painted since childhood in a self-taught manner, and in 1962 he won First Prize in Painting at the Third Salon for Students of the National Autonomous University of Mexico, at which Rufino Tamayo and Matias Goeritz, among others, were judges. In 1963 he participated in a collective exhibition held in Brussels, where he was awarded an Honorable Mention. At present he teaches painting at several schools. In 1965 he held his first one-man show at the Antonio Souza Gallery, an exhibition sponsored by the painter Jose Luis Cuevas. Hurtado will exhibit at the Gallery of the Pan-American Union in Washington, D. C. in 1966.

LOPEZ LOZA LUIS

Born in Mexico City in 1939. He studied painting, engraving and sculpture at the Higher Institute of Applied Arts in Mexico City and the Pratt Graphic Center in the United States. He also attended Juan Soriano's ceramics workshop, and at the same time studied engraving with Carlos Alvarado Lang and Isidoro Ocampo. He has held ten one-man exhibitions at the Visual Arts Gallery, the Mexico Gallery, the Proteo Gallery, the University Gallery, and the Antonio Souza Gallery, in Mexico City. He has also held exhibitions at Southampton University, the Jewish Museum (New York), the Chicago Art Center, the Pan American Gallery in Washington, D. C., the Phoenix Museum, the Martha Jackson Gallery (New York), in the United States; in Sao Paolo; and at the Museum of Modern Art in Colombia.

MARTINEZ RICARDO

Born in Mexico City in 1918. In 1927 he moved with his family to the United States. In 1930 he returned to Mexico and studied in the studio of his brother, Oliverio Martinez de Hoyos. He can, however, be considered a self-taught artist who has been drawing since early youth. In 1942 he took part in a collective exhibition of Mexican painters that was presented in Guadalajara, Jalisco; his works were hung alongside those of Orozco and Rivera. Since that date he has held eight one-man shows in the Gallery of Mexican Art, the last in 1964. In 1958, he went as a guest artist to the Venice Biennial. In 1960, New York's Contemporaries Gallery presented a personal showing of the artist's work. In 1952, he exhibited painting at the Carnegie International in Pittsburg as well as at the International Shows in Mainichi, Japan. At present, his works may be found in the following shows: "Moods of Lights" and "Mother and Child in Modern Art", both touring the United States. In 1961 and 1964. the works of this artist were exhibited at the Contemporaries Gallery with growing acclaim on the part of specialized critics. In 1963, he was the only Mexican painter invited to the Sao Paolo Biennial; there he won the Mohino Santista Prize. Martinez' canvases are found in the most important museums and private collections of the United States, Europe, and Mexico. He has taken part in more than two hundred collective exhibitions, both in Mexico and abroad. He has also illustrated books, among which "Death Without End" by Jose Gorostiza, and "Ghost Conclave" by Alfonso Reyes should be mentioned. In 1965, the Art Collection of the National Autonomous University of Mexico contained the monograph "Ricardo Martinez", written by the poet Ruben Bonifaz Nuno.

MAKA

Born in Paris in 1925, of a Russian-French father and a Mexican mother. Although she studied for a short time under Manuel Rodriguez Lozano, she can be considered a self-taught painter. She has held thirteen one-man shows: the first in 1955 at the Excelsior Gallery, and the last in 1965 at the Salon of Mexican Plastic Arts. Outstanding among this group of one-man shows were those held at Caracas, Venezuela in 1958; at Fort Worth, in 1960; at New York also in 1960; and those held at the Antonio Souza Gallery in 1962, and at the Juan Martin Gallery in 1963 and 1964. Her work has been selected for exhibitions of Mexican painting held at Tel-Aviv, Arizona, St. Louis, Los Angeles, New York, and Paris. Her painting has also been studied in the following books: "Contemporary Art" by Ida Rodriguez, and "Mexican Expressionism" by Margarita Nelken.

MESSEGUER BENITO

Born in Tarragona, Spain in 1930. He became a Mexican in 1950. From 1946 to 1951 he studied at "La Esmeralda" School of Painting and Sculpture, a dependency of the Ministry of Public Education. During his studies he was awarded one of the scholarships granted by the school. He was also awarded a scholarship to the graphic arts studio. He became known to the public in 1956 during the Exhibition of New Values at the Salon of Mexican Plastic Arts where he won First Prize. In 1957 he was again awarded First Prize in that competition. Since then he has taken part in collective shows such as the First National Salon of Painting (1959); the Second Inter-American Biennial in Mexico (1960); the Tokyo Biennial (1961); and the Paris Biennial of Young Artists (1965). He has won important prizes such as Honorable Mention in the Certamen de Honor a la Madre at the Casa del Arquitecto (1959); Honorable Mention at the First National Salon of Painting (1959); Gold Medal at the Graphic Arts exhibition (1961); and Second Prize and Silver Medal at the National Salon of Landscape Painting (1961). He has painted murals at the Hotel Casino de la Selva in Cuernavaca, Morelos; at the Narciso Bassols Auditorium of the School of Economics at University City; and he is currently working on a mural in the stairwell of the Mexican Institute of Audition and Language. He is a professor at "La Esmeralda" School of Painting and at the School for Foreign Students at the National University.

MORENO CAPDEVILA FRANCISCO

Born in Barcelona, Spain in 1926. He has been residing in Mexico since 1939. He studied painting at the School of Artistic Initiation N° 1, and engraving at the School of Book Arts, both in Mexico City. He has taken part in the following engraving exhibitions: Library of Congress, Washington, D. C. (1953, 1954, 1955); the "Xylon" in Yugoslavia (1956); the Tokyo Biennial (1957); at the Galliera Museum (1958); at the Inter-American Biennial in Mexico (1958, 1960); at the Internation Show in Lugano Switzerland (1960), and in other exhibitions of Mexican engraving in Japan, France, Italy, Poland and Latin America. He won prizes at the

Salons of Engraving in 1957 and 1959, and was awarded an Honorary Mention at the Inter-American Biennial in Mexico in 1960. In 1962 he presented his first works of painting at the annual competition at the Salon of Mexican Plastic Arts. There he won the Acquisition Prize for his work entitled "The Victim". In 1963 he held a one-man show with a numerous collection of oils at the Salon of Mexican Plastic Arts, and in 1964 he again exhibited his works at the Mer-Kup Gallery. That year he completed a mural on "The Destruction of Tenochtitlan" at the Mexico City Museum.

NIETO RODOLFO

Born in Oaxaca, Oaxaca in 1937. From 17 to 19 years of age he studied at "La Esmeralda" School of Painting and Sculpture. In 1961 he moved to France. Since then he has been living in Paris. In 1961 he held a one-man show at the famous France Gallery, which also represents Rufino Tamayo. In 1962 he had a one-man show in Oslo. That year he took part in the May Salon in Paris, and in 1963 he enteced the III Paris Biennial of Young Artists where he was awarded a First Prize. In 1964 and 1965 he again held exhibitions at the France Gallery, and in 1956 he showed a group of water-colors and gouaches at the Juan Martin Gallery in Mexico. He has taken part in several collective shows held in Europe, and illustrated "Fantastic Zoology" by Borges, edited by Gallimard.

PELAEZ ANTONIO

Born in Llanes, Asturias, Spain in 1921. He studied at the Perez Galdós Institute in Madrid. In 1936 he arrived in Mexico where his father was a resident, and the following year became a Mexican citizen. He studied at "La Esmeralda" School of Painting and Sculpture. In 1949 he took a long trip through Italy, Greece and Egypt. In 1952, on his return to Mexico, he held his first one-man show at the Gallery of Contemporary Art, an exhibition which Frida Kalho presented. He has held one-man shows at the Gallery of Mexican Art in 1956 and 1960; at the French Institute of Latin America in 1960; at Veracruz University in 1961. In Paris he has had one-man shows at the Edouard Loeb Gallery in 1959 and 1964. In Spain, he gave an exhibition of his paintings at the Santa Catalina Salon in the Madrid Atheneum. His work has been in collective exhibitions held in the United States, Europe and Mexico. In 1966 he will show at the Byron Gallery of New York. In 1956 Pelaez illustrated the book entitled "21 Women of Mexico", with text by Alfonso Reyes, Carlos Chavez, Diego Rivera, Rodolfo Usigli, Octavio Paz and Carlos Pellicer. Articles, as well as reproductions of his work, have appeared in the following magazines and newspapers: México en la Cultura, Bellas Artes, Hoy (Mexico); Cuadernos Americanos (Argentina); Time, Pictures on Exhibit (United States); ABC (Spain); Cahiers du Musée de Poche, Prisme des Arts, Chef d'Oeuvre de l'Art (France); The Arts Review (London).

RAMIREZ GABRIEL

Born in Merida, Yucatan in 1938. He is self-taught, having begun his professional painting in 1959. In 1965 he held a one-man show at the Juan Martin Gallery. That same year he was chosen to participate in the Paris Biennial of Young Artists. His form of expression links him spiritually to the COBRA group, although he introduces into his works a mood of irritating Baroque. His works are almost musical, a result of the range of colors he employs. His 1965 exhibition —in which he laid the base for a promising future —received great critical acclaim.

RAMOS PRIDA FERNANDO

Born in Mexico City in 1937. He studied at "La Esmeralda" School of Painting and Sculpture and at the San Carlos Academy. After two years he abandoned the academic approach to search for means of expression that harmonized more closely with his restless spirit. In 1958 he held an exhibition at the Gallery of Visual Arts. That same year he participated in the Biennial of Watercolor Painting in Philadelphia, United States. In 1965 he held a one-man show at the Gallery of Mexican Art, presenting a large collection of oils, water-colors, and drawings with great critical success. In 1965 his work was selected for the Paris Biennial of Young Artists.

ROJO VICENTE

Born in Barcelona, Spain in 1932. He has been living in Mexico since 1949, where he studied painting with Arturo Souto and typography with Miguel Prieto. He made study trips through Europe in 1953, 1955, 1960 and 1964. He has held one-man shows in Mexico in 1958, 1959 and 1961; in Miami in 1961; Again in Mexico City in 1962 and 1964; in Madrid and in Barcelona, Spain, in 1964. In 1965, he held two exhibitions simultaneously. one at the Juan Martin Gallery and another, of icons, myths and geometrical patterns, at the Casa del Lago Gallery of the National Autonomous University of Mexico. He has participated in many collective shows, outstanding among which are the following: 1958, Musee d'Art Moderne de la Ville in Paris; 1959, First National Salon of Painting in the Palace of Fine Arts in Mexico City; 1961, Sao Paolo Biennial; 1961, Tokyo Biennial; 1964, Exhibtion of Mexican Drawing at Bellas Artes, Mexico City; 1965, Contemporary Mexican Art, Phoenix Art Museum, United States; 1965, Paris Biennial of Young Artists. He was art director of the supplement "Mexico en la Cultura" and at present is art director of "La Cultura en Mexico" supplement of the magazine Siempre.

SANCHEZ CASTAÑEDA PILAR

Born in Mexico City in 1941. She took painting classes with private teachers from 1958 to 1960. From 1961 to the present she has been a student at Antonio Rodriguez Luna's Graphic Arts School. She has taken part in collective shows in Mexico as well as abroad. In 1962 she won the Exhibition Prize of the New Values competition at the Salon of Mexican Plastic Arts. In 1963 she was awarded the Acquisition Prize of the National Institute of Fine Arts, for the Museum of Modern Art, in the show held as a result of the aforementioned prize. She was accepted as a member of the Salon of Mexican Plastic Arts. In 1964 she won First Prize in Painting at the exhibition of the National School of Plastic Arts. That year she also won First Prize in Painting in a collective exhibition held at Guadalajara, Jalisco. She received the Press Prize at the Salon de Pintura 1964, which was held at Chihuahua, Chihuahua. She teaches painting in third year of Graphic Arts at the Ibero-American University. In 1966, she held an exhibition of paintings at the Salon of Mexican Plastic Arts.

SORIANO JUAN

Born in Guadalajara, Jalisco in 1920. At the age of fourteen he held his first exhibition in the Museum of Guadalajara, Jalisco. Influential in the formation of the artist was Jesús Reyes Ferreira, an outstanding painter. In 1935, Soriano moved to Mexico City, and a year later he took part in an exhibition organized by the League of Revolutionary Artists and Writers (LEAR). Later, he showed his works at the University Gallery (1941); at the Gallery of Mexican Art (1945); and at the Salon of Mexican Plastic Arts, a collection of portraits (1948). In 1951, he again exhibited at the Gallery of Mexican Art, this time a large collection of oils, watercolors, and drawings, which placed him among the most vigorous artists in Mexico. In 1951, he took a study trip through Italy. In 1954, he exhibited in Rome and the following year he had a show at the Gallery of Mexican Art. At the Antonio Souza Gallery in 1957, he exhibited oils and ceramics, the latter being a medium which had always attracted him. He has participated in collective shows, such as the International Exhibition in San Francisco (1938); as well as others of interest at the Museum of Modern Art in New York; the Philadelphia Museum; in Havana, Paris, London, Stockholm, Toronto and Tokyo. In 1959, the Museum of Modern Art of the Palace of Fine Arts in Mexico City presented a retrospective show of Soriano's work which embraced his 25 years as a painter; an exhibition organized in commemoration of the XXV anniversary of the Palace of Fine Arts. He is a teacher of ceramics, an engraver and a scene designer. His works for the theatre were for the group called "Poetry Read Aloud", and they demonstrate the ambitious and suggestive plastic combinations that this painter achieved for the national stage.

TOLEDO FRANCISCO

Born in Juchitan, Oaxaca in 1940. He is a self-taught painter. He became known to the public following an exhibition which the Antonio Souza Gallery held in 1959. In 1960 he showed at the Forth Worth Art Center. That year he travelled to Europe and exhibited in Paris at the Flinker Gallery; at the National Museum of Oslo; at the Hamilton Gallery in London; and later, in New York at the Saidenberg Gallery. From 1960 on he has exhibited his work frequently in Paris, Berne, Hamburg, London and New York. He has held a total of twenty one-man exhibitions, as far distant as India and Japan. In 1963, basing himself on the exhibition Soriano had held at the Flinker Gallery in Paris, Andre Pierre de Mandiaggues wrote a long poem about his work in the Twentieth Century Magazine. The French Minister of Culture, Andre Malraux, is among those who collect Toledo's work. His paintings are in the Museum of Modern Art in Paris, the Museum of Modern Art in New York, and in private collections in the United States, Europe, Asia and Mexico. In 1965 he gave an extensive show of his recent work (oils, gouaches, watercolors) at the Antonio Souza Gallery, where he will again exhibit in November 1966.

URUETA CORDELIA

Born in Coyoacan, Mexico in 1908. Daughter of the distinguished revolutionary, orator and man of letters, Jesus Urueta. Dr. Atl, on seeing her childhood drawings, encouraged her to follow a career of art. In 1925, she attended the Churubusco School of Open Air Art, directed by Alfredo Ramos Martinez. In 1930, during her stay in New York, she met Orozco and Tamayo at Alma Reed's Delphic Studios. Her drawings were hung in a collective exhibition of Mexican painters held at this gallery. In 1932 she taught drawing at primary schools in Mexico City. From 1938 to 1943, she travelled through Europe, commissioned by the Ministry of Foreign Affairs. On returning to Mexico she decided to paint professionally. Her first one-man show was held in 1950 at the Salon of Mexican Plastic Arts under the auspices of Margarita Nelken. In 1952 she exhibited her works in Paris at the Andre Weill Gallery. Since then her work has been sent with Mexican exhibits to London, Paris, Tokyo, South America, etc. In 1955, she was named Art Producer for the National Institute of Fine Arts. In 1957, she again exhibited at the Salon of Mexican Plastic Arts. In 1960, she presented a show at the Proteo Gallery. At the Mexico Biennial held in 1960, she was awarded Honorable Mention. In 1961, she held a one-man show at the Jacobo Glantz Gallery. The following year she won Honorable Mention at the VI International Biennial at Sao Paolo. In 1965 she exhibited at the Salon of Mexican Plastic Arts. Her work has been studied in the book "4 Subjective Attitudes" by Alfonso de Neuvillate.

URRUSTI LUCINDA

Born at Melilla, Spanish Morocco in 1929. In Mexico she studied at "La Esmeralda" School of Painting and Sculpture, and took lessons from Ricardo Martinez. In 1957, she won First Prize at the Annual New Values Exhibition at the Salon of Mexican Plastic Arts, an award that gave her the right to have a one-man show the following year. In 1959, she held a second show of her own at the Diana Gallery. In 1960, she took part in the Second Inter-American Biennial of Painting and Sculpture in Mexico in which she won Honorable Mention. She has taken part in many collective shows of Mexican painting held in Mexico as well as abroad. Lucinda Urrusti's work has always attracted attention for the finess of her textures and for her rich color which creates situations of unusual beauty. She is unquestionably one of the most subtle artists painting today.

VLADY

Born in Leningrad, Russia in 1920. From 1936 to 1939, he lived in Paris. Later he moved to Martinique, Santo Domingo, where he lived for two years. In 1941 he arrived in Mexico and later acquired Mexican nationality. He is a self-taught painter. His first one-man show was held in 1947 at the Gallery of the French Institute of Latin America; later he held exhibitions at the Juarez Bookstore (1951); at the Prisse Gallery (1953); and the Proteo Gallery (1956 and 1958). He has executed several murals in Mexico City and one of mosaics in the Hotel Cassino Hornos in Acapulco, Guerrero. In 1963 he presented a good collection of oils and drawings at the Misrachi Gallery. In 1965 he exhibited lithographs at the Salon of Mexican Plastic Arts.

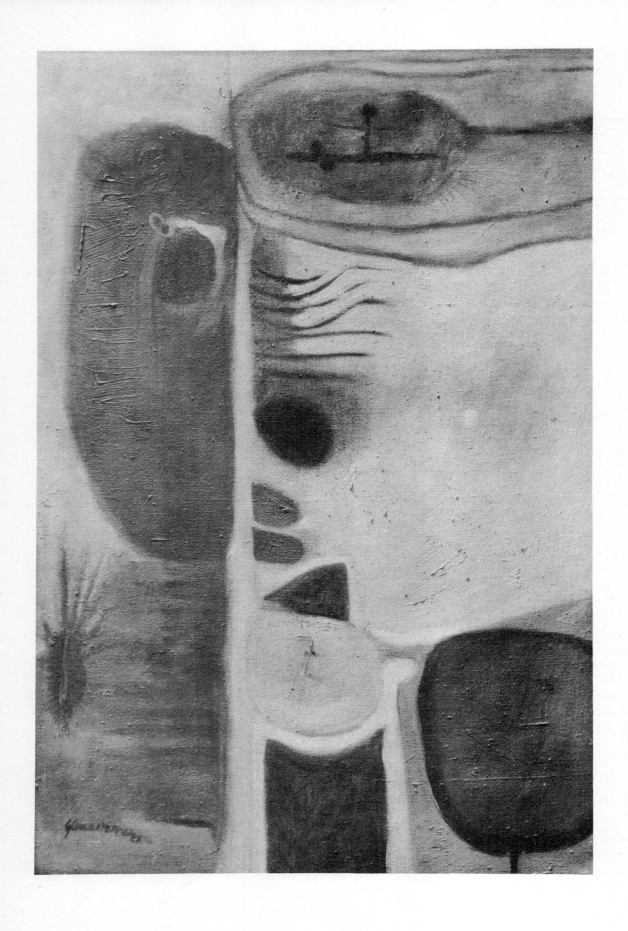

ACEVES NAVARRO GILBERTO. "Imagen de lo
Alucinante". Oleo sobre tela. Col. Sra. Olga Dondé.—
*"Image of Hallucination". Oil on canvas. Collection
Mrs. Olga Donde.*

ACEVES NAVARRO GILBERTO. "Carnaval de Nahuales". Oleo sobre tabla. Col. Salón de la Plástica Mexicana.— *"Carnival of Nahuals". Oil on wood. Salon of Mexican Plastic Art Collection.*

BELAUZARAN CARLOS. "Despliegue". Tinta sobre
papel. Col. Galería Mexicana de Arte.— *"Unfolding"*
Ink on paper. Mexican Gallery of Art Collection.

BELAUZARAN CARLOS: "Raskolnikov". Oleo y
collage sobre tela. Col. Galería Mexicana de Arte.—
*"Raskolnikov". Oil and collage on canvas. Mexican
Gallery of Art Collection.*

CARRILLO LILIA. "Niña Arcaica". Oleo sobre papel.
Col. Galería Juan Martín.— *"Old-fashioned Girl". Oil
on paper. Collection Juan Martin Gallery.*

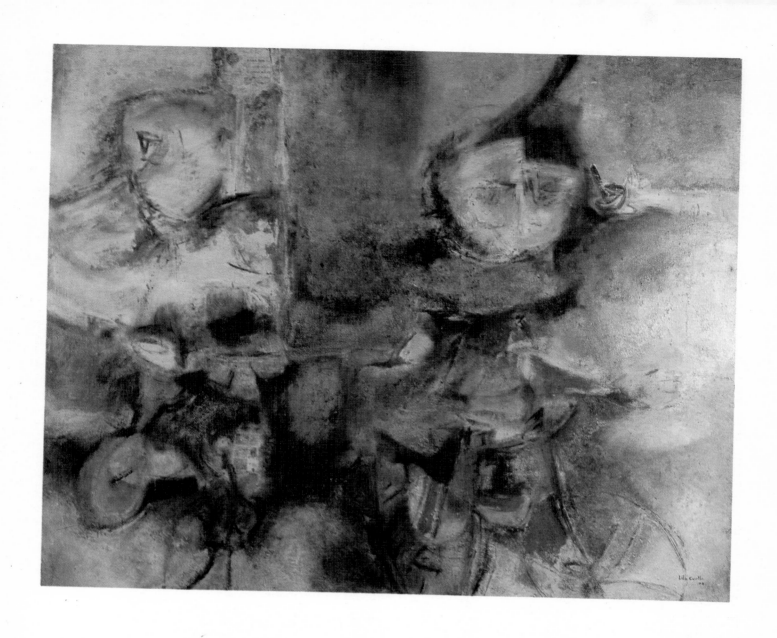

CARRILLO LILIA. "Niños en Triciclo". Oleo sobre
tela. Col. Galería Juan Martín.— *"Children on Tricy-
cle". Oil on canvas. Juan Martin Gallery Collection.*

CERVANTES PEDRO. "Hombre de Jazz". Tinta y
gouache sobre papel. Col. Galería Mexicana de Arte.—
*"Jazzman". Ink and gouache on paper. Collection Me-
xican Gallery of Art.*

CERVANTES PEDRO. "Cosmonauta". Oleo sobre
masonite. Col. Arq. Salvador Ortega.— *"Cosmonaut".
Oil on canvas. Salvador Ortega Collection.*

COEN ARNALDO. "El Futuro del Silencio". Oleo
sobre tela. Col. Galería Juan Martín.— *"The Future
of Silence" Oil on canvas. Collection Juan Martin
Gallery.*

COEN ARNALDO. "Sentimiento de Ausencia". Oleo sobre tela. Col. Galería Juan Martín.— *"Feeling of Absence". Oil on canvas. Juan Martin Gallery Collection.*

CORONEL PEDRO. "Hombre de la Rue de la Santé".
Oleo sobre tela. Col. Galería de Arte Mexicano.—
*"Man of la Rue de la Sante". Oil on canvas. Collection
Gallery of Mexican Art.*

CORONEL PEDRO. "El Llanto Desolado". Oleo sobre
tela. Col. Museo de Arte Moderno.— *"Anguished Weep-
ing". Oil on canvas. Museum of Modern Art Collection.*

CORONEL RAFAEL. "Monseñor". Oleo sobre tela.
Col. Galería de Arte Mexicano.— "Monsignor". Oil on
canvas. Collection Gallery of Mexican Art.

CORONEL RAFAEL. "Figura". Oleo sobre tela. Col.
Galería de Arte Mexicano.— "Figure". Oil on canvas.
Gallery of Mexican Art Collection.

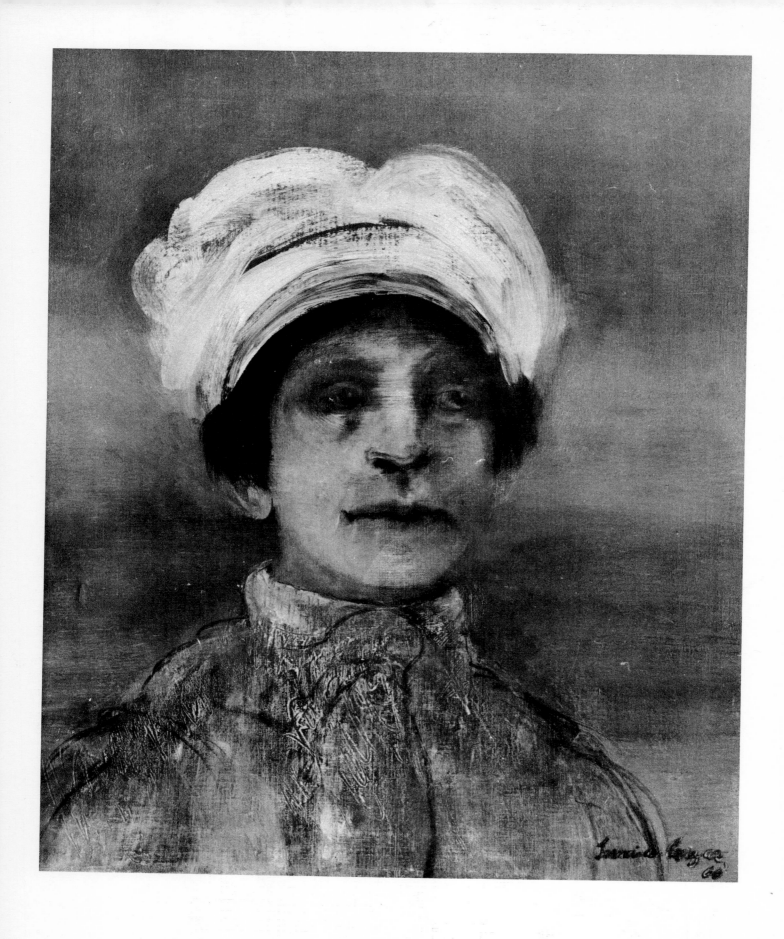

CORZAS FRANCISCO. "El Gran Alfredo". Oleo sobre tela. Col. Galería Juan Martín.— *"The Great Alfred". Oil on canvas. Collection Juan Martin Gallery.*

CORZAS FRANCISCO. "Desnudo". Oleo sobre tela.
Col. Galería Juan Martín.— *"Nude". Oil on canvas.*
Juan Martin Gallery Collection.

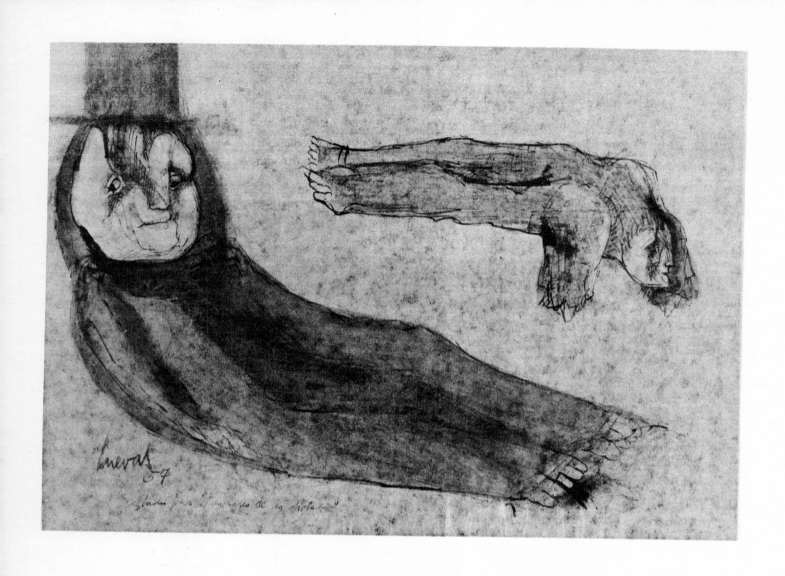

CUEVAS JOSE LUIS. "Estudio para Funerales de un
Dictador". Tinta sobre papel. Col. Particular.— *"Study
for a Dictator's Funeral". Ink on paper. Private collection.*

CUEVAS JOSE LUIS. "Museo del Hombre". Técnica
mixta sobre papel. Col. Mariana y Ximena Cuevas.—
"*Museum of Man*". *Oil on canvas. Mariana and
Ximena Cuevas Collection.*

DONIS ROBERTO. "Reminiscencia No. 2". Tinta y
acuarela sobre papel. Col. Galería de Arte Mexicano.—
"Reminiscence No. 2". Ink and watercolor on paper.
Collection Gallery of Mexican Art.

DONIS ROBERTO. "Amenaza Lírica". Oleo sobre
tela. Col. Particular.— *"Lyric Threat". Oil on canvas.
Private Collection.*

ECHEVERRIA ENRIQUE. "Pescado Frito". Oleo
sobre tela. Col. Galería de Arte Mexicano".— *"Fried
Fish". Oil on canvas. Collection Gallery of Mexican Art.*

ECHEVERRIA ENRIQUE. "Flores". Oleo sobre tela.
Col. Salón de la Plástica Mexicana.— *"Flowers". Oil
on canvas. Salon of Mexican Plastic Art Collection.*

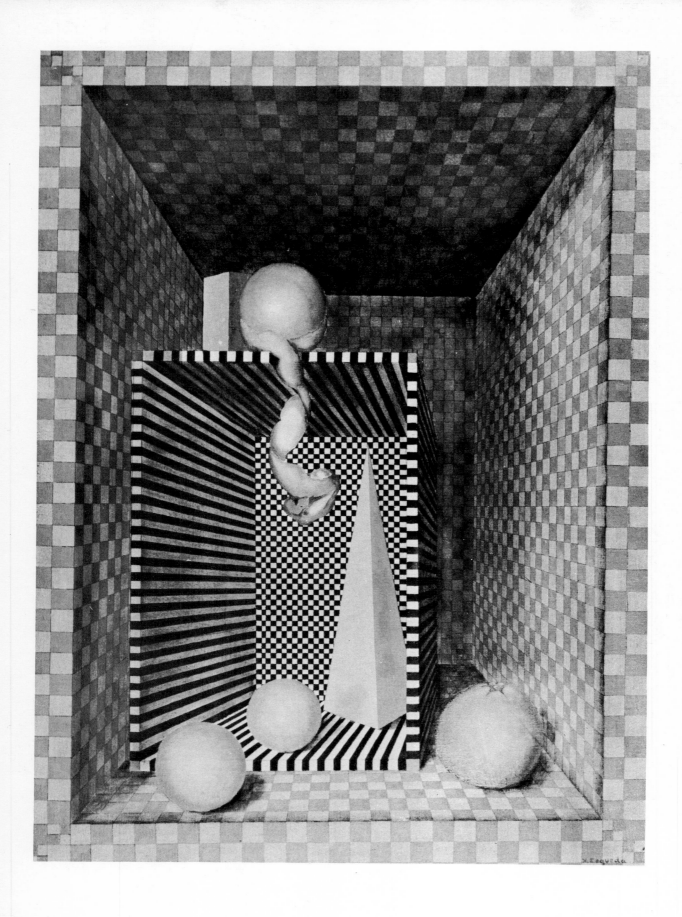

ESQUEDA XAVIER. "Naranjas Transformistas". Oleo
sobre tela. Col. del Autor.— *"Impersonator Oranges".*
Oil on canvas. Collection of the artist.

ESQUEDA XAVIER. "Inmanencia". Oleo sobre masonite. Col. particular.— *"Imanence". Oil on masonite. Private Collection.*

FELGUEREZ MANUEL. "Composición Dinámica".
Oleo sobre tela. Col. Galería Juan Martín.— *"Dynamic
Composition". Oil on canvas. Collection Juan Martin
Gallery.*

FELGUEREZ MANUEL. "Composición". Oleo sobre
tela. Col. Galería Juan Martín.— *"Composition". Oil
on canvas. Collection Juan Martin Gallery.*

FRIEDEBERG PEDRO. "My Secrets are not Your
Secrets". Gouache sobre papel. Col. Alfonso de Neuvillate.— *"My Secrets are not your Secrets". Gouache
on paper. Collection of Alfonso de Neuvillate.*

FRIEDEBERG PEDRO. "Melondrama". Gouache sobre papel. Col. Sra. Rosa Covarruvias.— *"Melondrama". Gouache on paper. Collection of Mrs. Rosa Covarruvias.*

GARCIA OCEJO JOSE. "Fauno y Bacantes". Tinta
sobre papel. Col. del autor.— *"Faun and Bacchantes".*
Ink on paper. Collection of the artist.

GARCIA OCEJO JOSE. "Preludio Intemporal". Oleo
sobre tela. Col. Galería Mexicana de Arte.— "*Atemporel
Prelude*". *Oil on canvas. Collection Mexican Gallery
of Art.*

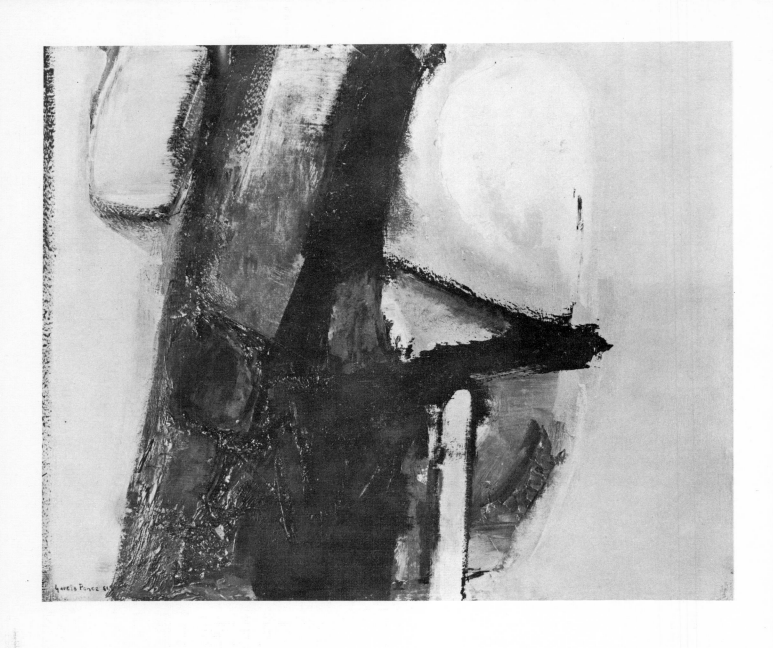

GARCIA PONCE FERNANDO. "Relieve Blanco".
Oleo sobre tela. Col. Galería Juan Martín.— *"White
Relief". Oil on canvas. Collection Juan Martin Gallery.*

GARCIA PONCE FERNANDO. "Búsqueda Cromática". Oleo sobre masonite.— *"Chromatic Search". Oil
on masonite. Collection Juan Martin Gallery.*

GIRONELLA ALBERTO. "Antonio el Inglés". Tinta.
Col. Particular.— *"Anthony the Englishman". Ink.*
Private collection.

GIRONELLA ALBERTO. "El Obrador de Francisco
Lezcano". Oleo sobre masonite. Col. Galería Juan Martín.— *"Francisco Lezcano's Workshop". Oil on masonite. Collection Juan Martin Gallery.*

HERNANDEZ DELGADILLO J O S E. "Personaje
1965". Oleo sobre tela. Col. Particular.— *"Character
1965". Oil on canvas. Private collection.*

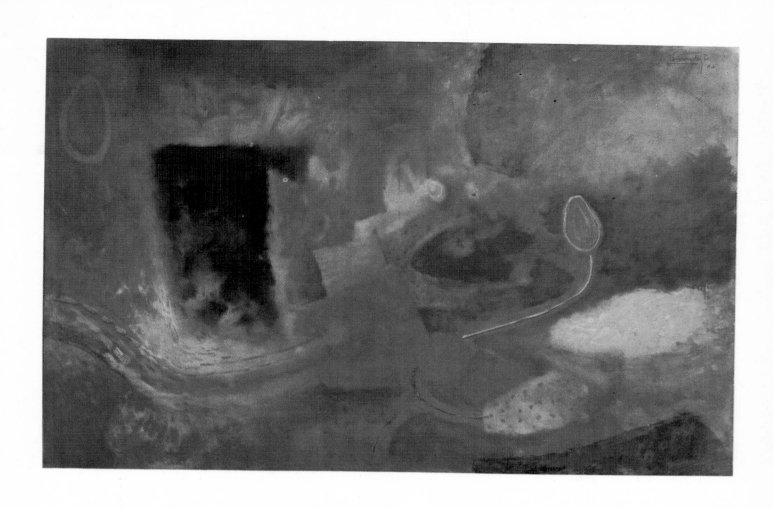

HERNANDEZ DELGADILLO JOSE. "Espacio 1966".
Oleo sobre tela. Col. Galería Mer-Kup.— *"Space 1966"*.
Oil on canvas. Collection Mer-Kup Gallery.

HURTADO RODOLFO. "Número 22". Oleo sobre
tela. Col. Galería de Antonio Souza.— *"Number 22".*
Oil on canvas. Collection Antonio Souza Gallery.

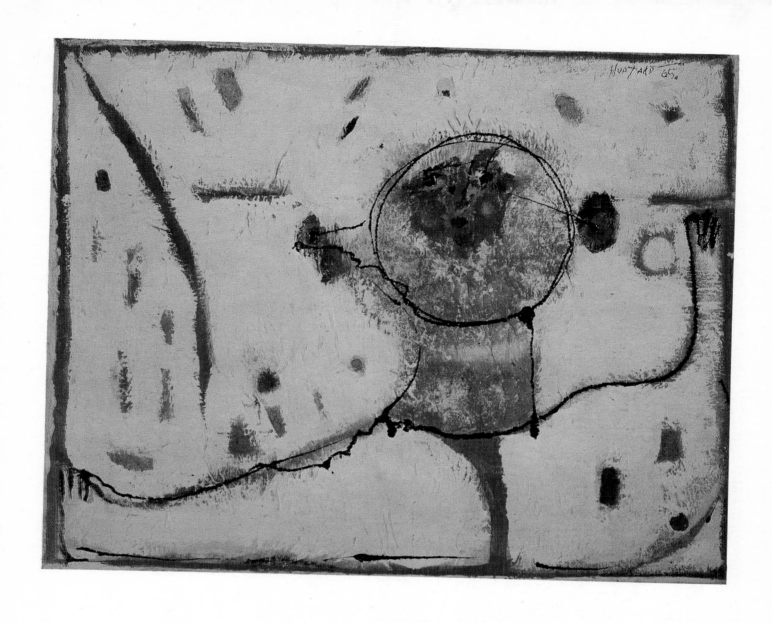

HURTADO RODOLFO. "Pintura No. 30". Oleo sobre
tela. Col. Galería de Antonio Souza.— "Painting No.
30". Oil on canvas. Collection Antonio Souza Gallery.

LOPEZ LOZA LUIS. "Araña". Oleo sobre tela. Col.
Galería de Antonio Souza.— *"Spider". Oil on canvas.*
Collection Antonio Souza Gallery.

LOPEZ LOZA LUIS. "Dora Mari". Oleo sobre tela. Col. Galería de Antonio Souza.— *"Dora Mari". Oil on canvas. Collection Antonio Souza Gallery.*

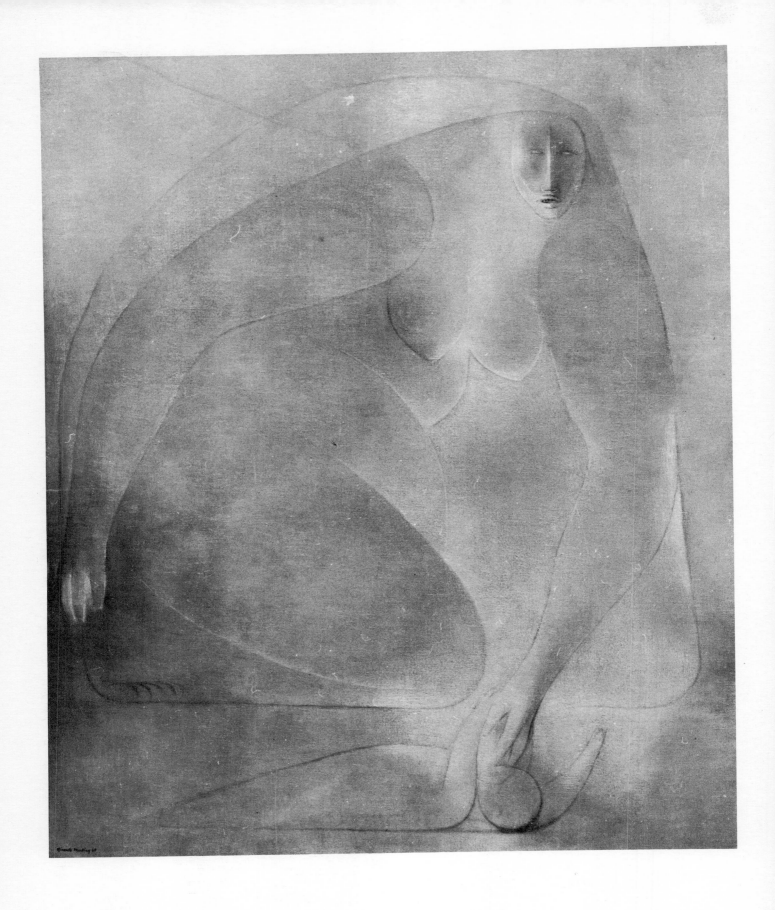

MARTINEZ RICARDO. "Maternidad'. Oleo sobre tela. Col. Galería de Arte Mexicano.— *"Maternity". Oil on canvas. Collection Gallery of Mexican Art.*

MARTINEZ RICARDO. "Grupo de Mujeres". Oleo
sobre tela. Col. Galería de Arte Mexicano.— *"Group
of Women". Oil on canvas. Collection Gallery of
Mexican Art.*

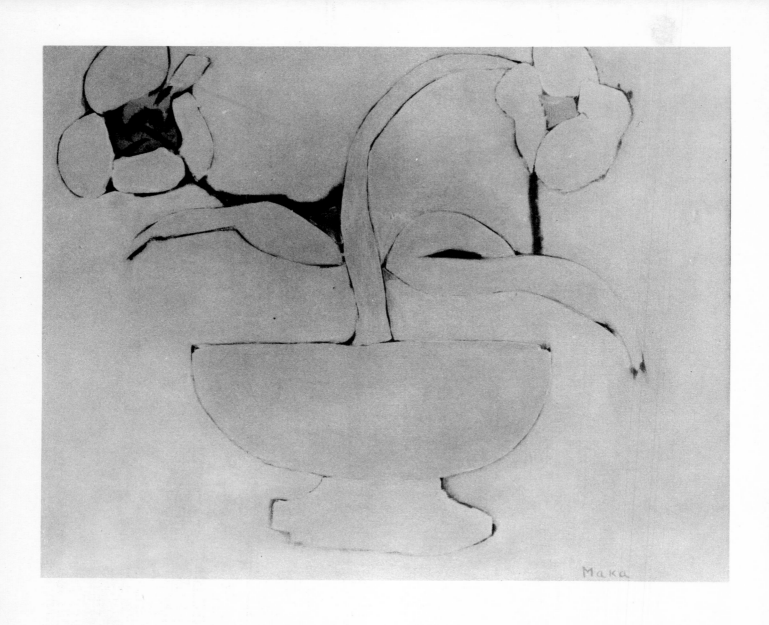

MAKA. "Flores". Oleo sobre tela. Col. Salón de la
Plástica Mexicana.— *"Flowers". Oil on canvas. Collection Salon de la Plastica Mexicana.*

MAKA. "Barca". Oleo sobre tela. Col. de la autora.—
"Boat". Oil on canvas. Collection of the artist.

MESSEGUER BENITO. "Patetismo". Oleo sobre tela.
Col. particular.— *"Patheticism". Oil on canvas. Private
collection.*

MESSEGUER BENITO. "Cozumel". Oleo sobre tela.
Col. del autor.— *"Cozumel". Oil on canvas. Collection
of the artist.*

MORENO CAPDEVILLA FRANCISCO. "Ahorca-
dos". Carbón sobre papel. Col. Particular.— *"Hanged
Men". Charcoal on paper. Private collection.*

MORENO CAPDEVILLA FRANCISCO. "Regreso".
Acrílico sobre tela. Col. Salón de la Plástica Mexicana.—
"Return". Acryllic on canvas. Collection Salón de la
Plastica Mexicana.

NIETO RODOLFO. "A-17". Acuarela sobre papel.
Col. Galería Juan Martín.— "A-17". Watercolor on
    paper. Collection Juan Martin Gallery.

NIETO RODOLFO. "Pintura". Oleo sobre tela. Col.
Arq. Jacobo Nicolayevski.— *"Painting". Oil on canvas.*
Collection of Jacobo Nicolayevski.

PELAEZ ANTONIO. "Reflejo Rojo". Oleo sobre tela.
Col. particular.— *"Red Reflection". Oil on canvas. Private collection.*

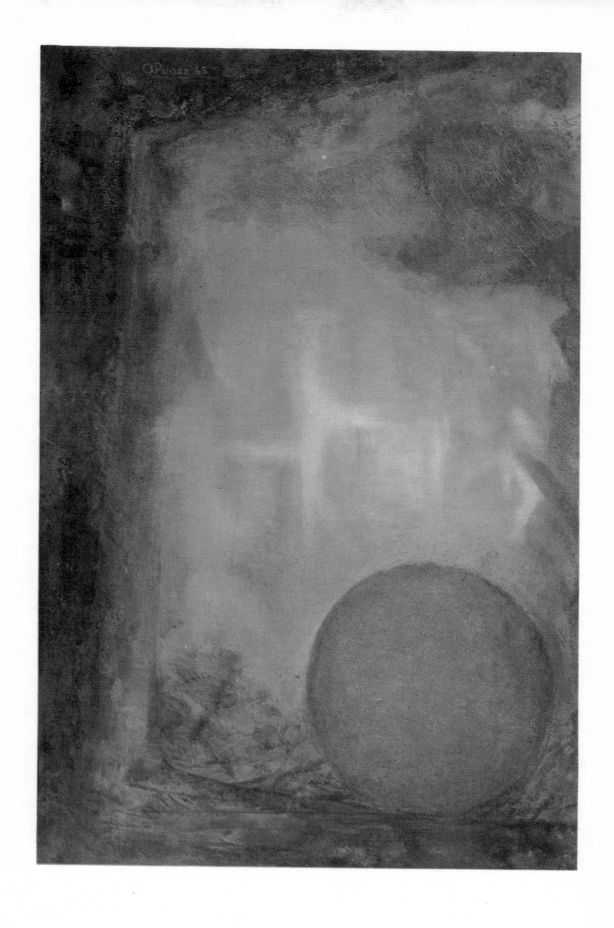

PELAEZ ANTONIO. "Esfera de Barro". Oleo sobre
tela. Col. del autor.— "Clay Sphere". Oil on canvas.
Collection of the artist.

RAMIREZ GABRIEL. "Lo que se Toca". Oleo sobre
tela. Col. Galería Juan Martín.— *"What is Touched".*
Oil on canvas. Collection Juan Martin Gallery.

RAMIREZ GABRIEL. "Semejante al Silencio". Oleo
sobre tela. Col. Galería Juan Martín.— *"Like Silence".*
Oil on canvas. Collection Juan Martin Gallery.

RAMOS PRIDA FERNANDO. "El Mundo de los Ni-
ños". Oleo sobre tela. Col. Galería de Arte Mexicano.—
*"The Children's World". Oil on canvas. Collection
Gallery of Mexican Art.*

RAMOS PRIDA FERNANDO. "Piedra de la Amistad". Oleo sobre tela. Col. Galería de Arte Mexicano.— *"Friendship Stone". Oil on canvas. Collection Gallery of Mexican Art.*

ROJO VICENTE. "Triángulo Sobre Rojo". Vinílica
y collage sobre tela. Col. Galería Juan Martín.—*"Triangle on Red". Vinyl and collage on canvas. Collection
Juan Martin Gallery.*

ROJO VICENTE. "Destrucción de un Orden". Oleo
sobre tela. Col. Galería Juan Martín.— *"Destruction
of an Order". Oil on canvas. Collection Juan Martin
Gallery.*

SANCHEZ CASTAÑEDA PILAR. "Mujer Pensativa".
Oleo sobre tela. Col. Salón de la Plástica Mexicana.—
"Pensive Woman". Oil on canvas. Collection Salon de la
Plástica Mexicana.

SANCHEZ CASTAÑEDA PILAR. "La Carta". Oleo sobre tela. Col. Salón de la Plástica Mexicana.— *"The Letter". Oil on canvas. Collection Salón de la Plastica Mexicana.*

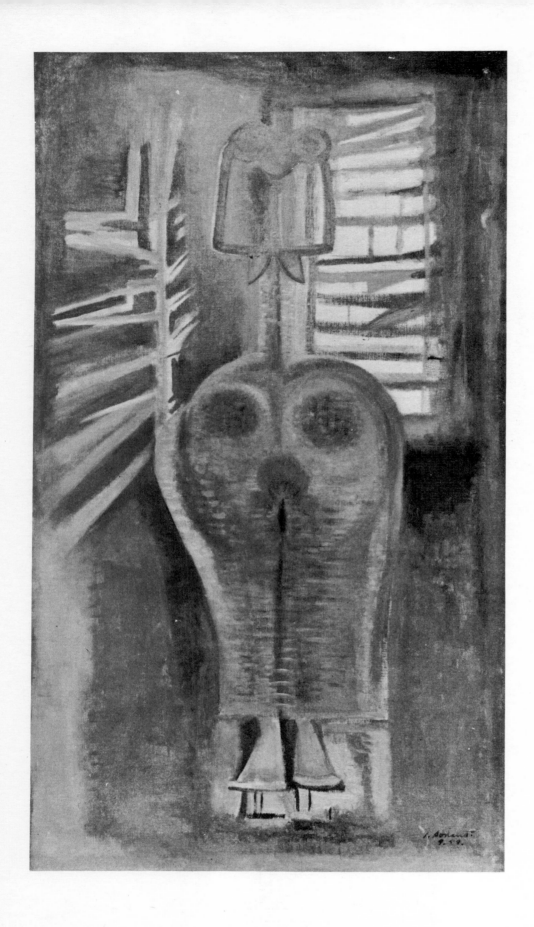

SORIANO JUAN. "La Madre". Oleo sobre tela. Col.
Galería Juan Martín.—*"The Mother". Oil on canvas.*
Collection Juan Martin Gallery.

SORIANO JUAN. "Lupe Marín". Oleo sobre tela. Col. Galería Juan Martín.— *"Lupe Marín". Oil on canvas. Collection Juan Martin Gallery.*

TOLEDO FRANCISCO. "Pintura". Oleo sobre tela.
Col. Galería Antonio Souza.—*"Painting". Oil on canvas. Collection Antonio Souza Gallery.*

TOLEDO FRANCISCO. "Pintura No. 1". Oleo sobre
tela. Col. Galería de Antonio Souza.— *Painting No. 1".
Oil on canvas. Collection Antonio Souza Gallery.*

URUETA CORDELIA. "Rotación". Oleo sobre tela.
Col. de la autora.—"Rotation". Oil on canvas.
Collection of the artist.

URUETA CORDELIA. "Al Filo de Obsidiana". Oleo sobre tela. Col. de la autora.— *"At the Edge of Obsidian". Oil on canvas. Collection of the artist.*

URRUSTI LUCINDA. "Piñas". Oleo sobre tela. Col.
Salón de la Plástica Mexicana.—*"Pineapples". Oil on
canvas. Collection Salon de la Plastica Mexicana.*

URRUSTI LUCINDA. "Trigo". Oleo sobre tela. Col. Salón de la Plástica Mexicana.— *"Wheat". Oil on canvas. Collection Salon de la Plastica Mexicana.*

VLADY. "Judith y Holofernes". Oleo sobre tela. Col.
particular.—*"Judith and Holofernes". Oil on canvas.
Private collection.*

VLADY. "Brillo Sobre la Playa". Oleo sobre tela. Col. Salón de la Plástica Mexicana.— *"Brilliance over the Beach". Oil on canvas. Collection Salon de la Plastica Mexicana.*